# Students With
# Mild Exceptionalities

*I dedicate this text to educators and practitioners working
with children with exceptionalities, who wish to be known
for all of their complexities of strengths and deficits, hopes, and fears.*

# Students With
# Mild Exceptionalities

## Characteristics
## and Applications

Sydney S. Zentall

*Purdue University, Indiana*

Los Angeles | London | New Delhi
Singapore | Washington DC

Los Angeles | London | New Delhi
Singapore | Washington DC

FOR INFORMATION:

SAGE Publications, Inc.
2455 Teller Road
Thousand Oaks, California 91320
E-mail: order@sagepub.com

SAGE Publications Ltd.
1 Oliver's Yard
55 City Road
London EC1Y 1SP
United Kingdom

SAGE Publications India Pvt. Ltd.
B 1/I 1 Mohan Cooperative Industrial Area
Mathura Road, New Delhi 110 044
India

SAGE Publications Asia-Pacific Pte. Ltd.
3 Church Street
#10-04 Samsung Hub
Singapore 049483

Acquisitions Editor:   Diane McDaniel
Editorial Assistant:   Megan Koraly
Production Editor:   Astrid Virding
Copy Editor:   Judy Selhorst
Typesetter:   C&M Digitals (P) Ltd.
Proofreader:   Ellen Brink
Indexer:   Kathleen Paparchontis
Cover Designer:   Gail Buschman
Marketing Manager:   Terra Schultz
Permissions Editor:   Adele Hutchinson

Illustrations by Susan Gilbert.

Printed in the United States of America

*A catalog record of this book is available from the Library of Congress.*

978-1-4129-7470-7

This book is printed on acid-free paper.

12 13 14 15 16 10 9 8 7 6 5 4 3 2 1

# Brief Contents

# Detailed Contents

### *Nonverbal Learning Disabilities*

# Preface

Student readers at all levels want succinctly presented information—information that is not wordy and not watered-down. They want a consumable set of understandings that are interesting and easy to navigate, that get to the point, and that can be used as a future resource. Using these guideposts, I have created this text with the intent of improving early identification and understanding of children with mild exceptionalities. Other available texts present information about special education more generally, the history of definitions, assessment, consulting/collaboration, legal cases, and so on—but with little information on the ways children with exceptionalities act, talk, think, perform, and respond socially in school settings.

This text involves a **change of content** in that it focuses primarily on the academic, behavioral, cognitive, social-emotional, and physical characteristics of children with a variety of exceptionalities, with a secondary emphasis on implications for accommodations and interventions. The text also includes "authentic activities" (case studies) that can provide the basis for independent, small-group, or whole-class problem solving. These are novel snapshot observations of real children using their actual wording and descriptions of their behavior, as well as the responses of their teachers, educational paraprofessionals, and peers. These cases may be especially important for undergraduate students who lack experience with children, but they also provide a rich source for graduates. The challenges of problem solving are highlighted in these cases through the inclusion of younger children who have not received diagnoses and of older students with special needs, whose incorrect labels or background information has sometimes resulted in incorrect conclusions or predictions about them. Some of these cases are complex, because most children attempt to hide their disabilities, and children with special needs typically have more than one disability, especially at older ages.

This text also represents a **change of form** and is similar to a field guide in its systematic presentation of information about a broad range of children with special needs. This will allow course instructors opportunities to rally their teachers (or prospective teachers) to think about and apply critical information across subtypes of students within categories of exceptionality. As one reviewer stated concisely about the format and related activities presented here: "The pedagogical features are the strength of the textbook and will prompt strong adoption. First, the end-of-chapter questions lend themselves to independent study for students who miss class or could be used to provide extra credit, to prepare for tests, and, most important, to structure students' learning. The case analyses encourage small cooperative learning group activities that are explicitly connected to textbook material. Third, the vocabulary focus alone is worth the purchase price" (Dr. Patricia O'Grady, University of Tampa).

# Acknowledgments

I am indebted to my graduate students for what they have taught me and will teach you about the complexities and interesting natures of children with exceptionalities. My contribution to this text is based primarily on evidence from the literature and from my own experiences as an educator of special needs children. However, my graduate students (and a few experienced undergraduates) told me about their experiences—the funny, the tragic, and the difficult. I never would have guessed that a child with traumatic brain injury might be characterized as a liar when in fact he was just filling in memory gaps with a narrative of what might or should have happened in his life (i.e., confabulation, which can occur after damage to an area in the frontal lobes of the brain; Garrett, 2011). For this text, I would like to credit the student authors of the case studies for chapters: 2 & 3, Jodi Hampton; 4 & 9, Konie Hughes; 5, Laura Bassett & Megan Vinh; 6, Jennifer Campbell Gant; 7, Julian Gates; 8, Heather Helmus-Nyman; 10, Becky Brodderick; 11, Jia Liu & Megan Lerch-Gordon; 12, Joy Cedarquist; 13, Melissa Savage-Bowling; 14, Karly Gibson; 15, Kate Kohder & Amy Wilson.

Throughout the text are original drawings by Susan Gilbert, which I have been privileged to obtain.

I also wish to thank Roselyn Bol, our administrative assistant, who tracked down references for me and located former graduate students to obtain permission from them to use their case studies.

Finally, I have been educated by a strong group of reviewers, who have enriched this text with their perspectives and careful review and suggestions:

Thomas J. Bierdz
Governors State University

Morgan Chitiyo
Southern Illinois University
Carbondale

Jeong-il Cho
Indiana University–Purdue University
Fort Wayne

Jeffrey T. Conklin
Columbus State University

Meenakshi Gajira
Saint Thomas Aquinas College

Dodi Hodges
Coastal Carolina University

Therese Hogan
Dominican University

Molly Kelly-Elliott
Miami University

Ann Maydosz
Old Dominion University

Ron Minge
Long Island University

Patricia O'Grady
University of Tampa

Kay C. Reeves
University of Memphis

Linda A. Revay
University of Akron

Joel Shapiro
Green Mountain College

Jennifer Shubin
Chapman University

Denise Skarbek
Indiana University
South Bend

Jerry Whitworth
Texas Woman's University

# Introduction to Mild Exceptionalities

**Chapter 1**
Formal Definitions and Federal Law

**Chapter 2**
Informal Analysis of the Characteristic Behavior of Individual Students

Chapter 1 begins with a societal look at exceptionality, focusing on categorizing and labeling *groups* and *subgroups* of children. A brief overview of the legal requirements that form the basis of disability categories is presented, followed by a discussion of the debate that surrounds identifying and labeling students and descriptions of how children differ in basic traits (e.g., in sensory and learning processes, personality) that form the basis for exceptionalities.

Labeling follows primarily from the legal and educational definitions of the Individuals with Disabilities Educational Act of 2004 (IDEA), with added information from the medical/psychological classification system of the *Diagnostic and Statistical Manual of Mental Disorders* (fourth text-revised edition), or *DSM-IV-TR*. In this text, the words *disability* and *disorder* may be viewed as interchangeable, although *disability* is used more often in education and *disorder* is primarily used in psychology. *Exceptionality* is an overarching term referring to children with either very high or very low abilities or both. The text also presents information about students at risk for disability, because these students often need identification or curriculum modifications. Furthermore, there is evidence that at-risk students are comparable to those who have been formally diagnosed in characteristics, skill deficits, and response to intervention (for example, students with

ADHD or with reading disabilities; see, e.g., Epstein, Shaywitz, Shaywitz, & Woolston, 1991; Fletcher, Blair, Scott, & Bolger, 2004; Shaywitz, Morris, & Shaywitz, 2008).

Overall, the IDEA categorical system is important because it provides the administrative and legal basis for funding services for these students. Individual disability categories are also important because differential effectiveness and need for specific interventions depend on the category of exceptionality. If category had no implications for intervention, there would be little need for "special" education or specialized services, since all strategies would work equally well for all students and the size of the group would be the only factor of importance. Still, it can be difficult to "place" a child within any one category of exceptionality, because (a) some children have overlapping characteristics, (b) characteristics change as the functional demands of living change at different ages and in different settings, and (c) some students learn ways to compensate. Because of these difficulties of differential diagnosis, special education and psychology are dependent on the observations, judgments, and sensitivities of its practitioners.

The main objective of Chapter 1 is to provide knowledge about categories and their legal basis and general traits in children that depart from "average." Inborn traits include, for example, personality types and learning abilities (e.g., perception and memory, executive functions). With this knowledge, the reader will be better able to recognize the expression of these traits within the different exceptionalities and their implications for intervention. As a follow-up to Chapter 1, this text is organized into the major divisions of academic learning disabilities (Section II), intelligence and adaptive behavior exceptionalities (Section III), attentional disorders (Section IV), social disorders (Section V), and motor disorders (Section VI); these reflect both the educational and the medical/psychological categories.

Chapter 2 differs from the above categorical approach by providing basic tools in understanding *individual children.* This noncategorical approach focuses on the behavior and the characteristics that can overlap disability areas. Chapter 2 reminds us that applying labels is not the only necessary step along a pathway of understanding individual students. To this purpose, the reader will learn to identify contributing attributes of tasks and settings (i.e., environmental factors) as well as the skills and goals that children bring to the performance of these tasks. From an understanding of the fit between what the child *must do* and what the child *can do,* the reader will be able to identify ways to provide empirically based practices (EBPs) or accommodations/interventions to improve social and/or academic performance.

As a follow-up to Chapter 2, each subsequent chapter presents at least one individual case of a child with functional impairments. It is these real cases that capture the actual behavior and responses of individual children and provide the reader with "problem-based" learning opportunities. This type of problem-solving activity has been described as "authentic" because the problem-solving strategies used are the same as those required in actual educational settings. It is for this reason that the cases are complex and often reflect the inconsistencies of individuals that differ from the apparent consistencies of categories of exceptionalities. The reader will observe that *not* all the characteristics of a disability will be seen in each student, and some characteristics from more than one disability may be present in any one child.

## LEARNING GOALS

In this section you will learn the following:

- A vocabulary that is related to the various exceptionalities and their underlying characteristics
- The legal requirements that form the basis of disability definitions and the nature of the debate that surrounds this labeling process
- How to recognize inborn childhood trait differences that form the basis of individual categories of exceptionality
- How to recognize the principles of response to intervention (RTI)
- How to recognize the principles of functional analysis (FA) and how to perform a simplified FA with goals that can be implemented as accommodations or interventions

# Chapter 1

## Formal Definitions and Federal Law

## FEDERAL LAWS

This introduction sets the stage for what follows in this volume by defining the legal requirements that guarantee children with mild disabilities the right to be identified and the right to an appropriate education. Two related federal laws (U.S. statutes), based on the U.S. Constitution, mainly the Bill of Rights, concern the rights of children with disabilities: the Individuals with Disabilities Education Act (**IDEA**) and **Section 504** of the Vocational Rehabilitation Act of 1973.

**IDEA:** The Individuals with Disabilities Educational Act of 2004, the main U.S. federal law for special education, which mandates schools to find, evaluate, and provide a free, appropriate program of education for each child with a disability.

## IDEA

IDEA has been chiseled out and transformed over time. Initially it was called Public Law 94-142, the Education for All Handicapped Children Act, when it was passed by Congress in 1975. Before 1975 there was no national legislation covering the evaluation and education of students with disabilities. P.L. 94-142 was later reinterpreted (reauthorized) in 1990 as IDEA; additional provisions were added in 1997 and most recently in 2004. The promise of these laws for students with mild exceptionalities has been summarized as follows:

> Before signing the Education for All Handicapped Children Act of 1975 (since reauthorized as the Individuals with Disabilities Education Act), President Ford expressed some concerns about the effect of the law. He worried that it would create new complexities and administrative challenges for public education. But ultimately it was hope and compassion that inspired him to sign the law. More than

---

**Figure 1.1**   When a student differs from the norm, that student may need the protection and guarantees of the Federal Law.

**FAPE:** Free, appropriate program of education, legally required under IDEA.

**IEP:** Individualized education program, a requirement of IDEA. An IEP is a written document with special instructions detailing related services designed for a student with a diagnosed disability.

**Accommodations:** Changes in the setting or task that are made by the teacher to bring out optimal responding from the child.

**Interventions:** Treatments used to change a child with disabilities (e.g., medications or skill training in weak areas, such as remedial phonics training for reading).

a quarter century later, we know that many of President Ford's concerns were realized. But we also know that IDEA has exceeded President Ford's greatest hopes. (President's Commission on Excellence in Special Education, 2002, p. 4).

IDEA is the main federal law for special education that provides funding for the education of disabled youth ages 3 to 21 years. IDEA delegates specific responsibilities to local school systems to locate and educate these children. If parents have submitted in writing to school officials that their child needs special education services or the school system has reason to suspect that a child has a disability (e.g., indicated by comments in the report card) but fails to act by referring the child for a comprehensive special education evaluation, the school officials have failed in their obligation to find and evaluate (the "child find mandate") and provide a free, appropriate program of education (**FAPE**) for a child with a disability. FAPE includes the rights of protection against discriminatory assessment (e.g., accounting for primary language differences) and of due process in procedures of assessment, placement, programming, and appropriate education (i.e., a program designed to provide "educational benefits" and related services, if necessary, in order for the student to benefit from specially designed instruction).

Appropriate education is translated to a written document called an individualized educational program (**IEP**). It is a legal document that represents the school's accountability to the student. IDEA requires an IEP for each student participating in special education programs. In addition, an individualized transition program (ITP) must be in place by the time the student is 16 years of age. A multidisciplinary team (including, e.g., special/general educators, speech and language pathologists, psychologists, nurses/physicians, administrators, social workers, school counselors, related service personnel, parents, the student) develops the IEP. It contains information about the child's current level of educational functioning; annual goals to be reevaluated every one to three years; a listing of special services to be provided (e.g., transportation, tutoring, occupational or speech therapy) and specifics of how, when, where, and by whom these services will be provided (e.g., by a special education teacher in a resource room); projected start and review dates for services; and details regarding how the child's progress will be measured. School systems often use goals that are based on their required state standards. When progress is not being made, different materials or methods must be implemented.

More generally, an IEP is a legal document that sets forth the duties and responsibilities of the school regarding that student and lists specially designed instruction and related services appropriate for the education of that student. The IEP represents accountability, and the school is legally bound to provide only the services, **accommodations,** and **interventions** listed in the IEP. Interventions based on functional analysis target high-frequency payoffs (e.g., needed stimulation). This might involve teaching the child to perform replacement behavior, such as, alternative nondisruptive behavior to get stimulation (Stahr, Cusing, Lane, & Fox, 2006). In contrast, accommodations change the task or setting. Some accommodations involve **assistive technology,** which can range from low-tech to light-tech (e.g., nonelectronic and inexpensive) to high-tech (Beard, Carpenter, & Johnston, 2007). Provisions for assistive technology are funded by grants to states from the Technology-Related Assistance to Individuals with Disabilities Act of 1968, amended as the Tech Act.

Once the plan has been developed, the team considers the best setting to achieve the goals listed. IDEA requires that the least restrictive environment (**LRE**) be selected for placement as much as possible, and this selection is then written into the IEP as part of the individualized goals. The U.S. Department of Education reported in 2006 that approximately half of all students with disabilities in the United States were being educated in general education settings for the majority of their day. More restrictive placement than the general education setting (e.g., special class, separate schooling) is to be selected only when it can be documented that the child cannot achieve learning satisfactorily in the general education environment, even with supplementary aids and services. The team also considers the degree to which the child's disruptiveness interferes with the education of other students with and without disabilities. In making their decision, team members must keep in mind that research has shown that average students in classrooms with students with disabilities achieve as well as students in classes without children with disabilities and have more positive attitudes toward students with disabilities. In addition, students with and without disabilities have been shown to improve their social and problem-solving skills and self-concepts when they share classrooms (for a review, see "Executive Summary," 1995, p. 5). If the setting selected is outside the general classroom, opportunities must exist for the student to interact with nondisabled peers to the maximum extent possible (i.e., in nonacademics, such as at lunch, at recess, and during physical education, and in subject areas such as art, math, and science).

General education teachers must have a copy of each student's IEP and comply with the terms of the IEP. General educators may not always be aware of the importance of compliance with the terms of the IEP. In one case, a general education teacher refused to do oral testing with a child as was specified within the child's IEP. The general education teacher was sued in civil court for failure to comply with the terms of the IEP, and the outcome was that the teacher had to pay $15,000 for his own legal fees and those of the complainants out of his own pocket (*Doe v. Withers,* 1992).

## Section 504

Section 504 of the Vocational Rehabilitation Act is a broad civil rights statute that includes all students with disabilities. For example, students who are currently

**Assistive technology:** "An item or piece of equipment or product system acquired commercially, off the shelf, modified, or customized, and used to increase, maintain, or improve functional capability for an individual with a disability" (Beard et al., 2007, p. 4).

**LRE:** Least restrictive environment. The LRE for a child is typically the general education classroom, in contrast to, for example, a self-contained classroom for students with disabilities.

receiving special education under IDEA are automatically Section 504 students. This law prohibits discrimination on the basis of disability in any program or activity that receives financial assistance from any federal agency (e.g., public school districts, institutions of higher education, other state and local education agencies). There are sanctions for *not* being in compliance (i.e., losing federal monies that support other educational programs). Section 504 is similar to the Americans with Disabilities Act (ADA) of 1990 (42 U.S.C. Sections 12101–12213), with provisions of equal educational opportunity, but differs in that ADA extended the benefits of 504 to non–federally funded agencies.

Section 504 was first important in public schools for those students needing physical access (e.g., ramps, elevators, larger bathrooms stalls) in the 1970s, although work continues today (e.g., installing automatic doors). Interpretations of this law have been extended to include activities related to instruction and to educational/social opportunities, such as field trips, recess, and evaluation procedures. Thus, a more recent impact of Section 504 has addressed access to the content of instructional programs for children with disabilities. This educational focus of Section 504 became nationally recognized with the need for services for students with attention deficit hyperactivity disorder (**ADHD**). Not allowing a student with ADHD (or with emotional/behavioral disorders) to go on a field trip because the student runs in the hall is an instance of punishing the child for his or her disability. In other words, the school cannot exclude a child from educational or social opportunities to punish the child for behavior that is a manifestation of a disability any more than the judicial system can unreasonably punish someone who is mentally deficient, legally insane, or a juvenile. This is known as **manifest determination**— that is, determining whether particular conduct is caused by or has a direct and substantial relationship to the child's disability or is the direct result of the failure of the local educational agency (**LEA**) to implement the IEP. Manifest determination is based on Section 504 of the Rehabilitation Act of 1973 (P.L. 93-112).

> No otherwise qualified individual with a disability . . . shall, solely by reason of his disability, be excluded from the participation in, or denied the benefits of, or be subjected to discrimination under any program or activity receiving federal assistance (29 U.S.C. 794[a] CFR Pt. 104).

Also guaranteed under IDEA is the principle that a school cannot change a student's placement (e.g., to an alternative educational setting) for more than 10 days without assessing whether the student's behavior is a manifestation of his or her disability and without conducting a functional assessment (see Chapter 2). An extension from 10 to 45 days can be made, without a manifest determination, if the student has weapons, illegal drugs, or has seriously injured another.

**ADHD:** Attention deficit hyperactivity disorder (see Section II).

**Manifest determination:** The determination of whether a child's "misconduct" is an outcome of the child's disability.

**LEA:** Local educational agency, such as a local school.

Unfortunately, Section 504 has fewer procedural safeguards than does IDEA, even though it sometimes references IDEA procedures as a way to meet its requirements. Section 504 also does not require an IEP, as IDEA does, but does require a "plan" of accommodations and related services, although this plan does *not* have to be written. It is recommended that those persons who are knowledgeable about the student (e.g., teachers, parents, counselors) convene and agree on a plan of services and accommodations that are "reasonable," decided on a case-by-case basis. Accommodations may involve changes, adaptations, or modifications to a policy, program, service, or workplace that will allow a qualified person with a disability to participate fully in a program, take advantage of a service, or perform a job (Code of Federal Regulations at 24 CFR Part 8). Section 504 also does *not* have a funding mechanism. However, in 2004, LEAs were authorized to use up to 15% of IDEA funds for students who have not been identified with disabilities but who require additional academic and/or behavioral support to succeed in general education settings.

Both IDEA and Section 504 include the requirement that a child with disabilities be placed in an LRE with the use of supplementary aids and services before placement in special education is considered. Both laws provide parents and students with grievance procedures and the rights to review records, to participate in hearings and be represented by counsel, and to due process at the local level.

## DISABILITY CATEGORIES DEFINED AND DEBATED

Also open to interpretation and possible reinterpretation are the "categories" of exceptionality. The categories have changed over time by (a) identifying more types of disabilities; (b) recognizing the importance of co-occurring disabilities and characteristics; (c) focusing more on the functional nature of characteristics as they are influenced by settings, tasks, and interventions (i.e., how students actually function in different settings); and (d) recognizing that an educational categorical system (IDEA) and a medical/psychological categorical system, the *Diagnostic and Statistical Manual of Mental Disorders* (**DSM-IV-TR**), provide valuable information.

**DSM-IV-TR:** The fourth edition, text revised, of the *Diagnostic and Statistical Manual of Mental Disorders*, which presents the most widely used medical/psychological classification system (APA, 2000).

Rather than selecting one type of categorical system, this text presents both IDEA and *DSM-IV-TR* categories, with the understanding that both will change over time for a variety of social, political, and scientific reasons. Furthermore, the two systems provide elaboration in different areas. For example, the psychological/medical system provides greater specification of emotional and behavioral disorders than the catchall IDEA category of "emotional and behavioral disorder" (EBD) and thus provides more information for Section V in this text. IDEA, in contrast, provides better information on the specific subtypes of learning disabilities for Section II. Finally, the area of giftedness is included in this text, even though it is not represented in either the educational or the psychological classification system, because of educators' difficulties identifying children who are diagnosed with two exceptionalities (the "twice exceptional," gifted and disabled; see Chapter 7 for more detail), especially those children from multicultural backgrounds.

## Educationally Defined Exceptionalities (IDEA and Section 504)

No categories are derived from Section 504; the law offers only a functional definition of disability ("handicap" was the original language in the law) as "a physical or mental impairment that substantially limits one or more major life activities." "Major life activities" include walking, seeing, hearing, speaking, sleeping, breathing, working, caring for oneself, performing manual tasks, and learning. Under Section 504, students can also be considered disabled if they (a) have a "history of" or past record of a physical or mental impairment (e.g., if labeled in high school, this label can be used in college) or (b) have been "regarded as" having a disability (e.g., are seen by parents as disabled). A student labeled as "disabled" under Section 504 may be eligible for special education services or not, depending on whether the student's team determines that services are necessary. The team must decide whether the student can perform standard skills without modifications or accommodations.

Similar to Section 504, IDEA makes a distinction between a diagnosis of disability and eligibility for services. If a child is diagnosed with a disability but can make educational progress in the general education classroom without services, that child is not covered by IDEA. Eligibility for special education is eligibility for a "service," not for a placement or diagnosis. For example, a child in a wheelchair can be labeled with a disability without requiring special services. A child evaluated in accordance with procedures outlined in IDEA must have a specified physical or mental impairment; that child can then receive special education and related services, if the child has been adversely affected in "educational performance," "even if the child has not failed or been retained in a course or grade" (Section 300.101[c][1]).

There are currently 14 IDEA disability categories:

1. Autism

2. Deaf-blindness

3. Deafness

4. Developmental delay

5. Emotional disturbance (ED)

6. Hearing impairment

7. Mental retardation

8. Multiple disabilities

9. Orthopedic impairment

10. Other health impairment (OHI)

11. Specific learning disabilities (**SLD/LD**)

12. Speech or language impairment

13. Traumatic brain injury (TBI)

14. Visual impairment including blindness

**SLD:** Specific learning disability (e.g., in math, reading).

**LD:** Learning disability, also termed *specific learning disability* (SLD) (see Section II).

(In 2008, the American Association on Intellectual and Developmental Disabilities, AAIDD), formerly the American Association on Mental Retardation, AAMR, and members of the community recommended a change in the term *mental retardation* to the use of the term *intellectual disability* or **ID.**) Some of the IDEA categories point to level of severity (e.g., hearing impairment versus deafness), whereas others span severity levels (e.g., visual impairment including blindness); some categories specify age level (*developmental delay* refers to children 3 through 9 years old with physical, cognitive, communicative, social/emotional, or adaptive behavioral delays) and some do not.

**ID and MID:** Intellectual disability and mild intellectual disability, previously labeled "mild mental retardation" or "educable mental retardation."

## Psychologically Defined (DSM-IV-TR)

The most widely accepted medical/clinical definition and assessment tool is the *Diagnostic and Statistical Manual of Mental Disorders,* or **DSM,** a manual published by the American Psychiatric Association (APA). The edition currently in use is the text-revised fourth edition, published in 2000, known as *DSM-IV-TR.* The fifth edition of the *DSM* is due out in 2013 and will be known as *DSM-V.* The *DSM*'s diagnostic categories of disorder are arranged by code numbers, which refer to type of disorder and level of severity (mild/moderate). Disorders first diagnosed in infancy, childhood, or adolescence are as follows:

1. Mental retardation

2. Learning disorders (e.g., reading, math, written expression)

3. Motor skill disorders (developmental coordination disorder, or DCD)

4. Communication disorders

5. Pervasive developmental disorders (autism, Rett syndrome, Asperger's)

6. Attention deficit hyperactivity disorder (ADHD) and disruptive behavior disorders (conduct disorder, or CD; oppositional defiant disorder, or ODD)

7. Feeding and eating disorders

8. Tic disorders (Tourette's syndrome)

9. Elimination disorders

10. Other disorders (e.g., anxiety disorders, selective mutism)

## Disability Categories Debated

Categories of disability are debated for a number of reasons, many of which are related to the difficulty of defining individual children, who may not fit neatly within a category, and to the definitions, which change over time in response to changing societal needs and attitudes. This task of distinguishing one disability category from another is termed **differential diagnosis.**

**Differential diagnosis:** The ability to identify a child at risk for a disability as different from related disabilities with similar or overlapping characteristics.

Problems differentially diagnosing children within a category are related to behavior, which can be normative (normal) at certain developmental periods (i.e., oppositionality at 2 years and adolescence). Furthermore, "dysfunction" for individuals with mild exceptionalities is not typically displayed across all settings. Dysfunction is defined within one or several settings or types of settings (e.g., math, noisy settings, changes of routine, nonchallenging or excessively challenging tasks). This is often misunderstood, even by professionals. As one asked, "Why, for example, does identification of ADD vary so widely from one social context to another?" He continued, "Unlike other medical disorders, such as diabetes or pneumonia, this is a disorder that pops up in one setting only to disappear in another" (Armstrong, 1995, p. 33). This kind of failure to understand the situational nature of mild exceptionalities could make it difficult to understand the reduced ability of these students. An incorrect assumption is that if a child can perform or behave adequately in situation A, then that child "should" be able to perform just as well in situation B. If not, perhaps that student is willful, lazy, bad, or poorly trained. Yet we have no difficulty understanding the setting conditions of a student with visual impairment. That is, the amount of light or the size of text can alter the student from sighted to blind.

There are also different levels of acceptance for labeling students. Labels can produce negative expectations and lead to an emphasis on problem characteristics and expectations of impaired functioning (stereotypes). Being "labeled" or singled out may lock an individual into a deviant role, especially when the child internalizes the negative reactions of others. Educators who believe that labels produce negative expectancies believe that students will behave in line with those expectations (e.g., using their disabilities as excuses). This has been called "enabling" students or "coddling" them. Enabling in this negative sense supports negative expectations (i.e., to disable) and occurs when expectations are lowered.

However, the positive meaning of the word *enable* is "to make able." This type of labeling increases expectations by providing accommodations to allow and require the child to perform at levels equivalent to peers. Furthermore, labeling can have important implications for instruction. For example, the primary information educators have when they are working with students with mild exceptionalities comes from the accumulated research on the characteristics of labeled children, as is summarized in this text. Although a diagnosis or a label does not substitute for good instructional programming, labels can be helpful in predicting how a child is likely to respond to interventions and to a variety of settings and tasks.

In addition, there are different attitudes and levels of acceptance of labeling specific groups of children, especially those with the "invisible disabilities" (i.e., where the children do not look different or are not easily assessed as different from their peers). For example, at one time there were a number of concerns about learning disabilities (LD): "The field quickly fell into a position where those who were alleged moderates claimed that 2–3% of the children had a significant learning disability; some claimed the condition to be a mere hoax, whereas others saw the prevalence to be well above 50%" (Senf, 1986, p. 28).

Evolving attitudes and new understandings change the interpretations of laws (i.e., reauthorizations), even though the original language of the laws that define disability remain the same. This happens because the federal laws define only the "boundaries," which must be interpreted and reinterpreted through judicial decisions in the U.S. courts, in each state court system, and again in each school district. Thus, interpretations of the laws differ widely today nationally and from state to state and will continue to change over time.

## GROUP NORMS: SOCIETAL DEFINITIONS

Most labels are derived from the extent to which a child's behavior deviates from the **norm.** If *norm* is defined as average, then abnormal, atypical, or deviant is that which occurs infrequently. The normal distribution or curve can be described as a hill with a gradual incline up and a gradual decline down. Most individuals (68%) cluster around the center of the hill, or the mean, as illustrated in Figure 1.1. The +1 and −1 in the figure represent the standard deviations (*SD* or σ), or significant departures from average functioning or behavior. These 1s and 2s represent the percentages of individuals falling below or above average functioning (the norm). Children with mild

**Norm:** A statistical average or the most frequently occurring score or response in a setting or during the performance of a task.

**Figure 1.2** Normal Distribution

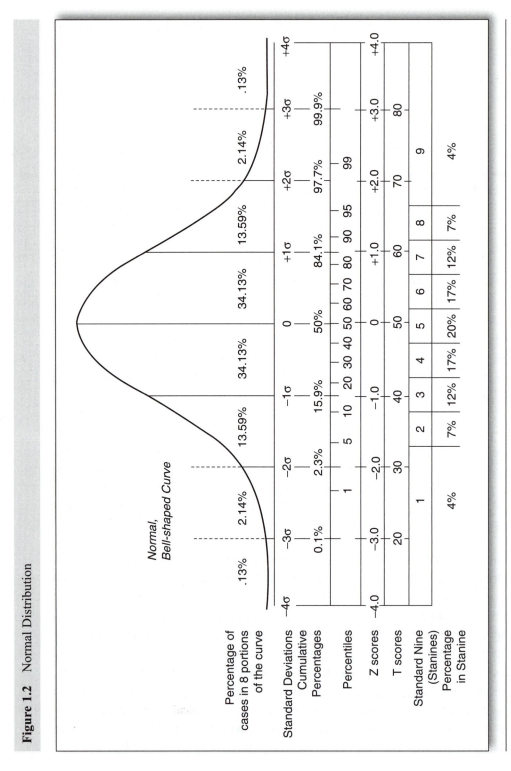

*Source:* Jeremy Kemp.

exceptionalities fall away from the mean, maybe 1 to 2 *SD* on a particular **trait,** and children with moderate exceptionalities fall closer to the "tails" of the distribution.

## Traits

These departures from average on specific traits can be used to categorize individuals; for example, the heights of most individuals cluster at the center of the distribution. Although height is not academically relevant, it is a stable trait once the individual has achieved a certain age. "Normal" height is defined as a height that falls close to and within a range of the most frequently occurring heights (which differs for men and women); deviant height (very short, very tall) is defined by the tails of the distribution. Even though scores at the extremes *are* statistically deviant (i.e., infrequent), not all extremes can be considered dysfunctional or educationally significant. That is, extremely high IQ and extremely tall can function better than average in specific settings (e.g., school and basketball). Thus, only when an extreme trait leads to loss of social or academic performance (i.e., **impairment** or loss of functioning) do we define disability or disorder. There are traits within all children that are more relevant to school functioning than height. These are the psychological processes or cognitive learning abilities of (a) sensory processes (e.g., seeing, hearing, touching, tasting), (b) learning processes (e.g., intelligence, memory, perception, attention, executive functions), and (c) personality (e.g., **introversion/extroversion** and ease of adaptation to change).

*Sensations* are the raw data of our experiences, which include the proximal senses of taste, smell, and tactile impressions (e.g., pain, pressure, temperature) and the distal senses of seeing and hearing. *Visual sensations* are the raw data of color, shape, and size. Children with sensory loss of vision and impaired functioning are called *visually impaired* (VI). Students with this disability can be recognized by the closeness or angle with which they hold their papers, by head tilting, squinting, headaches, differences in response to light (too much glare or not enough light), and by the failure to detect details (e.g., crossing of the letter *t,* observing exponents in math, reading small print, copying from the board). They may also fail to see the whole/gestalt, as with tunnel or pinhole vision, which can be observed in children who bump into things and who exhibit inconsistent or lack of social response. Students with corrected vision wearing glasses would not be considered impaired in that a disability label requires loss of function. For loss of function that is not correctable, there are low-tech accommodations, such as increasing the size of print or highlighting relevant information with markers, using the student's name and verbally describing objects or tasks, rather than pointing to things. For students with VI in today's technological world there are many high-tech accommodations, such as talking computers, scanners, calculators, and watches.

---

**Trait:** Habitual pattern of behavior that is associated with personality characteristics (e.g., extroversion) and is relatively enduring over time. Traits can also be physical, such as height and eye color.

---

**Impairment:** The outcome of a disability in terms of reduced functioning (academic or social).

---

**Introversion:** Demonstration of internalizing behavior (e.g., shyness, anxieties).

---

**Extroversion:** Demonstration of active, talkative, and acting-out types of behavior (e.g., hyperactivity).

*Auditory sensations* include pitch, frequency, intensity, and duration. We use these raw data primarily to understand language and to be warned of impending danger. Children with dysfunction in sensing sounds are called *hearing impaired* (HI). At the mild level of dysfunction, these children can be identified by speech that is too loud or is slurred. Many of these characteristics are addressed in the chapter on spoken language (Chapter 3), since speech (**expressive language**) is an output that directly reflects the accuracy of the input that an individual hears.

**Learning processes** are the second set of inborn traits. For these there is a cognitive transformation of raw sensory data into meaningful information. The first transformation is what is selected for processing (i.e., attention). Selective attention involves directing attention to important visual or verbal information (including thought). If a child is not attending to the *right* information and is attending to "nonrelevant" information, this can be described as an attentional bias. *Attention* is the primary basis for labeling children with ADHD. For example, children with ADHD are more likely to attend to novel stimuli and therefore have difficulty ignoring "distracting" or competing information (e.g., cartoons on TV monitors while attempting to do calculation tasks) (see Chapter 9). Finally, children with anxiety disorders selectively attend to information that signals danger (see Chapter 12) and so may have greater difficulty attending during evaluation activities, such as tests.

Sustained attention is the ability to maintain a consistent response over time, especially during a continuous or repetitive task or activity (Sohlberg & Mateer, 1989). If a child cannot sustain attention, then off-task responses will be observed. A related skill that requires sustained attention is the ability to hold verbal information in mind temporarily in order to plan, organize, or change that information (**working memory** or working attention; Zentall, 2005b). Working memory (WM) would be needed for such tasks as arithmetic problem solving, reading comprehension, and text generation (composition). Visual-working memory, which resides in the right frontal lobe (Stuss et al., 2001), involves identifying visual patterns, sequences, mapping, following visual directions, and other nonverbal skills. Overall WM is required to identify details, perform steps, plan, sequence, summarize, or reorganize that information. Without working memory, an individual would have difficulty carrying on an extended conversation, completing a long division problem, or planning a sequence of moves in chess (Garrett, 2011). Students with co-occurring LD (math as well as reading) are more likely to have greater deficits in WM than those with only one LD (Maehler & Schuchardt, 2009). Working attention deficits can be seen in many exceptionalities (e.g., children with ADHD, LD, or ID; Garner, 2009).

**Visual perception** is the ability to take what the eyes see (sensory data: color, size, form) and identify that object (an orange, round, ball—an orange). **Auditory perception** is the ability to transform the raw sensations of sound, pitch, and frequency into words and sentences or into other meaningful auditory events, such as birdcalls or

---

**Expressive language:** Talking (spoken language) and composition/spelling (written language).

**Learning processes:** Psychological processes or abilities that contribute to the learning of academic skills; these learning processes are intelligence, memory, perception/discrimination, and attention.

**Working memory (WM):** Memory that involves holding information in mind to bring hindsight and forethought into decision making (Greene, 2006), to consider personal history and possible future consequences for the purposes of planning, sequencing, summarizing, reorganizing, problem solving, and the like.

sirens. **Perception** is typically assessed through measurement of a child's ability to match and identify differences among similar letters, objects, sounds, or words. The ability to perceive accurately depends on how well the child receives a sensory signal, which in turn depends on the context. For example, it is easier to identify sounds or words if the words are not run together into strings of sounds with few pauses, and if the words are isolated from noisy background interference. By way of application, it would be more difficult for a child with auditory perceptual problems to listen to directions or a lecture where the teacher is addressing the whole group than it would be in a small-group or individual setting. In small-group and individual settings, the signal (teacher as the speaker) is louder than the noise in that setting (i.e., the signal-to-noise ratio). However, in large groups, the signal (teacher) is weaker, especially when there is more noise in the setting and the teacher is farther away. Visual perception also involves completing figures (identifying the whole from a part or blending parts into a whole) and finding a small part in a whole (visual analysis, such as identifying hidden pictures). Perceptual abilities can also involve translating from one sensory mode into to another (auditory to visual and visual to auditory). For example, perceptual difficulties can involve translating visual print symbols into sounds (reading) and sequences of sounds into visual print (spelling). Students with the types of perceptual problems described above are often students with learning disabilities.

**Memory** is either short- or long-term. Most school problems involve verbal memory, owing to the verbal nature of most school tasks and the difficulty of holding verbal information in mind. Assessment of verbal **short-term memory** involves measuring students' ability to hold about three to nine elements (words, digits, or letters) in mind (Miller, 1956). Short-term memory problems can be identified when children are unable to recall what the teacher said yesterday or just a few minutes earlier. Short-term memory differs from working memory in that working memory involves holding information in mind in order to reorganize, summarize, or change that information in some way (e.g., mental mathematics). **Long-term memory** involves the ability to recall information learned weeks, months, or years ago. For example, vocabulary and fact-retrieval skills depend on long-term memory. Visual memory is important in learning mathematics and in memorizing words based on their configuration. Children with memory difficulties are primarily students with LD, but memory difficulties are also found in children with auditory language difficulties, traumatic brain injury (TBI), and intellectual disabilities (ID).

Intelligence is defined broadly as the ability to adapt to the environment. However, a score on an intelligence test typically defines intelligence. Such a score is based on the assessment of (a) product (prior knowledge picked up from the environment, such as vocabulary) and (b) process (problem solving, abstract reasoning, symbolic thinking, planning, or new learning). Abstract thinking is the ability to move beyond the sensory/perceptual features of objects and beyond the specific functions of things to

---

**Visual perception:** The ability to take what the eyes see (color, form, and size) and give these visual sensations meaning (to identify objects, words).

---

**Auditory perception:** The ability to identify words/sentences from the sensations of sound. Perception can also require a synthesis or blending of sounds and an analysis or breaking of words into syllables.

---

**Short-term memory:** Immediate recall (within seconds when rehearsal is prevented) of from three to nine elements (words, digits, or letters) (Miller, 1956).

---

**Long-term memory:** The ability to recall information, such as math facts, learned last week, last month, or years earlier.

**GT:** Gifted and talented (see Section III).

**Executive functioning (EF):** Self-regulatory processes involved in such tasks as identifying problems, goal setting, developing plans, executing plans, and evaluating or self-monitoring the implementation of plans.

**Emotional intelligence (EQ):** The ability to identify and understand one's own and others' emotions by "reading" faces, gestures, and tones of voice—in essence to read between the lines of what is spoken.

alternative uses, symbols, categories, and interpretations. By way of application, the question "How is an orange similar to an apricot?" can be answered at the sensory/ perceptual level of "color," at the functional level of "both can be eaten," and at the more abstract level of "both are fruits." Symbols and categories are more abstract because they are not immediately apparent (i.e., the category of fruit cannot be seen). Children who are defined outside the range of "normal" intelligence are children categorized as gifted and talented (**GT**) and children with ID. Students with TBI also often have cognitive or intellectual deficits. Academic subjects that involve intelligent responding are those that require summarization and comprehension (reading comprehension, math problem solving). Students with ID will perform better with more concrete tasks, whereas GT students will perform optimally with more challenging tasks that require extrapolating, synthesizing, creating, or problem solving.

**Executive functioning (EF)** is another area related to intelligence that enables individuals to engage in goal-directed or problem-solving behavior, abstract thinking, and rule learning. EF also encompasses the cognitive flexibility, attention, and working memory systems that guide the individual throughout these regulatory processes. Common difficulties in EF are poor abilities in self-regulation, organization, planning, initiation, and monitoring (Deidrick & Farmer, 2005). Another type of intelligence is commonly known as **emotional intelligence (EQ)**. EQ can also be defined by the child's ability to generally or globally make sense of things (i.e., common sense) and to understand the emotional aspects of everyday social interactions (Stuss, Gallup, & Alexander, 2001). Students with low EQ are students with nonverbal learning disabilities (NVLD; see Chapter 4) and students with autism spectrum disorders, such as Asperger's syndrome (AS; see Chapter 13).

The third set of traits is expressed in personality as differences in inherited **temperament,** which include activity level, adaptability, approach/withdrawal, attention span and persistence, distractibility, intensity, mood quality, regularity, and responsiveness (Thomas & Chess, 1977). Most of these traits can be described in relation to functioning within the different parts of brain (see Figure 1.2).

The brain is made up of two halves (left and right hemispheres), each receiving sensory input from (and control over) the opposite side of the body (Garrett, 2011; this work is the basis for most of the following information on the brain). The two hemispheres have some identical functions, but each also specializes. In particular, the left hemisphere specializes in the language functions of receiving auditory input and generating spoken and written language in association with the motor cortex and Broca's area. Both social and math disabilities are **right-hemispheric functions** (i.e., functions of the right side of the brain; Semrud-Clikeman & Hynd, 1990), although some mathematics functioning can be located in the left frontal (calculations) and both parietal lobes (e.g., for estimating quantities, rank-ordering numbers. This area may be particularly important to the development of "theory of mind" or inferences about the

**Figure 1.3**  The Human Brain

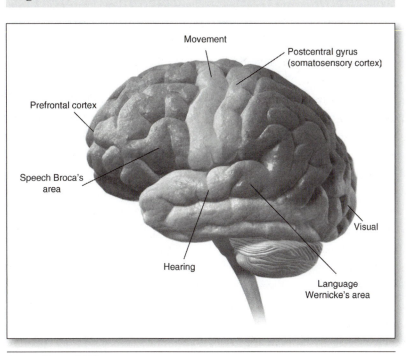

*Source:* Garrett (2011).

**Temperament:** Biologically based behavioral style that has a number of components, including (a) emotionality, or the degree to which a person can become upset; (b) sociability, or the degree to which a person prefers the presence of others; (c) activity, or the degree to which a person is restless; and (d) shyness, or the degree to which a person is uneasy in unfamiliar social situations (Masi et al., 2003).

**Right-hemispheric functions:** Functions of the right side of the brain. Damage to this area can impair pragmatics in language and in the nonverbal aspects of communication (e.g., understanding sarcasm, humor, irony).

intentions and feelings of others (empathy) (Stusset al., 2001). Students with problems in right-hemispheric functions are often those with nonverbal learning disabilities, traumatic brain injury, and autism.

In addition to the hemispheres, there are six layers in the cortex: The outer layer, which is wrinkled and convoluted, is called the gray matter; there is evidence that the second and third layers function to make associations by combining information, the fourth layer is the location of sensory functioning, and the fifth and sixth govern motor functions. The brain can also be divided into regions, with the prefrontal cortex the largest region.

Pennington (1991, pp. 3–31) was the first to suggest that areas of the brain that have evolved most recently in the history of the human species would be more likely to be affected by genetic and environmental variation. The areas implicated are the prefrontal cortex and the hemispheric functions (left frontal and temporal lobes) of language.

Less is known, perhaps, about brain chemistry—its activation and correlation with personality. Eysenck (1967) proposed that some personality traits (e.g., extroversion) are related to inherited properties in the brain, related to cortical arousal. **Arousal** or physiological activation is a trait that is also normally distributed; see Figure 1.4, which describes the range of activation. Arousal cannot be observed,

**Figure 1.4** Arousal: Normal Distribution

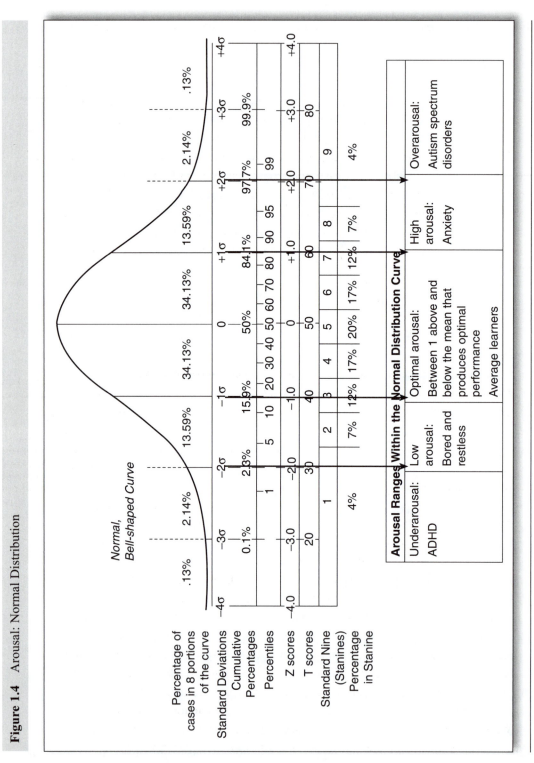

Normal, Bell-shaped Curve

| Percentage of cases in 8 portions of the curve | .13% | 2.14% | 13.59% | 34.13% | 34.13% | 13.59% | 2.14% | .13% |
|---|---|---|---|---|---|---|---|---|
| Standard Deviations | −4σ | −3σ | −2σ | −1σ | 0 | +1σ | +2σ | +3σ | +4σ |
| Cumulative Percentages | | 0.1% | 2.3% | 15.9% | 50% | 84.1% | 97.7% | 99.9% | |
| Percentiles | | 1 | 5 | 10 20 30 40 50 60 70 80 90 95 | 99 | |
| Z scores | −4.0 | −3.0 | −2.0 | −1.0 | 0 | +1.0 | +2.0 | +3.0 | +4.0 |
| T scores | | 20 | 30 | 40 | 50 | 60 | 70 | 80 | |
| Standard Nine (Stanines) | | 1 | 2 | 3 | 4 | 5 | 6 | 7 | 8 | 9 | |
| Percentage in Stanine | | 4% | 7% | 12% | 17% | 20% | 17% | 12% | 7% | 4% | |

**Arousal Ranges Within the Normal Distribution Curve**

| Underarousal: ADHD | Low arousal: Bored and restless | Optimal arousal: Between 1 above and below the mean that produces optimal performance Average learners | High arousal: Anxiety | Overarousal: Autism spectrum disorders |
|---|---|---|---|---|

*Source:* Jeremy Kemp.

but it can be assessed through psychophysiological measures, such as heart rate and skin conductance, and can be inferred from the amount of stimulation in the setting or the anxiety that the child communicates.

Eysenck suggested that introverts have high physiological arousal (to the right of the mean) and extroverts are underaroused (represented by the left extreme in Figure 1.4). Extreme levels of arousal could be placed at the opposite ends of this distribution (see Zentall & Zentall, 1983). When individuals are underaroused, they are more likely to feel bored and to seek out social interactions, excitement, stimulation, challenge, and change (e.g., ADHD). In general, underaroused children will approach, generate, or move closer to stimulation to increase their level of arousal and improve their own performance. In contrast, children who are overaroused or stressed will avoid change and prefer quiet, calm, nonstimulating settings and familiar people. Here students with autism spectrum disorder (ASD) are described at the far right end of this normal distribution and students with anxiety disorder are shown in the high average range.

**Arousal:** Physiological activation of the child, which has trait qualities (inborn individual differences) and state qualities that depend on setting conditions (e.g., number of people in a setting).

## States

Interacting with traits are task and setting variables, or **states.** The importance of states is that even average learners can be placed under conditions (states) that are too boring or too stressful. Thus, deviations from optimal arousal can occur for all learners. The **Yerkes-Dodson law** proposes that a certain level of arousal is needed for optimal performance. Arousal depends not only on a child's traits but also on type of task. Rote or repetitive practice tasks reduce arousal, whereas difficult tasks increase arousal. Thus, difficult tasks may require lower arousal, and repetitive tasks requiring persistence are performed better with higher arousal or activation. For example, an intellectually demanding task (e.g., composing stories) produces a higher state of arousal in an individual than does a less demanding task. Perhaps for this reason, an intellectually demanding task is performed better when the individual is less aroused (more relaxed) prior to beginning that difficult task. In contrast, a task requiring single-minded persistence with a simple response (e.g., long handwriting exercises) produces a lower state of arousal and is better performed at a higher state of arousal (e.g., with high-energy music).

**Yerkes-Dodson law:** Developed by psychologists Robert M. Yerkes and John D. Dodson (1908), this law posits that performance improves with increased alertness (arousal), but only up to a certain level, and when arousal is too high, performance decreases.

In applying this law to children with disabilities, one needs to consider not just the type of task but also the type of child. That is, we would expect simple, familiar, or boring tasks requiring persistence to be performed better by children with higher initial trait arousal (e.g., anxiety, autism) than by children with lower trait arousal (ADHD). Furthermore, if we want students with ADHD to perform optimally, we should *not* give them long tasks that are uninteresting, because it is more difficult for them to maintain sufficient arousal on and attention to these tasks.

When children are not optimally aroused to perform well on specific tasks, they will attempt to change their level of stimulation (arousal) through behavior.

**State:** Behavior, thinking, or mood that is temporary and depends on the conditions within the setting, such as time, task, persons, and amount of light or noise.

**Functional analysis or functional assessment (FA):** Assessment of a child's behavior in specific settings, tasks, or with specific persons produces a better understanding of how the child attempts to adapt his or her behavior to the immediately surrounding conditions.

Children who need additional stimulation and are underaroused will seek change and increase their level of variable activity, whereas children who are overaroused will avoid tasks and attempt to self-calm through repeated activities or ritualistic behavior. (Of course, if the child has already escaped from the task or is without a task, he or she may seek activities to replace lost task stimulation.)

Because we cannot measure a child's current physiological state of arousal on a specific task, we can only draw conclusions about what the student appears to need by observing and recording behavior and by describing current tasks and settings as performed in a **functional analysis.**

## Alternate Assessments of Traits

A number of tests and rating scales have been developed to assess traits. These can be classified into (a) semistructured interviews, (b) questionnaires or rating scales (using educators, peers, parents, or guardians as raters), and (c) tests (e.g., physiological measurements, such as heart rate, or achievement tests in reading, math, spelling). Scores on achievement tests are widely recognized within the field and are often compared with IQ scores. Children who achieve lower than they *should* achieve in reading (i.e., lower than their grade level or IQ would suggest), for example, may be labeled reading disabled (RD) or at risk for RD. However, these norm-based assessments are usually supplemented with assessments of how students respond immediately within various settings and to interventions, which are described in Section II.

### CHAPTER SUMMARY

- The legal requirements that form the basis of disability definitions are written into two federal laws: IDEA and Section 504 of the Vocational Rehabilitation Act. Both laws require placement of a child with disabilities in the least restrictive environment with the use of supplementary aids and services, and both laws provide parents and students with grievance procedures and the rights to review records, to participate in hearings and be represented by counsel, and to due process at the local level.

- IDEA is the main federal law for special education that provides funding for the education of disabled youth, 3–21 years of age, and that mandates schools to find, evaluate, and provide a free, appropriate program of education for any child with a disability. Appropriate education is translated to a written document, the IEP, which is a legal contract that spells out the planned accommodations and interventions. Placement decisions are also written into the IEP as part of individualized goals.

- Section 504 is an umbrella law initially written for students needing physical access and later modified to guarantee access to the content of instructional programs.

- The debate that surrounds the process of disability labeling includes issues of (a) behavior at one age being developmentally appropriate but at another age being atypical; (b) dysfunction that appears in some settings but not others; (c) acceptance of labeling, especially of the "invisible disabilities," whose dysfunction is less immediately apparent; and (d) interpretations of the laws, which change nationally over time and from state to state.

- Categories of exceptionality are based on IDEA, with further information provided by *DSM-IV-TR*'s medical/psychological system of classification. Differences or significant deviations from the norm form the basis of individual categories of exceptionality.

- The areas of deviation can be described as traits related to (a) sensory input (e.g., seeing, hearing, touching, tasting), (b) learning processes (e.g., intelligence, memory, perception, attention), and (c) personality (e.g., introversion/extroversion and ease of adaptation to change or novelty). These are often described as differences in temperament, which are related to structural or chemical differences in the brain. One inborn temperament difference found at extremes in children with disabilities is arousal, or physiological activation of the brain. This construct is an important one for understanding children with externalizing and internalizing behavior.

- In addition to inborn child traits, temporary states, which include responses to tasks and settings, must be taken into account. It is these setting variables that help us understand an individual child within a specific school setting, as discussed in Chapter 2.

## CHAPTER QUESTIONS

1. How are states and traits different?

2. Reducing the anxiety or stress on children may be particularly important for which types of tasks?

## TRUE/FALSE

1. If a person can do a task with an accommodation, then "disability" is not being used as an excuse.

2. Traits are habitual patterns of behavior that are associated with personality characteristics.

3. Interventions are changes in the tasks or settings that the teacher makes to improve student responding.

4. The language of laws changes over time.

5. The expression of mild exceptionalities changes as situations and tasks change.

6. Reading words (e.g., *pat* and *sat*) aloud to a student and asking if the words are the same or different is a way of assessing auditory perception.

7. When a teacher asks a student to give the meanings of the vocabulary words that he or she pronounces, this teacher is testing auditory comprehension.

8. Drawing one figure on the board and three similar figures below and asking a student to point to the one below that is just like the one on top is a way of assessing visual memory.

9. Asking a child to explain *why* the events occurred in a story just read is a way of assessing memory.

## SHORT ANSWER

1. "Reading" faces, gestures, and tones of voice is called _____.

2a. The prefix meaning "without"

2b. The prefix meaning "poor ability"

3. Working directly on weak areas is _____.

4. Using stronger skills to help with deficits is _____.

5. The ability to hold information in mind and recombine that information is called _____.

6. The acronym for attentional and hyperactive disabilities

7. Cause of disability

8. The medical manual of diagnosis

9. Anxiety, depression, shyness, and the like are called what kind of disorders?

10. The ability to judge similarities and differences, to match them with other similar objects, and to form understandable units

11. The funding law in special education

# Chapter 2

## Informal Analysis of the Characteristic Behavior of Individual Students

We turn now to the analysis of the actual behavior of the children we observe. This can be thought of as a cross-disability or noncategorical approach, because it goes beyond the label to the individual. It is important because labels or categories given to specific children can be inaccurate, may involve multiple categories, or may not yet have been determined. Furthermore, this analysis will provide a deeper understanding of a child's individualistic expression of disability within specific settings. Thus, this chapter complements the standardized test scores and normative comparisons discussed in Chapter 1.

There are two general methods related to the assessment of individuals. The first method is **response to intervention (RTI).** This approach examines a child's actual response to interventions that have been scientifically tested and found to be effective for most children; these interventions and accommodations are called evidence-based (or empirically based) practices (**EBP**s). RTI changes the definition of LD to those students who do not respond to EBPs and thus need more intense interventions; this places more responsibility on educators to provide EBPs before labeling children. The second method, often called an ABC analysis, examines the child's behavior (B) (e.g., the child fell off his chair) in response to setting **antecedents** (A) (e.g., group oral reading) and to consequences (C) (e.g., "peers laughed"). After we have conducted an ABC analysis, we can hypothesize "why" the child might have used this behavior (e.g., to get peer attention/relatedness and/or to avoid reading failure in a social context). These are called the child's *payoffs* (purposes or goals), whether conscious or not. With this in mind, we can attempt to improve the child's reading, especially in a social context.

**Response to intervention (RTI):** An assessment of achievement (e.g., reading) as it changes over time as the result of intervention.

**EBP:** Empirically based practice (also known as evidence-based practice)—that is, scientifically tested practice that has demonstrated effectiveness.

**Antecedents:** What precedes a particular behavior (time, setting, task, and so on).

**Figure 2.1** Observations of a student, whose individual expression of disability changes as a function of setting, task, and type of intervention

## RESPONSES TO INTERVENTIONS

RTI is a relatively new concept introduced to revise the identification of LD in response to the 2004 reauthorization of IDEA. It is also termed the "eligibility procedure" (Fuchs, Fuchs, & Speece, 2002). The assumption underlying this change is that poor instruction in general education settings cannot be a reason for a diagnosis (20 U.S.C. Section 1414). Such a change in definition (primarily for LD) places responsibility for failure more centrally within the instructional context, even though skill deficits can still be attributed to within-child disabilities.

The RTI model proposes to identify relatively poor performance and a slow rate of learning compared with peers and relative to grade-level benchmark expectations (i.e., measured using annual normative assessments or curriculum assessments). For this reason RTI could also be considered a prevention model. Initially, a screen should be made of a whole class. If the whole class is performing poorly or at a slow rate, then a total-class intervention may first need to be employed. In other words, this model assumes that the child has had instructional opportunities in a general education setting that are optimal at a Tier I level.

- *Tier I* implements academic and behavioral accommodations in general education settings before children have experienced significant failure. At Tier I, the goal is to determine how the student performs in comparison to others of the same age, gender, culture, and intelligence, as well as to identify the specific content that the child knows and does not know. Tier I addresses the needs of approximately 80% of students (Hawken, Vincent, & Schumann, 2008). However, if the child continues to perform worse than others and is considered at risk, he or she can be exposed to an additional more intense level of evidence-based interventions at the Tier II level.
- *Tier II* addresses the needs of 15% of students needing interventions, which are typically implemented in small groups (Hawken et al., 2008) for those at-risk students who are not responding to Tier I interventions.
- *Tier III* addresses the needs of 5% of students needing interventions (Hawken et al., 2008) for those students who do not show a significant response at Tier II. At this level individualized instruction is provided and a formal diagnosis and special education services are considered. That is, some schools consider special education a Tier III intervention.

Recent memos by the federal government require that U.S. states use RTI as only part of the criteria for determining whether a student has a learning disability (LD). In other words, the results of an RTI process constitute one component of the information reviewed in the required evaluation of possible disability status and cannot be the entire process or replace the need for a comprehensive evaluation. This caution is essential in the diagnosis of LD, the definition of which *excludes* ID and therefore requires normative assessments of intelligence. Normative assessments are also important for students with co-occurring giftedness (GT) or ADHD, who can perform at grade-level benchmarks under some conditions and thus need an assessment of cognitive potential relative to actual performance (Crepeau-Hobson & Bianco, 2010).

The full text of this assessment and applications is presented in most assessment and methods courses; what is important to know for purposes of this discussion is that the RTI model is intended to conserve special education resources by using a steplike progression of tiers. Progression up through tiers is determined through close monitoring of a student's degree of responsiveness to interventions. However, degree of responsiveness is not always clear and is typically not operationalized through a definition of a specific percentage of improvement. Some school districts do not specify degree of improvement but instead implement tier levels depending on how far behind a child scores in grade levels or in achievement test percentiles (i.e., in degree of impairment without the notion of degree of response). The principles of RTI are even less easily applied to social behavior than they are to academic behavior, primarily because behavioral standards are defined by the values of the community, school, and teacher and are not based on national standards or benchmarks of performance. Some schools use tardiness/attendance, school performance, and office disciplinary referrals as indicators of significant problems, with two to five such items indicating the need for Tier II interventions and six or more requiring Tier III (Hawken et al., 2008). Office referrals, however, could suggest as much about the incompatibility of the teacher-student relationship as about the child.

These difficulties in implementing a stepwise progression make the principles of **Universal Design for Learning** (**UDL**; see IDEA 2004 reauthorization) even more critical in Tier I accommodations (i.e., to offset the need for intervening with the large number of students who are placed in general education **inclusion classes**). Specific applications of UDL can be found under the subheadings "Implications for Accommodations in General Education Settings: Tier I" within the "Disability in the Classroom" sections that appear at the end-of-chapter discussions of most exceptionalities in Chapters 3–15. At the most general level, a preliminary step in UDL can be to provide "multiples": (a) multiple methods of *presenting content* within a curriculum that is both reasonable and challenging (e.g., graphics/videos/digital-input media); (b) multiple ways of *accepting responses* to demonstrate understanding that reduce language, cognitive processing, and motor barriers; and (c) multiple ways of *engaging students* with that content and with others (McGuire, Scott, & Shaw, 2006). UDL is concerned with the design of instructional materials, which should allow all children to access and respond to the curriculum. Thus, to

**UDL:** Universal Design for Learning, a philosophy related to designing and delivering products and services within a classroom that are usable by people with the widest range of capabilities. UDL should be in place before any student enters the classroom (Beard et al., 2007).

**Inclusion classes:** Classrooms in general education that include students who have disabilities or who are at risk for disabilities.

provide Tier I accommodations, educators must present tasks, accept responses, and engage students in learning activities in a variety of ways that take into consideration students who are at risk for disabilities. UDL should reduce some educators' overreliance on whole-class lecture, textbook reading materials, and independent workbook written assignments and tests.

**Task analysis:** The breaking down of a task (e.g., how to make a peanut butter-and-jelly sandwich) into its component parts, typically as they can be arranged sequentially, to achieve the overall task.

To accomplish the principles of UDL at a more specific level, an educator needs to understand the nature of the task and the types of abilities/disabilities that a child can bring to a task. For example, for the task of long division, the skills needed are (a) division, multiplication, and subtraction; (b) visual-motor skills for aligning and writing numbers; and (c) the ability to sequence the steps in task (e.g., for in a long division calculation). Finally, these task requirements must be aligned with the skills of the child (e.g., working memory, fine motor responses). Matching a child's skills to task components can be accomplished through a **task analysis** of subject areas, task-responding requirements (vocal, gesture, writing), task input provided (verbal or visual), and task learning process requirements (i.e., attention, perception, memory, and intelligence), as illustrated in Figure 2.2 and described in greater detail below.

*Subject areas.* The familiar academic subject areas of reading, math, social studies, writing, and science are not truly distinct. For example, math problem solving, social studies, and science all require reading; math and science both require an understanding of visual concepts and symbols.

**Figure 2.2**   Input/Processing/Output

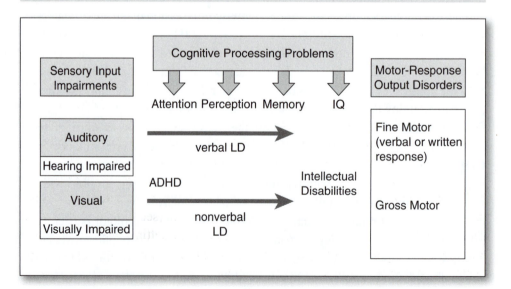

*Child inborn trait differences in relation to task requirements: Sensory input.* Infants "mouth" objects to learn about their environments. School-aged students use visual or auditory sensory input (see the left side of Figure 2.1). Students with impairments in the sensory area of hearing are hearing impaired (HI) and those with impairments of vision are visually impaired (VI). Even for children with mild losses of hearing, verbal instruction is usually faster and more variable in tone, pitch, and so on, and does not stay in place but fades as the speaker moves on to new content. Thus, the learner has little ability to stop and reexamine what has been presented. In contrast, a student can reexamine visual input, as long as it is not moving or rapidly being replaced with new images; this reanalysis mainly affects the speed of responding to visual stimuli. Although educators typically assume adequate functioning at the sensory level, many children have undetected mild to moderate sensory deficits, and some children do not use the hearing aids or glasses that they have (or they may have lost them and cannot afford replacements).

*Learning processes.* If children have difficulties in receiving sensory information, they will find it difficult to learn using the higher-level learning processes (see the middle section of Figure 2.1) of selectively attending, perceiving, remembering, or problem solving. In other words, sensory deficits will most certainly degrade academic performance that requires higher-level remembering and problem solving. More often there are cognitive process deficits that are not explained by sensory deficits. These learning processes (e.g., attention, perception, memory, intelligence), described more fully in Chapter 1, define a number of areas of exceptionality, as is depicted in Figure 2.1. That is, ADHD is defined by attentional disorders, LD is primarily accompanied by perceptual and memory problems (e.g., verbal LD by auditory perceptual and memory problems), and ID is defined primarily by problems in intellect and the application of problem solving to adaptive behavior.

*Response output requirements.* The last set of requirements involves motor responding (e.g., speaking, writing, moving, gesturing), which may be defined as response output, as on the right-hand side of Figure 2.1. Most of these responses involve fine motor movements of the hand, but some involve planning fine motor responses of the mouth and of large muscles (DCD, or developmental coordination disorder). For example, tasks in the subject areas of reading and social studies often involve extended writing. Such response requirements are difficult for children with visual-motor and coordination difficulties or for children with little control over their own motor responses (see Chapter 15). Subject areas also tend to rely on specific instructional formatting with set response requirements (e.g., worksheets, labs, computer practice, group instruction), which may alter the child's ability to respond.

An analysis of these input/process/output variables makes it clear how important it is to provide multiple methods of instruction for an inclusion classroom. Changes in the setting or task that the teacher makes to produce improved responding are called *accommodations*. When children respond positively to the accommodations provided, this does not mean that the disability at-risk factors were never present. Most mild disabilities are situational and respond positively to optimal conditions. The child is not "cured" and will revert back to difficult behavior and poor performance in nonoptimal settings and tasks. Even with accommodations, the child may still experience academic or social failure, at which time an additional individual analysis of the child's behavior is often needed for Tier II interventions.

In the selection of interventions at this level, EBPs are the standard. These are defined as practices that have produced *statistically significant* improvements in student outcomes, such as achievement or behavior. However, the concept of statistical significance has changed, since significance can almost always be found when an intervention study has a large number of participants and uses accurate measures (Harrison, Thompson, & Vannest, 2009). Thus, the field now considers the *educational significance* of a finding—asking whether such an outcome is likely for individual students (i.e., that controls for the number of participants in the study). If an intervention study shows statistical as well as educational significance, and the findings have been demonstrated repeatedly (i.e., have been replicated), the intervention is likely to be an EBP.

## FUNCTIONAL ANALYSIS OF ANTECEDENTS, BEHAVIOR, CONSEQUENCES, AND PAYOFFS

The second individualized method of analysis is the ABC analysis, which can be used to understand why some children behave or perform poorly (dysfunctionally) within specific settings. Most of us will show "abnormal" responding when we are placed in "abnormal" settings or presented with difficult circumstances. For example, Taylor, whose father died less than a year ago, has been attending a new preschool. Under these conditions, Taylor exhibited the following behavior:

1. Pushed a girl and made her cry because she touched his snack

2. Protected his painting from other kids and put it into a box carefully

3. Grabbed a book from a boy's hand and said, "It's my book!"

4. Yelled at a boy who got on Taylor's bicycle and tried to get the boy off the bike

5. Argued with another boy who wanted to get on his bike

For these events, Taylor's "abnormal" responding may have been quite normal, given the loss of his father, as reported by the observer:

> This is a huge emotional cost to a little boy. I still can remember his face when he saw other children's fathers taking their children home. From the data you can see that he is very concerned about his own things—nothing can be touched or used by others. Perhaps it's because he just lost one of the most precious persons in his life and he cannot afford further loss.

Beyond such reactions to abnormal circumstances, children with exceptionalities are more sensitive to environmental conditions, such as settings that are too loud or crowded; new or unpredictable social experiences; difficult tasks; possible loss, pain, or failure; requirements to speak or write; repetitive or nonchallenging tasks; light that is too bright or too dim; and instructions that are too rapid or too long. Task and setting conditions that most of us would find acceptable without a loss of functioning may cause a child with an exceptionality to appear to overreact; such a reaction can provide an educator with cues about the elements within the setting that need to be changed to produce optimal responding. A simple analysis requiring less time than most FAs (see Hawken et al., 2008) is presented below. This involves a brief discussion of antecedent settings and task requirements, an examination of behavior and consequences, and finally an assessment of possible behavioral goals (needs or payoffs, as was observed for Taylor, whose need was to avoid loss in his preschool setting). These are the constructs necessary to an understanding of the procedures of a functional analysis.

## Antecedents

*Settings analysis.* Settings are defined by the numbers and types of objects (e.g., resources) and persons within a spatial area. The spatial area can be further defined by the order (e.g., small predefined areas), colors and patterns, and the amount of change inherent to those physical objects, such as pictures versus windows (i.e., the more change, the more stimulation). The physical presence of adults and children within a setting can also contribute to the overall amount and change (or ordering) of stimulation. Some setting variables have been documented to produce adverse responding by specific groups of children, as shown in Table 2.1.

**Table 2.1**  Setting Conditions That Increase the Problem Behavior of Children With Specific Exceptionalities

| Exceptionality | Setting conditions |
| --- | --- |
| Aggression | These children may be more aggressive when conditions are crowded, noisy, and with few resources. |
| Social anxiety | These children may demonstrate considerable avoidance behavior in any social setting but especially in those that are unpredictable and where ongoing conversations are taking place (e.g., hallways). |
| Autism spectrum disorders | These children are likely to avoid loud noises, crowding, and lack of predictability. |
| Reading difficulties | These children may be more disruptive prior to and during reading time and find their reading tasks even more difficult with background conversations. |
| ADHD | These children may have greater difficulty in nonchanging, nonactive environments with overly familiar persons, especially as the year or the classroom period progresses over time. |
| Giftedness | These children may have greater difficulty in nonchallenging school contexts that focus on basic skills. |

## Procedures in a Functional Analysis

The educator must first observe the behavior and record positive and negative incidents within specific setting and task requirements. Here are several bits of interactive behavior (the child, the setting, and the task) that provide a glimpse into the child. This is a particularly good description of behavior because we *can see or hear the behavior* of the child:

- Jumped out of his chair, hopped on one foot, and shouted, "Ouch!"
- Cut through entire newspaper when he was supposed to cut out one picture
- Spun scissors around one finger, scissors flew off and landed on the desk
- Sat glue stick on end and tipped it over with finger (four times)
- Laid his head on the paraprofessional's arm when the paraprofessional was helping another student
- Asked what to do next

Usually behavior alone is insufficient to allow an educator to understand a child, but in this example most readers can readily understand what the child is attempting. In contrast, off-task behavior, aggression, and excessive verbal behavior, for example, are more likely to have a number of possible purposes. For example, children may talk a lot (a) to avoid handwriting (**dysgraphia**), (b) as a means to gain verbal/social stimulation (ADHD), or (c) as a **compensatory behavior** (NVLD). In other words, "Behavior is a message, not a diagnosis" (Silver, 2004, p. 19). This does not mean that the child uses behavior in a conscious way.

In another example the student's goals are only somewhat clear to the observer: "We have a student who sits where he can look out the window, but he just sits and stares and doesn't get his work done. It is only a problem at math time" (Zentall, 2006, p. 185). Is this a problem of the window distracting the child or the child avoiding the task? In other words, would moving this child to the front of the room eliminate the child's problem when the purpose of this child's behavior is to avoid math?

If we understand how behavior functions in that context for this child, we can teach the child to substitute behavior that will achieve the same function or purpose (e.g., replacement ways to get help when math is difficult). We can also change the task to produce more optimal responses by using accommodations that reduce task difficulty, increase active responding, and increase the relevance/interest of the math task, or we can implement interventions that teach math strategies. Thus, FA is a system of recording behavior with the objective of determining appropriate accommodations (changes of task and setting made by teachers) and interventions (changes of skills and behavior taught to children) (see Step 4 below).

**Dysgraphia:** Difficulty with the task of handwriting (see Section VI).

**Compensatory behavior:** Individuals may work around their weak areas by relying on their stronger areas of functioning. For example, difficulties understanding gestures, tones of voice, and facial expressions can be offset by stronger verbal skills.

**Table 2.2**   ABC Coding Criteria

| *Antecedents* | *Behavior Observed* | *Consequences* | *Payoffs* |
|---|---|---|---|
| *Settings* and types of *tasks* and *activities, persons,* instructional *groupings,* and when: *time* on task or during the day | Descriptions of observable behavior without interpretations | How others respond to the behavior or what happens as a result of the behavior | To what purpose— get or avoid |

The elements of an ABC analysis are the identification of behavior, antecedents, consequences and payoffs (see Table 2.2), which can be accomplished through the following four simple steps:

*Step 1: Create a log of positive and "negative" behavioral incidents.* Accurately describe behavior, settings, and tasks while avoiding interpretations and labels such as "acts up," "impulsive," or "lazy" and inferred states (e.g., being anxious, angry). See the behavioral log in the case study of Jason at the end of this chapter.

*Step 2: Analyze the log* by using the word-processing functions of cutting and pasting to place all the behavioral incidents that were initially recorded chronologically into an "antecedent behavior consequence/payoff table" (ABC-P)—some tables of this type are organized with behavior first (BAC-P), because that is what the teacher notices first. See the ABC-P for the case study of Elliot at the end of Chapter 5. Note that some teachers record the behavior directly in an ABC-P table to avoid this cutting-and-pasting task.

*Payoffs* are our best guesses about the goals/purposes of the child's behavior (i.e., "the message"). This is the greatest challenge and where interpretation comes into play. It is based on the assumption that all behavior has a purpose, regardless of whether that behavior looks rational to us. The child is attempting to get a need met or avoid a possible undesirable outcome. The need or payoff is usually reasonable, but perhaps the child's way of meeting the need is inappropriate. Children often have more than one payoff for a specific behavior. For example, many children attempt to get social attention or establish relatedness with others, but they go about getting this attention differently—through showing us their achievements (getting competence), through humor (getting fun stimulation), or through making others angry (getting emotional social stimulation). In these examples, *getting attention does not tell us as much as how the child attempts to get attention.* This is important because teachers usually have difficulty seeing beyond the "getting attention" payoff. So look deeper and record the *way* the child is getting attention as the higher-order payoff. Furthermore, many payoffs are two sides of the same coin. That is, a child may be attempting to get stimulation while also avoiding boredom (e.g., when performing repetitive, nonchallenging worksheets). (The above information, references, and Table 2.3 are updated and adapted from Zentall, 2006, pp. 65–66.)

*Step 3: Summarize the data* by using an Excel graph or by listing percentages. In an Excel graph, *get payoffs* can be entered as positive values (e.g., 5) and *avoid payoffs* as negative values (e.g., –5). The result will display get payoffs to the right of the center and negative avoid values to the left of center, as illustrated in Figure 2.2.

*Step 4: Select at least two goals that address the child's frequently occurring payoffs* (in the example in Figure 2.3, the high-frequency payoff is to avoid work). Remember that it is the payoffs that must be targeted, *not* the behavior! If we address the payoffs, the behavior should change on its own and for a longer time period, since the child is now getting more of what he or she needs. In other words, the first goal should be to involve the teacher in changing the tasks or setting conditions to *address the high-frequency payoffs* (e.g., in the above case, to increase the fun or challenge or to decrease the difficulty of the task to decrease the work-avoidance payoff) or provide accommodations, such as peer tutoring, since this child attempts to get social stimulation. A second goal would be to design an intervention that identifies replacement behavior for the child to learn that involves a more appropriate way to avoid the task or get help (i.e., teach the child how to ask questions). Interventions that attempt to change child behavior are often more difficult to implement than accommodations that the teacher can immediately make to the setting or task.

**Table 2.3**   Payoffs (Child Goals) Coding Criteria

| Get payoffs | Avoid payoffs (some of which may be related to future possible outcomes) |
| --- | --- |
| **Children attempt to get competence (mastery or achievement) by** Talking about or demonstrating accomplishments or interests in reading, projects, after-school clubs, and the like. Asking for help or making statements such as "I don't get this." Alternatively, any statement of "I know this. . . ." Creating or collecting objects, stories, or records of accomplishments. Reading by subvocalizing (whispering or reading out loud) to help them perform optimally. | **Children attempt to avoid possible social punishment or failure from specific** Subject areas (e.g., math). Response requirements (e.g., handwriting, talking). Worksheets, listening, group contexts. |
| **Children attempt to get relatedness from** Peer attention or interactions. Adult attention, proximity, or interactions. | **Children attempt to avoid social experiences with** Peers. Teacher attention or possible reprimands (e.g., by blaming others, making excuses, lying). |
| **Children attempt to get self-determination or control by** Controlling (correcting, choosing, bossing, leading). Continuing an activity or task that is preferred. Maintaining independent action, opinion, or feelings (arguing, debating). | **Children attempt to avoid possible lack of control or predictability by** Preferring familiar settings and resisting new social situations (e.g., during transitions at the beginning and ending of class). Resisting specific tasks (e.g., difficult, independent, nonpreferred tasks). |

*(Continued)*

**Table 2.3** (Continued)

| Get payoffs | Avoid payoffs (some of which may be related to future possible outcomes) |
|---|---|
| **Children attempt to get different types of stimulation:**<br><br>Emotional stimulation (intense or negative social reactions, e.g., shock, anger, disgust).<br><br>Activity or kinesthetic stimulation (physical contact).<br><br>Sensory and tangible stimulation (sights, objects, tastes/food, smells, sounds).<br><br>Change (fun, excitement, play, risks, unusual projects or activities).<br><br>Cognitive stimulation (thinking, problem solving, daydreaming, creating). | **Children attempt to avoid boredom by**<br><br>Avoiding routine or basic tasks (e.g., computations, phonics workbook activities, handwriting)<br><br>Avoiding repetitive activities such as morning calendar time |

*Source:* Zentall, S. S. (2006). Adapted from p. 65–66.

**Figure 2.3**   Writing Activity Bar Graph

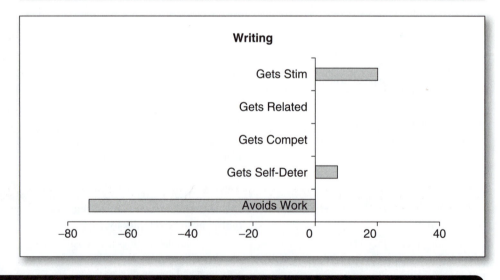

# CHAPTER SUMMARY

- Chapter 1 provided a brief overview of the federal legal requirements that form the cultural basis of disability categories. Deviation from average (norms) provides a way to understand performance and behavior. To understand individual students so that we can program for intervention, we use the noncategorical approach described in this chapter, observing the responses of each child to tasks/settings and to increasingly intense interventions. Thus, this chapter has presented discussion of the *analysis of individual children* within a local context (specific settings and tasks). The methods described are not used to make comparisons among different children; rather, they are used to make comparisons of one child in several settings or under different task conditions. There are essentially two such methods: RTI and FA.

- RTI involves assessing the *effects of interventions on the performance and behavior* of children. These interventions increase in intensity and are provided to determine whether additional special education services may be needed. RTI does not replace the need for a comprehensive evaluation; rather, it is considered one component of the information reviewed in the required evaluation process.

- FA is typically applied to provide a better *understanding of individual children's behavior* in specific settings and with tasks that occasion disruptive behavior and poor performance. This is often considered a Tier II strategy. Defining antecedents includes noting the (a) social conditions (persons, resources available, and familiarity/predictability of the setting); (b) task variables (subject area, visual or auditory modality input); (c) task responses required; and (d) learning processes (attention, perception, memory, problem solving) that may be required.

- In this FA process, the procedural steps in understanding the behavioral message are to observe the behavior and informally record appropriate and inappropriate behavior, the task or setting conditions that came before these responses (antecedents), and what followed these responses from the environment (consequences, i.e., what did the child get or avoid in that setting). With these elements in mind, the educator can hypothesize what the probable goals of the child might be in terms of getting or avoiding social relatedness, competence, control, or stimulation (payoffs)

## CHAPTER QUESTIONS

*Description 1.* From a log—the child exhibited the following behavior:

- Jumped out of his chair, hopped on one foot, and shouted "Ouch!"
- Cut through entire newspaper when he was supposed to cut out one picture
- Spun scissors around one finger, scissors flew off and landed on the desk
- Sat glue stick on end and tipped it over with finger (four times)
- Laid his head on the paraprofessional's arm when the paraprofessional was helping another student

- Asked what to do next
  1. How would you describe the "problem behavior" of this child?
  2. Can you tell which specific tasks or instructions elicit problem behavior in this child?
  3. Can you tell whether the child is attempting to get something or avoid something?
  4. What are the possible exceptionalities of this child?

*Description 2.* The student was directed to color with the pink crayon because pink was the "color of the day." She did not want to use a pink crayon; she wanted to use red. She was extremely persistent in using the red crayon, and the paraprofessional had a difficult time getting her to understand the directions. The child threw herself on the floor and had to be persuaded to get back up to the table and continue working. When she got back up to the table, she deliberately broke her pink crayon in half.

1. How would you describe the "problem behavior" of this child?
2. Can you tell which specific tasks or instructions elicit problem behavior in this child?
3. Can you tell whether the child is attempting to get something or avoid something?

## Other Chapter Questions

1. Which types of children do you think would be easier to work with—those who attempt to get things (competence, stimulation, and so on) or those who are attempting to avoid (possible failure, social interactions, and the like), and why?

2. If a child becomes verbally aggressive when you ask him to start his math, how are his payoffs different from those of a child who becomes verbally aggressive on the playground when he is attempting to enter an ongoing game?

3. Why is it important to target children's payoffs rather than their behavior?

### TRUE/FALSE

1. A child with a high frequency of needs to get relatedness could perform well in peer tutoring.

2. A child with a high frequency of needs for self-determination would perform well if told exactly how and when to do a task.

3. A child with a high frequency of avoidance types of behavior would respond well to punishment.

4. A child with a high frequency of needs to avoid boredom would respond well to unusual approaches to tasks.

5. Impulsivity is an observable action.

6. RTI focuses intervention on inherited behavioral characteristics.

7. UDL is considered a Tier II intervention strategy

8. Characteristics of both the child and the task interact to produce optimal or less-than-optimal performance.

9. LD is typically accompanied by intellectual deficits.

10. Setting variables are called antecedents.

## PROBLEM-BASED CASE APPLICATIONS AND QUESTIONS

### CASE STUDY 2.1: JASON

*"Talk to the hand, 'cause the face ain't listening."*
(adapted from a report submitted by Jodi Hampton)

*Background.* Jason is a 13-year-old boy in sixth grade at K. Middle School. He was diagnosed with an emotional disability 3 years ago. Jason has a history of depression, verbal and physical aggression, low self-esteem, difficulty making friends, and non-compliance. He also has difficulty hearing. Some background information reveals that Jason was born to two teenage parents, with no complications during the pregnancy. Jason's parents are highly supportive and work closely with the school to follow through on disciplinary actions as well as reinforcement. Jason exhibited demanding, outgoing, and high-energy levels of behavior as an infant and toddler. He was diagnosed with ADHD 6 years ago. He has a history of anger, temper loss, suicide attempts, and defiant behavior at home, as well as at school. Currently, Jason spends half of the school day at the Academic Center and the other half at K. School. Reports show that Jason works very well at the Academic Center with mainly one-on-one individualized attention. When he is at K. School, he works best with computers. Jason shows consistent outbursts in unstructured settings and thrives in one-on-one situations, where he exhibits a friendly, courteous, and eager-to-learn attitude.

*Behavioral Log*

*January 26 (15 minutes of discussion lecture)*

- Jason was observed in his life skills class, where two special education teachers team teach. While the class was waiting for the bell to ring, Jason was constantly yelling out loud. The other students were talking to each other, but none were as loud as Jason. The teacher and peers ignored the volume of Jason's voice.

- When the bell rang, Jason was told to please get to his seat. He was sitting at a table in the middle of the classroom. He yelled, "Too bad! This is my seat now, and I'm going to sit where I want." The teacher replied that he had two choices of where to sit, one being his assigned seat and the second being the time-out room.

- Teacher turned back to the discussion to begin instruction and to give Jason a chance to think about his choices. The class was discussing car insurance. Jason yelled out (still in wrong seat) three times that he doesn't even have car insurance. This was ignored. Teacher then stated that girls' car insurance is cheaper than insurance for boys, and Jason yelled out that this is not fair.

- Teacher then turned to Jason and gave him his two choices of where to sit again. Jason yelled, "Bull crap, I have already yelled 'Bite me' to my first-hour class so I don't have to do anything." But Jason did walk over to his assigned seat. He kicked his chair and was told that he had now "lost" his chair for that action, so he was not able to sit, he had to stand. He kicked the chair again and threw his books on the floor. He yelled, "I don't give a darn about this chair. Don't even make me yell because they will hear me clear across the building." This was ignored.

- Teacher then started talking about checks and paying bills. The class was doing a role-play unit on jobs, where they had to work, get paid, and pay bills. As the other teacher began talking, Jason sang out loudly, "Nah, nah, nah" as she was talking. He then yelled that he had already paid his bill for misbehaving when he got charged $45 for misbehaving at the Academic Center. (He goes to the Academic Center every day in the mornings.) He then stated that he was not paying any more. He then proceeded to put his necklace over his mouth and said to the class, "Hey everyone, look, I have a mustache!" Everyone ignored him. During the rest of this particular discussion, Jason yelled out seven more times that he had already paid his bills, and then mocked what the teacher was saying under his breath.

- Both teachers told me that when they began independent seatwork, not even 10 minutes later, Jason sat down in his own seat and began quietly working.

### *January 29 (15 minutes discussion)*

- When the bell rang to begin class, Jason was in his assigned seat. Only one teacher was in the room. Teacher yelled for everyone to sit down, and Jason finished her sentence with a "and Shut Up!" He was told that that isn't a nice way to say that, and maybe next time it would be more appropriate to say "be quiet." The class was supposed to go to the computer lab today, but we had a two-hour delay, and there wouldn't have been enough time. So they had a discussion on computers. During this discussion, Jason put down another student and said he was lying and that that student always lied. Someone else yelled out that Jason is the one that always lies. Jason and the teachers ignored this interaction. Two other students kept yelling out negative comments toward Jason, and he ignored these. Jason was very quiet during this conversation, and kept rubbing his arm. He contributed a little to the conversation here and there, but he mainly focused on his arm. I later found out from another teacher that he had written on his arm and was trying to get it off before his mom saw it.

- After about five minutes, he stopped playing with his arm and began singing out a rap song quite loudly. This was ignored. Teacher was telling another student to look up the word *ethics* in the dictionary. Jason yelled out that this student can't even spell his own name. Teacher told Jason that it is not nice to put others down. Jason asked the entire class why anyone wants to talk about ethics when they can talk about women.

- At this time, the second teacher came into the classroom and called Jason out. Jason got defensive right away because he knew it was because of something he did earlier that day. He began yelling out that there was no way he was going out to the hallway. He kept repeating, "Talk to the hand, 'cause the face ain't listening." He screamed that he didn't want to go out in the hallway and began to get verbally aggressive. Eventually, he got up and went to the hallway by himself, while yelling.

### *January 29 (7th period, movie)*

- The class happened to be watching a movie about animals, so I also used this time to interview Mrs. B. about Jason. She said that this was an all-around bad day for Jason. He was almost involved in a fight when he first came to school, then he yelled, "Bite me" in 5th period and got sent to the office. He received five noon detentions within one hour of being at school. Mrs. B. also told me that he has a hearing loss in one ear, which she believes may contribute a little to his loudness, but overall, he knows when he is raising his voice. She said that in 7th period he loves doing well and rarely is a behavior problem.

### January 30 (6th period, end of day)

- Jason was disruptive as soon as he came into the classroom. He was obviously not in a good mood. Within 5 minutes, he called someone a name and got sent to the time-out room. He spent his entire time in the time-out room yelling, singing rap songs, and pounding on the glass window and door.
- Eventually, he came out because his mom happened to call to see how he was doing, so he got to talk on the phone with her. He took the phone and yelled into it without putting his ear on the receiver that he hated school, that it sucked, and that he is going to kill himself, and then he began singing "La, la, la" into the phone.
- His mother came to school to pick him up. Jason and the class were supposed to go to the computer lab today, and he really enjoys this activity, so when he was put into time-out and knew that he wasn't going to the computer lab, he didn't have any reason to cool down.

### January 31 (7th period, computer class)

- Jason was working on the computer. He was totally involved with what he was doing, and didn't talk out at all. He raised his hand, and waited to be called on. When Mr. H. called on him, he very appropriately asked about when he could make up the rest of his missed assignment. He also asked if he should go ahead and log off the computer or start another section. He was told to log off, and that he could come during any study time to finish his work. After he logged off, he got in line and talked at an appropriate volume, and very respectfully.

### January 31 (chalkboard game)

- Jason was playing a game with the class on the chalkboard. The two teachers reported that he was great the entire period. He was talking and laughing with the class.

### February 2

- Report from teacher: Jason came into class and called someone a name. He immediately got sent into the time-out room. He slammed the door to the time-out room, then kept opening and shutting the door while yelling out comments to the class and teacher. Within 5 minutes, he calmed down and came out to sit at his desk. He then stayed quiet and did his seatwork beautifully.

### February 3 (class discussion)

- Someone mentioned reading *Charlie and the Chocolate Factory,* and Jason then sang out the Oompa Loompa song. When it got to be Jason's turn, he said that he got ungrounded. He said also that he had on his lucky shirt that makes him stay out of trouble. The teacher smiled and asked him if she can buy some more of those shirts. He said that he already has more and he will wear them so that he can act better.

- Another student then made fun of Jason. He yelled out that he got all his work done today after another student said that they got their work done. He then said he got all checks this morning on his behavior card (good thing), and that two girls like him. The teacher then asked him if he wants people to like him. She reminded him that people look at the way others act, and that behavior is always remembered. So if he wants people to like him, he should act appropriately. He started punching his binder and laughing. Someone then made fun of him. Jason laughed and said that it doesn't matter when he gets made fun of—he just laughs along with them or ignores it.

- The teacher then asked the class why they thought she just made everyone go around and say something positive about the class. Jason said that it was because 90% of the average person's day is good while only 10% of their day is bad. Jason then said that wasn't true for him, and that his was about half-and-half.

- So, Mrs. B. asked him to go through every part of his day today, including bus ride and before school. She logged everything he said, and when they totaled it up together, it ended up that 90% of his day so far was good. He then stated that he hadn't gone home yet, and he knew that his brother would get on his nerves and he would have to beat him up. So Mrs. B. said that now is the time to think about a way to make his evening a good one. She asked him what he could do to avoid his brother. He said he would try. I had to leave at this point.

## Case Questions

Conduct steps 2–4 as described earlier in this chapter to address the following questions:

1: Describe the settings and task analysis involved in this log. Create two columns, with positive settings in one and negative settings in the other. How do the data collected affect your overall impression?

2: What traits does Jason have in the areas of: (a) sensory processes (e.g., seeing, hearing), (b) learning processes (e.g., intelligence, memory), and (c) personality? What is your evidence?

3: What payoffs does Jason desire?

4 (problem-based small-group assignment): Assuming that Jason is currently at a Tier II or III intervention level because of his diagnosis, and based on your understanding of his traits and responses to tasks/interventions, how would you monitor Jason's progress in these settings and what changes would you recommend for other subject areas?

# SECTION II

## Verbal and Nonverbal Learning Disabilities

LD is often described as an "invisible disability," since the children do not look disabled and typically respond normally. Within the context of such apparent normality and in otherwise smart children, it is the unexpectedness of their learning problems that makes them appear unwilling rather than less able. LD presents a fractured picture of abilities and disabilities that cannot be explained by lack of vision or hearing, low intelligence, or emotional disturbance, because these causes are disqualified through exclusionary clauses in the definition (also called "rule-outs").

LD is presented early in this text because LD represents the majority of children with disabilities, with 80% of these students experiencing language, reading, and/or spelling disabilities, and another 20% experiencing mathematical disabilities (Hay, Elias, Fielding-Barnsley, Homel, & Freiberg, 2007). Although spoken language disorders are typically categorized as communication (speech/language) disorders under IDEA, disorders of spoken language provide the developmental basis of written language problems, and thus they are presented early in this section on LD.

A comprehensive picture of this LD group involves two major divisions: verbal LD (VLD), discussed in Chapters 3 and 4, which can include spoken language as well as written language disabilities; and nonverbal LD (NVLD), addressed in Chapter 5, which also includes children with math disabilities (MLD). Research on the characteristics of these disabilities and the interventions used typically focus on the specific learning disabilities (SLD) of reading, spelling, math, and written language, as represented in Figure II.1.

The flow of this section begins with Chapter 3 and VLD—specifically the receptive language disorders of listening and the expressive language disorders of talking (but not speech disorders, which are presented in Chapter 15 as motor disorders); this section continues in Chapter 4 with written language disorders, which are often called the academic learning disabilities (e.g., reading, composition). Chapter 5 begins with math learning disabilities (MLD). Children with MLD can have difficulties in verbal learning, nonverbal learning, or both. Thus, Figure II.1 shows that math performance specifically involves the reading

**Figure II.1**  Learning Disabilities Subtypes

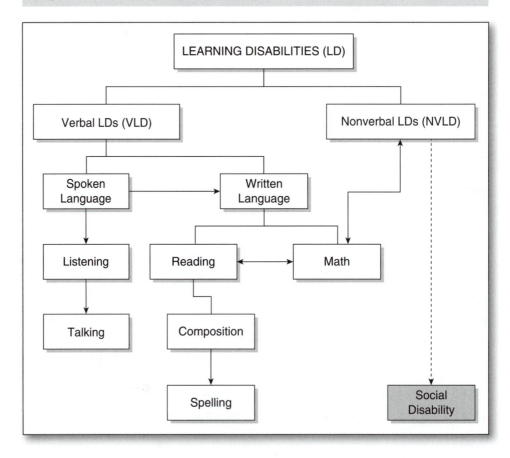

comprehension of word problems, as well as an understanding of nonverbal or visual information (understanding numerosity).

There is group of children with math problems associated with a failure to understand visual information, even though they can count, memorize facts, and generally understand the verbal information presented. This group is labeled NVLD. Students with NVLD often have math deficits that stem from failure to understand visual concepts (greater than, estimations, and so on) and mathematical symbols (+, −, ¾) that represent quantities, operations, or expressions. They also have difficulties interacting with other children, since they lack an understanding of social communication (e.g., gesture, tone of voice, emotion, facial expressions). Most children learn to understand social communication on their own and figure out relationships and rules that (a) are useful for their own behavior (e.g., self-help skills); (b) underlie actions (e.g., cause and effect, if-then relationships); and (c) can be expected from others (e.g., from younger versus older students versus adults). A child with an NVLD has difficulty making these connections and may have difficulty anticipating actions/reactions in social settings.

## LEARNING GOALS

In this section you will learn the following:

- The vocabulary associated with LD
- How learning disabilities are *formally defined* by IDEA in such a way as to be inclusive of all the subtypes and how this definition has changed to now include both (a) achievement that is below IQ expectancy and (b) unexpectedly low achievement in response to levels of empirically based intervention and accommodations
- The etiology and prevalence of each subtype and how age, culture, and gender alter LD
- How educators can *informally identify* these children through observations of their (a) behavior, (b) responses to social and communication settings, (c) responses to academic tasks, and (d) responses to motor and physical tasks
- The possible implications of understanding LD characteristics in the selection of treatments for these children (interventions and accommodations)
- How to apply the information you have learned to observations of case studies of real children who have spoken and written language disabilities

# Chapter 3

## Disorders of Spoken Language

Language develops in an individual from spoken language (listening and talking) to written language (reading, math, and composition). First you listen and then you talk, and first you learn to read about ideas and then you learn to write ideas. Language is first a receptive skill that involves taking in information; it then progresses to expressive language or conveying spoken and written information. Difficulties at the early developmental levels will affect later skills. For this reason, this chapter focuses on spoken language disorders of listening and talking.

Children with disorders in **receptive language** will have difficulty when the speakers they are listening to have different styles or accents, when they speak too rapidly, or when background noise is loud or includes conversations. In addition, they will have difficulty responding appropriately to instructions or directions, especially when instructions have multiple parts. When speaking, these students may have difficulty finding the right words, forming sentences, and organizing ideas to express their intended meanings. They may avoid talking in class. The difficulties here can be separated into three components of expressive language: form (e.g., grammar, **phonetics**), content (e.g., meaning or **semantics**), and everyday use (**pragmatics**) (Bloom & Lahey, 1978). Phonology is the study of how sounds are organized and used within and across languages. In contrast, phonics involves awareness or sensitivity to the sound structure within words (hearing individual beginning, middle, and ending sounds within words) and making discriminations between words and their sounds (rhyming or finding similar words), blending sounds, and separating sounds into segments. More generally, it concerns the ability to translate visual symbols into sounds in order to pronounce words. In addition to difficulties with phonics, students with LD show deficiencies in the

> **Receptive language skills:** Listening skills (in the area of spoken language) and reading and math skills (in the area of written language).

**Figure 3.1**   Spoken Language Disorders are demonstrated when Jeff attempts to communicate to Jenny

49

**Phonetics:** Phonetics deals with the physical production of sounds.

areas of pragmatics, which include the use of nonspecific referents and ambiguous messages, failure to take the perspectives of others, nonassertive responding, and difficulty asking questions or seeking clarification.

Overall, students with spoken communication impairments struggle to find ways to understand and be understood. It can be difficult to identify these children, because they are likely to hide their disabilities from others, especially when they are asked to perform in their weak areas—listening during classroom discussions, responding to verbal instructions, giving oral reports, reading aloud, writing compositions. In some cases, they disrupt to create a distraction from their disabilities; in other cases, they shy away from social interactions that could highlight their disabilities and cause social rejection. A good example of a verbal LD student is Jason, whose case study appears in Chapter 2. Jason said to his teacher, "Talk to the hand 'cause the face ain't listening." Jason's problems are clearly displayed in his inability to understand classroom discussions and his disruptive behavior only in those settings.

## FORMAL IDENTIFICATION

### Definitions

#### IDEA

IDEA 2004 defines a language disorder as a *communication disorder:*

**Semantics:** The meanings underlying verbalizations (substance).

[A] speech or language impairment means a communication disorder, such as stuttering, impaired articulation, a language impairment, or a voice impairment, that adversely affects a child's educational performance. (34 CFR Section 300.7[a][c][11])

IDEA also defines a specific learning disability as

**Pragmatics:** Everyday, practical language that is used for social communication. For students with LD, deficient areas of pragmatics include the use of nonspecific referents and ambiguous messages, failure to take the perspectives of others, nonassertive responding, and difficulty asking questions or seeking clarification.

a disorder in one or more of the basic psychological processes involved in *understanding or using language,* spoken or written, which may manifest itself in an imperfect ability to listen, think, speak, read, write, spell, or do mathematical calculations; this includes perceptual handicaps, brain injury, minimal brain dysfunction, dyslexia, and *developmental aphasia,* but does not include learning problems resulting from visual, hearing, or motor disabilities, of mental retardation, of emotional disturbance, or of environmental, cultural, or economic disadvantage. (H.R. 1350, Section 602 [30]; italics added to indicate overlap with spoken language deficits)

However, the 2004 IDEA revisions for specific learning disabilities added an RTI criterion. The following changes and clarifications were made concerning the identification of spoken and written language disabilities and of specific learning disabilities:

1. When determining whether a child has a specific learning disability, a local educational agency shall not be required to take into consideration whether a child has a severe discrepancy between achievement and intellectual disability *in oral expression, listening comprehension, written expression, basic reading skill, reading comprehension, mathematical calculation, or mathematical reasoning.*

2. In determining whether a child has a specific learning disability, a local educational agency may use a process that determines if the child responds to scientific, research-based intervention as a part of the evaluation procedures. (Section 614[b][6]; italics added)

### *DSM-IV-TR*

*DSM-IV-TR* (APA, 2000, p. 61) defines language disorders as expressive (diagnostic criteria 315.31) and mixed receptive/expressive (diagnostic criteria 315.32):

*Defining characteristics:*

- Expressive language symptoms: limited vocabulary, errors in tense, difficulty in recalling words or in "producing sentences with developmentally appropriate length or complexity."
- Receptive language symptoms: "difficulty understanding words, sentences, or specific types of words, such as spatial terms."

*Impairment:* "The difficulties with receptive and expressive language significantly interfere with academic or occupational achievement or with social communication."

*Exclusions:* Not pervasive developmental disorder, and if there is co-occurring ID, speech-motor, sensory deficit, or environmental "deprivation," the language symptoms must be in excess of those that are typically present with those disabilities.

### *Frequently Occurring Subtypes*

Specific expressive language disorders are as follows:

> **Circumlocution:** Saying something in a roundabout way (e.g., by describing an object or saying it is like something else rather than actually naming it).

> *Anomia/dysnomia:* Poor verbal memory that produces a poor ability to speak or produce words. In place of words, individuals may use nonverbal sounds, pantomime, delayed responses, **circumlocutions,** or written responses. These children can read silently but cannot read aloud, because they cannot recall the names of words, even though they can recognize the words.

*Aphasia:* Poor or limited working memory or holding information in mind, so that these children confuse word order in sentences and confuse verb tenses.

*Cluttering:* "A disturbance in fluency and language formulation involving an abnormally rapid rate and erratic rhythm of speech and disturbances in language structure" (APA, 2000, p. 59). Children with cluttering may have many thoughts at once, may make constant self-interruptions and revisions, and may seem unclear about what they want to say. Cluttering may also occur in older children who attempt to avoid stuttering by speaking rapidly. Cluttering is different from hesitations in language that can be seen in stammering or stuttering and different from rapid speech that can be seen in the manic phase of bipolar disorder (see Section V). (Disorders of articulation are described in Chapter 15 as motor disorders.)

### Possible Co-Occurring Conditions and Differences Among Related Disabilities

Difficulties with language, similar to difficulties with social behavior, characterize most every area of exceptionality. ADHD is one of the most commonly co-occurring conditions; it has been estimated that ADHD co-occurs in about half the population of those with verbal language disorders (for a review, see Freer, Hayden, Lorch, & Milich, 2011). For example, individuals with ADHD spontaneously talk more and change conversational topics more often. Probably because they talk more, they are also more dysfluent and poorly organized (Zentall, 1988). They are less likely than typical peers to tell coherent stories (i.e., with goal plans, attempts at resolution, and outcomes) unless they are provided with picture cues (Freer et al., 2011; Zentall, 1988). However, when asked to talk about a specific topic, they talk less and request less information from others, especially when asking for more information also involves getting more delays. Their social or pragmatic language is negative/competitive and includes more exclamations and commands.

The evidence also indicates that about half of those students with oral language difficulties also have RD (Snowling, 2009). The estimated co-occurrence of language disorders with LD is 35–60% (Schoenbrodt, Kumin, & Sloan, 1997). Children with LD produce less language (shorter mean utterances) and use poorer pragmatics (e.g., failure to provide specific information to the listener, more negative/competitive, less assertive, and less persuasive—"I want it because" without providing a rationale). Expressive language and phonological awareness symptoms co-occur with and persist longer in those students with childhood apraxia of speech (Velleman, 2011). (See Chapter 15 for discussion of speech impairments.) Children with emotional and behavioral disorders (EBD) have language disorders (71%) and about half of children with language disorders have been labeled EBD or oppositional defiant disorder (Benner, Nelson, & Epstein, 2002; Greene, 2006). In general, children with EBD talk less (e.g., shorter length of statements) and use language lacking in pragmatics—with poor turn taking, more frequent topic changes, and failure to provide specific information to the listener. Students with ID have receptive and expressive language delay that increases in relation to lower levels of IQ, with problems in production, **syntax,** and social use or pragmatics (Roberts, Price, & Malkin, 2007).

Selective mutism and acquired aphasia may be mistaken for language disabilities. Although these disabilities have language outcomes, they are not long-term, cross-setting, or primary in their definition or description of these groups. Selective mutism (see Section V) includes limited expressive output. Interviews with parents and observation can determine whether normal language exists in home settings, as would be observed for selective mutism but not with a general language disorder. Acquired aphasia is a language disorder that may be temporarily associated with a medical condition (e.g., head trauma, viral infection), but a true language disability persists beyond the **acute** recovery period of a medical condition. Autism spectrum disorders (ASD; see Section V) also involve language impairment but may be distinguished by "communication impairment (e.g., stereotyped use of language) and by the presence of a qualitative impairment in social interaction and restricted, repetitive, and stereotyped patterns of behavior" (APA, 2000, pp. 60–61). Children with these disorders produce language that has good structure but has different features, such as echoing, repeating, monotone intonation, and poor pragmatics.

> **Syntax:** Grammar and sentence construction, or the correctness of the form of language. Syntax includes rules of morphology, such as how plurals and possessives are formed.

> **Acute:** Immediate and typically short-term.

> **Developmental expressive language disorders:** Children with such disorders "often begin speaking late and progress more slowly than usual through the various stages of expressive language development" (APA, 2000, p. 59).

## Etiology

*Biogenetic.* **Developmental expressive language disorders** and other disorders involving language delay are more likely to occur in individuals with family histories of communication or learning disorders (APA, 2000).

*Environmental.* A smaller percentage of children have **acquired language disorders,** such as Jason in Chapter 2, who has a hearing loss possibly due to **exogenous factors,** such as insult to the brain or environmental disadvantage (lack of exposure to language or opportunities to speak).

*Functional.* Jason in Chapter 2 is disruptive in an environment that involves discussion, but he is compliant in environments that involve visual input, as the following observations reveal:

> **Acquired language disorder:** A type of language disorder in which an impairment occurs after a period of normal development as the result of a neurological or other general medical condition (e.g., encephalitis, irradiation, TBI) (APA, 2000).

> **Exogenous factors:** Factors in a disability that have their etiology outside the person (acquired).

1. "As the other teacher began talking, Jason sang out loudly, 'Nah, nah, nah.'"
2. Computer work: "He was totally involved with what he was doing, and didn't talk out at all."

**Language production:** The quantity or amount of language spoken or written.

Functional assessment of children with decreased **language production** might also document that some children avoid talking as a way to decrease social contact. In other words, talking increases social interactions, which some children wish to avoid (see the section headed "Social Phobia" in Chapter 12).

## Prevalence, Gender, Age, and Cultural Factors

*Prevalence.* "In children under 3, language delays are quite common, occurring in 10%–15% of children" (APA, 2000, p. 60).

*Gender.* Expressive language disorders are more common in boys than in girls.

*Age.* The identification of spoken language disorders occurs at earlier ages than the recognition of written language problems. *Preschool:* Severe forms of mixed receptive-expressive language disorders are usually apparent by age 2, but most are identified before age 4. *Elementary school:* Milder forms of verbal language disorders may not be recognized until elementary school (APA, 2000).

*Culture.* Students with language disabilities that stem from learning English (i.e., second-language learners) cannot be diagnosed with language disabilities. However, students who have difficulties in their primary language are more likely to have difficulties learning another language, such as English (Artiles, Rueda, Salazar, & Higareda, 2005). This makes differential diagnosis more difficult without an assessment in the child's primary language.

# INFORMAL EDUCATOR IDENTIFICATION OF CHARACTERISTICS

**Verbal LD (VLD):** Verbal learning disability; difficulty with language-based subject areas of reading, spelling, and composition. Problems with talking and listening may be early indicators. Children with VLD are sometimes referred to as having language learning disabilities (LLD).

## Behavioral

Children with **verbal LD, or VLD,** are often viewed by teachers as inattentive or unaware, limited in their ability to comprehend or follow directions, making irrelevant responses, and appearing uncommunicative or withdrawn (Reeves, 1980). Alternatively, children with VLD may show acting-out types of behavior, such as disruption, especially during classroom discussions.

## Social-Emotional

Children with verbal language disorders are also likely to have emotional and social problems (Cherry & Rubinstein, 2006). Emotional dysregulation can be seen in (a) depression and low self-esteem, related to past failures; (b) frustration and anger, related to current failures; and (c) anxiety disorders, related to anticipated failure.

The social problems of these students can create even more difficulties than the language problems. These students are more likely to have negative social communications than are typical comparison peers—specifically more competitive and rejection statements to others and fewer helpful and considerate statements (Bryan, Burstein, & Ergul, 2004). They also tend to receive fewer considerate and more rejection statements from their peers. Sometimes these children try to avoid the appearance of not understanding, as does Bart, whose case study appears at the end of this chapter:

> Bart also has problems understanding people who speak too quickly. When his classmate would speak too quickly, he would act like he was just ignoring them, when in fact they were speaking too quickly for him to understand.

In addition, teachers can view these children, *incorrectly,* as unmotivated and not willing to learn (DiSarno, Schowalter, & Grassa, 2002). For example, in Chapter 2's case study, Jason's teacher did not recognize how much Jason's hearing loss was affecting his social behavior in classroom discussions. Perhaps educators' failure to recognize the difficulties of children with VLD makes it even easier for these children to become socially isolated or to associate with younger children, whose language skills are closer to their level.

## Cognitive

Problems in thinking and recall may be reflected in failure to understand or use **abstract verbal language,** moving from the use of concrete to more abstract language. That is, students with VLD have been found to perform worse than equivalent-IQ peers on thinking tasks (hypothesis testing or rule identification) when they had no alternatives to choose from but to perform as well as their peers when choice options were available and they did not need to recall or have memorized responses (Masterson, 1993). This suggests that difficulties holding information in mind can contribute to lack of verbal comprehension.

## Communication

Communication requires language, and language can be verbal or nonverbal (gestural). See Figure 3.2. Verbal language can be broken down into the categories of receptive language and expressive language.

**Abstract verbal language:** The degree to which language involves more than the concrete naming of things and moves to descriptions of objects (adjectives), descriptions of actions (adverbs), and use of abstract prepositions, along this continuum: (a) single words— nouns (objects, concepts, categories), verbs (simple verbs, verb tense), adjectives, prepositions; (b) phrases and sentences (following directions); (c) paragraphs and stories; (d) cause and effect; (e) drawing of inferences; (f) fact versus opinion; (g) absurdities and humor; (h) idioms and figures of speech ("on the rocks," "over the hill").

**Figure 3.2**   Language: A Rule System

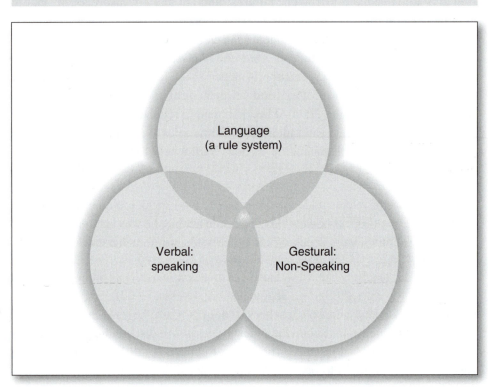

---

**Central auditory processing disorders:** Listening disorders that are severe and involve, for example, poor awareness of, attention to, and discrimination of sounds; poor association of sounds with symbols; poor recall of sound sequences; and overall slowed processing rate.

*Receptive language problems* (listening skill deficits or more severe **central auditory processing disorders**) may be indicated if a child (a) takes 5–10 seconds longer than other children to process information (Saunders, 2001), (b) asks for repetitions, or (c) is overly loud. Difficulties in listening tasks may include (a) hearing words or questions incorrectly, as indicated by inappropriate responses, such as answering "Do you buy your lunch at school?" with "Spaghetti"; (b) insensitivity to rhyming, as indicated by failure to select the rhyming pair from the following three options—fat/cat/sit (auditory perception/discrimination); (c) failure to recall or follow directions (auditory memory); and (d) failure to understand word meanings or complex logic ("if-then" sentences) (auditory reasoning, abstract language, or verbal IQ).

---

**Language quality:** The content, structure, and pragmatic social (everyday) use of language.

*Expressive language* (speaking) refers to the amount of language produced and the **language quality.** There may be differences in the quantity or production of language (fewer words, fewer different words, and shorter sentences; Redmond, 2004). An example of reduced language production comes from Jason's case study in Chapter 2, when the class activity changed from working on computers to a group discussion about computers:

> The class was supposed to go to the computer lab today, but we had a two-hour delay, and there wouldn't have been enough time. So they [the class] had a discussion on computers. During this discussion, he [Jason] put down another student and said he was lying and that that student always lied. . . . Jason was very quiet during this conversation.

In addition to production deficiencies, there may also be difference in the quality of the language: (a) less complex syntax—limited types of sentences (e.g., imperatives, questions); (b) talking later or using less mature grammar than peers (developmental delay), with omissions of parts of sentences and unusual word order; (c) difficulties with semantics (e.g., making inaccurate statements such as "I'm hot. I want my sweater on" when meaning to say, "I'm hot. I want my sweater off"); and (d) difficulties with pragmatic use (e.g., providing less information when asked, requesting less information when needed, making topic changes without warning listeners). In addition, children with expressive language problems may confuse similar words, such as *borrow* and *tomorrow,* or make new words, like *bomorrow.* (For a review of assessments, see Stichter, Conroy, & Kauffman, 2008.)

## Academic

In general, students with VLD have difficulty in the classroom following oral directions, comprehending reading materials and math word problems, and understanding rapid or distorted speech (Cherry & Rubinstein, 2006). VLD can affect all academic subjects (Camahalan, 2006) and can change over time. That is, problems in spoken language at age 5 can show up again as reading problems at age 8 and as problems in written expression (composition) at age 14 (Lerner & Kline, 2006). Students with VLD also tend to be slower in verbally responding, take longer in completing tasks, and tell less complex stories (e.g., Klecan-Aker & Kelty, 1990). The case study for this chapter, Bart, provides a good example of a VLD that affects reading. Bart has particular trouble when he attempts to read in a noisy environment:

> His teacher commented that sometimes when Bart reads, he covers up his ears to block out the background noise so that he can concentrate on his reading. So if there is too much background noise for him to concentrate, he just does not read.

## SUMMARY OF STRENGTHS AND NEEDS

| Probable strengths | Probable needs |
|---|---|
| • Nonverbal areas of math, science, art, computers <br> • Social or motor skills | • Alternative ways to demonstrate competence and understandings that do not involve language <br> • Assistance in small-group work, such as taking turns as speaker, assignment of a group member to take notes, or scripted assignments or outlines, all of which increase the clarity of the signal or reduce the need to understand verbal directions |

## DISABILITY IN THE CLASSROOM

### Implications for Accommodations in General Education Settings: Tier I

*For poor receptive language:*

1. Decrease the rate and quantity of verbal instruction.

**Graphic organizers:** Tools such as mind maps and outlines that allow students to visualize their ideas.

2. Use technology. Provide digital recorders or free iPad apps for playback of instructions. To make information assimilation faster, use **graphic organizers** (flowcharts, semantic or concept maps, Venn diagrams, webs and guided notes) that offer students outlines of information that will be presented during class. Concept maps "help students sort, simplify, show relationships, make meaning, and manage data quickly and easily" (Gallivan & Kottler, 2007, p. 117). A study of middle school students with LD using graphic organizers produced more understanding of relationships on written essays (DiCecco & Gleason, 2002).

**Cuing/prompting:** The use of cues that precede the desired behavior in time and act as reminders of what is required.

3. Use pictures or cue cards (**cuing** or **prompting**) whenever multiple-step instructions are given.

*For poor expressive language* that involves insufficient production and poor organization or goal structure, use picture cues, story maps, or self-questioning techniques (for a review, see Freer et al., 2011).

### Implications for Interventions in Small-Group and Individual Settings: Tiers II and III

*For failure to comprehend spoken language,* teach students single words, phrases, paragraphs, and simple stories that progress from concrete to more abstract.

*For failure to produce language:*

1. Use shared book reading (parent/child and teacher/child), which is associated with increased vocabulary and use of abstract language (Crain-Thoreson, 1999).

2. Use light-tech devices that require no power source, such as "gestures, necklace photos, communication boards, eye-gazing objects, choice boards, props, and voice output devices" (Beard et al., 2007, p. 110).

3. Use high-tech augmentative and alternative communication (**AAC**) devices, such as text-to-speech, single- or multiple-level voice output that can record several messages, which the student can use throughout the day, and screen display devices. (For information on additional AAC communication devices, see Beard et al., 2007, p. 116.)

*For anomia/dysnomia,* give concrete experiences and pictures paired with objects to be named within categories, pairs, and associations. Also use sentence-completion tasks and rapid, timed naming drills.

*For syntactical aphasia* and more severe language disorders, teach natural language within meaningful play experiences, with the use of pictures (e.g., "Tell me a story about this picture" or about this experience) and by using sentence-building exercises (noun-verb to more complex constructions).

**For pragmatics:**

1. Train children to request needed objects in their natural environments (Hatton, 1998).

2. Use pretend play (e.g., "Pretend you are an 'X' and show me what you would do").

3. Provide opportunities for interaction with multiple partners in dyadic interactions (DeKroon, Kyte, & Johnson, 2002).

## Long-Term Outcomes

The school dropout rate for students with verbal LD is almost 40% (APA, 2000). Of those children with speech-language disorders in preschool, 70% will continue to experience language difficulties at age 9 (Riccio & Hynd, 1993). "By school age, prevalence estimates range from 3% to 7%" (APA, 2000, p. 60). In other words, students can "catch up" on some language functions given time.

**AAC:** Augmentative and alternative communication. AAC devices provide technological support for the language that the child has: verbal (speech) or nonverbal/gestural modes of communication (pointing or mechanical output systems) and alternative communication methods that bypass the oral system of communication.

Even though these children may have language problems that become less noticeable as they age, other verbal learning disabilities (e.g., reading disabilities) may replace earlier language disorders.

## CHAPTER SUMMARY

- The parts of IDEA's formal definition of LD that relate to this chapter describe problems in understanding or using spoken language, which can be observed as an "imperfect" ability to listen, think, and speak that is not caused by sensory, emotional, or intellectual disabilities or cultural differences. The RTI criterion that has been added does not replace the definition, but it adds a new context of assessment.

- Subtypes of spoken language disorders include anomia/dysnomia, aphasia, and cluttering. Co-occurring disabilities of ADHD and EBD have spoken language difficulties, and autism is characterized by the poor social use of language and by stereotyped, repetitive language. Subtypes of language disorder can be assessed through functional analysis designed to determine whether the disability is cross-setting (e.g., aphasia) or specific to social settings (e.g., selective mutism, hearing impairments).

- The etiology of language disorders is based in biology or nature (e.g., developmental delays), although some can be acquired (e.g., hearing loss, environmental disadvantage). Spoken language disorders are readily identified at the preschool and early elementary ages; at older age levels written language disabilities are more frequently identified. These disorders are more prevalent in boys than girls.

- Educators can informally identify receptive language disorders through observations of students' unusual behavioral responses to directions/statements and their acting out rather than "using words." Careful listening to students' spoken language—the syntax, meanings conveyed, and social uses of language—will reveal most of these differences. In response to the often negative or "odd" social responses of children with language disorders, peers are more negative and rejecting, especially toward older elementary students. Academic difficulties will occur primarily when the learning tasks are verbal (group discussions, lectures) and disappear when the context is primarily visual (computers, handwriting). Spoken language problems usually develop into problems with written language, such as reading and composition.

- Interventions that remediate language disorders include sentence-building activities and shared book reading. Accommodations that can help these children compensate include the use of pictures and meaningful experiences paired with language. Educators can also provide verbal input while increasing the use of visuals (flowcharts, schedules, and the like).

## CHAPTER QUESTIONS

1. Assume that it is your responsibility to present a summarization of language disorders to other educators. In your summary, describe the possible long-term effects of early language problems.

2. How does the fact that some children cannot hold information in mind affect their performance in school?

3. How would you accommodate students with auditory processing problems, who are involved in small-group instruction at older age levels?

## TRUE/FALSE AND MULTIPLE-CHOICE

1. When students are identified at earlier ages as having language disorders, this typically indicates more severe disability.    F

2. Girls are more likely than boys to have early expressive language disorders.   F

3. Indicator(s) of auditory problems are
   A. speaking in shorter sentences
   B. difficulty following directions
   C. making up words or combining words
   D. misordering words in a sentence
   E. all of the above

4. In learning single words, the developmental order is
   A. verbs, nouns, prepositions, adjectives
   B. prepositions, adjectives, verbs, nouns
   C. nouns, verbs, adjectives, prepositions
   D. nouns, adjectives, verbs, prepositions

5. Children who have long pauses before speaking or who have difficulty reading aloud (although they can read silently) may have
   A. cluttering
   B. dyspraxia
   C. syntactical aphasia
   D. dysnomia

6. What deficit areas exist across almost all mild disability categories?

   A. reading and math
   B. speaking and listening
   C. memory and IQ
   D. language and social skills

## SHORT ANSWER

1. Language that goes beyond concrete examples of nouns, verbs, and so on is called _____language.

2. Speaking without inflection, similar to students with autism

3. Talking in circles means coming up with another long way to say something that you cannot recall

4. Poor ability to retrieve names of objects when speaking or reading out loud

5. Rapid rush of words and ideas that need to be revised

6. The quantity (length and amount) of language

## PROBLEM-BASED CASE APPLICATIONS AND QUESTIONS

### CASE STUDY 3.1: BART

*"The computer is great for him, but he does not get a lot accomplished because he is worried about what is happening around him."*
(adapted from a report submitted by Jodi Hampton)

*Background.* Bart is a 17-year-old junior at a small high school. He had a fairly complicated birth, during which he stopped breathing and was given oxygen. He was diagnosed with an auditory processing/communication disorder 3 years ago. Bart's parents are supportive and frequently meet with his teachers to discuss his progress.

### Behavioral Log

*First hour, Agriculture Mechanics.* This class is taught by one teacher and is part lab work and part class work. Midterms are due on this day, so the students are working on a reading comprehension assignment dealing with Hurricane Katrina. They are to read a short news article and answer questions about what they have read. It is currently midterm time, so instead of the teacher filling out the midterm grades, she yells out the grade for each student while the students are reading to themselves.

- While the teacher is explaining the assignment, she asks for attention a couple of times. Bart ignores her and continues to talk to his friends. Since he missed the directions, he asks his neighbor for help.
- Bart begins to read the newspaper article. While reading he is constantly tapping his fingers. He continues to tap his fingers the entire time he is reading the article. When it is time to begin answering the questions, he realizes that he does not have a pen. He has to borrow a pen from a classmate. Bart seems very concerned about whether or not the assignment is for a grade.
- After maybe a minute of looking at the questions, Bart again begins to talk to his classmates.
- Bart begins to work on the task after the teacher reminds the class what they should be doing. He works on the task with a partner. He also helps out another student with one of the questions.
- The teacher announces that class is almost over and that they need to turn in their work. Bart is the last one to leave the class; he has to recheck is midterm grade because he forgot to write it down. Teacher's comment: "Bart is great child with a really good attitude."

*Second hour, English.* Bart's second hour is English. On this day, there is a substitute teacher.

- Bart opens his silent reading book to read and then closes it, ignoring the directions. In the next minutes he still is not reading; he rubs his eyes and also continues to talk to his classmates. Bart during this time keeps playing with/touching whatever is near him, from the writing utensil on his desk to his classmates seated near him.
- After about 20 minutes, Bart decides that instead of reading he is going to shred his notebook paper and throw it at his classmates.
- He continues to take part in the paper-throwing fight until the substitute teacher calls him up to the front to receive his grade. Bart goes up to the front when called.
- After receiving his grade Bart tries once again to read, and he is bothered by one of his classmates, who is trying to talk to him about after-school plans. Bart spends the rest of the class period talking to his classmates, banging his pencil or

tapping his fingers on his desk. Bart is constantly moving his hands. Finally, in the last 5 minutes of class, Bart begins to read but closes his book quickly. He is the last to leave class.

*Third hour, Physical Education.* Teacher comments that Bart is enrolled in advanced Physical Education. The teacher says the class will be very unstructured today because the teacher has to fill in the midterms, and the students have a free period during which they can play games or just sit and talk with friends.

- Bart is playing Ping-Pong with a classmate. He and his partner are the only ones doing anything active. He plays Ping-Pong for the entire hour. Bart seems to get along well with his classmates. This is the first class in which he seems very at ease, and very busy.

*Fifth hour, World History—after lunch.*

- The teacher is passing out a test from a week before. Bart seems quite proud of his grade on the exam, even showing it to many of his classmates seated around him. He even remarks to the teacher about how well he did, though he says that he did not study.
- The teacher announces to the class that they are going to watch more of the movie that they have been watching while he fills in the midterms. He reminds the class that no one likes it when people talk during movies.
- While watching the movie, Bart constantly taps his fingers on his desk. He also rolls up his test and bangs on his desk while watching the movie.
- Bart ignores the teacher's instructions and talks to the classmates seated around him. For the rest of the class period Bart is either tapping his fingers on his desk while watching the movie or talking to his classmates. At the end of the period he is once again the last student out of the classroom.

*Sixth hour, Computer Lab.* Since he has to make up two credits in math, Bart participates in Plato lab, which is a self-paced math tutorial. On this day, the students are to turn in their logs so that the teacher can give them their midterm grades. Bart cannot find his log, because it appears his work folder is very disorganized.

- Bart argues with the teacher, who has to give him a lower grade because he cannot find his log.
- While the teacher is double-checking her records, Bart walks around the room, basically stopping by everyone's workstation, interrupting every student in the class. He does not start working on his assignment. He gets out of his seat again

and starts arguing with the teacher because she wants to place him in a general education math class. The teacher says that he is a very nice child but he is very disorganized. He has a hard time focusing on his work. The computer is great for him, but he does not get a lot accomplished because he is worried about what is happening around him.

## High-Frequency Payoffs

A graphing of the observations of Bart recorded in the behavioral log shows that one of his *most frequent payoffs* is avoiding the task of listening, which he does 11% of the time (see the bars to the left of the midpoint in Figure 3.3). Bart tries hard to grasp what the teacher is saying, but by the time he processes the first step the teacher has already moved on and he has missed the rest of the directions. He avoids listening the most when the teacher is addressing the whole class. Bart also avoids reading 11% of the time. When he is given a reading task, he does not complete it. Instead, he usually talks to his classmates around him or even throws paper instead of reading. When given a reading comprehension task, he will complete the task after a while, but when

**Figure 3.3**  Avoid Payoffs and Get Payoffs

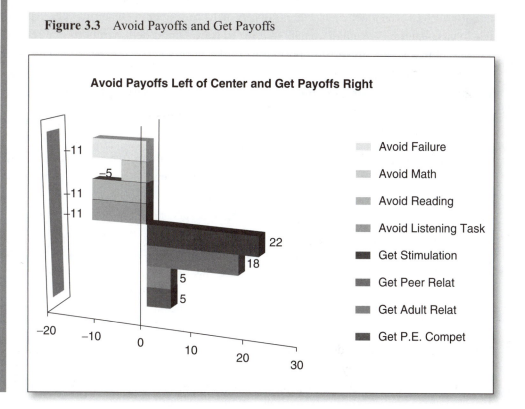

given a simple silent reading task, he will not read. The difference might be that one task is for a grade while the other is not.

Bart avoids many tasks about 11% of the time so that he will not appear incompetent (avoids failure). He covers up not being prepared for class by quietly asking for a pen so as not to appear to be different. He forgets to write down his midterm grade, but does not admit that he forgot.

Bart also behaves to avoid punishment—there is a lot of pressure put on Bart to succeed in school so that he can participate in sports and avoid disappointment from his parents. Bart avoids the task of math only 5% of the time. According to his IEP, Bart is being taught math on the computer through an online tutorial called Plato. Instead of completing his online sessions, he goes and helps another student, because Bart also struggles in math. He is currently making up credits in math from the year before.

Bart also has many payoffs of getting relatedness from peers (18% of the time) and from teachers (5%). He touches or talks to his classmates on many occasions. About 22% of his payoffs are to get stimulation, which he appears to need constantly. He is always tapping his fingers on his desk and often touches his classmates. Bart does this mostly when the teacher is giving directions.

Bart's least-frequent payoffs are during PE; Bart seems to really want to have the attention of his PE teacher. He does this by behaving very well during PE. His PE teacher is also the basketball coach, so a lot of Bart's good behavior could be related to the fact that sports are very important to Bart's family.

## Diagnosis Versus ABC Analysis

Bart has been labeled with an auditory processing disorder. He has trouble listening and following directions, especially when people speak too quickly. When his classmates speak too quickly, he acts like he is just ignoring them, when in fact they are speaking too quickly for him to understand. Another characteristic is that sometimes he speaks too loudly. At one point during his independent study time, the classroom was completely quiet, so Bart tried to whisper, but everyone could hear every word he was saying; this indicates his inability to gauge volume. Bart also seems to have problems with auditory memory. For example, in Bart's agriculture mechanics class, the teacher gave multistep directions about how the students were supposed to obtain and check their midterm grades, but Bart was unable to follow the directions.

It is a struggle for Bart to understand directions, especially when they are given in a setting with background noise (e.g., students having their tutorials read to them, the teacher talking to other classmates), so he simply stops listening. His teacher commented that sometimes when Bart reads, he covers up his ears to block out the background noise so that he can concentrate on his reading. So if there is too much background noise for him to concentrate, he just does not read.

Bart is behind in math and avoids doing math; this may be because it is hard for him to remember or use math vocabulary. Bart does math on a computer. He cannot do well in a normal math classroom because he cannot process what the math teacher is saying, and he does not understand the language of mathematics or how to solve math problems that involve problem solving or multistep directions. Bart's independent study teacher said that Bart just *did not want* to do his work.

## Case Questions

1: How does Bart's problem in listening end up as a problem in reading and then in math by the time he is 17 years old?

2: Why did it take so long to identify Bart's problems?

3 (problem-based small-group assignment): Construct a table of Bart's strengths and areas needing development for the purposes of communicating succinctly with a team that includes his parents.

4 (problem-based small-group assignment): Construct a list of accommodations that could be helpful for Bart.

# Chapter 4

## Disorders of Written Language

Written language is the substance of most academic learning. Within this category are reading disabilities and spelling and composition disabilities.

## READING DISABILITIES OR DYSLEXIA

Of all the skills children learn prior to and during their school years, reading is probably the most essential. Reading can enrich children's lives by opening up new worlds of people and places—worlds of adventure, sports, relationships, and knowledge. At a practical level, reading is the most efficient way to learn new subject matter, such as science and social studies, and more generally to understand a world that is broader than the child's own small world. Middle school children who read well are estimated to read about 10 million words during a school year; children with reading difficulties read fewer than 100,000 words during that same period of time (Lyon, 2003). Exposure to fewer words leads to a narrowing of perspective and of understanding, and specifically it leads to reduced vocabulary and reduced background knowledge (Lyon et al., 2003).

   **Reading disability** (**RD**) is a broad category that includes problems in decoding and encoding. Children who have difficulty with reading single words accurately and fluently (speed) are also described with the term **dyslexia**. The name in Greek means "difficulty with words." The main problem for those diagnosed with the disorder in English-speaking countries is there difficulty understanding of how sounds fit together to make words (Lyon et al., 2003). Dyslexia is specifically identified as inaccurate **decoding**, which persists from childhood to adulthood as slower reading fluency, and is usually associated with impairments of phonological processing,

**RD:** Reading disability. This broad term is used to refer to many problems associated with reading, including reading comprehension problems or hyperlexia, but most often it refers to dyslexia.

**Dyslexia:** A disorder of reading or decoding that is often accompanied by spelling problems.

---

**Figure 4.1**   A child with reading disabilities struggles with her assignment

**Decoding:** The process of translating visual symbols (letters) into auditory equivalents (sounds and words) or the achievement of accurate and/or fluent word recognition.

**Reading comprehension:** The ability to gain meaning from text that is read (understanding or encoding).

verbal processing speed, and verbal short-term memory (Snowling, 2009). Because it persists over time, it cannot be considered a developmental delay. Reading also involves encoding or **reading comprehension**—that is, understanding what has been read. The ability to encode depends on decoding skills, since it is impossible for children to understand printed text unless they can first decode the symbols.

Learning to read is complex, especially for the young child learning to decode English, because it involves an integrated series of steps. As Silver (2004) notes: "A child must recognize each unit of sound or *phoneme*, and connect it to the correct . . . [visual symbols or characters]. There are 44 phonemes in the English language. Each letter has a sound, vowels have a short and a long sound, and certain combinations (e.g., *sh, th, ch*) have their own sounds. There are 36 characters in the English language (i.e., the letters *a* through *z* and the numbers 0 to 9)" (p. 15). To learn to read, a child must learn to break this code by learning which visual symbols go with which sounds (i.e., sounding out words). "Spelling is the reverse process" (Silver, 2004, p. 15) of translating sounds into visual symbols.

It is important to remember at this point that reading comprehension or encoding is the main purpose of reading, and reading aloud is *not*. Reading aloud has little relevance for students with RD, but it does have specific purposes in individual assessments of errors, in dramatics, for storytelling, and in improving comprehension for children with ADHD (see Chapter 9). Although reading aloud may help some children comprehend when they receive their own auditory feedback, it is embarrassing for students with RD to read aloud in public. Furthermore, if a child has dysnomia, reading aloud is impossible, whereas reading silently produces good comprehension. Thus, if a child comprehends correctly while reading silently or reading aloud to him- or herself, decoding errors are of little functional importance.

## FORMAL IDENTIFICATION

### Definitions

#### IDEA

IDEA's definition of SLD (presented in total in Chapter 3) also defines written language disabilities. The relevant part is repeated here (with italics added) to emphasize reading disability as

a disorder in one or more of the basic psychological processes involved in *understanding* or using language, spoken or written, which may manifest itself in an imperfect ability to listen, think, speak, *read*, write, spell, or do mathematical calculations. (H.R. 1350, Section 602 [30])

## DSM-IV-TR

*DSM-IV-TR* (APA, 2000) defines reading disability as follows:

*Defining characteristics:* Reading accuracy, speed, or comprehension scores that fall substantially below what would be expected given the individual's age, intelligence, and age-appropriate education.

*Procedures:* Achievement and intelligence are measured individually on standardized assessments. "Substantially below" is defined as a discrepancy of more than 2 *SD* between achievement and IQ. A 1–2 *SD* smaller discrepancy between achievement and IQ can be used if a child's performance on an IQ test could have been compromised by "an associated disorder in cognitive processing, a comorbid mental disorder or general medical condition, or the individual's ethnic or cultural background."

*Exclusions:* If a sensory deficit is present, the reading difficulties must be in excess of those typically associated with that sensory deficit.

## Frequently Occurring Subtypes

**Dyslexia:** This subtype is identified by decoding problems that typically result from a deficit in the phonological component of language; dyslexia is an unexpected disability given a child's good cognitive abilities (IQ) and probable exposure to effective classroom instruction. Reading comprehension or encoding difficulties are usually secondary consequences of dyslexia. That is, if children struggle to read, it will be difficult—if not impossible—for them to concentrate on understanding, since all their effort is expended on the decoding task. When children with decoding problems are eventually taught to read, they *should* be able to understand what they have read. Similarly, if they are read to, they should understand that material (i.e., unless there are co-occurring intellectual disabilities). *Spelling* is associated with dyslexia. Most children with dyslexia have both reading and spelling disabilities; when children are good readers but poor spellers, they are thought to have a milder form of dyslexia (Mather, 2003).

**Hyperlexia:** Children who can decode fairly easily but do not comprehend what they have read fall within this subtype. For example, they are unable to paraphrase or summarize the materials read. When children have this encoding problem, instruction should begin with comprehension of spoken language, which is a prerequisite skill to reading comprehension.

## Possible Co-Occurring Conditions and Difference Among Related Disabilities

About 15% to almost 50% of students with RD have other disorders (Cardon et al., 2005; Lyon, 1996). For example, ADHD is found at twice the rate in students with RD compared with the general population (15% versus 7%; Lyon 1996). Children with RD plus ADHD have greater problems in attention and more difficulty with reading than either group singly (Lyon, 1996). As well, about half of students with math disability also have RD (Geary, 2003), which may be due to shared verbal deficits (Snowling, 2009). Anxiety, depression, withdrawal, and low self-esteem are more prevalent in RD groups than in the general population, especially in girls (Willcutt & Pennington, 2000).

ADHD-inattentive subtype can be confused with children with RD. However, inattention is a secondary characteristic of children with RD, who show inattention (off-task) only during tasks that require reading (e.g., social studies, science, math word problems).

## Etiology

**Endowment:** The abilities an individual is born with (congenital).

Both genetics/**endowment** and educational experiences can determine reading abilities, and the better the child's innate endowment, the easier it is for the child to profit from educational experiences (Vellutino et al., 1996).

**Heritability:** The percentage of a characteristic that can be explained by genetics.

*Biogenetic.* RD is highly heritable; it runs in families and may be seen in a child's parents, grandparents, aunts, and uncles. RD is found in 23–65% of children whose parents are dyslexic and 40% of their siblings (Shaywitz et al., 2008). Genetics account for 50–60% of cases of RD (for a review, see Wenar & Kerig, 2006). More children with dyslexia than without dyslexia have been found to have had fathers who were manual laborers, which may "reflect reading difficulties and educational failure" in the fathers (Heiervang, Stevenson, Lund, & Hugdahl., 2001, p. 255). A deficit in sound/symbol awareness is the best predictor of reading difficulties (Vellutino et al., 1996) and reflects the greatest degree of **heritability** (reviewed in Lyon, 1996). What is surprising is that inheritance of RD is more often found in high-IQ than in average-IQ students (Shaywitz et al., 2008).

**fMRI:** Functional magnetic resonance imaging, a type of neuroimaging technology that is used to conduct assessments. An individual performs a task requiring specific skills while undergoing an MRI, and the brain activity associated with performing the task can be nonintrusively assessed.

What is inherited are brain differences, as has been illustrated by **fMRI** (functional magnetic resonance imaging) studies. These studies show that the left-hemisphere, posterior brain systems of individuals with RD do not function as they "should" during reading (Lyon, 2003). According to Shaywitz et al. (2008), "Neurobiological evidence is beginning to emerge to support behavioral data indicating that many dyslexics are not able to make good use of sound-symbol linkages as they mature, and instead, they come to rely on memorized words" (p. 460).

*Environmental.* At least half the variance associated with RD has been found to be related to environmental factors (see Olson & Byrne, 2005, cited by Shaywitz et al., 2008). The risk factors associated with reading disabilities include pre-natal risk factors (e.g., loss of oxygen, poor nutrition) and the educational and economic background of the family; for example, RD is more prevalent among poor families and schools, small-town families, and families of low socio-economic status (**SES**) (Berninger, 2001; Sideridis, 2009). However, even in middle-SES families, children can be exposed to poor teaching and miss impor-tant prereading experiences.

**SES:** Socioeconomic status; that is, the economic class of an individual.

*Functional.* Functional assessments of children with dyslexia find that these chil-dren avoid assignments that involve reading, especially reading aloud, but they do *not* avoid other areas, such as math calculations, physical education, theater, or art. "Because reading is an effortful activity that involves the element of choice" (Sideridis, 2009, p. 605), motivation to approach or avoid can be observed. For example, students with hyperlexia will volunteer to show off their excellent decoding skills but avoid answering questions about the meaning of what they have read.

## Prevalence, Gender, Age, and Cultural Factors

*Prevalence.* Reading disabilty is one of the most common diagnoses in school-age children (Bental & Tirosh, 2007) at about 18% of students (defined by an IQ/achievement discrepancy when assessed on individual achievement tests; Shaywitz et al., 2008). When RD is defined as "significant difficulties in read-ing single words accurately and fluently, in combination with deficits in pho-nological awareness," prevalence estimates of dyslexia are similarly 17% (Lyon, 1996, p. 61). Recent changes in definition such as RTI (see Chapter 2) have altered current prevalence rates of students with RD to 5% of students (i.e., after intervention attempts have failed) (Shaywitz et al., 2008). Although the definitions used may result in the categorization of different samples of children, what they all have in common is *early failure* in reading. Furthermore, skill deficits and responsiveness to intervention are similar for children with reading problems and for the more severe clinically defined RD group (e.g., Shaywitz et al., 2008).

*Gender.* Overall, 10–15-year-old boys underperform in reading achievement more than do girls (Machin & Pekkarinen, 2008). In U.S. schools, three to four times more boys than girls were identified (Lyon, 1996). Even in population studies in Norway, dyslexia occurred in boys at four times the rate for girls (Heiervang et al., 2001). Perhaps the slower maturation of language functions in the left hemisphere of the brain in boys, in comparison with girls (Semrud-Clikeman & Hynd, 1990), explains the greater prevalence of *verbal* LD in boys and the greater prevalence of *nonverbal* LD in girls (see Chapter 5). In other words, girls mature faster in left-hemispheric language functions at the cost of right-hemispheric nonlanguage functions, and the reverse is true for boys.

*Age. Preschool and early elementary school:* It is important that early language delay is identified and interventions planned, because such delay is predictive of later reading failure (for a review, see Heiervang et al., 2001). As early as 3.5 years, it is possible to predict who will develop reading problems by using a small set of measures: tests of letter knowledge and rapid naming, a measure of phonological skill, and an assessment of family risk status (for a review, see Snowling, 2009). *Elementary school:* Children with RD are diagnosed around age 7 after failing in response to initial reading instruction (Vogel, 1998). Students with RD are also more likely to have difficulties solving mathematical word problems. *Secondary school:* Difficulties understanding social studies and science texts and learning a foreign language are often observed in high school students with dyslexia (Shaywitz et al., 2008).

*Culture.* Prevalence rates for reading failure are higher for children living in poverty, who come to kindergarten exposed to less than half the number of words known by middle-class children of the same age (Lyon, 2003). Economic differences can also be seen in the language delays of preschoolers; such delays act as predictors of later reading failure (Heiervang et al., 2001).

## INFORMAL EDUCATOR IDENTIFICATION CHARACTERISTICS

The following characteristics are often, but not always, found in children with RD.

### Behavioral

**Clinical range:** The level at which a child's disability is severe enough for the child to be labeled and to receive services.

Fourth-grade students with RD, especially boys, have been found to have higher behavior problem scores than typical peers (44% in the **clinical range**) according to parent and teacher ratings (Heiervang et al., 2001). In classrooms, these children may appear insensitive and offensive (Cicci, 1984) or aggressive, clownish, and difficult to control (Humphrey, 2002). Doug, whose case study appears at the end of this chapter, shows a range of disruptive behavior and avoidance types of behavior: "Problematic behavior includes not keeping his hands to himself, not paying attention, not following directions."

## Social-Emotional

Many students with RD exhibit a number of emotional characteristics, such as poor emotion recognition (Most & Greenbank, 2000; Nabuzoka & Smith, 1995), poor academic self-concept (Settle & Milich, 1999), anxiety, depression, **learned helplessness,** and feelings of self-dissatisfaction (Durrant, Cunningham, & Voelker, 1990; Settle & Milich, 1999). Peers, parents, and teachers rate children with dyslexia, especially girls, as having more shyness, anxiety, and depression than other children (Heiervang et al., 2001). Most of these outcomes are the result of a history of failure in school. This conclusion is supported by research findings showing effective reading intervention in first grade to be associated with decreased levels of behavioral and emotional problems by middle school (Kellam, Rebok, Mayer, Ialongo, & Kalodner, 1994).

**Learned helplessness:** A condition in which individuals attribute their successes to external factors (not to their own efforts) and their failures to their lack of ability (not to lack of effort).

The social behavior of students with RD ranges from disruptive and **antisocial** to passive and withdrawn; both types of social behavior attempt to protect the child's self-image (McNulty, 2003). Perhaps it is not surprising that these children are unpopular (Vaughn, Hogan, Kouzekanani, & Shapiro, 1990). Doug shows negative verbal behavior with others, makes negative self-statements, and has negative perceptions of academic tasks, as stated by his teacher:

**Antisocial:** Against the social order (e.g., breaking social rules).

> Doug's lying about an incident with a classmate that included name-calling, negative comments ("You don't trust me," "No one likes me," "I can't do this."), not trying (lethargic), resistance to her help (at times). . . . He does not like to be ignored, has a negative attitude in all subject areas, though his skills are better in math.

Peer responses to students with RD are typically negative: 75% are teased or bullied and 60% are rejected in early elementary school (Singer, 2005). More recent research indicates that students with LD have as many friends and belong to as many peer groups, but these friendships are with others with LD (e.g., Estell, Jones, Pearl, & Van Acker, 2009).

## Cognitive

*Attention.* Students with RD and ADHD show poorer selective and sustained attention performance than their peers (Willcutt, Pennington, Olson, Chhabildas, & Hulslander, 2005; Bever, 2005). However, the off-task attention of students with RD is likely due to lack of motivation to attend to reading.

*Intellectual.* LD is defined by excluding children with lower-than-average intelligence; thus, by definition, children with RD have average to above-average intelligence. However, verbal intelligence also includes executive functions (working memory, self-monitoring of comprehension, and selection of strategies, such as skimming and the use of headings). These aspects of intelligence (not measured by IQ tests) are applied in the reading of texts, novels, and instructions, and they appear to be weaker in students with RD than in their peers (Martinussen & Tannock, 2006; Siegler, 1991). Educators can observe indicators of intelligence in students' listening comprehension. Doug, who is 7 years old, appears to be intelligent—he clearly understands what he hears. He cannot understand what he reads, however, and that is because, in fact, he cannot read. "His avoidance behavior was absent in listening settings, particularly during story time. . . . (His strength is in listening comprehension.)"

Even though IQ is typically average to above average in students with RD, higher verbal intelligence *is* associated with greater gains in reading performance (Stage, Abbott, Jenkins, & Berninger, 2003). High verbal IQ may help students learn the inconsistent sound/symbol rules in the English language or to use context cues to "figure out" words. As noted above, a higher heritability for dyslexia has been reported in children with higher IQ (Shaywitz, et al., 2008, p. 458). Students with intellectual disabilities (ID) appear to have more difficulty learning these rules as reported by their teachers, who eventually teach these students through the **sight approach** rather than by using phonetic rules. In contrast, in Spanish, Finnish, and Italian, there is no association between verbal IQ and reading, perhaps because these languages have consistent relationships between letters and sounds, making it the easier for children to learn to read and to spell (Jiménez, Siegel, & López, 2003; Shaywitz et al., 2008).

**Sight approach:** A method of teaching reading that relies on visually based retrieval (sometimes called the basal reading approach). Children are taught to recognize and associate meanings with whole words or word pictures, often using high-frequency grade-level words.

*Auditory memory.* To be good readers, children must hold in mind sounds, syllables, words, and ideas and associate letter symbols with sounds (phonics) (Berninger, 2001; Camahalan, 2006; McGee, Brodeur, Symons, Andrade, & Fahie, 2004). Reading comprehension is related to working memory, which is poor in students with RD (Bental & Tirosh, 2007; Dahlin, 2011). Long-term memory is also weak in students with RD, who have been found to perform more slowly than normal-achieving students in the rapid naming of letters, digits, colors, and objects but not in naming animals or foods (Bental & Tirosh, 2007). It has been suggested that students with RD might have more difficulty storing and retrieving symbolic verbal information (e.g., letters, digits).

*Visual memory.* Visual working memory is less strongly associated with reading decoding than is verbal working memory (Martinussen, Hayden, Hogg-Johnson, & Tannock, 2005). Even so, RD (and ADHD) students perform worse than typical peers in visual-spatial working memory (e.g., recalling the placement of objects) (Martinussen & Tannock, 2006; Marzocchi et al., 2008), visual short-term memory, and visual perceptual speed of coding and matching symbols (Willcutt, Pennington, et al., 2005). These specific visual deficits, however, are more likely to contribute to difficulties reading pictographs in languages such as Chinese. That is, in China, students must translate whole words rather than translate symbols to sounds. Thus, students with RD in China are more likely to have deficits in visual memory of whole pictographs (e.g., 鸟, the pictograph for "bird") and in visual discrimination between similar-looking characters or pictographs (e.g., 戍 [*shu*] means to guard the frontier, 戊 [*wu*] can mean the center or the earth, and 戌 [*xu*] can mean the period in the day from 7:00 to 9:00 P.M.) (Chan, Hung, Liu, & Lee, 2008; Ho, Chan, Leung, Lee, & Tsang, 2005).

Thus, reading disability depends on the strengths/weaknesses of the learner in relation to the "reading requirements" of a language. However, among RD students, long-term verbal and visual and visual-spatial memory abilities are below those of typical readers, indicating that dyslexia has cognitive contributors that extend beyond verbal learning (Menghini, Carlesimo, Marotta, Finzi, & Vicari, 2010). Specifically, there appears to be a generalized memory deficit that goes beyond a phonological disorder as the sole explanation of dyslexia.

## Communication

Language development in children with RD appears normal (Berninger, 2001), as in the case of Doug, whose "current individualized education program indicated normal language development." However, for many of these students, there may be language delay, as indicated by poor organization of thought (Cicci, 1984).

## Motor, Physical, and Somatic

Students with RD demonstrate more severe problems than typical peers (and than students with ADHD) in gross motor skills, fine motor skills (e.g., tapping tasks), and visual-motor integration (Kooistra, Crawford, Dewey, Cantell, & Kaplan, 2005; Shanahan et al., 2006; Tiffin-Richards, Hasselhorn, Richards, Banaschewski, & Rothenberger, 2004).

## Academic

Students with RD perform worse than peers in the areas of basic word recognition and general reading achievement (Bental & Tirosh, 2007; Ghelani, Sidhu, Jain, & Tannock, 2004; Shanahan et al., 2006; Willcutt, Pennington, et al., 2005). Verbal learning disabilities affect not only reading but also spelling and composition (Camahalan, 2006). Students with RD can become progressively less engaged academically, in a snowballing of negative outcomes that has been called the **Mathew effect** (Cunningham & Stanovich, 1997). This is often characterized as "the rich get richer and the poor get poorer" (Cunningham &

**Mathew effect:** The spreading of reading difficulties to other subject areas (e.g., math problem solving), accompanied by a cyclical downward spiral of motivation.

Stanovich, 1997). Doug will never fully "catch up" and will have continued difficulty reading fluently:

- "When it was Doug's turn, he could read few words. For unknown words, he didn't use any decoding strategies; rather, he looked to his partner for help."
- "During an interview with Doug's teacher, she had many concerns in both academic and behavior areas. His grades were failing in reading, math, and spelling."

Specific academic problems observed in the classroom among students with RD include the following:

<table>
<tr><td>

**Fluency:** The ability to read text accurately and quickly (automatically).

---

**Context cues:** The meanings of words and pictures that surround unknown words, which children may use to decode the unknown words and capture meaning.

---

**Visual errors in, composition, and spelling:** Students spell words exactly the way they sound and not the way they look.

</td><td>

1. Poor **fluency** (speed reading) and a dependence on guessing and **context cues** (e.g., pictures)
2. Difficulty with new vocabulary and a dislike of reading aloud (Singer, 2005)
3. **Visual errors,** particularly in the form of letter reversals—*b* for *d*, *w* for *m*, *p* for *q*, *tip* for *pit*; *felt* for *left*—when reading, spelling, or writing (e.g., multiple-choice exams can pose difficulties when the choices include b and d); punctuation and capitalization errors, and spelling that reflects poor recall of sound/symbol inconsistencies with a reliance on good sound analysis (e.g., writing "nite" for the word *knight*).
4. **Auditory errors** as seen in the misreading of phonetically consistent "nonwords" (*fong, tat*) and poor performance in syllable and phoneme counting games, detection of rhyme, and phoneme or syllable manipulation (e.g., phoneme deletion— "Say this word without this sound") (for a review, see Mann & Brady, 1988)

</td></tr>
</table>

In the English language it is primarily auditory errors or difficulties with phonics (i.e., the connection of letters to sounds) that explain dyslexia. (For further discussion of the assessment of spelling and handwriting errors and standardized reading achievement, see Stichter et al., 2008.)

## SUMMARY OF STRENGTHS AND NEEDS

| *Probable strengths* | *Probable needs* |
|---|---|
| • Good talking skills.<br>• Good listening comprehension skills.<br>• May have well-developed skills in visual-spatial areas—an ability to think three-dimensionally (e.g., think about an object from many different angles) and in pictures rather than words; may see solutions in the "mind's eye" (for a review, see Silverman, 2003). | • Early intervention—prior to second grade.<br>• High-interest books.<br>• Help with learning replacement behavior to avoid social embarrassment (e.g., asking to be allowed to skip reading aloud in class) rather than withdrawing or disrupting reading tasks. |

| Probable strengths | Probable needs |
|---|---|
| • May have good social skills and peer relationships.<br>• May develop alternate strength areas, such as math skills (Berninger, 2001).<br>• May develop the ability to use verbal context cues and pictures to figure out the meaning of printed text.<br>• May learn strategies that involve focusing on the gestalt, for example, by reading only the headings and the topic sentences in each paragraph. | • Assessment of the degree of spread of RD to other areas (e.g., math).<br>• Reduced emphasis on reading speed and reading aloud.<br>• At the upper elementary level, comprehension remains the primary objective, but the accumulation of knowledge takes precedence at advanced age levels. "Learning to read" in elementary school becomes the challenge of "reading to learn" at advanced grades. |

**Auditory errors in composition and spelling:** Errors in which the words within sentences, sentences within paragraphs, and ideas within compositions are out of order or poorly organized. Also, sounds, syllables, and words are missing or have omissions, additions, substitutions, or ending errors (agreement, tense, plural, possessives).

# DISABILITY IN THE CLASSROOM

## Implications for Accommodations in General Education Settings: Tier I

Important for all students in general education settings is differentiated instruction, which varies in time, content, and degree of scaffolding (based on group assessments of students' skills; Gersten, Compton, et al., 2009). However, in this setting there is a controversy over which method of teaching reading is best for children. Comparison studies suggest that the context-enriched **whole language approach** produces gains primarily for general education students, whereas young students with disabilities perform best in basal or sight approach reading programs and with **phonological code systems** (e.g., Drecktrah & Chiang, 1997). Phonological code systems of teaching reading are empirically based and highly structured and "explicitly teach application of phonological rules to print" with continuous monitoring of progress (Lyon, 1996, p. 65); they are often first tier in RTI. Lyon (1996) has suggested the following developmental sequence: (a) phonological awareness, which predicts reading in prekindergarten; (2) letter patterns taught in first and second grades; (c) fluency stressed in second and third grades; and (d) vocabulary (background knowledge) stressed in fourth grade. Such training can be implemented in peer-assisted learning programs, with coach-reader pairs, or in small groups (Gersten, Compton, et al., 2009). Typically, after a word has been learned through a phonological method, it is placed in long-term memory and recalled visually as the whole word, which produces reading that is fluent; phonics is then used as a backup strategy (i.e., when a child forgets a word or encounters a new word).

*Technologies.* Low-tech accommodations include the traditional approach of providing students with additional time, but of greater use are technologies that bypass reading, such as auditory translations of texts in the form of talking storybooks, books on tape, and electronic books. (For a list of possible resources, see Beard

**Whole language approach:** A method of teaching reading that involves using a context of meaningful experiences, which are dictated by the child, written by the adult, illustrated by the child, and subsequently reread by the child. This method is often used with older students who have been unable to make gains through the phonics method.

**Phonological code system:** A method of teaching children to read in which they learn the visual letter symbols, their corresponding sounds, and their governing rules in order to decode words and to spell (hundreds of component graphemes, phonemes, syllable types, prefixes, suffixes, and roots).

et al., 2007, p. 75.) *Reading-assistive technologies* are also available that present highlighted and magnified visual versions of text and pictures paired with words (e.g., Elder-Hinshaw, Manset-Williamson, Nelson, & Dunn, 2006). Additional assistive technologies include the Quicktionary Reading Pen II, which has been found to be an effective compensatory device for improving reading comprehension for an LD group, ages 10–18, with reading difficulties (Higgins & Raskind, 2005). Among college students with attentional problems and very poor reading comprehension, combining visual and auditory text input with highlighting and note-taking options has been found to promote faster reading for longer periods of time and with less fatigue (Hecker, Burns, Elkind, Elkind, & Katz, 2002).

## Implications for Interventions in Small-Group and Individual Settings: Tiers II and III

When early intervention is implemented, children with dyslexia *can* learn to read, although more slowly than their non-RD peers. Children with reading failure (RD, reading problems, or at risk for RD) represent varying degrees of severity that require similar interventions (Shaywitz et al., 2008). For example, computers should be provided for students to use to organize and reorganize written assignments and to check spelling. (For a list of spelling-assistive technological resources, see Beard et al., 2007, p. 77.)

Age may be an important factor in selecting reading approaches. Most research has focused on primary grades (Gersten, Compton, et al., 2009), and most of the resulting EBPs have focused on sound-symbol correspondence as well as fluency, comprehension, and vocabulary. Such interventions have been implemented three to five times per week for 20 to 40 minutes at a time in small groups, with progress monitored monthly and for at least 5 weeks (Gersten, Compton, et al., 2009). However, some children do not respond to these intensive interventions (Dahlin, 2011). For these students, listening and reading comprehension and vocabulary development should be a major component of Tier II interventions (Gersten, Compton, et al., 2009). Older students with RD should focus on learning a functional set of sight words within a meaningful context or be placed in a functional curriculum with text-to-speech accommodations (Shaywitz et al., 2008). Functional interventions can improve two types of literacy:

1. *Prose literacy:* the knowledge and skills needed to understand and use information from texts, including editorials, news stories, poems, and fiction

2. *Document literacy:* the knowledge and skills required to locate and use information contained in various formats, including job applications, payroll forms, transportation schedules, maps, tables, and graphs (Leuven, Oosterbeek, & van Ophem, 2004, p. 470)

In addition, at the upper elementary levels, interventions involving motivational priming may be important. Significantly improved reading comprehension and fluency were found in a recent study in which students were provided with positive feedback about reading level attained and then challenged to perform better than previously and better than another student identified as "clever" (Zentall & Lee, 2012). The intervention condition described a positive label (e.g., "clever," "good reader") associated with specific reading behavior (e.g., "a person who answers questions with few errors and understands what they read"). This EBP is practical because it requires only brief reading text to be used for within-child comparisons of performance (e.g., using portfolios or bar graphs). The labels used can be varied (e.g., "hard worker," "careful reader"), as long as they are tied to behavior (e.g., "are good at answering questions about reading").

Tier III interventions might involve daily instruction through one-on-one tutoring, which Vellutino et al. (1996) found helped 67% of poor readers to achieve at an average to above-average level after only one semester of tutoring—33% of the subjects in that study were considered severe RD and did not make gains. Over time, about half the children with RD in that study who had early high-quality instruction later became successful in school.

Also found to be effective for learners with reading and attentional problems is computerized training focusing on working memory. A 5-week training program that included reinforcement was found to improve working memory and reading comprehension (but not word decoding; Dahlin, 2011). Also for students with RD and at risk for RD, the use of reading materials designed to be "interesting" (novel, action-oriented, surprising, scary) has been found to improve reading comprehension (Richards, Thatcher, Shreeves, Timmons, & Barker, 1999; Beike & Zentall, 2012).

Several interventions for hyperlexia focus on encoding and have produced promising results. Most interventions for hyperlexia should begin at the level of understanding spoken language. In addition, students can be taught to use cognitive maps to visualize images in order to reduce their cognitive load; cognitive mapping has been shown to be effective in improving the reading comprehension of adolescents with behavior disorders (in a single-subject study design; Blankenship, Ayres, & Langone, 2005). Also, explicit strategy-based approaches have been successful (see Shaywitz et al., 2008); for example, story mapping of characters, setting, problem, events, and outcomes can improve recall and comprehension for students with behavioral difficulties (see Babyak, Koorland, & Mathes, 2000).

## Long-Term Outcomes

It has been estimated that 74% of children who are RD in third grade continue to read below grade level by ninth grade (Lyon, 1996). In other words, most children do not outgrow RD. Improvements in word recognition accuracy can be achieved, but deficits in fluency remain (Shaywitz et al., 2008). Statistics show that 35% of those who do not complete high school are RD, which is twice the rate of nondisabled peers (Blackorby & Wagner, 1996), and only 17% of individuals with RD enroll in any postsecondary courses (Fairweather & Shaver, 1990). Overall, prose literacy (e.g., the ability to understand and use text information) also predicts the attainment of better jobs and higher wages (Leuven et al., 2004). Youths who drop out generally experience negative outcomes—unemployment, underemployment, and incarceration.

However, with early intervention using evidence-based practices, an 18% incidence of RD was reduced to 1.4–5.4% (Lyon et al., 2003). Well-designed practices can alter the "neural systems that serve skilled reading" (Shaywitz et al., 2008, p. 459). Without these practices, performance differences between children with and without LD (not specifically identified as RD) increase as children progress through school (Deshler et al., 2001). This may be due to the spreading effects of reading disability into other areas of academic performance (e.g., social studies and science). The ability to read in the first grade is directly related to long-term outcomes in student achievement (reading comprehension, vocabulary, and general knowledge), even with IQ controlled (Cunningham & Stanovich, 1997).

## COMPOSITION AND SPELLING DISABILITIES

Composition is a way of expressing what has been learned. Writing also involves an active process of integrating knowledge. Thus, we learn as we write. In this process, the child brings personal experiences, feelings, and ideas into play to understand an external topic (e.g., through research and synthesis of information). Writers can also create permanent products that can be compared with other products and analyzed by the teacher for specific interests or creativity, or for skill deficits in spelling, handwriting, or sentence structure. Through journaling, writing can even lead to improved self-understanding.

Although learning gains can be achieved through the process of writing, composition itself is the most complex of all academic areas to perform, because it requires all the skills of language production, reading, handwriting, grammar, and spelling. This cumulative difficulty can be overwhelming to a child with intellectual difficulties, as in the case of Rex, whose case study appears at the end of Chapter 6:

> [Rex] has more breakdowns during writing than any other time of the day. He has shouted out that his mom needs to help him and started crying on more than one occasion. . . . This is another time of day when he will revert to baby talk. He will say, "Me done." When he has finished a paragraph or assignment, he will say, "Me done."

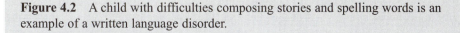

**Figure 4.2**   A child with difficulties composing stories and spelling words is an example of a written language disorder.

Stated differently, writing requires the skills of generating content, which includes amassing background knowledge, and then planning, organizing the content, translating, revising, and improving the writing (Graham & Harris, 2003). The first part is the generation of verbal content, followed by a whole set of lower-level skills of keeping ideas in mind to arrange them in logical sequence and inter-relationship, as well as translating these ideas into visual symbols and placing them physically on paper. See Figure 4.2. As Graham and Harris (2003; 2009) observe, students with LD focus primarily on rapidly generating ideas and on the formalities of spelling and neat writing rather than on the processes of planning, organizing, and reviewing.

Spelling, a subcomponent of written language, involves the ability to translate sounds and spoken words into visual symbols that represent words. See Figure 4.2. English-speaking children with spelling disorders probably either have not made sense of the rules for relationships between sounds and the visual letters that represent sounds (Hann, Penney, & Power, 1999) or have not visually memorized the inconsistencies in the English language.

For example, here is a paraphrase of an e-mail received from the mother of a student:

7-year-old high-achieving student who loves math, is a strong reader, a born story-teller and has good comprehension of what she reads, but has consistent spelling difficulties. She does perform at an average level on her weekly spelling but does not apply what she has learned in her free writing. Her teacher assumed that she would mature and spelling would catch up, but she has not made progress. The teacher has never had a student who performs so poorly in spelling without improving yet performs so well in other areas. These were the types of errors she made: "muther" rather than "mother," "grate" rather than "great," "vare" rather than "very." She is also very sensitive to others' emotions, has no social or behavioral problems at school, but when she returns home she shows bouts of intense anger.

Response to the mother:

She is using her strong auditory sense to spell. Her spelling is very accurate phonetically—also she is a good storyteller (an auditory-based task). I would guess that she has weaker visual memory. She does not recall things she has seen (although she can for *short* periods of time on her weekly tests). It appears that she needs accommodations for written language production, for example by submitting oral reports on a computer that translate her spoken words into written sentences. It does sound like she has good understanding of visual symbols, math, and emotional communications. It is the visual long-term memory of words where she appears to have difficulty. Her intense emotions at home could simply be that home is the place she feels most comfortable letting it out, which could show you how much she is struggling with specific visual memorizing tasks at school.

## FORMAL IDENTIFICATION

### Definitions

#### IDEA

IDEA's definition of SLD (presented in total in Chapter 3) also defines written language disabilities. The relevant part is repeated here (with italics added) to emphasize written language disability as

a disorder in one or more of the basic psychological processes involved in understanding or using *language*, spoken or *written*, which may manifest itself in an imperfect ability to listen, think, speak, read, *write, spell*, or do mathematical calculations. (H.R. 1350, Section 602 [30])

#### DSM-IV-TR

*DSM-IV-TR* (APA, 2000, p. 61) supplies the following definition for SLD (diagnostic criteria for 315.2, Disorder of Written Expression):

*Defining characteristics:* "Writing skills, as measured by individually administered standardized tests (or functional assessments of writing skills), are substantially below those expected given the person's chronological age, measured intelligence, and age-appropriate education."

*Impairment:* "interferes with academic achievement or activities of daily living that require the composition of written texts (e.g., writing grammatically correct sentences and organized paragraphs)."

*Exclusions and conditions:* If a sensory deficit is present, the difficulties in writing skills are in excess of those usually associated with it." A diagnosis of "Disorder of Written Expression is generally not given if there is only poor handwriting (or spelling)."

### Frequently Occurring Subtypes

Poor writing can be categorized into problems of content, form, and clarity.

*Content* is the generation of ideas, which are drawn from prior experiences and a general motivation to write. Writing follows a developmental sequence that begins with *knowledge telling* (Siegler, 1991). That is, a child in the second, third, or fourth grade will organize a story around a topic and then retrieve from memory things about that topic in a sort of unorganized grocery list. By the sixth grade, the child will refer to more than the topic sentence and create internal connections; these rich interconnections depend on the child's ability to keep more of the story in mind. That is, children's written language reflects the quality and organization of their spoken language. As students develop, they move from a knowledge-telling to a *knowledge-transforming* goal, in which they take a position or make a case with their knowledge. The process of writing itself increases the writer's knowledge (Siegler, 1991).

*Form* encompasses grammar, punctuation, spelling, and handwriting. These are the mechanical aspects of writing. Children create their best writing when they can dictate stories at their normal speaking rate; their second-best compositions are created when they slow their dictation down for a scribe, and the poorest-quality compositions result when children must apply their skills using the mechanical aspects of form (see Bereiter & Scardamalia, 1982, cited in Siegler, 1991).

*Clarity* of written communications is assessed in the process of revision. Revision requires the detection of errors of consistency, organization, and form (e.g., grammatical errors, missing sentences, contradictory information) and errors of perspective (i.e., separating what the writer knows from what he or she can expect the reader to know) (Siegler, 1991). The ability to detect and repair these types of errors increases with age and with the flexibility and ability to hold multiple perspectives, as well as the story line, in mind.

### Possible Co-Occurring Conditions and Differences Among Related Disabilities

*DSM-IV-TR* states that a "Disorder of Written Expression is commonly found in combination with Reading Disorder or Mathematics Disorder" (APA, 2000, p. 55). Writing composition is built on the lower-level skills of reading and language, so it is not surprising that about three-fourths of students with composition disabilities also have reading problems. Students with ADHD (see Section IV) have difficulty with planning, organizing, and revising written materials, due to deficits in working memory and avoidance of repetitive editing, and difficulty with handwriting, due to their poorer fine motor skills (for a review, see Zentall, 2006). Students with dysgraphia (see Chapter 15) (and possibly NVLD; see Chapter 5) also may avoid written compositions due to poor-quality handwriting and poor visual-motor skills. However, these children should be able to create good spoken narratives and possibly good typed stories.

## Etiology

*Biogenetic.* The biogenetic factor associated with composition and spelling disabilities is similar to that documented for children with reading deficits—that is, heritability. Twin studies have indicated that reading disability is heritable, with a 33% overlap between reading disability and mathematics disability (Snowling, 2009). Spelling difficulties have an even greater degree of heritability than reading difficulties (see Mather, 2003).

*Environmental.* These factors include poor living conditions, poor instruction at school, and lack of significant verbal interactions or reading experiences during early childhood.

*Functional.* Functional assessments of students with written language disorders find that they avoid or perform poorly on long assignments that require planning, especially in comparison to other areas, such as math, physical education, art. Unfortunately, handwriting and spelling difficulties can lead "children to avoid writing and to the development of the mind-set that they cannot write" (Weintraub & Graham, 1998, p. 146).

## Prevalence, Gender, and Age Factors

*Prevalence.* Around 8% to 15% of the school population is estimated to have written expression or composition disabilities (Lyon, 2003), and two of every five students with LD have IEP goals related to written language (Kavale & Forness, 1995).

*Gender.* Writing problems are identified more frequently in boys than in girls.

*Age.* "Although difficulty in writing (e.g., particularly poor handwriting or copying ability or inability to remember letter sequences in common words) may appear as early as the first grade, disorders of written expression are seldom diagnosed before the end of first grade, because sufficient formal writing instruction has usually not occurred until this point in most school settings. The disorder is usually apparent by second grade" (APA, 2000, p. 55).

Between the ages of 10 and 12, good spellers make a transition from reliance on sound/symbol correspondence to reliance on previously stored visual representations of words (Mather, 2003). In other words, most learners begin with sound analysis but progress to using visual memory of whole words and thereby increase speed.

# INFORMAL EDUCATOR IDENTIFICATION OF CHARACTERISTICS

## Behavioral

Behavioral problems, such as disruptiveness and off-task actions, would be expected in students with writing disabilities only when they attempt to avoid those written tasks on which they typically fail.

## Social-Emotional

Similarly, social-emotional problems, such as low academic self-concept or passivity, would be expected when students fail in the production of written work and when teachers grade only on form (spelling, handwriting, grammar) but not on content or substance.

## Cognitive

*Intellectual.* Those students in the lower ranges of verbal IQ will produce compositions of low abstract quality; their compositions will primarily involve naming and describing concrete objects and events. Levels of abstraction can be scored informally from low (1 to 3) to high (4 and 5) using the following list adapted from Myklebust's Picture Story Language Test (1965):

1. Names or lists items (naming)

2. Describes quality or action by using adjectives, adverbs (describing)

3. Produces inferences about feelings or relations (interpreting)

4. Infers preceding action or outcome (past/future) (narrative interpreting)

5. Generalizes, moralizes (evaluative interpreting)

The ability to generate content is impaired when a child has underlying difficulties with spoken verbal language or in reading, as is the case with Doug:

> Students were at their desks finishing a paragraph. As in other subjects, he [Doug] didn't work until the teacher came to him. Rather than writing, Doug talked to his neighbor and looked around. In one instance, the teacher repeated instructions and asked him what he was to do. He looked at her and held up both fists and said, "I don't know." While she helped others, he did not work and played with pencils and an eraser. She came over, threw the broken pencils away, and read aloud his writing. . . . Doug wrote only two words: "We go."

Although reading comprehension and composition are typically related to intelligence, spelling is not.

*Memory and organization.* Working memory deficits contribute to math, reading, and composition disabilities (Swanson & Sáez, 2003) and affect the ability to organize thought and translate that thought into a sequence of sentences, topics, and interconnected ideas. Working memory deficits can be seen in written work that is brief, incomplete, lacking in development and organization, and reflective of difficulty managing time (e.g., long-term projects, term papers).

*Perception. Auditory errors* can be seen in sentences with poor structure or word order and in the omission or addition of words, the substitutions of sounds in words, and word-ending errors (agreement, tense, plural, possessives). When spelling errors are caused by auditory errors, the resulting words bear little resemblance to the words intended; the vowel sounds of the words may differ (*late* spelled *loud*), possible real-word replacements may be used (*cat* spelled *come*), sounds or syllables may be missing (*beginning* spelled *being*), or endings of words may be missing (*spotted* spelled *spot*). *Visual errors* can be seen in spelling (punctuation and capitalization errors) and in handwriting wherein the eye attempts to guide the hand.

When a child does not realize that his or her handwriting is poor, a visual and not a motor problem is indicated, but if the child constantly erases, the problem is likely in the failure of the hand to meet the standards of the visual system.

## Communication

Spoken language lies at the base of written language. If a child has difficulty with composing written language, it is important to determine his or her adequacy in spoken language. Evidence indicates that about half of students with RD also have oral or spoken language difficulties (Snowling, 2009). If the child shows similar poor organization and lack of production in speaking, then the fault lies in spoken language, and this is where remediation should be begin. However, if the child can speak clearly and at length on a subject area but cannot write about that topic, then the problem lies in the written translation of thought sequences.

## Motor, Physical, and Somatic

Children with poor fine motor skills will have poor handwriting (dysgraphia; see Chapter 15), which could reduce their production of written compositions. However, these students should also be able to tell good stories and engage in lengthy conversations.

## Academic

Children with written language disabilities produce fewer written sentences, fewer words that are seven letters or more, and more spelling and capitalization errors than typically developing peers (Houck & Billingsley, 1989; Shanahan et al., 2006). Their written work may lack quantity and form/organization, similar to the spoken narratives of students with ADHD, which lack goals, attempts at resolution, and outcomes (Freer et al., 2011).

## SUMMARY OF STRENGTHS AND NEEDS

| Possible strengths | Probable needs |
|---|---|
| • Good spoken language and sometimes talkative<br>• May have good keyboarding skills<br>• May have good gross motor skills | • Alternate ways to integrate information that do not involve written language or spelling (e.g., through verbal communication, through audio recordings, through debates)<br>• Alternate ways to express knowledge (e.g., verbally, pictorially)<br>• Help in developing strategies for revising/organizing text<br>• Additional time and breaks between written assignments |

## DISABILITY IN THE CLASSROOM

### Implications for Accommodations in General Education Settings: Tier I

Weintraub and Graham (1998) found that it took students with LD an additional 20 to 50 minutes to write what their non-LD classmates wrote in 30 minutes. Thus, added time is a useful accommodation. To address problems of too little quantity of written work, it can be helpful to (a) reduce the required length of compositions or allow students to present verbal narratives; (b) provide word processors, which allow writers to focus on their ideas and later make revisions without recopying; and (c) use **mnemonics,** prompt cards, and "think sheets" to aid the writing process (Englert et al., 1995). Students may need instruction in keyboarding and in how to revise (MacArthur, 1996). The current use of word processing programs is unknown, although in 1994 only 55% of teachers reported the use of word processing in the classroom, and fewer used this software for composing (Zimmerman & Conant, 1994).

**Mnemonics:** Memory "tricks" such as acronyms, crazy phrases, or cartoons that act as global or abbreviated cues and can be used to recall more complex and detailed verbal information.

*To address problems of organization,* concept mapping and other assistive technology adaptations have been found to be useful (see Beard et al., 2007, p. 79). The following approaches have also been shown to be helpful:

1. Provide a deck of cards with template sentence openings (e.g., "Similarly," "For example," "On the other hand"); this can lead to more richly interconnected stories, even though the prompts do not specify content (Bereiter & Scardamalia, 1982, cited in Siegler, 1991).

2. Have students draw pictures and sequence those pictures prior to writing from them.

3. Use cuing steps: who (characters, feelings), where (setting), what (goal, problem), and how (plan, solution).

4. Use graphic organizers, such as mind maps and outlines, that allow students to visualize their ideas and to make "associations between [and among] concepts" (Beach, Appleman, & Dorsey, 1994, p. 703).

5. Provide feedback from teachers and peers (pair student-writers with student-critic/editors and then have them reverse roles).

6. Use self-monitoring checklists (Graves & Hauge, 1993). For example, on a card listed in one column are the words *characters, setting, problem, plan,* and *ending.* Next to each of these words are two other columns headed

"Check as I plan" and "Check as I write." The student is instructed to write down ideas for each part, and then, during the actual writing, check to see if all the ideas are included in the composition.

*To address handwriting, grammar, and spelling,* use computer-assisted composition (CAC), which specifically accommodates with tools such as editing for spelling and grammar and relistening to auditory input. Use programs that involve speech feedback to enable the less accomplished reader to hear and read along with the program (Montague & Fonseca, 1993).

*Overall motivational strategies* that have proven successful with students who have written language disabilities have been summarized by Pintrich and Schunk (1996, pp. 248–251) as follows:

1. Focusing on meaningful learning activities
2. Designing tasks for novelty, variety, diversity, and interest
3. Designing tasks that are challenging but reasonable
4. Providing opportunities for students to have some choice and control over activities in the classroom
5. Focusing on individual improvements and not comparisons with others
6. Making evaluation private, *not* public
7. Recognizing student effort
8. Helping students see mistakes as opportunities for learning

## Implications for Interventions in Small-Group and Individual Settings: Tiers II and III

If a child has poor spoken language as well as poor written language, it is advisable to begin instruction by targeting spoken language. If the child has only poor writing, the educator should explicitly teach the different components in the writing process (a basic outline for planning, writing, and revising), and provide feedback related to the explicit steps taught earlier (Harris & Graham, 1999). Critical in this process is an integrated assessment model that ties the outcomes of writing assessments (e.g., ratings, observations, permanent products) to specific skill training (for review see Parker, Burns, & McMaster, 2012). In addition, the following strategies are useful:

**Modeling:** When a child observes an adult or another child with characteristics similar to his or her own who is interacting with a feared object or in a feared situation, the observing child learns responses from the behavior modeled.

1. Teach academic strategies (a) by **modeling** and with a checklist, while pretending to be a naive writer talking aloud about the process; (b) by using a template for the structure of different styles (descriptive and argumentative) (Harris & Graham, 1999); and (c) by using self-instructions, self-reinforcement, goal setting, and self-monitoring (e.g., Linemann & Reid, 2008).

2. Teach editing by using peer editors, with each student taking turns as a student-critic and a student-writer. The student-critic asks the student-writer to explain any sentence or idea in the student-writer's composition that needs to be further refined. Revisions are then made by the student-writer, and the students switch roles (Wong, Butler, Ficzere, & Kuperis, 1996).

3. Teach cognitive flexibility by using jokes and riddles and different types of writing, such as opinion essays and personal narratives (Wong et al., 1996).

*To address spelling:*

1. Use peer tutoring, with student tutor and student tutee paired with a "script" of spelling words. The tutor dictates the items and the tutee responds orally. The tutor awards the tutee two points for each correct response or gives the correction and awards one point after the tutee practices the correct response three times. Improved spelling has been shown to be related to active responding, frequent and immediate feedback, and the presentation of material at a student-controlled pace (DuPaul & Henningson, 1993). This technique is also appropriate for typically developing adolescent boys, who have been shown to be willing to allow same-gender peers with LD to participate without rejection, as long as there are no performance costs to their inclusion (Plata, Trusty, & Glasgow, 2005).

2. Use self-correction. In one tested method, students with LD placed checkmarks next to their correctly spelled words; for the words they spelled incorrectly, they copied their misspellings and then wrote out the correct spellings. They then circled in red the parts they had misspelled on both the error imitations and the corrected words. Improvements in spelling were found to result when students' attention was focused on the parts of words they had spelled incorrectly (Gettinger, 1985);

3. Use finger spelling to practice spelling words for children with LD. For example, students have been taught the sign language alphabet to practice spelling words with a partner.

## Long-Term Outcomes

According to *DSM-IV-TR,* "Disorders of Written Expression may occasionally be seen in older children or adults, and little is known about its long-term prognosis" (APA, 2000, p. 55). What has been shown is that document literacy (e.g., filling out job applications, payroll forms) is a significant predictor of attaining good jobs, full-time employment, and higher wages (Leuven et al., 2004).

## CHAPTER SUMMARY

- Written language disabilities are included in the one formal definition of LD by IDEA, which now includes the RTI criterion. *DSM-IV-TR* separately categorizes RD as unexpected underachievement relative to IQ.

- The overlapping subtypes of written language disorders are reading, composition, and spelling. Reading can be further categorized into decoding and encoding. Decoding problems are labeled *dyslexia;* encoding difficulties are either the result of the decoding problem or caused by poor understanding of spoken language. Spelling involves a reverse process to that of reading (reading = symbol to sound; spelling = sound to symbol). Composition performance problems can be categorized into those involving content and those involving form (grammar, punctuation).

- Co-occurring anxiety and depression are observed especially among older students who have experienced school failure. A frequently co-occurring disability is ADHD. Both groups will show inattention, but students with LD will show attentional difficulties primarily in the specific academic area(s) of their LD, whereas students with ADHD will show inattention across a range of subject areas that depend on the length, passive nature, and familiarity of the task (nonnovel and nonactive tasks and settings).

- The etiology of written language disabilities is genetic. Spelling disabilities have greater heritability than RD. Although children come to school with a genetically based mix of perceptual skills (phonemic awareness), intersensory skills (symbol to sound), and memory abilities, environmental influences can alter these abilities (e.g., enriched or impoverished learning experiences at home and in school). Antecedents that are clues to type of written language disability are the presence/absence of problems in specific areas (e.g., writing or spelling assignments but not math, reading aloud versus reading silently) that the child attempts to avoid or disrupt.

- Written language disabilities are more prevalent in boys than in girls. RD is one of the most common childhood disorders and is identified earlier than composition or spelling disabilities. The negative effects of written language disabilities spread at older age levels to science, social studies, and learning foreign languages. Both listening comprehension and reading comprehension can also affect math problem solving.

- Written language disorders can be informally identified from observations of behavioral and attentional responses to reading and writing assignments. Often, children with such disorders will attempt to avoid looking "dumb" in front of peers by disrupting or clowning. However, these attempts are not successful in helping them achieve popular acceptance, and most of these children select similar friends with LD. Emotional responses include depression/anxiety, low academic self-concept, and passivity.

- Dyslexia depends on the strengths/weaknesses of the learner in relation to the "reading requirements" of a language. Lower verbal intelligence, especially in the executive functions of selecting and monitoring reading strategies, can make reading comprehension more difficult. Poor working memory—that is, poor ability to hold sounds, syllables, words, and sequences of ideas in mind—contributes to poor reading comprehension and poorly sequenced writing. Spelling is not related to level of intelligence. Most processing problems related to spelling are perceptual, intersensory, and memory deficits. Short- and long-term verbal and visual memory deficits are common in students with LD; such deficits contribute to difficulty in storing and retrieving symbols (e.g., letters, digits, words). Deficits in small motor skills (discussed in Chapter 15) may contribute to poor written compositions and spelling performance.

- The academic difficulties of students with written language disabilities can be assessed during oral reading tasks, composition assignments, and spelling tests. Specifically, assignments in each area can offer clues about visual or auditory errors. Performance on compositions can offer additional clues about whether the child can (a) hold information in mind (length produced), (b) plan and sequence that information (organization), and (c) think abstractly. Since composition is built upon the lower-level skills of reading and language, the majority of students with composition disabilities will also have reading problems, and some of these children will speak little or speak with poor organization.

- Early interventions that remediate and teach the application of phonological rules to print are especially important for young children at risk for RD. Students who have failed in those systematic programs may do well by memorizing sight words that are relevant to upcoming lessons and that are personally meaningful and functionally important. Learning strategy-based approaches for composition include setting goals and developing outlines for planning and the use of checklists with self-reinforcement and self-monitoring strategies for revising. If a child has poor listening comprehension as well as poor reading comprehension, intervention should begin at the lower level of listening.

- Accommodations provided by the educator should include reading-assistive technologies, optional aloud or silent reading, private (not public) feedback, interesting reading and written language assignments, and choices of methods/materials. For producing compositions, useful accommodations include extensions of time, assignments of reduced length, writing technologies to replace handwriting and that catch grammar/spelling mistakes, teacher-provided verbal cue cards or child-produced small pictures to help with organization, and peer-assisted techniques for spelling.

## CHAPTER QUESTIONS

### Reading

1. What is the relationship between attention disorders and reading disabilities?

2. If comprehension is the ultimate goal of reading and a child comprehends well, does it matter if the child reads out loud poorly? What are the purposes of asking children to read aloud?

3. If a child can decode but not encode, where should intervention begin?

4. If a child has dyslexia but needs to understand social studies or science texts, what kinds of accommodations are appropriate?

5. What is an important variable to keep in mind when teaching reading to children who have already experienced failure?

6. What are the effects of economic poverty on reading?

7. What approach might be taken to help the child described here by a parent?

We have a younger daughter who is 8 years old and in third grade who is having some reading struggles. She is still above where the school would intervene and have her tested for a learning disability, because she is on point in subjects other than reading. She is very confident, outgoing, and artistic. However, something is not "clicking" with reading—she is about a grade level behind. We are working one-on-one at home, in addition to her pullout reading group at school. I have scheduled an eye exam as well, just to be sure there is no vision issue.

## TRUE/FALSE AND MULTIPLE-CHOICE

1. Reading is primarily a visual task.

2. A child with reading disabilities or dyslexia will **most likely** have difficulty with

   A. memory skills
   B. sound-symbol associations
   C. visual skills

3. If a child cannot comprehend when reading independently, what is the **first** question you should ask? Can the child

   A. decode?
   B. write?
   C. hear?

4. Computer-assisted composition is a good strategy for children with poor
   A. fine motor skills
   B. spelling
   C. reasoning skills
   D. A & B
   E. All of the above

5. For children with RD which is the **least** correct—that they will be
   A. delayed in reading but will "catch up"
   B. continued delayed reading speed
   C. delayed in reading comprehension

## Composition and Spelling

1. Why is it important to evaluate the ideas produced in a composition separately from the mechanics (writing, grammar, and spelling)?

2. What are some ways in which children can monitor their own progress in writing?

3. What have you learned in this chapter that was new or interesting for you?

## TRUE/FALSE

1. Written work that is brief, incomplete, and poorly organized suggests problems in working memory.

2. Spelling errors that have missing sounds or syllables reflect visual errors.

3. Document literacy includes the functional skills of filling out job applications and understanding how to read transportation schedules, maps, tables, and graphs.

## SHORT ANSWER

1. Errors of punctuation, capitalization, and the like are _____ errors.

2. Using pictures in a story as _____ _____ to figure out what particular words are is a compensatory type of skill.

3. Memory skills that are useful in helping us speak or write for an extended time and help us organize what we say are called _____ _____.

4. The understanding of written text is called _____.

5. Errors of word order, verb tense, omissions, and substitutions of words are _____ errors.

6. _____ language provides the basis for written language.

## PROBLEM-BASED CASE APPLICATIONS AND QUESTIONS

### CASE STUDY 4.1: DOUG

*"I'm dying here."*
(adapted from a report submitted by Konie Hughes)

*Background.* Doug is a 7-year-old boy who is placed full-time in a first-grade general education classroom. He has been diagnosed with a mild communication disorder—specifically, his articulation errors with *l* and *r*. His current IEP indicates normal language development and states that his communication disorder will probably *not affect* him academically. He receives 20 minutes of speech services twice a week and daily intervention (40 minutes) in phonics.

During an interview with Doug's teacher, she expressed many concerns for him in both academic and behavior areas. In the classroom he exhibits problematic behavior: difficulty staying on task, inappropriate off-task behaviors, and staring into space—even during one-on-one instruction. Problematic behavior includes not keeping his hands to himself, not paying attention, not following directions, not working well with others, and displaying few social skills. Doug does not like to be ignored, and he has a negative attitude in all subject areas, though his skills are better in math than in other areas. He is receiving failing grades in reading, math, and spelling. Some current emotional statements and behaviors that the teacher has concerns about: Doug's lying about an incident with a classmate that included name-calling, his negative comments ("You don't trust me," "No one likes me," "I can't do this"), his not trying, and his resistance to her help (at times).

Doug's mother reports behavioral problems at home: He is easily distracted, hyperactive, and homework takes "hours." There is a family history of ADHD. Behavior rating scales have been requested.

Doug does have positive attributes—at times he is kind to classmates, he has shown he is capable of expressing his feelings, and he is generally compliant. His interests are social rewards (attention and praise), drawing, Legos, daydreaming, sleeping, and recess. His strength is comprehension of stories read aloud.

The general education classroom has 15 students. Doug's teacher has a calm and positive demeanor, and she models a courteous manner and provides positive feedback. When the noise level or behavioral disruptions in the classroom begin to increase, she begins quietly counting backward from five to one—aloud and using her fingers. Her students understand this cue to stop and listen.

## Behavioral Log

*Reading.* Observations were made during partner reading: Students sat on the floor with a partner and took turns reading a page in the story assigned for the week from their text.

- The teacher assigned an independent reader to partner with Doug. When the other student read, Doug did not follow along and looked elsewhere. When it was Doug's turn, he could read few words. For unknown words, he didn't use any decoding strategies; rather, he looked to his partner for help.
- One partner encouraged Doug to sound out words by beginning the first sound, but Doug wouldn't try, and eventually the student told him the word.
- Another time, the partner simply ignored Doug and talked to her neighbor. Whenever the teacher noticed Doug not reading, she'd help him. His response to one of these instances was, "I don't know what to do."
- Because he wasn't paying attention, when it was his turn to read, he would look to his partner and ask, "Which page am I on?"
- During a multiple-choice test, the teacher read each question aloud and the students marked their answers on their test sheets. (Doug's test performance is generally poor because the teacher does not read the multiple-choice answers aloud as well.) In one instance, after the teacher read the question, Doug placed his hands on his cheeks, yawning and staring. The teacher came over to his desk, placed her finger on the number of the question on his paper, and read again; then he looked at the page and marked his answer.
- Throughout the remainder of the test, this routine continued; only when the teacher came to his desk, pointed at the number, and read again did Doug look at his paper and mark an answer.
- The last question required that students both write a sentence and create a drawing. In the amount of time given, compared to his peers, Doug was the only student to complete only one of these two (the picture). His drawing was not relevant to the question, but compared to those of his peers, it had more details.

*Math.* The teacher stood at the chalkboard giving whole-group math instructions; students sat at their desks with their workbooks. Instructions were given; students then worked a problem either on the board or in the workbook.

- Doug did not follow along. During observations, he laid down his head and stared, rummaged in his pencil box, or talked aloud (others ignored him).
- In one instance, the teacher came over to Doug's desk and pointed to the problem in his workbook, and he said that he couldn't find a pencil.
- She got a pencil and asked what number comes after 21. Doug responded, "I hate math," but wrote the number. The teacher reminded him that he knew this.
- When she came to him again, because he wasn't working but playing with crayons, she pointed to the number to color (to count by twos). He responded, "I'm dying here."
- As the teacher gave the class further instructions to color numbers as they counted by fives, Doug first put his arms inside his shirt then pulled his desk toward him and scooted down, tipping his chair. He said, "I'm done. When do I get to sleep?"
- As students continued working, the student in front of Doug turned to look at him. Doug said, "What are you looking at?" He continued to balance his chair and rocked it while the teacher asked the class questions.
- When Doug laid down his head and the teacher came over, he closed his eyes. She asked him where they were in the lesson, and he didn't know. She told him what to do, and he did it.
- When the teacher asked the classroom a question, Doug raised his hand but didn't get called on; he said, "Aw . . ." and turned in his chair to face the back of the room. He fell off the chair, sat on the floor, and said, "Help me, I'm dying." Neighbors looked but didn't say anything. As the teacher went around the room, he said again, "I'm dying. Good night," and sat under his desk. After the teacher came over, he colored the correct bear in his workbook with the wrong color and then went under his desk again.

*Writing.* During one observation, students worked in groups at different stations.

- Doug was with a group of three others and was to complete a worksheet (writing the word under the matching blended sound). As soon as he sat down, he asked, "Help me? I don't know what to do." He looked at me and I suggested he ask the group again, and he responded, "They're mean, they're girls."
- He then copied another's paper and began sticking his pencil lead underneath his fingernail.
- When one of the girls said something, Doug said, "You're my worst enemy. Be quiet."
- During another observation, students were at their desks finishing a paragraph. As in other subjects, Doug didn't work until the teacher came to him. Rather than writing, he talked to his neighbor and looked around.
- In one instance, the teacher repeated instructions and asked him what he was to do. He looked at her and held up both fists and said, "I don't know."

- While the teacher helped others, Doug did not work and played with pencils and an eraser. She came over, threw the broken pencils away, and read aloud his writing. During this observation, Doug wrote only two words: "We go."

*Listening.* Observations in this setting were done while the children were sitting on the floor listening to instructions during calendar time, listening to directions for an upcoming activity, during story time (teacher reading a story aloud), or during transitions.

- During calendar time, when the students were counting coins as a group, Doug used his fingers to figure out the answer. He raised his hand and was called on. At times he just stared, and after a while, he began to hit his head against a chair.
- When students were watching the teacher as she read aloud a paragraph posted on the wall, Doug kept his eyes on her. This focused attention was also observed while the teacher read a story aloud to the group; initially, he was sitting underneath the table and was asked to come out from under it.
- He then, at the periphery of the group, walked on his knees, with legs crossed and hands on his feet, all the while keeping his eyes on the book. After a while, he was asked to sit on his bottom; he grinned wide and sat for the remainder of the story.
- He remained relatively still for about 12 minutes, then quietly untied his shoes.

## ABC Analysis

Overall, Doug's highest-frequency payoffs are avoiding failure and getting competence (combined with self-determination) in each subject area. His next-highest payoff is getting stimulation, which he did almost 50% of the time during listening, when it was difficult for him to be still. During math he was stimulated with his pencil and crayons; during writing he was stimulated with drawing (drawing pictures usually accompanied writing).

## Diagnosis Versus ABC Analysis

Doug is in first-grade general education full-time, but he has been diagnosed with a mild communication disorder—specifically speech. His current IEP indicates normal language development and suggests that his communication disorder will probably not affect him academically. However, throughout all three subject areas, Doug had behavioral occurrences of avoiding failure. In each setting, the routine between the teacher and Doug remained the same: He avoided doing any work until the teacher came to him. She then repeated instructions and he got back on task. But as soon as she moved away, he returned to off-task behaviors. Thus, both teacher and students reinforce his avoidance behavior. Probable skill deficits in reading and writing contribute to the payoffs observed. Doug's negative statements suggest that he usually does not understand instructions. And when his attempts for help go unanswered, he doesn't know how to act appropriately. When Doug did ask for help, these usually were *indirect* attempts: "I'm dying here" (repeated many times during math); "You're my worst enemy. Be quiet" was the frustration voiced to peers who didn't help him during a group writing activity. Examples of his *direct* attempts to get help are when he said, "I don't know," while holding up both fists in frustration (during writing, responding to teacher); and "Help me? I don't know what to do," addressed to his peers as soon as he sat down to do a worksheet in a group.

Doug did not display avoidance behavior and was more actively engaged for longer periods in settings that required only listening (see Figure 4.3), especially during story time, when he could get stimulation by moving around. (His strength is in listening comprehension.) Interestingly, he was a more active participant during listening to math, where his skills are average, and he shows little interactive behavior (only avoids) during reading, where is skills are below average. Thus, his behavior functions to avoid failing mainly in areas of deficit. His behavior also functions to get competence or self-determination (control) by seeking help from anybody, which he continually does not get.

## Intervention Derived From ABC Analysis

Doug's work samples during reading and writing suggest that he has more difficulty in these two subjects. The academic area selected for intervention is reading. His work samples and behavior in reading indicate that a skill problem exists. Therefore, if his skill deficit is addressed, his negative avoidance behavior should decrease, and he should begin to achieve some competence. The intervention during partner reading will be to increase his reading vocabulary, such that he can experience success.

First, on Monday, Doug will listen to a story with the teacher and class choral reading. Doug will then choose five words that he wants to learn and write them on cards. Each week, Doug can choose more words to learn.

Next, Tuesday through Thursday, Doug will listen to the same story on tape. Doug will practice memorizing word cards with a peer assistant. Words that he has learned will go in one envelope, labeled "Words I know"; words that he is still learning will go into another envelope, "Words I am learning." Doug will chart his progress by coloring in squares on a self-regulation chart. As an incentive, after practicing Doug will be allowed time to draw or daydream.

**Figure 4.3**   Doug's High-Frequency Payoffs

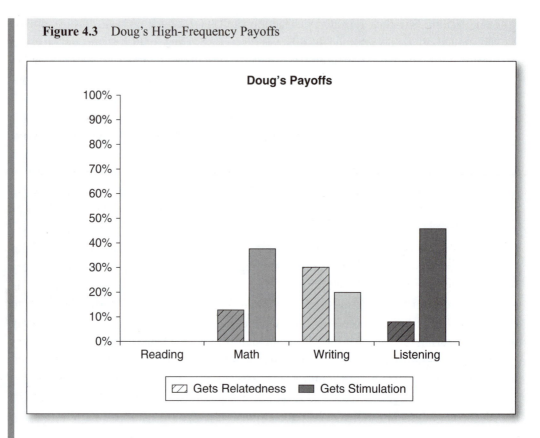

*Use and results of the intervention.* The purpose of the intervention and the steps involved were explained to Doug; after listening to the story, he selected three words to learn and wrote them on cards. As motivation, he was allowed to draw with new markers (something he likes to do very much) only after he had practiced reading his words three times. He had no problem reading his word cards. He also charted, with a marker, each time he practiced. The next day, the peer assistant read while Doug listened, stopping whenever he came to one of the words that Doug had learned. However, Doug was not paying attention; instead, he was rolling all over the floor and attempting to talk to other students.

Doug drew while he listened to the peer assistant read. He then chose five words to practice, which he wrote on cards with a red marker, his favorite color. Then he practiced his words with the peer assistant. He had problems reading one of these words, *Cecil,* the name of the robot from the story. He continued to practice both weeks' words (eight words), and the chart continued to motivate him to see how many words he read, as did the growing pile of word cards. After practicing the cards three times, he got to draw. By the end of the second week, he could read *Cecil.*

At the beginning of the third week, Doug chose six words. During practice he had trouble remembering two of these words, but he didn't get frustrated, and he really wanted to put all of these six cards into the "Words I have learned" envelope. He practiced until he knew this week's six words and continued to practice and chart the previous weeks' words, for a total of fourteen words. One day he practiced by playing a game with the cards with the peer assistant, which he really enjoyed, and the teacher said this went very well. On the last day of the intervention, I had him practice his words; by this time he was reading fourteen cards. Once in a while he would forget a word, but for the first time, he attempted to sound the word out rather than just guess. He wanted to complete a line of ten squares on the chart, so he kept practicing. Although after practicing three times he gets to draw, he didn't want to stop! As he went through the stack each time (total of fourteen words), he was beginning to be able to read the words more fluently and at a faster pace. This was very motivating to him, and he finished coloring the row on the chart. Then when I began reading the story, without my prompting, he began choral reading with me. Although he read mostly by echoing me, I stopped at any words on his cards, and he read them correctly. He even corrected me when I read "was" wrong, and he truly enjoyed pointing out my mistake.

The hypothesis was that if the intervention addressed his skill deficit, Doug's negative avoidance behavior would decrease, and he would begin to achieve some competence. Did his avoidance behavior diminish? Yes, he was more often engaged while listening to the story on tape and actively engaged by actually reading the word cards himself. This intervention was successful, because he was getting some competence and success from being able to read the cards fluently, and by the last week, he wanted to continue to practice them *beyond* the three times to get to draw. I had been observing him for many weeks and had never before seen him even try to read along. He always looked around while the other student(s) read, and only attempted to read when it was his turn, and then required a lot of help. During this last week, when he read, he did not ask for, or need, help to read any of "his" words. When I praised him for jumping in to read with me, he said, "I like reading." Additionally, Doug's end-of-story test scores improved once the intervention began. The teacher seemed pleased and wants to continue this approach.

What didn't go well was mostly during the "practice" week. Originally, Doug was going to listen to a peer assistant read the story. But Doug's behavior was too difficult for another student to deal with, and his own reading was interrupted too much. The alternative of having him listen to the story on tape worked better. Keeping all of the cards, charts, and markers organized in a folder was something that Doug couldn't do. Either I or the teacher had to put them back in the folder and put it elsewhere than in his desk, as he shreds or breaks things. Also, the intervention required more time from the teacher than originally planned, but she didn't seem to mind, perhaps since he was keeping out of trouble.

The next step to add to this intervention, eventually, as Doug continues to become more competent, is the whole language approach, for him to begin writing sentences or stories (along with his pictures) using these words he has learned. Since he doesn't work well independently, writing with a tutor or an older student would work well. When he has completed his story, he could then read it aloud to the class, giving him competence and social recognition in front of his peers.

## Case Questions

1 (problem-based small-group assignment): What reading approach was used in the past to teach Doug and why was this approach unsuccessful? Create an alternative plan that also presents your data tactfully to a team, including the classroom teacher.

2 (problem-based small-group assignment): Make a list of the elements of the intervention that was finally used with Doug. Which payoffs did this approach target?

3: Plan a strategy to teach Doug how to ask for help more appropriately and more specifically, rather than saying, "I'm dying here" (a phrase he repeated many times during math). In other words, how would you help Doug to verbalize his problems in math, as well?

# Chapter 5

## Math Disabilities and Nonverbal Communication Disabilities

To understand children with nonverbal or visual communication deficits, it is important to *watch* them (a) when they estimate money, time, objects, and space (e.g., how much/many, how far, how often, what age); (b) when they attempt to follow patterns of movements (e.g., how to make a bed, understand and play games, understand dangerous situations) or to control motor sequences (e.g., tearing tape); and (c) while they interact socially with other children. Some of these children have both a math LD (MLD) and a nonverbal LD (NVLD) and some have only an MLD (also termed **dyscalculia,** which is similar to the word *dyslexia* that characterizes most children with RD).

> **Dyscalculia:** A specific learning disability (SLD) in math; also called a math disability (MD) or math learning disability (MLD).

## MATH LEARNING DISABILITIES OR DYSCALCULIA

Mathematics is presented initially in this chapter and at the end of the discussion of verbal LD as a bridge, because math involves both verbal requirements (e.g., reading math word problems, math vocabulary) and quantitative thinking (e.g., numeric symbols, distance, time). Math is of practical use for individuals in their everyday adaptation to the environment, for example, in making comparisons and estimations for purchasing and for planning of time, distance, and resources. Human infants, as early as 3 months, and animals (e.g., primates, birds) have a built-in sense of **numerosity** (how many) and magnitude estimations (e.g., more and less than) that does not rely on counting or measuring (Boysen & Capaldi, 1993; Piazza et al., 2010). This indicates the universality of these underlying math skills.

> **Numerosity:** Number sense, or the ability to understand the properties of numerical problems or expressions without doing precise computations, such as would be involved in estimations of quantity (Gersten & Chard, 1999).

**Figure 5.1**   A child with math learning disabilities is confused by numbers and numerosity

Note that difficulty with numerosity is considered the core deficit of MLD, similar to the core phonological deficit in RD (Butterworth, Varma, & Laurillard, 2011). On number comparison tasks, 10-year-old children with MLD score similar to 5-year-old typical learners matched in IQ (Piazza et al., 2010). Students with MLD do not seem to grasp the meaningfulness of numbers, their size and value relative to other numbers (Butterworth et al., 2011). This often takes the form of an overreliance on finger counting (Piazza et al., 2010).

Unfortunately, math and MLD have received less scientific study than have reading and RD. This may be because fewer children are affected by MLD, or it may be the result of a cultural attitude that proficiency in math is not as important for an educated individual as is proficiency in reading. This attitude is changing, however. The ratio of reading studies to math studies was 100 to 1 in the period 1966–1975, whereas in 1996–2005 the ratio was 14 to 1 (Siegler, 2007). Thus, concern about children with MLD is becoming more common in today's classrooms.

## FORMAL IDENTIFICATION

### Definitions

#### IDEA

IDEA's definition of SLD (presented in total in Chapter 3) also defines math disabilities. The relevant part is repeated here (with italics added) to emphasize math disability as

> a disorder in one or more of the basic psychological processes involved in *understanding* or using language, spoken or written, which may manifest itself in an imperfect ability to listen, think, speak read, write, spell, or do *mathematical calculations*. (H.R. 1350, Section 602 [30])

#### DSM-IV-TR

*DSM-IV-TR* (APA, 2000, p. 53) supplies the following definition for math disability(diagnostic criteria 315.1):

> *Defining characteristics:* Math skill "is substantially below that expected given the person's chronological age, measured intelligence, and age-appropriate education," which is measured individually on standardized tests.

> *Impairment:* Poor math skills must significantly interfere with academic functioning and daily living tasks that require math.

*Exclusions and conditions:* "If a sensory deficit is present, the difficulties in mathematical ability are in excess of those usually associated with it."

### Frequently Occurring Subtypes

*DSM-IV-TR* groups math deficits into problems in various skill categories:

"linguistic" skills (e.g., understanding or naming mathematical terms, operations, or concepts, and decoding written problems into mathematical symbols); "perceptual" skills (e.g., recognizing or reading numerical symbols or arithmetic signs, and clustering objects into groups); "attention" skills (e.g., copying numbers or figures correctly, remembering to add in "carried" numbers, and observing operational signs); and "mathematical" skills (e.g., following sequences of mathematical steps, counting objects, and learning multiplication tables). (APA, 2000, p. 53)

Math disabilities can also be categorized into problems related to concrete versus abstract skills. Calculations typically rely on memory, whereas higher-level math problem solving relies on the selection of strategies and concepts. Problem-solving skills can be further classified into "procedural" skills, or knowing sequences of actions and strategies; "conceptual" skills, or understanding the principles underlying those actions and strategies; and "utilization" skills, or knowing when to apply those actions (Siegler, 1991).

Having a variety of strategies and selecting advanced strategies can be delayed in students with LD. For example, such students may not have moved from counting unit by unit on their fingers to a more advanced "counting on" strategy (i.e., beginning with the highest number and adding on; for example, taking 6 and adding 3 by counting 6, 7, 8, 9). We can see that Doug, whose case study appears in Chapter 4, is still functioning at a very concrete stage of addition:

During calendar time, when the students were counting coins as a group, Doug used his fingers to figure out the answer.

### Possible Co-Occurring Conditions and Differences Among Related Disabilities

MLD is frequently found in neurological disorders, such as ADHD, epilepsy, and fragile X syndrome (Shalev, 2004). The evidence of co-occurrence is particularly strong in the combined and inattentive subtypes (IN) of ADHD (see Chapter 9). For example, students with the IN subtype have lower math achievement than children with the hyperactive/impulsive subtype (HI) of ADHD (Marshall, Schafer,

O'Donnell, Elliott, & Handwerk, 1999), and 32% of students with MLD have attention problems (Dietz & Montague, 2006; Shalev et al., 2001). For this reason, children with MLD are frequently misdiagnosed as ADHD. Although "higher rates of MLD are reported for students with ADHD (31%) than are reported for the general population (6%–7%)" (Zentall, 2007, p. 220), children with only MLD will show behavioral problems primarily during math, as an initial avoidance of math, or during later task performance when their greater effort leaves them less able to sustain further attention to difficult math problems (**disability fatigue**).

**Disability fatigue:**
The tiredness or lack of energy a child with a disability feels as the result of the effort he or she must expend in attempting to overcome skill deficits or to conform with school requirements.

There is also considerable overlap between MLD and RD. It has been estimated that more than 50% of students with MLD also have RD (Geary, 2003). Doug is an example of a child with RD who also finds math a difficult subject. Note that it was in his math class where he repeatedly stated, "I'm dying here." Although some overlap between RD and MLD can be explained by difficulties with reading word problems, number sense (numerosity and the ability to estimate) is a stronger predictor of mathematics ability than is reading (Jordan, 2007). Giftedness can sometimes **mask** or hide MLD. As *DSM-IV-TR* states, "Particularly when Mathematics Disorder is associated with high IQ, the child may be able to function at or near grade level in the early grades, and Mathematics Disorder may not be apparent until the fifth grade or later" (APA, 2000, p. 54). A child with MLD may also have a nonverbal LD—a broader-based disability described later in this chapter.

**Masking:** The hiding of a disability by giftedness or of giftedness by a disability.

## Etiology

*Biogenetic.* Like other learning disabilities, MLD is a brain-based disorder with a strong genetic component (Rubinsten & Tannock, 2010). Shalev et al. (2001) have estimated that 66% of mothers, 40% of fathers, 53% of siblings, and 44% of second-degree relatives of a child with dyscalculia have dyscalculia themselves, with prevalence within families almost 10 times higher than expected in the general population.

*Environmental.* Prematurity and low birth weight are associated with MLD, and poor teaching can also be a contributor (Shalev, 2004; Shalev et al., 2001).

*Functional.* Functional assessments of students with MLD have documented that antecedents are assignments involving mathematics, especially when the children are frustrated or when their failure is public. In fact, there is evidence of an association between disruptive classroom behavior and children's lack of knowledge of basic mathematical principles (Finn, 1989).

## Prevalence, Gender, Age, and Cultural Factors

*Prevalence.* It is estimated that 5–8% of children in the general school population have some form of MLD (Geary, 2004; Butterworth et al., 2011), and about 25% of students with LD receive services in math (Rivera, 1997).

*Gender.* There is multinational evidence that boys and girls achieve in math at similar rates through the fifth grade, but after that boys outperform girls in standardized math and **aptitude** tests (Machin & Pekkarinen, 2008; VanTassel-Baska, 1998c). However, dyscalculia affects both genders fairly equally (Shalev, Auerbach, Manor, & Gross-Tsur, 2000; for a review, see Ashcraft, Krause, & Hopko, 2007).

*Age.* "Although symptoms of difficulty in mathematics (e.g., confusion in number concepts or inability to count accurately) may appear as early as kindergarten or first grade, Mathematics Disorder is seldom diagnosed before the end of first grade because sufficient formal mathematics instruction has usually not occurred until this point in most school settings. It usually becomes apparent during second or third grade" (APA, 2000, p. 54). Problems accumulate? such that by age 12, students with MLD can recall one-third fewer basic math facts than typical learners (Hasselbring et al., 1988). Achievement in mathematics is different from achievement in reading in its dependence on grade and the instruction provided in particular grades. Furthermore, mathematics becomes more abstract as children advance in grade level, such that difficulties with math reasoning may not show up until fourth grade or later.

*Culture.* Culture is a major environmental factor in math achievement, with students in Asian cultures such as Korea and Japan significantly outperforming those in England, Norway, Denmark, and the United States (Leuven et al., 2004).

**Aptitude:** A natural ability or intelligence. Different types of aptitude can be assessed, such as verbal-linguistic, logical-mathematical, musical, spatial, bodily-kinesthetic, interpersonal, intrapersonal, and naturalistic (Gardner, 1983).

# INFORMAL EDUCATOR IDENTIFICATION OF CHARACTERISTICS

## Behavioral

As Covington (1992) found, students with MLD often engage in externalizing disruptive behavior in order to avoid doing assigned work, in the hope of deflecting attention away from their academic difficulties. Doug in Chapter 4 expressed his frustration:

As the teacher gave the class further instructions to color numbers as they counted by fives, Doug first put his arms inside his shirt then pulled his desk toward him and scooted down, tipping his chair. He said, "I'm done."

## Social-Emotional

Children judge their own and others' intelligence by math performance (Stipek & Mac Iver, 1989). Thus, children with MLD may cover up "being stupid" by withdrawing effort, giving up easily, or pointing out the academic faults of their peers, or they may show aggression toward peers as a result of frustration. Jane, whose case study appears later in this chapter, responds aggressively to her teacher and to her peers during math instruction. For example, she "argues with the teacher about having already done the math problems assigned."

There is also the independent phenomenon of *math anxiety,* which exists when fear interferes with an individual's manipulation of numbers and solving math problems. Math anxiety is a separate disorder experienced by 4% of high school students, more commonly in girls than in boys. Math anxiety can result from past negative experiences with math that create feelings that interfere with a person's ability to make connections among numerical concepts (Rubinsten & Tannock, 2010). Although poor math skill and low IQ can also contribute to math anxiety, this disorder can exist without general anxiety, test anxiety, or low intelligence (Rubinsten & Tannock, 2010).

Students with math anxiety typically focus on fast rather than accurate performance, especially when problems involve carrying or borrowing. When the speed with which students do math problems is emphasized, math anxiety levels are likely to increase. Math performance also worsens when these students are asked to work out problems at the board in front of peers (similar to when students with RD are asked to read aloud) and when teachers have high demands for correctness (see the review by Ashcraft et al., 2007; see also Section V for additional information on specific anxiety disorders).

## Cognitive

Math involves a wide range of cognitive skills, including intelligence, working memory, receptive language, and spatial understandings (Butterworth et al., 2011).

*Intellectual.* Students with MLD use the same range of strategies as normally developing children, but they more often use strategies employed by younger children (e.g., finger counting) rather than verbal strategies (mental calculations) (Geary, Hoard, Nugent, & Byrd-Craven, 2007). Although children with low IQ are excluded by definition from the category of LD, these students do have more difficulties with the nonverbal concepts of weight and measurement (Derr, 1985), and the learning of math strategies also may require verbal intelligence.

*Memory/perception.* Children who perform poorly on tasks requiring working memory also tend to perform poorly at problem solving, recalling text information, and computations (Passolunghi & Pazzagliab, 2004). Even so, MLD can affect those with normal working memory (Butterworth et al., 2011), and when working memory is involved it is visual-spatial more than verbal working memory that is associated with math (for a review, see Martinussen et al., 2005). Poor working memory contributes to the use of less advanced math strategies (for a review, see Zentall, 2007). For example, finger counting may be an outcome of poor memory of facts or a cause of poor memory for math facts (Butterworth & Reigosa, 2007). Additional working memory deficits seen in the classroom are those related to the following skills: (a) handling multiple steps and recalling the sequence of steps, (b) handling the mixed ordering of events (e.g., with a question at the beginning rather than at the end of the problem), (c) carrying and borrowing numbers, (d) doing mental math, and (e) organizing information or eliminating irrelevant information or numbers. Students with MLD perform worse than average students when they must deal with nonrelevant numbers and objects more than with irrelevant words (see Zentall, 2007). Knowledge of mathematical *procedures* does improve as children with MLD age; however, *long-term memory* of facts does not (Geary et al., 2007; Jordan, 2007).

*Short-term memory* deficits do not characterize students with MLD as a group (Butterworth & Reigosa, 2007). However, the case study of Jane shows evidence of poor verbal memory: "For one of the assignments Jane was expected to memorize a passage, which the teacher knew she would have trouble with."

Students with MLD may also have *visual perception deficits* and problems with *inattention* that result in careless errors (omitting numbers, not noticing changes of operations), failure with left/right orientation, difficulty visualizing objects in space, and confusing numbers (e.g., 7 and 9, 3 and 8). There is also evidence that their search for visual information is confined to a smaller than normal area, which may affect performance with geometry and other detailed visual tasks (Cotugno, 1987).

## Academic

Students with MLD have been found to show only 1 year of academic growth for every 2–3 years of schooling (for a review, see Zentall, 2007). Common academic problems for students with MLD include difficulties comparing numbers, making estimations for answers, and the overuse of fingers when counting (beyond the age when this is normal) (Butterworth et al., 2011). To understand these difficulties, we need to examine both the verbal and the visual factors that contribute to math performance. For example, <u>children with verbal LD have dif-ficulty with math story problems and with understanding the language of math</u>. Bart, whose case study appears in Chapter 3, has problems with spoken language, and he also demonstrates difficulties in math problem solving:

> Bart is behind in math and avoids doing math; this may be because it is hard for him to remember or use math vocabulary. . . . He cannot process what the math teacher is saying, and he does not understand the language of mathematics or how to solve math problems that involve problem solving or multistep directions.

In other words, some difficulties with word problems reflect *verbal* or *language-based problems* of reading or understanding and recalling terms that represent quantitative concepts, such as translating numbers and visual symbols into language equivalents (e.g., > into "greater than"). These language-based problems occur for students with MLD when they are reading math problems and show up as poor fact accuracy, slower speed than that of typical students (especially while doing times tables), and transposition of numbers when taking down verbally given sequences of numbers, such as phone numbers (for a review, see Zentall, 2007).

**Nonverbal (visual) communication:** Communication without verbal language, through gestures, postures, facial expressions, visual symbols, and concepts.

Students with MLD also have difficulties with ***nonverbal (visual) communication,*** particularly in the recognition and understanding of patterns, relationships, and symbols (e.g., understanding variables or symbols to express relationships, such as plus and minus signs, variable $X$ or $Y$ designators) and in understanding and estimating nonverbal concepts (time, space/distance/measurement, money, weight, quantity/conservation) (Dehaene, 1992). In contrast to Bart and his verbal learning disability, Rex, diagnosed as MID (see the case study in Chapter 6), has more problems with the visual concepts in math:

> Rex has a hard time in math. He doesn't understand time or money. He will play with his number line or math manipulatives instead of doing math practice. Rex will pound his pencil into his desk and attempt to speak over the teacher. . . . He also argues that his answers are right. He will even pull out his number line and show the teacher how he got his answer. Once he is corrected, he will comply.

In the classroom, teachers report that students with MLD differ from their peers in (a) their knowledge about counting, which depends on long-term memory and use of a verbal notation system (1, 2, 3, . . .); (b) their understanding of place value, which is needed for multidigit calculation and depends on knowledge of the Arabic notation of place value; and (c) their ability to compare and estimate, which is based in preverbal number sense or numerosity skills (for a review, see Geary et al., 2007).

# SUMMARY OF STRENGTHS AND NEEDS

| *Probable strengths* | *Probable needs* |
|---|---|
| • Compensatory academic areas: reading, writing, spelling, art<br>• Good spoken language and sometimes talkative | • Verbally based math deficits require additional instruction in the language of math and reduced problem verbiage<br>• Visually based math deficits require verbal instruction paired with visual concepts. |

# DISABILITY IN THE CLASSROOM

## Implications for Accommodations in General Education Settings: Tier I

Although there is no agreement on the characteristics of high-quality instruction in general education settings for children with or at risk for math disability (Gersten, Beckmann, et al., 2009), educational reforms recommended by the National Council of Teachers of Mathematics (2000) have stressed *math problem solving* (for a review, see Woodward, 2004). In line with these reforms, a whole-class evidence-based math curriculum for students at risk for MLD includes real-world problems, visual supports, guided practice with new items, and application of new concepts (for a review, see Woodward & Brown, 2006). Real-world problems with divergent solutions that describe relationships among quantities using text, tables, or graphs are effective, as is asking children to justify and predict why one procedure or solution has advantages over others (Lesh & Doerr, 1998).

Additional components involve the use of technology such as the FLYPen, produced by LeapFrog Enterprises, which can improve the problem-solving accuracy of middle school special needs students by providing audio feedback via a "pentop" computer (Bouck, Bassette, Taber-Doughty, Flanagan, & Szwed, 2009). Students also need challenges, which include momentary failures, in order to learn persistence (Woodward & Brown, 2006). Math problem solving by students with MLD can also be improved through the use of software programs that visually or concretely represent math problems (e.g., Scheuermann, Deshler, & Schumaker, 2009; for a review, see Woodward & Brown, 2006); visually enhancing representations within problems can be helpful for students with ADHD (Kang & Zentall, 2011). A sketching software package has been used effectively to teach concepts to students in kindergarten through the fourth grade and may have applications for students with disabilities, because the process involves the hands-on construction of an object and then exploring that object by dragging the object with a mouse

(Furner & Marinas, 2007). Also related to technology, a clicker system, with each student "betting" on the answers, increases participation and decreases fearfulness of making mistakes (math anxiety). More broadly, it can get students to expose their faulty math concepts (Sparks, 2011).

Although the EBPs described above have been shown to be effective, it should be noted that contradictory research indicates that those teachers who questioned their students about their strategies and who listened to their explanations had students with greater gains in achievement over those teachers randomly assigned to implement advanced knowledge of the "best" math strategies (Peterson, Carpenter, & Fennema, 1989). This evidence is consistent with current thinking that instruction should provide models, but also that students should "think aloud" (i.e., self-report ongoing strategies) (Gersten, Beckmann, et al., 2009).

For teaching *computations* to students with MLD in large-group settings, EBPs involve maintaining a rapid pace, with varied activities, high levels of engagement, challenging standards for achievement, and peer-assisted learning strategies (Fuchs & Fuchs, 2001). Note that math anxiety is made worse by an emphasis on speed and on finding the one perfect solution, as previously described. Software programs that provide extended practice have been adapted for the purpose of teaching computations (Butterworth et al., 2011), possibly without public pressure to perform rapidly. For slowed calculations, the use of computers with games and talking on-screen calculators has been shown to improve the attention and performance of students with MLD; competitive games are effective for students with ADHD (Zentall, 2007). (For a more complete listing of assistive technology in math, see Beard et al., 2007, p. 81.)

*Specifically for reading problems* that can contribute to difficulties with math, accommodations may include reducing the amount of math language, reading the problem to the child, or matching reading level to instructional materials. Especially for students with RD, initial strategies should address their memory abilities and their reading comprehension of multiple-step problems (for review, see Zentall & Ferkis, 1993; Xin, 2008). *For working memory problems,* the following can be helpful: (a) using checklists with the steps to follow in doing word problems, (b) using drawings to help the child visualize, (c) reducing the amount of information in problems, and (d) using calculators (currently only half of special educators and 36% of secondary educators allow students to use calculators; see Maccini & Gagnon, 2006). To address students' *failure to attend to important information,* color can be added to materials, especially to relevant factors such as signs and steps; also, active and novel learning environments can be created through the use of small groups and the addition of music (for a review, see Zentall, 2007).

## Implications for Interventions in Small-Group and Individual Settings: Tiers II and III

Tier II students may receive supplemental small-group math instruction aimed at building targeted mathematics proficiencies, typically provided in sessions of 20–40 minutes, 4–5 times per week, with monthly progress monitored (Gersten, Beckmann, et al., 2009). Also at a Tier II level, self-monitoring and goal setting with graphs have been shown to be effective for improving computational accuracy and fluency for students with LD and ADHD (Konrad, Fowler, Walker, Test, & Wood, 2007); the strongest effects have been produced by goal-setting interventions. Dyadic interactions can also be useful. Bottage (2002) found that having students work in pairs to solve a problem after watching an instructional video produced better results than teacher-led instruction; for those students with disabilities, improvements were seen primarily with easier types of problems.

Tier III typically involves one-on-one instruction. Butterworth and colleagues (2011) have concluded that there is a "serious lack of evidence-based approaches to dyscalculia intervention" (p. 1053). For years, concrete materials (e.g., Cuisenaire rods, number cards) have been used to make number concepts meaningful. In recent years, conceptual model-based problem-solving instruction (COMPS) has been implemented in individual sessions to help children represent math concepts in models and with transitions to equations (e.g., Xin, Wiles, & Lin, 2008; Xin & Zhang, 2009). Recent empirical reviews also recommend building upon the foundation of numerosity and number concepts (Butterworth et al., 2011). In agreement, Woodward (2002) proposes that students with LD are likely to benefit from instruction beyond basic facts and simple word problems.

## Long-Term Outcomes

Dyscalculia is a stable learning disability that persists for approximately half of the students diagnosed (Shalev et al., 2001). The long-term impairment is related to the usefulness of math for everyday functioning. This can be labeled *quantitative literacy,* which "involves the knowledge and skills required to apply arithmetic materials, such as balancing a checkbook, figuring out a tip, completing a form or determining the interest on a loan from an advertisement" (Leuven et al., 2004, p. 470). Quantitative literacy is a significant predictor of attaining good jobs, full-time employment, and higher wages (Leuven et al., 2004). At more advanced levels, we use math to *reduce* the amount of information we need to examine trends related to advertising, government planning, research conclusions, and scientific projections.

Because of these outcomes, high-quality instruction in the early years is critical; it can reduce the frequency of MLD by 36% at the end of first grade (Fuchs et al., 2005). Furthermore, effective math (and reading) interventions in first grade have been found to be associated with decreased levels of behavioral and emotional problems by middle school (Kellam et al., 1994). However, the lasting effects of these interventions are unknown.

## NONVERBAL LEARNING DISABILITIES

What makes children with NVLD distinctive in school settings are their broad-based social and math disabilities. If a child has both social and math disabilities, it is probable that he or she has an NVLD, because both social functioning and math ability are associated with the right hemisphere of the brain (Semrud-Clikeman & Hynd, 1990). However, the disabilities of many of these children go undetected because the children have good verbal skills, even though they lack what we may call common sense See Figure 5.2. On repeatedly hearing a description of herself as having little common sense, a girl with NVLD responded with perfect verbal logic: "It's not common sense, if it is not common to me."

Mild cases of NVLD present some of the most interesting and challenging disabilities to identify. The markers of children with mild NVLD are social problems (they are not engaged with or complain about other children) and difficulty with

**Figure 5.2**   The puzzlement experienced by a student with nonverbal learning
disabilities

math (e.g., they do not want to understand how to do math problems, but just want to know or memorize the answers) as well as compensatory strengths of very high interest in reading and high need for adult verbal interaction (talkative). Students with more severe NVLD may appear tactless and even bizarre in the inappropriateness of their responses to their social environments. Many of these children do have some awareness of their visual communication difficulties, as stated by Elliot, a bright and active 5-year-old boy who knowingly said, "My eyes are on backwards." (Elliot's case study is presented at the end of this chapter.) David Goldstein (n.d.) has developed a rating scale that parents can use to screen their children for NVLD. It includes statements such as, "My child has difficulty remembering and organizing visual or spatial information (e.g., has difficulty lining up numbers to do a math problem or lining up words neatly on a page)," along with the possible responses of "never/rarely," "sometimes," and "always/often."

## FORMAL IDENTIFICATION

### Definitions

#### *IDEA*

IDEA's definition of SLD (presented in total in Chapter 3) can be used to define NVLD when we interpret "understanding or using language" to include nonverbal communication. The relevant part is repeated here (with italics added) to emphasize nonverbal learning disability as

> a disorder in one or more of the basic psychological processes involved *in understanding or using language,* spoken or written, which may manifest itself in an imperfect ability to listen, think, speak, read, write, spell, or do mathematical calculations. (H.R. 1350, Section 602 [30])

#### *DSM-IV-TR*

*DSM-IV-TR* does not provide a definition of nonverbal learning disabilities.

#### *Frequently Occurring Subtypes*

NVLD subtypes include the following:

*Motoric deficits:* lack of or delayed coordination, balance problems, graphomotor skills

*Visual-spatial-organizational difficulties:* poor visual recall, faulty spatial perception, and difficulty with spatial relations

*Social problems:* poorer comprehension of nonverbal communication (facial expression and gestures), difficulty adjusting to transitions and novel situations, and deficits in social judgments (For a review, see Semrud-Clikeman, Walkowiak, Wilkinson, & Christopher, 2010.)

## Possible Co-Occurring Conditions and Differences Among Related Disabilities

Some children with NVLD have a wide range of co-occurring disorders, including Asperger's syndrome, autism, TBI, and ID (see the case study of Andy in Chapter 8). Often it is difficult to make a differential primary diagnosis, as in the case of Elliot: "Elliot's IEP makes it clear that Elliot is a source of confusion for the team of people who have been brought together to evaluate his placement options." It is perhaps for this reason that these children are frequently misdiagnosed with one of the following:

> *Giftedness* (GT), due to their mature vocabulary, rote memory skills, and reading ability. However, parents realize early that something is wrong in a comparison between the children's strong verbal skills and their visual weaknesses. Students with GT do not characteristically have visual deficits.

> *Asperger's syndrome* (AS), because social skill deficits overlap between NVLD and AS. The two disorders are similar in that the children display odd social behavior and preference for routines. However, the verbal behavior of children with AS is used less frequently to maintain contact with the listener (Semrud-Clikeman & Hynd, 1990); in contrast, children with NVLD desire and enjoy verbal social interactions with adults (Morris, 2002). Furthermore, children with AS typically have good math/science skills that students with NVLD do not have, at least in the elementary years. Furthermore, students with NVLD do *not* have repetitive patterns of behavior or interests that students with AS have, although students with NVLD may have obsessive interests in reading.

> *Dyspraxia and/or dysgraphia,* due to their early problems with coordination and motor control and to their difficulties with fine motor tasks, such as illegible handwriting (Palombo, 1996).

> *Communication disorder,* because during preschool ages, students with NVLD can have speech or articulation problems (Cornoldi, Rigoni, Tressoldi, & Vio, 1999). Differential diagnosis is made easier by the fact that the language skills of students with NVLD are very good, even though they may have speech problems.

*Intellectual disabilities* (ID), due to the fact that both groups could have low visual (or performance) IQ. However, students with NVLD will have average to above-average verbal IQ, whereas those with ID will typically show lower verbal IQ. Thus, differences between groups can be found in the uneven performance in verbal versus nonverbal IQ test performance found primarily for NVLD.

*Narcissistic or borderline personality disorders* (Palombo, 1996), because individuals with NVLD can appear to be self-centered. Differences here are that, unlike children with these disorders, students with NVLD are honest, nonaggressive, and have a clear sense of who they are.

## Etiology

*Biogenetic.* NVLD involves a neuropsychological deficit in brain development and/or brain function that originates in the right hemisphere of the brain. Disruptions in **perinatal** development may influence right-hemispheric functioning (Semrud-Clikeman & Hynd, 1990). Right-hemispheric dysfunction causes problems with visual-spatial, intuitive, organizational, evaluative, and holistic processing and with the ability to understand context cues and nonverbal social cues (Hahn, 2004; Petti, Voelker, Shore, & Hayman-Abello, 2003). The right hemisphere also specializes in processing social-emotional and non-verbal information in a more global fashion—differently from the step-by-step analytic fashion of the left hemisphere, which specializes in language (Semrud-Clikeman & Hynd, 1990). A genetic influence is suggested by higher rates of bipolar disorder in the extended family members of children with NVLD (Antshel & Khan, 2008).

**Perinatal:** During the time of childbirth.

*Environmental.* Adults can make this disorder worse by responding with sarcasm. That is, parents may assume that a verbally smart child should know the answers to apparently "stupid" questions, for example, about the meanings of nonverbal actions of others.

*Functional.* Functional assessments of these students should document specific antecedents that set the occasion for NVLD, such as new situations and transitions, mathematics, social interactions, and motor-coordination tasks (Palombo, 1996). In these situations, students with NVLD use verbal interactions and questioning, or they simply avoid or disrupt these tasks. Elliot was observed in situ with difficulties transitioning from one subject to another, an activity that is relatively unstructured and typically lacks specific instructions:

During this time, Elliot has to independently figure out what is expected of him either by following the other students or by watching the teacher. This poses a problem, because he does not understand subtle cues and body language. He has trouble learning through observation of other students, and he typically needs very direct instruction. Elliot has done much better during transitions when his caseworker directly tells him what is expected of him.

## Prevalence, Gender, and Age Factors

*Prevalence.* NVLD represents about 0.1% to 1% of the general population. The disorder is most likely underreported because of failure to identify individuals with NVLD due to their strong verbal skills, or they may be misidentified as having Asperger's syndrome. Furthermore, less than 10% of individuals with LD have NVLD (Little, 2001, cited by Burkhardt, 2005)—a figure that may also reflect underreporting of NVLD.

*Gender.* There is a higher prevalence of NVLD disabilities in girls than in boys. This has been explained by the faster maturation of the left hemisphere (i.e., language functions) in girls. That is, the dominance of the left hemisphere may contribute to the slowed development of the right hemisphere (nonverbal functions) in girls (Semrud-Clikeman & Hynd, 1990).

*Age.* The fact that some children with NVLD do relatively well in their early elementary years by handling academic demands requiring memorization (e.g., reading, decoding) (Palombo, 1996) also makes diagnosis difficult. Early symptoms of NVLD may also be less noticeable in later years if the child learns to compensate with excellent verbal memory skills.

# INFORMAL EDUCATOR IDENTIFICATION OF CHARACTERISTICS

## Behavioral

Adults often say that they feel like they are constantly punishing and correcting these children (Palombo, 1996). Children with NVLD are often confused and frustrated and unsure of how to express their needs, and thus may exhibit aggressive behavior (Morris, 2002). This is illustrated in Elliot's case: During transition back to his desk, Elliot "pushed a child standing at his desk and began to yell, 'It's cleanup time!'" More typically, students with NVLD are hardworking, persistent, goal oriented, and incredibly honest. When behavioral problems are *not* apparent, it has been observed that some children with NVLD have learned to rely on verbal rules of conduct (Silverman, 2003).

## Social-Emotional

In kindergarten, students with NVLD appear smart but are unable to make friends. They are likely to develop an overdependence on adults, usually their parents. Developing friendships is something these children crave, even though they have difficulty understanding how to negotiate and sustain relatedness. They will often reach out to other children, but when they do they are typically misread and come across as rude and insensitive, or they simply look socially awkward and have difficulty understanding and responding appropriately to social-emotional signals (Foss, 2001; Palombo, 1996). The social problems of these children can be explained by lack of *social understanding*—a hallmark of NVLD (Hahn, 2004). From the case study description of 5-year-old Elliot:

> Emotional stimulation and provoking may be ways that Elliot has found to have people attend to him. For example, Elliot began to say "butt" to try to get a reaction from the people in his group. It is probable that Elliot does not know what kind of reaction he will get based on what he is doing; he just understands that he will get a reaction. When he said "butt," the children in his group laughed.

Specific social indicators are that they cannot detect when they are being lied to (gullible), they cannot "read between the lines," and they have difficulty judging the moods/attitudes of others from tone of voice, facial expression, physical contact, or gesture. In social situations they are likely to "apply a previous experience in a rote but inappropriate fashion" (Dobbins, Sunder, & Soltys, 2007, p. 3). They do not have deficits in social visual perception (i.e., they can recognize faces); rather, they have deficits in their ability to understand the expressions on the faces of others (Semrud-Clikeman & Hynd, 1990). It is difficult for them to sense subtle changes in situations and in other people's emotions, and they cannot predict others' possible emotional reactions or intentions. For example, they may judge all intentions as positive (i.e., gullibility). Children with NVLD do not have a real sense of body awareness; they typically do not respect social distance (e.g., they may intrude physically) and do not understand social boundaries (Palombo, 1996). Taken from Elliot's case:

> He keeps touching the other students or sitting too close to them. In this situation, Elliot is using the sense of touch to feel a sense of closeness with his classmates and other people.

Especially when these children enter the upper elementary grades or begin middle school, teachers and peers continually misunderstand them. They are accused of being lazy, rude, and uncooperative. If a child with NVLD has not benefited from diagnosis and an intervention plan at this point, the cognitive, social, and emotional demands of high school can be overwhelming. Because of these social difficulties at older ages, additional disorders of *depression* and *anxiety* are more likely to develop—with anxiety expressed in public settings and anger more often expressed at home (Palombo, 1996; Petti et al., 2003). For these reasons early identification of this disorder is especially important.

## Cognitive

*Attention/perception.* The attentional difficulties that are often observed in children with NVLD have been explained by the deficits in visual perceptual skills seen in these children and are not related to ADHD (Semrud-Clikeman et al., 2010). Visual perceptual skill deficits make it difficult for an individual to locate objects spatially in complex settings (e.g., to find a bird in a tree) and to orient left/ right, up/down, and north/south.

*Intellectual.* Students who have difficulty reasoning with visual pictures, objects, or symbols have difficulty understanding absurdities or humor in pictures or understanding the function of objects, such as "What does this object do?" (e.g., a screwdriver). At home they will show deficits with pretending and anticipating (Semrud-Clikeman & Hynd, 1990), which are typically seen in the play of young children. Children with NVLD also will have difficulty grasping the "big picture," especially if it requires some understanding of how physical things relate (e.g., how to organize a desk, which depends on understanding objects in space). They have difficulty with the whole (the gestalt) of a situation, even though they may recall the details. Understanding the gestalt is important for social understanding as well as for everyday functioning. Their deficits with getting the big picture and understanding some basic nonverbal concepts (e.g., quantity, age) may lead them to be incorrectly classified as intellectually disabled. This is true in the case of Elliot, who

> was given services based on a diagnosis of developmental delay (DD). He was referred for reevaluation of his DD diagnosis to determine a placement and transition to kindergarten. After testing, it was determined that Elliot fell into the average range for adaptive functioning and that services based on a label of DD were unnecessary.

*Memory.* Typically students with NVLD score higher on tests of verbal memory than on tests of visual memory (Little, 2001, cited by Burkhardt, 2005). They do not form or hold visual images in mind, therefore they cannot recall visually what they have seen; they are not skilled at **revisualization** (e.g., they cannot draw something previously seen but can draw a still life of objects that remain present). They may need to write everything down or translate visual information to verbal information. In the absence of a visual gestalt, the left hemisphere, which is the verbal meaning-making hemisphere of the brain, uses bits and pieces of experience to attempt to make a whole. Sometimes these children are accused of lying when in fact they are not lying but engaging in **confabulation** to fill in the gaps of visual information that are missing. Confabulation is a way that people with TBI fill in for losses in memory that typically occur in cases involving damage to the frontal lobes of the brain (Garrett, 2011).

**Revisualization:** Seeing something again in one's mind (visual memory).

**Confabulation:** The reporting of events that never happened (e.g., false memories) although the individual describing them believes them to be true events.

## Communication

Children with NVLD often show excellent auditory skills and speak at an early age (Semrud-Clikeman & Hynd, 1990), and they can be hyperverbal to compensate for poor visual skills. Toddlers may show greater interest in labeling objects than in manipulating them, often asking, "What's that?" and *not* showing a preference to learn through mouthing, touching, and throwing, which are more typical of average toddlers. Older students with NVLD will focus on the verbal content of what is said (the words) and not the intonation or the surrounding context within which it is said (Semrud-Clikeman & Hynd, 1990). When interpreting the words of others, they will sometimes use past experience that is unrelated to their current context (Palombo, 1996). An example from Elliot's case study:

> Many times he answered questions inappropriately, because he did not understand the context of the situation or question. For instance, when Elliot was asked where his library book was, he said it was in the library. . . . He presented his view of reality, which made perfect personal sense to him.

Elliot simply understands that books are always held in the library even when he takes them out of the library (change of context). For children with NVLD, even the verbal context of speech (i.e., intonation) may be difficult to "read," and all types of music (e.g., classical, jazz, country) may sound the same.

In addition to their deficits in the receptive skills discussed above, children with NVLD do not communicate their own needs well and show specific difficulty with the pragmatic or social forms of language. Characteristic of their expressive language are high quantity (talkativeness) and the frequent asking of "dumb" questions. For example, when a child with NVLD saw other children on in-line skates go by, he asked, "What is that?" On seeing someone replacing a lightbulb or turning on a light switch, an older upper elementary student with NVLD might ask, "What are you doing?" When an adolescent with NVLD was offered the opportunity to watch a movie, she asked, "Will I understand this movie?"

## Motor, Physical, and Somatic

Preschool and elementary-aged students with NVLD have difficulty with independent activities and self-help skills, and they fail to have a clear sense of their own bodies in space (Semrud-Clikeman & Hynd, 1990). Parents may notice that they have trouble tying shoes and buttoning. They also have difficulty understanding hazards, nonverbal routines (e.g., preparing for bedtime), and games. Preschool educators note that these children rarely play with puzzles, blocks, or construction toys (Semrud-Clikeman & Hynd, 1990). Students with NVLD typically have poor fine motor coordination and difficulties in the patterning or sequencing of movements, which are observable in such actions as manipulating a pencil when learning to write, learning to play the piano, or learning to dance. They also can have poor gross motor coordination, such as clumsiness—they may fall down frequently, have poor balance, and have difficulty learning to ride a bike or kick a ball. This is not always the case; for example, Elliot is described as "very active."

## Academic

Because of their motor difficulties, children with NVLD are easily identified in school by their poor performance on handwriting tasks (Cornoldi et al., 1999; Palombo, 1996). Across the age span these children have difficulties with the fine motor skills necessary for copying work and forming numbers. Numbers make "no sense" to them, especially when patternings of numbers are required (e.g., for making change, balancing a checkbook, counting, following a recipe). These children also have difficulty with independence skills and frequently get lost, forget to do homework, seem unprepared for class, and have difficulty following directions unless they are very explicit and given verbally. These classroom problems are especially noticeable when these children first enter new settings. This can be contrasted to average children, who when presented with new setting requirements will observe others and figure out the meanings of the actions they observe.

Although children with NVLD may recall all or most of the steps in an action sequence, they are less likely to understand cause and effect or the relationships among the steps (unless someone has explained them) (Semrud-Clikeman et al., 2010). This is illustrated by the case of a 16-year-old boy with NVLD: He went out with his family in their boat, and when he was asked to anchor the boat, he threw the anchor overboard without first making sure it was tied to the boat. The same boy heated some soup on the stove, and when it had finished cooking, he emptied the pan into his soup bowl and placed the pan back on the burner without turning the burner off.

Educators may observe that they have unusual difficulties with **number concepts,** such as quantity and more/less (relative magnitude) and the use of visual symbols (e.g., size, shape). Here is an example:

**Number concepts:** Quantity, more/less (relative magnitude)—related to numerosity.

> Elliot is beginning to have problems with more abstract concepts such as sorting by shape and not color. He has problems disregarding the color of a particular shape when he is asked to sort on shape.

Most will have difficulties in school with math, telling time, understanding spatial concepts (e.g., geometry, angles), aligning numbers, map reading, compass orientation, and directionality (left, right). More broadly, they will have difficulties with *estimations* of time ("How long have we been sitting here?" or "How long is recess?"), distance, size and volume, number, money ("How much is a piece of candy versus a TV?"), and age ("How old do you think I am?").

However, not all children with NVLD have math disabilities (von Aster, 2000) and older students with mild NVLD can learn to achieve in mathematics using their strong verbal memory skills. Furthermore, these students usually do very well academically with language-based subjects and show early speech development, excellent vocabulary and auditory memory, and early reading and spelling (e.g., reading cereal boxes at 3 years old and by fourth grade reading at college level). Their well-developed rote *verbal* memory also allows them to read well once they have learned phonetic rules (Fisher & DeLuca, 1997; Palombo, 1996), as observed in Elliot:

> Elliot is a verbally bright 5-year-old boy who has a passion for reading and loves singing. . . . Elliot is also a very good reader who understands how to break down words; he understands the rules of reading.

Students with NVLD are likely to learn word recognition skills (phonetic rules), but by the fourth or fifth grade, they can encounter reading comprehension difficulties, especially when inferential thinking is required or when understanding of visual concepts or social actions is referenced in their reading materials (some may show features of hyperlexia; see Chapter 4). As Semrud-Clikeman et al.

(2010) note, children with NVLD "often show excellent single word reading skills and spelling ability but have difficulty with inferential thinking, complex reading comprehension, and mathematics" (p. 583).

Older elementary and high school students with NVLD may have areas of knowledge expertise or gaps in knowledge that depend on whether or not they have had information explained to them verbally or have read and memorized information. That is, NVLD can lead children to compensate with strengths in verbal areas (decoding, spelling, talking) (see Harnadek & Rourke, 1994). For example, gifted children with NVLD can be "whizzes" with words (obsessive readers and also talkative, but talking *at* rather than *with* the listener or asking questions), with speech that is often **monotone** (Silverman, 2003, p. 537). Many of these students rely on memorizing but have difficulty paraphrasing what they have memorized.

**Monotone:** Speech without inflection.

## SUMMARY OF STRENGTHS AND NEEDS

| *Probable strengths* | *Probable needs* |
| --- | --- |
| • Verbal academic areas: reading, writing, spelling<br>• Good spoken language and sometimes talkative<br>• Verbal memory<br>• Ability to adapt to difficulties (e.g., by using a "talking" clock or by placing tape on dials of a clock or on a set number on a speedometer; or by using a physical attribute, such as a scar, to tell left from right) | • Help with mathematics, especially understanding symbols and problem meanings<br>• Scripted responses to social situations and provided verbal explanations of events, especially in new contexts<br>• Fine motor skill development or accommodations involving assistive technologies<br>• Help with spatial understandings that are necessary for organization of objects, determining left from right, telling time (e.g., talking clocks)<br>• Help with paraphrasing<br>• Emphasis on strengths and developing reasonable bypass strategies (Dobbins et al., 2007)<br>• Social interactions with peers (e.g., online peer-based book clubs) to reduce their overreliance on adults |

## DISABILITY IN THE CLASSROOM

### Implications for Accommodations in General Education Settings: Tier I

Educators can offer the following kinds of accommodations to help students with NVLD:

1. Use **simultaneous verbalizations**—that is, pair visual information with verbal explanations.

2. Encourage the child's questioning (Rourke, 1995).

3. Break tasks down with step-by-step instructions, verbally discuss the tasks, and ask the student to repeat directions and understandings.

4. Give explicit feedback. That is, telling a child to "be more careful" will not help the situation, because the child will not understand what that means unless it has previously been explained (Palombo, 1996).

5. Use the child's strengths, such as reading and rote memory, to compensate for weaknesses, such as organizational ability and the ability to understand contextual cues (Fisher & DeLuca, 1997).

**Simultaneous verbalizations:** Verbal explanations presented concurrently with visuals.

## Implications for Interventions in Small-Group and Individual Settings: Tiers II and III

1. Use direct verbal instruction to improve social outcomes: At older ages, assign the child homework of making a phone call a week, and provide a script of what to say. At younger age levels a caseworker may be needed, as in Elliot's case: "Elliot does really well when someone is in his classroom to guide him on what to do to make friends and to help him remember his manners. Since his caseworker has been coming to visit, Elliot has made a close friend in his group."

2. Practice interpreting facial expressions, voice tone, and body language using gestures, charades, sequences of pictures, and movies.

## Long-Term Outcomes

NVLD affects the academic, social, and economic functioning of individuals (Petti et al., 2003). For those individuals with advanced verbal IQ, there is improved functioning (Cornoldi et al., 1999; Semrud-Clikeman et al., 2010). However, adults with NVLD are likely to avoid social relationships because they fear people will realize how many things they cannot do. They retain feelings of social inadequacy and depression and do not work at jobs commensurate with their level of education (Semrud-Clikeman & Hynd, 1990). Even when they find employment, they continue to show impairment. For example, a teacher with seemingly mild NVLD had a relatively successful career. However, when she retired, she physically withdrew all her retirement money from her bank, and the cash was stolen from her as she walked home from the bank. She did not consider alternative ways to get access to her money that might involve less risk.

## CHAPTER SUMMARY

- Learning disabilities, both verbal and nonverbal, are formally defined by IDEA to include (a) achievement that is below IQ expectancy and (b) low achievement in response to empirically based treatments (RTI). *DSM-IV-TR* defines math learning disability but does not define NVLD. Math disabilities/difficulties co-occur with ADHD, NVLD, and RD. However, children with ADHD show attentional problems across more subject areas, and children with RD typically do not show math problems as long as the problems are read to them. The social deficits of children with NVLD sometimes lead to confusions in diagnosis (e.g., as autistic or as having Asperger's syndrome, social anxiety disorders), but correct diagnoses are possible based on the positive responses of children with NVLD to verbal instruction and the often hyper-verbal behavior of these students.

- The etiology of MLD and NVLD is biogenetic, with some environmental factors contributing to MLD (e.g., prematurity, missing or inadequate math instruction). Of course, specific math tasks and public exposure of math failure are antecedents to math frustration. In contrast, for NVLD new situations, transitions, mathematics, social interactions, and motor-coordination tasks are antecedents to difficulties.

- In contrast to reading, the level of math achievement in students with MLD is dependent on grade level of math instruction, which at young ages involves math facts and at older ages typically involves abstract math reasoning.

- Dyscalculia affects boys and girls at the same rate, but boys have higher achievement in mathematics, especially at older age levels. NVLD is identified more often in girls than in boys, making it unusual compared with other learning disabilities and their prevalence in males.

- Children with MLD can be informally identified through observations of disruptive and avoidant behavior during math. Their verbal IQ is often average, but their abilities to understand visual concepts of quantity, measurement, and so on are likely to be impaired. Difficulties using advanced math procedures (multiple steps, mixed ordering of events, carrying and borrowing numbers, mental math) may be related to poor working verbal memory skills, and careless errors are often due to visual perceptual and inattention problems.

- The deficits of students with NVLD are social, motor, and visual-spatial organization and patterning. Verbal IQ and verbal memory are considerably higher than nonverbal IQ and memory. Characteristics of the language of these students are talkativeness and asking what appear to be "dumb" questions. Similar to children with MLD, students with NVLD have difficulty understanding and estimating nonverbal concepts (e.g., quantity, age). Although the verbal communication of children with NVLD is often excellent, their social problems can be severe. That is, they do not correctly read social nonverbal communication and have difficulty getting the big picture. For these reasons, they do not respond appropriately in social settings.

- The academic problems of children with MLD are related to one or several underlying factors. Language problems will affect their understanding of math terms and word problems, perceptual problems will affect their ability to copy numbers, and their understanding of basic mathematics concepts will be compromised by their failure to understand symbols and nonverbal relationships and patterns. Students with NVLD show academic strengths in reading, spelling, and language arts, and their academic weaknesses lie in motor control, organization and patterning, and mathematics (e.g., geometry).

- Interventions for children with MLD depend on the nature of underlying skill deficits. For language problems, initial strategies should address memory and reading comprehension of multiple-step problems. For difficulties with number concepts, direct verbal instruction on an individual basis may be needed that builds on concepts of numerosity. Children with NVLD respond especially well to verbal rules of conduct and direct verbal instruction from adults.

- Accommodations for children with MLD include peer-assisted strategies in math, checklists for problems with sequences of steps, permission to use calculators, and the use of interesting, real-world problems. Accommodations for students with NVLD include instruction that pairs verbal explanations with context and the encouragement of questioning and verbal memory skills to compensate for poor understandings.

## CHAPTER QUESTIONS

### Math Learning Disabilities

1. Why is MLD often mistaken for ADHD?

2. Do the public aspects of math performance (e.g., working at the board in front of the class) affect some children more than others?

3. What are some categories of math problems?

4. What are some visual concepts in math?

5. What are some appropriate strategies for dealing with the disruptive behavior of children with MLD?

6. What have you learned in this chapter that was new or interesting for you?

## TRUE/FALSE AND MULTIPLE-CHOICE

1. Contributors to MLD can be either visual or verbal difficulties.

2. A poor understanding of number concepts and the number system can be characteristics of
   A. dyscalculia
   B. VLD
   C. RD

3. Poor ability to recall math steps or math terms or perform mental math involves
   A. verbal working memory skills
   B. visual perception and visual orientation skills
   C. both A & B

4. Which type of disorder is most likely to cause a child to suffer from an emphasis on speed in curriculum-based assessments?
   A. MLD
   B. RD
   C. math anxiety disorder

### Nonverbal Learning Disabilities

1. Why are math difficulties and social-emotional difficulties often found together?

2. Why are children with NVLD so rarely identified compared to children with verbal LD?

3. How are children with Asperger's and intellectual disabilities similar to and different from those with NVLD?

4. Why do children with NVLD ask so many questions? Should they be discouraged from doing so?

5. Why do children with NVLD have more problems than their non-NVLD peers when they enter new situations?

6. Why are children with NVLD, even with their problems, sometimes identified as gifted?

7. In your opinion, which is more appropriate for students with NVLD—compensation or **remediation training**? Why?

**Remediation training:** Intervention that takes the form of asking the child directly to practice or learn skills in his or her weak areas of functioning.

## MULTIPLE-CHOICE

1. Identify the disability: My child seems clumsy and has difficulty lining up numbers to do math problems. She appears disoriented or confused when entering a new situation and gets lost easily. She doesn't seem to get the humor in a joke that she hears or in silly pictures, but she talks and questions me a lot and has a good memory.

   A. NVLD
   B. RD
   C. dysgraphia
   D. dyscalculia

2. What game might a student with NVLD describe with the following information?

   - ball flying around
   - people running to and fro
   - nobody knows what to do next
   - men stand in line in order to hold long sticks

   A. soccer
   B. football
   C. baseball

## SHORT ANSWER

1. The ability to see again in the "mind's eye"

2. The best way to teach children with NVLD is through _____ instruction.

3. A child's ability to compensate could _____ identification of a disability.

4. To understand "how many" without counting is the concept of _____.

## PROBLEM-BASED CASE APPLICATIONS AND QUESTIONS

### CASE STUDY 5.1: JANE

*"I am not going to be in your math class next week."*
(from a report submitted by Laura Bassette)

*Background.* Jane is a 15-year-old female who is in tenth grade at a local high school. She lives with her mother and father. Jane has been placed in a resource room math class as a child identified with an emotional disability. She receives special education services in order to help her understand the content in her classes and to help her behave appropriately. Jane is included with general education students in all her other classes, which are earth science, computer, gym, English, and theater arts. Jane's strengths are that she has a great personality and a good sense of humor. She is very willing to participate in class and wants to please her teachers. She can be a hard worker when she puts her mind to it and does not allow herself to get distracted. Jane also typically works to get along with her peers in the classroom and tends to seek out friendships with other girls.

Jane's weaknesses are that she can be disruptive, inappropriate, and disrespectful to others around her. She can be verbally aggressive to her peers and can get easily angered or annoyed when frustrated. She also sometimes argues with her teachers when she is asked to do work or when she is redirected.

The theater arts teacher has commented that Jane's behavior had been problematic and that during Jane's freshman year she was very needy and clingy. Additionally, the teacher mentioned there had been a discussion about Jane being put into Theater Arts II instead of Theater Arts I again during her sophomore year. However, she was placed in the introductory class again for her sophomore year. The teacher then went on to say that this year Jane has been expressing much more appropriate behaviors during the class and also has expressed more confidence. She also noted that she was surprised that Jane volunteered to paint during the one observation, because in the past she had not readily volunteered.

## Behavioral Log

### Wednesday, September 12, 1:00–1:35 p.m., Math

- Plays with scissors during math lesson. Teacher asks her to put them down and she does.
- When asked to open book to page 47, she says, "I never heard of that page."
- Sings to herself unnoticed by others.
- When directed to do problems 8–20, she says, "I don't know how to do those."
- Bangs her hand on the desk and laughs. Then puts her head down on the desk laughing.
- Opens a drawer undirected by the teacher and pulls out note cards and taps on the desk with them. Teacher asks her to put the cards away and she does.
- Pulls chair over to her with her foot and puts her hand on her leg and laughs.

### Monday, September 17, 12:45–1:35 p.m., Math

- Talks out loud apparently to herself about girls getting into a fight during lunch.
- Works quietly on math problems.

- Turns in assignment and puts head down on desk. Teacher asks if she has anything else to do. Do you want to play with some Play-Doh? She puts her head back down.
- Holds up notebook and makes an obscene hand gesture toward another student, which is unnoticed by the teacher.
- Says, "That bell needs to ring." Makes another obscene gesture to the same student, sings briefly, and laughs to herself.

### Friday, September 21, 12:48–1:17 p.m., Math

- Closes eyes and puts head down on her desk while teacher is instructing math class.
- Raises hand and says she wants a harder state achievement test.
- Mocks teacher about a problem they were working on and laughs, saying, "I was just doing that to trick you."
- Laughs, fidgets in seat, and pulls desk forward.
- Puts head down on desk.
- Raises hand and gives a correct answer and laughs.

### Friday, September 21, 1:20–2:15 p.m., Theater Arts

- Sits quietly by herself.
- Puts head down on the desk.
- Plays with her hair, puts it up and down.
- Talks to a male student about the pep rally and says, "I've been here last year so I know."
- Stands by the door waiting for the bell to ring and looks at the pictures.

### Monday, September 24, 12:44–1:35 p.m., Math

- Turns around, points to an empty desk, and says, "This kid needs to stop pushing my desk."
- Tells the teacher, "I am not going to be in your math class next week." Teacher responds, "You always say that."
- Places book on the empty desk behind her and says, "This kid behind me keeps taking my book."
- Calls out teacher's name in a singsong voice, and then when teacher responds says it wasn't her calling, "it was Jacob back there" (again indicating the empty desk).
- Argues with the teacher about having already done the math problems assigned.
- Discusses out loud to herself the classes she took last year and states what she had each period last year.

### Wednesday, September 26, 12:57–1:35 p.m., Math

- Throws paper clip across room unnoticed by teacher.
- Rummages through her notebook, ignoring teacher instructions, and the teacher asks that she look up.
- Teacher assigns problems and she stares into space and laughs and complains about the work.
- Raises hand and says, "I know what it is," and answers problem correctly.
- Laughs and claps when the teacher discusses how the class did much better understanding the algebraic concept than her class last year.
- Asks the teacher to let her do a big problem on the board; teacher redirects her to do the assigned problems.
- Bell rings and she goes to exit the class, leaving the calculator and book on her desk; the teacher redirects her to put them away properly.

### Wednesday, September 26, 1:40–2:30 p.m. —Theater Arts

- Before the teacher arrives, stands by and listens to a conversation between two female students.
- Teacher asks for volunteers to paint the set and she raises her hand.
- Paints quietly and does not talk with the other students who are painting.
- Asks teacher if she can open the door so they can hear the bell ring and the teacher says yes so she opens the door.
- Stands and waits for bell to ring and does not talk to anyone.

## Diagnosis Versus ABC Analysis

Jane was diagnosed with an emotional/behavioral disability. However, Jane may have an undiagnosed MLD. On her math state achievement test, Jane received a score of 280, and she needed a score of 521 to pass. Overall, Jane expressed her most significant behavioral problems in her math class during direct instruction and independent work. Jane engaged in behaviors that would allow her to get attention particularly from the teacher; however, by doing this she also avoided doing math. During the math group work Jane demonstrated more appropriate behavior, and this led to better responses from her teacher. One of the math classes involved working hands-on with a scale to demonstrate the equality of an equation. During this observation Jane was actively engaged in the task and answered a question correctly, prompting the teacher to tell the class how well they were learning the concept. These behaviors allowed Jane to get recognition for her competence in math.

During the theater arts class, Jane did not feel the need to act out, and an emotional disability became apparent (i.e., isolation from her peers). However, this isolation could be secondary to her math LD. The math teacher also commented that Jane does not act out as much in her other classes.

## Case Questions

1: Can you identify Jane's specific problems in math?

2: What would you want Jane to learn to help herself in the future?

3 (problem-based small-group assignment): List two to three settings in math and in the teacher's behavior that work for Jane. What could you do to expand on these to provide accommodations for Jane in the general education setting?

4 (problem-based small-group assignment): Select a word problem from a math book. List those parts of the problem that require reading comprehension. List those parts of the problem that could involve working memory. List the parts of the problem that require mathematics. Convert the word problem to a numerical sentence that has no words, only symbols and numbers. Which form of the problem (the one expressed in words or the one expressed numerically) would be easier for students with NVLD to solve? Which problem would be easier for student with only reading comprehension difficulties?

5 (problem-based small-group assignment): It appears that Jane would be categorized as Tier II, because she is involved in small-group math instruction aimed at building targeted mathematics proficiencies. This instruction is typically provided in sessions of 20 to 40 minutes, 4–5 times per week, with monthly progress monitored. Specifically what would you monitor to assess Jane's response to intervention in math to determine whether she might need more intensive (one-on-one) Tier III interventions and a possible diagnosis of MLD?

## CASE STUDY 5.2: ELLIOT

*"My eyes are on backwards."*
(adapted from an assignment submitted by Megan Vinh)

*Background.* Elliot is a verbally bright 5-year-old boy who has a passion for reading and loves singing. He is very active. However, Elliot's IEP makes it clear that Elliot is a source of confusion for the team of people who have been brought together to evaluate his placement options. He has been placed in a general education classroom with four other students with disabilities and seven students whose first language is not English. In preschool, Elliot was given services based on a diagnosis of developmental delay (DD). He was referred for reevaluation of his DD diagnosis to determine a placement and transition to kindergarten. After testing, it was determined that Elliot fell into the average range for adaptive functioning and that services based on a label of DD were unnecessary.

However, new services were seen as necessary because of Elliot's deficits in language. He has problems discussing abstract ideas. Elliot is beginning to have problems with more abstract concepts, such as sorting by shape and not color. He has problems disregarding the color of a particular shape when he is asked to sort on shape. However, Elliot is also a very good reader who understands how to break down words; he understands the rules of reading. Many of his communication problems are related to the fact that he does not know how to communicate that he wants to be friends and just does not understand what other students are communicating to him.

During 7 days of direct observation, it became clear that Elliot was displaying inappropriate behavior in his kindergarten classroom. The types of behavior included singing and humming while the teacher was talking, yelling at the other students, ordering other children around, and calling out answers. His behaviors, along with their antecedents, consequences, and payoffs, are listed in the following ABC table.

## ABC Table

### Centers/Stations Antecedents

| Antecedent | Behavior | Consequence | Payoff |
|---|---|---|---|
| Day 1:<br>Coloring the "A" ditto | Elliot would not use color to color his picture, despite what the directions said.<br>He pointed to each student in his group and told them they were boring.<br>Began to sing about the letter *A*.<br>Yelled at a girl in his group. | Verbal reminder: Helper asked him to use color.<br>Another student told Elliot he was being mean.<br>He was allowed to sing because he had finished his work.<br>Verbal reminder: The teacher told him not to yell. | Gain self-determination.<br>Gain emotional stimulation.<br>Avoid boredom and gain competence.<br>Gain emotional stimulation. |
| Day 1:<br>New ditto | Stood up 6 times during individual seatwork.<br>Put his head directly in front of the university helper's face to get the helper to speak to him.<br>Ran from station to station. | No one said anything because he was finished working.<br>The helper talked to Elliot.<br>No one said anything to him. | Gain activity/sensory stimulation.<br>Gain relatedness.<br>Gain activity/sensory stimulation. |
| Day 1:<br>Center 2:<br>Legos | Yelled at another student and banged his fists on the desk.<br>Hummed while he played with the Legos.<br>Yelled at the university student from across the room. | Teacher reprimand.<br>No one said anything because he was doing his work.<br>Teacher reprimand. | Gain emotional stimulation.<br>Gain activity/sensory stimulation.<br>Gain relatedness. |

| Antecedent | Behavior | Consequence | Payoff |
|---|---|---|---|
| Day 3:<br>Independent ditto | He yelled, "Look out it's a bumblebee." (There was no bumblebee.)<br>He brought a chair over for his caseworker to sit next to him. | Caseworker said, "Elliot you're so silly."<br>Elliot's caseworker sat down and thanked him. | Gain relatedness.<br>Gain relatedness (appropriate). |
| Day 5:<br>Independent ditto<br>The teacher told everyone to put away the papers they were working on. | Elliot was rushing through the paper and not taking his time coloring.<br>He tried to give his crayon to his caseworker to finish his paper.<br>Elliot screamed, "NO!" | The teacher came over and talked to him about taking his time.<br>The caseworker told him to finish his paper himself.<br>The teacher gave him the choice to finish his paper and then move to the next station. | Gain self-determination.<br>Avoid failure.<br>Gain self-determination. |
| Day 5:<br>Sorting shapes | Elliot began to say "butt" over and over again. | His caseworker gave him a verbal reprimand and the children laughed. | Gain emotional stimulation and relatedness. |
| Day 6:<br>Independent ditto | Made vomiting noises. | The university student helper reprimanded him. | Gain emotional stimulation. |
| Day 7:<br>Coloring ditto | He yelled at a girl.<br>Elliot began coloring his paper very fast. | His caseworker told him to stop yelling.<br>His caseworker told him to slow down. | Gain emotional stimulation.<br>Gain self-determination. |

## Transitions Antecedents

| Antecedent | Behavior | Consequence | Payoff |
|---|---|---|---|
| Day 1:<br>Directions:<br>Transition from stations back to his desk | Played with glue inside of his desk.<br>Pushed a child standing at his desk and began to yell, "It's cleanup time!"<br>Sang on his way to the carpet. | Teacher took away his glue stick.<br>Teacher reprimand.<br>Teacher reprimand. | Gain activity/sensory stimulation.<br>Gain self-determination.<br>Gain cognitive stimulation and gain competence. |
| Day 2:<br>Transition from snack to instruction | Talked to himself and sang the days of the week song.<br>He yelled at the teacher and said he did not want to participate in centers.<br>He put his head down on his desk. | An aide reprimanded him.<br>Teacher gave him a choice. | Gain cognitive stimulation and gain competence.<br>Gain self-determination. |

(Continued)

| Antecedent | Behavior | Consequence | Payoff |
|---|---|---|---|
| Day 2: Transition from centers back to class | Hummed on his way back to his seat. Sat on his knees and began talking to the people around him. | Teacher reprimand. Teacher reprimand. | Gain activity/sensory stimulation. Gain relatedness. |
| Day 3: Transition from centers to seat | Yelled on his way back to his seat. He got in a girl's face and yelled at her. | Teacher reprimand. Teacher reprimand. | Gain emotional stimulation. Gain emotional stimulation. |
| Day 3: Waiting in line | He sang a song he learned in class. He got out of line. | Another child began to sing with him. He was sent to the end of the line. | Gain competence and cognitive stimulation. Gain activity/sensory stimulation. |
| Day 5: Transition from the puppet show to class | He was touching another boy in line. He began counting to ten on his way to his seat. He began telling the other children to be quiet. | The boy told him to stop and he moved away from Elliot. No one said anything to him. Teacher reprimand. | Gain social/kinesthetic stimulation. Gain competence. Gain self-determination. |

## Circle Time/Story Antecedents

| Antecedent | Behavior | Consequence | Payoff |
|---|---|---|---|
| Day 1: Circle time | Called out twice. | Teacher reprimand. | Gain competence. |
| Day 1: Story | Touched other children. | Teacher reprimand. | Gain social/kinesthetic stimulation. |
| Day 2: Circle time | Elliot remembered how to spell the color purple. Called out what he liked and disliked despite what the directions of the activity were. Called out, saying that he was tired. Made noises. Talked to another student while the teacher was talking. | Teacher praise. Teacher reprimand. Teacher responded, "You should go to bed earlier." Teacher reprimand. Teacher reprimand. | Gain competence (appropriate). Gain competence. Avoid failure. Gain sensory/activity stimulation. Get relatedness. |

| Antecedent | Behavior | Consequence | Payoff |
|---|---|---|---|
| Day 3: Circle time | Hummed. Moved around and hummed. | Teacher reprimand. His caseworker asked him if he was paying attention. | Gain activity/sensory stimulation. Gain activity/sensory stimulation. |
| Day 4: Circle time | Sang to himself. He began moving around, humming, and clapping. | Teacher reprimand. No one said anything. | Gain competence. Gain activity/sensory stimulation. |
| Day 5: Circle time | He stood up and lifted his shirt and tried to get something from his pocket. He read the title of the book for the class. | The teacher had her back turned to him. Teacher praise. | Gain activity/sensory stimulation and tangible stimulation. Gain competence (appropriate). |
| Day 5: Story | Elliot turned around to touch other children. He put his face in front of the book. Stood up and began counting. | His caseworker told him to turn around. His caseworker told him to sit back. Teacher reprimand. | Gain social/kinesthetic stimulation. Gain sensory/activity stimulation. Gain competence. |
| Day 6: Circle time | He sat down very close to and leaned on the university helper. Hummed. | The university helper told him he needed to sit up. No one said anything | Gain social/kinesthetic stimulation. Gain sensory and activity stimulation. |

## ABC Analysis

*Centers/stations.* This situation is specifically problematic for Elliot, because in three of four stations there is a lack of supervision and lack of direct verbal instruction. During centers, Elliot seems to want some form of relatedness or some social/kinesthetic stimulation, yet does not know how to express this need appropriately.

In Figure 5.3, gain relatedness is the second bar next to the rightmost bar, and gaining relatedness in an emotional negative manner is the second bar from the leftmost bar. Elliot will yell at his peers or order them around to try to fulfill his needs. However, when reminded that his behavior is inappropriate, he will apologize without prompting. Emotional stimulation and provoking may be ways that Elliot has found to have people attend to him. For example, Elliot began to say "butt" to try to get a reaction from the people in his group. It is probable that Elliot does not know what kind of reaction he will get based on what he is doing; he just understands that he will get a reaction. When he said "butt," the children in his group laughed.

Elliot began to have more one-on-one help from his caseworker, who began coming to the classroom every day to sit with Elliot and to offer more verbal direction. The results of his interactions with his caseworker made it clear that Elliot needed to have this kind of verbal help to learn appropriate and inappropriate behavior. Elliot does really

**Figure 5.3**  Elliot's Payoffs

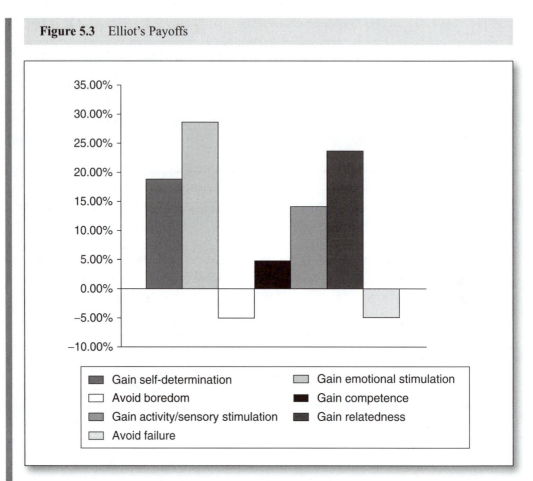

well when someone is in his classroom to guide him on what to do to make friends and to help him remember his manners. Since his caseworker has been coming to visit, Elliot has made a close friend in his group. His behaviors directed at trying to gain emotional stimulation have diminished, because he is being cued on how to address other students in a way that promotes relatedness. However, his behaviors directed toward activity/sensory stimulation have continued. Specifically, Elliot will sing songs he has learned in class or will hum to himself. These may reflect a second disability of ADHD or anxiety (i.e., they may be his way of calming himself). A more detailed analysis of when this behavior occurs would be necessary to determine the cause.

*Transitions.* The next situation that is difficult for Elliot is transitioning from one activity to the next. During this time, Elliot has to independently figure out what is expected of him either by following the other students or by watching the teacher. This poses a problem, because he does not understand subtle cues and body language. He has trouble learning through observation of other students, and he typically needs very direct instruction. Elliot has done much better during transitions when his caseworker directly tells him what is expected of him. Elliot is usually running from one station to the next, singing or humming, and occasionally he orders the other students around. He is seemingly trying to control situations where he feels control is lost. Elliot will also cry during transitions and will become helpless when he does not want to switch between activities. This can usually be remedied by giving Elliot a choice to finish what he was doing or to move on.

*Circle time/story.* The children are supposed to sit on the carpet and listen while the class goes over the date and the weather. Elliot seeks competence in this setting by calling out answers. He is the top reader in his class and seems to enjoy reading, and his teacher has utilized this strength by allowing him to read the title of the book for story time to the class each day. When Elliot does not have a chance to read the title, he begins to call out. When he is told to stop calling out, he will stop what he is doing, but his behavior aimed at seeking activity/sensory stimulation increase. He keeps touching the other students or sitting too close to them. In this situation, Elliot is using the sense of touch to feel a sense of closeness with his classmates and other people.

## Diagnosis Versus ABC Analysis

Elliot lacks the ability to comprehend nonverbal communication and has problems with social judgment and with socially interacting. Elliot does not do well with transitions or with new situations. Many times he answers questions inappropriately because he does not understand the context of the situation or question. For instance, when Elliot was asked where his library book was, he said it was in the library (lack of understanding of change of context). He presented his view of reality, which made perfect personal sense to him.

Elliot initially had problems with decoding words and letters. However, when he gained an understanding of the rules of language, he began to read quite well. It is likely that Elliot has an NVLD. This may be reflected in his saying, "My eyes are on backwards."

Elliot may also have co-occurring ADHD, hyperactive/impulsive subtype (ADHD-HI). In support, the payoffs of most of Elliot's behaviors were to gain some type of stimulation. Elliot gets out of his seat, moves around, runs around the room, blurts out answers, and hums and sings to himself quite frequently. However, in the long view Elliot does not seem to fit the profile for a student with ADHD. His NVLD would need to be addressed first.

## Interventions Derived From ABC Analysis

Elliot needs to find appropriate ways to gain competence, stimulation, and relatedness. Teaching Elliot how to make friends and then pairing him up with a peer helper or peer buddy may be beneficial. Elliot could take on a teaching role, which could allow him to utilize his strengths as a reader to help the other child read. Specific and repeated verbal instructions should be given to him. He needs to be taught that he should keep an appropriate distance between himself and other students and that yelling, controlling, bossing, and touching other children are inappropriate ways to try to gain friendships. It became apparent during circle time that Elliot's behavior seeking sensory/activity stimulation was reduced when he was given a job and felt a sense of competence.

Lastly, his teacher needs to be educated about NVLD. She should understand that Elliot's rote memory and his verbal abilities are high, but that his ability to understand abstract meaning and visual and inferential concepts, such as cause and effect, are not as high and that he will struggle with mathematical concepts. Elliot needs to be taught how to ask for help appropriately. His self-esteem is typically very fragile (e.g., Elliot will cry for no apparent reason). He also does not do well with new situations and transitions, which should be made more verbally structured to help him to prepare and cope. His teacher needs to help him use his reading skills and rote memory to compensate for his weaknesses in organization and understanding context.

## Case Questions

1: Make a pie chart that displays the frequencies of consequences that Elliot receives from teachers for his behavior. Develop a change plan for the teacher based on your interpretation of how well these consequences are working. Come up with a method to analyze responses by this student to the teacher's change in consequences (RTI).

2: What are Elliot's strengths? How might each of his strengths be used to help him?

3: Develop two strategies to teach a child with NVLD to understand cause and effect.

4: If Elliot has two disabilities, which one is most important to target initially?

5 (problem-based small-group assignment): Transitioning is an activity that is less structured and typically lacks specific instructions. During this time, "Elliot has to independently figure out what is expected of him either by following the other students or by watching the teacher." Since Elliot has difficulty with transitioning and a caseworker cannot be there to interpret each transition, how could you help him identify relevant cues? Describe several different transition settings and the cues to which Elliot should attend.

# SECTION III

# Cognitive Exceptionalities

Intelligence reflects a broad mental capacity to solve problems and to understand, yet it is typically measured by performance on intelligence tests. Most scores on these tests cluster around the middle within a normal range. The term *cognitive exceptionalities* refers to extreme scores on intelligence tests—both very high and very low scores. Students with high IQ scores of 130 and up define the first cutoff for gifted and talented. Students with GT have wide-ranging capacities to solve problems, reason, plan, handle abstract ideas, learn quickly, and profit from experience (Lubinski, 2009). Unfortunately, the potential of students with GT and co-occurring disabilities ("twice-exceptional" students) is typically not identified, because their disabilities mask their giftedness. Alternatively, neither their disabilities nor their giftedness is recognized, and they just appear average.

At the other end of the normal IQ distribution are low scores and poor functioning on everyday life skills, which define students who have intellectual disabilities (ID). The focus here is on mild ID, or MID. Students with MID have a wide range of impairments that can affect attention, language, verbal learning, visual learning, problem solving, social interactions, physical functions, and motor skills (i.e., adaptive behavior in addition to low scores). Figure III.1 displays IQ ranges and students significantly above or below the mean, indicated by standard deviations (*SD* or σ) or percentages of students above or below.

Also addressed in this section, in Chapter 8, are students with traumatic brain injury (TBI), with a focus on mild traumatic brain injury (MTBI). See Figure III.2. Students with MTBI have specific cognitive impairments in the areas of attention/concentration, impulsivity, speed of information processing, memory, and communication; they may also have social or mental health problems and sleep problems (Gerberding & Binder, 2003; Nampiaparampil, 2008). These students are included in this section because they have deficits in executive functioning that in some ways are similar to those found in students with LD (described in Chapters 3, 4, and 5). However, students with LD generally follow a smooth developmental course that is less frequently observed in students with MTBI.

## LEARNING GOALS

In this section you will learn the following:

- The vocabulary associated with cognitive exceptionalities
- How children with intellectual and traumatic brain injuries are formally defined by IDEA and *DSM-IV-TR*
- How the level of intellectual impairment or of co-occurring giftedness defines each subtype but is expressed with considerably more variability in students whose cognitive processing has been altered from brain injury
- The etiology and prevalence of each disability and how age, culture, and gender modify the outcomes
- How educators can informally identify these children through observations of their (a) behavior, (b) responses to social and communication settings, (c) responses to academic tasks, and (d) responses to motor and physical tasks
- Possible implications for interventions and accommodations for such children
- How to apply the information you have learned to case applications of students with cognitive exceptionalities

**Figure III.1** Normal Distribution of IQ Scores

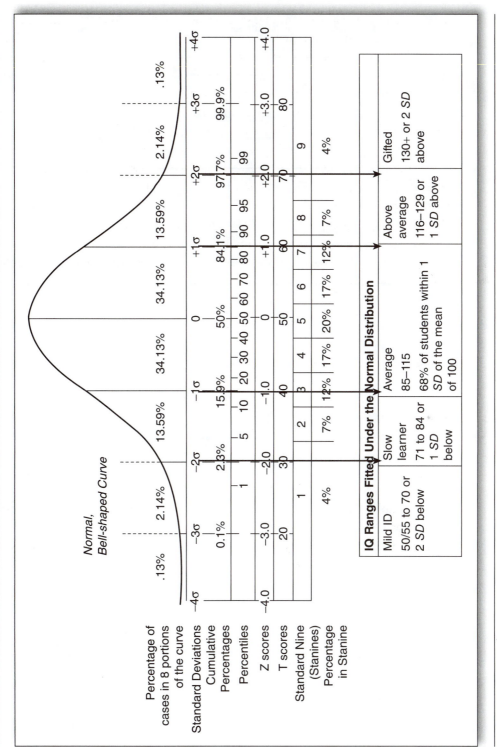

*Source:* Jeremy Kemp.

**Figure III.2**   Cognitive Exceptionalities

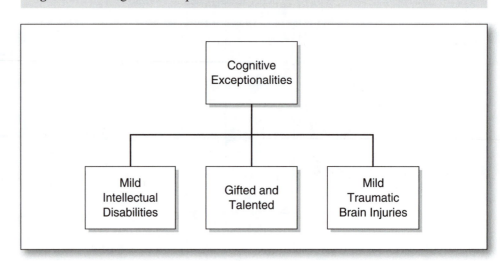

# Chapter 6

## Mild Intellectual Disabilities

Mild intellectual disability (**MID**), the focus of this chapter, is defined as having an intelligence quotient (IQ) score within a range below 70–75, although U.S. states differ in their application of IQ criteria and definitions (Polloway, Patton, Smith, Lubin, & Antoine, 2009). Two types of intelligence are generally assessed: performance intelligence, using novel visual stimuli (pictures, blocks, objects, mazes); and verbal intelligence, using auditory stimuli (vocabulary, statements. The Wechsler Intelligence Scale for Children (WISC) incudes both verbal and performance scales. Scores from this test are normally distributed, typically with a mean score of 100 and a range that defines "average" from 85 to 115. Typically, cognitive limitations will cause a child with MID to develop more slowly than a typical child (e.g., taking longer to learn to speak, walk, care for personal needs) and will cause difficulties in learning. This chapter also addresses information relevant to slow learners (71 to 84 IQ), who do not qualify for special education services but are considered at risk. In other words, there are many K–12 students in the schools who function above the 70 IQ cutoff and do not have IEPs but exhibit many characteristics of MID. Even though we use these ranges of IQ to define these students, the field of ID has moved beyond IQ to a comprehensive look at how individuals apply **intelligence** to functioning (**adaptive behavior**). So students with ID must have limitations in cognitive functions that affect their adaptive behavior (e.g., communicating, self-care, social skills).

For example, Rex, whose case study appears at the end of this chapter, shows difficulty with abstract verbal and visual concepts (making connections between actions

**MID:** Mild intellectual disability, previously labeled "mild mental retardation" or "educable mental retardation."

**Intelligence:** When the verbal and performance intelligence scales are combined they form a single score, called an intelligence quotient (IQ) or the full-scale IQ.

---

**Figure 6.1**    A student with Mild Intellectual Disabilities

**Adaptive behavior:**
Behavior in the areas of practical everyday functioning that are needed to live independently, care for oneself, and interact with others. Adaptive areas include communication, community use, functional academics, school/home living, health and safety, leisure, self-care, self-direction, social interaction, and work.

and their causes, specifically "why a character in a story ran from another character," "making the connection that 10 pennies equal one dime"). In other words, Rex shows difficulties in thinking with symbols, such as money, and with abstractions (e.g., "if-then" thinking). However, Rex could do well with the concrete task of recalling the events in an interesting story or in counting the number of dimes that he has for spending. His cognitive difficulties affect a broad range of academic and adaptive behavior, so the primary question is what adaptive behavior and functional academic skills will be most important for him to learn. Rex does have the capacity to learn some abstractions if he is taught through a systematic approach, which generally should be rule based and involve direct instruction, multiple exemplars, and repetition. However, it is also important that educators working with children such as Rex apply the principles of discrimination learning, that they teach skills that can be transferred to new settings and tasks, and that they encourage the children's independence of opinion and action.

# FORMAL IDENTIFICATION

## Definitions

### IDEA

IDEA's definition of intellectual disability (ID) is "significantly subaverage general intellectual functioning existing concurrently with deficits in adaptive behavior and manifested during the developmental period that adversely affects a child's educational performance" (34 C.F.R. Section 300.8[c]). "Subaverage" means 70–75 IQ or below (about 2 SD below the mean) and "developmental period" means that the disability is present prior to 18 years of age.

### DSM-IV-TR

DSM-IV-TR defines mild mental retardation as significantly below-average intellectual functioning within an IQ range of 50–69 (APA, 2000). This includes more students within the moderate range of ID.

### Frequently Occurring Subtypes

*Down syndrome* is a genetic condition characterized by additional chromosomes and the presence of an extra 21st chromosome.

*Fragile X syndrome* is the most commonly inherited cause of ID and is associated with symptoms of autism.

*Fetal alcohol syndrome* is a medical condition characterized by physical and behavioral disabilities in a child resulting from the mother's heavy exposure to alcohol during pregnancy; it is considered a leading "known" cause of intellectual disability (Burgess & Streissguth, 1990). Individuals with FAS can exhibit a wide range of IQ scores, from 20 to 120, with an average score of 65 (Green & Gillen, 2002). Deficits in verbal learning have also been linked to FAS (Kerns, Don, Mateer, & Streissguth, 1997).

### Possible Co-Occurring Conditions

Populations such as students with LD and ADHD exclude students with ID and define only students with average to above-average IQ scores. Even so, children with ID may have significant verbal or nonverbal disabilities. Rex, for example, also appears to have a reading disability ("Rex has a hard time discriminating and remembering sounds, and may have a reading and spelling disorder") and a non-verbal LD, as indicated by his difficulties with the concept of time, his poor fine motor skills, and his inability to understand some social cues:

> He does not understand sarcasm at all. When someone says something sarcastic, he laughs only after others do. If he is in a one-on-one, he will ask what did the teacher mean. He often cannot tell if someone is angry or joking around by the person's facial expression.

### Differences Among Related Disabilities

Sabornie, Evans, and Cullinan (2006) compared students with emotional and behavioral disorders (EBD) and MID and found that students with EBD have higher IQ scores and better academic skills but more behavioral problems. Students with MID have broader areas of dysfunction than students with LD, who have specific areas of limited functioning (MacMillan, Siperstein, & Gresham, 1996). Separating youngsters with MID from those with ADHD, the inattentive and combined subtypes, requires determining whether hyperactivity and off-task behavior remain even when their tasks are made more appropriate for the children's mental ages or abilities. Although ID and ADHD can co-occur, students with ADHD typically demonstrate more **impulsivity** than do students with ID alone (Pearson, Yaffee, Loveland, & Lewis, 1996).

**Impulsivity:** Personality trait that involves overly fast responding, difficulty waiting to respond or inhibiting responses, and acting without considering possible consequences. (Section III)

## Etiology

Although we can identify the causes of ID in many students, the etiologies are unknown for approximately 40–50%. Those etiologies that are identifiable range widely in type.

*Biogenetic.* Genetics plays a significant role in IQ, with an influence that increases with age (Garrett, 2011). Single-gene abnormalities account for 25% of cases of ID.

**Abreaction:** The release of emotions by acting out; often a reaction against a set of circumstances.

For example, children with Down syndrome have 47 instead of the usual 46 chromosomes and the presence of part or all of an extra 21st chromosome. Fragile X syndrome is also genetically based and associated with ID. More than 1,000 additional biological causes have been found to explain ID (Wenar & Kerig, 2006).

**Transference:** The implementation of what has been learned in one setting, context, or task in another setting, context, or task (e.g., from a school to a work environment, from reading to social studies).

*Environmental.* Environmental effects on the central nervous system associated with ID include prenatal and postnatal problems. During pregnancy, infections (such as German measles), severe maternal stress, and malnutrition can affect the developing fetus. For example, FAS is caused by prenatal alcohol exposure of 5 to 6 drinks per occasion, 45 drinks per month, and daily consumption. The timing of this drinking can lead to permanent brain damage as the fetus develops. Premature birth can be a problem, as can postbirth infections (meningitis, encephalitis) and exposure to environmental toxins (e.g., lead). More difficult to identify are psychosocial factors related to deprivation in early childhood (e.g., inadequate social and/or linguistic stimulation), which can be an outcome of poverty. Such deprivation also contributes to intellectual disability and to the disabilities seen in slow learners (those with IQ scores in the 60–70 range).

**Generalization:** The application of information, elements, or problem-solving processes to novel situations or tasks (e.g., from addition to multiplication).

*Functional.* Functional assessments of children with ID generally find that these children show academic difficulties and behavioral **abreactions** when tasks are abstract and require **transference,** fast responding, independent thinking, application of information (**generalization**), **incidental learning,** or problem solving. Transference is often considered to have the same meaning as *generalization,* but the two can be distinguished according to the level of abstraction that is required. Transference is the direct application (copying) of a skill across contexts, whereas generalization is more broadly the application of elements, such as those used in problem solving or in "if-then" thinking. Children who fail to generalize fail to extract commonalities across prior learning experiences, tasks, or settings.

**Incidental learning:** Gains in knowledge that are unplanned or unintended; informal learning. Most children with average IQs "pick up" information from their own observations and from direct experiences. Children with ID are unlikely to experience much incidental learning; they need direct instruction with relevant information highlighted.

## Prevalence, Gender, Age, and Cultural Factors

*Prevalence.* According to the American Association on Intellectual and Developmental Disabilities (2010), 1 out of every 10 families in the United States has a family member with ID. It is the third-largest disability category, with about 85% of those in this category having a mild disability (APA, 2000).

*Gender.* ID is three times more prevalent in males than in females (see Wenar & Kerig, 2006), which may reflect the fact that boys also show more variability in the expression of IQ and therefore are overrepresented in the lower extremes of IQ (and the higher extremes of giftedness) (Gottfredson, 2003). The reasons for this greater variability in males are unclear.

*Age.* As a group, children with mild ID are often not distinguishable from children without ID until after preschool (APA, 2000).

*Culture.* Environmental factors associated with lower IQ in children include inadequate housing, nutrition, and health care; poor parental mental health; low parental educational level and occupational level; high levels of stress; and high numbers of children within a family (for a review, see Rosenberg, Westling, & McLeskey, 2008). Poverty and low economic status are factors because these are associated with lack of access to resources, understimulating home environments, and lack of parental education (Wenar & Kerig, 2006). It has been found that IQ runs about 20–30 points lower in the lowest economic classes than in the highest, but there is little evidence of racial differences that are not better explained by culture and motivation (Garrett, 2011). In addition, data from the U.S. Department of Education (2006) indicate that over the past four decades there has been a decrease in students receiving special education services within the category of ID at the same time that services for LD have increased. Some of this shift in diagnoses is the result of a trend toward different interpretations of IQ cutoffs (Polloway et al., 2009) in response to social/cultural pressures and preferences for labeling students with LD rather than ID.

## INFORMAL EDUCATOR IDENTIFICATION OF CHARACTERISTICS

### Behavioral

The prevalence of problem behavior in students with ID is three times greater than that in average students (Soenen, van Berckelaer-Onnes, & Scholte, 2009). Some of this can be explained by co-occurring disabilities. For example, there are more students with ADHD symptoms among lower-IQ students, and the lower the IQ, the higher are parent and teacher ratings of ADHD symptoms (Simonoff, Pickles, Wood, Gringras, & Chadwick, 2007). Problem behavior can be brought out in individual children by unexpected classroom changes, such as making a transition to a new activity or task; moving to a new environment; or change of school, grade level, or teacher. Most often, however, these children show behavioral problems in response to difficult tasks, as the example of Rex illustrates:

**FAS:** Fetal alcohol syndrome.

Rex's difficulty is paying attention and focusing on the task at hand. He will tell stories, ask to leave the room, sharpen his pencil, state that work is too hard, and talk over the teacher.

Although most students with ID will learn behavioral ways to avoid tasks that are difficult, students with Down syndrome more readily learn that it is okay to avoid a task and often show less task persistence; these students can also exhibit stubbornness and strong-willed personalities (Fidler, 2006). For students with **fetal alcohol syndrome (FAS),** there are associated behavioral characteristics of aggression, lack of inhibition, hyperactivity, impulsivity, poor judgment, misreading of social cues, difficulty learning from consequences, and inappropriate sexual behavior and talk.

**Social interpersonal problem solving:** The generation of multiple strategies for responding in a social situation and the selection of a good strategy that is more effective than others (Edeh, 2006); also could be termed *social brainstorming.*

## Social-Emotional

Not all students with low IQ have poor social skills; this may be an area of adaptive functioning for some students. However, social functioning is typically related to level of cognitive development (de Bildt et al., 2005) and can be a major contributor to the poor **social interpersonal problem solving** and lower social competence of children with ID (Edeh, 2006). For example, many students with ID are gullible, easily manipulated by their peers, and more likely than non-ID students to be rejected or neglected at school and to have high levels of stress during social exchanges (Hartley & MacLean, 2005). Under these conditions, they are more likely to internalize their difficulties into anxiety, depression, and withdrawal (Didden, Korzilius, van Oorsouw, Sturmey, & Bodfish, 2006). In fact, for children with ID the risk of developing a co-occurring psychiatric disorder is three to four times that for normally developing children (Wenar & Kerig, 2006).

Depression is one of the most common disorders in this population and is more common in students with milder ID than in those with more severe ID—probably because of the greater self-reflection that is possible for students with higher IQ (Myrbakk & von Tetzchner, 2008). The specific disorder of FAS brings depression, anxiety, and sleep disorders. Down syndrome is associated with both positive and negative social/emotional characteristics. On the positive side, such children can be affectionate, eager to make friends, cheerful, fun, generous, and very sensitive to their own needs and those of others. The negative characteristics are depression, low social status compared with others, and feelings of frustration that arise from not being understood because of communication problems. Some behavior displayed by these children, especially aggression, is related to their difficulty in recognizing their own emotional states of fear, sadness, or anger (Matheson & Jahoda, 2005), and other socially inappropriate behavior can occur while they are seeking acceptance from others (Bouras, 1999). An example from Rex's case:

> Rex can act very bossy during recess. He tends to say, "Let me show you" and "You do this." He wants to be the one in charge. Rex wants to get self-determination in 75% of the observed recess behaviors. This is one time of day that he feels equal to his peers, and he wants to show that he belongs by asserting his personality.

# Cognitive

Children with MID can exhibit deficits in most all cognitive process areas (intelligence, memory, attention) (Fletcher et al., 2004).

*Intellectual performance.* For infants and toddlers with MID, there is a failure to meet intellectual age milestones (e.g., walking, talking). For school-aged children, problem-solving performance is typically deficient (Huffman, Fletcher, Bray, & Grupe, 2004), with poor **abstract thinking** (thinking about nonphysical ideas such as love, fairness, and kindness, rather than concrete objects/events), poor symbolic thought (words, gestures, pictures, numbers), and poor ability to categorize information. Some of these areas might be described as problems in executive functioning (e.g., planning, sequencing, concept formation, problem solving). Problem-solving performance is typically deficient in children with MID (Huffman et al., 2004) and can be summarized as (a) poor learning from experience in the absence of direct instruction (i.e., poor incidental learning); (b) lack of ability to transfer skills they have learned to new settings/tasks (poor transference); (c) failure to draw on all their knowledge to solve problems (poor generalization); and (d) inflexibility given changing task or setting conditions (Siegler, 1991). Failure to transfer occurs unless there is practice of the same skill in each new situation. In other words, these students might have sufficient skills or knowledge, but they are unable to use what they know because they do not transfer what they know to new settings/tasks. In the case study, Rex "is unable to recognize spelling or vocabulary words in text, even after completing a 20-minute task that involves those words only."

*Working memory, attention, and short-term memory.* Children with MID show deficits in selective and sustained attention, seen, for example, as off-task glancing and reliance on others while doing both simple and complex tasks (Pearson et al., 1996). Interestingly, these children may be slow to attend to and identify the relevant dimension or question in a task and may fixate on nonrelevant dimensions, but once they "catch on," they can learn rapidly (Wenar & Kerig, 2006). Individuals with MID require 20% more brain neural activity to perform a task that demands attention than do individuals with an IQ of 115 or higher—this is an example of inefficient processing (Garrett, 2011). They also have difficulties with working memory and in using short-term **memory strategies** (e.g., rehearsal, clustering, associational) (Huffman et al., 2004; Numminen, Service, & MacLean, 2002). For example, a special educator observed what appeared to be working memory deficits in a 15-year-old student as she watched him work pre-algebra math problems on a whiteboard. He could perform each step within the

**Abstract thinking:** The ability to go beyond visually based concrete events or objects to form visual concepts, such as greater than, and symbols, such as understanding that one thing can represent many. For example, a picture of a chair can represent a chair and a color (e.g., red and green) can represent an action (stop/go). Verbal abstract processing involves making categories, such that a word or group of words can represent an idea (e.g., fairness).

**Memory strategies:** Strategies for retaining material in memory. These include rehearsal or repetition; clustering, or grouping similar items to make recall easier (all animals, all things that are red); and associational learning, or the pairing of the meaning of the items to be recalled with past experiences (using the situation or setting as a cue to recall behavior, such as an acronym with each letter representing a word or a mental picture prompting the recall of a word).

problem, but he could not connect three or four of these steps in a row to complete the problem.

These types of attention and memory problems make learning slow and inefficient. A child with MID may need 20–30 trials of learning with feedback, whereas the typical child needs 2–3 trials. Rex, for example, "does not remember what happened to characters at the beginning of a story listened to on compact disc or through oral reading." Children with Down syndrome have an auditory short-term memory span of only two to four numbers, whereas typical children can recall five numbers. The use of visual (instead of only auditory) presentation of numbers can increase the span of recall for children with MID.

*Perception.* Minimal impairment has been recorded in visual perceptual areas for students with MID (APA, 2000, p. 43). However, Rex clearly has difficulties with auditory discrimination, as noted by his teacher (e.g., "I will say 'drip' and he will say 'trip,' thinking he has said the same word. He also does this with ending sounds.").

## Communication

Infants with Down syndrome are delayed in shifting from babbling to speech, and toddlers are delayed in expressive verbal language and nonverbal requesting of objects and often have unintelligible speech. Toddlers with ID usually do not learn to speak with words until around the age of 3 years; they may not form their first sentences until they are 5 years old. This delayed language is associated with lower academic achievement, especially reading (Torgesen, 2000). As well, these children's slower processing speed and delayed responding can result in their missing some instruction and losing opportunities to participate. Instruction may need to be slowed down for such children, and the time allotted for processing may need to be increased. For these reasons, it is common to find that students with MID do not speak in their general education classes, but they do speak outside. This was observed in the case of Rex, whose general education teachers were surprised by his behavior in the cross-categorical room. They all mentioned that Rex was quiet and kept to himself. They were also concerned, because he seemed to stay away from social interaction within the general education room but then seek it during special activities.

## Motor, Physical, and Somatic

In the main, the population of students with MID is heterogeneous, and few physical differences characterize the group. However, such students may be prone to more injuries and illnesses than their non-MID peers (Vanlint & Nugent, 2006). Other physical/sensory characteristics can include seizure disorders, hearing impairment, and fine motor immaturity that causes difficulties with dressing (buttons and snaps, tying shoes), handwriting, and speech (Taylor, Richards, & Brady, 2005). For example, Rex shows good large motor skills but poorer small motor skills, as reported by his teacher:

> He is very sporty and has excellent gross motor coordination. However, he has slower fine motor skills. For example, he has a hard time tying his shoes. Writing is most difficult for Rex, and writing small is even more difficult, though he is getting better. Rex also has a hard time copying items from one page to another and an even harder time copying from the board. He writes one letter at a time.

In contrast to most students with MID, students with FAS exhibit several physical diagnostic characteristics. These children are low in weight at birth and thereafter experience growth deficiency for height and weight, with slender builds into adolescence. They also have distinctive facial features: small, closely set eyes; long smoother area between nose and lips; thin upper lip; and flat midface. Other characteristics of FAS are poor coordination of large muscles and problems with response inhibition and spatial learning (Streissguth et al., 1994). Students with Down syndrome also have distinctive facial features (folds over the eyes, underdeveloped nasal bridge), as well as other physical differences, including small ear canals that retain water and cause frequent ear infections; small jawbone, teeth, and mouth, with less space for the tongue; small hands and feet; and short arms and legs. These children often have visual impairments and congenital heart defects that result in reduced blood supply to the body, which is associated with fatigue and breathing problems. Some Down syndrome children have sleep apnea, digestive problems, and weak immune systems.

## Academic

In general, children with MID demonstrate an inability to meet the educational demands of school at the same rate as typical peers. *DSM-IV-TR* states that "by their late teens, they can acquire academic skills up to approximately the sixth-grade level" (APA, 2000, p. 43). However, this projection is based on averages, like most information about categories of exceptionalities, and does not represent all individuals. Academics difficulties more frequently occur for students with MID across subject areas, especially in those areas requiring comprehension and application, whereas students with LD are more likely to have difficulties in a few particular subject areas (Gresham, MacMillan, & Bocian, 1996).

*Reading.* Children with MID can develop basic skills in reading (decoding) and comprehension (defined as recall of events, characters, and so on), but they show weaknesses in inferential comprehension (e.g., causal thinking, what is the problem for the main character in this story, what is the best title). Rex says that he likes reading, but he attempts to avoid failure in reading 38% of the time in a number of ways. He is usually the first one to ask to go to the bathroom or get a drink. . . . Rex has trouble sounding out words and reading fluently. He will often stop in the middle of a sentence and attempt to tell a story about his mother. He will also stop reading to ask a question about the pictures on the page or about something new on the wall.

Thus, Rex has some problems decoding, but his major problem is in comprehension of what he hears and what he reads:

Rex answers with responses that do not correspond to the questions presented to him. When I ask him why a character in a story ran from another character, he responds by talking about something they are wearing or something that happens in another part of the story.

*Math.* Children with MID can develop basic math and **functional math skills** and will use a similar range of strategies in the computation of addition but will show weaknesses in higher-level math problem solving (Beirne-Smith, Patton, & Kim, 2006; Huffman et al., 2004). For example, Rex has difficulty with understanding visual concepts, such as money and time:

"He has a hard time . . . making the connection that 10 pennies equal one dime. . . . He has a hard time putting meaning to time. He is currently working on labeling clocks in math. He can find the time on a paper clock, but cannot apply this skill to a wall clock. He cannot understand that something happens today instead of yesterday. He doesn't understand how much things cost. He asked if a pop costs more than 10 dollars. . . . He does not know his left from his right and has a hard time reading a map in social studies.

It is also generally observed that these children learn to expect failure and are more likely than their non-MID peers to rely on external control and the rewards associated with a task (i.e., **extrinsic motivation** rather than **intrinsic motivation**) (Taylor et al., 2005). This external focus can be seen in off-task glancing and a reliance on others for help with both simple and complex tasks (Pearson et al., 1996). **Self-determination** theory proposes that human beings begin life with intrinsic motivation (Deci & Ryan, 1985); when a child experiences academic failures and adults pressure the child to perform at a higher level, the child's achievement motivation changes to become externally directed (Vansteenkiste, Lens, & Deci, 2006), with the child attempting to please others. Rex often relies on adults: "Rex is very dependent on all adults. He seeks approval on a daily basis. He will randomly hug

**Functional math skills and curriculum:** Skills and curriculum related to the use of money, time, and measurement. Functional reading involves basic word recognition and comprehension of literal meanings. Functional skills in general might be considered the skills necessary for adaptive behavior.

**Extrinsic motivation:** Impetus to action that is directed toward the goals of others; the evaluation of progress in relation to others' standards.

**Intrinsic motivation:** Impetus to action that is directed toward self-selected interests and goals; the evaluation of progress in relation to one's own standards or past performance.

**Self-determination:** The state of feeling in control (empowered) and able to make one's own decisions and have one's own plans. This is the opposite of learned helplessness, which was described in Section II.

any adult in the room." The problem-solving performance and independence training of a child such as Rex can be improved through a strategy that makes use of his interests (Edeh, 2006) to encourage intrinsic motivation. As Rex's teacher observed about his reading: "He is still unable to do this task even after 4 days of reading the same story, unless the story is of high interest to him."

## SUMMARY OF STRENGTHS AND NEEDS

| *Probable strengths* | *Probable needs* |
|---|---|
| • Can improve reading performance by focusing on interest areas.<br>• Ability to learn rapidly after identifying relevant dimensions of a task.<br>• May be skilled socially. | • Instruction that uses areas of high interest and individual strengths (meaningful experiences) to help students learn new materials, to generalize, and to recall old materials.<br>• Direct instruction on relevant dimensions of a setting or highlighting relevant dimensions of a task.<br>• Training in transfer from one setting to other real-world settings.<br>• Independence training involving direct instruction in the skills of communicating with others; taking care of personal needs, health, and safety; and home living.<br>• Additional time to process and respond.<br>• Instruction that takes into account the three types of coping: active, distraction, and avoidant. Only active coping (gaining control over a stressful situation or over one's emotions) decreases social stress in students with MID (Hartley & MacLean, 2005). Distraction and avoidant coping are associated with aggression, depression, anxiety, and delinquency.<br>• A functional curriculum that addresses friendships and social skills and that places emphasis on adaptive living skills. Note that this alternative curriculum may prevent a student from attaining high school graduation in those states that require a qualifying exam or completion of specific courses. The legality of such restrictions has yet to be tested in the justice system.<br>• Language instruction that is presented at the level of the student, with a simple, concrete structure. |

## DISABILITY IN THE CLASSROOM

### Implications for Accommodations in General Education Settings: Tier I

The inclusion of students with MID in general education classrooms (heterogeneous grouping) provides these children with "social advantages from positive peer modeling and greater achievement" (Freeman & Alkin, 2000, p. 3). In these settings, educators should do the following to ensure maximum benefit for students with MID:

1. *Encourage self-determination* by providing choices (Nota, Ferrari, Soresi, & Wehmeyer, 2007). It is important that individuals with MID are (a) treated in a nondiscriminatory manner and (b) listened to and given choices in decisions that concern them (Cook, Cooper, Miller, & Petch, 2008).

2. *Improve the rate and accuracy of task performance and improve self-determination by encouraging goal setting* (for a review, see Copeland & Hughes, 2002). An "equity principle" of the National Council of Teachers of Mathematics (2000) is that all students can learn problem solving and math concepts, and opportunities should be presented to these students.

3. *Encourage social success* by asking students to set goals, which leads to higher self-determination. Peer tutoring tasks can improve social opportunities and build friendships for these students, as well as teach them the importance of interdependence.

4. *Improve memory* by providing additional practice using computers (see the specific academic areas previously discussed).

5. *Reduce disruptive behavior* by requiring exercise at various intervals throughout the day (for a review, see Allison, Faith, & Franklin, 1995). Also, reinforced compliance training, using modeling, role play, and positive feedback (e.g., hugs), has been found to be more useful than time-out. (Compliance was defined as an appropriate child response to a request within 10 seconds and performance completed within 40 seconds; Ducharme, Harris, Milligan, & Pontes, 2003.)

## Implications for Interventions in Small-Group and Individual Settings: Tiers II and III

**Social skills training:** Direct instruction in the subcomponents of individual social skills (e.g., social greetings involve eye contact, smiling, handshake, verbal statement), which are modeled and reinforced for each step that approximates correct achievement (successive approximation).

*For social skills,* interventions should begin with cognitively simple tasks (e.g., greeting someone who enters the room) rather than with more demanding tasks such as understanding humor or another's perspective (de Bildt et al., 2005). Educators can encourage long-term maintenance of skills by teaching problem solving based on students' interests, which has been found to result in better independent problem solving performance over time (Edeh, 2006). In other words, meaningful materials improve recall and generalization. Traditional interventions aimed at **social skills training** have not been successful in producing socially important, long-term, or generalizable changes in social competence for any of the mild disability categories, including MID (see Gresham et al., cited by Edeh, 2006).

*For improving task performance,* the principles of **discrimination learning and training** are useful. In this method, students are presented with stimuli with few irrelevant details and a few relevant dimensions, and their attention is directed to these relevant dimensions or they can be taught rules for identifying relevant dimensions. The difficulty/complexity of the task can then be increased over time (Beirne-Smith et al., 2006). For example, a teacher asked a student with MID to compare the letters *T* and *F*. When the student noticed the cross in the middle of the *F*, he had little difficulty thereafter writing the word *Friday.*

**Discrimination learning and training:** Discrimination learning involves the ability to perceive differences between two stimuli presented for comparison.

*For improving sequential processing* in multistep algebraic problems, helpful interventions include teaching students to use each step in a math problem as a prompt for remembering the next step, focusing on verbs (e.g., give away, end up with) to indicate the operations, and translating problem information into equations (Neef, Nelles, Iwata, & Page, 2003).

*For improving communication skills,* interventions should focus first on the understanding of spoken language (Torgesen, 2000) and then on expressive communication.

*Tier III.* Children with MID can learn academics as well as functional life skills through structured lessons in actual settings. Such **community-based learning** (e.g., in life skills such as cooking, dressing, practicing job tasks, and community mobility) has been shown to produce more success than learning in a restrictive classroom (Katsiyannis, Zhang, & Archwamety, 2002) and better independent living after completion of school (Wehmeyer & Agran, 2005). A functional curriculum is useful when it focuses on applied money concepts, applied time concepts, and health and safety concepts.

**Community-based learning:** Method of education that uses structured lessons in actual settings (e.g., workplace, home).

## Long-Term Outcomes

Students with MID are less likely than their non-MID peers to make a transition to adult status and live independently. However, "during their adult years, they usually achieve social and vocational skills adequate for minimum self-support, but may need supervision, guidance, and assistance, especially when under unusual social or economic stress" (APA, 2000, p. 43). Students with MID, especially secondary-level students, who have been educated in general education settings have better achievement, language, prosocial behavior, flexibility, and social relations (engagement, interaction, adjustment, and contacts) than do those who have been educated in special classes, even though these children are less accepted and receive lower rankings than their average peers (for a review, see Freeman & Alkin, 2000). As adults, individuals with MID feel less of a sense of purpose and less autonomy and find fewer opportunities for personal growth than do their non-MID peers (see Rosenberg et al., 2008).

For individuals with FAS, long-term outcomes are more serious and remain throughout the lifetime: intellectual problems, poor age-appropriate life skills, and behavior problems stemming from central nervous system damage. Individuals with FAS have a high incidence of mental illness, major depression, alcohol or drug dependence, school failure, legal problems, and difficulties with employment and with independent living (Famy, Streissguth, & Unis, 1998).

## CHAPTER SUMMARY

- IDEA and *DSM-IV-TR* formally define children with MID by their subaverage intelligence. The definitions also specify educational impairment and deficits in adaptive behavior. Frequently occurring subtypes are Down, fragile X, and fetal alcohol syndromes.

- Definitions of children with EBD, LD, and ADHD exclude children who have ID. Thus, a primary exceptionality would always be ID, with co-occurring conditions of EBD, LD, or ADHD considered as secondary disabilities. To differentiate among these mild disability categories: EBD would have more behavioral problems, ADHD would have more impulsivity, and the attentional problems of MID would be found mainly during the performance of difficult tasks that require abstract thinking (e.g., tasks that require applications or generalization from old learning or problem solving in new learning settings).

- ID is the third-largest disability category, typically identified after the preschool age, and in males three times more often than in females.

- The etiology of ID is often unknown, but under some circumstances it can be traced to genetic or to prenatal/postnatal causes (nutrition, infections, toxins, and inadequate social/linguistic stimulation).

- Students with ID can be informally identified by educators from observations of their behavior during the performance of demanding tasks and in social interpersonal communication settings. These students exhibit behavioral problems at three times the rate of students without ID. Cognitive performance provides an easy marker for students with MID, who often have difficulty identifying relevant dimensions within tasks (e.g., how a *t* differs from an *f*), immature memory strategies, poor working memory, and greater difficulty understanding that symbols can represent objects, ideas, operations, or quantities. Their academic areas of dysfunction are delayed language and a slower rate of developing academic skills, with lower achievement especially in reading comprehension and math problem solving.

- Interventions include instruction in functional life skills and in math, literacy, and communication. Discrimination training—helping students compare and contrast and highlighting what is relevant—can increase the speed of learning.

- Accommodations for students with MID take into account their slower processing speed, delayed responding, and poor fine motor skills by including additional time, practice in areas of interest, and verbal response opportunities. Accommodations for depression and low self-efficacy include interdependence training with goal setting, choices, and peer learning opportunities.

## CHAPTER QUESTIONS

1. On which types of tasks can students with MID be expected to perform adequately?

2. Why are children with MID identified later in elementary school rather than earlier?

3. If students with MID are typically dependent on the judgments and standards of others, how can educators help them learn independence?

4. How can educators change learning tasks so that children with MID will learn more rapidly?

## TRUE/FALSE AND MULTIPLE-CHOICE

1. Method(s) to help students with MID:
    A. discrimination training through emphasis on relevant task features
    B. practice of skills in different real-word contexts (transfer training)
    C. repetition and slower rate
    D. all of the above

2. Factor(s) contributing to intellectual disability:
    A. poverty
    B. race
    C. neither of the above
    D. both A & B

3. Instruction that focuses on the use of skills in real-world settings:
    A. discrimination training
    B. functional curriculum

4. The classroom condition most likely to bring out disruptive behavior in students with MID:

   A. crowding
   B. changes in schedule
   C. difficult tasks

5. Which of the following statements would be easiest for students with MID to understand?

   A. We must all be fair and share cookies.
   B. Everyone must have a cookie.
   C. It is not kind to take all the cookies.

6. Observation of which of the following enables differentiation among ADHD, LD, and MID?

   A. abstract nature of the task
   B. narrow versus broad areas of dysfunction
   C. presence/absence of impulsivity
   D. all of the above
   E. A and C

7. Students with MID are more likely to have large-muscle difficulties than small-muscle problems.

8. Depression is more common among higher-IQ students with MID than among lower-IQ students.

9. Boys in general show more variability in IQ and thus more are found at both extremes of the IQ distribution (intellectually gifted and intellectually disabled).

10. Children with MID are better with incidental learning than other types of learning.

## SHORT ANSWER

1. Problems during pregnancy occur during the_____ period.

2. Using reinforcement when children perform as requested is called _____ training.

3. Teaching students how to use the same skill (e.g., how to get help) across different settings or tasks by showing them elements in common in the different settings or tasks (e.g., looking for an adult in charge, written directions, a buddy) is called _____ training.

4. Using children's interests and goals to engage them in the learning context is appealing to their _____ motivation.

# PROBLEM-BASED CASE APPLICATIONS AND QUESTIONS

## CASE STUDY 6.1: REX

*"How do you know?" "Why did you do that?"*
(adapted from an assignment submitted by Jennifer McCampbell Gant)

*Background.* Rex is an 8-year-old student in the third grade. He attends school for 2 hours and 15 minutes every day in a Title I building in a cross-category classroom as stipulated by his IEP. His IEP states that he has an ID with a secondary disability of a communication disorder. He attends speech class weekly to work on expressive language. The rest of his time is spent in a general education setting. He attends all special activities, such as gym, music, and art, with his general education class. He also learns with a modified science and social studies curriculum within his general education classroom. His teacher is a veteran teacher and works well with him. Rex is introduced to reading, language arts, spelling, and math curriculum in his cross-categorical classroom in small-group settings.

Rex has a difficult home life. His parents, who are divorced, have both served time in jail (they have never been incarcerated at the same time). Rex lives primarily with his dad but does go back and forth with his mother. It has been documented by past teachers that Rex performs better in school on those days after he has stayed with his father the night before.

**Figure 6.2**  Rex's Overall Payoffs

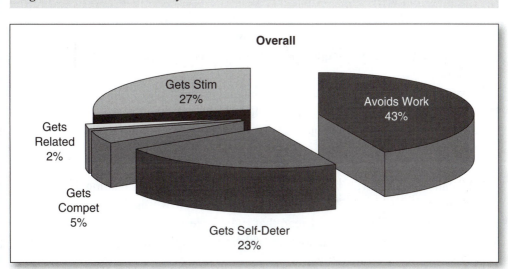

## ABC Analysis

From 39 instances of behavior, it was determined that Rex's main difficulty is paying attention and focusing on the task at hand. He will tell stories, ask to leave the room, sharpen his pencil, state that work is too hard, and talk over the teacher. In response to this behavior Rex was often redirected or refocused. For example, on September 10, Rex was reminded five times to keep working. This all took place during one math lesson. Rex has never been sent to the hall, but he has had to take written notes home about his lack of focus. He does not like this because he is constantly seeking to please.

### *Reading*

| Behavior | Antecedent | Consequence | Payoffs |
|---|---|---|---|
| Stated that he can't open his book to the right page | Reading orally | Teacher said nothing but gave stern look | Gets self-determination and control over class |
| Asked to get a drink several times | Reading orally | Teacher allows drink | Avoids reading |
| Walks slowly back to seat | Reading orally | Teacher said nothing | Gets activity stimulation |
| When reading, speaks in baby talk | Reading orally | Teacher said nothing | Gets play stimulation |
| Reprimands another student for not following along | Reading orally | Teacher stated that she could handle the class herself | Gets competence |

Rex stated that he likes reading. However, Rex attempts to avoid failure in reading 38% of the time in a number of ways. He is usually the first one to ask to go to the bathroom or get a drink. Rex likes to move around the room and take short breaks. He is allowed to do so frequently because he tends to come back ready to continue working.

Rex has trouble sounding out words and reading fluently. He will often stop in the middle of a sentence and attempt to tell a story about his mother. He will also stop reading to ask a question about the pictures on the page or about something new on the wall. Reading instruction is a challenging time for Rex, but it offers rewards for his hard work. He is allowed to read with the principal and to a kindergarten student if he can read his stories with at least 85% accuracy. He likes reading to adults, so he will strive for this goal. He works hard to master new words. Rex wants competence in reading; he will ask, "Did I read that right?" He is also the first one to reprimand another child for not following along. This is another attempt at getting competence.

## *Writing*

| Behavior | Antecedent | Consequence | Payoffs |
|---|---|---|---|
| Threw pencil at floor | Writing lesson | Teacher did not notice | Avoids writing |
| Stated that he already did this several times | Reading orally; writing brainstorm | Teacher redirected to continue reading | Avoids reading |
| Had to be reminded to keep working | Beginning of writing paragraphs | Teacher redirected to continue writing | Avoids writing |
| Had to be told to get to work five times | During writing lesson | Teacher redirected to continue writing | Avoids writing |
| Asked to sharpen pencil three times | During writing lesson | Teacher told him to stop sharpening pencils | Avoids writing |
| Stated that he wasn't messing with it | During writing lesson | Teacher told him to begin working | Avoids writing |
| Began tipping back in his chair | Writing lesson | Teacher directed class to put all legs of chairs on the floor | Gets stimulation-activity/play or avoids writing |
| Began chewing on shirt | During writing lesson | Teacher ignored behavior | Gets activity stimulation |
| Plays with pencil | Beginning of writing paragraphs | Teacher redirected to continue writing | Avoids writing |
| Had to be told to get to work three times | During writing lesson | Teacher redirected him to continue writing. | Avoids writing |
| Began to cry and stated, "My mom needs to help me!" | During writing lesson | Teacher said I understand but she is not here and we need to finish our paragraph | Gets social stimulation |
| Asked to sharpen pencil before work even began | Writing lesson | Teacher tells him to hurry so we can all get started | Avoids writing/self-determination and maintains preferred activity |
| Asked to use bathroom several times | During writing proofreading | Teacher allows him to go | Avoids writing |
| Got caught playing in bathroom | During writing proofreading | Teacher writes note to parents | Avoids writing |
| Continuously scratching knee | During writing lesson | Teacher ignores | Avoids writing |

Rex tries to avoid writing 73% of the time. He has stated that he doesn't like writing because he can't spell words. Writing is a time when all students are working independently and are often at different stages in their writings. The teacher has to divide her attention to meet the needs of all students. If Rex has not completed his assignment or if another student is having difficulties, he does not get a lot of individualized attention. Rex has to be reminded to get to work and to stay focused on his work. He will try to delay writing by asking to sharpen his pencil or use the restroom before instruction time has even begun. He has more breakdowns during writing than any other time of the day. He has shouted out that his mom needs to help him and started crying on more than one occasion. This is another time of day when he will revert to baby talk. He will say, "Me done." When he has finished a paragraph or assignment, he will say, "Me done."

## Math

| Behavior | Antecedent | Consequence | Payoffs |
|---|---|---|---|
| States that work is too hard | Math facts | Teacher redirected to continue working | Avoids math |
| Plays with number tape | Math practice | Teacher ignores behavior | Gets stimulation-activity/play or avoids math fact practice |
| Reminded to focus three times | Independent math lesson | Teacher redirected to continue working | Avoids math |
| Left seat and began hugging adults in room | Independent math fact practice | Teacher asked him to sit back down and get to work | Gets social stimulation and avoids math |
| Asked for help during work after it was already finished | Math lesson | Teacher gave assistance and praise but reminded to wait until whole page is completed | Gets social stimulation and gets competence |
| Begins pounding pencil into desk | During math lesson | Teacher told him to stop pounding pencil into desk | Gets self-determination and power over teacher |
| Begins talking over teacher | During math lesson | Teacher told him to stop talking and to get to work | Avoids math and gets social stimulation |
| Argues with teacher over answers on math page | During math lesson | Told by teacher to stop arguing and redo the questions | Gets self-determination |

Rex has a hard time in math. He doesn't understand time or money. He will play with his number line or math manipulatives instead of doing math practice. Rex will pound his pencil into his desk and attempt to speak over the teacher as a way of seeking self-determination and social stimulation. He also argues that his answers are right. He will even pull out his number line and show the teacher how he got his answer. Once he is corrected, he will comply and often hug the teacher before returning to his general education classroom. In fact, Rex tries very hard to please all adults that he sees in the school setting. He will leave his seat and hug adults that come in and out of the room. This is providing him social stimulation and allowing him to avoid his work for a short time.

### Recess

| Behavior | Antecedent | Consequence | Payoffs |
|---|---|---|---|
| Acts bossy toward others at recess | Recess | Teacher did not redirect | Gets self-determination and power |
| States "Let me show you" several times | Recess | Teacher reminded him to share with others | Gets self-determination and power |
| Asks "Why did you do that?" when students walk away | Recess | Teacher did not redirect | Gets social stimulation-relatedness |
| During cleanup, directed others by saying "You do this." | Recess | Teacher reminded him to help clean up because he plays too | Gets self-determination and power |

Rex can act very bossy during recess. He tends to say, "Let me show you" and "You do this." He wants to be the one in charge. Rex wants to get self-determination in 75% of the observed recess behaviors. This is one time of day that he feels equal to his peers, and he wants to show that he belongs by asserting his personality. He will also ask others, "Why did you do that?" This comes after peers walk away from him. Recess is a highly unstructured setting and does not require academic skills. Rex has stated that he likes recess the most next to lunch and gym. When asked why, he responds by saying that he gets to be with everyone else.

### Lunch

| Behavior | Antecedent | Consequence | Payoffs |
|---|---|---|---|
| Tries to trade sandwich to other students | Lunch | Teacher did not notice | Gets stimulation-activity/play |

*(Continued)*

(Continued)

| Behavior | Antecedent | Consequence | Payoffs |
|---|---|---|---|
| Stated that he ate all his vegetables several times | Lunch | Staff praised him | Gets competence |
| Asked several students for their desserts | Lunch | Teacher did not notice | Gets self-determination |
| Throws cookies on floor and crushes them | Lunch | Teacher did not redirect | Gets peer relatedness |

Lunch is another time of day when Rex is in an unstructured environment. Supervision is limited and Rex is left with his peers. He seeks social stimulation a majority of the time. He asks to trade sandwiches and snacks with his peers. He knows this is against the rules, but he also knows that no one is watching him. He will approach adult staff members and state that he ate all his vegetables. This gets him praise. He will also throw cookies on the floor and crush them as a way to get peer attention and relatedness. He tends to spend lunchtime with students who have negative behaviors, who will accept him and approve of his bossy behavior toward others.

## Diagnosis Versus ABC Analysis

ID was Rex's diagnosis, with a secondary disability of a communication disorder.

*Verbal disability.* Rex answers with responses that do not correspond to questions presented to him. When I ask him why a character in a story ran from another character, he responds by talking about something they are wearing or something that happens in another part of the story. He does not remember what happened to characters at the beginning of a story listened to on compact disc or through oral reading. His comprehension when reading by himself is low. He is still unable to do this task even after 4 days of reading the same story, unless the story is of high interest to him. He is talkative, but still uses some baby talk. He says things like "Mines time to go" often. I make him say phrases correctly but often get a "That is what I said" response.

His verbal problems are also seen in poor auditory skills in reading and spelling. Rex has a hard time discriminating and remembering sounds, and may have a reading and spelling disability. For example, he has a very hard time sounding out words. Once he does sound it out correctly, he cannot hold the sounds together to say the word correctly. I will say "drip" and he will say "trip," thinking he has said the same word. He also does this with ending sounds. For example, the story will have the word "here's" in it, and Rex will read it "here." I will correct him and say, "here's." He then repeats "here" and says, "That is what I said." He also does this is the "'d" ending and occasionally with the "ing" ending. Rex will also mispronounce letters, mostly *t, h, s, d,* and *p,* thinking he is pronouncing another letter in that set. He does not know the difference between short and long vowel sounds. Everything comes out the same. When he is spelling, almost every vowel is an *i* and most words end in *e.* He can recall many individual letter sounds, but not all. He also has a difficult time when asked to see the word inside his head before he tries to spell it. He is unable to recognize spelling or vocabulary words in text, even after completing a 20-minute task that involves those words only.

*Nonverbal disability.* Rex may also have a nonverbal disability. He does not understand sarcasm at all. When someone says something sarcastic, he laughs only after others do. If he is in a one-on-one, he will ask what did the teacher mean. He often cannot tell if someone is angry or joking around by the person's facial expression. He will ask, "Are you upset?" even if you have a smile on your face. He is very sporty and has excellent gross motor coordination. However, he has slower fine motor skills. For example, he has a hard time tying his shoes. Writing is most difficult for Rex, and writing small is even more difficult, though he is getting better. Rex also has a hard time copying items from one page to another and an even harder time copying from the board. He writes one letter at a time. (This might also be explained by his memory disability.)

Related to an NVLD, Rex has poor visual comprehension. He has a hard time remembering his basic math facts and counting and making the connection that 10 pennies equal one dime. He will also ask questions that could be called "dumb." He will ask, "What time is it?" When he is given the response, he will reply with, "How do you know?" He is referred to the clock and he responds with "Oh." He has a hard time putting meaning to time. He is currently working on labeling clocks in math. He can find the time on a paper clock, but cannot apply this skill to a wall clock. He cannot understand that something happens today instead of yesterday. He doesn't understand how much things cost. He asked if a pop costs more than 10 dollars. He was told that it costs 50 cents, and he replied with "Okay." He does not know his left from his right and has a hard time reading a map in social studies.

*Dependence.* Rex is very dependent on all adults. He seeks approval on a daily basis. He will randomly hug any adult in the room with whom he has interaction regularly. He is very attentive to his little sister and will ask to leave the room to hug her when he can see her in the hallway. He often chews on his shirtsleeves and zips himself all the way up in a sweatshirt. This could be an attempt to self-comfort or hide.

He whines often and comments that he needs his mom to help him. He tells stories of events with his mother and father often. When he is in trouble or frustrated, he will often cry. When someone else is hurt or crying, he is the first to try to comfort and will often cry with him or her. He is very sensitive to what you say and takes things very literally.

*ADHD.* Rex's inability to focus may at first look like ADHD. He likes to walk around the classroom, does not like to repeat tasks, and has a hard time getting along with peers in an unstructured environment. He also has a hard time maintaining control of his emotions. However, these problems appear to be secondary to his ID.

Overall, there is more information about Rex than a diagnosis of ID specifies. He has more general problems that bridge verbal and nonverbal intelligence, memory, and auditory perception, as well as emotional difficulties associated with failure (dependence) and behavioral problems in the cross-category room.

## Interventions Derived From ABC Analysis

Though both of his parents are supportive of what happens with Rex at school, there is not much carryover to the home. Avoidance of schoolwork is his most frequently occurring payoff. The creation of fun learning activities that lead to success for Rex instead of failure can target this payoff and reduce his avoidance behavior. He wants to work hard and spell words correctly. This helps him stayed focused on the task. He enjoys learning new spelling words. One way to help Rex improve his phonetics skills is to do repeated practice. However, Rex does not thrive using repetition, so the curriculum can be repeated, but the tasks need to change. Furthermore, the application of phonetic rules may be more difficult in their abstract requirements, whereas memorizing a set of interesting sight words may be more useful for Rex. Peer tutoring can also be used to help improve his memory and social skills, because Rex likes interacting with other students.

## Case Questions

1: Note the low percentage of Rex's attempts to get competence. Why is this important and how would you increase this percentage?

2: If Rex avoids writing because he can't spell, what accommodations would you recommend?

3: What does it tell you that Rex behaves differently in the special education classroom from the way he behaves in general education settings?

4: What is your opinion about (a) sending notes home about Rex's failure to "focus" and (b) reminding Rex to pay attention?

5 (problem-based small-group assignment): As noted above, Rex shows difficulty with abstract verbal concepts (making connections between actions and their causes, specifically "why a character in a story ran from another character") and with visual concepts ("making the connection that 10 pennies equal one dime"). In other words, Rex shows difficulties in thinking with symbols. However, Rex could do well with the concrete tasks of recalling the events in an interesting story or in counting the number of dimes that he has for spending. Given this information, what adaptive behavior and functional academic skills are most important for him to learn? Why? How would you go about teaching Rex these higher-level skills?

6 (problem-based small-group assignment): Rex spends approximately three-fourths of his time during written assignments avoiding the task. How would you determine the degree to which this behavior is or is not related to a handwriting or fine-motor problem?

# Chapter 7

## Exceptionalities Co-Occurring With Gifted and Talented

### *The Twice Exceptional*

Twice-exceptional students are often overlooked in the American education system (Assouline, Foley Nicpon, & Whiteman, 2010), and perhaps this occurs because we do not understand the nature of intelligence. General intelligence is more than book learning or test-taking skills. It reflects a deep capacity for comprehending the environment, solving problems, handling abstract ideas, learning quickly, and profiting from experience (Lubinski, 2009). Although it involves broad capacity, it is typically measured by an intelligence test and an IQ score. A high score of 130 is the cutoff for gifted and talented, with 160 as the cutoff for highly gifted children. In fact there is evidence of a significant "bump" on the normal IQ curve at about 160, with scores up to 200; this suggests that the normal curve is not as smooth as once thought (Webb et al., 2005). The highly gifted and talented fall in this tail end of the IQ distribution, but their scores are so high that they could be described as qualitatively different in intelligence (i.e., they are outside the range of normal experiences; Gottfredson, 2003).

It may be surprising that many of these GT and highly GT children have co-occurring mild disabilities (i.e., typically with LD and ADHD). The relationship between intelligence and disability is complex—not only is higher intelligence associated with better reading performance (Stage et al., 2003), but it is also associated with higher heritability for poor reading ability and reading disability (Shaywitz et al., 2008).

Given the overlap between extreme ability and disability, it is important to understand giftedness as a single trait. Giftedness shows up early in toddlers as differences in attention (alertness, long span, and preference for novel over

---

**Figure 7.1**  A student who is both gifted and twice-exceptional

174 SECTION III: COGNITIVE EXCEPTIONALITIES

familiar stimuli), excellent memory, and advanced language development and vocabulary. Infants with GT, compared with typical infants, often need less sleep, are more active, smile or recognize caretakers earlier, and have a marked need for stimulation that appears different from their intense reactions to pain, noise, and frustration (Silverman, 1998). "Gifted infants tend to be both highly active and highly reactive—intense balls of energy who have as great an impact on their environment as their environment has on them" (see Robinson, 1993, cited in Silverman, 1998).

However, in order for these innate predispositions or traits to produce extraordinary achievement, additional child qualities are needed. These include task commitment (zeal, tenacity, grit), creativity, and perhaps verbal, quantitative, spatial, musical, or other talent (Gottfredson, 2003; Renzulli, 1979). According to Renzulli (1979), certain environments, opportunities, and encouragements are also necessary for the development of giftedness. Such challenging opportunities are less frequently provided when the child has a co-occurring disability (twice exceptional) or when the child comes from an underrepresented group or culture. It is thus important to recognize giftedness associated with disability and within different cultures. That is, the stereotype of a gifted child as a Caucasian girl who knows all the answers, is behaviorally compliant, and wears glasses (as in the drawing at the beginning of this chapter) does not represent the diversity of this group of students.

## FORMAL IDENTIFICATION

### Definitions

Gifted/talented is not a category under IDEA and is not defined in *DSM-IV-TR*. It is an area of exceptionality rather than of disability. The federal government does not require services for GT students or fund gifted educational programs; however, some states do recognize these children as having special needs and provide them with GT services (Bianco & Leech, 2010). Teacher referral of GT students is considerably less than it is for academic or behavioral problems in children, and teacher referral of twice-exceptional students is particularly low (Bianco & Leech, 2010). When GT students are referred, the referrals are typically based on intellectual ability. An IQ score of 130 is the standard cutoff for entrance into gifted programs (although this score may vary by state); this score indicates that the child is performing better than 96% of the population on that test (Taylor, Smiley, & Richards, 2009). Fortunately, the field of giftedness has supplemented the use of just one cutoff full-scale IQ score with such important indicators of GT as high levels of task commitment or of creativity (Crepeau-Hobson & Bianco, 2010).

The National Association for Gifted Children defines a student with GT as someone who shows or has the potential for showing an exceptional level of performance in one or more areas of expression (a **talent**). This is consistent with recent emphasis on intelligence as multiply determined (i.e., verbal-linguistic, logical-mathematical, musical, spatial, bodily-kinesthetic, interpersonal, intrapersonal, and naturalistic; see Gardner, 1983).

### Frequently Occurring Subtypes

Students with GT have been categorized into the following subtypes: (a) creative, (b) academic, (c) intellectual, (d) underachievers, (e) economically disadvantaged, and the (f) highly talented with specific aptitudes (Gardner, 1983). GT students can also be subdivided into those who are creative and those who are not (Webb et al., 2005). **Creativity** can be assessed as a child's production of products useful to the self or to society (see Csikszentmihalyi, 1996, cited by Gallagher, 2003). Creative individuals are typically independent, nonconventional, flexible, and sufficiently introverted to allow for reflective thinking (see Simonton, 1999, cited by Gallagher, 2003). Table 7.1 presents a comparison between creative and academic/intellectual subtypes.

The **underachiever** can be defined by (a) uneven academic performance, (b) discrepancies in performance between high ability and lower school performance, and (c) discrepancies between investment of effort and performance with

**Talent:** Exceptional level of performance in verbal-linguistic, logical-mathematical, musical, spatial, bodily-kinesthetic, interpersonal, intrapersonal, and naturalistic areas of functioning. Talent is less heritable than the g factor.

**Creativity:** The ability to sustain a wide array of interests, openness to novel experiences and to tangential ideas, and the ability to apply existing knowledge to novel problems.

**Underachiever:** A child for whom there are discrepancies between aptitude or IQ and actual performance on everyday schoolwork.

**Table 7.1**  Academic/Intellectual and Creative Subtypes of GT Students

| Intellectual and academic subtype *(analytic intelligence)* | Creative subtype *(synthetic intelligence)* |
|---|---|
| Excels in intelligence, has a very high IQ, outstanding grades, exceptional analytical ability | Earns good grades but scores low on aptitude tests |
| Superior at acquiring knowledge | Good at acquiring knowledge |
| Very good at solving problems | Very good at "finding" problems |
| Tests well | Does not test well (and thus has an "underachiever" label) |
| Excels in planning, monitoring, evaluating, and implementing problem solving | Excels in coping with novelty, in seeing old problems in new ways |
| May see the trees but not the forest | Can identify which problems are most important (i.e., sees the gestalt) |

self-selected readings or topics of interest versus with everyday schoolwork. This could be described as significant variability in school performance and significant subtest scatter when tested. These students often hear statements such as, "You are so good in math, why can't you do better in all your other subjects?" (Seely, 1998b, p. 88).

### Possible Co-Occurring Conditions

In addition to environmental influences that decrease achievement, many children with GT have co-occurring disabilities. These children, the **twice exceptional,** are often not identified as gifted. Silverman (2003) has concluded that "a major cause of underachievement in the gifted appears to be undetected learning disabilities" (p. 533). Students with GT + LD are more likely to show creative potential but also to behave disruptively and underachieve, which reduces their opportunities to be identified as gifted (Moon & Reis, 2004). Rather than being accelerated, which they should be, about half of these students are retained one grade in school, which is a considerable source of shame for them (Reis et al., 1995, cited in Moon & Reis, 2004). The "incidence of learning disabilities in the gifted population is at least as high as the incidence in the general population (10–15%)" (Silverman, 2003, p. 533). When gifted children have learning disabilities, their giftedness is typically missed or not identified until third or fourth grade, and for many not until middle or high school (Webb et al., 2005). In these cases, the disability masks the giftedness such that the disability is recognized but GT is not; alternatively, giftedness can mask the disability, such that the child looks average and the disability is not recognized. This happens when the child uses intelligence to compensate for weaknesses. For example, giftedness can hide reading disabilities, because the abstract reasoning ability of these children (e.g., using context cues) allows them to fill in missing sounds and words when listening and when decoding (Silverman, 2003). However, these twice-exceptional children are still performing significantly below where they could be performing, which contributes to the appearance that they are lazy, undisciplined, or unmotivated.

**Twice exceptional:** Having both giftedness and co-occurring disabilities, such as LD or ADHD.

### Differences Among Related Disabilities

Students with GT are often placed in repetitive and boring school contexts, which contributes to the expression of social/behavioral disabilities in these children. For example, gifted children typically spend one-fourth to one-half of their time in general education classrooms waiting for other students to catch up with their classroom assignments (Webb et al., 2005, pp. 23–24). Under these conditions, they become bored and unmotivated and may become disruptive, displaying behavior that looks like ADHD, conduct disorder (CD), or oppositional defiant disorder (ODD). For example, Simone was an enthusiastic preschooler who was quite curious and appeared to be interested in preschool. However, during story time, she would start by listening, but before long she would be lying on the floor, generally disrupting the lesson by playing with nearby objects or talking. When the teacher questioned her, it became clear that she was an advanced reader and had already heard or read most of the stories available in class. Furthermore, when the teacher gave directions, she could pretty quickly figure out what was required, and so did not need to pay attention to additional details from the teacher.

Students with GT and emotional disorders (ED) are regularly overlooked for referral for GT special services, because their behavior does not conform to common stereotypes of giftedness (Bianco & Leech, 2010). Similarly, professionals are confused by the overlapping characteristics between ADHD and GT during elementary school years: emotional intensity, high levels of energy and activity, creativity, and an attraction to novelty (e.g., avoiding repetition and doing things differently) (Clark, 2002; Zentall, Moon, Hall, & Grskovic, 2001). These two groups are also similar in their engagement with sports and social activities. Chris, whose case study appears at the end of this chapter, shows signs of co-occurring ADHD, but ADHD might never have been considered if this child had been challenged:

> Chris may not be ADHD-HI; he is a highly gifted child who has never really been stimulated academically, at least not at school. His lack of cognitive stimulation (challenge) may well have caused him to behave disruptively in class and garnered him a diagnosis of ADHD. . . . No other members of his family have an ADHD diagnosis.

ADHD can be distinguished from GT in that some of the overlapping characteristics noted above are not markers for ADHD (e.g., extraordinary memory, long attention span, advanced language development, questioning of traditions). More definitively, students with pure GT do not show impulsivity (e.g., blurting out incorrect answers) more than other children of the same age and do not show social problems unless they are highly gifted. Nor do these GT students avoid homework, unless it is very repetitive and nonchallenging. Flint (2001) has documented that students with both GT and ADHD often demonstrate creativity, but students with GT without ADHD are better able to organize and finish their creative projects. Students with GT are emotionally intense and have a clear sense of justice, which may result in their being incorrectly identified as oppositional defiant disordered. However, unlike students with ODD, students with GT demonstrate intense emotions of all types (positive and negative), and their anger, when expressed, is more often a response to perceived larger social injustices (Webb et al., 2005). Further, in the identification of GT students, a distinction must be made between bright children and gifted children. Table 7.2 lists the characteristics of these two kinds of children (see "Bright Child," n.d.).

**Table 7.2**   Comparison of the Characteristics of Gifted and Bright Children

| Gifted children | Bright children |
| --- | --- |
| Are beyond the group | Are in the top group |
| Are highly curious | Are interested |
| Construct abstractions | Understand ideas |
| Create new designs | Understand visual abstractions |
| Are mentally and physically involved | Are attentive |
| Play around, yet test well | Work hard |
| Discuss in detail | Answer the questions |
| Ask questions | Know answers |
| Are good at "guessing" by synthesizing information | Are good at memorizing |
| Show strong feelings and opinions | Listen with interest |
| Are intense | Are receptive |
| Prefer the company of adults or other smart peers | Enjoy the company of peers |

*Source:* http://gleigh.tripod.com/brightvG.htm.

## Etiology

*Biogenetic.* Genetics plays a major role in determining intelligence (see Taylor et al., 2009). This is reflected in statements about Chris: "His father is highly gifted, and his other siblings are gifted as well. Giftedness is clearly a family trait."

*Environmental.* Children from low-SES backgrounds tend to have lower IQ than higher-SES peers, most likely owing to lack of environmental stimulation, inadequate resources (e.g., adults, health services), and limited opportunities for expression or development.

*Functional.* The antecedents that increase disruptive/avoidance behavior in GT students are nonchallenging tasks, inflexible educator demands for routine, rote task performance, and an emphasis on form rather than substance, on compliance rather than invention, and on dependence rather than independence.

## Prevalence, Gender, Age, and Cultural Factors

*Prevalence.* Over the past several years, 3–5% of school-age children have been assessed as GT. If the highly talented are included, the estimate could be as high as 10–15% (Taylor et al., 2009). Furthermore, it is estimated that there are 300,000 twice-exceptional students in the U.S. educational system (Foley Nicpon, Allmon, Sieck, & Stinson, 2011).

*Gender.* Gifted boys and girls are often more **androgynous** than other children (see Kerr & Cohn, 2001, cited by Webb et al., 2005), and gifted girls have broader interests and adopt nontraditional roles more often than other girls. Boys outnumber girls at the extremes of giftedness (Gottfredson, 2003). However, at the elementary level, where there is more emphasis on achievement and grades than on possible talent, girls outnumber boys in gifted programs. In contrast, at the secondary level, in talent-search and on-campus programs, boys outnumber girls (VanTassel-Baska, 1998c). This could be interpreted biologically, that boys are underrepresented at the early grades or culturally, or that high school girls may be more likely to avoid expressing their giftedness in order to fit in with other girls (Silverman, 1998; VanTassel-Baska, 1998c).

> **Androgynous:** Having the behavioral or social/emotional characteristics of both gender groups (male and female).

*Age.* Screening for giftedness in early learners involves the assessment of abstract reasoning and problem-solving skills as well as screening for the GT characteristics of high curiosity, early language development, enjoyment and speed of learning, excellent sense of humor, high activity level, intensity, long attention span, vivid imagination, and extraordinary memory. As might be expected, smart children become smart adolescents. However, for all individuals there is a decline in mental power beginning in early adulthood (ages 18 and up). Although the **g factor** declines, knowledge continues to grow until old age and then declines with very old age (Gottfredson, 2003).

> **G factor:** General intelligence factor. A measure of efficient processing across a number of brain areas, distributed across the frontal, parietal, and temporal lobes, which involves the brain's ability to pull together different functions and types of processing. G is more heritable than specific talents (Garrett, 2011).

*Culture.* Students with GT are found in every ethnic, SES, and cultural group (Reis & Renzulli, 2010). However, there is evidence that Jewish and Asian Americans are more frequently identified as gifted, whereas students who are African American are underrepresented (i.e., using current IQ-based selection procedures that assess verbal skills and accumulated knowledge; Gottfredson, 2003). Teachers typically refer "high-achieving, well-behaved, Caucasian, English-speaking, male students from upper middle class families" (Bianco & Leech, 2010, p. 322). Furthermore, standardized assessments of IQ with seventh and eighth graders from a community sample documented that only about 16% were from lower-SES backgrounds (VanTassel-Baska, 1998a). That is, children from economically disadvantaged families, especially minorities and those who are linguistically different, are infrequently identified as gifted (Seely, 1998b). Part of this is due to referral bias and some is due to environmental factors (Plomin & Price, 2003). For example, looking "smart" may be less acceptable for boys from lower-SES neighborhoods, thus their likelihood of identification is reduced. Family and other environmental factors that contribute to poor motivation and inadequate opportunities are frequent school changes, teacher indifference, and family disruptions (e.g., divorce).

---

**Underrepresented GT:** Gifted children whose families are economically disadvantaged or are members of a minority or linguistically different culture.

---

Even though **underrepresented GT** children see themselves as less academically competent, they also see themselves as more socially competent and with clear strengths in creativity. VanTassel-Baska (1998a) has summarized some of the indicators of creativity for children from underrepresented cultures as follows: the ability to express feelings, to be emotionally responsive, and to be expressive through role play, storytelling, the visual arts (drawing, sculpture), creative movement (dance, dramatics), and expressive speech, body language/gesture, and humor. These children also exhibit enhanced enjoyment of music/rhythm and of group activities and problem-solving activities. They can improvise with commonplace materials/objects; have rich imagery in their informal language; are quick to warm up; and are original, problem centered, and persistent.

## INFORMAL EDUCATOR IDENTIFICATION OF CHARACTERISTICS

### Behavioral

Gifted children, given the right encouragement and circumstances, exhibit many positive behavioral characteristics. For example, two early behavioral indicators of giftedness are creative play and a sense of humor (Seeley, 1998a). However, given less encouraging environments, these students may exhibit negative characteristics in the classroom. Students at the *elementary school* level may be glib in their responses to teacher inquiries, dominate classroom discussions or disrupt lessons, become impatient to move on to the next task, and become frustrated with tasks that seemingly have no meaning or relevance for them (Webb, 2000). During *middle school,* when other children are concerned about following rules, these students question rules (Silverman, 1998). Students with GT often have a clear perception of what they believe to be correct and struggle with inflexible classroom rules, emphasis on basic skills, and standardized procedures (Webb et al., 2005).

## Social-Emotional

Most group comparison studies indicate that children with high intelligence are as well adjusted as or better adjusted than children of average intelligence (Gallagher, 2003). In fact, early indicators of giftedness are advanced social skills and social ethics; these include choice of advanced-level friends, advanced play interests, and advanced moral judgments of fairness, justice, altruism, idealism, aesthetics, and issues related to mortality (Seeley, 1998a; Silverman, 1998). GT children can also be very socially sensitive to the needs of others, seek to contribute to the enjoyment of others and themselves, and have strong personal attachments and commitments to human rights and other global issues (Silverman, 1998).

However, the *judgment* of these children often falls behind their intellectual development. They may criticize or make other remarks that appear less mature or rude than might be expected given their cognitive skills and talents. For example, Peterson and Ray (2006) examined a specific indicator of social adjustment, bullying (defined to include name-calling and teasing), and found that rates for eighth-grade GT children were as follows: 67% had experienced bullying, 11% had been frequently bullied, and 28% had been the bully. These were similar to the rates of typical children: 75–89% had been bullied; 10–37% had been frequently bullied; and 24% had been the bully. These statistics were more likely to characterize boys, and the bullying occurred most often during the sixth grade. Because judgment depends on experiences/ insights and on maturation of the brain's **frontal lobes,** it is more likely to be age appropriate than are other characteristics of the gifted child (Webb et al., 2005). "In general the brighter the child, the greater is the gap between judgment and intellect. However, each passing year, the gap narrows" (Webb et al., 2005, p. 27).

There is further evidence of greater alienation and social problems for many of those GT children with IQ of 180 or greater (Webb et al., 2005), with co-occurring LD (Olenchak, 1994) and ADHD (Moon, Zentall, Grskovic, Hall, & Stormont, 2001), and from low-SES groups. For example, children with the underachievement type of giftedness are low in motivation and have poor self-esteem (Seeley, 1998b). The lower self-esteem may be caused by these children's difficulties in juggling two exceptionalities, especially when others view them in terms of their disabilities rather than in terms of their abilities (Baum, Rizza, & Renzulli, 2006) or when teachers believe that these children must first master basic tasks before being challenged by complex tasks. Low self-esteem can also be produced by expectations that are too high because they are based only on

**Frontal lobes:** That part of the brain that plays an important role in human behavior, with damage to that region affecting high-level cognitive functions (intelligence) as well as social behavior, personality, personal memories, and self-awareness (for a review, see Stuss et al., 2001).

aptitude without accommodating for disabilities. In the case study of Chris, it is unclear what contributes to the magnitude of his social-emotional difficulties:

> Chris is a very sensitive child who is prone to outbursts that can become violent. He is very bright and often tries to manipulate the circumstances to meet his needs. When he is unable to do so, he does not seem to be able to handle the emotional aspect of not getting his own way or gaining power. Chris has a difficult time relating to his peers.

Chris shows evidence of narcissism, but these characteristics could be in response to the loss of significant others. (Narcissism is further described in Chapter 11.) Alternatively, or in addition, Chris demonstrates characteristics of social phobia (see Chapter 12):

> His largest avoid payoff . . . is the avoidance of social relatedness. . . . Chris does not engage his peers unless he absolutely has to. He knows he has alienated them and seems to have no idea how (no ability or no desire) to bridge the gap in relatedness.

In many GT students, low self-esteem and disruptive behavior may be attributed to the fact that they are more aware, sensitive, and idealistic than typically developing children (Clark, 2002). Such students may experience deviance fatigue—that is, the exhaustion that comes with constantly expending the energy required to "make a giraffe act more like a horse" in order to fit in (Webb et al., 2005, p. 64).

## Cognitive

*Intellectual.* An overall score on an intelligence test defines intelligence; this global score represents accumulated knowledge and reasoning abilities. When a test assesses multiple aptitudes (e.g., verbal, spatial, visual), students who are high in one mental aptitude tend to be higher on all aptitudes. This is considered a general intelligence factor—the g factor (Gottfredson, 2003). Even though subtest scores are related, most studies that have assessed GT students have reported higher verbal IQ scores than performance IQ scores (e.g., 27% with at least 20 points between verbal and performance scales) and greater within-child variability or subtest scatter (Webb et al., 2005). Unfortunately, intelligence tests seldom assess creativity or "talent" (e.g., musical, leadership, or physical aptitudes). There is surprising evidence of increased rates of LD and ADHD as IQ increases, especially above 160 (Silverman, 2003).

*Attention, memory, and organization.* Early indicators of giftedness are attention and memory abilities (Seeley, 1998a). GT students require little to no repetition in order to retain information, and repetition may actually interfere with their retention of information (Tannenbaum, 1992).

## Communication

Early indicators of giftedness are advanced language development, advanced vocabulary, and frequent questioning (Seeley, 1998a). Children with GT may produce messy writing as their hands attempt to keep pace with the fluency of their ideas (Webb et al., 2005). However, children with GT and co-occurring verbal LD may not display advanced language development.

## Motor, Sensory, and Somatic

Although failing to meet early motor and language developmental milestones can be an early indicator of ID (see Chapter 6), the reverse of meeting milestones of motor coordination, memory, or discrimination is not predictive of the IQ scores of youth at 16–17 years of age (Seeley, 1998a). In other words, motor skills and lower-level cognitive skills do not predict later IQ performance.

## Academic

Parents may observe early reading by children with GT during preschool and early elementary school ages. At school, these children score at the 95th percentile or higher on any group-administered achievement test, and they already know 60–75% of the material that would be presented in a year at their chronological age level (Neihart, 1999, cited in Webb et al., 2005). Early cognitive indicators of giftedness are high task motivation and persistence, which can be observed in children with innate talent areas, such as in music, chess, mathematics, creative writing, or language, but rarely are these observed early in the areas of visual arts, science, or leadership (Seeley, 1998a). In the case study for this chapter, Chris shows these early indicators of talent and interest:

> Chris tends to work on his own in the resource room. He enjoys working on math problem solving and problem-based learning. . . . Chris is a very accomplished student. He loves math and when introduced to square roots was able to do most of them in his head. He was very proud of this. When Chris engages in individual work he seems to enjoy the process. He likes to prove that he can accomplish a task on his own and seems to gain enjoyment and self-efficacy from it.

These children are self-motivated, persistent, adept at expressing their ideas, and able to move through information at a rapid pace (Renzulli, 1979), and many work to broaden their own knowledge through leisure reading, hobbies, and projects. As would be expected, their academic self-concept is higher than that of the average student (for a review, see Taylor et al., 2009).

It should also be noted that children with GT are more variable in their academic abilities and behavior than are typical children (Webb et al., 2005). This is most often reported in students with SLD/LD, who are frequently found in this population (Assouline et al., 2010). For example, written language disabilities occurred in 74% of a referred GT sample, and higher IQ was more likely to be associated with inattention, hyperactivity, emotional difficulties, and visual-motor problems in GT students than in those with lower IQ. These associated factors can mask giftedness and mistakenly be labeled as laziness by educators (Assouline et al., 2010).

## SUMMARY OF STRENGTHS AND NEEDS

| Possible strengths | Probable needs |
|---|---|
| • High **metacognitive skills** (reflective skills), which enable these students to select their own goals, tasks, schedules, resources, and so on.<br>• Enjoyment of problem solving and problem-based learning opportunities.<br>• The ability to grasp concepts of fair play, justice, kindness, conservation, and the like.<br>  ○ Possibility of multiple talents (although some GT children are talented only in certain areas, such as math, written composition, or music, and care should be taken to limit advanced expectations to these areas). | **For GT students:**<br>• Training in how to be leaders without being bossy.<br>• Empathy training to reduce possible bullying behavior and judgment errors.<br>• Training in how to negotiate with teachers who believe that basics (rote skills) come first.<br><br>**From teachers:**<br>• Understanding of the need to refer gifted children with co-occurring disabilities for GT services. That is, special education teachers have been found to be less likely than general educators to refer children with disabilities and GT; special education teachers tend to focus on weaknesses (remediation) rather than on strengths (compensation) (Bianco & Leech, 2010).<br>• Flexibility to emphasize substance over correctness of form, invention and observation over production, and independence over dependence.<br>• Expectations that do not mean quantitatively just more of the same type of work.<br>• Recognition of alternative types of giftedness (e.g., social, creative, humor, visual arts, dance, storytelling).<br>• Opportunities to work faster and nonsequentially without needing to write down steps or procedures.<br>• Products that involve advanced readings or themes/issues that can be tied to real-world problems (e.g., tropical rain forests, weather patterns). |

| Possible strengths | Probable needs |
|---|---|
| | **From school systems:** |
| | • Dually differentiated programs for giftedness (focusing on strength and compensation) and disability (focusing on remediation) (Crepeau-Hobson & Bianco, 2010). In fact it may be important to identify GT as primary and disability as secondary (Foley Nicpon et al., 2011). Unfortunately, even programs that focus singly on students with GT are rare, occurring only 16% of the time; further, evidence indicates that more than 60% of teachers do not have training in GT (Reis & Renzulli, 2010). |
| | • Specialized instruction for GT students that is highly effective in increasing achievement (for a review, see Reis & Renzulli, 2010), includes programs in which students are grouped with similar high-IQ peers and have advanced curricular choices (unfortunately, homogeneous groupings are offered only 21% of the time; Reis & Renzulli, 2010). Even more effective are pullout programs, separate classes for GT, and special schools (Delcourt, Cornell, & Goldberg, 2007). |
| | **From parents:** |
| | • An understanding of early childhood development (i.e., parents are good judges of giftedness in their preschool children; Silverman, 1998). |
| | • Encouragement of older girls with GT: holding high expectations, encouraging high levels of activity, avoiding overprotectiveness, supporting interests and capabilities, encouraging achievement in mathematics, finding female role models, and so on (VanTassel-Baska, 1998c). |
| | • An understanding that a child raised in a verbally rich environment or a child with NVLD may not be GT, even when the child tests high in verbal IQ. Placing unrealistic expectations on a child *to be* gifted can produce excessive pressure. |

# DISABILITY IN THE CLASSROOM

## Implications for Accommodations in General Education Settings: Tier I

Educators can use a number of accommodations to make sure that twice-exceptional students achieve to their capabilities, many of which should be in place in classrooms defined by UDL principles. Environmental opportunities include specific characteristics of the adults who interact with twice-exceptional students. For example, there is evidence that effective teachers of students with GT from underrepresented populations are more likely than less effective teachers to include student ideas, use praise and encouragement, verbally recognize student feelings, promote time on task, and use multiple activities per unit of time. Teachers who model enthusiasm for a subject of study have profound effects on students' intrinsic motivation to learn about that subject (Feldhusen, 1998c). Helping students set their own goals and manage time is also important, since many of these students are multitalented and have difficulty setting priorities.

Two methodological approaches have been found to be effective with twice-exceptional learners. One is to use strengths to compensate for weaknesses (Seeley, 1998b). With an emphasis on strengths and a de-emphasis on disability, children can learn to compensate (Moon & Reis, 2004). This emphasis on strengths is particularly important for girls with giftedness, who sometimes have low expectancies, avoid challenge, and blame themselves for failures (VanTassel-Baska, 1998c).

No less important are accommodations and interventions specifically for reading and math, since many of these children are already doing their best to compensate. These accommodations are described as Tier I and II strategies in the chapters in Section II, in the specific academic areas where students may have learning disabilities. The differences for GT students, in comparison with a typical LD curriculum for math and reading, are presented below.

The reading requirements and homework for GT students should involve more complex, abstract materials (e.g., primary rather than secondary sources, advanced readings and analysis of readings, solving complex verbal problems, answering divergent questions, conducting empirical research) that are available in more contexts (e.g., libraries, studios, computer labs, meeting places, online) and can be responded to in multiple way (e.g., written essays, small-group projects, seminars, debates, e-mail discussion groups, Listservs) (Feldhusen, 1998c). For mathematics, the curriculum for GT students should be fast paced (unless the child has an MLD or math anxiety), with an emphasis on concepts, mathematical models, and multiple solutions to one problem rather than multiple problems with one solution for each. One important accommodation across subject areas is to "accept correct answers, even if the child cannot show his or her work" (Silverman, 2003, p. 541). That is, these children's written work should be graded on content and advanced concepts and not on mechanics or compliance with step-by-step procedures (spelling, grammar, written math steps). According to Silverman (2003), nonsequentiality is a common ingredient in the profiles of gifted children with LD, and most do not learn in a step-by-step fashion. (For a complete menu of instructional activities for the GT child in reading, writing, verbal expression, math, science, social studies, and leadership/social skills, see VanTassel-Baska, 1998b.)

## Implications for Interventions in Small-Group and Individual Settings: Tiers II and III

Inclusion, which is widely used in collaboration between general and special education, does not typically provide or know how to provide the specialized programming needed for giftedness (Seeley, 1998b). At a Tier II level, there needs to be a differentiated curriculum for twice-exceptional learners that focuses on remediation of a problem (e.g., a reading disability) as well as on the strengths of GT in specialized instructional groupings. Thus, for the disability, there needs to be appropriate Tier II interventions, and for the giftedness, specialized programs are needed, such as cluster grouping of GT students within classrooms, **homogeneous groupings** for subject-matter acceleration, and cross-grade groupings in nongraded classrooms (for a full description, see Feldhusen, 1998a, 1998b). Although few studies have been done on these twice-exceptional children (Moon & Reis, 2004), the research undertaken so far indicates that acceleration of GT students should include twice-exceptional students (i.e., students with GT should not be retained in grade with their age-mates for social reasons). When students with GT plus ADHD are accelerated, they achieve at the level suggested by their abilities, even though they still have difficulties in group work, peer interactions, and long-term projects (Moon et al., 2001; Zentall, Moon, et al., 2001). These specific social difficulties may require additional specialized interventions effective for students with ADHD. For Tier III, enrichment pullout programs and full-time gifted programs are appropriate, again with specific remediation for co-occurring disabilities.

> **Homogeneous groupings:** Groupings of students who are similar in one or more characteristic(s). For example, in the gifted area, groups that encourage the development and achievement of gifted students are those "cluster" groups with the most advanced learners.

At the secondary level, the major offerings for GT students are advanced/honors classes, special academic classes, target schools, and classes at local colleges and universities. Many of these opportunities are available only in larger school systems or cities (Feldhusen, 1998b), but distance education can provide additional opportunities.

## Long-Term Outcomes

Advanced information-processing skills allow individuals to meet the everyday environmental demands and opportunities of life. "IQ is strongly related, probably more so than any other single measurable human trait, to many important educational, occupational, economic, and social outcomes" (Gottfredson, 2003, p. 34).

The g factor is strongest at predicting school achievement, moderately so for job performance, and least for law-abidingness. (Low g, as would be found in the ID population, predicts higher health costs, higher numbers of auto accidents, poverty, illegitimacy, school dropout, and so on).

*Continuance.* The heritability of IQ increases with age. That is, about 20% of IQ scores are closely related to parental intelligence in infancy, 40% in preschool, 60% in adolescence, and 80% by adulthood (see Plomin et al., 2001, cited by Gottfredson, 2003). In other words, the effects of the environment (family advantage, child-rearing style) decrease as children age and the effects of inheritance increase. However, inheritance and environmental opportunities interact. That is, gifted children will seek out and adapt environments to be in line with their inherited abilities, especially as they age (Bouhard et al., 1994, cited in Gottfredson, 2003). For example, bright children select bright playmates; they read more, ask more questions, are more curious, and think more. They engage in more cognitively directed activity. This can be described as evidence that intelligence may be more of an appetite than an aptitude (Plomin & Price, 2003).

## CHAPTER SUMMARY

- IDEA and *DSM-IV-TR* do not formally define GT. What are formally defined are co-occurring disabilities. However, the strengths that accompany giftedness may mask a disability or the disability may be so noticeable that the giftedness is undetected (e.g., with ADHD, behavioral disorders).

- Educators can informally identify GT children through observations of their behavior, which is often intense, with high levels of activity and reactivity to the environment. Early indicators are alertness, excellent memory, and advanced language development. These basic skills are often expressed through early reading achievement and leisure reading experiences. However, variability in academic abilities is often noted, such that persistence in talent areas may be a better indicator.

- Subtypes are talented, creative, academic, and intellectual, typically from high-SES backgrounds and cultures. Some GT students, however, are underachievers or economically disadvantaged. Underachievement in students with GT can be a result of differences in language, culture, or behavior. It is interesting that children who are highly gifted are also more likely than average-IQ children to have co-occurring disabilities. Educators may detect GT in these students by noting discrepancies between children's interests in self-selected readings and projects versus performance on schoolwork. GT is also expressed differently in underrepresented groups and cultures (e.g., storytelling, socially, performing arts).

- GT and ADHD have similar energy and intensity, but students with GT generally do not show impulsivity or social problems and usually finish their homework and the projects they initiate. Creative play, social skills, social sensitivity, and a sense of humor are positive indicators. However, GT students also show emotional immaturity relative to their IQ. This can be seen in the social characteristics of bossiness, bullying, impatience, and insistence on "what is right" (advanced moral judgment).

- The etiology of high intelligence/talent is genetic, but GT can be increased when the child selects challenging experiences and when the environment provides opportunities for expression. A functional assessment would find that the expression of GT is reduced in school contexts that provide nonchallenging, noncreative tasks with an emphasis on form over substance, basic over advanced skills, and correctness and production over ideas and independence of thought.

- Suggested accommodations for GT students are listed under the heading "Summary of Strengths and Needs" earlier in this chapter.

## CHAPTER QUESTIONS

1. Why are GT students often mistakenly identified as children who have disruptive behavior disorders?

2. "Intelligence is more of an appetite than an aptitude." What does this statement mean?

3. How can educators identify GT children from underrepresented populations?

4. If a child is high in the g factor, what additional factors might he or she need to produce extraordinary achievement?

5. What have you learned about the GT population from this chapter that you find interesting?

## TRUE/FALSE AND MULTIPLE-CHOICE

1. It is better to keep students at their social level with age-mates than to accelerate them to work with peers at their intellectual level.

2. Creatively GT students perform better with sequential step-by-step procedures than with unorganized issues.

3. Young gifted students are typically similar to same age peers in

   A. judgment and bullying behavior
   B. knowledge of facts
   C. creativity and divergent thinking

4. Children with GT are unlikely to show uneven academic performance, to perform lower than their IQs would suggest they should, or to be disruptive in classes.

5. Children at the extremes of high IQ are more likely also to have

   A. excellent social skills
   B. social problems and RD
   C. ADHD

6. A major contributor to disruptive behavior in general educational classes for GT students:

   A. nonchallenging and extra work
   B. time spent waiting for others to catch up
   C. all of the above

7. GT students differ from students with ADHD in their long memory, persistence, and finishing of projects.

8. GT can be similar to ADHD in

   A. intensity and activity
   B. questioning of rules
   C. impulsivity

## SHORT ANSWER

1. A child who knows all the right answers, works hard, answers questions, and learns with ease is considered _____.

2. A type of grouping in which all members are similar with respect to at least one trait (achievement level, interest, etc.)

3. The ability to put together ideas of parts of objects to form a whole

4. Takes information apart in order to understand it better (e.g., breaks down a large task into individual steps)

## PROBLEM-BASED CASE APPLICATIONS AND QUESTIONS

### CASE STUDY 7.1: CHRIS

*"He finishes reading a chapter in a book and stops reading; the teacher tells him he needs to read until 8:45 A.M."*
(adapted from an assignment submitted by Jillian Gates)

*Background.* Chris is a 7-year-old highly gifted student in the second grade at an urban elementary school. He is also diagnosed with ADHD, hyperactive subtype, along with co-occurring ED. Chris was removed from the general education gifted cluster classroom and placed full-time in the resource room. Chris is a very sensitive child who is prone to outbursts that can become violent. He is very bright and often tries to manipulate the circumstances to meet his needs. When he is unable to do so, he does not seem to be able to handle the emotional aspect of not getting his own way or gaining power. Chris has a difficult time relating to his peers. He spends a large part of his time in the general education classroom being very disruptive and sometimes violent. When the class sits on the carpet with the teacher, Chris often pulls another child's hair, wanders around the classroom, throws a fit if he is not chosen for a task, or sometimes walks to the front of the classroom and interrupts the teacher. If a classmate antagonizes him or stands up to him, he has been known to lash out, once attempting to stab a child with a sharpened pencil. He has also thrown things at classmates and pulled things out of others' hands. He has thoroughly alienated his classmates to the point that they do not want to sit next to him or anywhere near him at all. Some of the girls are actually frightened of him.

Chris comes from a home where he had a very controlling father. His father divorced his mother very suddenly and left; this affected him greatly. He also had a godfather who was his surrogate father after the divorce. They were very close. His godfather died of a heart attack last spring, so again Chris is fatherless. He seemingly has little control over people leaving him.

### Behavioral Log

| Behavior | Antecedent | Consequence | Payoff |
|---|---|---|---|
| **Wednesday, September 5** | | | |
| Drops bag on floor | Morning routine | Teacher redirects him to complete the routine | Gets competence (power) |

*(Continued)*

(Continued)

| Behavior | Antecedent | Consequence | Payoff |
|---|---|---|---|
| Throws papers | Drops papers on the floor while looking for book in desk, leaves them on the floor | Teacher asks him to pick up papers | Avoids task, gets emotional stimulation |
| Begins to read with papers still on floor | Teacher asks him to pick up papers | Teacher comes over to desk to ask him again | Gets relatedness |
| Throws papers | Teacher asks him to pick up papers | Teacher stops him pushing desk | Gets emotional stimulation, avoids task, gains competence (power) |
| Finishes reading chapter in book and stops reading | Reading time | Teacher tells him he needs to read until 8:45 A.M. | Avoids task, gets competence (power) |
| Refuses to read | Teacher tells him he needs to read until 8:45 A.M. | Teacher turns card to red and sends him to "time-out" | Avoids task |
| Cuts corners running around gym | Warm-ups for gym class | Teacher yells at him across gym | Gets competence (power) |
| Continues to cut corners | Teacher yells at him across gym | Teacher yells at him across gym | Gets competence (power) |
| Shoves boy in front of him in line | Waiting in line for his turn | Boy shoves back, teacher does not notice | Gets competence (power), gets emotional stimulation |
| Stands on foot of boy behind him | Waiting in line for his turn | Child pulls foot away and ignores him | Gets competence (power), gets emotional stimulation |
| Cuts corners running around gym | Trips while running backwards | Teacher yells at him across gym | Avoids failure, avoids social failure |
| **Thursday, September 13** | | | |
| Leaves board game on floor after picking up pieces | End of recess | Aide asks him to put game away | Avoids task, gets competence (power) |
| Growls at aide | Aide asks him to put game away | Aide does not respond | Gets self-determination, gets competence (power) |

| Behavior | Antecedent | Consequence | Payoff |
|---|---|---|---|
| Walks on all dark squares in hallway | Walking in line to chess class | Teacher warns him to walk in line | Gets self-determination, avoids social failure |
| Boy behind him in line shoves him | Getting back in line after being reprimanded | He shoves boy | Gets competence (power), gets tangible stimulation |
| He shoves boy | Boy behind him in line shoves him | Teacher pulls him out of line and reprimands him | Gets competence (power), gets tangible stimulation |
| Teacher pulls him out of line and reprimands him | He shoves boy | Pulls his arm away from teacher | Avoids social failure, gets self-determination |
| Continually corrects chess partner | Chess class | Partner gets upset | Gets competence (power), gets relatedness |
| Tries to help partner | Partner gets upset | Yells at partner | Gets competence (power), gets relatedness |
| Yells at partner | Partner gets upset | Teacher removes him from the class | Avoids failure, gets self-determination |
| **Friday, September 14** | | | |
| Plays with pillows in reading corner | Reading time | Teacher reminds him of task | Gets self-determination, gets competence (power) |
| Falls asleep in reading corner | Reading time | Teacher does not notice | Gets self-determination, gets competence (power), avoids task |
| Wakes up, but refuses to open eyes | Reading time on pillows | Teacher gives warning | Gets competence (power), avoids task |
| Refuses to change card or follow instructions | Teacher gives warning | Teacher changes card for him | Avoids failure, avoids task, gets competence (power) |
| Tries to lie down again | Given warning and card color changed | Teacher sits him up | Avoids failure, avoids task |
| Refuses to change card and starts throwing pillows at the teacher | Not following instructions to sit up | Teacher changes card for him and stands him up to move him to time-out | Avoids failure, gets self-determination |

*(Continued)*

(Continued)

| Behavior | Antecedent | Consequence | Payoff |
|---|---|---|---|
| Screams and falls to floor kicking | Teacher stands him up to move him to time-out | Teacher tells him to get up | Avoids failure, avoids task |
| Opens one eye and kicks teacher | Teacher tells him to get up | Teacher calls for help, evacuates other students from the room | Avoids task, avoids failure, gets self-determination, gets kinesthetic stimulation |
| Continues to kick | Teacher calls for help | Teacher ignores him | Gets self-determination, gets kinesthetic stimulation |
| Stands up and runs to desks and starts to push them over | Teacher ignores him | Teacher places him in small child restraint | Gets sensory stimulation, gets emotional stimulation, gets kinesthetic stimulation |
| Frees himself from restraint and runs to classroom door | Teacher places him in small child restraint | Teacher holds door closed | Gets self-determination, gets kinesthetic stimulation, gets self-determination |
| Attempts to crawl under computer table | Assistant principal tries to talk to him | Assistant principal pulls him out from under table | Avoids failure, gets self-determination, avoids sensory stimulation |
| Kicks assistant principal | Assistant principal pulls him out from under table | He is placed in full restraint | Gets sensory stimulation, gets kinesthetic stimulation |
| **Tuesday, September 18—Teacher Interview** | | | |
| Released from restraint | Calmed down | Ran and climbed under computer table | Gets self-determination, avoids failure, avoids sensory stimulation |
| Spoke with mother on phone and began to cry | Would not communicate with staff or come out | Mother told him she loved him, but he had lost his video game reward | Gets emotional stimulation, avoids failure, gets relatedness |
| Would not stop crying | Mom told him he lost his video game reward | Mom came and picked him up | Gets self-determination, gets emotional stimulation, gets relatedness |

| Behavior | Antecedent | Consequence | Payoff |
|---|---|---|---|
| **Friday, September 21** | | | |
| Pushes other students aside so he can work on project at their table | Told to work on violin project | Students will not move | Gets competence (power), gets self-determination |
| Tells students that this is where he always works on his project | Students will not move | Students will not move, teacher redirects him to another table | Gets competence (power), gets self-determination |
| Growls, moves to another table, and begins to sing loudly | Teacher redirects him to another table | Teacher asks him to be quiet | Gets competence (power), gets self-determination, avoids social failure |
| Breaks pencil in half | Teacher notices that he is copying notes word-for-word, and not making own sentences | Teacher send him to "time-out" | Gets emotional stimulation, gets kinesthetic stimulation |
| Ignores teacher | Told computer time is up | Teacher removes his headset and tells him again | Gets self-determination, gets competence (power) |
| Ignores teacher again | Teacher removes his headset and repeats instructions to log off computer | Teacher logs him off midgame | Gets self-determination, gets competence (power) |
| Yells, "No!" Flings himself out of chair trying to overturn it | Teacher logs him off computer midgame | Teacher reminds him that he has a reward coming if he can keep it together | Gets self-determination, gets competence (power) |
| Bumps into several desks on the way to his own, gets work out, but does not begin | Teacher reminds him that he has a reward coming if he can keep it together | Teacher reminds him to gets started | Gets competence (power), gets self-determination, avoids task |
| Continues to sit doing nothing, says he has no pencil | Teacher reminds him to gets started | Teacher tells him to figure it out and problem solve | Gets self-determination, gets competence (power) |

## ABC Analysis

*Resource room.* Chris has been placed in the resource room on a full-time basis except for special events and some special classes such as PE and music. He is the only high-ability student in the resource room, so he does not participate in group activities, as his level of work is far higher than that of the other students. Chris tends to work on his own in the resource room. He enjoys working on math problem solving and problem-based learning. He also enjoys reading, if it is his choice of reading. He is working on the *Chronicles of Narnia*. If Chris is able to choose the order of tasks, then he is able to complete a task without a fuss. It is only when a schedule is imposed on him that he rebels. The resource room staff tries to keep him on the same schedule as his general education classroom so that he will be finished with a task in time to attend PE or music or to be able to attend special events such as chess class. This is also done for ease of transition back into the general education classroom in the event that this does occur.

The vast majority of Chris's payoffs in the resource room are get payoffs. He is determined to gain power and self-determination. He has been removed from his class-room and he is in a room he does not particularly enjoy. His activities are monitored by at least four adults at all times, and he has very little control over what he does. While the ultimate goal is to provide Chris with the opportunity to make appropriate choices, in order to be able to keep him in his least restrictive environment, the school needs to have him adhere to a stringent schedule. If too much self-determination is given to Chris before he learns the skills to cope with it, then his behavior is such that a more restrictive environment will be chosen for him.

*General education.* When Chris attends chess class and PE class he has very little interaction with his peers. While Chris is trying to establish himself in the group and gain relatedness to some degree, he has also learned behavior in the general education classroom that he uses to distance himself from the other students and avoid social failure. He knows he has already isolated himself from his peers, so he continues the pattern in his interactions with them. This can be seen very clearly in PE when he chooses to play by himself in the corner rather than interact with his classmates, whom he has not seen in several days.

*Independent work.* Chris is a very accomplished student. He loves math and when introduced to square roots was able to do most of them in his head. He was very proud of this. When Chris engages in individual work he seems to enjoy the process. He likes to prove that he can accomplish a task on his own and seems to gain enjoyment and self-efficacy from it. Chris does not like to rely on the help of others and tends to take over a group when he does interact. What Chris reacts to is the amount to which he can self-direct his activity. These are self-determination payoffs as well as power payoffs. Again, Chris is not avoiding the task per se, but trying to exert his will on the situation.

*Group work.* The only time Chris has really worked in a group was in a pair at chess. His behaviors were most often power seeking in that setting. He also showed power-seeking behavior when he did not greet his peers when he joined them in line and they did not greet him. He made no attempt at all to engage his peers in an appropriate manner; he merely resorted to the power-seeking behaviors of shoving and standing on toes. Again, this shows an avoidance of close interaction

Before the observation, it appeared that Chris was avoiding work, interaction, and stimulation. However, the observation data show that his get payoffs were higher than his avoid payoffs (see Figure 7.2). Many of his behaviors were double and even triple coded. For example, even when Chris chose to avoid something, the ultimate goal was a get payoff—most often get self-determination (42%) or get competence (56%) (see Figure 7.3).

Chris's largest get payoff is to get competence, with 55% of his get payoffs for this alone; his second greatest is to get self-determination, with about 40% (the fourth positive-value bar from the left in Figure 7.3). (Remember that some behaviors had several payoffs.) His largest avoid payoff, at 30%, is the avoidance of task (the largest negative-value bar below the line). This is primarily avoidance of reading. However, Chris's reading assignments are not related to his interests or even to classroom requirements (e.g., he finishes reading the chapter in the assigned book and stops reading, but his teacher tells him that he needs to read until 8:45 A.M.). Furthermore, his avoidance of task often co-occurs with his need for self-determination and selecting his own task.

**Figure 7.2** Chris's Overall Payoffs

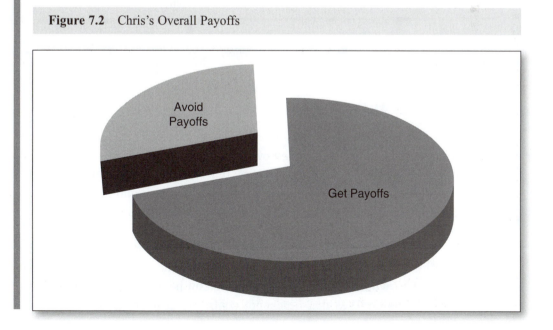

**Figure 7.3**  Chris's Payoff Percentages

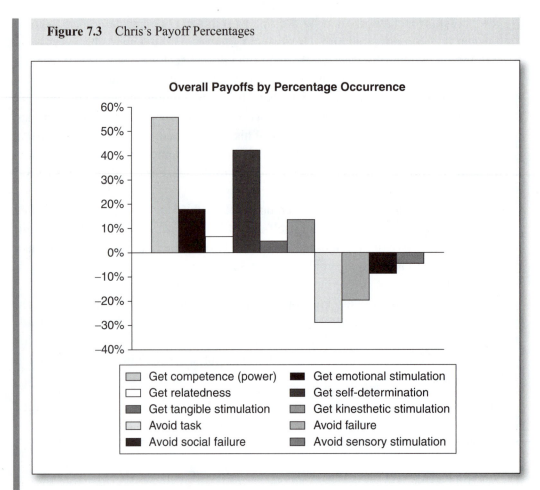

## Diagnosis Versus ABC Analysis

Chris is a 7-year-old highly gifted student in an urban elementary school who has also been diagnosed with ADHD with co-occurring EBD. Most of this social disability is the result of control seeking. Apparently very few children in the neighborhood like Chris, and his sister does not like him either. He has dug himself into such a deep hole, socially speaking, that he may not know how to rectify the situation. He may well fear giving up his power-seeking behaviors.

Chris's mother is very dependent on him having his medications. She added Risperdal to his Concerta toward the end of last year. Whenever she missed giving Chris his meds she would rush to school to be certain he got them. It has gotten to the point that Chris believes that he cannot control his own behavior without the medication, and he has voiced this belief many times. This belief may add to Chris's feelings of lack of self-determination or lack of control. If he truly believes that he can behave appropriately only with chemical intervention, then again power and self-determination are removed from him.

However, Chris may not be ADHD-HI; he is a highly gifted child who has never really been stimulated academically, at least not at school. His lack of cognitive stimulation (challenge) may well have caused him to behave disruptively in class and garnered him a diagnosis of ADHD. His father is highly gifted, and his other siblings are gifted as well. Giftedness is clearly a family trait. No other members of his family have an ADHD diagnosis. Chris is a highly gifted child who may well be able to grasp cognitively what is happening to him? but is unable to deal with it emotionally. He has moved through three counselors in the last year because of issues his mom had with them and is provided no counseling services in school since the school he attends does not have a counselor.

## Interventions Derived From ABC Analysis

Chris has not had the opportunity to really show his giftedness (need for competence and control). If given the right challenging environment, Chris may well show a decrease in his negative behavior and an increase in his "gifted" behaviors, as is often the case with bored gifted students. It may be important to see Chris in a medication-free state in order to be able to assess his behavioral issues properly (i.e., the meds are not reducing his negative social behavior). Chris needs to be included in setting up his own behavior plan, which would include goal setting. Gifted students have high metacognitive skills and can become part of their own teams. Chris should be a part of determining his own schedule for the day and monitoring it, using pictures or words or even writing his activities in his daily planner. This will also allow Chris to gain some self-determination and power. He can then monitor what is going to happen in a given day and cross off tasks as he accomplishes them.

Chris should be given choices within limits. I believe that the educational reaction to his violent outbursts in the past has been to remove all choices from him. This seems only to have exacerbated his behavioral problems. If Chris perceives some choices in his day-to-day tasks he may feel more in control and respond better to being told what to do. For reading time, Chris should be allowed to choose the book he wants to read or a place in the room where he would like to read and a length of time to read. All of these choices still accomplish what the teacher needs him to do, but they also allow him to determine a few things for himself within the framework of his school day.

## Case Questions

1: Given that Chris has multiple possible diagnoses (ODD, EBD, GT, ADHD), for which diagnosis should accommodations begin?

2 (problem-based small-group assignment): If Chris has a high need for control/self-determination, how could you teach him more appropriate replacement behavior so that he could express control more positively?

3: In what ways is requiring a child to conform to a standardized schedule (rather than including choice and self-determination in the curriculum) similar to enforcing a mastery of basic skills as an entry requirement into advanced assignments?

# Chapter 8

# Traumatic Brain Injuries

**TBI** and mild traumatic brain injury (**MTBI**) are defined by an injury to the brain caused by an external physical force, resulting in physical, cognitive, and emotional impairment that adversely affects a child's educational performance and/or independent living. (This category does not include students who are born with brain damage, such as damage to motor areas of brain documented in cerebral palsy). Children with TBI typically have impairments related to specific functions or across a range of cognitive functions, such as language, memory, attention, reasoning, abstract thinking, judgment, and problem solving, as well as in information acquisition, social behavior, and sensory and perceptual processing. Some children have physical trauma to just one part of the brain, such as the motor cortex (see the discussion of the brain's anatomy in Chapter 1), with outcomes in gross and fine motor skills.

**TBI and MTBI:**
Traumatic brain injury and mild traumatic brain injury. TBI can result from severe injuries to the brain that cause long periods of loss of consciousness, including lengthy periods of coma and frequent seizures. MTBI can result from less severe or more focal injuries to the brain.

What makes students with TBI distinctive is the high variability in their behavior and performance, in contrast to other exceptionalities, which represent extremes at one end of a normal distribution of traits. That is, in the preceding chapters, we have considered relative extremes in IQ and of learning abilities. In addition, in Chapters 9–15, extremes in activity, temperament (introversion/extroversion), and anxiety are presented. These extremes interact with individual personalities and cultures in fairly predictable ways (e.g., high activity can produce greater societal punishment and may result in greater child anger/aggression or depression). Some of these traits can change over time but in relatively predictable ways and during specific developmental periods (e.g., gross motor

**Figure 8.1** A student with a mild traumatic brain injury

hyperactivity becomes restlessness during adolescence); such changes are different from the unexpected and highly variable changes in the cognitive performance and adaptive behavior of children with TBI.

The case study for TBI is Andy, whose history indicates that he suffered some brain damage in a drowning accident. Loss of oxygen to the developing brain produces unclear outcomes, especially since some brain functions of young children can be reprogrammed to other areas of the brain (i.e., **plasticity** of brain functions). In other words, when there is permanent damage to brain cells, new connections can form. For this reason, we cannot predict with accuracy what specific outcomes to expect in the case of brain injury to young children. However, it is the outcomes that educators must address, and whether a child follows a normal developmental sequence or not may be of less importance than the current cognitive functioning of the child.

**Plasticity:** The ability of the brain, especially the brain of a young child, to form new connections between intact areas, with uninjured brain tissue taking over the functions of lost neurons.

## FORMAL IDENTIFICATION

### Definitions

#### IDEA

IDEA defines traumatic brain injury as

an acquired injury to the brain caused by an external physical force, resulting in total or partial functional disability or psychosocial impairment, or both, that adversely affects a child's educational performance. The term applies to open or closed head injuries resulting in impairments in one or more areas, such as cognition; language; memory; attention; reasoning; abstract thinking; judgment; problem-solving; sensory, perceptual, and motor abilities; psycho-social behavior; physical functions; information processing; and speech. The term does not apply to brain injuries that are congenital or degenerative, or to brain injuries induced by birth trauma. (34 C.F.R. Section 300.8[c][12])

#### DSM-IV-TR

*DSM-IV-TR* does not define TBI.

#### Frequently Occurring Subtypes

The severity of the injury in TBI can range from mild, which is loss of consciousness (i.e., MTBI), to severe damage leading to severe mental changes. Types of physical damage to the brain can be used to indicate injury severity:

1. **Concussion,** which has focal effects that can be recovered, typically with no damage to tissue unless there are repeated concussions

2. **Contusion,** which involves focal damage to brain cells

3. **Shearing,** during which layers of the brain ride up on each other, producing global damage

There is a primary injury, which occurs at the moment of impact, and then the brain undergoes secondary effects of altered cerebral blood flow and metabolism, swelling, and inflammatory reactions (Morris, 2010). The outcomes can be coma, permanent damage, and death. The resulting impairments are often compounded when these students have multiple concussions or TBIs. That is, a single TBI doubles the risk of a second TBI, which in turn increases the risk of a third TBI at eight times the rate (McKinlay et al., 2008).

Subtypes can also be derived from the various kinds of causes of TBI. These are external forces, opposing forces, and lack of oxygen to the brain. Lack of oxygen occurs, for example, during drowning and as a result of strokes. Of those individuals in the United States who suffer TBI caused by external force, one-fourth are less than 2 years of age (e.g., shaken or tossed babies) at the time of their injuries. Approximately 10% of brain injuries from external damage are caused by firearms, but 90% of this 10% die. Falls are another major cause of external-force TBIs, especially in children younger than 5. Opposing-force injuries are usually sustained during vehicle accidents (car, bike, pedestrian); these account for one-half of TBIs in adolescents. Contact sports are another major contributor during adolescence, accounting for about 63,000 cases of MTBI annually in high school varsity athletics; football accounts for 63% of these cases (Powell, 2000).

The severity of a brain injury, from MTBI to TBI, is typically based on ratings of the presence or extent of loss of consciousness and posttraumatic **amnesia** (Morris, 2010). Cognitive outcomes can also be related to whether the brain has incurred **focal damage,** such as might be produced by a sharp object, which causes relatively mild cognitive characteristics, or **global damage,** which might involve the prefrontal cortex. Injuries resulting in global damage, such as might be caused by a car accident or major fall, are accompanied by more severe cognitive outcomes. Both types of damage are likely to affect attention/concentration and visual perceptual skills. Focal damage may produce unexpected judgment errors and short-term memory losses of new learning. Global damage is more likely to affect major functions of intelligence, including problem solving and organization, and long-term recall of old learning.

**Concussion:** The most common brain injury, which generally occurs either when the head accelerates rapidly and then is stopped suddenly or when the head is shaken.

**Contusion:** Bruising of brain tissues. Contusions of the brain can cause bleeding and toxic effects.

**Shearing:** A form of damage to the brain resulting from cut nerve pathways.

**Amnesia:** Loss of memory of immediate or distal events.

**Focal damage:** Damage affecting specific areas of the brain.

**Global damage:** Damage affecting large areas of the brain and causing major changes in cognitive functions and adaptive behavior.

### Possible Co-Occurring Conditions

Students with TBI often have co-occurring disabilities, because children with prior disabilities typically experience TBIs. For example, the prevalence of ADHD in children with a TBI is 20–50% (Yeates et al., 2005). Which comes first, TBI or ADHD, is often a question. That is, children who have ADHD are more likely than other children to suffer from a TBI because of their heightened activity and risk taking (Mayfield & Homack, 2005). TBIs can make any prior condition worse by creating a sudden onset of new learning or emotional/behavioral problems. Alternatively, TBIs can cause ADHD by specifically damaging the frontostriatal and cerebellar regions of the brain, which are the areas implicated in ADHD (Mayfield & Homack, 2005). These children are actually more like children with Asperger's syndrome—showing difficulties responding to change and overstimulation. Next to ADHD, depression is the most common and persistent of new diagnoses in students with TBI (Wenar & Kerig, 2006).

Finally, the rate of emotional and behavioral disorders in students with TBI has been reported to be 34%, compared with other physical disabilities (epilepsy, cerebral palsy) at 11%, which is a rate twice that of children without physical disabilities (Wenar & Kerig, 2006).

### Differences Among Related Disabilities

The differentiation of TBI from MTBI is often based on where a child initially received medical treatment. That is, children who were initially treated for their brain injuries in emergency care settings or in nonhospital medical centers are typically considered to have MTBI; those who were hospitalized with their injuries are classified has having TBI.

## Etiology

*Biogenetic.* Although collisions with the environment are the "first cause" in the etiology of TBI, there is evidence that about half the children with TBI have previously met the criteria for biologically based disorders. That is, some disabilities with a known biogenetic basis (e.g., ADHD) have an active and risk-taking style, and others (e.g., LD and ID) result in children's having difficulty anticipating possible risks and consequences, either of which may contribute to the likelihood of later brain injuries.

*Environmental.* Of course, the damage in TBI is caused by environmental conditions (falls, bike accidents). However, there are also family risk factors that increase the probability that children will be exposed to dangerous conditions.

That is, in many families parents have so many responsibilities and are so overwhelmed and disorganized that they do not sufficiently monitor their children or protect them with safety gear (Wenar & Kerig, 2006).

*Functional.* Functional assessments of these students should document specific antecedents of task complexity or difficulties in handling change.

## Prevalence, Gender, Age, and Cultural Factors

*Prevalence.* Of all pediatric injuries each year, 25% are brain injuries. Individuals with TBI make up the fastest-growing disability group in the United States, in part because survival rates are continually improving. The majority of these (70–90%) are classified as MTBI (McKinlay et al., 2008), which may *not* be identified at the time of the injury. Furthermore, by the age of 25 more than 30% of individuals have self-reported a brain injury (McKinlay et al., 2008). Perhaps for this reason, MTBI has been called the "silent epidemic" (Murray-Leslie, 2000). Sports-related injuries accounted for 20% of TBIs in the United States in 1991 (Gerberding & Binder, 2003).

*Gender.* Among children with TBI, the ratio of males to females is two to one, with differences between gender rates increasing during adolescence, such that by adulthood the rate for men is two to three times that of women (Abelson-Mitchell, 2008).

*Age.* Brain injuries are most likely at two peak age groups: birth to 4 years old and 15 to 19 years old. Falls are the most common causes from birth to 14 years of age and in older adults; vehicle accidents and sports injuries are most common for ages 15–25 (McKinlay et al., 2008). Infants and very young children respond to brain injuries with vomiting; older children report headaches and dizziness. Both age levels respond with irritability and lethargy or fatigue.

*Culture.* Hospital admissions for TBI are highest among lower-SES groups (Gerberding & Binder, 2003).

## INFORMAL EDUCATOR IDENTIFICATION OF CHARACTERISTICS

Most initial reactions of a child with MTBI or TBI come in adjusting to physical changes. After the injury, a new onset of behavioral and social problems may develop. Typically these later developments are related to damage of the prefrontal brain region, which is involved in judgment and planning (executive functions).

## Behavioral

*Preschool to early elementary school.* Difficult behavior can be the direct result of brain injury and is often seen in children with TBI between the ages of 3 and 10. For example, prefrontal damage can result in increased hyperactivity (or greatly reduced activity), distractibility, impulsivity, and temper tantrums. The behavioral changes of students with TBI can be disturbing, because insults to the brain are unpredictable; they can produce extreme behavior or they can cause mild but unexpected responses in specific situations. For example, Dee had specific visual-spatial, directionality, and timing problems, which caused impairment in such tasks as crossing streets. Even as a 10-year-old, Dee could not recall which direction to look first when he crossed two-lane streets, so he would stand on the curb for a long time, looking repeatedly back and forth without crossing. Dee sang his own version of the song "America" (written by Samuel Francis Smith); instead of "My country, 'tis of thee, sweet land of liberty," he sang, "My country's busy street, sweet land of liberty."

*Older elementary school to secondary school.* Behavioral problems are also seen from the age of 10 through adolescence, often involving inappropriate comments and actions, such as drug abuse, sexual promiscuity, crude language, and violence (Mayfield & Homack, 2005). Andy's case study indicates that he is within this age range, and although he can be violent when frustrated, his behavior mainly looks like hyperactivity and inattention. Because these types of behavior appear to have followed his brain injury and are accompanied by high levels of performance anxiety and perfectionism, interventions would probably include the reduction of noise and crowding, difficulty, and unpredictability; such interventions are described in Chapter 13's discussion of autism spectrum disorders.

## Social-Emotional

Some of the social and emotional problems that are outcomes of TBI are related to direct damage to specific parts of the brain and to specific parts of the body (i.e., limb injuries have four to six times the rate of depression and psychiatric disorder; Gould, Johnston, Ponsford, & Schonberger, 2011). "Families actually rate behavior disturbances and personality change as the most troublesome and persistent problem following injury" (Clark, 1996, p. 550). However, from the perspective of the child, the greatest problem is a profound sense of loss (Dykeman, 2003). When children with TBI initially return to school after they have been injured, their educational and emotional needs are often very different from those they had before the injury. Often they recall how they were before, and this carries with it many emotional and social problems. These children's families, friends, and teachers also recall what they were like before their injuries, and these individuals may have trouble changing or adjusting their expectations.

Students who can no longer perform social skills will become withdrawn. As they become withdrawn, they are five times more likely to develop secondary internalizing disorders, such as depression, anxiety, sleep disturbances, and difficulty regulating emotions (moodiness) (Mayfield & Homack, 2005). In other words, if a child has a social deficit before a TBI, that deficit will intensify after the injury; aggressive and violent children tend to be more violent, and timid children tend to be even more withdrawn (Benedict, 1997). An example is a 15-year-old girl with a history of anorexia nervosa who sustained a head injury from a bicycle fall. Initially she was drowsy, slow to respond, and disoriented in time. During the following 3 weeks, she was tired, lost interest in activities, had poor hygiene, slept excessively, and worried about not being able to remember the accident. Then she had difficulties in thinking and began hearing voices and was finally diagnosed with bipolar disorder (Sayal, 2000).

For children with TBI whose injuries occurred before they entered school, the picture is different, because there is no loss of a prior personality or set of skills. This is similar to children with LD, who do not have a readjustment to make. Even so, such children with TBI are likely to display emotional overreactions, such as impatience, irritability, and low frustration tolerance (Mayfield & Homack, 2005). Andy's injuries occurred prior to school entry, and for him we observe anxiety and perfectionism. Examples of this are his continual self-monitoring and self-criticalness:

> The procedure for the pretest was discussed, and Andy called out two times, "Oh, shoot. I just caught myself." . . . Throughout this [writing] process he often fussed with his eraser, which he always held in his nonwriting hand. He also fussed with his skin. When he came to a word that gave him trouble, he would write and erase several times.

Furthermore, Andy's emotional responses to perceived failure are unpredictable and often violent, as illustrated by this description of his behavior during a poetry lesson:

> Challenging words in the poem were reviewed in order to prepare the students for a successful reading. The students were asked to read through the poem silently, and then each would have a turn reading it aloud. One student read aloud, and then it was Andy's turn. He continued to move the paper around, put his head on his desk, wrapped his arms around his head, and made a lot of noise. He was sent to his desk with the suggestion that he cool down and take

a couple of deep breaths. At his desk, he took all of the materials out, putting folders up to hide himself. He had a pen with which he scribbled on a piece of paper. A short time later he shoved all of those materials to another desk and then, putting his hands around his head, laid his head on his desk. His behavior continued to escalate as he yelled, "Shut up! I hate you!" to teachers and other adults in the room. Then he was asked to leave the room because of this behavior. . . . He yelled, "No!" and would not move out of his chair. He clung to his desk with his feet and, with his hands around his head, continued to yell, "No!" The principal was involved next; Andy would not get up for him, either. The principal physically removed Andy by picking him up at the armpits. Andy kicked and screamed—flailing his arms and legs about.

Although Andy can be emotionally unstable when frustrated, he can also be very aware of others' anxieties and needs for inclusion:

As Nick was passing out letters, he became flustered when trying to get them out of the small compartment. Andy reassured Nick by telling him, "Take your time, Nick." . . . during the end of journal time he said, "I am going to write about Bryan next," and wrote "Bryan" on the next clean page. Bryan smiled at him.

Andy's emotional difficulties cannot be explained as poor awareness of his own and others' vocal emotions, facial expressions, and other nonverbal social cues, as may be found for some students with TBI (Bowen, 2005; Schmidt, Hanten, Li, Orsten, & Levin, 2010). (For this latter group, damage may have occurred to the right hemisphere of the brain.)

Also related and often observed in students with TBI is impulsive responding, which may contribute to difficulties in planning and organizing. Although Andy is an example of a student with such planning and impulsivity problems, he does not have difficulties initiating and completing work or working at a fast enough pace, which can also be a part of TBI/MTBI (Deidrick & Farmer, 2005, p. 24).

## Cognitive

Commonly associated with TBI are difficulties with reasoning, information processing, attention or staying on task, memory, planning, concentration, and understanding the connection between behavioral actions and their conse-quences (Coulter & Jantz, 2007; Mayfield & Homack, 2005). As described earlier, these executive functions organize, direct, and manage other cognitive functions, emotional responses, and behavior (Morris, 2010). Overall, in stu-dents with TBI "cognitive performance is often uneven. Children may exhibit intact basic intellectual and cognitive skills in some areas in contrast to weaknesses in other cognitive domains" (Deidrick & Farmer, 2005, p. 24).

*Intellectual.* IQ tests are traditionally used to assess cognitive impairment in individuals with TBI (Tsaousides & Gordon, 2009), as a decline in general intelligence, especially in nonverbal abilities, can continue for up to 5 years postinjury. **Nonverbal IQ** is often assessed with speeded processing when manipulating novel stimuli (Wenar & Kerig, 2006), and these children show slowed processing, thinking, and response speed and increased task completion time (Tsaousides & Gordon, 2009). In contrast, verbal abilities represent well-rehearsed knowledge (old learnings), and these are less likely to be compromised unless the child was very young at the time of injury and had not already accumulated sufficient language skills. As well, children with TBI may display cognitive fatigue and attention/concentration deficits.

More disturbing to Andy's teacher, however, are his **cognitive distortions;** Andy believes that "first and fast are best," and anything less than perfection produces an emotional meltdown:

> Andy has cognitive distortions: Fast is good. Slow is bad. I appear dumb if I get help, therefore I must do things by myself. This is typical of someone who thinks only in black-and-white terms, a quality of perfectionism.

*Attention, memory, and organization.* Generally children with TBI show problems in maintaining attention, focusing, and dividing their attention among several tasks (i.e., multitasking; Yeates et al., 2005). Common complaints include mental slowing, trouble following conversations, losing a train of thought, and difficulty attending to several things at the same time (Morris, 2010). Memory is also one of the most common deficits, which can reduce the rate of new learning and lead to feelings of dependence, isolation, and loss of a sense of history (Tsaousides & Gordon, 2009). Types of memory, as discussed in Chapter 1, include working memory, short-term memory, and long-term memory. Lesions of the prefrontal cortex following accidental injury can result in loss of working memory (Stuss et al., 2001).

*Visual-spatial perception.* Depending on the site of brain damage, visual problems may result, such as blurred or double vision, cuts in the visual field, or even low vision or blindness. More often observed are visual-spatial processing deficits. Children with TBI may have trouble realizing the positions of large objects around them and may consequently run into things (Mayfield & Homack, 2005). They may have difficulty navigating their physical surroundings, especially in new settings (e.g., motor limitations, spatial deficits) and show difficulties with writing or drawing tasks. Andy has some these visual types of errors. His handwriting marks "do not stay within the confines of the lines" and "include very few punctuation marks."

**Nonverbal IQ:** Performance IQ, which is often assessed through testing that involves speeded processing during the manipulation of novel stimuli (mazes, blocks).

**Cognitive distortion:** A bias in interpreting events, typically produced by a set of past experiences (e.g., an expectation of negative or hostile interactions, or failure experiences). This is included within the category of cognitive characteristics because it is a thinking bias.

Although Andy did show good auditory perception of sounds in his spelling, poor visual memory can be seen in his failure to memorize the inconsistencies in the English language: "About the third or fourth word they were asked to write the word *soak*. I said the word, used it in a sentence. . . . Andy spelled *soak* like this: 'soke.'"

## Communication

Students with MTBI have problems understanding language, expressing their own meanings through language (Nampiaparampil, 2008), and maintaining conversation (pragmatics) (Deidrick & Farmer, 2005). When the damage occurs at a young age, there can be problems using vocabulary and naming objects (memory) or difficulty with multiple-step instructions (Mayfield & Homack, 2005). Students may say inappropriate things, may have difficulty understanding the perspectives of others, or may have **dysarthria** (unintelligible speech) or confused language.

**Dysarthria:** A condition that results in unintelligible speech that sounds like gibberish.

## Motor, Physical, and Somatic

At the motor level, students with TBI may have spasticity (sudden contraction of muscles), may be completely or partially paralyzed on one or both sides, may have low physical stamina (fatigue), or may have difficulty with balance, walking in a straight line, or throwing a ball. Although motor functions are the first to recover, including speech (Clark, 1996), and 73% of TBI patients have good and relatively speedy recovery of these functions, those with severe TBI may still require wheelchairs.

Students with TBI can also experience difficulties with fine motor skills (Bowen, 2005), and assessments of the degree of difference between performance of the dominant versus the nondominant hand can be used to assess how generalized their injuries are (Tsaousides & Gordon, 2009). At the somatic level, children with TBI can have dizziness, insomnia, nausea, headaches, seizures, or sensory losses of smell or taste. Sometimes TBI results in increased perception of sensory events, such as an **aura** that often precedes a seizure and acts as warning of this upcoming event.

**Aura:** A somatic or sensory feeling or a motor response that precedes a seizure and acts as a kind of warning.

Another common outcome of TBI is chronic pain, which also contributes to poorer recovery especially when not identified (Nampiaparampil, 2008). One of the most common physical complaints following brain injury is headache, which can continue for up to 6 years postinjury (Clark, 1996). A small number of children with TBI are medically fragile and are homebound for periods of time (Deidrick & Farmer, 2005).

## Academic

Cognitive difficulties can inhibit children with TBI from learning new information, causing them difficulties in keeping up academically (Deidrick & Farmer, 2005). Specific academic difficulties for these children are math problem solving, reading comprehension and composition, planning, and understanding the order of events. Tests of math (requiring attention/memory and visual processing) and of written expression (requiring verbal skills across academic areas) appear to be especially useful for identifying TBI in children (Taylor et al., 2002). In the area of written language, Andy's verbal problems are clearly in evidence. That is, Andy's writings "consist of very simple sentences with repeated phrases such as 'It was cool,' 'It was fun,' 'It was the best.'"

Although single-word reading (from long-term memory) often remains intact (for a review, see Deidrick & Farmer, 2005), reading decoding may be affected when eye movements are impaired, which occurs in 90% of those with MTBI (Ciuffreda et al., 2007). These individuals make gains in reading comfort, efficiency, and attention when they are provided training in eye-tracking exercises with feedback. Difficulties with comprehension can be seen in the monotonous way that Andy reads: "Andy reads with little expression, very monotone and quite quickly." Along the pathway of recovery, "plateauing" can occur (i.e., a child makes rapid progress, then seems to stay the same for a period of time, and then suddenly makes another improvement). This plateauing can affect one function but not another, and that lack of predictability can be frustrating to teachers.

## SUMMARY OF STRENGTHS AND NEEDS

| *Probable strengths* | *Probable needs* |
|---|---|
| • Strengths are often dependent on preinjury personality and skills. Thus, higher IQ and fewer pretrauma psychological problems are positive indicators. | • The initial greatest concern for students with TBI is early identification of intracranial bleeding, with possible indicators of seizures, vomiting, and amnesia (Bazarian & Townend, 2009).<br>• Help with figuring out ways to make their lives more predictable (schedules, assistive technology).<br>• Skills in how to handle change.<br>• Skills in planning and self-monitoring.<br>• A school buddy system to reintegrate the child into the classroom. |

## DISABILITY IN THE CLASSROOM

### Implications for Accommodations in General Education Settings: Tier I

Not all students with MTBI require collaboration among specialized services, and some students can be served with a Section 504 plan (see Chapter 1). However, in most cases staff inservice will be a needed component (Clark, 1996).

*Low-tech accommodations* that educators might offer include the following:

- Give more time to finish schoolwork and tests and be flexible about expectations to maximize the student's chances for success.
- Give directions one step at a time or provide written directions demonstrating how to perform new tasks.
- Arrange the classroom physically. Children with spatial difficulties will need more room to maneuver (Bowen, 2005). If a child is hypersensitive to stimulation, at least part of the classroom should be designed to reduce stimulation; if a student gets tired quickly, a resting area should be provided for frequent breaks. Alternating periods of instruction, activity, and rest is also recommended (Bowen, 2005).
- Establish and maintain consistent routines. If a routine is going to change, let the student know beforehand. Use advance organizers, such as drawing maps in planning the day, creating outlines prior to lessons, and listing possible solutions when giving the student a problem.
- Provide specific accommodations for the learning process affected. For example, for a child with memory deficits, use reviewing, opportunities to practice new skills, and a consistent routine; for a student with comprehension problems, emphasize main points on a consistent basis (Keyser-Marcus et al., 2002); for a child with inattention issues, break down large assignments into smaller tasks and provide breaks.
- Supervise students carefully, especially those with disabilities, and provide safety rules and education.

*High-tech accommodations.* Assistive technologies can be very useful, especially computers, voice recorders, pagers, iPads, and smart phones, which can provide prompts, alarms, schedules, and even photos of people and locations to help students with TBI in the management of everyday of tasks.

**Self-monitoring:** The focusing of attention on aspects of the self (e.g., thoughts, behavior, feelings). In an intervention with a child with disabilities, auditory signals (e.g., taped beeps) may be used to cue the child to self-monitor by recording current behavior or feelings at the sound of each signal.

## Implications for Interventions in Small-Group and Individual Settings: Tiers II and III

From 43% to 73% of children with TBI receive special education services for at least 4 years (Deidrick & Farmer, 2005, p. 24). In addition, a number of medical, speech/language, psychological, and educational professionals may be involved in interventions with such children. It is recommended that students with TBI be taught how to use assignment books and daily schedules. They should also be trained in **self-monitoring,** which alone can produce behavioral change (Dykeman, 2003).

## Long-Term Outcomes

TBIs are the main cause of death and disability in youth in the United States (Gerberding & Binder, 2003). Common immediate outcomes are relatively rapid progress in the first 3 months followed by a slow recovery rate (for a review, see Clark, 1996). The outcomes of TBI/MTBI depend on (a) preinjury skills and abilities, (b) socioeconomic status and levels of stress on the family, and (c) the extent of damage, assessed, for example, by the number of co-occurring disabilities and the duration of time experiencing seizures, amnesia, and comas (Taylor et al., 2002; Wenar & Kerig, 2006). Severity of damage is a good predictor of hyperactivity (Clark, 1996), and there are worse outcomes when a coma lasts 14 days or more versus 7 days. Duration of coma and of loss of memory (amnesia) posttrauma are two predictors of poor outcome (Clark, 1996). However, even among those for whom coma lasts "only" 24 hours, many die, become vegetative, or have moderate disabilities. Although many individuals recover from their injuries, it is estimated that 5.3 million American are living with lifelong disabilities as a result of brain injury (Morris, 2010, p. 17). Recent research shows that even MTBI that results from repeated closed-head concussions has greater cumulative consequences than previously assumed (Morris, 2010).

*Infancy through kindergarten.* The outcomes of TBI also depend on the child's age at the time of trauma. It is widely recognized that recovery does not follow a predictable course and that the brain is relatively plastic and can recover functions, especially in younger persons. Thus, younger children may be more responsive to treatment, may adapt socially/emotionally, and could resemble children with LD.

*Elementary and secondary levels.* Children who are older at the time of their injuries realize their losses and adapt less well socially and emotionally. For example, children 9 years of age and over self-report more negative emotions and an awareness of how their lives have been affected by their injuries (Wenar & Kerig, 2006). However, older children also have more "old learning" to rely on postinjury.

## CHAPTER SUMMARY

- TBI is formally defined by IDEA but not by *DSM-IV-TR*. Subtypes are defined by level of severity (MTBI versus TBI). TBI often presents with a broad range of impairments, whereas MTBI more often presents with only some areas of dysfunction. Co-occurring conditions are ADHD, ID, LD, and emotional and behavioral disorders; these may predate TBI or develop as new diagnoses. Most often, depression and the behavioral characteristics of ADHD follow TBI.

- Age is a factor in identification, with a quarter of children identified with TBI at less than 2 years (such as shaken babies) and falls being a major cause in children younger than 5. Vehicle accidents and contact sports are largely responsible for TBIs incurred between the ages of 15 and 25. Younger children who have suffered a brain injury may vomit, while older children will report headaches/dizziness; all children will respond with irritability or fatigue. Children identified very young with TBI may look more like children with LD as they age; older children are more likely to recall their losses of skills and friends, resulting in psychosocial adjustment difficulties.

- Individuals with TBI make up the fastest-growing disability group in the United States. TBI is identified twice as often in boys as in girls, and hospital admissions for TBI are highest among lower-SES groups.

- The etiology of TBI is damage to the brain; however, some children have risk factors (e.g., high activity, intellectual disability, inadequate family supervision) that make them more likely than others to incur brain injuries. In the classroom, task difficulty and change may trigger negative or avoidant responses from children with TBI.

- Educators can informally identify these children through observations of their highly variable and "unexpected" behavior and their changes in social responses. The social changes look like acting out (inappropriate crude comments, drug abuse, sexual promiscuity, aggression) or take the form of internalizing emotional responses (withdrawal, moodiness, anxiety, perfectionism). Communication changes can include socially inappropriate statements as well as unintelligible or dysnomic speech. Depression and variability in academic performance are often identified later. Family members are most distressed by changes in the child's personality and behavior.

- Changes in cognitive processing depend on where the damage occurred in the brain and the extent of damage. Memory is one of the most common losses, which can contribute to slower thinking and responding. Focal damage, most often associated with MTBI, may produce unexpected judgment errors and losses of new learning; global damage, associated with TBI, is more likely to affect intelligence, including recall of old learnings, problem solving, understanding connections between actions and consequences, and organization (executive functions). Nonverbal intelligence can decline for up to 5 years after injury, whereas verbal intelligence, especially the old learning of older children, is typically more stable. Both global and focal types of damage are likely to affect attention/concentration and visual-spatial skills involved in mobility and handwriting. Motor skills, both gross and fine, recover earlier than other functions. Academic difficulties depend on whether old or new learning has been affected. Generally, higher-level skills involving comprehension and problem solving (e.g., math word problems, compositions) are likely to be affected.

- Interventions should initially target the skills of handling change, planning, self-monitoring, and safety.

- Accommodations include establishing routines to help the children schedule their lives, as well as providing additional time, step-by-step directions, adequate physical space, and reduced noise and other stimulation.

## CHAPTER QUESTIONS

1. What risk factors are present in some children and their families that make the children more likely to incur brain injuries?

2. How does age of onset of a brain insult affect the long-term course of the individual's resulting disability?

3. If abrupt changes in personality, language, or behavior can signal even a mild TBI, what somatic cues might you look for?

4. Why may a child have decreased academic functioning after he or she has apparently recovered physically from a TBI?

5. Why are there changes in social functioning after a child has apparently recovered physically from a TBI?

6. Why are vocabulary and verbal IQ poor indicators of TBI?

7. What have you learned in this chapter that you found interesting or have a question about?

## TRUE/FALSE AND MULTIPLE-CHOICE

1. Children's responses to MTBI and TBI are relatively unpredictable.

2. Children with TBI have more difficulties with the lower-level skills of calculations and decoding than with the higher-level skills of problem solving.

3. Children with MTBI/TBI often develop over time with worsened
   A. motor disorders
   B. verbal deficits
   C. attention/memory problems
   D. social problems

4. The most immediate and sustained deficits in children with MTBI/TBI:
   A. motor disorders
   B. IQ deficits
   C. attention/memory problems

5. After brain injury, the first functions to recover are typically language deficits.

6. Global damage to the brain is more likely than focal damage to affect old memories and old learnings.

7. When a child sustains damage to a local area in the frontal area of the brain, the child may make up stories to complete his or her missing memories. This is called

   A. abstract thinking
   B. dysarthria
   C. plasticity
   D. confabulation

8. Hyperactivity and inattention that occur *prior to* a brain injury suggest interventions related to

   A. ADHD (Chapter 9)
   B. autism spectrum disorders (Chapter 13)
   C. externalizing behavioral disorders (Chapter 11)

9. Hyperactivity and inattention that occur *after* a brain injury suggest interventions related to

   A. ADHD (Chapter 9)
   B. autism spectrum disorders (Chapter 13)
   C. externalizing behavioral disorders (Chapter 11)

10. Very young children respond to a head injury with

   A. headaches
   B. vomiting
   C. dizziness

## SHORT ANSWER

1. Condition in which brain layers ride up on each other and therefore cut nerve pathways

2. Bleeding into the brain, which is toxic to brain cells

3. Bruising of the brain

4. A state of prolonged unconsciousness

5. Speed of responses to novel stimuli (e.g., block designs) is measured in the assessment of _____ IQ.

## PROBLEM-BASED CASE APPLICATIONS AND QUESTIONS

### CASE STUDY 8.1: ANDY

***"I like dirt and mud because they are slippery."***
(adapted from a report submitted by Heather Helmus-Nyman)

*Background.* At the age of 4, Andy suffered from a critical drowning incident and required resuscitation. Andy began preschool under the handicapping label of communication disorder. Two years later, in kindergarten, his qualifying area was other health impairment (OHI), specifically ADHD. Apparently, at this very young age, Andy displayed a great number of behavior problems. Andy was medicated at that time, and still is, at age 11. Those who have seen him both on and off the medication agree that it makes a difference in his ability to attend.

Andy has been given the following labels, from toddler to the present:

- Age 3: communication disorder
- Age 5: OHI (ADHD), communication disordered
- Age 7: LD, OHI (ADHD), communication disordered
- Age 10: OHI (ADHD), communication disordered
- Age 11: OHI (ADHD)

When Andy was 7 years old, a discrepancy was detected between his achievement and his intelligence, therefore, his qualifying conditions for special education were changed to learning disabled, other health impaired, with a communication disorder. Yet, 3 years later, as part of the mandated reevaluation process, Andy went through a second round of intelligence and achievement testing and the discrepancy was lost—and so was the label of LD. His scores on the Wechsler Intelligence Scale for Children (WISC-III) at that time were as follows: verbal score, 73; performance score, 90; and full-scale IQ score, 79.

At some point in his very young life, Andy obtained second-degree burns on his hands and was hospitalized for about a week. Still today he has scarring on his hands, and fine motor control is an issue for him. He receives occupational therapy services for 30 minutes weekly.

Andy's parents divorced when he was about 2–3 years old. For the next several years, Andy resided with his mother, making occasional visits to his father. Since Andy's mother remarried, Andy has lived with both her and his stepfather. His mother is up and off to work early every morning, leaving before her family is awake. Overall, she appears distant from her son, and there is little evidence of follow-through or academic support coming from her concerning Andy's homework or special projects.

Andy's stepfather, on the other hand, appears stern, strict, rough, and gruff. Although Andy has lived with his stepfather for only two years, the stepfather's personality may, in part, influence Andy's self-critical behaviors. Andy is a student who has significant learning challenges, who may never achieve academic excellence. This may be difficult for his stepfather to understand and accept, as he may have high expectations for Andy. Yet, fortunately, Andy and his stepfather do share a common interest: go-cart racing. From the discussions that take place in the classroom, it seems as though the two of them enjoy every aspect: tires, tune-ups, and an afternoon at the track. In addition to Andy, his stepfather and mother have one other son, Andy's younger brother by just one year. Hard competitive battles, with computer games in particular, occur between these two boys. It would seem that the older brother would most often come out on top, but Andy does not have the visual-motor agility of his younger brother. This, in part, may explain Andy's deep-rooted need to be first, fast, and fantastic at all that he does. Since he often falls short of being better than his younger brother, he arrives at school each morning ready to beat somebody at something, to be the winner, the best.

Andy's strengths, according to his stepfather, include his strong desire to learn and to succeed. He is personable, inquisitive, and energetic, with a zest for life. The areas in which Andy faces challenges, according to his stepfather, are patience, slowing down, persisting and not being so easily discouraged, and neatness.

Andy was asked to respond to two questions: "What do you like?" and "What gives you trouble?" He stated each and every response quickly, using very few words. He reported that he enjoys his two dogs a great deal. In addition, Andy likes go-cart racing and likes dirt and mud "because they are slippery." He also spends time playing a variety of sports, such as basketball, soccer, and football. Last, Andy communicated that he delights in helping people. Based on his responses, Andy's interests and strengths can be summarized as follows: animals, speed, competition, relationships, and fun.

## Behavioral Log (abbreviated)

### Monday, January 21

Andy reads with little expression, very monotone and quite quickly. His written pieces (a) do not stay within the confines of the lines; (b) consist of very simple sentences with repeated phrases such as "It was cool," "It was fun," "It was the best"; and (c) include very few punctuation marks.

The procedure for the pretest was discussed, and Andy called out two times, "Oh, shoot. I just caught myself." He erased to fix the words both times. Throughout this process he often fussed with his eraser, which he always held in his nonwriting hand.

He also fussed with his skin. When he came to a word that gave him trouble, he would write and erase several times. It seemed like he wanted it to look just so. At one point he said, "I'll come back to it." We ran out of time to make the corrections, so I asked the students to help me problem solve the situation. Andy suggested that we finish the pretest tomorrow. That was the consensus, and I thanked him for being a problem solver.

### Tuesday, January 22

I reminded each student that cursive is expected for rewriting. Andy groaned when he heard this. I ignored his noise, and he began to write in cursive. The first word, *Friday,* gave Andy trouble. He raised his hand and asked for help. I complimented him for asking for help instead of getting frustrated. I asked Andy to point to letter *T.* Then, I asked him to compare it to letter *F.* He noticed that the only different piece was the cross in the middle. Andy had little difficulty writing the word *Friday* after that point, and I made mention of how proud of him I was that he asked for help.

The next activity involved manipulating letters in order to make words. It was Nick's turn to pass out the letters. When I handed the letters to Nick, Andy questioned me on this. I reminded Andy that he put the letters away last time, so now it is Nick's turn. Andy nodded, and we moved on. As Nick was passing out letters, he became flustered when trying to get them out of the small compartment. Andy reassured Nick by telling him, "Take your time, Nick." I told Andy that he was very thoughtful to say that and showed good use of people smart. At one point during the "make and break" process Andy asked his neighbor, Brandon, to be quiet. Later, in asking the boys to spell the word *oak,* I noticed that this word was giving them trouble. Next, I asked them to think of another word that has the same vowel sound as *oak.* Andy suggested the word *boat.* I used his example as a teaching point.

### Wednesday, January 23

I passed out the stack of letters and asked each of them to spread them out in front of them. Andy did this, and Brandon asked him how many letters were needed. I asked Andy to count his letters and tell Brandon. He did. Brandon thanked Andy for helping him. About the third or fourth word they were asked to make was the word *soak.* I said the word, used it in a sentence, and gave them this helpful hint: Remember what you know about the word *oak,* which we made yesterday. Andy spelled *soak* like this: "soke." I told him that I understood why he chose the bossy *e* at the end, but this word uses another long *o* chunk, like *oak.* Then Andy remembered the connection we made with *oak* earlier. He said, "Oh, like boat." "Yes," I answered. "Good thinking!"

### Thursday, January 24

Andy began with the spelling practice test. The paper was in front of him when he arrived at our table, and he immediately began to number it and write his name. His paper was complete and he was finished first. He numbered very quickly and vocalized sounds while he did so. At one point another student asked, "What do we number it to?" Andy helped by saying, "Sixteen." The other boy continued to number his paper and knew when to stop. Another boy in the group asked, "Where is Brian?" Andy responded with, "Brian is right there," and Brian was walking in the door. The other boy said, "Oh." Then, Andy made a comment about my vest. He said it was neat.

### Friday, January 25

When Andy was writing in his journal I noted that he wrote the letters for words very quickly. Perhaps he writes quickly in hopes of getting finished first. The sentences were again very simple: Nick is cool. Nick is nice. Nick is the bomb. While writing, he often moved his mouth around. He used manuscript and occasionally looked up at Nick and smiled since he was the topic. After about a 5-minute writing period, he stopped and said, "C'mon, c'mon, c'mon" and shook his journal around in front of him. Then he said, "C'mon, one more!" I did not respond. He then shook his hands around in front of him. He added one more sentence. Next, I asked the boys to reread what they had written. Andy did so after about a minute of looking around the room. He wanted to do it when he wanted to. At one point while rereading silently he erased and fixed something. While doing this he said, "I caught myself." When finished, he put his pencil in his mouth and chewed on it a bit. I let him do this. Last, during the end of journal time he said, "I am going to write about Brian next," and wrote "Brian" on the next clean page. Brian smiled at him.

### Monday, January 28

Andy began frustrated. Previously, in his reading group, he was frustrated and angry because there were several words in a poem that they were working on that gave him trouble. He sat with his head down on the table. I asked him how he was feeling. He responded, "Mad."

### Friday, February 1

Poetry was next. The paper with the poem was passed out to each student. The poem is practiced each day of the week with choral reading and silent reading, and students receive a copy each Monday in their home folder. Andy began to fuss with the paper immediately, moving it all around the table. Challenging words in the poem were reviewed in order to prepare the students for a successful reading. The students were asked to read through the poem silently, and then each would have a turn reading it aloud. One student read aloud, and then it was Andy's turn. He continued to move the paper around, put his head on his desk, wrapped his arms around his head, and made a lot of noise. He was sent to his desk with the suggestion that he cool down and take a couple of deep breaths. At his desk, he took all of the materials out, putting folders up to hide himself. He had a pen with which he scribbled on a piece of paper. A short time later he shoved all of those materials to another desk and then, putting his hands around his head, laid his head on his desk. His behavior continued to escalate as he yelled, "Shut up! I hate you!" to teachers and other adults in the room. Then he was asked to leave the room because of this behavior. He was told that he was not invited to stay because the room is for learning, and others cannot learn when he is shouting. He yelled, "No!" and would not move out of his chair. He clung to his desk with his feet and, with his hands around his head, continued to yell, "No!" The principal was involved next; Andy would not get up for him, either. The principal physically removed Andy by picking him up at the armpits. Andy kicked and screamed—flailing his arms and legs about. He was taken to the office. A couple of hours later, he returned. I asked him if he was ready to learn, because we were about to take our spelling and dictation test. He told me that he could do it, and I told him that I was glad. He grabbed his pencil and eraser and joined us at the table. He numbered his paper right away. During the test he wrote in cursive but often moved his mouth and lips around while writing.

### Tuesday, February 5

Andy came to the table without his homework folder. Before I even had a chance to ask, he said that he left it at home. I told him that surprised me because he is always responsible with his homework. I also assured him that it was okay and that I forget things at home too sometimes, like my lunch. Andy said that he did the homework; he just left it at home. I asked him to please remember it tomorrow. Next, Andy helped Brandon, the boy sitting next to him, by handing Brandon's homework to me. Shortly after that, Brandon used the word *sexy* in a sentence. That got the others laughing. I told Brandon that it may be okay for him to use that word at home, but it is inappropriate for school. Then Andy lightly slapped himself on the cheek and said, "I need to slap myself." I asked Andy why he did this, and he shrugged his shoulders and said, "I don't know." I did not pursue it from there.

### Friday, February 8

Andy wrote words for the spelling test in cursive. He attempted the first word and right away erased it. He said, "Shoot." The first word was *buy.* Andy spelled it "by" and asked me if I could tell that what he wrote was a *B Y*. I told him that I could certainly tell it was a *B Y*. He told me he was really going to do each of the words in cursive, the whole test. I told him that I appreciated his efforts because I know that cursive sometimes gives him trouble.

## ABC Analysis

Analyzing Andy's behaviors in the log proved most interesting; after examination of just a few days, the results became very apparent. Specifically, 86% of Andy's behaviors were for the purpose of getting something, while just 14% were for avoidance of some sort (see Figure 8.2). Beginning with the highest-frequency payoff, get competence at 51%, the majority of his behaviors displayed a high need for mastery and recognition. This makes complete sense given the fact that Andy longs to be first and fast. In addition, Andy finds it necessary to achieve without any help from peers or adults. For example, when asked to number a paper, Andy typically goes like a shot, writing the numbers as a fast as his hand will go and, at the conclusion of this process, announcing aloud, "I beat!" Not only does he have an urge to finish the quickest, but he also wants everyone involved to know it. A second example: When the students are dismissed, Andy reacts with physical signs of agony and discomfort when he is not first to leave the room. In peeking out the doorway, I notice him running to catch up to or beat the student ahead. Another example: When asked to write in his journal, he immediately begins to write, generally announcing to all the title of his entry.

**Figure 8.2**   Andy's Avoids and Gets

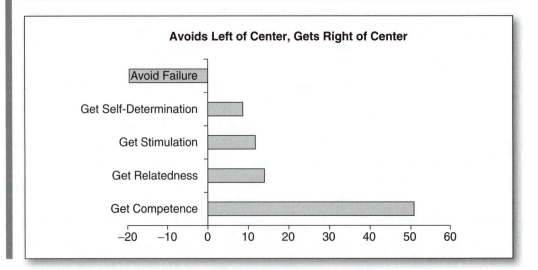

He typically writes a few pages' worth of information in a very rushed manner and is sure to share how many pages he ended up with. He is not the least bit concerned about the quality of his piece; instead, he focuses on the quantity.

Andy has cognitive distortions: Fast is good. Slow is bad. I appear dumb if I get help, therefore I must do things by myself. This is typical of someone who thinks only in black-and-white terms, a quality of perfectionism.

A second payoff for Andy, which in most cases overlaps and connects with getting competence, is tied for second in frequency and is the only avoid payoff, avoid failure at 14%. A task that nearly always triggers Andy is writing, cursive in particular. When asked to write words, sentences, or paragraphs in cursive, Andy writes quickly, which fulfills his competence need. However, writing quickly may reduce Andy's anxiety, but he does not achieve the mastery he expects from himself, therefore he erases and erases and erases. Perfectionism is associated with exaggerated anxiety-based reactions to mistakes (i.e., self-criticalness).

## Diagnosis Versus ABC Analysis

Andy's intelligence scores are consistent with a slow learner, which would be consistent with minimal TBI. In particular his verbal intelligence is low; this could explain his early diagnosis of communication disordered and also explain why he reads in a monotonous voice (i.e., without comprehension). As well, the hyperactivity is most likely an outcome of MTBI and so are the fine motor problems of handwriting and not staying "within the confines of the line." He also makes mistakes that cause anxiety and a need to erase and redo. Overall, my conclusion is that because Andy did not receive the correct diagnosis of TBI, a number of his problems associated with TBI have gone unrecognized.

## Interventions Derived From ABC Analysis

Andy's cognitive distortion is such that he believes "I will appear incompetent if I ask for or receive help from an adult, so I am going to struggle through this myself."

### Intervention 1: Asking for Help

*Purpose.* Provide Andy with "get competence" opportunities and make tasks he usually seeks to avoid more pleasurable.

- Provide fun, alternate ways to ask for help.
- Provide handwriting choices based on purpose of task to decrease erasures.
- Provide reinforcement for slow and careful work.
- Teach the value of speed and its place.

*Method.* Rather than raising his hand, Andy will utilize the following materials: toy car, stuffed dog, or making a question mark with clay.

*Results See Figure 8.3.* Andy asked for help only twice in 3 days during baseline, or on average less than once a day. After intervention, Andy requested help 20 times in 5 days, or 4 times a day. Who would have thought a lump of clay would have done all that?

**Figure 8.3**  Andy's Requests for Help Before and After Intervention 1

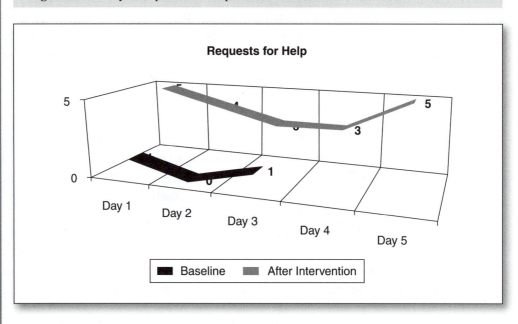

### Intervention 2: Decrease Erasures

The focus of this intervention was twofold—slowing Andy's motor movements and removing the anxiety that writing in cursive causes him. Since his ability to print is in the mastery phase, Andy was allowed to use this style of writing. Simply speaking with Andy about writing more slowly produced fewer erasures. This involved a lot of positive reinforcement and tutorials on the importance of various levels of speed for different dog breeds, because Andy likes dogs. Andy shared the information that we gathered by presenting it to a small group of his peers. This activity brought about social interaction with grade-level peers and also gave Andy an opportunity to express himself verbally in a meaningful context. This intervention also reduced his number of erasures. See Figure 8.4.

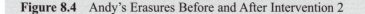

**Figure 8.4** Andy's Erasures Before and After Intervention 2

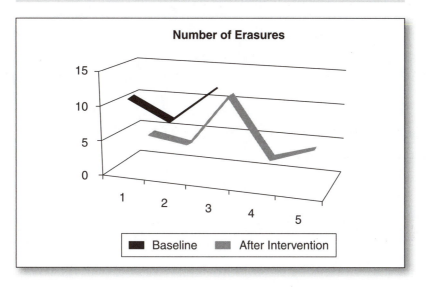

## Case Questions

1: Is there evidence that Andy has a handwriting problem that contributes to his low production of writing?

2: What disability label did Andy never receive? Would receiving that label have made a difference for him? Why or why not?

3: Is there evidence that Andy has a language disability?

4: What kinds of deficits does Andy have that indicate the diagnosis of TBI?

5: Andy is on medication, but have accommodations been made for his ADHD?

6: Can you list some of the values of Andy's teacher?

7: Andy's teacher concludes after a brief interview with him that his interests are "animals, speed, competition, relationships, and fun" and that "his comprehension when reading by himself is low. He is still unable to do this task even after 4 days of reading the same story, unless the story is of high interest to him." Specifically how would you use Andy's interests to help him with reading comprehension?

8 (problem-based small-group assignment): Create a list of the skills you would recommend for Andy, who will be moving on from the elementary school program (i.e., a safe and secure place with caring, familiar faces) to a middle school environment, with its demands for high levels of responsibility, independence, and self-control.

# Attentional Disorders

**Chapter 9**

Attention Deficit Hyperactivity Disorder: Inattentive and Combined Subtypes

**Chapter 10**

Attention Deficit Hyperactivity Disorder: Hyperactive/ Impulsive Subtype

The IDEA category of other health impairment (OHI; see Figure IV.1) provides the umbrella under which the subtypes of attention deficit hyperactivity disorder (ADHD) are defined. These subtypes are ADHD-IN, the inattentive subtype; ADHD-C, the combined subtype; and ADHD-HI, the hyperactive/impulsive subtype. (Note that Figure IV. 1 includes other disabilities, in addition to ADHD, that fall under the OHI category. These include Tourette's syndrome, which is discussed in Chapter 15 on motor disorders.)

The percentages of the subtypes, as shown in Figure IV.2, indicate that the majority of children with ADHD (inattentive subtype plus the combined subtype) are characterized with inattention, and most research into ADHD has been conducted with the combined subtype (Wilens, Biederman, & Spencer, 2002). Young children express the hyperactive/impulsive subtype, which develops into the inattentive or combined subtype in later years. Evidence for this transition is supported by findings of an increase in identifying the inattentive subtype and a decrease in hyperactivity/impulsivity symptomology over a period of 8 years (Lahey, Pelham, Loney, Lee, & Willcutt, 2005). Information on the HI subtype follows in Chapter 10 to suggest a bridge to the externalizing behavioral disorders, presented in Section V, which addresses social disorders.

**Figure IV.1**   OHI Subtypes

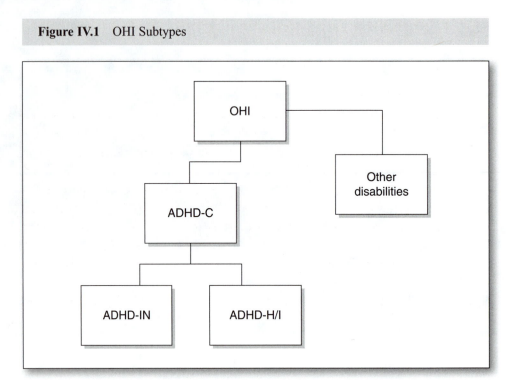

**Figure IV.2**   ADHD Subtypes

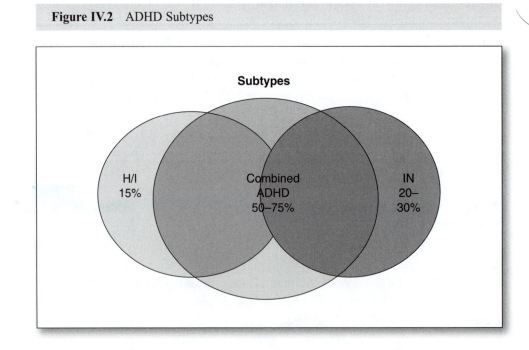

# LEARNING GOALS

In this section you will learn the following:

- The vocabulary associated with attentional disorders
- The subtypes of ADHD and how each is formally defined by IDEA and *DSM-IV-TR*
- The etiology and prevalence of ADHD and how age, culture, and gender can influence outcome
- How educators can informally identify children with the two subtypes of ADHD through observations of their (a) behavior, (b) responses to social and communication settings, (c) responses to academic tasks, and (d) responses to motor and physical tasks
- Possible implications for accommodations in Tier I settings and for interventions appropriate for Tiers II and III
- How to apply the information you have learned to a case study of a student with ADHD

# Chapter 9

## Attention Deficit Hyperactivity Disorder

*Inattentive and Combined Subtypes*

Students with the inattentive subtype of ADHD, or **ADHD-IN,** have been compared to children who play baseball but are unaware of the score or who is up and are just as likely to wander off to somebody else's game when there is little action in their own. This is often characterized as daydreaming in classroom contexts (as Figure 9.1 depicts and a couch-potato at home). These children's attentional problems can be summarized as difficulty in selecting and sustaining attention to **relevant informa-tion** (e.g., the baseball game, who is batting, who is on base, the score) while ignoring what is not relevant (e.g., the beetle in the field, itchy pants, what to eat for lunch). In most cases, the nonrelevant information is novel (e.g., the beetle) and therefore more interesting and attention captivating (distracting) for children who prefer novelty.

Relevant information, which is typically less interesting, includes the content of spoken or written language (the words) and the details within tasks (e.g., changes in mathematical process signs in a mixed-operation worksheet). Directing attention to this relevant information is difficult for children with ADHD-IN because their atten-tion is captured by what is moving, colorful, funny, or emotional, rather than what is relevant. A child with ADHD-IN may understand that you are angry (emotion) or notice the mole on the left side of your face but have no idea what you have said that explains your anger. Perhaps these children should be better described as having an **attentional bias** toward novelty rather than a deficit of attention, given that all chil-dren attend to something at all times, unless they are sleeping.

In addition to difficulties directing attention to relevant information, children with ADHD-IN also have problems with **sustained attention.** This is frequently observed as off-task behavior. Teachers respond to this behavior by "calling" these

**ADHD-IN:** Attention deficit hyperactivity disorder, inattentive subtype.

**Relevant information:** Information that is important to correct task performance.

**Attentional bias:** Preference for certain types of stimuli. All humans selectively attend to their own names, and most attend to information that signals potential danger (e.g., loud sounds). Students with the inattentive subtype of ADHD are more likely than their peers to selectively attend to novelty (movement, color, emotion, and so on).

**Figure 9.1**   A student with the ADHD–Inattentive subtype

231

children back for whatever short period of time that might be achieved (i.e., by redirecting their attention). Ken was such a child—he would drift off and constantly be called out by his teacher. One day his teacher said to him, "You must get tired of hearing your own name all the time." He replied, "Yeah—I wish I could change my name to Dylan!"

## FORMAL IDENTIFICATION

### Definitions

#### *IDEA*

Typically students with ADHD-IN will receive services under LD, if there is a co-occurring LD. Students who do *not* qualify for any co-occurring disability fall within the category of **OHI,** which is the umbrella under which ADHD is defined in IDEA, with approximately 20% identified in this category (U.S. Department of Education, 2006). The IDEA definition of OHI follows, with italics added to indicate those parts with specific relevance to this chapter:

> Other health impairment means having limited strength, vitality, or alertness, including a heightened alertness to environmental stimuli, that results in limited alertness with respect to the educational environment, that (i) is due to chronic or acute health problems such as asthma, *attention deficit disorder or attention deficit hyperactivity disorder,* diabetes, epilepsy, a heart condition, hemophilia, lead poisoning, leukemia, nephritis, rheumatic fever, sickle cell anemia, and Tourette syndrome; and (ii) adversely affects a child's educational performance. (34 CFR Section 300.8[c][9]; see National Dissemination Center for Children With Disabilities, 2012)

> *Rule-outs or exclusions:* Excluded from a diagnosis of **ADHD-HI** are children who are low IQ or gifted and children with LD or a transient emotional disorder (e.g., a child with parents divorcing).

> *Placements:* Under the OHI category students receive accommodations in general education under Section 504 (if their ADHD adversely affects their major life functions of learning or socialization).

#### *DSM-IV-TR*

*DSM-IV-TR* (APA, 2000, p. 92) defines ADHD-IN as follows:

> *Defining characteristics:* Six (or more) of the following symptoms of inattention have persisted for at least 6 months to a degree that is maladaptive and inconsistent with developmental level:

*Inattention:*

- Often fails to give close attention to details or makes careless mistakes in schoolwork, work, or other activities
- Often has difficulty sustaining attention in tasks or play activities
- Often does not seem to listen when spoken to directly
- Often does not follow through on instructions and fails to finish school-work, chores, or duties in the workplace (not due to oppositional behavior or failure to understand instructions)
- Often has difficulty organizing tasks and activities
- Often avoids, dislikes, or is reluctant to engage in tasks that require sustained mental effort (such as schoolwork or homework)
- Often loses things necessary for tasks or activities (e.g., toys, school assignments, pencils, books, or tools)
- Is often easily distracted by extraneous stimuli
- Is often forgetful in daily activities

*Impairment:* Social or academic.

*Conditions:* "Some characteristic must be present before age 7 years and some impairment must be present in two or more settings" (e.g., school, home).

## Frequently Occurring Subtypes

*DSM-IV-TR* (APA, 2000, p. 93) describes the subtypes of ADHD:

*Attention deficit hyperactivity disorder, predominantly inattentive type:* Diagnosis of this subtype requires that the criteria listed above are met for the past 6 months

*Attention deficit hyperactivity disorder, combined type:* Diagnosis of this subtype requires that both the criteria for hyperactive/impulsive subtype listed in Chapter 10 and the criteria for predominantly inattentive subtype listed above are met for the past 6 months.

## Possible Co-Occurring Conditions and Differences Among Related Disorders

Inattention is observed in almost every mild disability category (Krupski, 1980) and is associated with significant school failure and co-occurring conditions (Rowland, Lesesne, & Abramowitz, 2002). For example, students with the IN subtype of ADHD are more likely also to have RD (36%) than students in the general population (17%) (Lyon, 2003) and to have an **internalizing disorder:** 10–40% have co-occurring anxiety and 20–30% have co-occurring depression.

**Internalizing disorders:** Disorders that cause individuals to express feelings inwardly and thus increase the likelihood of anxiety and/or depression.

Students with ADHD plus anxiety may have lower tolerance for both stress and boredom (i.e., a narrow window of arousal).

However, it is important to consider the evidence that symptoms of inattention (off-task behavior or task avoidance) would be expected for any child placed in an academic setting that is inappropriate for his or her (a) high IQ (giftedness), (b) low IQ (ID), (c) divergent perceptual or memory skills (LD or TBI), (d) high stress or anxiety level, or (e) need for familiarity and sameness (autism spectrum disorders). Because inattention (like social deficits and language disorders) is a marker variable for so many mild disabilities, it is important to examine the nature of the task the child is avoiding. Table 9.1 provides a comparative analysis that may help with this differential diagnostic task:

**Marker variable:** Distinguishing characteristic.

**Table 9.1**  Differential Diagnosis of Inattention

| | | | | |
|---|---|---|---|---|
| | *Characteristics for ADHD, LD, ID, GT, ODD, and ASD* | | | |
| | *Inattention behavior observed* | *Problems in performance and persistence observed* | *Attention and behavior improved with* | *Differential assessment* |
| ADHD | Variable, sensation-seeking activity, impulsivity, or inattention during wait time when no active responses are available, especially in familiar settings or with familiar people and tasks. | Performance deficits demonstrated by less production and slower, more variable performance that decreases over time, especially during boring, familiar, or repetitive tasks or later in the day or in the school year. | Novel, emotional, colorful, animated themes and tasks, presented with computers or in game formatting, that are self-paced with little wait time. | Assess behavior and persistence during short, novel, self-paced tasks versus longer rote tasks (for a review, see Zentall et al., in press). |
| LD | More activity (away from seat) and/or inattention during tasks within the child's SLD (e.g., reading but not math, or for all subject areas that involve reading, but not during lab time). | Skill deficits are seen initially in performance and later due to fatigue. Teachers report that these students are easier to redirect back to their tasks than students with ADHD. | Areas where a child can demonstrate competence outside the child's SLD. | Assess academic activities that produce task avoidance and off-task behavior and contrast these with activities during which the child seeks competence. |

| | | | | |
|---|---|---|---|---|
| *Characteristics for ADHD, LD, ID, GT, ODD, and ASD* | | | | |
| | *Inattention behavior observed* | *Problems in performance and persistence observed* | *Attention and behavior improved with* | *Differential assessment* |
| ID | "ADHD symptoms are increased in children with ID" (Simonoff et al., 2007, p. 595). The lower the IQ, the higher the rating of ADHD symptoms (e.g., more activity during tasks of greater difficulty). However, there is less impulsivity in the ID population than in the ADHD population (Pearson et al., 1996). | Less persistence when students with ID are exhausted by tasks that are cognitively complex, involve concepts, or require comprehension but not during tasks assessing basic skills. | Familiar tasks or when the task is of moderate difficulty. | "In children with Mental Retardation, an additional diagnosis ADHD should be made only if the symptoms of inattention or hyperactivity are excessive for the child's mental age" (APA, 2000, p. 91). |
| GT | High-energy behavior characterized as intense and busy (Beljan et al., 2006). Disruptive activity may also occur during wait time, where these students spend much time waiting for others to catch up. | Less persistence and more possible disruption when tasks are at a basic level or when tasks are nonchallenging and in "academically understimulating environments" (APA, 2000, p. 91). | Challenging and complex tasks. | Assess off-task behavior in problem-solving tasks versus basic skill tasks. |
| ODD | Due to high rates of co-occurring ADHD, these students can be active but can also exhibit more withdrawn, anxious, aggressive, and depressed behavior (Carlson, Tamm, & Gaub, 1997). Children with ODD have less inattention than those with ADHD but have higher rates than typical children (Carlson et al., 1997). | Assigned tasks with little choice in type of task, response mode, materials, and so on. Often less compliance getting started on an assigned task. | Self-selected or choice tasks. | Assess noncompliance or off-task behavior in self-selected or choice tasks versus in assigned tasks. |
| ASD | Children with ASD and anxiety disorders are generally passive and typically show repetitive activity, repeated topics of conversation, and avoidance of specific persons, tasks, settings, or events (e.g., tractors or storms in close proximity). | A change in schedule, novel tasks or settings, and social tasks (e.g., crowding) elicit avoidance and poorer performance. | Greater persistence on tasks of special interest and on repetitive tasks, due to their familiarity. | Assess off-task behavior in areas of child's special interests (familiar tasks) versus in novel topic areas. |

## Etiology

Similar to most mild disabilities, ADHD has no single causative factor. The biogenetic explanation is favored and could account for any number of possible cognitive and academic outcomes.

*Biogenetic.* The combined subtype of ADHD that includes both inattention and hyperactivity/impulsivity has higher heritability than either of the pure subtypes. For example, heritability for identical twins is .91 compared to .75 for fraternal twins, which suggests that genetics is more important than environment (for a review, see Wenar & Kerig, 2006). One specific gene that has been identified is the D4 receptor gene. Also associated with biogenetic factors are differences in the chemistry and structure of the brain. At the chemical level, there is evidence of deficient **dopamine** and norepinephrine, which are involved in the transmission of information among nerve cells. Furthermore, there is evidence that psychostimulants such as Ritalin (methylphenidate) can increase the availability of dopamine at the synapses of cells in the brain (McNab et al., 2009). Finally, at the structural level, some individuals with ADHD have reduced total brain size (3–4%) and smaller prefrontal cortex (8%) and lower activity in the frontal lobes (for a review of this evidence, see Castellanos et al., 2002). This does not cause ADHD symptoms but is associated with it, in the same way that a larger brain size at birth and in early development is associated with autism (Redcay & Courchesne, 2005).

The academic deficits reported for the IN and combined subtypes have also been explained by biogenetic differences in executive functions. Barkley (2006) has suggested that executive functions are needed to self-regulate effort, and poor EF can be used to explain ADHD. However, executive dysfunctions (a) are common to many disability groups, (b) do not explain the severity of academic impairment (Barry, Lyman, & Klinger, 2002), and (c) are not necessarily responsive to psychostimulants (Swanson, Baler, & Volkow, 2011). In other words, descriptions of biogenetic EF differences cannot explain the primary characteristics of ADHD (activity, impulsivity, inattention) (for critiques, see Nigg, 2001; Willcutt, Doyle, Nigg, Faraone, & Pennington, 2005), since evidence of EF deficits does not explain why these characteristics exist.

*Environmental.* Prenatal factors, such as maternal smoking, and postnatal contributors, brain injury, and ingestion of toxins, such as lead, can account for about one in five children with clinically defined ADHD. In addition, as few as 3–5% of preschoolers with ADHD may be sensitive to food dyes or sugar, and 40% may have deficiencies in essential fatty acids compared with 10% of typical children (Stevens et al., 1996).

**Dopamine:** A chemical that helps transmit signals from one nerve cell in the brain to the next.

*Functional.* Functional analysis would find that the antecedents that encourage inattentive behavior for students with ADHD are are nonmeaningful, nonstimulating, or **rote tasks** with too much delay-time between responses. Examples of this would be during listening tasks, especially when active responses are not available, and during tasks that require delay to examine detail or that require **sustained attention** or working memory. During these times, inattention or "distraction" functions to create novelty or change for a child who has difficulty maintaining sufficient activation and may be considered easily bored. These functional responses are explained by the optimal stimulation theory (i.e., inattention, activity, and impulsivity all serve to increase stimulation in an underactivated/underaroused child) (for discussion of the theory and a review, see Zentall & Zentall, 1983; for a review of a related biochemical dopamine deficiency hypothesis, see Swanson et al., 2011).

Overall, there is a mismatch between the arousal state of the child with ADHD (biogenetic) and the arousal state required for the child to perform a long or effortful task (environmental) (Wu, Anderson, & Castiello, 2006). This functional dependence of ADHD on the amount of stimulation available in different task and setting conditions is well elaborated in *DSM-IV-TR* (APA, 2000, pp. 86–87):

> Symptoms typically worsen in situations that require sustained attention or mental effort or that lack intrinsic appeal or novelty (e.g., listening to classroom teachers, doing class assignments, listening to or reading lengthy materials, or working on monotonous, repetitive tasks). Signs of the disorder may be minimal or absent when the person is receiving frequent rewards for appropriate behavior, is under close supervision, is in a novel setting, is engaged in especially interesting activities, or is in a one-to-one situation (e.g., the clinician's office). The symptoms are more likely to occur in group situations (e.g., in playgroups, classrooms, or work environments) where waiting is required.

In contrast, good attention is likely to be observed in children with ADHD when they are engaged in novel tasks (tasks involving color/light, sound, movement, emotion, meaningfulness/interest).

## Prevalence, Gender, Age, and Cultural Factors

*Prevalence.* ADHD, inclusive of all subtypes (the combined, inattentive, and hyperactive/impulsive), is the most frequently identified disorder in school-aged children (e.g., Willcutt et al., 2001). Although 8–20% of community samples would receive a diagnosis of ADHD based only on behavioral indicators (two to six students per class), only 3–7% of children have a severe enough disorder with

**Rote tasks:** Repetitive tasks that lack variation or novelty, such as math calculations, spelling drills, and handwriting practice.

**Sustained attention:** The ability to maintain a consistent behavioral or cognitive response during continuous or repetitive activity (Sohlberg & Mateer, 1989). Damage to the right frontal lobe of the brain has been reported to produce deficits in sustained attention (for a review, see Stuss et al., 2001).

significant impairment to warrant services (one or two students per class) (see, e.g., Shaywitz & Shaywitz, 1988). That is, the prevalence rate drops when students must also show evidence of social or academic dysfunction. Thus, about 44% of students with ADHD are receiving special education services, and the other 56% could be found in inclusion settings receiving accommodations if they have Section 504 plans (e.g., Bussing, Zima, Perwien, Belin, & Widawski, 1998).

*Gender.* Boys and girls are identified at equivalent rates within the pure inattentive subtype of ADHD (see Wenar & Kerig, 2006). For the ADHD combined subtype in the general population, around 9% of males and 3% of females are found, with a ratio of about four boys to one girl (e.g., August, Realmuto, MacDonald, Nugent, & Crosby, 1996).

*Age.* Children with the inattentive type of ADHD tend to be identified during elementary school, when the attentional demands of task performance are needed (Barkley, 2003).

*Culture.* There is consistent evidence of associations between high levels of ADHD characteristics and low parental education, single-parent and stepparent families, and low economic status (for a review and evidence, see Rydell, 2010). Girls, in particular, have been found to be vulnerable to these family stressors.

## INFORMAL EDUCATOR IDENTIFICATION OF CHARACTERISTICS

**CD:** Conduct disorder.

### Behavioral

Students with the IN subtype of ADHD are less disruptive and less likely to have ODD or **CD** than students with the HI subtype. Casey, for example, "did not display disruptive behavior but instead began avoiding assignments and teachers." This behavior may be specific to Casey, since girls with ADHD more typically solicit attention and assistance from their teachers (for a review, see DuPaul et al., 2006).

**Internalizing symptoms:** Symptoms that are directed inward. Somatic internalizing symptoms include stomachache, insomnia, and nausea; mood symptoms include worrying and depression; and behavioral symptoms include crying, withdrawal, and phobias.

### Social-Emotional

Students with ADHD-IN display fewer externalizing types of behavior and have more internalizing emotional problems, such as anxiety, depression, and social passivity, all of which contribute to neglect by peers and to decreased popularity. Girls, who more often represent the IN subtype, have more **internalizing symptoms** of depression and anxiety than do boys (DuPaul et al., 2006).

Cognitive distortions are another part of the social profile of older children with ADHD (combined subtype). That is, they are less optimistic about what might happen socially next week (Zentall, Cassady, & Javorsky, 2001). This attitude can be explained by their history, which has been self-reported as more negative and as having more failure experiences in their everyday lives, and by their emotional overreaction to both the good and bad events in their lives (this the case especially in adolescent girls with ADHD) (Abikoff et al., 2002; Grskovic & Zentall, 2010). Casey at the age of 13 has characteristics of inattention (failure to organize and complete tasks) and of emotional overreactions to distress: "She has daily contact with a case manager who works with Casey on basic skills involving organization, task completion and managing stress and emotions." These emotional overreactions in students with ADHD-C are similar to the reactions of younger children (i.e., emotional immaturity).

While keeping in mind the information presented above, we must also take into account the social and emotional resilience of some children with ADHD, even those with co-occurring LD, and of their resource room teachers. For example:

> Now Justin had already been in the resource room to have a 100-question final in English read to him earlier that day. It wasn't easy but I did manage to keep him on-task. . . . Around 1:00 p.m. Justin walked into my room again with a 187-question final in Earth and Space. At this point it was apparent that he was worn out and not at all happy. . . . Well I started reading the final and he stopped me close to the middle of the final. He looked at me and said "Ms. Y I only have two brain cells left right now, and I just want you to know that they are fighting over which one of them is going to survive. I'm just not sure that the surviving brain cell is going to be able to handle the rest of this final." I just looked at him, and we started laughing hysterically, because it was such a true statement, and I was feeling the same way (Zentall, 2006, p. 121).

## Cognitive

*Intellectual.* Overall, the IQ scores of the population of students with ADHD vary from severely ID into the gifted range. However, individuals selected from clinics do have lower IQ scores than students drawn from school-based samples, and children who have ADHD plus LD have lower verbal IQ scores than their peers (e.g., Andreou, Agapitou, & Karapetsas, 2005). In addition, girls more than boys with ADHD have intellectual impairments associated with their inattentive symptoms (DuPaul et al., 2006). There is further evidence that IQ scores decline as students get older (Nussbaum, Grant, Roman, Poole, & Bigler, 1990), perhaps because problem-solving speed is emphasized on IQ tests at advanced age levels (Silverman, 2003). Furthermore, IQ tests may underestimate intelligence in school-based samples of students with ADHD, because *some* IQ subtests (e.g., mental math and digit span) also require working attention and attention, which can lower IQ from 2 to 5 full-scale IQ points (Jepsen & Mortensen, 2009).

Some types of problem solving may be advanced. For example, research has found that students with ADHD (a) scored higher on tests of creative thinking than similar-IQ peers without ADHD (Brandau et al., 2007; Shaw & Brown, 1990), (b) told more creative stories with novel themes and plots (Zentall, 1988), (c) used more nonverbal information and strategies during problem solving in response to high states of arousal (videos and games; Lawrence et al., 2002; Shaw & Brown, 1999), and (d) contributed to higher percentages of correct problem solutions in cooperative groups than were observed in groups without these students (Kuester & Zentall, 2012; Zentall, Kuester, & Craig, 2011). Casey fits this evidence of creative intelligence: "Casey is a creative young girl. She loves to draw and write. Her artistic talent is impressive and she hopes to do something within the art industry after high school." It has been suggested that the attentional bias seen in ADHD (i.e., attraction to novelty/originality) may be a contributor to creativity (Zentall, 2005b), and Hallowell and Ratey (1995) have suggested that individuals with ADHD have a higher tolerance for ambiguity.

Executive functions are another aspect of intelligence (defined in Section I and discussed in the subsection on biogenetic etiologies in this chapter). There is evidence of EF deficits in many children with ADHD. However, EF deficits are also documented for many students with mild disabilities (reported in the chapters on LD and ID) and thus fail to provide an explanation of ADHD as different from LD and ID.

*Attention.* **Selective attention** is the failure to "get on track," especially with added details and descriptions (e.g., adjectives/adverbs, overlapping visual or conversational backgrounds). Selective attention makes it difficult for students with ADHD to pay attention to **neutral cues,** to the underlying structure of a task, and to details. This attentional bias contributes to these children getting lost in the beginnings of things and in transitions between settings or tasks or when there is a complex task (visual or auditory) and relevant information is covered up in some way (e.g., conversations that overlap a listening or a difficult reading task for young children). Average children find it easier to selectively attend to relevant task information—to the underlying structure of a task, the details, the relevant information in directions. The implications of this attentional bias in the classroom are a failure to pay attention to important information, especially neutral information that occurs early in a task, setting, or social experience, and a failure to attend to **internal cues,** such as feelings.

*Sustained inattention* is the failure to "stay on track," especially on tasks that are long or repetitive, or that require holding information in mind, such as mental math, multiple-step directions, organizing, or planning. In the classroom, difficulty sustaining attention is seen as: (a) visual off-task behavior, (b) changes in activities and failure to

**Selective attention:** Preference for attending to some things. For students with ADHD, selective attention is directed toward external stimulating sights, sounds, smells, tastes, movement, emotion, and aggression, and internally to exciting daydreaming, thought, and emotionality. This can be called an attentional bias rather than an attentional deficit.

**Neutral cues:** Information that is not salient and is difficult to notice, such as the organization of a room or the structure of an assignment.

**Internal cues:** Thoughts, feelings, strategies, values, and the like.

maintain routines (i.e., routines require repetition of the same behavior), (c) verbal changes in topics of conversations, and (d) cognitive off-task behavior, such as reading or daydreaming. Daydreaming is often observed in children with the IN subtype:

> He's not a child really that disturbs other children as far as he doesn't run around the room or necessarily talk a lot or anything. He just tends to daydream a lot and just be in another world. So it's not that he's disturbing to other children (Zentall, 2006, p. 112).

And as stated by a parent:

> I am a mother of four children. My second child, Damon, age 7, has been diagnosed as ADD. He does have a limited memory and is a daydreamer; however, he also reads on a 6th grade level and has a very big imagination (Zentall, 2006, p. 146).

Failure to stay on task reduces work speed and production. However, attending to "distractions" does *not* increase errors unless the distractions are very tempting (e.g., cartoons, toys, animals; Freer et al., 2011). For example, students with ADHD performed more poorly than peers when required to walk along a path and follow a series of instructions (touching or looking at objects at a series of checkpoints in a zoo) in the presence of distracting animals (Lawrence et al., 2002). Surprisingly, "distractions" may actually help the child perform in the classroom, especially when tasks are long and tedious. That is, off-task looking may provide "doses" of environmental stimulation that the child needs. Thus, being distracted does not necessarily mean performing poorly, and placing the child away from windows is not an appropriate accommodation, although it is often incorrectly recommended. For individual children, performance should be assessed with and without "distractions" and with different types of tasks that offer varying levels of engagement.

*Memory.* The memory characteristics of children with inattention are typically related to the length of the material to be memorized. In other words, attention and memory are related. If a child has difficulty attending to repetitive information, the child will have difficulty recalling that information. *Working memory* involves the ability to hold information in mind (sustain attention) and ignore nonrelevant interfering information. Poor WM is seen in the slower, more variable performance with more errors for children with ADHD than for their peers (Wu et al., 2006). Students with ADHD may have little difficulty with math until they are in high school algebra with multiple step problems to perform. Deficiencies in WM have been explained as the outcome of insufficient arousal or brain activation (dopamine neurotransmission) (McNab et al., 2009). Tasks that are fun (e.g., video games) release dopamine, which temporarily increases arousal and can improve the cognitive functions of WM (Lawrence et al., 2002).

Students with ADHD recall fewer items in *short-term memory* tasks, but they also spend less time rehearsing and do not select efficient memory strategies (i.e., they fail to categorize information). When information is precategorized or they have practice in sorting, they can recall as much as their peers (e.g., Kerns, Eso, & Thomson, 1999). Verbal *long-term memory* of children with ADHD has been assessed in studies asking students to name common objects rapidly. For example, when asked to name letter/number symbols and objects/colors, children with ADHD show impairment primarily when naming colors and objects, whereas children with RD show impairment with the more abstract letter/number symbols (Bental & Tirosh, 2007; Ghelani et al., 2004).

Perceptual skills involve attending to visual detail in tasks, and students with ADHD attend for less time and respond faster, but they are as able as non-ADHD peers to search for global themes in pictures and respond as well in listening tasks when presented with **global or gestalt cues** (e.g., it looks like a giraffe) (Zentall & Gohs, 1984). Research has also found that *perceptual speed* is slower than average for RD, ADHD, and RD + ADHD groups (Willcutt, Pennington, et al., 2005), with the RD group the slowest (Shanahan et al., 2006). It has been suggested that the speed of processing visual detail may depend on the type of stimuli, and some variables (e.g., the addition of color) can slow down that speed (Kercood, Zentall, Vinh, & Tom-Wright, 2012).

> **Global or gestalt cues:** Cues to the big picture that can be presented as advance organizers, concept maps, general descriptions, or comparisons (e.g., "It is like X").

## Communication

Teachers and parents often complain about the *listening skills* of children with ADHD. This could be explained by observations that these children *look like* they are not listening or they fail to comply over time to verbal requests to "be quiet," "pay attention," and so on. However, these students *can* get major points from conversations and stories, as long as their listening task is not too long or interrupted, and the material listened to is not boring, too detailed, or too descriptive (with irrelevant information) (for a review, see Zentall, 2006).

In expressive skills, children with the combined subtype of ADHD in general education typically *talk more* than other children (showing verbal hyperactivity; see Chapter 10), but more relevant to this chapter on attention is the *quality* of their language. Language impairment exists in 35–50% of children at risk for ADHD and in about 90% of children with ADHD selected from clinical populations (see Redmond, 2004). Some of these deficits can be described as the social or pragmatic aspects of language. Compared with typical students, students with ADHD make more off-task comments, interrupt more often, are poorer at turn taking, and show poorer organization in their language. They also make more sequencing errors, use more ambiguous referents, and make more changes in the focus of their play and their conversational topics. However, these children also produce less language with fewer idea units, provide insufficient information, and make fewer requests for information when they are asked to talk about a specific topic. Decreased language can be explained by the difficulties children with ADHD have with holding sequences of related information in mind (e.g., while waiting for a turn to talk). We do know that picture cues and TV programs (without toy distractors) can improve their storytelling performance (e.g., in production and in relaying story goals and outcomes) to the level of typical peers (Freer et al., 2011; Zentall, 1988). That is, cues and visual prompts may reduce the requirements for verbal working memory; this has implications for accommodations.

## Academic

Academic deficits and school-related problems tend to be most pronounced in the subtypes of ADHD marked by inattention (APA, 2000, p. 88), and the more severe the behavioral/attentional symptoms, the greater the reading/math difficulties (Barry et al., 2002). Inattention could also explain the lower achievement test scores of girls with the inattentive subtype (but not those of boys) (DuPaul et al., 2006).

Most researchers agree that poor academic performance is secondary to the attention problems of students with ADHD. Primary academic problems are more typical of students with LD or ID. Students with ADHD have academic difficulties (a) starting tasks (often seen as noncompliance), (b) organizing task information and materials, (c) accuracy (grades), (d) persisting, and (e) producing sufficient work—a set of problems represented by the acronym SOAPP (Zentall, 2006). These difficulties contribute to findings that 80% of these children have learning problems severe enough to cause them to lag several years behind their peers in school, and about a quarter of them have learning disorders severe enough to receive a codiagnosis of LD (Barkley, 2006). Difficulties maintaining attention further reduce their ability to memorize calculations or read long books/stories and reduce the time they spend studying or rereading materials (Lorch et al., 2004). Difficulty attending to **detailed cues** contributes to spelling problems and careless errors in many tasks, such as mathematics.

**Detailed cue:** A part of the whole (e.g., a tree that is one of many that make up the forest).

*Composition, reading, and spelling.* Overall, disorders of written language are twice as common as reading, math, or spelling disabilities (Mayes, Calhoun, & Crowell, 2000), partly because writing compositions requires the use of reading, spelling, handwriting, and spoken language skills. Similar outcomes would be expected from students with ADHD, who score lower than peers in both recall and recognition spelling tests, and 38% of these students have significant spelling disabilities (for a review, see Zentall, 2006). In the area of reading, ADHD and RD co-occur in about 34% of the combined subtype of ADHD (Willcutt, Pennington, et al., 2005). For this ADHD + RD group, reading difficulties are similar to those seen in students with RD (decoding problems leading to comprehension problems), but the problems are magnified (Mayes et al., 2000) due to attentional difficulties. In contrast, students with ADHD *without* RD are as accurate as their peers in reading aloud, but they are slower and more variable in their silent reading (for a review, see Zentall, Tom-Wright, & Lee, in press). In the area of reading comprehension, students with ADHD have problems during the performance of long, descriptive reading passages that have interruptions in the sequence of the narrative and that require keeping events in mind related to "if-then" causality.

*Math.* MLD has been found in children with ADHD (31–60%) at about five times the rate of students in the general population (6–7%) (Zentall et al., in press). Even without LD in math, students with ADHD are less accurate at younger ages with addition and subtraction computational facts when required to "borrow" and with multiplication facts. Among the types of math procedures that are difficult for these children are those that require holding information in mind (e.g., for borrowing, negative numbers) and a greater reliance on finger counting (Zentall et al., in press). More specifically, through middle school, their retrieval speed of math calculations is slower and more variable and is the best predictor of attentional problems. These children also attempt fewer problems than do typical peers, even when the problems are self-paced using a computer, with accuracy and speed feedback, and when there are statistical controls for slower typing speed.

Slower math problem-solving performance can be explained by the poor reading recognition and reading comprehension of many children with co-occurring ADHD and RD. When these factors have been controlled, poorer performance can be explained by requirements to shift sets between two types of operations or actions (e.g., mixed operations) and to work with the nonverbal concepts of time, distance, and sets (for a review, see Zentall, 2007). These students are also less accurate when irrelevant verbal information is added, in contrast to students with math LD, who are more likely to be confused by nonrelevant numbers added to problems (Passolunghi, Marzocchi, & Fiorillo, 2005). Working memory problems are also a significant contributor to multi-step problem performance.

**Skill deficit:** Lack of ability or lack of educational experience in "how" to do something.

*Handwriting.* The typically illegible handwriting of students with ADHD appears to be the result of visual-motor **skill deficits.** Visual-motor skills are less well developed in children with the inattentive subtype than in typical peers and can be assessed as early as preschool (Resta & Eliot, 1994). Poor fine motor skills contribute to slower and less accurate typing, although failure to sustain attention to repetitive practice is

also a factor. The handwriting of students at risk for ADHD has been found to deterio-
rate over time and practice more rapidly than that of peers who were matched on initial
handwriting (Zentall, Falkenberg, & Smith, 1985). The handwriting of students with
the HI subtype has been shown to be even poorer than that of those with the IN subtype
(Resta & Eliot, 1994). In particular, boys develop gross motor skills earlier and often
at the expense of early fine motor skill development, which may explain why students
with the HI subtype have poorer fine motor skills than their IN subtype counterparts.

## SUMMARY OF STRENGTHS AND NEEDS

| *Probable strengths* | *Probable needs* |
|---|---|
| <ul><li>Attention to global or gestalt cues ("big picture" cues)</li><li>Attention to novelty (color, movement, high interest); can be good at multitasking</li><li>Good memory when there are visual cues and when information is precategorized</li><li>Greater performance and persistence on problem solving, divergent thinking, and creative storytelling tasks than peers with similar IQs</li><li>Prefer doing their best on academic tasks (i.e., more competitive goals than students with RD and than peers without disabilities)</li><li>Prefer to learn through their own interests and curiosities and to make independent judgments more than do students with reading problems (Zentall & Beike, 2012)</li></ul> | <ul><li>Accommodations that highlight neutral cues, detail in tasks (e.g., spelling), and the underlying organization of tasks and settings</li><li>Interventions that teach ways to reduce anxiety and emotional overreaction, especially in adolescent girls</li><li>Interventions that teach students how to categorize information for easier recall</li><li>Interventions that teach students how to use visual cues and pictures to reorganize or plan</li><li>Accommodations that allow for breaks or active responding during rote or long tasks</li><li>Accommodations that allow for alternatives to handwriting, such as typing or verbal responding</li><li>Accommodations that tell students exactly what behavior is expected ("do rules") and under what circumstances (structure), while also providing variation in teaching methods, materials, and response opportunities</li><li>Interventions for high school and college students that teach study strategies, note and test taking, outlining, and time management (see Reaser, Prevatt, Petscher, & Proctor, 2007)</li><li>Accommodations in schoolwide homework guidelines that include the amount of time students are expected to work on homework and consequences for failure to complete homework (e.g., turn it in the following day or by Friday without consequence or with a loss of points)</li><li>Accommodations in grading policies based on equivalent content (e.g., information, performance objectives) but with changes in directions, responses required, amount of content per unit time (e.g., breaking assignments into smaller parts) (see Beyda & Zentall, 1998)</li></ul> |

# DISABILITY IN THE CLASSROOM

A case conferencing committee may place a child with ADHD who is eligible for services within the OHI category of IDEA. However, the OHI category is not tied to teacher licensure or funding. Thus, a student with ADHD could be placed with a teacher certified with any exceptionality in any categorical or a multicategorical setting; these placement decisions often vary by state. When categorical placement is needed, students with inattentiveness but not hyperactivity are more often placed in LD classes or in resource rooms (Barkley, DuPaul, & McMurray, 1990). Regardless of placement, school systems spend "approximately $15 to $22 billion per year to educate children with ADHD," some of which may be related to co-occurring conditions (Hart, Massetti, Fabiano, Pariseau, & Pelham, 2011, p. 55).

## Implications for Accommodations in General Education Settings: Tier I

In the past, schools have attempted to change or "normalize" the child with ADHD; this can be seen in studies implementing behavior modification interventions (for a review, see Hart et al., 2011). More recently, the principles of Universal Design for Learning in have been applied in general education settings, where most of these students are educated (Loe &Feldman, 2007). Applications of the principles of UDL have been labeled "antecedent interventions." Typically these involve task or instructional modifications that form the basis of the activity- and novelty-based curriculum (ANBC), which has been field-tested by teachers with effectiveness documented (Zentall & Javorsky, 1997).

The primary components of ANBC are aimed at providing an active and interactive curriculum:

- *Use technology* (e.g., allow use of calculators, especially for multiple step problems in math, and use of computers for keyboarding of compositions). Use computer-paced instruction to improve math and *computer-assisted instruction* (CAI) that involves combinations of stimulation (individual rapid pacing, active engagement, practice with multiple sensory input) and increased information (instructional objectives, incentives, immediate feedback/reinforcement, small chunks of academic material).
- *Provide active responding opportunities.* For example, children with and without ADHD have been found to attempt more words and to read with greater accuracy in an active condition (holding and flipping word cards to be read) than in a passive condition (teacher control of word cards) (Zentall & Meyer, 1987). Furthermore, in that study improved attention and behavioral gains (impulsive errors, talking/noisemaking, activity) were seen in the active

conditions only for the ADHD group. In addition, *reading aloud* has been shown to improve the comprehension performance of students with ADHD relative to reading silently (for a review, see Zentall et al., in press).

- *Increase opportunities for activity* (recess) *between lessons* to improve duration and focus of attention and reduce fidgeting (for a review of the empirical data, see Ridgway, Northup, Pellegrin, LaRue, & Hightshoe, 2003).
- *Reduce delays* by providing self-paced instruction (Tseng, Henderson, Chow, & Yao, 2004).
- *Use classwide peer tutoring* (CWPT), with the entire class divided into two teams and individuals taking turns tutoring one another (e.g., Greenwood, Horton, & Utley, 2002). Correct responding on the first attempt achieves two points, whereas incorrect responding achieves feedback and another chance to answer the question for one point (for a review, see DuPaul et al., 2006).

The secondary components of the ANBC are intended to alter the nature and timing of task performance:

- *For selective attention tasks,* increased practice helps, but since these students avoid repetition, provide opportunities to practice tasks at different time periods or days (distributed practice), or change the nature of the information by chunking or grouping similar categories of information, using global cues (e.g., analogies), or by visually highlighting important information. For example, these students performed better on spelling with color added to inconsistent sound/symbol letters (e.g., in the word *receipt*) than when added randomly (Zentall, 1989; Zentall & Kruczek, 1988). Similarly, color-highlighted operation signs have been found to improve math accuracy relative to a nonhighlighted condition (Kercood & Grskovic, 2009).
- *For working memory,* visual cues (e.g., pictures) can be used as prompts to tell or write stories. It is also helpful to reduce the demands of sustained attention through the use of interesting or action-oriented books, chapters rather than whole reports, and short poetry rather than long narratives. For multi-step math problems, students will need ordered steps that can be checked off. For tests, they may need to memorize these steps with single words that are set to a favorite tune, such as Twinkle twinkle little star.
- *For sustained attention,* reduce time on task (e.g., completing small components of an exam or a composition on successive days) and reduce the length of instruction and repetition. Add novelty directly to parts of tasks. For example, research has found that children with ADHD produced more correct addition problems with computer-administered colored numbers and movement than with black numbers on a gray computer screen and when problems were printed on brightly colored cards relative to performance on

gray cards (Lee & Zentall, 2002). When information from a light source (e.g., contrasts, transparencies, shadows) was added to geometric figures to be calculated and compared to geometric figures presented with only a single value and no input from the light source, students with ADHD actually performed better than their peers (Kang & Zentall, 2011). The addition of auditory stimulation (but not conversational noise) may also be useful: Boys with ADHD have been found to perform more problems with greater accuracy with background music than with silence (or with speech)—effects not found for comparison peers (Abikoff, Courtney, Szeibel, & Koplewicz, 1996). In reading tasks, active verbs, unfamiliar characters, surprising story endings, and vivid adjectives have been shown to improve the reading comprehension of boys with ADHD but not that of their classmates (Beike & Zentall, 2012). Casey is a good example of this: "Casey's behaviors avoid reading comprehensions tasks (head hanging and ignoring the teacher) . . . [yet] Casey also loves to read, when the content is interesting to her. She likes reading romance and adventure stories."

A third component of ANBC involves altering the environment and the consequences to the child from the environment:

- *For behavioral management,* reward effort and persistence and gradually increase expectations with self-graphing (self-monitoring/self-instruction) for skills that are inconsistently performed (i.e., **performance deficits**). For middle school students with ADHD, mirrors in a "homework station" improved homework production to levels equivalent to their peers (Hall & Zentall, 2000). Mirrors were especially beneficial for those children with ADHD who looked at the mirrors (i.e., were "distracted") and less beneficial for those who did not, relative to comparison children (Zentall, Hall, & Lee, 1998). Applications of this research could be made in small-group settings. Mirrors increase attention to the self and also appear to bring a child's own behavioral standards to the forefront, but they are effective only when the student knows what to do or knows the relevant standards (Zentall et al., 1998).

**Performance deficit:** Lack of motivation or attentional ability to sustain effort to an area the child already has the skills to perform.

## Implications for Interventions in Small-Group and Individual Settings: Tiers II and III

### Tier II

- *For working memory,* use technology or intensive computer training with graduated practice involving holding information in mind (e.g., 5 weeks of practice). This approach has been shown to improve verbal and visual-spatial WM capacity and to improve (a) listening capacity relative to a control condition, (b) math reasoning at a 6-month follow-up to baseline, and (c) reading comprehension. However, no improvements in IQ or reading recognition have been seen with this technique (Dahlin, 2011; Holmes, Gathercole, & Dunning, 2009). Assistive reading software (Kurzweil 3000) that presents a combined visual and auditory input of text with highlighting and provides note-taking options has been found to produce faster reading for longer periods of time and with less fatigue for college students with attentional problems, but only those students with very poor comprehension improved their reading comprehension (Hecker et al., 2002).

- *To improve memory,* giving students brief experience sorting words they need to remember has been found beneficial, with performance improving to a level equivalent to non-ADHD peers (August, 1987). The use of materials that are precategorized by time chronology, topics, or cause-and-effect relationships has also shown some success.

- *For off-task behavior,* teach self-monitoring strategies. Asking children to self-monitor their task-unrelated thoughts as they proceed through a practice task has been shown to improve their immediate memory scores (French, Zentall, & Bennett, 2003). That is, when students know they need to report their numbers of task-unrelated thoughts (internal interferences), this appears to act as a form of self-monitoring. Self-monitoring also has applications for producing improved quality of written language (Linemann & Reid, 2008).

*Tier III.* Psychostimulant medication increases neurotransmission of impulses (DuPaul, Ervin, Hook, & McGoey, 1998), specifically through increases in dopamine, which produce sufficient brain activation needed for sustaining attention and working memory (McNab et al., 2009). This intervention is considered Tier III because most students with characteristics of ADHD can be successfully accommodated in the classroom without medication. However, for those students currently taking medication, teachers can help by monitoring the effects and side effects of medication, such as irritability, sadness, tics, and stress, in collaboration with other personnel and parents. While it is important to remember that each student has a right to privacy about his or her medications, it is also important to communicate to the child that the pill can improve attention, but it is the child's effort and not the pill that is responsible for improved skills. Table 9.2 presents the pros and cons associated with the use of medications by children with ADHD.

Assessments of the use of medication and behavioral interventions, singly and in combination, have initially shown promising findings, but they have failed to show greater long-term gains than routine care. In the 1990s, the National Institute of Mental Health's Collaborative Multisite Multimodal Treatment Study of Children with ADHD (known as the MTA study) compared three treatment groups: a group that received carefully managed and monitored medication treatment, a

**Table 9.2**    Pros and Cons of the Use of Medications as an Intervention for ADHD

| Pros | Cons |
|---|---|
| • Medication is the single and most effective intervention for inattention and excessive behavior for 75–80% of ADHD students, with performance improvements on rote practice tasks.<br>• Children with co-occurring behavioral disorders or LD show gains in reading and math achievement with medication (Zentall et al., in press), but medication must be used in conjunction with effective instruction and behavioral strategies and cannot be considered a "magic pill."<br>  ○ Use of medications has been associated with decreased absenteeism and retention in grade (Advokat, 2009). However, these findings could be related to sample bias. | • Approximately 25–35% of students are nonresponders, and some have risk factors (e.g., heart issues, possible stimulant abuse) that preclude the use of some types of medications. (Nonstimulant medications include atomoxetine, clonidine, guanfacine, desipramine, deprenyl, and bupropion.)<br>• Children without co-occurring learning or behavioral disabilities have *not* demonstrated gains in math or reading achievement in response to medication (Zentall et al., in press).<br>• No long-term gains in social or vocational outcomes have been documented.<br>• In general, long-term compliance with medication regimens is poor. |

group that received intensive behavior therapy, and a group that received a combination of the two. The control group received routine community care. Some of the study's findings were as follows:

- At 36 months (22 months after treatments stopped), there were no longer any treatment group differences in ADHD/ODD symptoms or in any other aspects of children's functioning.
- An 8-year follow-up study of 21 different measures was assessed for 436 of the original 579 participants, who now ranged in age from 13 to 18. Findings were that all treatment groups of children maintained improvements relative to baseline? but that none of the treatment groups was more or less successful than any of the others. In addition, there was a steady decline in the use of medication by the children over time.

However, more recent studies (conducted in 2008 and 2009) have reported higher math and reading achievement for students with ADHD who had self-selected to continue the use of medication beyond a year. Unfortunately, these effects could be explained by initial differences between those students who continued to use medication versus those who discontinued (e.g., in IQ or initial response to medication; for a review, see Zentall et al., in press). Thus, the gains in achievement documented from the use of stimulant medication are short-term and primarily for those students with co-occurring LD.

## Long-Term Outcomes

Clinically referred students are three to seven times more likely than typical peers to be retained at grade level, to be suspended/expelled, or to eventually require special education services (LeFever, Villers, Morrow, & Vaughn, 2002), with significantly higher dropout rates and increased frequency of failure. For example, it is estimated that 37% of students with ADHD do not finish high school versus 9% of teenagers in the general population, and only 5% of students with ADHD get a college degree in comparison with 35–40% of typical students (Barkley, 1998). (Retention in grade has been reported for 72% of the IN subtype versus 17% of the HI subtype; Lahey et al., 1994.) Students with the combined subtype typically obtain about 2 years less schooling than their peers and have poorer vocational outcomes, such as lower-ranking positions (APA, 2000, p. 88). On the positive side, those children with only the IN subtype are *less* likely than those with the HI subtype to develop **delinquency,** to be expelled from school, or to become substance abusers (see Wenar & Kerig, 2006).

**Delinquency:** Involvement with the legal system.

Adults with the combined subtype are more likely to make changes of vocation, residence, and schools attended than comparison populations; they are more likely to be fired and do not rise up the economic or employment ladder as quickly as others from the same neighborhoods with the same IQ and educational level. Many adults with ADHD need vocational support, such as job coaches.

*Continuance.* For those with the combined subtype who are identified in elementary age levels, ADHD persists into adolescence for 35–80% and into adulthood for 49–66% (Advokat, 2009).

## CHAPTER SUMMARY

- ADHD is separated into two subtypes: inattentive (ADHD-IN) and hyperactive/impulsive (ADHD-HI); a third combined group is also recognized (ADHD-C). Each of these is formally defined by *DSM-IV-TR,* whereas IDEA defines only ADHD-C under the category of OHI. This chapter summarizes information on ADHD-IN and ADHD-C subtypes, which frequently co-occur with LD and internalizing disorders, such as depression.

- The prevalence of this disability is 8–20% of students within general education settings. Elementary school boys and girls with the inattentive subtype are identified at similar rates, whereas the ADHD-C subtype overrepresents boys four to one.

- The etiology of ADHD is genetic, with environmental factors (e.g., maternal smoking, ingestion of lead), explaining only one in five cases. Genetics may specifically contribute to the temperament trait of underarousal in these children, which results in their seeking stimulation through changes in attentional focus of thought, task, and activity. Functional assessments reveal that the triggers or antecedents of inattention for this group are (a) long, repetitive, familiar, and "boring" tasks; (b) tasks that require delays, sustained attention, and holding information in mind; and (c) tasks involving visual search within an embedded context. Students with other types of disabilities will also show inattention (e.g., GT, ID, LD), but only when their tasks are too easy (GT) or too difficult (ID, LD).

- Educators can informally identify children with ADHD through observations of their behavior, which is often off task and task avoidant at the start of assignments and especially over time. Language is another indicator, with more frequent changes of conversational topics. Also, these children produce less information when asked to talk about one subject but they talk too much or too loudly when freely conversing and associating ideas.

- Children with the IN subtype are more likely to show internalizing social behavior than are those with the HI subtype. In addition, those with the IN subtype are more likely to overreact emotionally.

- Lower intellectual functioning is not common to these students, unless they have been identified in clinical settings or have co-occurring LD. EF deficits have been documented and may contribute to these children's difficulties in planning and anticipating the consequences of their actions, similar to other mild disability categories. Creativity and originality have also been documented.

- Academic failure is a common outcome of attention problems. Generally, students with ADHD have difficulty starting tasks, organizing task information, accurately responding to and persisting on tasks, and producing sufficient work. In both math facts and reading decoding, they exhibit slower and more variable performance than their non-ADHD peers. Whereas accuracy of reading aloud is not a problem for students with ADHD (without RD), accuracy of basic math calculations is. Math problem-solving difficulties are typically explained by verbal factors related to reading, although some deficits may be found with nonverbal concepts of time, distance, and the like. Finally, even more severe problems may be found in written compositions; some of this is due to poor handwriting, organizational problems, and the need to sustain focus on one topic.

- Accommodations should include active response opportunities, novel assignments, frequent feedback, computers for keyboarding and performing rote operations, highlighted or reduced directions, picture cue prompts, and shortened or subdivided assignments.

Educational interventions include training aimed at improving working memory, categorization strategies, and self-monitoring of attention and of performance.

## CHAPTER QUESTIONS

1. Create an accommodation plan for a second grader who daydreams so much that she cannot complete the spelling of a single word without being redirected—she even daydreams in small teacher-led groups.

2. How can you identify what is relevant within a task or skill to be achieved? For example, what is the relevant distinction between bossiness and leadership, and how could you highlight these differences for a child with combined ADHD?

3. Why are students with the IN subtype of ADHD and students with LD more likely than other children to experience anxiety and depression?

4. Inattention seems to be a marker of children with mild disabilities; can you explain why this is so?

5. What kinds of tasks increase the likelihood of inattention for students with the IN subtype?

6. How is working memory related to sustained attention?

7. How can educators help children to get "on track"?

8. How can educators help children to stay "on track"?

## TRUE/FALSE AND MULTIPLE-CHOICE

1. Children with ADHD produce better work in handwriting when they are asked to redo it immediately.

2. An educator's knowledge about the heritability or genetic basis of a disability is more important than his or her knowledge about the situational dependence and response to intervention of that disability.

3. Talking too much when asked to talk and talking too little spontaneously are typical for ADHD.

4. Children who have problems with sustained inattention
   A. get bored faster than other children
   B. have difficulty with repetitive and long tasks
   C. have difficulty directing their attention to neutral cues

    D. have difficulty directing their attention to internal cues

    E. A & B

    F. C & D

5. Children who have difficulty with selectively attending

    A. change activities frequently

    B. have problems with maintaining routines

    C. are less aware of feelings, strategies, intentions, and so on

6. Students with the inattentive subtype of ADHD, more than the hyperactive-impulsive subtype

    A. have academic skill problems

    B. are less likely to be disruptive

    C. are more likely to have specific learning disabilities

    D. all of the above

7. Preferred activities offered as rewards for students with the inattentive type of ADHD might include

    A. time to daydream

    B. talking time

    C. creative projects

    D. all of the above

8. Psychostimulant medication is especially useful for ADHD students who have problems with

    A. selective attention tasks that have embedded information, like spelling

    B. sustained attention tasks that are rote and repetitive, like math facts

    C. neither A nor B

    D. A & B

9. Placing students with ADHD away from windows and doors is a *not* a good accommodation, since these students need additional stimulation, especially during repetitive tasks.

## SHORT ANSWER

1. Ignores important stimuli and _____ attends to what is novel

2. Inattention is a *primary* characteristic of ADHD and a _____ characteristics of LD.

3. Loss of function (academic/social/vocational) is also termed an _____.

4. "Rule-outs" in a definition, which describe what a disability is not, are also termed _____.

5. A child who gets bored quickly may fail to _____ attention.

## PROBLEM-BASED CASE APPLICATIONS AND QUESTIONS

### CASE STUDY 9.1: ZEB

*"Watching the frog."*
(adapted from a report submitted by Konie Hughes)

*Background.* Zeb is an 8-year-old male in second grade at a local elementary school. He is diagnosed with LD in reading, math, and written language. He is also labeled ADHD–inattentive subtype. His mother has withdrawn his medication, preferring that he spend more time receiving special educational services without medication. The general education teacher has complained about Zeb's lack of attention, arguing, and disturbances during whole-class instructions, not knowing the homework assignments, and not completing these assignments.

Zeb's positive attributes are his outgoing personality, his personableness, and his desire to please the teacher. Teachers and students generally like him. Although he struggles in all academic areas, he likes math. He is an active participant, particularly during instruction in math, and continually attempts to complete his work. He likes the computer and recess, and he was very interested in a frog that was in the classroom.

### Behavioral Observation

The general education classroom contains approximately 24 students, with student desks grouped in rows of two. Generally the teacher is calm, has a good rapport with students, and encourages engagement. The resource room is divided into sections, with desks and bookshelves delineating teaching areas. The special education teacher works with one group in one area; in another, a child works at a group of desks with a paraprofessional; and two corners are arranged for small groups, with a paraprofessional working with each one. Zeb works in one of these groups at a table with one other student and a paraprofessional.

*Setting 1: Transitions*

Transitioning into a task or waiting is difficult for Zeb, whether he's at his seat or in the hallway. He's in constant motion (getting out of his seat, playing with things, moving his desk, touching the walls) or talking and having fun (using a book as a puppet, turning on a water faucet by leaning into it). As students from other classes enter the room for ability-group lessons, Zeb acts as the class greeter (he sits nearest the door).

| Behavior | Antecedent | Response | Payoff |
|---|---|---|---|
| He puts paper into folder and puts it away. | Transition: end of task | | Get competence |
| While waiting to go to resource room and sitting at desk, he gets out of seat and plays with math manipulatives in cart. | Transition | | Get stimulation: activity |
| The teacher tells kids to sit down and wait; he pushes his desk and seat around. | Transition | Peer response | Get self-determination: control |
| As soon as he sits down, he asks to go to bathroom. Told no and told to listen. He follows directions. | Transition | | Avoid task |
| Sitting in hallway. Folds up book and uses it as puppet's mouth talking to others and students exiting bathroom. | Transition | Peer response | Get stimulation: fun Get relatedness |
| Standing in line, he leans on the water faucet, turning it on. | Transition | | Get stimulation: fun |

## Setting 2: Whole Group

Whole-group instruction of the Daily Oral Language (DOL) worksheet (total of 10 short problems in language and math); math occurs with the teacher at the front of the room going over the assignment and asking questions. Zeb appears not to be listening, because he is constantly moving in his seat, playing with objects, talking, or making noises. However, he does hear more than is at first apparent, because he raises his hand at times in response to questions and follows *some* of the instructions. He isn't able to stay with the teacher step by step. I have noticed in math that he will go ahead and write an answer to a problem he can do, which is further down the worksheet, while the teacher and class work on an earlier problem. When he finally notices that the class has finished the earlier problem, he simply looks at his neighbor's sheet and copies. Of course this disrupts that student, because Zeb is talking and leaning into him. If he needs an eraser, he'll grab the pencil from the neighbor's hand or talk out about needing an eraser, disturbing everyone around him. They don't complain and quickly accommodate him! When he starts talking inappropriately (about lunch or whether he likes another student) during a lesson, his neighbors will turn to him but largely don't respond.

During a whole-group instruction of writing, the teacher stands at the front of the class as she goes over sentences, asking students what corrections are needed. The students have the assignment on their desks; they make the corrections on their papers as the teacher guides them. Again, this requires a lot of attention, listening, and waiting. Zeb's behavior—whistling, singing, and pushing his desk around—serves two purposes: avoidance of the prolonged listening and waiting task, and getting stimulation, both sensory and activity. Unless he disrupts the entire class (singing or whistling), the teacher ignores most of his behavior. When he does disrupt the class, he gets a consequence (pulls a card), but this seems ineffective.

| *Behavior* | *Antecedent* | *Response* | *Payoff* |
|---|---|---|---|
| Throws down pencil and talks to neighbor: given a warning. | Daily Oral Language worksheet | Teacher response | Avoid task |
| As the teacher talks and asks questions, he whistles and is told to pull a card. | Correcting sentences | Teacher response and punishment | Avoid task <br> Get stimulation: sensory |
| Plays with desk, picks it up, and slides around on chair. Starts singing and is told to pull second card. | Correcting sentences | Teacher response and punishment | Avoid task <br> Get stimulation: activity |
| Raises his hand and tries to answer question but answers incorrectly. As the teacher talks with other students, he sticks his pencil into a crayon and waves it around. | Daily Oral Language worksheet | | Get competence <br> Get stimulation: sensory |
| Follows direction to get dry-erase board. | Following directions | | Get competence |
| Talks to neighbor and sits on knees as he is told to clear the board; instead plays with manipulatives. | Math calculations | | Get self-determination: control |
| Told to count with teacher; he has marker top in his mouth and watches an adult on the computer in the corner. | Math oral calculation | | Avoid task <br> Get stimulation: sensory |

NOTE: All activities involve listening.

### Setting 3: One-on-One

In the resource room Zeb gets structured reading and writing. The paraprofessional guides him in a reading program that begins with sounds or words that she models, followed with responses from Zeb. Next he reads aloud a short story and then independently completes a worksheet while she helps another student at the table. I notice that he can sit still for longer periods of time even during these shorter and more varied lessons, and there isn't anything to play with other than a pencil. Generally, there is nothing on the table for him to grab. However, one day a teacher placed a frog in a container on the table; he kept touching it and asking questions about it until the teacher threatened to take it away.

The paraprofessional continually has to redirect him, as he still likes to talk and initiate inappropriate conversations with her (questioning whether she smokes, wanting to get on the computer when someone else has earned it). As he completes one worksheet, she gives him positive reinforcement and gives him another worksheet. He is still easily distracted by anyone entering the room and by changes in the music. In this setting he really doesn't have to be organized because he sits at a table and the teacher places the necessary materials in front of him.

| Behavior | Antecedent | Response | Payoff |
|---|---|---|---|
| He follows paraprofessional's directions as she points to words. | Guided reading | | Get competence |
| Told to sit down and do work after getting Kleenex. He begins talking to paraprofessional. | Worksheet | Teacher response | Avoid task<br>Get self-determination: control |
| After three more prompts to begin a second page, he keeps touching the frog container, asks paraprofessional if she smokes, and asks again about the frog. | Worksheet | Teacher response | Avoid task<br>Get self-determination: control |
| Gets reminder to get back to work; asks if he can get on computer when he's finished after hearing another student has earned it. | Worksheet | Teacher response | Avoid task<br>Get self-determination: control |
| Paraprofessional working with another student; he talks out, giving the answer. | Worksheet | | Get competence |

## ABC Analysis

### Consequences

Effective strategies:

- One-on-one/personal attention
- Frequent verbal reinforcement
- Short segments of instruction
- Incentives (recess, computer)

Ineffective strategies:

- Punishing bad behavior (pulling card)
- Ignoring bad behavior
- Responding to bad behavior (reminders)

Zeb's overall payoffs were 71% gets and 31% avoids (some behaviors had more than one payoff (see Figure 9.2). Whole-group instruction was the setting where Zeb had the highest frequency of payoffs—avoiding and escaping tasks that required a lot of listening, waiting, and sustained attention. He successfully avoided most of these tasks and replaced task performance with seeking stimulation.

**Figure 9.2** Zeb's Payoffs Within Three Settings

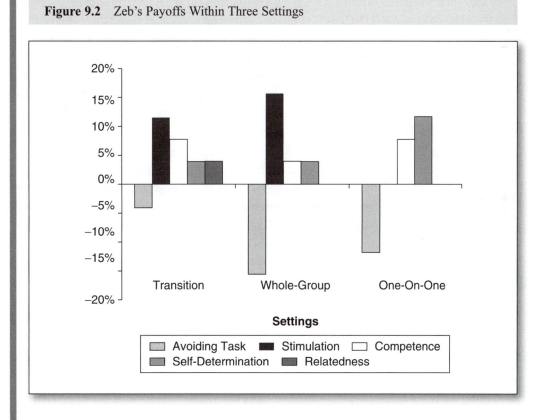

Zeb's high-frequency payoffs were as follows:

1. Avoiding tasks (leftmost bar in Figure 9.2) that required sustained listening, attention, or waiting and also at the same time getting stimulation: sensory (whistling), activity (pushing his desk around, playing with objects), and fun (using book as a puppet, turning on water faucet).

2. Getting self-determination: control (talking, asking questions).

3. Getting competence: mastery (attempting to answer questions, following directions, giving answers out of turn).

## Diagnosis Versus ABC Analysis

Zeb's behavior meets the six minimum criteria of *DSM-IV-TR* for ADHD-IN. Zeb has problems, particularly in the general education classroom. He is unable to stay focused on instructions and tasks and completing his work, as other children are able to do. He struggles to sustain attention on a task in the resource room until an adults gives him a direct reminder to return to his task. During transitions, he continually needs and finds stimulation to get through difficult waiting times. Another requirement for a diagnosis of ADHD-IN is that the behaviors be present in more than one setting; Zeb does have behavior problems at home, and his mother would rather have the school address these difficulties. Furthermore, teacher interviews support the criterion that his disability affects his social and academic functioning. Zeb does exhibit emotional outbursts, has poor academic performance, and has conflicts with adults and peers. Though other children seem to like Zeb, perhaps they are also afraid of him because he can be aggressive.

Zeb's negative behavior increases during instruction in subject areas that give him the most trouble (math and writing) and when he must listen during group discussions. Sustained attention problems are also apparent in math, even though Zeb likes math. In the observation period, he avoided counting with the class, instead getting stimulation from the marker top in his mouth (and watching an adult using the computer). During writing his need for stimulation (and avoiding the writing task) increased, and he reacted by disrupting the class and getting negative teacher responses (and pulling two cards).

Zeb accomplished more and was not disruptive in the resource room even with difficult subjects. The difference was getting one-on-one instruction and shorter amounts of instruction (which, in turn, required shorter amounts of listening). Immediate incentives were in place for him—smiley faces for good behavior, a reward of recess for finishing his homework, getting to use the computer when he finished work, and watching the frog.

Zeb avoided transitioning into a lesson by (a) asking to go to the bathroom right at the start of the lesson, (b) trying to get control by asking to do something else, or (c) by talking to the teacher or to students around him. Transitions allow him to get needed stimulation, without getting into trouble, through activity (getting out of his seat or moving his seat back and forth, going over and playing with the math manipulatives). Sitting and waiting in the hallway for 15 minutes to go into the library wasn't boring for Zeb; he stimulated himself and got others' attention by using his book as a puppet. Standing in line next to the doorway, he had some last-minute excitement by leaning into the water faucet and turning it on.

## Interventions

Interventions with Zeb are aimed at teaching him replacement behavior so that he can get stimulation appropriately (social stimulation from peer tutoring) and at increasing his approach behaviors in subjects that he avoids (writing). Zeb needs to change his behavior in small steps and receive incentives that he enjoys. Possible incentives include opportunities for adult and peer social interactions, time on the computers, and time with the classroom's frog. He is active, so he might respond to earning activity time to draw or play with manipulatives, clay, or Legos. Finally, he likes getting smiley faces, so earning stickers toward a longer-term goal would be worthwhile. Giving Zeb a job to be in charge of some classroom supplies will help him feel important and successful and help him learn skills in organization.

> *Step 1:* Zeb will complete a self-monitoring chart of on-task behavior during one lesson of his choice (DOL, writing, or math). Reinforcement with smiley faces will be given for appropriate behavior—to be defined for him.

> *Step 2:* Zeb will be assigned a peer tutor during lessons to help him check his work.

> *Step 3:* Zeb will spend time with the teacher learning to identify the times he is frustrated, learning appropriate ways to deal with those times, and learning to ask for help.

> *Step 4:* Zeb will be in charge of supplies (pencils and erasers) for the classroom.

A peer tutor for Zeb will not only make it easier for the teacher to spend time helping other children but will also address Zeb's copying and disruption (talking and grabbing). A peer tutor should be a good role model for Zeb, and since he is very sociable, he should do well with this personal attention. The self-monitoring chart of on-task behavior has been shown to be helpful for students with ADHD and should reduce troublesome behaviors and allow frequent feedback. Zeb will be in charge of handing out or collecting papers during assignments or transitions to allow activity for him.

## Case Questions

1: Under what conditions does Zeb show the greatest amount of disruptive behavior? What might explain Zeb's relatively high level of avoiding tasks, even in a one-on-one setting? What specific tasks are difficult for Zeb?

2: In what ways does Zeb show creativity/originality?

3: What is the focus of Zeb's teacher's writing instruction?

4: What is a topic that Zeb might enjoy learning and writing about? How might a teacher accommodate and intervene in the instruction of composition to improve Zeb's writing difficulties?

5: How might a teacher accommodate for Zeb's reading difficulties beyond teacher or peer individual tutoring?

## Chapter 10

# Attention Deficit Hyperactivity Disorder

## Hyperactive/ Impulsive Subtype

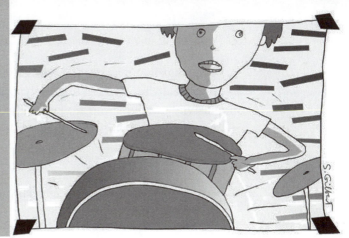

Children with hyperactivity and impulsivity are easy to notice, interesting to watch, and difficult to ignore; they are labeled the hyperactive/impulsive (HI) subtype of ADHD (ADHD-HI). They are often identified at an early age as children who bounce higher and faster than other children and typically against rather than with the natural flow and order of situations. One teacher described a student with ADHD-HI as "having enough energy to light a city." However, in classrooms, they can be disruptive and at increased risk for developing aggression. If they have the combined subtype, they may have both social and academic impairments, but those with the pure HI subtype are more likely to have social impairments. Of course, there are some children with milder forms of ADHD who have no impairment or who are able to compensate and do not receive services.

## FORMAL IDENTIFICATION

### Definitions

#### IDEA

A case conferencing committee may place a child with ADHD-HI who is eligible for services under the OHI category of IDEA, as stated in Chapter 9. In practice, students with HI, especially when there is aggression, are often placed in classes for students with behavioral disorders (Barkley et al., 1990). If eligibility is first assessed and the student fails to qualify under IDEA, he or she will be referred to a Section 504 committee for accommodations to be provided within the

**Figure 10.1** A child with ADHD–Hyperactive/Impulsive Subtype performs well when actively responding.

general education classroom. There are no specific tests for this disorder; assessment is usually based on ratings of the primary characteristics of hyperactivity and impulsivity by adults who are familiar with the child (teachers and parents) across settings and in comparison to other children of the same age (Neef et al., 2005).

### DSM-IV-TR

*DSM-IV-TR* (APA, 2000, p. 92) defines ADHD-HI as follows:

*Defining characteristics:* Six (or more) of the following symptoms of hyperactivity/impulsivity that have persisted for at least 6 months to a degree that is maladaptive and inconsistent with developmental level:

*Hyperactivity:*

- Often fidgets with hands or feet or squirms in seat
- Often leaves seat in classroom or in other situations in which remaining seated is expected
- Often runs about or climbs excessively in situations in which it is inappropriate (in adolescents or adults, may be limited to subjective feelings of restlessness)
- Often has difficulty playing or engaging in leisure activities quietly
- Is often "on the go" or often acts as if "driven by a motor"
- Often talks excessively

*Impulsivity:*

- Often blurts out answers before questions have been completed
- Often has difficulty awaiting turn
- Often interrupts or intrudes on others (e.g., butts into conversations or games)
- *Impairment:* Social or academic

*Exclusions and conditions:*

- Characteristics observed before 7 years of age and observed in two or more settings (usually home and school)
- ADHD "is not diagnosed if the symptoms are better accounted for by *another mental disorder* (e.g., Mood Disorder [especially Bipolar Disorder], Anxiety Disorder, Dissociative Disorder, Personality Disorder, Personality Change Due to a General Medical Condition, or a Substance-Related Disorder)" (APA, 2000, p. 91).

## Frequently Occurring Subtypes

*DSM-IV-TR* (APA, 2000, p. 93) describes the subtypes of ADHD:

> *Attention deficit hyperactivity disorder, predominantly hyperactive/impulsive subtype:* Diagnosis of this subtype requires that criteria listed above are met for the past 6 months.

> *Attention deficit hyperactivity disorder, combined type:* See Chapter 9.

## Possible Co-Occurring Conditions

The characteristics of ADHD can be found in more than 30 disorders ranging from sensory disorders to academic, psychological, social, and medical problems. By age 7, 54–67% of children referred to clinics with ADHD are also diagnosed with ODD, and by adolescence, 44–50% may also be diagnosed with CD (Greene, 2006; Loeber, Burke, & Pardini, 2009).

Internalizing symptoms are also present. That is, about one-third of students with ADHD have co-occurring anxiety disorders (Jensen et al., 2001), although such disorders are less frequently observed in students with only HI. Willcutt, Pennington, et al. (2005) found that approximately 34% of students with ADHD–combined subtype had RD, but they found no students with only the HI subtype without RD. In other words, RD is associated with the inattention of the combined subtype.

## Differences Among Related Disabilities

Activity is a better marker in the identification of ADHD than is attention, because inattention characterizes so many other children with mild disabilities. For students with ADHD, it is the degree and **chronic** nature of activity that differentiates it from the appropriate activity of young typical children.

> Toddlers and preschoolers with this disorder differ from normally active young children by being constantly on the go and into everything; they dart back and forth, are "out of the door before their coat is on," jump or climb on furniture, run through the house, and have difficulty participating in sedentary group activities in preschool classes (e.g., listening to a story). (APA, 2000, p. 86)

**Chronic:** Persisting over time. Chronic behavioral problems differ from short-term acute behavioral difficulties.

Sometimes the sports participation of a child will mask HI, as stated by one teacher: "I don't think there's hyperactivity. I don't see that at all. But he's in so many athletic activities, I don't know" (Zentall, 2006, p. 105).

In comparison with children with the IN subtype, those with the HI subtype display more impulsivity and aggressiveness; therefore, students with HI are more likely to be rejected, whereas students with the IN subtype are more often socially neglected. Children who are neglected are just ignored by their peers, whereas children who are rejected receive negative peer feedback, teasing, or abuse. Children with the HI subtype are also more assertive (rather than passive) and more competitive—needing to "best" others and with less of a need to please teachers than students with the inattentive subtype (Carlson, Booth, Shin, & Canu, 2002). (See Table 10.1 for a summary of the differences between the subtypes.) When students with ADHD-HI are given an IDEA-based EBD label as an outcome of these social problems, it is essential that teachers understand the differences between students with ADHD and students with EBD in the types of interventions that are needed. That is, students with ADHD exhibit **sensation-seeking behavior** and have learned inappropriate ways to get the stimulation they need. This is not true of students with CD, who have learned that bullying is a means to achieve competence in a world in which they feel powerless, or for students with ODD, who have learned to avoid task and setting demands.

**Sensation-seeking behavior:** Behavior that is highly variable and produces additional stimulation for the child.

Gifted children are often labeled ADHD because they show similar characteristics of intensity, energy/activity, and task and homework avoidance, especially when presented with nonchallenging/uninteresting tasks (e.g., Beljan et al., 2006) or when they are in "academically understimulating environments" (APA, 2000, p. 91). However, impulsivity, social disorder, and schoolwork problems are not

**Table 10.1**  Comparison of ADHD Subtypes

| Inattentive subtype (IN) | Hyperactive/impulsive subtype (HI)[a] | Combined subtype |
|---|---|---|
| Passivity<br>Cooperativeness<br>Social neglect<br>Learning problems and co-occurring learning disabilities<br>Fine motor problems greater than typical peers<br>Attentional and working memory problems | Hyperactivity (variable activity) and more spontaneous talk<br>Impulsivity and risk taking<br>Aggression<br>Emotional intensity<br>Competitiveness<br>Possible dislike or rejection by peers<br>Fine motor problems (more than IN)<br>Gross motor problems (50%) | Combination of the social and academic problems of the IN and HI subtypes |

a. It should be noted that if the HI subtype is a developmental precursor of the combined and IN subtypes (Lahey et al., 2005), then some of the characteristics observed may reflect developmental differences.

typical of students with pure GT (Zentall, Moon, et al., 2001). (The highly gifted may appear asocial but will interact well with older peers and adults.) Furthermore, the memory, long attention span, advanced language development, and preferences for cognitive and language stimulation found in gifted children do not characterize students with ADHD, unless they have co-occurring GT. (For further information on differential diagnosis, see Chapter 7.)

Observers often mistake the hyperactivity in ADHD-HI students for the repetitive activity of students with anxiety disorders or with autism spectrum disorders; this is because they fail to note the directionality of activity. For students with hyperactivity, activity is approach (moving toward others) and variable (not repetitive, unless there is a co-occurring anxiety disorder or the child is taking high doses of psychostimulant medication), in contrast to the repetitive and often socially avoidant activity of children with ASD or children with anxiety disorders. Students with ADHD seek change (novelty), whereas students with ASD seek sameness and familiarity, even though they can demonstrate periods of rage and aggression when placed in crowded, noisy, or unstructured contexts (cafeteria, recess, hallways, assemblies). Thus, taking into account context and type of activity should make differential diagnosis easier.

ADHD is also diagnosed in at least half the number of clinic-referred individuals with Tourette's syndrome (see Chapter 15). This may be the case because TS often presents with disturbing sounds and repeated motor movements in classroom contexts. When the two disorders do coexist, the onset of ADHD often precedes TS (APA, 2000, p. 88). For example, the tics of children with ADHD that appear in later school years can be an outcome of high medication doses co-occurring with stressful tasks. In addition, traumatic brain injury can be misdiagnosed as ADHD (see Chapter 8), because hyperactivity and impulsivity often accompany TBI and MTBI.

## Etiology

*Biogenetic* (see also Chapter 9's discussion of the inattentive subtype of ADHD). The frontal regions of the brain are often involved in ADHD, and in adults there is preliminary evidence of reduced dopamine release in the hippocampus and amygdala (Volkow et al., 2007). The heritability of activity level is even higher than that of IQ (Willerman, 1973; Wood, Saudino, Rogers, Asherson, & Kuntsi, 2007). ADHD-HI is also strongly linked to CD, with a shared genetic heritability of 37%, and to ODD, with shared genetic heritability of 42%. However, lower correlations of shared heritability have been found for the combined and IN subtypes (Martin, Levy, Pieka, & Hay, 2006).

*Environmental.* Hyperactivity and impulsivity do not result from the management techniques of families, because the siblings of children with ADHD infrequently have such poor outcomes. That is, children with ADHD are more antisocial and have poorer careers (45%) than their non-ADHD brothers (18%). However, "family, school, and peer influences are also crucial in determining the extent of impairments and comorbidity" (APA, 2000, p. 90). For example, in research with community (nonclinical) samples, preschoolers with hyperactivity and aggression, more than preschoolers with only hyperactivity, had (a) fathers who were more restrictive with their preschoolers and more permissive with their school-age children, (b) siblings who retaliated aggressively, and (c) mothers who reported more physical aggression directed to partners and more verbal aggression received from partners during conflict, and who were less protective of their children (Stormont-Spurgin & Zentall, 1995, 1996). Findings such as these indicate that in families with children who have ADHD, fathers need to learn how to redirect their children's activity rather than restrict or permit it, mothers need to monitor their children closely and even overprotect them from strangers and potential harm, and all family members need to understand that retaliation does not reduce the inappropriate behavior of students with ADHD and can make it worse.

*Functional.* Functional assessments show that the antecedents that trigger sensation-seeking activity, risk-taking behavior, aggression, and increased emotionality (in addition to the attentional biases described in Chapter 9) are as follows: (a) activities and tasks that require *delayed* responding, such as baseball but not soccer, multiple-choice tests, and planning or organizing; (b) *sitting and listening* that do not have active task-response opportunities, even to fidget or doodle while seated, or possibilities for the child to move out of his or her seat; (c) *repetition or overfamiliarity of verbal information;* (d) presentation of material *later* in a day or school year, after a length of time in a given setting, or in a task when novelty has decreased; (e) *familiarity* of a person to whom the child has adapted (e.g., with female more than male teachers); and (f) a setting that allows the child *few opportunities to interact and talk* with others (large groups versus one-on-one) (for recent evidence, see Zentall, 2005b, 2006). These types of **setting-specific responses** support the optimal stimulation theory (see Chapter 9). Briefly, the trait of lower arousal places students with ADHD at the tail end of the arousal distribution as physiologically underactivated (see Chapter 1). Students with ADHD with low arousal will increase sensation-seeking activity, talkativeness, and disruptiveness while also attempting to avoid delays by responding impulsively. Thus, each of their primary characteristics of activity and impulsivity (for inattention, see Chapter 9) functions by self-generating a more optimal state of arousal for the child.

**Setting-specific responses:** Responses that occur only at certain times or in certain situations.

## Prevalence, Gender, Age, and Cultural Factors

*Prevalence.* The pure HI subtype is more typically observed in younger children and represents about 15–18% of the total number of children with ADHD.

*Gender.* Boys are identified more often than girls (a ratio of three or four to one) for the combined subtype; however, 12% of boys and only 2.4% of girls meet the diagnostic criteria for the HI subtype (August et al., 1996; DuPaul et al., 2006). ADHD is missed or misdiagnosed often in girls, and girls with ADHD are often referred to as having a "hidden disorder" (Quinn, 2005, p. 579). Girls' ADHD-related behavior manifests differently from that of boys. For example, boys with ADHD exhibit more gross motor behavior (e.g., running and climbing) than their typical peers, whereas girls with ADHD may not differ from their female peers in gross motor activity in school but are more likely to exhibit small motor movements, such as doodling and being emotional and hypertalkative, with more interrupting, swearing, and changing of conversational topics. "Verbal impulsivity within the social context was the single most defining characteristic of girls with ADHD, in contrast to the motor activity of boys" (Grskovic & Zentall, 2010, p. 181).

*Age.* Identification of ADHD typically occurs in response to **developmental tasks:** (a) during *preschool,* inhibiting activity is a major developmental task; (b) during *elementary school,* attending to tasks is the developmental task; and (c) during *middle and high school,* social development is the major task. For this reason, HI subtype is often identified in preschool and kindergarten, with possible identification of social impairment following later in time.

> **Developmental tasks:** Accomplishments at specific ages (e.g., inhibition of activity, attention, establishing peer networks, developing autonomy).

*Culture.* Underrepresentation of African Americans in the ADHD category has been documented in clinical samples (Jarvinen & Sprague, 1995), but overrepresentation has been reported in school-identified or community samples (Lambert, Sandoval, & Sassone, 1978). One possible explanation is rater bias; alternatively or cojointly, clinical samples represent families of higher economic status with better access to these resources.

# INFORMAL EDUCATOR IDENTIFICATION OF CHARACTERISTICS

## Behavioral

Characteristically, these children move up and down and out of their seats more often at home and at school. Compared with typical children, children with ADHD-HI move their bodies three times more often, move their heads twice as often, and cover four times the area in their movements (Teicher, Ito, Glod, & Barber, 1996). However during their middle school years, gross motor activity declines; at this age these children are characterized by restlessness. In the case study for this chapter, John is a good example:

> Most of his behaviors were throwing or playing with objects, writing either on himself or paper and moving around either at his seat or in the room. John seemed to play with his pencil, book, cell phone, or anything else he could get his hands on. He constantly wanted to be touching, throwing, or playing with anything near him.

Thus, the essential behavioral marker for this subtype is a high rate of sensation-seeking verbal and motor activity (i.e., hyperactivity, hyperverbal). "Talking and moving are related forms of hyperactivity, even though some children talk more and some move more" (Zentall, 2006, p. 89). Until the 1970s, the activity of these children was consistently described in the literature as purposeless, random, undifferentiated, and undirected (for a review, see Zentall, 1975). In current writings, however, words such as, *purposeless* are rarely seen. It is now widely accepted that the activity of these children is functional or goal-directed, even though the child's goal (e.g., to watch a bug) may be different from the goals of the teacher. Subsequently, the label *hyperactivity* changed to *attention disordered* as the field began to examine the second primary characteristic of ADHD.

Currently, difficulty withholding active responses (i.e., impulsivity) has become popular as the third primary characteristic. Impulsivity does contribute to risk taking and "may lead to accidents (e.g., knocking over objects, banging into people, grabbing a hot pan) and to engagement in potentially dangerous activities without consideration of possible consequences (e.g., repeatedly climbing to **precarious** positions or riding a skateboard over extremely rough terrain)" (APA, 2000, p. 86). Minor home accidents often become serious auto accidents when these students are teens.

**Precarious:**
Dangerous or risky.

Barkley (e.g., 2006) has described impulsivity as self-regulatory problems caused by EF deficits (see the subsection on cognitive characteristics of ADHD-IN in Chapter 9). Impulsivity has also been described as "delay aversion" (e.g., Sonuga-Barke, Williams, Hall, & Saxton, 1996)—that is, avoidance of the unpleasantness of delay and its requirement to withhold active responding and therefore to delay access to needed kinesthetic stimulation. Children with ADHD experience time intervals with "nothing to do" as longer than their peers. In the final analysis, it should be noted that only about 35–50% of children have impulsivity (e.g., Willcutt, Doyle, et al., 2005), and thus impulsivity does not explain ADHD but is one of the three primary characteristics of ADHD.

## Social-Emotional

ADHD-HI can lead to social problems, as reported by Peter:

I am 12 years old and I have ADHD, which basically means I'm more aggressive than others. I have very unique qualities, such as I am able to speak out to say what I feel. I like to write letters; I wrote to the President twice and got two letters back and a picture of him. I want to be a lawyer when I grow up, but I think I started too early, because I got in trouble a lot last year for arguing. I like to get to the bottom of things. I try to understand everything.

And I have quicker reactions; I just automatically say something I am thinking. I'm not letting people that call me names get to me right now, because I have a lot more life to go through. I handle a lot of rejection. . . .

I like to travel, play soccer, basketball; I like games and puzzles. I hope to go to Yale when I get to college. . . . I'm not very patient. Well that's me. (quoted in Zentall, 2006, p. 90)

In line with their greater needs for stimulation, children with HI subtype as early as 15 months of age have strong needs for social stimulation (attention, participation, and recognition). However, many of these children *do not know how* to achieve their social goals in school. For example, students with ADHD have been found to have more difficulty than their peers identifying the *nature* of social problems (e.g., child sat alone) and to recall fewer socially appropriate solutions for joining, sharing, resolving conflict, and maintaining relationships (Zentall, Cassady, & Javorsky, 2001). Thus, some specific types of social problems (e.g., being excluded, conflict resolution, maintaining friendships) may be difficult for these students, who do not recognize the underlying variable (e.g., of exclusion).

At least in their early elementary years, they are seen as equally desirable play partners as non-ADHD peers but as less desirable schoolwork partners (less friendly, less considerate, and more aggressive), possibly because they may seek negative, emotional attention and reactions when they do not know how to achieve positive social attention. This can involve noncompliant behavior (see the discussion of co-occurring ODD in Chapter 11 and the case study, John, in this chapter) and the disruptions, interruptions, impatience, bossiness, and argumentative or socially provocative behavior (e.g., negative, assertive, competitive, aggressive). In general, this behavior is *not* relationship enhancing, and children with HI are more often disliked and rejected by their peers than children with the IN subtype (Wheeler & Carlson, 1994). Thus, friendships are at risk; in one study, 30% of teens with ADHD-HI reported that they had no steady friends; for those with co-occurring aggression, 60% had no friends in class. Compared with their non-ADHD peers, these children have more problems during adolescence, with more time spent alone, fewer interpersonal interactions, and less satisfaction with peer, sibling, and adult relationships. Poor social outcomes appear to be even greater for girls. Girls with ADHD-HI do *not* have difficulty initiating friendships, but they do have difficulty sustaining them (for evidence related to the above summary, see Mrug, Hoza, & Gerdes, 2001).

## Cognitive

Information on the IQ, memory, and working memory problems that typically occur for children with IN is presented in Chapter 9. The focus here, in regard to students with HI, is on adaptive intelligence. Sternberg (1985) describes this as "contextual intelligence," which is the ability of an individual to adapt to or to reshape an environment so that it better fits with his or her skills, interests, and values. Students with ADHD do not have the option of selecting more optimal school environments, and young children rarely have control to reshape their environments. When students with ADHD attempt to adapt to their classroom environments, they are successful for short periods of time, but more often their adaptations cause disruption. For example, during research tasks with delays, students with ADHD were observed to have "dived under the table that held the apparatus, danced while watching their reflection in the observation window, and twirled their chairs," in contrast to typical children, who "sat in their chairs waiting for each trial to begin" (Schweitzer & Sulzer-Azaroff, 1995, p. 682). When intelligence is defined as problem solving, children with the HI subtype typically do not have difficulties. For example, students with ADHD used "remarkable" divergent thinking to outwit a computer in a stimulating problem-solving task, and those in a second study used more visual strategies than peers to avoid hazardous consequences in an exciting video game (for a review of evidence, see Zentall, 2006). In other research, students with ADHD contributed to more correct problem solutions in cooperative groups than were observed in groups without these students (Zentall et al., 2011).

## Communication

It has been frequently observed that children with ADHD have *difficulty listening,* especially to lectures. Of course, it is the observer's assumption that a child is not listening simply because the child is moving and does not "look like" he or she is paying attention. As one 6-year-old student with ADHD and giftedness stated, "Mom, if I wasn't paying attention, how come I got all the answers right on the test?" (Zentall, 2006, p. 225).

Although these children may have adequate receptive language skills, as long as the input is short, there is considerable evidence that they differ from other children in *expressive language.* For example, talking out is a frequently observed problem for children with the HI subtype. Compared with peers, they speak at a faster pace and are more talkative, noisier, louder, and more intense (higher and less uniform pitch, with exclamations, swearing, and commands) (for a review and data, see Zentall, 1988, 2006). Talkativeness is especially characteristic of girls (Grskovic & Zentall, 2010). When students with ADHD speak spontaneously, they do not stay on topic; their conversation is steered by associational memory (whatever comes to mind through associations) or visual stimuli within the immediate environment. These children often use their own spontaneous and excessive talking to self-guide their immediate responding by repeating cues, commenting on their own choices, and so on. The *content* of the speech of students with ADHD includes more dysfluencies (substitution errors, revisions), which could be due to the rate and quantity of language produced and is very different from the quantity produced when they are asked to talk (see Chapter 9 for discussion of the communication characteristics of children with the IN subtype).

## Motor, Physical, and Somatic

Children with ADHD or at risk for ADHD have difficulties performing sequences of *fine motor* movements; this characteristic is more often observed in the HI subtype than in the IN subtype (Resta & Eliot, 1994). Fine motor difficulties would explain slower performance on many classroom tasks. Additionally, about half the number of students with ADHD have *gross motor*-coordination dysfunction (Tseng et al., 2004).

## Academic

The behavior of children within the combined subtype of ADHD is often so disruptive that their academic problems are hidden. This is a problem particularly for students with the combined subtype who are similar to the IN subtype, with more learning problems or LD. Overall, it is important to remember that children with HI can learn, and they learn especially well while being active, as long as they are not required to channel energy away from learning to sitting still (which can lead to "disability fatigue").

In addition to needing an active curriculum, these children seek to avoid repetitive activity. This can be a problem in school, because repetitive activity is necessary for the maintenance of routines (e.g., routines of object placement, organization for long-term projects, homework production). Impulsivity (i.e., delay avoidance) has more negative academic outcomes than activity. To the degree that children with HI avoid tasks with delays (e.g., Sonuga-Barke et al., 1996) and have difficulty withholding active responses, they will also have difficulty (a) passively listening, (b) asking for help, (c) choosing among alternative responses (e.g., multiple-choice tests), and (d) planning within a time frame. Repetitive and nonactive tasks contribute to their lack of production in some academic areas and overall lack of motivation in many classroom settings.

## SUMMARY OF STRENGTHS AND NEEDS

| *Possible strengths* | *Probable needs* |
|---|---|
| • Productive, busy, enthusiastic<br>• Sociable, unless they have already received considerable social punishment<br>• Helpful<br>• Spontaneous and funny<br>• Skilled in creative thinking; contribute to creative solutions in small-group problem-solving tasks | • Reinforcement of and interventions for showing good manners<br>• Accommodations during sitting and listening tasks, tasks with repetition and with little movement possible, and tasks that are presented later in the day or are longer<br>• Strategies to handle their own emotional intensity<br>• Strategies to help them learn how to plan and anticipate consequences that do not require added wait time or response repetition<br>• Strategies to help them speak and write in a linear sequence without changing topics<br>• Social interactive stimulation (groups), which can motivate them to listen to their teachers and do as asked<br>• Schoolwide discipline policies that distinguish between serious offenses (fighting) and minor offenses related to the nature of the disability (impulsivity, talking back, running in the halls) (see Beyda & Zentall, 1998) |

## DISABILITY IN THE CLASSROOM

### Implications for Accommodations in General Education Settings: Tier I

Children with the HI subtype without serious social or emotional problems or co-occurring ODD or CD or LD should receive accommodations for ADHD in their general education classroom. Both schoolwide and classroom accommodations are needed:

*Schoolwide:* To the extent possible, time-out should occur in an area of the classroom and not in the hall, in the principal's office, or by taking away recess, unless for safety reasons.

*Classroom:* The principles of the activity- and novelty-based curriculum (ANBC) have been presented in Chapter 9. Accommodations that relate to hyperactivity and impulsivity are generally designed to *redirect* an active behavioral style in the following ways:

- Cognitively (offer choices, provide reasonable challenges)
- Verbally and socially (provide opportunities to talk and engage with peers in line with UDL principles)
- Physically (e.g., allow standing or kneeling to work, movement opportunities in class, from center to center, from seat to seat, and performing class jobs inside the classroom and delivering messages outside of class) (Note that 8-year-old students with and without ADHD have been found to show less appropriate behavior on days without recess than on recess days; Ridgway et al., 2003.)
- Through incorporation of active tasks, with flash cards or response boards, peer tutoring, cooperative groups (Zentall et al., 2011) (For discussion of accommodations for fine motor difficulties, see the section on dysgraphia in Chapter 15.)
- Through teaching of rules about handling delay (e.g., during groups take turns by passing a stick for the "talker"), encouraging the drawing of small pictures to plan compositions or projects, and using fun routines
- Through providing ways for handling delays by allowing students to play with "toys" such as fuzzy pipe cleaners during delay (As one undergraduate, who was student teaching at the time, described: "[She] noticed how well a teenager with ADHD attended to his reading when he could also 'play-with' a small collapsible ruler. When the teacher took away his ruler, he spent the remainder of the period disrupting students around him, and his teacher spent the remainder of her time yelling at him"; Zentall, 2006, p. 81.)

In addition to redirecting, self-monitoring is an EBP. Specifically, three behaviors can be monitored for positive behavioral support: sitting in seat, raising a hand before speaking, and using materials appropriately (Cole, Marder, & McCann, 2000), which can be combined with training in the use of self-monitoring sheets (Gureasko-Moore, DuPaul, & White, 2007). Similarly, using daily report cards involves recording two to three positive goals for the day. Then teachers rate the child's goal attainment following each academic period rather than make summary judgments at the end of the day; the ratings reports are sent home to parents. Frequent early communications with the parent(s) about a child's *positive* gains are essential (for reviews, see Reid, Trout, & Schartz, 2005; Wilens et al., 2002).

**Strategic reprimands:** Short, firm, immediate, and consistent reprimands.

**Behavior modification:** Strategies aimed at changing behavior that involve the application of learning principles, such as the use of reward.

*Behavior modification.* Consequences that are delivered after behavior occurs represent one of the most frequently used educational techniques to produce immediate, short-term gains. Students with ADHD require more intensive consequences (frequent and immediate) than their non-ADHD peers, probably because consequences provide not only social feedback and rewards but also stimulation for these students. Thus, they need a combination of intense positive reinforcers and **strategic reprimands** (short, firm, nonemotional, immediate, and consistent). Table 10.2 provides a summary of guidelines for the use of **behavior modification** with students with ADHD.

**Table 10.2**    Guidelines for Applying the Principles of Behavior Modification for ADHD

| Positive consequences | Negative consequences |
|---|---|
| Note that rewards are by definition those consequences that increase behavior. Stimulation can be very rewarding for these students. Therefore: <br><br> • Praise—with emotion!!!! <br> • Use menus of rewards (i.e., change rewards frequently) as these children more readily habituate to the same rewards. <br> • Provide preferred activities (e.g., classroom jobs) that are **contingent** on appropriate behavior (e.g., you do X and you get Y). <br> • Use charts and self-check lists. <br> • Do not select rewards that are too appealing (distracting), because they become too important (small stickers have been described as "rewarding"). <br> • Positive reinforcement should occur three times more often than negative consequences (DuPaul, 2007) and should follow prosocial behavior. <br> • Low-interest tasks need reinforcement for students with ADHD, whereas for high-interest tasks additional reinforcement is unnecessary. | • Negative consequences (taking away positives or giving negatives) should be used sparingly. It is estimated that 74% of preschool teachers' statements to children with HI are verbal reprimands and task redirections (Alessandri, 1992). <br> • Do *not* use loud or emotional reprimands following aggressive behavior (e.g., no yelling or loud public reprimands), as even viewing these emotional responses can increase aggression specifically in children with ADHD (Meyer & Zentall, 1995). <br> • Use **inclusionary time-out** inside the classroom. Do *not* withdraw activities, such as recess, gym time, or extracurricular activities. <br> • Do *not* punish task-avoidance behavior; it will increase task avoidance. |

## Implications for Interventions in Small-Group and Individual Settings: Tiers II and III

Children with ADHD plus anxiety are more responsive to interventions than are students with pure ADHD or ADHD with co-occurring CD/ODD; students with ADHD plus ODD/CD are more responsive to interventions with medication (Jensen et al., 2001).

Interventions with these students should include direct instruction in the following:

- *Handling delays:* Teach interesting academic routines before tasks (ordering of tasks, pencils) and the rule of "wait a day" before responding to emotional or interpersonal situations or disagreements.
- *Understanding directions:* Teach verbal self-statements: Exactly what are the instructions? Can I restate or rewrite the directions? Do I have a plan to use with these directions?
- *Developing a plan of action or goals:* Do I have a "picture" of the end product?
- *Repairing social interactions:* Teach social routines or manners (e.g., excuse me for interrupting; please; thank you; could I also hold this squeeze ball while I'm listening; I really like to help this way, thanks).
- *Selecting appropriate activity:* Teach **replacement activities** for getting attention or activity stimulation.

**Replacement activities:** Different and socially more appropriate ways to achieve the same goals (e.g., asking questions rather than talking excessively).

*To reduce negative verbal and off-task behavior* in small groups, educators can ask each group member to take turns and justify his or her contribution or solution, and then arrive at a group consensus (teaching rules about when—and how—to interact) (Kuester & Zentall, 2012).

*When monitoring children who are on medication* for behavioral gains, in addition to the attentional gains presented for the IN subtype in Chapter 9, educators should look for short-term gains in peer interactions and in their own interactions with these students (e.g., reduced negative or directive behavior). Other possible short-term gains include less disruption and better child compliance and lower teacher ratings of active/impulsive behavior. (No long-term improvements in social/peer relationships have been associated with the use of medications.)

## Long-Term Outcomes

The long-term outcomes for children with the HI subtype are more likely to be social, whereas the outcomes for children with the inattentive subtype are more likely to be academic and possibly vocational. Some children with the HI subtype are likely to be expelled from school or to develop delinquencies or substance abuse (Wenar & Kerig, 2006). When this subtype also develops aggression or CD, we find greater aggression, rejection, and lower achievement than either group without co-occurring disorders. However, research suggests that ADHD does not predict CD, unless there is already early evidence of CD (Loeber et al., 2009).

It is only at the extremes of the distribution of activity where qualitative differences in functionality (impairment) are generally observed. Thus, it is possible for many children with ADHD-HI to function well socially and academically in the inclusion classroom with few modifications. Furthermore, many of these children learn to channel their needs for activity into sports or other ways of being actively engaged. For girls with ADHD, engagement in extracurricular activities and sports during and after school appears to reduce dysfunction, including delinquent behavior (Booth, Farrell, & Varano, 2008; Grskovic & Zentall, 2010).

*Continuance.* Activity levels change as children with ADHD-HI grow older (e.g., from gross motor movements to restlessness). However, children with high activity will be adults with high activity. Protective long-term factors for both genders include finding occupations that make use of their active style (sales, music, dance/ art, self-employed business, or active roles in fields such as teaching or medicine).

## CHAPTER SUMMARY

- This chapter describes the HI subtype of ADHD, which is formally defined by *DSM-IV-TR* using characteristics related in hyperactivity and impulsivity. IDEA does not separately define the HI subtype, although this subtype can be classified under EBD if the behavioral manifestations include aggression. Internalizing symptoms can also be present. The HI subtype differs from the IN subtype in that it involves more activity, impulsivity, aggressive/assertiveness, and competitiveness. Students with ADHD are similar to students with GT in intensity and activity-disruptiveness during the performance of nonchallenging tasks, but they differ from GT students in impulsivity and social disorder. Differences in the variability of activity and seeking of change that characterize ADHD distinguish it from the repetitive and avoidant activity of ASD and from tic disorders and TS.

- Significant heritability explains activity as a temperament trait. The prevalence of ADHD-HI within the total population of ADHD is only 15–20%. It is identified earlier (preschool) than the IN subtype and at three to four times the rate in boys as in girls. Girls express ADHD somewhat differently from boys, with more small motor movements, talkativeness, verbal impulsivity, and changes of conversational topics.

- Educators can informally identify students with the HI subtype through observations of their activity, which involves two to four times the rate of activity of typical students. These children are also more talkative, noisier, louder, and more intense than their peers. The social responses of these students can be aggressive, disruptive, impatient, bossy, argumentative, and noncompliant. This behavior gets negative social reactions, making it difficult for these children, especially girls, to maintain friendships; the result can be social isolation. Social intelligence may also be less well developed in these children, as indicated by their failure to generate or employ socially appropriate solutions for joining, sharing, resolving conflicts, or maintaining relationships.

- Intellectually, the HI subtype can be found across the normal distribution of IQ from GT to ID, but children with ADHD-HI are typically excluded by definition if they are also ID. Recent evidence indicates that their problem-solving skills may be advanced, especially when problems are presented in novel settings using computers or games. These children also have deficits in fine motor skills that contribute to slowed performance on many academic tasks, and approximately half of students with the HI subtype also have gross motor problems. Because those students with this subtype do not have inattention, they have fewer academic problems than children with the IN subtype, beyond those of handwriting and an avoidance of delays and academic routines. However, overall achievement test scores still indicate specific problems in academic performance (e.g., mathematics).

- Accommodations and Tier I treatments for children with ADHD-HI include adding novelty to the environment and providing an active-response curriculum that is self-paced without delays, with more intense and positive consequences and strategic non-emotional reprimands. Some situations can worsen the disability: (a) child management techniques that involve punishment, modeling aggression, or retaliation; (b) antecedent settings of low novelty with activity restrictions; and (c) delays that also require students to cease responding.

- Interventions and Tier II and III treatments should focus on teaching academic routines with checklists and self-monitoring, social routines (thank you, excuse me), and activity replacement behavior, rather than on attempting to reduce behavior.

## CHAPTER QUESTIONS

1. Does the activity of students with ADHD differ from that of students with ASD?

2. How does the HI subtype differ from the inattentive subtype?

3. How is the behavior of girls with ADHD different from that of boys with ADHD?

4. Describe a situation in which you have felt restless and wanted to get up and move around. Is that situation different from those tasks/setting that elicit hyperactive behavior in children?

5. Which of the accommodations discussed in this chapter have you seen in the classroom?

6. What have you learned in this chapter that is new or interesting to you?

## TRUE/FALSE AND MULTIPLE-CHOICE

1. Preferred activities to use as rewards for students with hyperactivity include providing extra time for

   A. errands
   B. talking
   C. recess
   D. all of the above

2. For students with ADHD, the need to stay still and be quiet in classroom settings produces

   A. disability fatigue
   B. replacement behavior
   C. better learning
   D. none of the above

3. Waiting for directions, asking for help, selecting multiple-choice options, and planning all involve

   A. executive functions
   B. assertiveness
   C. wait time

4. Restlessness is more characteristic of younger children with ADHD than is out-of-seat behavior.

5. The social behavior of students with ADHD is more difficult for their peers to tolerate in classroom settings than in play settings.

6. The social difficulties of most students with ADHD include

   A. social avoidance of and negative interactions with others from an early age
   B. lack of knowing how to join groups, share, resolve conflicts, and maintain relationships

7. Teachers often assume that because a child is not looking at them and is being active, the child is not listening.

8. Girls with ADHD are more talkative and impulsive with what they say, whereas boys with ADHD are more impulsive with what they do.

9. Children with ADHD are less likely than their peers to have handwriting problems.

10. ADHD should be one of the last disorders considered when a child exhibits off-task behavior.

## SHORT ANSWER

1. The mother's smile was _____ on (i.e., dependent on) the baby's gaze at the mother.

2. Restrictive and permissive parenting styles are often seen in the _____ of these children.

3. Another way of describing impulsivity is as delay _____.

4. Commands that have objective outcomes specified

5. Reprimands that are firm, consistent, and immediate

## PROBLEM-BASED CASE APPLICATIONS AND QUESTIONS

### CASE STUDY 10.1: JOHN

*"He poked the student next to him with his finger."*
(adapted from a report submitted by Becky Brodderick)

*Background.* John is a student in the seventh grade at C. Junior High School. He has been defined as a student with other health impairment for his ADHD. His test scores show no discrepancy between his full-scale IQ and his achievement scores, and his IQ is average. John attends a resource study hall and two inclusion classes as well as general education classes. John lives with his grandfather, grandmother, and younger brother. His grandparents have guardianship, and John sees his birth mother and father on occasion. They are divorced and the birth father has remarried twice. John has been moved around among all three homes for many years, which means he has gone to different schools, as well.

In the past John has been on a few different medications; at this time, he is not on medication. John and his grandfather felt the last meds were making him tired, and John felt like he was never hungry and would try to eat but then would get sick because of the meds, so he stopped taking his meds. John has stated that he felt the meds helped him concentrate a little better in class, but the sleepiness and nausea that came with them were not worth it.

John is not passing any of his current classes except for PE and art. The primary behavior of concern is John's lack of motivation to do his work. He has turned in only 5 assignments out of 25 in math, and the 5 he turned in were incomplete, with the work done randomly. He did some of the work correctly but didn't even get close to finishing. He has not turned in enough for his teacher to know if he understands the material. In English he has not turned in any work at all. John has no concern about whether he passes classes or passes on to the next grade, or about what kind of trouble he gets into on occasion. The secondary concern is John's ability to sit still during lectures. John is constantly moving or doing something rather than listening in class.

### Behavioral Log

### Tuesday, August 28, 1:15–1:55

- John played with pencil during math lecture. Teacher reminded him to pay attention.
- After given homework assignment in math, John pushed the paper on the floor. Teacher picked it up and gave it back to John and told him to get started.
- Sat at his desk and did nothing. Teacher asked him to come back to his desk to talk to her.
- John refused to do his work because it was too hard. Teacher offered to help him.
- Told teacher he didn't need her help. Teacher wanted to know why he felt this way.
- He told her he wasn't going to do the work. Teacher asked him why he wasn't going to do the work.
- He left the room. Spent the rest of the day in ISS (in-school suspension).

### Wednesday, August 29, 9:10–9:40

- John did not get out his materials when he was asked to during a science lab. Teacher reminded him to get the materials out.
- John and his partner played with their scale. Teacher reminded them that it wasn't a toy.

### Friday, August 31, 10:00–10:50

- John played with his cell phone during English lecture.
- John got up to get tissue and returned to his seat by walking behind the teacher. When he walked behind the teacher he made a face behind her back, so the rest of the class could see the face.

- John threw a wadded-up piece of paper at the trash can. Teacher told him not to throw paper in her room.
- He told her he didn't throw it. Teacher warned him next time he would go to the office.
- John threw a paper wad at a student after the teacher handed out a writing assignment. Teacher told him to go to the office.
- John threw the paper away on his way out the door.

### Wednesday, September 5, 2:05–2:45

- John brought nothing to do with him to study hall. He was told to go back to his locker and get something to do in study hall.
- He returned 10 minutes later with a book to read. The teacher told him to read the book.
- John just sat there and didn't read. Teacher didn't say anything; she was helping other students with homework.
- He fell asleep. Teacher told him to get up.
- John refused to get up. Teacher sent him to the office.

### Thursday, September 6, 10:15–10:45

- John was touching another member of the group while presenting a play in English class. Teacher reminded him to take the play seriously because it was for a grade.
- He laughed obnoxiously at other play members when they messed up their parts. The teacher told him it wasn't funny and to continue with the play.
- John started laughing when it was his turn to speak. The teacher warned him if he acted out again he would not be allowed to participate in the play any longer.

### Friday, September 7, 9:20–10:00

- John was making a drawing on his paper during a large-group science lecture. The teacher did not notice he was doing anything.
- He started tossing his pencil up in the air and catching it. The teacher asked him to make sure he was paying attention to the lecture.
- John was writing on his arm with a marker. Teacher did not notice.
- He passed a note to another student. Teacher asked for the note and told John to pay attention, along with the other student.
- John laid his head down on his desk like he was going to try to sleep. Teacher told him to sit up.
- He poked the student next to him with his finger. The kid told him to stop. Teacher told him to stop touching other students.

*Monday, September 10, 1:25–2:00*

- John laid his head down like he was going to sleep during a large-group math lecture. The teacher asked him to sit up.
- He played with his cell phone under his desk. Teacher did not notice.
- John passed a note back and forth with a student. Teacher did not notice.
- He drew a picture on his forearm. Teacher asked him to pay attention.
- John played with his book. He was opening it, closing it, and flipping through the pages. The teacher did not notice.
- After getting his homework, he sat at his desk and did nothing. The teacher did not notice because she was helping other students.

*Tuesday, September 11, 2:30–3:00*

- John was talking off subject while reading a social studies assignment with another student. The teacher reminded to stay on task.
- He was looking at a magazine on his lap. He was told to get back to reading the social studies book and give the teacher the magazine until the end of the class.
- John tried to talk to the student next to the group. The student told John he was trying to work and to leave him alone. The teacher told him it was his last warning before he would have to read on his own.

## ABC Analysis

*High-frequency payoffs.* The largest percentages of payoffs for John are get stimulation and avoid boredom, followed by get control and avoid work.

*Overall payoffs* (percentages noted out of 52 payoffs). John's attempts to get control may be an outcome of his having been moved frequently between parents and grandparents; he doesn't get to choose where he lives or where he wants to be—the adults in his life just decide for him. I believe he feels he needs some control in his life, and he can get that by telling the teacher what work he is and isn't going to do.

There are two reasons he may be avoiding work. One is that he has moved so much that he hasn't gotten the education he needs and it is hard for him; second, he gets bored with the work and doesn't want to do it. However, an assessment of John's academics is needed.

*Large lecture.* John's lecture/large-group classes include math, science, and English lectures and resource study hall. During lecture/large group, John had a payoff of stimulation 58% of the time. See Figure 10.2. John did not want to do work or listen to what was going on during the lecture. He wanted to avoid work and thereby needed additional stimulation.

**Figure 10.2**   John's Payoffs During Large Lecture

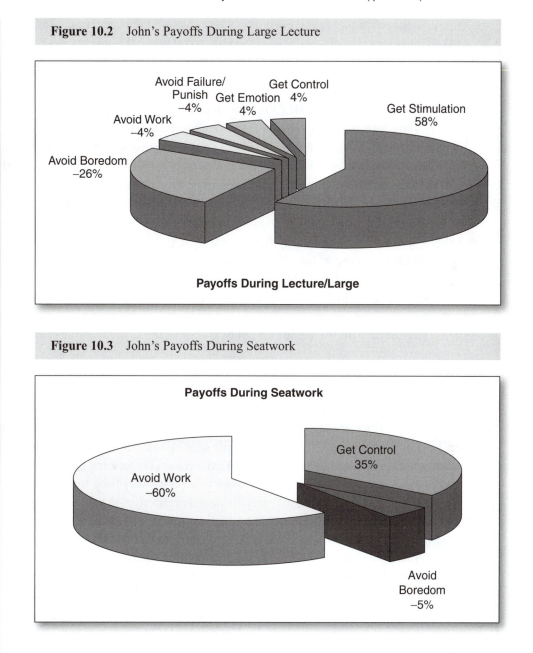

Avoid Failure/
Punish
−4%

Get Emotion
4%

Get Control
4%

Get Stimulation
58%

Avoid Work
−4%

Avoid Boredom
−26%

**Payoffs During Lecture/Large**

**Figure 10.3**   John's Payoffs During Seatwork

**Payoffs During Seatwork**

Get Control
35%

Avoid Work
−60%

Avoid
Boredom
−5%

John avoids seatwork; it did not matter if he was in math, English, science, or study hall, he had the same behaviors. See Figure 10.3. John is more capable of handling small groups and partners, in situations where he doesn't just have to sit in a chair and listen but has more freedom to move around. He also does fine in PE and art, where he gets to be moving around and doesn't have to just sit. It appears he enjoys both classes, which are are hands-on and not so structured. He paid attention and asked questions. He did not have to be redirected and did not refuse to do work.

## Diagnosis Versus ABC Analysis

John was diagnosed with ADHD. From the functional analysis and in support, most of his behaviors were throwing or playing with objects, writing on himself or paper, and moving around either at his seat or in the room. John seemed to play with his pencil, book, cell phone, or anything else he could get his hands on. He constantly wanted to be touching, throwing, or playing with anything near him. He would throw paper wads at people and across the room. He would throw his pencil up in the air and catch it. John also wrote on objects and would write notes to another student and continue doing this until he was told by the teacher to stop. If he was told by the teacher to stop he would just write on himself. He would also draw pictures on his papers. This behavior is consistent with ADHD, the HI subtype.

John also refused to do any kind of work, which could be related to ODD, specific undiagnosed learning disabilities or learning gaps from frequent moves, or attentional problems associated with the combined subtype of ADHD. ODD is supported by the fact that John would actually tell the teacher he would not do the work. He would throw his work away in the trash can. John would also just sit and do nothing during homework time. The teacher would ask him if he needed help, but he never accepted. He purposely did not bring materials to his resource study hall class, so he could go back to his locker and get materials. It took him 10 minutes to go to his locker and come back. This trip should have only taken a couple of minutes. Another example is when he walked all the way around his classroom to get a tissue. He took the roundabout way and then walked behind his teacher and made a face on his way back to his seat.

However, John's "oppositionality" was displayed primarily during large lecture and seatwork. While in lecture/large-group and seatwork settings he ended up being sent to the office. The teacher would try to redirect John in the large-group settings, but it did not usually work. John would not listen to the redirection and would be sent to the office. An example: John threw a wad of paper at the trash can. The teacher told him not the throw paper in her room. John told her he did not throw the paper, and the teacher told him next time he would be in the office. After she handed out the assignment for the day, John threw a paper wad at a student. The teacher sent him to the office. He knew he would have to go to the office, but he didn't care. However, in small-group and partner settings he responded to redirection. John's teacher only needed to redirect his behavior in small groups and partner settings. He did not want to miss any of the time spent doing these activities, so he would listen to the teacher and do as she asked. He was asked to cooperate or he would not be able to continue in the activity, and he then followed the directions.

Clearly John is showing noncompliance and setting avoidance in large groups. So this is not a case of broad-based ODD. John has difficulties in these specific settings, and he responds the only way he knows how.

## Interventions Derived From ABC Analysis

There are two settings in which John needs help. The first is the large-group or lecture setting: During the observation period, 58% of John's payoffs during lectures were to get stimulation. His other big payoff during lecture was to avoid boredom at 26%. I believe that for John, getting stimulation and avoiding boredom go hand in hand. The other setting is seatwork, where he has a payoff of 60% in avoiding work and a payoff of 35% in getting control. He actually said to a teacher during observation that he didn't do his work because it was too hard. He needs an educational assessment. Until that has been completed, he may profit from a reduction in assignment quantity. By doing only half of the assignment he is avoiding work, and the teacher can see what he is capable of doing. I would give him control by allowing him to pick the even- or odd-numbered problems, or the problems on the top half of the page or the bottom half of the page, or the easy versus hard problems. He would also have the choice of going to the resource room for help when he gets his assignment. This choice would also give him control of where he is doing his assignment. Right now John is not doing any of his work, so even assignments of reduced quantity will be a start and will address his ADHD until he can be assessed to determine whether there is LD or gaps in learning or simply a nonactive curriculum in those settings.

## Case Questions

1 (problem-based small-group assignment): John does fine in some settings and poorly in others. Summarize these differences (e.g., between large-group settings and seatwork). What do the payoffs that John needs suggest to you in terms of interventions or accommodations?

2: If you were the teacher and had to wait for an educational evaluation of John, how might you get some informal understanding of his academic skills before that evaluation?

3: What is important to John that could be used as a motivator in addition to what was noted by the observer?

# SECTION V

# Social Disorders

In previous sections of this book, you have learned how disability affects academic functioning. For those sections, you needed to understand task requirements that involved (a) selective and sustained attention (and working memory) for students with ADHD, (b) perception/memory for students with LD, and (c) thinking and problem solving for students with ID, TBI, and GT–twice exceptional. Many of these children with attentional, learning, and cognitive exceptionalities do have social disorders. However, their social characteristics are secondary to their failure experiences or to their excessive activity/impulsivity. In the current section, the focus is on children whose *primary* disability is social.

*DSM-IV-TR* breaks social disorders into a number of distinct disorders and presents information about each. In contrast, IDEA provides one umbrella term combining ED and BD with one definition (EBD) that is used for all. Figure V.1 shows the chronology of the presentation of these social disorders in this section: behavioral disorders (Chapter 11), emotional disorders (Chapter 12), autism spectrum disorders (Chapter 13), and addictions and abuse (Chapter 14). Figure V.1 also categorizes the two major temperament differences as behavioral disorders (BD), often associated with inadequate behavioral inhibition (**disinhibition**) and

**Disinhibition:** The inability to stop verbal or motor responses that are often socially inappropriate (e.g., cursing, removing all clothes after a seizure).

externalizing behavior, including aggression; and emotional disorders (ED), typically associated with early inhibited or internalizing behavior, and with anxiety disorders and depression (for a review, see Nigg, 2001). These major emotional and behavioral disorder categories are based on personality traits (i.e., inborn temperament; Eysenck, 1967). Most of us fall within a normal range along a "personality" continuum from being socially shy (introverted and inhibited) to socially bold (outgoing/extroverted). Typical children have some flexibility in expressing introversion/extroversion, such that they are bold in one situation and shy in another. At the extremes of this continuum we find students with behavioral and emotional disorders, who have temperaments with a more restricted range of expression.

Although Figure V.1 separates social disorders in a categorical way, differences are often in degree rather than in type (see Moffitt et al., 2008). For example, children can have behavioral disorders and emotional disorders or both internalizing and externalizing characteristics, especially at older age levels. In other words, temperament is genetically determined but is modified in expression through accumulated life experiences. For example, most aggression is within the behavioral disorders category, but some of the most severe instances of aggression can be observed in children within the autism spectrum disorder category. This group of students is represented to the right of ED, with core deficits in social reciprocity (White, Keonig, & Scahill, 2007), with subtypes of Asperger's, autism, and

**Figure V.1**  Social Disorders of EBD and ASD

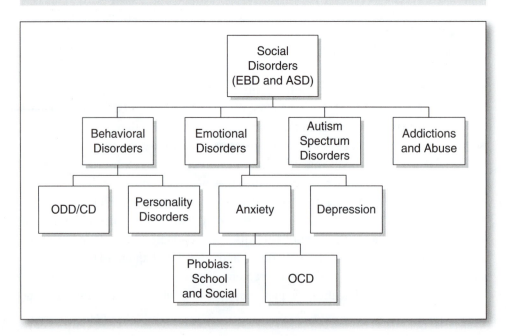

pervasive developmental disorder (not otherwise specified). The aggression observed in these students is typically a defensive response to change or over-stimulation (e.g., perceived social threat). Children with ED and ASD can use aggression as a defensive response (to avoid); children with BD are more likely to use aggression instrumentally to get resources, control, or social status, and some children may learn to use aggression both to get and to avoid. This is why a functional assessment is often necessary in selecting Tier II interventions for aggression. Finally, this section includes information about children who have been or who currently are addicted or abused. The experiences of these children contribute to secondary emotional disorders and to outcomes of inadequate social interactions.

## LEARNING GOALS

In this section you will learn the following:

- The vocabulary that is associated with social disorders
- How each category of children is formally defined by IDEA (which combines them within one category of EBD) and by *DSM-IV-TR* (which separates them into distinct categories, subtypes, and co-occurring conditions and how they differ from others in related categories)
- The etiology of behavior disabilities and how age, culture, and gender can influence outcome
- How educators can informally identify children with externalizing behavioral disorders through observations of their (a) behavior, (b) responses to social and communication settings, (c) responses to academic tasks, and (d) responses to motor and physical tasks
- Possible implications for treatment (interventions and accommodations)
- How to apply the information you have learned to case studies of children with behavioral and/or emotional disorders

# Chapter 11

## Externalizing Behavioral Disorders

Most children with externalizing behavioral disorders seek interactions with others, often through aggression and risk-taking behavior. However, it is important to remember that aggression, like anxiety, is not necessarily disordered and can be adaptive for individuals and for society. For example, assertive behavior, risk-taking, rebellion, and nonconformity can be important in achieving resources, self-protection, innovation, and independence. In fact, popular children use aggression in **instrumental** ways to enjoy certain social advantages of attention and control over resources (Hawley, 2002). In contrast to these possible advantages, children with BD and aggression typically have too little anxiety, empathy, and guilt (see Wenar & Kerig, 2006), which makes it more difficult for them to learn from negative experiences and social consequences.

**Instrumental:** Directed toward obtaining a goal.

BD and ED are represented as one disability in the IDEA definition below. What is common between ED and BD is found in the first three listed impairments (A, B, and C). In contrast, characteristics D and E are more often associated with ED (discussed in Chapter 12). According to IDEA, children with **EBD** exhibit

**ED and EBD:** Emotional disturbance and emotional behavioral disorder; the latter is the more commonly used term.

one or more of the following characteristics over a long period of time and to a marked degree that adversely affects a child's educational performance:

(A) An inability to learn that cannot be explained by intellectual, sensory, or health factors.

(B) An inability to build or maintain satisfactory interpersonal relationships with peers and teachers.

**Figure 11.1**   A classic example of a child with Oppositional Defiant Disorder

(C)  Inappropriate types of behavior or feelings under normal circumstances.

(D)  A general pervasive mood of unhappiness or depression.

(E)  A tendency to develop physical symptoms or fears associated with personal or school problems.(ii) Emotional disturbance includes schizophrenia. The term does not apply to children who are socially maladjusted. (34 C.F.R. Section 300.7[c][4][i])

The last sentence of this definition, excluding students with social "maladjustment," historically referred to those children who had learned behavior inappropriate to the dominant school culture. Excluding children from minority cultures from the definition was expected to reduce the overrepresentation of African American children with an EBD diagnosis. However, it is discriminatory to include *or* exclude students from special services based on culture, race, gender, sexual orientation, or the like (Cartledge, 1999). Thus, this particular exclusionary clause remains as a reminder that it is important to consider culture for its possible effects on social behavior. For example, individuals within particular subcultures may learn aggressive behavior to survive (e.g., in a threatening neighborhood, a gang, or in high school, to renegotiate one's popularity by teasing or bullying same-gender social rivals) (Faris & Felmlee, 2011).

If children can learn aggression as a way of surviving or advancing in a subculture ("socially maladjusted"), they can relearn cooperative behavior if they are given a change of environment or a change of rewards. For example, we all learn to act differently depending on our environments, whether at home, at work, with our parents, with our children, or with our peers. Thus, children can relearn appropriate behavior when they are provided with appropriate rewards and incentives for doing so. Furthermore, if a child has learned behavior to adapt to a subculture, that behavior cannot be considered "disturbed." The case of David, an African American 8 year-old student, offers an example. David was placed in a special school for children with EBD. He probably was gifted because he quickly relearned appropriate school behavior and was returned to his local school system. In little time, however, David reclaimed his original "difficult" behavior in that public school after he was repeatedly assaulted by his peers for demonstrating this new pattern of behavior. The point is that educators must consider cultural context before labeling a child as behaviorally disordered.

It is probable that children like David will challenge authority. This can be especially difficult for educators to handle, especially when students are smart in the ways they make such challenges. Adults may be tempted to meet the challenges with retaliation or punishment to reassert control and power. However, negative teacher behavior (e.g., reprimands, suspensions) further encourages disruptive behavior in students with BD, as well as in typical students (Beyda, Zentall, & Ferko, 2002). Of course, aggression cannot be allowed to continue, since the more that behavior produces rewards (secondary gains) for the child (e.g., avoiding requirements or obtaining resources), the more quickly the child learns that aggression "works." Thus, educators must be particularly vigilant in responding appropriately to these children. They should also keep in mind that at least half the number of children with aggression have heredity as a contributing factor (Garrett, 2011), and perhaps many others have learned aggression or are aggressive in response to feelings of helplessness and lack of power.

The first question an educator should ask is, What type of aggression is the child showing? Types of aggression can be framed broadly into offensive (proactive) versus defensive (reactive). Defensive aggression is aggression that protects the child against (a) excessive demands (e.g., noise or crowding, as would be seen in anxiety disorder and **Asperger syndrome, or AS**), (b) difficult task demands (e.g., reading aloud, as in the case of children with RD or ODD), or (c) threats to "image" or "loss of face," as in the case of narcissistic personality disorder (**NPD**). All of these defensive types of aggression have the underlying message that the best defense is a good offense. Children who are reactively aggressive are more likely than their peers to show high states of physiological arousal in response to threat (i.e., they are sensitive to threat and respond impulsively). This is different from students who later might be identified as CD, who attempt to advance their own interests at significant cost to the rights of others (proactive aggression) and who may show little in the way of stress in response to threat or in remorse for their behavior (guilt).

Children with **ODD** are often the youngest group to be identified. They challenge authority by being oppositional (saying no) and possibly argumentative and hostile. From these children's perspective, they are responding to unreasonable demands placed on them by their families or teachers. In contrast, children with CD have more severe forms of proactive aggression. Those in this group are hostile, unable to delay gratification, and demonstrate aggression by violating not only the norms of their own subcultures (family and school) but also those of society at large (e.g., through **vandalism,** fire setting) (Hawley, 2002). A **correlation** is also found between aggression and NPD (Ang & Yusof, 2005). Children with CD and NPD see themselves as capable and feel they are just responding to the hostile provocations of others; this is different from children with ODD, who see themselves as "put upon."

**Asperger syndrome (AS):** A syndrome within the autism spectrum disorders category that has been considered a mild form of autism (high-functioning autism). Children with AS have a greater capacity to achieve normal-like behavior and functioning than do children with autism.

**NPD:** Narcissistic personality disorder.

**ODD:** Oppositional defiant disorder.

**Vandalism:** The destruction of another's property.

**Correlation:** The positive association of one factor, *A,* with another, *B,* such that the higher the amount of factor *A* (e.g., intelligence), the higher the amount of factor *B* (e.g., achievement). One factor does not necessarily cause the other; the two are simply related.

## OPPOSITIONAL DEFIANT DISORDER

Children with ODD have been described as uncooperative, defiant, and hostile toward adults (e.g., parents, school staff, teachers/assistants), but their behavior does not involve major social violations (McKinney & Renk, 2006). "Usually individuals with this disorder do not regard themselves as oppositional or defiant, but justify their behavior as a response to unreasonable demands or circumstances" (APA, 2000, p. 100). These perceptions could be accurate when activity restrictions and rules are imposed on a child who has a high need for activity, or when task demands are unreasonable given the child's perceived or real ability level. These would be understandable reasons for oppositional behavior. However, it is more difficult to use this deficit-based explanation for the peer problems also shown by children with ODD (Greene, 2006).

## FORMAL IDENTIFICATION

### Definitions

#### IDEA

IDEA defines this group of children under the category of EBD (see the Section V overview).

#### DSM-IV-TR

*DSM-IV-TR* (APA, 2000, p. 102) defines ODD as follows:

*Defining characteristics:* A recurrent pattern of negativistic, defiant, disobedient, and hostile behavior toward authority figures that persists for at least 6 months and is characterized by the frequent occurrence of at least four of the following behaviors:

- Often loses temper
- Often argues with adults
- Often actively defies or refuses to comply with adults' requests or rules
- Often deliberately annoys people
- Often blames others for his or her mistakes or misbehavior
- Is often touchy or easily annoyed by others
- Is often angry and resentful
- Is often spiteful or vindictive

*Impairment:* Social or academic

*Exclusions and conditions:* "Only if the behavior occurs more frequently than is typically observed in individuals of comparable age and developmental level." Not a psychotic or mood disorder or conduct disorder.

### Frequently Occurring Subtypes

The main type of ODD is predominantly *actively* oppositional; a child with this type says no frequently or argues and gives excuses and finally does the exact opposite of what was requested. The *passive* subtype ignores or delays responding to requests and shows passive resistance (not *really* doing exactly what was requested). (Table 11.1 lists the characteristics that differentiate the passive and active subtypes of ODD.) Children with the *passive-aggressive* subtype may have a perpetual sarcastic smile while carrying out hostilities and may apologize with a sweet smile and appear guilt free and innocent (Long & Long, 2001). These children's negativism is based on feelings of self-importance (they feel misunderstood and unappreciated)—no one has the right to ask them to do anything, and they have no obligations toward others (Fossati et al., 2000).

Children with passive aggression often have the attitude that life is full of people who will take advantage, and therefore it is better *not* to put yourself out for people (Millon & Radovanov, 1995). Children with the passive-aggressive personality type do not alternate between passive and aggressive behavior; rather, they combine the two kinds of behavior into quarrelsome and submissive, manipulative and charming, conforming and irritating to others (Lilienfeld & Penna, 2001). This subtype can be identified by their ongoing whining and grumbling, complaints of being misunderstood by others, and antiauthority critical comments (Fossati et al., 2000). When parents have overly high expectations and standards, their children may be anxious and fearful about the expression of their own anger and not know how to be assertive (Long & Long, 2001).

**Table 11.1**   Characteristics of the Passive and Active Subtypes of ODD

| *Passive type* | *Active type* |
|---|---|
| • Ignores a request<br>• Delays complying<br>• Doesn't do exactly what was asked | • Argues<br>• Gives excuses for finally doing the very opposite<br>• Provocative in stirring up controversy |

## Possible Co-Occurring Conditions and Differences Among Related Disabilities

ODD rarely travels alone; it is often related to depression, anxiety, ADHD, LD, and CD (Greene et al., 2002). ODD might also be a symptom of underlying mood disorders—depressive and bipolar disorders (Rowe, Maughan, Costello, & Angold, 2005). In fact, rates of ODD/CD have been found to be about four to ten times higher in depressed students than in nondepressed students (for a review, see Skoulos & Tryon, 2007), and approximately 40% of students with ODD also meet criteria for anxiety disorder (Drabick, Ollendick, & Bubier, 2010). Among children with ADHD, 65% also have ODD, and 80–93% of children with ODD also have ADHD (Greene, 2006; Mayes & Calhoun, 2006). Some consider ODD a subtype of ADHD (Poulton, 2011), possibly because of the active style of children with ADHD, which produces frequent "stop" and "no" commands by parents, which are volleyed back by the children.

ODD also overlaps with CD in the expression of aggressive behavior (Rowe et al., 2005). Although these two disorders are related, students with ODD do *not* show patterns of aggression toward animals or people, deceit/theft, or destruction of property. Furthermore, CD more often than ODD involves individuals outside the family, such as peers, teachers, and individuals in the community, whereas ODD typically involves family members.

Some children with learning problems (e.g., ID, LD) show oppositionality, but this behavior is specific to failure-producing tasks and setting demands. Thus, ODD can occur as a systematic way to avoid difficult tasks. These avoidant and oppositional children may also attempt to deal with anxiety by controlling tasks and others (Wenar & Kerig, 2006). Lily (whose case study data appear in Appendix II) shows this type of behavior:

> She often did what she wanted to do instead of what she was asked to do. . . . if she was unhappy with a boy holding a piece of paper, she would shout, "Put it down" and even scratched him.

Finally, some children with giftedness may also show oppositionality when the setting requirements are controlling and demand conformity (e.g., in token economy systems) or when they are inflexible and do not reward divergent thinking or questioning (Webb et al., 2005).

ODD can be a difficult disorder to identify accurately because of its overlap with other disorders and because some oppositional behavior is typical in the normal development of all children. As *DSM-IV-TR* states: "Because transient oppositional behavior is very common in preschool children and in adolescents, caution should be exercised in making the diagnosis of Oppositional Defiant Disorder especially during these developmental periods" (APA, 2000, p. 101). Even typical children, especially toddlers, comply with parental requests only two-thirds of the time (see Wenar & Kerig, 2006). In sum, all children will show some oppositional behavior at these stages, but children with ODD will show this behavior more frequently, at greater intensities, and for longer periods over time (i.e., it is not just a phase).

## Etiology

In this disability, there appears to be an incompatibility between the negative qualities of the child and those of the parent. That is, the child's difficult qualities (e.g., hyperactivity, irritability/negativity, language processing problems, LD, anxiety, need for control) worsen the parent's difficult qualities (e.g., anxiety, feelings of helplessness, need for control). Thus, both biological and environmental factors must be considered.

*Biological.* Many parents of children with ODD report that these children were more rigid and demanding and more active than other children from an early age. "In males, the disorder has been shown to be more prevalent among those who, in the preschool years, have problematic temperaments (e.g., high reactivity, difficulty being soothed) or high motor activity" (APA, 2000, p. 100). Thus, there is some evidence of genetics as a factor. At the physical and behavioral levels, there is also evidence that children with co-occurring ADHD and ODD respond to provocation differently, with a greater increase in arousal and more retaliatory behavior (Waschbusch et al., 2002).

*Environmental.* Family dysfunction is reported more often in families with children with ODD than in typical families (Greene et al., 2002); these families use an inconsistent style of discipline that is irritable, explosive, and inflexible. The parents are more likely to be **insular,** low in supervision and involvement with their children, highly stressed, with marital problems, physically abused or abusing, and from low-income and/or poor educational backgrounds (Greene, 2006; McKinney & Renk, 2006). There is evidence that these parents may also have ADHD, CD, substances abuse, or depression (APA, 2000). In such cases, many of the children in these families may have learned inappropriate behavior from inadequate parental models.

**Insular:** Isolated socially.

*Functional.* Oppositional behavior is developmentally correct in children who have a need for self-determination or independence (e.g., in 2-year-olds or adolescents). When this pattern of behavior is expressed at other age levels, functional assessments can determine whether the antecedents for oppositional behavior are commands/demands/requests, as is often the case in ODD. The presence of these antecedents would indicate a function to avoid possible failure or loss of control or to gain these very elements of control, competence, or access to preferred activities.

## Prevalence, Gender, Age, and Cultural Factors

**Epidemiological samples:** In research studies, groups of individuals recruited from the general population or from community samples and not from special schools or mental health clinics.

*Prevalence.* From **epidemiological samples,** 3–16% of children can be classified as ODD. From clinical populations, one-third to 65% receive the diagnosis of ODD (Loeber et al., 2009; McKinney & Renk, 2006).

*Gender.* Girls are defined as ODD less frequently than are boys (1% to 4%) (Munkvold, Lundervold, & Manger, 2011), but girls express ODD differently, showing more withdrawn behavior than males (McKinney & Renk, 2006).

*Age.* ODD occurs before the age of 8 and no later than adolescence. However, ODD is typically *not* an early developmental expression of CD (Diamantopoulou, Verhulst, & van der Ende, 2011).

*Culture.* Families with a combined income of less than $20,000 per year have higher rates of children with ODD (Lanza & Drabick, 2011). Furthermore, punitive disciplinary practices and lower levels of maternal support are strongly correlated with a child's defiant and oppositional behaviors, which are more common in low-income, mother-headed families (Olson, Ceballo, & Park, 2002).

**Protective factors:** Those events, attitudes, life experiences, or individual traits that are associated with positive long-term outcomes (e.g., sense of humor).

**Protective factors** include family routines (consistency and organization), as shown by research that examined the strategies of parents in low-SES urban neighborhoods that were associated with low levels of ODD characteristics (Lanza & Drabick, 2011).

# INFORMAL EDUCATOR IDENTIFICATION OF CHARACTERISTICS

## Behavioral

Generally, students with ODD can be described as being more confrontational than their peers and than students with other types of disabilities (Skoulos &

Tryon, 2007). Typically they adapt poorly to new situations and transitions and are resistant or actively defiant (Greene, 2006). Lily demonstrates this:

> When other children wanted to play with her toys or see what she was playing
> . . . her way of refusing is usually shouting, "NO!" and grabbing the toys in her arms, or stretching out her arms to keep others away.

According to *DSM-IV-TR:* "During the school years, there may be . . . swearing, and the precocious use of alcohol, tobacco, or illicit drugs" (APA, 2000, p. 100). Adolescents with ODD more frequently lose their tempers, argue and refuse to comply with adults, blame others, annoy others, and are easily annoyed by others (Skoulos & Tryon, 2007). Students with ODD also have more risk-taking behavior than typical peers and more than students with only ADHD (Humphreys & Lee, 2011).

## Social-Emotional

Students with ODD are more likely to avoid social interactions, except with friends who have similar aggressive tendencies. These students also have poor relations with teachers because they ignore requests, delay responding, or argue and give excuses for doing the opposite of what was requested. They put significant others under high stress, especially anyone with authority and especially familiar persons (usually the parents) (Greene et al 2002; McKinney & Renk, 2006).

Many students with ODD lack **empathy** (Hanna, Hanna, & Keys, 1999). Children with ODD also struggle with analyzing the emotions they themselves are feeling (Greene, 2006). They may have "low self-esteem (or overly inflated self-esteem), **mood lability,** and low frustration tolerance" (APA, 2000, p. 100). For example, instead of responding in a healthy way to their own frustration or sadness, they respond immediately with aggression or opposition. Lily refused others' initiations even though she attempted interactions with others:

**Empathy:** The ability to feel or identify with the feelings of another.

**Mood lability:** Ups and downs in feelings that appear to be unpredictable.

> It is interesting to see that on the playground when she wants to relate with others, and even though her help was refused by the girl, she still tries to grab her arms or shoulders. In contrast, she avoids what others initiate. When someone came to the ladder and wanted to climb after her, she would shout to him, get his hands off the ladder or even kick him. She seems to be bossy on the playground and does not like others getting in her way and interrupting her.

## Cognitive

What has been documented is that children with ODD have problem-solving deficits (Greene, 2006), which may be related to their lack of flexibility (shifting sets) as well as their difficulty inhibiting responses (deficits in the executive functions of self-regulation; Greene, 2006). Specifically, children with ODD have difficulty in one or more of these stages of social problem solving: "interpretation of cues, clarification of cues, access of responses and response decision" (Kempes, Walter, Han, & Engeland, 2005, p. 14). Deficits in working memory have also been documented (Greene, 2006).

## Academic

Children with ODD show significantly lower academic confidence and lower school adjustment than peers (Skoulos & Tryon, 2007). This area requires further research to determine the specific nature of their academic problems.

## DISABILITY IN THE CLASSROOM

### Implications for Accommodations in General Education Settings: Tier I

**Alpha commands:** Commands that have a clearly stated outcome (e.g., "When you have finished your math homework, you may select one TV program to watch").

**Compliance:** The capacity to delay achieving one's own goals in response to the implicit or stated goals/standards of authority figures (Greene et al., 2002).

Students with ODD are most often found in general education settings, where they often overrespond to loss of control, unpredictable/unexpected changes, and punishment such as response cost or the loss of objects or activities (Humphreys & Lee, 2011). For these reasons, they have a greater need for choice and for routines accompanied by advance warnings and organizers. At a minimum, accommodations should provide students with specific feedback about what to do. When children are oppositional, it is important for adults to use **alpha commands** but to first obtain and then sustain eye contact (20–30 seconds after a request), which will increase **compliance** (see Kapalka, 2004). Accommodations must also provide sufficient reinforcement of appropriate behavior (Hawken et al., 2008). However, general educators may need some training in how to give positive reinforcement, how to pick their battles, how to enforce rule-based consequences fairly and consistently, how to get support from other professionals, and how to encourage family collaboration and communication.

## Implications for Interventions in Small-Group and Individual Settings: Tiers II and III

Even though primary responsibility for diagnosis will not fall to educators, educators can help with the functional analysis (FA), which is critical to understanding environmental contributors (Greene, 2006). The Tier II interventions described below should be carried out by a support team that includes a special educator, a behavioral consultant, a therapist or school counselor, and so on.

At a *behavioral* level, children with ODD can be taught the difference between aggressive behavior and assertive behavior (i.e., to express anger in a verbal, non-blaming, respectful way) (Long & Long, 2001). For example, training in the use of positive words (e.g., "You have a different opinion—that's okay") has been found to produce fewer aggressive responses in children than training with neutral words (see Combs & Slaby, 1977). This training may be needed in conjunction with or before some children with ODD are placed in general education settings (Skoulos & Tryon, 2007).

At a *cognitive* level, a cognitive-behavioral model of intervention (collaborative problem solving, or CPS) can be used to focus on triggers of aggression (e.g., frustration), strategies for handling unmet expectations, and collaborative methods to resolve parent-child disputes. CPS has been found to produce greater gains than parent training at a 4-month follow-up assessment (Greene et al., 2004). Children who are self-centered lack an understanding of the perspectives of others, but their views may be broadened through exposure to others' different but strongly felt emotions, opinions, experiences, and strategies (e.g., in discussion groups). In addition, repeated prompting with verbal statements such as "What appears to be fair to you may not be fair to others" and "You cannot expect everything to go your way" can be effective. Interventions that involve self-monitoring can also be effective with children with ODD, because it empowers them to judge their own behavior by graphing.

Interventions that focus on emotions may also be useful. Because some of these children have little empathy, it is important to help them recognize their own feelings and to recognize and respond to others' emotions. Research has found that preschoolers who can accurately identify puppets' emotions (i.e., happy, sad, angry, fearful) and who emotionally respond to videotaped distressed actors are more likely to show prosocial and "helping" behavior and less likely to show aggression in later years (e.g., Denham et al., 2002).

*Tier III.* Tier III interventions include medication to reduce oppositional behavior in children with ADHD (for a review, see Greene, 2006). In addition to the support of school personnel described above, *parent education* is the intervention often selected to reduce oppositional behavior, which usually occurs at higher rates at home and is often related to adult-child incompatibility (Greene, 2006). This includes teaching parents how to build on the positives of the student through positive attending, appropriate commands, "contingent attention, reinforcement, and use of time-out procedure" (Greene, 2006, p. 291). Parents can also be instructed in how to make alpha commands (Wenar & Kerig, 2006). Note that research has documented that when oppositional behavior decreases at home, it tends to increase at school (Wahler, Vigilante, & Strand, 2004). Perhaps techniques that focus only on compliance fail to take into account the child's needs for independence, control, and self-determination (Hanna et al., 1999).

## Long-Term Outcomes

Children with ODD and co-occurring mood disorders may be at increased risk for long-term poor outcomes, including school failure and academic difficulties, poor relations with peers, and increased risk for mental disorders in adulthood (Greene et al., 2004; van Lier, Muthén, van der Sar, & Crijnen, 2004).

*Continuance.* "ODD is one of the most stable diagnoses and one with the poorest rate of recovery" (Wenar & Kerig, 2006, p. 173). However, only one-third of children with ODD develop CD, often during middle childhood, and level of aggression appears to be the best predictor of continuance (Wenar & Kerig, 2006).

## CONDUCT DISORDER

Children with CD are defined by behavior that violates the rights of persons or property. See Figure 11.2. These children transgress not only the rules of the family and school (as is the case in ODD) but also those of society (APA, 2000). Their behavior, in turn, evokes responses from parents and teachers that include harsh and erratic discipline, which reinforces or increases the original behavior (Lynam & Henry, 2001). These children do not perceive themselves as aggressive; rather, they see others as hostile (in line with their history), which justifies their own retaliatory aggression. Their projecting of blame can be seen in the serious warning of an aggressive child who stated to his teachers, "You guys are on my last nerve!"

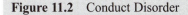

**Figure 11.2** Conduct Disorder

## FORMAL IDENTIFICATION

### Definitions

#### *IDEA*

IDEA defines this group of children under the category of EBD (see the Section V overview).

#### *DSM-IV-TR*

*DSM-IV-TR* (APA, 2000, pp. 98–99) defines conduct disorder as follow:

*Defining characteristics:* A repetitive and persistent pattern of behavior in which the basic rights of others or major age-appropriate societal norms or rules are violated, as manifested by the presence of three (or more) of the following criteria in the past 12 months, with at least one criterion present in the past 6 months:

- *Aggression to people and animals*
  1. Often bullies, threatens, or intimidates others
  2. Often initiates physical fights
  3. Has used a weapon that can cause serious physical harm to others (e.g., a bat, brick, broken bottle, knife, gun)
  4. Has been physically cruel to people
  5. Has been physically cruel to animals
  6. Has stolen while confronting a victim (e.g., mugging, purse snatching, extortion, armed robbery)
  7. Has forced someone into sexual activity

- *Destruction of property*
  8. Has deliberately engaged in fire setting with the intention of causing serious damage
  9. Has deliberately destroyed others' property (other than by fire setting)

- *Deceitfulness or theft*
  10. Has broken into someone else's house, building, or car
  11. Often lies to obtain goods or favors or to avoid obligations (i.e., "cons" others)
  12. Has stolen items of nontrivial value without confronting a victim (e.g., shoplifting, but without breaking and entering; forgery)

- *Serious violations of rules*
  13. Often stays out at night despite parental prohibitions, beginning before age 13 years
  14. Has run away from home overnight at least twice while living in parental or parental surrogate home (or once without returning for a lengthy period)
  15. Is often truant from school, beginning before age 13 years

*Impairment:* Social and academic

### Frequently Occurring Subtypes

Intermittent explosive disorder (see APA, 2000, p. 667) is an infrequently occurring disorder that involves "behavioral earthquakes." It is relatively rare and different from CD in that it is not a reaction to specific provocations (Greene & Ablon, 2006) and therefore cannot be seen as truly a subtype of CD.

---

"Explosive Disorder is not preceded by an event. It is described by the individual as 'spells' or 'attacks' preceded by a sense of tension or arousal," with irritability, rage, racing thoughts, increased energy during the aggressive acts, followed immediately by a sense of relief, fatigue, and possible feelings of remorse, regret, or embarrassment about the aggressive behavior (APA, 2000, p. 664).

### Possible Co-Occurring Conditions and Differences Among Related Disabilities

CD may co-occur with a number of different externalizing and internalizing disabilities. Rates of CD and ODD have been found to be about four to ten times higher in depressed children than in typical children (Angold & Costello, 1993). When depression co-occurs with CD, it typically predicts suicide, especially when combined with substance abuse. Youth with CD may also have co-occurring narcissism, anxiety disorders, or addictions. Co-occurring anxiety may be a protective factor in CD, as children with both disabilities have lower rates of aggression and violent crime (Angold & Costello, 2001). Lily is a good example of ODD at her young age, but she hangs on the border between the two groups because her aggressive behavior involves not just yelling but also hitting:

> Free play time occupies more time than other activities, so it is the phase during which most of her inappropriate behaviors are observed, which include yelling at others, grabbing toys, touching and hitting others and disobeying teachers' orders and requests.

CD and ADHD can co-occur. For example, approximately 45–70% of students with ADHD learn aggressive behavior, in contrast to only about 4–10% of typical children (for a review, see Meyer & Zentall, 1995). When CD and ADHD do co-occur, the results are greater disturbance and poorer outcomes than are found for either disorder alone (e.g., physical aggression, social rejection, low achievement especially in reading, poor motor coordination; Angold & Costello, 2001; Lynam & Henry, 2001). As well, these students with co-occurring disorders self-report fewer goals related to being fair and more goals related to *getting into trouble* than do children with only ADHD, whereas children with only ADHD report more goals related to *stirring up trouble.* Both groups report goals related to having fun (Barron, Evans, Baranik, Serpell, & Buvinger, 2006; Zentall, 2005a).

## Etiology

The contributions of genetic and environmental influences to CD appear to be similar to those for ODD (Loeber et al., 2009). That is, inborn temperament characteristics of children with CD bring out negative responses from parents who are not well prepared to deal with this type of behavior. This negative interaction pattern is continued in schools with teachers.

*Biogenetic.* There is evidence that genetic factors are related to the lower physiological arousal (measured by heart rate and galvanic skin resistance) seen in students with CD (Larkby, Goldschmidt, Hanusa, & Day, 2011), which is associated with reduced reactivity to punishment (for a review, see APA, 2000) as well as reduced capacity to take in emotional information from the social environment (Herpertz et al., 2008). Furthermore, "the disorder . . . appears to be more common in children of biological parents with Alcohol Dependence, Mood Disorders, or Schizophrenia or biological parents who have a history of Attention-Deficit/ Hyperactivity Disorder or Conduct Disorder" (APA, 2000, p. 98). The overlap among CD, ODD, and ADHD is primarily the result of shared genetic influences (Dick, Viken, Kaprio, Pulikkinen, & Rose, 2005).

*Environmental.* Prenatal maternal smoking (more than 10 cigarettes per day) and especially maternal exposure to alcohol in the first trimester predict CD at a rate three to four times higher than that found in the general population (Larkby et al., 2011). Thus, the environment in the womb can contribute to CD. Similar to ODD, family dysfunction is more often reported in children with CD than in typical families (Greene et al., 2002). Overall, parental antisocial behavior and low education predict CD (Loeber et al., 2009), and harsh discipline and low parental warmth predict an increase in CD symptoms over time (for a review, see Berkout, Young, & Gross, 2011). Additional factors are "parental rejection and neglect, difficult infant temperament, inconsistent child-rearing practices with harsh discipline, physical or sexual abuse or other traumatic life events, lack of supervision, early institutional living, frequent changes of caregivers, large family size, history of maternal smoking during pregnancy, peer rejection, association with a delinquent peer group, neighborhood exposure to violence, and certain kinds of familial psychopathology (e.g., Antisocial Personality Disorder, Substance Dependence or Abuse)" (APA, 2000, p. 96). Negative peers also influence or are correlated with CD or aggression, as are preferences for viewing violent TV programs. Similarly, a school environment of conflict (e.g., frequent student fighting and defiance, teachers unable to maintain order) has been found to be related to an increase in CD over a 2-year period (see Kasen et al., 1990, cited in Wenar &

Kerig, 2006). Thus, children with genetic factors that predispose them to CD are more vulnerable to difficult environmental conditions.

*Functional.* Functional analysis shows that aggressive behavior can function to advance self-interest or to avoid and self-protect. Children who are unskilled are more likely to use aggression to avoid demands or requirements. Antecedent settings that occasion protective aggression include settings that are active and overcrowded, that have low levels of structure coupled with difficult tasks, and that allow little flexibility in responses (e.g., Milich & Landau, 1988). In contrast, those children who use aggression to get power or control (e.g., bullies) have learned to use aggression when their peers refuse to interact with them and when peers cry, whine, back down, and allow them to get what they want (van Lier et al., 2004). For students with ADHD and aggression, antecedents to aggression are entering new groups and situations in which resources and adults are scarce (Stormont-Spurgin & Zentall, 1995).

## Prevalence, Gender, Age, and Cultural Factors

*Prevalence/gender.* CD is found more often in males (about 4%) than in females (about 1%) (Boden, Fergusson, & Horwood, 2010; Loeber et al., 2009). However, these differences can be partially explained by the fact that harsh discipline is administered to boys more than to girls (Berkout et al., 2011). More often documented are differences between boys and girls in the expression of CD: "Girls were more likely to endorse non-confrontational stealing, lying, and running away than boys, whereas boys were more likely to endorse staying out late and breaking and entering than girls" (Berkout et al., 2011, p. 506). Boys, more than girls, are competitive, dominating, and aggressive (fighting in the halls, overtly violating rules, vandalizing property) and less cooperative, verbally supportive, or conflict avoidant (Maccoby, 1998). Girls are more likely to respond with aggression when attempting to enter groups and boys are more likely to respond with aggression to peer provocations (Feldman & Dodge, 1987). Girls in general have greater pressure to conform to social norms than do boys, which explains the fact that there are few behavioral differences early in development and more differences as children age (Lynam & Henry, 2001). Girls with CD use negative verbal behavior and relational aggression (e.g., gossiping, excluding other girls or "icing") and covert rather than overt aggression.

*Age.* Aggressive and defiant behavior emerges developmentally at about 3 years (e.g., Tremblay et al., 1999). Thus, the onset of CD can occur as early as preschool. However, ODD is typically identified earlier, at an average onset age of 6, whereas CD is identified from middle childhood through middle adolescence, at around 9 years (Wenar & Kerig, 2006). Recent evidence indicates that early CD symptoms (not ODD) are the best predictor for later CD symptoms (Diamantopoulou et al., 2011). The significant symptoms of CD usually emerge first with less severe behavior (e.g., lying, shoplifting, physical fighting) and more extreme behavior (e.g., burglary) emerging later. The most severe conduct problems (e.g., rape, theft while confronting a victim) emerge last. CD takes precedence over the diagnosis of ODD or ADHD (APA, 2000), probably because CD has more serious outcomes.

Age of onset of CD can be used to determine subtypes, according to *DSM-IV-TR* criteria (e.g., childhood-onset type and adolescent-onset type). *Early starters* are more likely to have a biological basis, neurocognitive deficits, low IQ, parental antisocial behavior, and severe family adversity (Moffitt et al., 2008). Students with *late onset* of aggression are more likely than early starters to be responders to difficult environments and have higher rates of substance abuse, impulsivity, psychological problems, and poor long-term vocational outcomes.

*Culture.* CD is more often identified in urban than in rural areas and in Western cultures (Foltz, 2008).

## INFORMAL EDUCATOR IDENTIFICATION OF CHARACTERISTICS

### Behavioral

Aggression can be overt (verbal negative statements) or covert (lying, stealing) (Little, Jones, Henrich, & Hawley, 2003), although the two types of aggression are correlated (i.e., a child who shows more of one type will also show more of the other; for a review, see Wenar & Kerig, 2006). Two behavioral predictors of CD are early substance abuse and antisocial behavior (Moffitt et al., 2008).

### Social-Emotional

Aggressive behavior differs on the social basis of why it is initiated—proactively versus reactively (offensively versus defensively) (Little et al., 2003). Children with CD show both proactive and reactive aggression, but their reactive aggression is interpreted by others as "mean" and appears to be related to impulsivity and poor frustration tolerance (i.e., it is sometimes a reaction to a history of abuse). Proactive aggression is more goal oriented or instrumental (i.e., to obtain resources) and is related to higher social competence (Little et al., 2003).

Children with **externalizing disorders** pay less attention than their peers to subtle emotions, as demonstrated by their (a) self-reporting fewer feelings of fear or sadness in difficult social situations, (b) greater difficulty recognizing facial sadness than other emotions, (c) interpreting their own fear or sadness as anger or general arousal, (d) recalling fewer social cues, and (e) selectively attending to the salient cue of hostility in ambiguous situations (e.g., Braaten & Rosen, 2000). In other words, when students fail to identify their own or others' subtle emotions, they feel unprepared for coping with social situations and with the emotions involved. Children with ADHD plus aggression also misidentify the emotions of others; for example, they tend to misinterpret sadness as anger (Kats-Gold, Besser, & Priel, 2007). Children with CD are often described as having callous or unemotional characteristics that are useful in predicting severe and persistent delinquency (Pardini & Fite, 2010).

**Externalizing disorders:** Disorders that cause children to act out emotions through aggressive or disruptive behavior.

## Cognitive

Documented in students with CD are difficulties sustaining attention, planning, and verbal memory (e.g., repeating sentences; Olvera, Semrud-Clikeman, Pliszka, & O'Donnell, 2005). Considerable research links lower-than-average verbal intelligence to antisocial behavior (APA, 2000; Lahey, Moffitt, & Caspi, 2003). Also documented are deficits in EF, especially on assessments of cognitive flexibility (Olvera et al., 2005), and cognitive distortions or misinterpretations of ambiguous social events (e.g., being bumped into, other children laughing) as indicating hostile intentions (Little et al., 2003). This bias in interpretations can be explained as a child's learning from past experiences (as a victim and a bully) to expect hostility and aggression from others (for a review, see Zentall, Cassady, & Javorsky, 2001).

## Communication

Verbal deficits are found at high rates in children with CD, delinquent adolescents, and adult criminals; in fact, research has found that 26% of delinquents but only 2% of comparisons scored two or more *SD* below the mean on language skills (Lynam & Henry, 2001). In addition, poor language test performance has been shown to be associated with more verbal aggression in class (swearing, name-calling, and rude language) (Olvera et al., 2005).

## Academic

Among children with CD, reading and other verbal skills are often lower than what would be expected based on their age and intelligence, although older students may show poorer academic functioning explained by their skipping school or being expelled. Long-term research suggests that co-occurring ADHD also predicts academic problems in boys (Pardini & Fite, 2010).

## DISABILITY IN THE CLASSROOM

### Implications for Accommodations in General Education Settings: Tier I

Children with CD, especially at older age levels, are rarely found in general education settings and are often placed in alternative educational settings. However, IDEA specifies principles that relate to the suspension of students with aggression. For example, a school cannot expel or suspend a student for more than 10 days in any one school year and has no obligation to offer services to the suspended student. If a school determines that a student's unacceptable behavior is unrelated to a previously defined disability, it may discipline the student in the same way it would the student's peers.

Because of the seriousness of outcomes for children who are "discipline problems" with or without a disability label, accommodations are suggested to prevent aggressive behavior without punitive or suppressive efforts (Foltz, 2008). Because these children typically justify their own anger and aggression based on others' hostility, it is important for educators *not* to meet hostile behavior from the child with hostile punishment. That is, adult aggression reinforces the child's perception of the world as hostile. More appropriate accommodations for children with CD do the following:

- Encourage routines, appeal to the students' interests, and prompt them prior to difficult settings that could elicit aggression (e.g., crowding, entering groups). Giving children choices does not mean giving them positive things after they have tantrums; offering choices is a preventive measure.
- Include as many adults as possible in the setting and increase the numbers of available materials, supplies, and spaces within which the children can play and learn. It is important that educators *not* yell at or use loud public reprimands for children with ADHD plus aggression, as these responses can increase aggressive and off-task behavior (for a review, see Zentall, 2006). In other words, it is important to increase emotional reactions to prosocial behavior and decrease emotional responses to inappropriate behavior (i.e., the reverse of what is typically done). Asking children to restate verbally the prior events of a social interaction is an effective way to handle a challenging conflict interaction (Zentall, Cassady, & Javorsky, 2001).

- Respond to aggression with a nonemotional consequence- and rules-based system (i.e., rules with reasons about safety, comfort, learning, communication, fairness, life, health, and so on) that includes high doses of positive feedback. In fact, one study found that only 11% of teachers' behavior reinforced the appropriate behavior in disruptive children, in contrast to 82% of teachers' behavior reinforcing the positive responses of appropriate behavior of nondisruptive classmates (van Lier et al., 2004). In addition, it may be important to teach the peers of children with CD to respond with disapproval in low tones or with nonverbal, nonemotional reactions (e.g., by walking away) when confronted by aggressive social behavior, because asking peers to ignore aggressive behavior is difficult and seems to communicate to students with ADHD and aggression that aggressive behavior is acceptable (Meyer & Zentall, 1995).

## Implications for Interventions in Small-Group and Individual Settings: Tiers II and III

At a minimum, Tier II interventions should involve FA to assess for environmental triggers of aggressive behavior and should be supported by a team that includes a special educator, a behavioral consultant, a therapist or school counselor, and the like. Tier II interventions should take the following approaches:

- Use cognitive-behavioral therapy, the goals of which are to improve problem-solving skills, communication, impulse control, and anger management skills.
- Teach adolescents to use a "hassle log" to record aggressive or emotional reactions in their daily lives so that they can begin to understand what events trigger anger (Feindler & Ecton, 1986). Younger students might make drawings of difficult situations.
- Train students with aggression to use small notebooks during free time to tally their negative and positive behavior, report the results, and receive feedback from the teacher for improved positive social interactions and reduced negative interactions with peers (Gumpel & David, 2000).
- Teach boys with aggression to ask questions rather than make demands when entering new groups (Tryon & Keane, 1991).

Although medication can be useful for ODD, it should be noted that medication is *not* considered effective in the treatment of CD (Wenar & Kerig, 2006).

## Long-Term Outcomes

Oppositional behavior and aggression are two problem behaviors that result in referral for special education services. Early onset predicts poorer long-term outcomes (e.g., violence in the home, criminality, personality and other mental disorders, substance abuse, work and family life problems, physical health problems, and low income; Hodgins, Cree, Alderton, & Mak, 2008; Moffitt et al., 2008). There is *continuity* of CD from preschool to adolescence and from adolescence to adulthood, with only 14% of children improving. Co-occurrence with ADHD makes CD problems more resistant to change (for a review, see Wenar & Kerig, 2006), but girls show less continuity or greater response to intervention and more often show late-onset CD (Moffitt et al., 2008). However, girls also show an increased dropout rate and pregnancy (Loeber et al., 2009). Some children with CD go on to develop schizophrenia, and schizophrenia is more common in CD than it is in the general population (for a review, see Hodgins et al., 2008). For those with late onset the outcomes are relatively better, with less impairment in work, education, and health, but negative outcomes do include substance abuse and undetected crimes (Moffitt et al., 2008).

## PERSONALITY DISORDERS: NARCISSISM

**Figure 11.3**  An Older Student with Characteristics of Narcissistic Personality Disorder

Marcos, a fourth-grade boy, had trouble playing with his peers at recess and always wanted to be the hero and the winner. When not the boss of the game, he would quit, saying that he was bored. Playing *his* way was something he was very passionate and proud of, because he thought he *was* the best. While playing cars one day with two other boys, who were not following his rules, he hit one of them and verbally attacked the other. After that, he just walked away and went to tell on the other boys, because in his opinion they had offended him by not listening. Marcos was very demanding and wanted to get everything he asked for, or else he threatened his parents and his teacher. When he did something he was asked to do, he expected a payback even if what he did was his responsibility.

The term *narcissism* has its origins in the ancient Greek myth about a man named Narcissus who rejected the advances of a nymph named Echo. Echo punished Narcissus by dooming him to fall in love with his own reflection in a pool of water. The NPD pattern represents an obsession with one's own gratification and dominance over others. It does not indicate a random (nonpersonal) pattern of aggression but only instrumental aggression in the service of the self. Even though the American Psychiatric Association is considering eliminating NPD as a diagnostic category in *DSM-V,* the behavior associated with NPD can still be recognized as a characteristic pattern of responding.

## FORMAL IDENTIFICATION

### Definitions

#### IDEA

IDEA defines this group of children under the category of EBD (see the Section V overview).

#### DSM-IV-TR

*DSM-IV-TR* (APA, 2000, p. 714) defines NPD as follows:

*Defining characteristics:* At least five of the following are necessary:

- Grandiose sense of self-importance
- Fantasies of unlimited success, power, brilliance, beauty, or ideal love
- Believe that they are superior, special, or unique and expect others to recognize them as such
- Generally require excessive admiration

- A sense of entitlement . . . [with] unreasonable expectation of especially favorable treatment
- The conscious or unwitting exploitation of others
- Lack of empathy and difficulty recognizing the desires, subjective experiences, and feelings of others
- Often envious of others or believes that others are envious of them

### Frequently Occurring Subtypes and Differences Among Related Disorders

There are two subtypes of NPD: narcissistic grandiosity and narcissistic vulnerability. Individuals with the grandiosity subtype repress negative aspects of self, have an inflated self-image, fantasize about power and wealth, and exhibit harsh envy and aggression; this is the subtype that will be discussed here. Individuals with the vulnerability subtype have a diminished self-image, are shameful and depressed, and are socially withdrawn (Pincus & Lukowitsky 2009).

Narcissists appear to have high self-regard. Healthy nonaggressive individuals also have a healthy self-regard, but they differ from those with NPD in that narcissists have *inflated* views of themselves along with accompanying aggression. Narcissists wish to have status over others, a characteristic associated with low self-esteem, not high self-esteem (Barry, Frick, & Killian, 2003). In other words, we must all take into account the total fabric of who we are—including the negatives. Individuals with NPD, however, view themselves as only positive and as "entitled" to rights (**positive entitlement**) and protected from wrongs (**negative entitlement**). Arrogance (defined as expressing one's own abilities regardless of the opinions of others) can be seen in children with giftedness, but in these children, unlike in those with NPD, it is not a cover for internal emptiness. Gifted children truly are competent and do have empathy for others.

**Positive entitlement:** The feeling that one is "owed" good things, such as respect and positive outcomes.

**Negative entitlement:** The feeling that one "deserves" to be protected from bad outcomes or unpleasant experiences because one is special.

## Prevalence, Gender, Age, and Cultural Factors

*Prevalence.* Although NPD used to be associated primarily with adults, characteristics of the disorder may be seen in children. Some of these are developmentally appropriate, as can be seen in 2-year-olds and in adolescents: "Narcissistic traits may be particularly common in adolescents and do not necessarily indicate that the individual will go on to have Narcissistic Personality Disorder" (APA, 2000, p. 716). However, some children do not outgrow this selfishness and seem to view the world without regard for others' needs or rights. Around 1% of the general population suffers from NPD; in clinical groups, the proportion is 2–16% (APA, 2000).

*Gender.* Males represent about 75% of those diagnosed with NPD.

*Age.* Since many adolescents have characteristics of NPD, it may be important to note the degree to which a child manifests these characteristics rather than to diagnose NPD.

*Culture.* Children of parents with NPD, adopted children, children of successful parents, coddled and wealthy children, and children of divorce are more likely than other children to have NPD (Bardenstein, 2009).

## INFORMAL EDUCATOR IDENTIFICATION OF CHARACTERISTICS

### Behavioral

Adolescent narcissists admit to participating in delinquent behavior: 72% say they misuse illicit drugs and 69% say they misuse alcohol, and 88% say they are sexually overseductive or proactive (Westen, Dutra, & Shedler, 2005). The most visible behavior in the disorder is the way a child with NPD deals with peers and authority figures when thwarted. The child feels entitled and when denied will respond with rage or by holding grudges and retaliating later. The child forms a false self (image and memories) and spends most behavioral energy protecting this false self-image by being useful (charming, simulated emotions, attends to others' superficial needs). Self-protection can also involve delinquent behavior, lying, and bossiness. Jack, whose case study appears at the end of this chapter, has some of these qualities:

> When handling a lot of these situations, Jack yelled as loud as he could to get others to pay attention to him. Many times throughout free time, Jack was yelling . . . when he was upset that things weren't going his way.

### Social-Emotional

The impairment of these children is social, as indicated by their lack of true concern for the needs of others (i.e., they attend to others' needs only to get something in return), poor moral development, and orientation toward immediate rewards. They also have a preference for being alone or physically distant rather than for social relatedness. For the most part, the primary emotional characteristic is anger, which often lies just below the surface. These children have suffered humiliation and embarrassment at not being loved originally for who they were, and as a defense they are **apathetic** and without true feelings beyond anger.

**Apathetic:** Indifferent (without emotion).

**Grandiosity:**
Feelings of superiority and entitlement often accompanied by fantasies of winning, becoming powerful, or gaining revenge for perceived injustice.

Low self-esteem makes individuals with NPD very sensitive to criticism or defeat. Although they may not show it outwardly, criticism may haunt them and may leave them feeling humiliated. They may react with disdain, rage, envy, or defiant counterattacks to any perceived attack to protect their **grandiosity** and feelings of entitlement. Seeing oneself as "better than others" justifies manipulating others to satisfy needs. This can be seen in Jack:

> When free time is about to end, the students are responsible for cleaning up their area and helping their peers. Jack tried the best he could to avoid cleaning up. Instead of cleaning up, Jack continued to sit at a table and color. When reminded to help clean up, he got up and threw his paper on the floor instead of putting it in his cubby.

## Cognitive and Communication

Cognitive distortions are common in children with NPD and include distortions related to entitlement about the self, the world, and the future (Ronningstam, 2005). Jack's case illustrates this: "One day, he got up and started telling the other students that he was ET and was going to get everyone." His feelings of "specialness" were reflected in his seeing himself as ET. These children's view of communicating with another person is that of getting something out of someone; they believe in tit for tat and "I won't do that unless I get something for it." More frequently, children with NPD issue commands or demands, such as "Give it to me," "I said I want it!," "Buy me . . . ," "Take me . . . ." This type of communication was observed in Jack:

> Each morning, the children are served breakfast. Jack would usually come running down the stairs in the morning, scream to everyone that he was there, and start running around. . . . When it was announced that breakfast was ready, Jack would run as fast as he could to make sure he was the first in line. If he wasn't, he would throw a fit. A few mornings, Jack did not like what was being served for breakfast. He would tell his teacher he didn't like it, and would yell as loud as he could that he was not going to eat it. He would also demand that she get him something else to eat.

## Academic

The implications of NPD for academic achievement are minimal, because many of these students have considerable ambition and academic self-confidence (APA, 2000). Children with NPD are more likely to perform well under pressure

(Vogel, 2006), and they also have an extreme need for success. Achievement for these children is getting admiration rather than gaining knowledge. For example, Jack's need for a positive image was always at the forefront: "At one point, his teacher gave him a smiley face on his paper, and that was not good enough for him. He made sure she also put a star on his paper." Thus, for the narcissist "how things appear is more important than how things really are" (Webb et al., 2005, p. 81). There are, however, negative implications for classroom performance by children with NPD "due to intolerance of criticism or defeat" (APA, 2000, p. 716). This and the fact that they do not acknowledge the rights of others contribute to their poor performance in classroom small groups (Vogel, 2006).

## DISABILITY IN THE CLASSROOM

### Implications for Accommodations in General Education Settings: Tier I

The people surrounding the narcissist typically do the changing, because it is so difficult for individuals with NPD to change. Some ideas for accommodations for children with NPD include (a) "buttering them up" and letting them be the center of attention, because they do well under pressure; (b) making contracts with them that specify they are not going to get praise/resources until the teacher gets what he or she is looking for; and (c) using competition to motivate them to learn, because they always have to be the best (Barry et al., 2003).

### Implications for Interventions in Small-Group and Individual Settings: Tiers II and III

A support team (including a special educator, behavioral consultant, therapist, school counselor, and so on) is especially important for the student with NPD. Interventions with these students should take the following into account:

- Students with NPD need an understanding of the distorted belief that "I am special." Cognitive-behavioral treatment helps with such cognitive distortions and can help subdue the disorder temporarily (for a review, see Loeber et al., 2009). However, it is very rarely cured—getting rid of narcissism is similar to getting rid of one's personality.
- Students with NPD need to learn empathy and to see things from others' perspectives, to understand the difference between true friendship and using people to get recognition/resources, and to focus on key emotions and constructs such as pain, sympathy, duty, fairness, and self-control.

## Long-Term Outcomes

Most narcissists have trouble regulating their behavior but may be less aggressive when they have more guilt, role-taking or perspective-taking abilities, and self-awareness. In those with NPD, "sometimes vocational functioning can be very low, reflecting an unwillingness to take a risk in competitive or other situations in which defeat is possible" (APA, 2000, p. 716).

## CHAPTER SUMMARY

- The social disorders that fall within the behaviorally disordered category are often associated with aggression (active or passive). Behavioral disorders often co-occur with ADHD or with the emotional disorders of anxiety and depression. It can be difficult to distinguish among related disabilities, since oppositional behavior occurs normally at around 2 years and during adolescence, and narcissism (inflated self-centeredness) is characteristic of most children. However, NPD is also characterized by entitlement, and CD is relatively easy to spot as it includes the violation of persons, animals, or property.

- The etiology of these disorders appears in the poor match between the inborn difficult qualities of the child (e.g., irritable, explosive, inflexible) and the negative qualities of the parent, family, or school (e.g., low supervision and involvement, harsh discipline, conflict, physical abuse, low income, and/or poor educational background). Immediate antecedents are often demands/requests. Noncompliance and aggression often function to avoid possible failure, loss of control, or loss of esteem. Aggression can also function to get resources.

- Aggressive and defiant behavior emerges at about 3 years. ODD occurs before the age of 8, and symptoms may change during elementary school with increased use of drugs. NPD and CD are most often identified during adolescence. Rates of ODD are similar in boys and girls, especially in young children; girls often express oppositionality through passivity and express aggression through negative social behavior (gossiping). NPD and CD are found at much higher rates in boys than in girls. Cultural effects are related to SES, with low income and single parenting risk factors for the development of oppositionality.

- Educators can easily observe externalizing behavior of refusal, noncompliance, and aggression in children with ODD and CD. They may have greater difficulty identifying the lying, rage, oversensitivity, and feelings of entitlement that characterize children with NPD; the lack of empathy in children with NPD and CD is also difficult to identify.

- Cognitively, young children with these disorders show difficulty adapting to new settings and respond with aggression. Children with NPD see others as failing to recognize their "specialness." Children with ODD and CD often have lower verbal IQ than their peers and poor language skills, which contribute to their acting-out behavior. In line with their past experiences, these children have biased interpretations that others are making unreasonable demands or are hostile. For those children who are highly active or who have limited skills, behavior or performance requirements/demands may be unreasonable.

- Low academic achievement is common in children with behavioral disorders, especially in the area of language arts (reading). This is not the case for students with NPD, who mainly perform well in academic settings but may have difficulty in classroom small groups.

- Appropriate interventions for children with externalizing behavioral disorders include behavior modification with positive consequences and contracts (teaching cooperative and assertive behavior) and functional analysis to identify whether the behavior is offensive or defensive and specifically what the child "needs" (e.g., avoidance of failure or getting control).

## CHAPTER QUESTIONS

### Oppositional Defiant Disorder

1. Oppositionality can function to either get or achieve certain outcomes or to avoid certain outcomes. Can you give an example of each of these?

2. Although popularity may not be essential for children with mild disabilities, what social outcome might be essential for any child?

3. How is the behavior of girls with ODD different from that of boys with ODD?

4. What part do families play in the expression of ODD?

5. At which two age levels is oppositionality developmentally appropriate?

6. Can children with ODD become physically aggressive?

### Aggression/Conduct Disorders

1. How is aggressive behavior different from a diagnosis of conduct disorder?

2. Why is aggression so difficult to change once it has been learned?

3. How might poor verbal skills contribute to children's aggressiveness?

4. Why do yelling and using loud public reprimands make aggression worse in children with ADHD?

5. How does the school environment increase the expression of aggression in children?

6. Present an argument to respond to a teacher who says, "Why bother to invest time in a student with CD, since you cannot change the student's home environment?"

## Narcissistic Personality Disorder

1. How can it be that children feel entitled even when they have low self-esteem?

2. What kinds of things would you look for that would indicate that a child lacks empathy, especially when some children will copy others' facial expressions of feelings in social settings?

3. Are children with NPD likely to be high achievers?

## Multiple-Choice

1. ODD can be generally categorized as behavior that functions

   A. to get self-determination/control
   B. to avoid tasks
   C. A & B

2. Parents or guardians who infrequently monitor or supervise their children are likely to increase the children's probability of

   A. delinquency
   B. depression
   C. anxiety

3. Parental factor(s) contributing to CD in children:

   A. punitiveness
   B. permissiveness
   C. mental illness
   D. all of the above

4. Children who violate persons, animals, and the property of others have

   A. ODD
   B. ADHD
   C. CD
   D. all of the above

5. Risk taking is a behavior found in

   A. NPD
   B. ADHD
   C. CD
   D. B & C
   E. All of the above

6. Girls express aggression differently from boys, through

   A. physical aggression
   B. gossip and "icing"
   C. verbal threats
   D. A & B

7. Which of the following factors does *not* increase aggression in school?

   A. teacher or peer models who are aggressive
   B. noisy situations
   C. competitive activities and crowding
   D. self-paced transitions from one activity or another

8. Some individuals think that things should go their way and turn out well for them and that they should not encounter bad things. This is called

   A. entitlement
   B. dysphoria
   C. perseverative thinking

## SHORT ANSWER

1. Responding to others' perceived threats with aggression is what type of aggression?

2. The type of entitlement in which a person feels that no bad things should ever happen to him or her is _____ entitlement.

3. A disorder wherein a person violates the person or property of another

4. Bullying to obtain resources is an example of _____ aggression.

5. An appropriate accommodation for children with ODD is to provide _____.

6. A response that depends on the behavior of another is called a _____ response.

**PROBLEM-BASED CASE APPLICATIONS AND QUESTIONS**

## CASE STUDY 11.1: LILY

*("She shouted, 'NO!'")*
(adapted from an assignment submitted by Jia Liu)

See Appendix II for this case study's data.

## Case Questions

1: Under what conditions (settings/tasks/peer interactions) does Lily show appropriate social responses?

2: What are Lily's preferred activities that could be made contingent on specific behavior?

3: What are Lily's strengths?

4: Lily has many possible diagnoses and a language difference. Where would you begin helping her?

5: In what setting would you begin your interventions? Why?

6: What are some accommodations that should be made for Lily's need for activity, and in which settings are they needed?

## CASE STUDY 11.2: JACK

*("Look everybody, its me—Jack.")*
(adapted from a report submitted by Megan Lerch-Gordon)

*Background.* Jack is a 6-year-old student who attends a general education classroom in a local elementary school. Jack is above average in the areas of both math and reading. He reads at a second-grade level and loves to read but sometimes has a hard time staying on task. His teacher says some of his off-task behavior is due to assignments that are too easy. He can breeze through an assignment and then gets bored. His teacher feels that sometimes he has a hard time making and keeping friends. Jack can be very loud and likes to scream, which scares his peers.

The behavior that Jack displayed most often during the observation period was not following directions. See Figure 11.4. Many times, Jack would start an assignment without listening, not pick up during cleanup time, and not do what was asked of him.

**Figure 11.4**   Jack's Behaviors

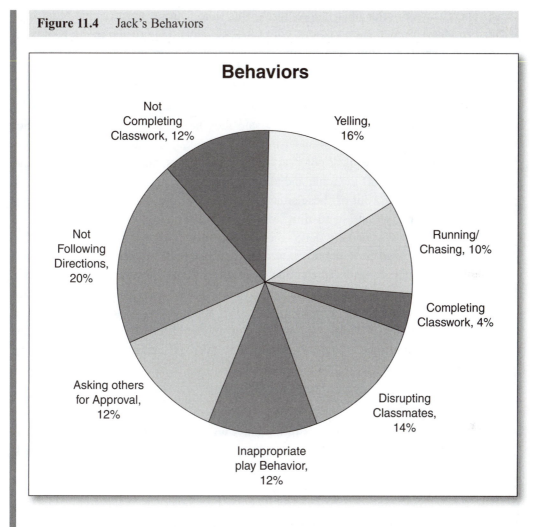

# Behaviors

- Not Completing Classwork, 12%
- Yelling, 16%
- Running/Chasing, 10%
- Completing Classwork, 4%
- Disrupting Classmates, 14%
- Inappropriate play Behavior, 12%
- Asking others for Approval, 12%
- Not Following Directions, 20%

Another very common behavior for Jack was yelling. Yelling occurred mainly during actitivies with little to no structure, such as at breakfast or lunch and during free time. Jack also had a difficult time playing with his peers. He would engage in name-calling and bossing them around. Another high-percentage behavior was disrupting classmates. When others were supposed to be working, Jack would be trying to talk to them, reading out loud, telling them to watch him do his work, or telling them to copy off him.

## Behavioral Log

### Free Time

During free time the students were allowed to play with table activities—such as blocks, dolls, card and board games, and cars—play in the kitchen area, or have free art. There was not a lot of structure during this time. During most of this time, Jack liked to play card and board games with other students. One of the many behaviors observed during this time were continual conflicts with his peers.

- During a game of Bingo, Jack decided to get under a table when he was the number caller. Because he could not see his peers' cards when he was under the table, he did not believe when they said they had a number he had called. So, instead of getting out from under the table to look, he began to call them names.
- In another instance, Jack got mad at one of his peers, and he took his hand and wiped the cards off the table and all over the floor.
- When handling a lot of these situations, Jack yelled as loud as he could to get others to pay attention to him. Many times throughout free time, Jack was yelling. This was usually done when he was upset that things weren't going his way and he wanted to get an emotional response from his peers.
- When free time is about to end, the students are responsible for cleaning up their area and helping their peers. Jack tried the best he could to avoid cleaning up. Instead of cleaning up, Jack continued to sit at a table and color.
- When reminded to help clean up, he got up and threw his paper on the floor instead of putting it in his cubby. He would also get up and wander around the room instead of helping clean up.

### Seatwork, Coloring

During this period each student in the class was given a coloring sheet related to weather to complete. During this antecedent, several different behaviors from Jack were observed.

- When given this coloring activity, Jack decided to take his red crayon and scribble all over his paper. He told his teacher that the reason he did this was because coloring would take way too long to do if he took his time.
- His teacher gave him another sheet, and he began to take his time.
- He also told the other students that he would steal the day care's crayons when the teacher wasn't looking and that she would not ever know that he had taken them.
- Finally, when he handed in his coloring activity, his teacher gave him praise and put a sticker on it. He did not think he had done a very good job on it, so he started drawing sad faces all over his project.

### Seatwork, Math

Math is a very strong subject for Jack. He is further advanced in math than the other four students in his day-care group. Individual math is done at a long table, and each student has an assigned seat at the table. The students are spaced apart to help decrease distraction when they are completing their work. During the individual seatwork in math antecedent, adding one-digit numbers and skip counting were the primary focuses.

- During math-related activities, Jack had a very hard time staying in his seat and working. He would often tell the other students what they were supposed to be doing and at one point even told them they could copy off of his work.
- One day, he got up and started telling the other students that he was ET and was going to get everyone.

### Seatwork, Writing

Writing was done individually at the same table where individual math was conducted. Jack is a very good writer.

- When working on writing assignments, he would go off on his own without listening to the teacher's instructions.
- He would sound out words all on his own, and help others spell words. However, he made it very clear to other students when they had made spelling mistakes.
- Many times, Jack would talk out loud as he wrote. This would sometimes make his peers mad, because it would distract them from their own work.
- He would also ask the other students to watch him write, so they could see how to write the right way.

### Seatwork, Reading

Reading is probably Jack's strongest area. As stated before, he reads at about a second-grade level and is a lot further ahead than the rest of his peers. He enjoys reading out loud and to his peers. While reading is his favorite subject, several different behaviors were still seen during this antecedent.

- When given a reading-related assignment and asked to put his name on the paper, he said he was not going to because the assignment would be way too easy for him and he didn't need to do it. Since reading is something he is very good at, he likes to make sure he is doing a good job. This seems to allow for him to get competence in something he is good at and makes him feel good about himself.
- During reading, he asked his teacher several times if he was doing a good job, and when she told him yes, he would let his peers know that the teacher had told him he was.
- At one point, his teacher gave him a smiley face on his paper, and that was not good enough for him. He made sure she also put a star on his paper.

- Jack would breeze through reading activities, so this would lead him to activities that would get him into trouble, such as standing up and running around, disrupting his peers, and being loud.

## Group Work, Math

A math lesson was conducted in a group setting at a round table where students were given assigned seats. During the observations of math in a group work setting, the students were working on estimation.

- Whenever the teacher asked the students to write down an estimate, Jack would automatically yell his answers out loud.
- The group was estimating using manipulatives. Jack would continually try to remove the manipulatives from the table and hide them. This would instantly make his peers upset and cause a fight.
- Also, every time Jack's estimation was correct or close to the correct answer, he would stand up and shake his bottom and dance around. When he was not correct, he would slam his hand down on the table or yell out loud.

## Breakfast/Lunch

Each morning, the children are served breakfast.

- Jack would usually come running down the stairs in the morning, scream to everyone that he was there, and start running around. Students are to sit at a table and do table activities, such as draw, play with games, play with blocks, or work on homework. When it is announced that breakfast is ready, the students may get in line to get their breakfast.
- When it was announced that breakfast was ready, Jack would run as fast as he could to make sure he was the first in line. If he wasn't, he would throw a fit.
- A few mornings, Jack did not like what was being served for breakfast. He would tell his teacher he didn't like it, and would yell as loud as he could that he was not going to eat it. He would also demand that she get him something else to eat. When he was frustrated about breakfast, he would sit at the table and cry and sometimes scream at the other students. His peers would get very frustrated with him and get away from him. Students would even cover their ears and ask the teacher to make him stop yelling.
- At lunchtime, the kindergarten students are the only students at the day care. The five of them sit at a table together to eat lunch. The students may choose where they sit at the table. During lunch, Jack would always fight about whom he would want to sit by. This would cause a great debate between him and his peers.

- While Jack was eating, he would take his hand and wipe all of his trash onto the floor. He would also just randomly get up, run around the table, and come back and sit down. On one occasion, he stuffed his mouth full of food and told all of his peers to look at him and then began to spit it out all over.

## ABC Analysis

For the most part, Jack would do what he was told to do after receiving a verbal warning (36% of the time). See Figure 11.5. However, there were a few instances in which he continued to do what he was not supposed to be doing. Some of these instances led to Jack having to serve a time-out. Another significant consequence of Jack's behavior was being rejected by his peers. When Jack would act up, scream, name-call, or chase his peers, they would walk away from him or tell him they did not want to be his friend. Sometimes peer rejection would lead to another student telling on him. This would always make him very upset.

**Figure 11.5** Jack's Consequences

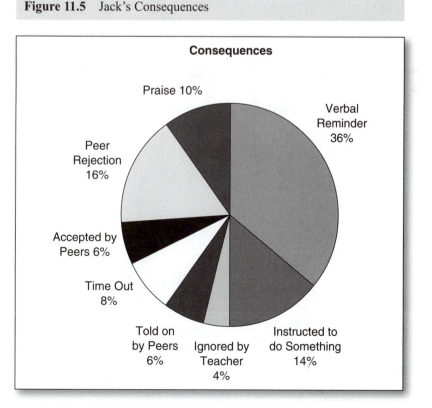

When his teacher would give him praise, he wanted his peers to know he had received praise. Praise is something Jack loves. Sometimes, Jack's behaviors would be ignored by his teacher and his peers, and he did not like being ignored, and this would usually lead him to act out more.

*High-frequency payoffs.* The payoffs for Jack's behaviors (see Figure 11.7) show that he has a very high need to get negative emotional stimulation from his peers. He also likes to get self-determination or control.

## Diagnosis Versus ABC Analysis

Jack is very outgoing, and he can get very loud and aggressive with his peers. He attempts to control situations to his advantage (self-determination and competence), especially when he has direct contact with his peers (e.g., transitions, free time, during breakfast and lunch). Across all settings (see Figure 11.6), Jack's 18% payoff of getting competence or "looking good," was often at the expense of others. Jack is currently showing aggressive behavior, with some behavior that is consistent with NPD characteristics.

**Figure 11.6** Jack's Payoffs

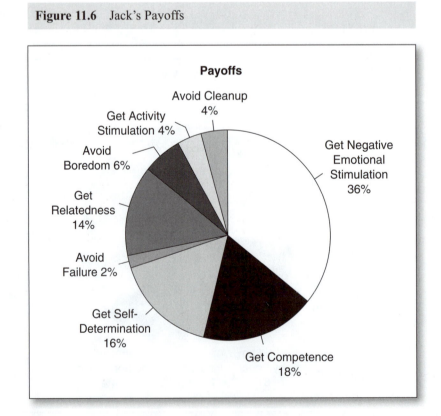

## Interventions Derived From ABC Analysis

Jack has a very hard time maintaining friendships. His peers do not see him as the very intelligent student he is, but as the student who comes up and screams in their ears or the one who seems to be bossing them around. For the purpose of intervention, I am going to focus on Jack's most frequent needs for getting negative emotional stimulation and getting competence. Jack really enjoys reading. He finds great joy in being able to pick out the book that the teacher is going to read for the day. He is also a very good reader. To address the payoff of getting emotional stimulation through dramatic reading, scary stoires will be used. Scary stories "deliver an emotional punch" (Richards et al., 1999). Jack has a very high need for emotional stimulation, and through reading scary stories, he can get the emotional stimulation that he needs and can relay that emotion to me or his peers in a way that is not negative and will not get him into trouble.

At the start of the week, Jack will be provided with the book *Disney's Classic Scary Story Book*. The stories within this book are based on Disney animated films and contain original Disney characters, such as Mickey Mouse and Nemo. On Day 1, Jack will be allowed to pick one scary story to focus on for a two-day period. On the first day with the new story, I will read the story to Jack, using intonation and different voices to act out the story. After I finish reading the story to him, he and I will take turns reading the story together, due to the fact that some of the stories are a little bit longer. During this time, I will continue to use different types of intonation to "act out" the story. I will ask Jack to read like he is "acting out" the story too in a scary way.

On Day 2, Jack will be able to pick a friend to read at least part of the story to. I will remind him that when he is reading with his peer, he needs to read the story and try to "act it out" for them. After the first two days, Jack will be allowed to pick out another story. We will again follow the same routine. On Day 2 he will pick a new peer and read the story.

The goal of this intervention is to decrease Jack's need to get negative emotional stimulation. Each day, I will monitor his behaviors during free time and breakfast and lunch. I will record any behavior that relates to his payoff of getting negative emotional stimulation. The ultimate goal is that Jack's yelling will decrease by 50% from the baseline mean. If it does, he will be able to pick out our next scary story. However, on days that the occurrences of yelling do not decrease, Jack will not be able to pick out another story; rather, I will pick it for him. On the very last day of the 3-week intervention period, Jack will be allowed to read a scary story to the whole class.

### Baseline Data

- Baseline mean: 14.7
- Intervention mean: 9.1

*Summary of results.* Reading is something Jack loves to do. When I explained to him at the beginning of the intervention how each day was going to operate, he seemed very excited and wanted to start right away. Each morning, he would come running to me, asking if it was time to read. For him, this reading time was more than just being able to read and act out scary stories using his voice. It was a time for him to work one-on-one with an individual, whether an adult or one of his peers. When working with his peers, he treated them with respect and always made sure they were paying attention to him read. Out of the seven days that Jack was eligible to pick out a story to read, he earned the privilege on five days. On the days he did not get to pick out the story, he became very discouraged and complained that he did not really like the story that I had picked out for him. This seemed to give him some encouragement to remember not to scream with talking with his peers.

On days Jack got to read with his peers, he was even more eager. He worked really well with his peers. Not one time during paired reading did he yell or display any behaviors aimed at getting negative emotional stimulation. He used a variety of skills, such as using different types of intonation, when reading to his peers. While the overall mean of the number of times Jack yelled during unstructured activities did not decrease by 50% from the baseline mean, on the last day of the intervention, Jack yelled only five times during these activities. This is 75% less than the baseline mean. Jack began to utilize the time during reading with me or reading with a peer to gain positive emotional reactions instead of getting negative emotional stimulation.

This change was meaningful not only to Jack but also to his peers. They began to come up to him and want to play with him. They would argue over whom he would get to read to. His peers also seemed to benefit from this intervention and began to build relationships with him. Through this intervention using dramatic reading with scary stories, Jack seemed to gain an understanding of the meaning of obtaining emotional responses in appropriate ways.

## Case Questions

1: Jack was only 6 at the time of this observation. Why was it important to target his behavior at such a young age?

2: To what degree do you think the verbal reminders (consequences) were helpful to Jack? How do you know?

3 (problem-based small-group assignment): Design an alternative whole-class accommodations plan to help Jack feel competent. Design a Tier II intervention to teach Jack how to handle being ignored and bored.

# Chapter 12

## Internalizing Emotional Disorders

Healthy emotional development requires the ability to communicate feelings and needs (Greene, 2006, p. 287). Emotional disorders could be described as characterized by failing to communicate needs proactively, as well as overreacting or underreacting emotionally to setting conditions. Students within the ED category are children who have difficulty damping down the anxiety they feel and who overreact to situations of possible threat from the environment (e.g., anxiety about negative feedback from peers or teachers).

However, we all need some level of anxiety, which is important generally for the survival of the individual and of the species (i.e., anxiety contributes to the human ability to anticipate and prepare for extreme conditions of danger by attacking or escaping—fight/flight). Subjective anxiety (emotion) serves as a warning signal to prepare us for stressful conditions, which include difficult social requirements. We also require a certain level of arousal to motivate us to learn and to persist when faced with challenging or long tasks. However, humans are not suited to be in a constant state of alertness in preparation for attack. When alertness becomes a steady state, individuals are more likely to avoid tasks and social experiences, and when the anxiety is so intense and chronic that it interferes with functionality, it can be described as an anxiety disorder. Avoidance of particular tasks and situations can reduce learning, because learning involves taking some risk of failure while abandoning what is familiar, safe, and successful.

The IDEA definition combining BD and ED, presented in Chapter 11, is repeated below. In addition to the learning and social impairments described in A, B, and C, which are common for both ED and BD, criteria D and E are more

---

**Figure 12.1** A child with an Internalizing Emotional Disorder

characteristics of children with ED, the focus of this chapter. According to IDEA children with EBD exhibit

one or more of the following characteristics over a long period of time and to a marked degree that adversely affects a child's educational performance:

(A) An inability to learn that cannot be explained by intellectual, sensory, or health factors.

(B) An inability to build or maintain satisfactory interpersonal relationships with peers and teachers.

(C) Inappropriate types of behavior or feelings under normal circumstances.

(D) A general pervasive mood of unhappiness or depression.

(E) A tendency to develop physical symptoms or fears associated with personal or school problems. . . . Emotional disturbance includes schizophrenia. The term does not apply to children who are socially maladjusted. (34 C.F.R. Section 300.7[c][4][i])

These children can be difficult to identify because they are less able than other children to express their worries or their pain verbally. When pain exceeds a child's capacity for understanding how to cope with pain, as in Max's case, there may be a very direct reaction:

Max Blake was 7 the first time he tried to kill himself. He wrote a four-page will bequeathing his toys to his friends and jumped out of his ground-floor bedroom window, falling six feet into his backyard, bruised but in one piece. Children don't really know what death is . . . but they know what unhappiness is and what it means to suffer. (Carmichael, 2008, p. 33)

Some of these students will have externalizing behavior. For example, older children will mask sadness with acting-out, aggressive, and angry types of behavior (e.g., Hyde & Forsyth, 2002; Quinn, 1997). Younger children express sadness by playing less, and some children mask anxiety with stomachaches or headaches, which are experienced as real (Annemieke, de Wit, de Bruyn, Riksen-Walraven, & Rost, 2000). Some educators do not want to see or feel these distressing emotions in children. However, ignoring these signals decreases educational possibilities for these children.

The specific disorders that are presented in this ED category are interrelated through anxiety and heightened arousal. Anxiety involves (a) cognitive responses (i.e., subjective apprehension, worry, and thoughts about future danger or threat, selective attention to threatening stimuli when presented with ambiguous events),

(b) physiological responses that accompany fear (e.g., increased heart rate), and (c) behavioral responses that are typically avoidant (Drabick et al., 2010; Ollendick, Grills, & Alexander, 2001). Most important to understand are the different ways in which children in each subgroup *deal* with anxiety. For example, students with specific anxiety avoid types of events or persons associated with fear. Children with **obsessions** attempt to *control* their excessive anxiety through rituals or **compulsions,** and children with depressive disorders are generally passive and feel they have little control. Some people say that anxiety and depression are two sides of the same coin. Clearly there is evidence that anxiety identified in childhood predicts later depressive episodes (Cole et al., 1998). Because differential diagnosis will be a task assigned to a psychologist, it is most important for the educator to be able to identify the characteristics of anxiety and depression, even when these feelings are disguised as acting-out behavior and somatic complaints. Figure 12.2 provides more details about social disorders than were initially presented in Figure V.1 in the Section V overview.

**Obsessions:** Repeated unwanted thoughts involving feelings, images, or experiences that cause anxiety (e.g., "I am going to drive into the river").

**Compulsions:** Seemingly purposeful types of behavior that individuals perform to relieve, prevent, or undo the anxiety or discomfort created by their obsessions or to "magically" prevent some dreaded event or situation (Adams, 2004).

**Figure 12.2** Emotional Disorders

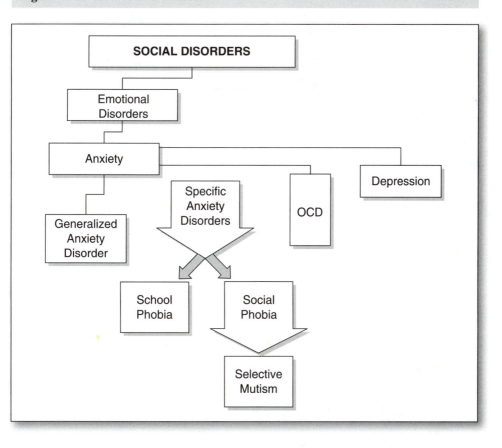

## GENERALIZED AND SPECIFIC ANXIETY DISORDERS

High levels of anxiety can be broadly based, across situations (generalized anxiety disorder), or specific to settings (e.g., school, social exchanges) or to more concrete stimuli (e.g., elevators, heights). See Figure 12.3. Each of these types of anxiety disorder is associated with distressing internal symptoms and avoidance behavior.

**Figure 12.3**   A Student with a Specific Anxiety Disorder Related to Spiders

## FORMAL IDENTIFICATION

### Definitions

#### *IDEA*

IDEA defines this group of children under the category of EBD (see the Section V overview).

#### *DSM-IV-TR*

*DSM-IV-TR* (APA, 2000) defines generalized anxiety disorder as follows:

*Defining characteristic:* Chronic anxiety is present, even when there is a little to no stress at hand, that is marked by irritability, fatigue, headaches, excessive sweating, etc.

- Excessive anxiety and worry (apprehension expectation), occurring more days than not for at least 6 months, about a number of events or activities (such as work or school performance).
- The person finds it difficult to control the worry.
- [In children] the anxiety and worry are associated with one or more of the following six symptoms (with at least some symptoms present for more days than not for the past 6 months): (1) restlessness or feeling keyed up or on edge, (2) being easily fatigued, (3) difficulty concentrating or mind going blank, (4) irritability, (5) muscle tension, and (6) sleep disturbance (difficulty falling or staying asleep, or restless, unsatisfying sleep).
- The focus of anxiety and worry is not confined to a particular situation or event (as in other anxiety disorders).

*Impairment:* "The anxiety, worry, or physical symptoms cause clinically significant distress or impairment in social, occupational, or other important areas of functioning [school or sports]."

### Frequently Occurring Subtypes

Specific anxiety disorders include social phobia (social anxiety disorder) and school phobia, both of which are discussed below. Within social anxiety disorders, there are additional subtypes (e.g., selective mutism). Additional disorders that are not classified above and less frequently seen in children include posttraumatic stress disorder and panic disorder.

**Posttraumatic stress disorder (PTSD)** is the result of experiencing, witnessing, or being confronted with an event involving actual or threatened serious injury or death that creates a response involving intense fear, helplessness, or horror. For an individual with PTSD, the reexperiencing of such a past event may be triggered by sounds, smells, or visual details associated with the event, and reexperiencing the event might occur in symbolic form during nightmares. Children with PTSD are hypervigilant (overly sensitive to possible threat) and may show startle reactions in response to unexpected sights or sounds. Although repetitive behavior (e.g., seen in compulsive disorders) usually relieves the anxiety associated with PTSD, reenactments of trauma through play do not reduce and may increase the level of anxiety for these students unless there is an element of repair imposed (Wenar & Kerig, 2006). In a sense, anxiety stemming from trauma is rationally based and might be considered an example of conditioned responding.

**Posttraumatic stress disorder (PTSD):** A condition characterized by continual reexperiencing of an earlier traumatic experience that involved death or serious injury or threat to the self or others. In children, behavioral responses to trauma include agitation or disorganization (APA, 2000).

Panic disorder is characterized by the abrupt onset of episodes of intense fear or discomfort, which peak in approximately 10 minutes and include a feeling of imminent danger or doom and the need to escape, with physical/somatic symptoms: palpitations, sweating, shortness of breath or feelings of smothering or of

**Agoraphobia:** A condition causing fear and avoidance of leaving one's home.

choking, chest pain or discomfort, nausea or abdominal discomfort, dizziness or lightheadedness, tingling sensations, chills or hot flushes, trembling, a sense of things being unreal, and a fear of losing control, "going crazy," or dying. These symptoms can occur with or without **agoraphobia.**

### Possible Co-Occurring Conditions and Differences Among Related Disabilities

Approximately 33% of children with anxiety disorders have met the criteria for two or more different subtypes of anxiety disorders (for a review, see Tannock, 2000). For students with a history of LD, there is a 92% incidence of anxiety disorders. Anxiety differs from fear in that it anticipates threat, whereas fear responds to immediately fearful conditions. Children who are *anxious* may be described as "worrying forward," anticipating something dangerous or difficult; in contrast, children with *depression* "worry backward," focusing on past actions, events, or persons (see Figure 12.4). That is, anxiety can be "characterized as a future-oriented emotion" (Silverman & Ollendick, 2005, p. 381); anxious children worry about themselves and others' reactions to them, whereas children with depression have already formed a negative self-concept (for a review, see Wenar & Kerig, 2006).

## Etiology

There is an interaction between a child's negative experiences and a child's more sensitive physiological reactions to these experiences (biogenetics plus history).

*Biogenetic.* For all individuals there are normal developmental stages of anxiety, described below under age factors. Differences from the "norm" are inherited differences in temperament (inhibited/shy, avoidant of novelty and challenge). Overall, heritability accounts for one-third of anxiety disorders, with many of these children's parents also reporting anxiety disorders (Wenar & Kerig, 2006).

**Figure 12.4**   Interrelations Among Fear, Anxiety, and Depression

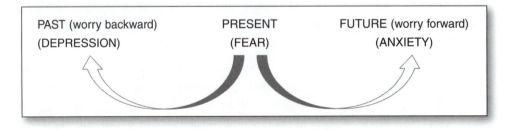

There are also locations in the brain that correspond to negative emotions, such as sadness and anxiety (left hemisphere), and to positive emotions (right hemisphere, including the nonverbal aspects of recognizing emotion, tone of voice, and conveying emotion through tone of voice) (Garrett, 2011).

*Environmental.* Some fears are based on one's own life experiences; for example, failure in school can lead to anticipation of future failure. Observation learning (e.g., of a dog biting another person or of a parent's response to dogs) can also create a focus for anxiety. In these ways anxiety is "contagious" and "children often 'catch it' from their parents" (Webb et al., 2005, p. 91). These would be called **conditioned fears** and not phobias, as these anxieties are rationally based on prior experience.

> **Conditioned fear:** Fear that is learned from observing another person's fearful or avoidant response or from direct experience with a traumatic event (e.g., being bitten by a dog).

*Functional.* In functional assessments, we would expect anxiety disorders to worsen under stress. However, there may be different stressors for different children (e.g., family problems, abuse, bullying, academic difficulties). Children cope with stressors in a variety of ways (e.g., upset stomachs or headaches, anger, aggression, regression), and these coping mechanisms usually work in the short term by enabling children to destroy or avoid stressors (fight or flight).

## Prevalence, Gender, Age, and Cultural Factors

*Prevalence.* Anxiety disorders are among the most common childhood emotional disorders, with prevalence rates from 10–21% in school-age populations (Dadds & Barrett, 2001) and as high as 45% in clinic populations (Wenar & Kerig, 2006). Anxiety disorders become more easily identifiable as children reach middle childhood and older. That is, prevalence rates increase from 8% (11-year-olds) to 20% (21-year-olds) (Wenar & Kerig, 2006).

*Gender.* By the age of 6, girls are twice as likely as boys to have an anxiety disorder; this difference increases over age levels (Ollendick et al., 2001; Wenar & Kerig, 2006).

*Age.* Normal fears begin with an infant's startle response (**Moro reflex**) and progress to fears of separation, followed by fears of imaginary creatures, animals, and the dark. In new situations, with new people, or with unpredictable events, children with trait anxiety will be more inhibited, physiologically aroused, and anxious than other children (Ollendick et al., 2001). Specific fears, such as fear of spiders, are more common in young children than in older children. For students of school age, fears are related to school, and during adolescence, fears are related

> **Moro reflex:** The inherited startle reflex.

to social and evaluative settings (Ollendick et al., 2001). In addition, as children age, the focus of anxiety may change or spread—for example, from fear of new situations to agoraphobia.

*Culture.* Race, culture, and/or ethnicity may contribute to anxiety disorders. For example, African Americans experience more **phobias,** panic disorders, and sleep problems relative to the general population; and individuals from Asian cultures are more likely to express anxiety of the somatic form (e.g., muscle tension) than the cognitive form (worrying) (see Wenar & Kerig, 2006).

**Phobia:** Irrational fear, such as fear of snakes or of the dark, that is *not* based on direct or observed experiences and may be associated with, or representative of, a past experience that was fear inducing (e.g., passing too near a cliff edge while driving). Some phobias are temporary and specific to a normal developmental period (e.g., fear of going into the attic).

# INFORMAL EDUCATOR IDENTIFICATION OF CHARACTERISTICS

## Behavioral

Anxiety is usually associated with introverted and avoidance types of behavior. There are some positive coping responses to anxiety, such as problem-focused coping that is related to long-term health, as well as excessive talking, physical exercise, sleeping, and emoting (laughing, crying, cursing). In addition, there are some negative coping responses, such as eating and drug use (alcohol, smoking), and neutral responses (pacing, finger tapping, hand rubbing, and retreating into fantasy and daydreaming to resolve problems) (for a review, see Penley, Tomaka, & Wiebe, 2002). Young children may have tantrums when confronted with anxiety-producing stimuli. Older children often show repetitive behavior; they are more likely to repeat statements or topics that relate to their concerns and/or to show nervous twitches/tics, habits, rituals, and routines. Some of these children are able to verbalize their fears, as was Pete, the case study in this chapter, who said "he was scared of new things."

## Social-Emotional

High anxiety has been linked with poor social adjustment. "Research suggests that approximately 10%–21% of children report clinical levels of anxiety that can impact [academic achievement], . . . social and peer relations, and future emotional health" (Kendall, Pimentel, Rynn, Angelosante, & Webb, 2004, p. 277). Pete reported some of these social and performance avoidance problems:

While there were times when he seemed to love attention, there were certainly other conditions when he wanted to be socially invisible (avoiding the social attention he might receive as a [probable] result of his failure). He was frequently down on himself. ("I'm not smart at all," "I can't do it, it's timed," "There's just so many problems with me.")

## Cognitive

Although anxious students are equivalent to others in basic intelligence and memory, there may be a link between high anxiety (high physiological arousal) and impaired cognitive functioning (Kendall et al., 2004). In addition, children with anxiety are more likely to misinterpret ambiguous situations by overestimating danger and underestimating their ability to cope (Bogels & Zigterman, 2000). Compared to typical children, anxious children are more likely to attend to threatening cues, become distracted by worry, focus on negative outcomes, recall threatening information, and interpret ambiguous information as threatening (Eisen, Brien, Bowers, & Strudler, 2001; Daleiden, 1998). That is, these children selectively attend to and recall threatening experiences, and form a cognitive picture of the world as a dangerous place.

## Communication

Anxiety can be reflected in the negative quality of statements that children make. For example, high levels of anxiety are related to statements about the self that are negative (e.g., "I thought I would fail") as well as overall negative statements ("Life is terrible") (Ollendick et al., 2001, p. 10). Some of the statements are subvocal negative self-statements. For example, a potentially threatening event (giving a speech) is often accompanied by exaggerated negative self-statements and warnings (be careful of this, don't do that, talk loud enough, look at the crowd/make eye contact) (Bogels & Zigterman, 2000; Kopecky, Sawyer, & Behnke, 2004).

## Academic

For all children, the performance of simple tasks can be improved by anxiety, but the performance of complex tasks is made worse (see Chapter 1). Complex tasks include those with multistep problems, those that require greater amounts of reading or communication, and those that are group or teacher paced. It is for this reason that impaired academic functioning has been reported at a significantly higher rate for students with high anxiety (Kendall et al., 2004). In the classroom, anxieties preoccupy a child's attention, such that less attention can be devoted to learning. For example, a young child with a spider phobia was intent upon investigating each corner and window of a room before he could be reassured that it was safe for her to begin her work. See Figure 12.3.

# SCHOOL REFUSAL

**School phobia:** A specific disorder of school refusal wherein children avoid school in favor of staying home because of an irrational fear of separation from parents or caregivers.

Many children avoid school occasionally, but children with **school phobia** avoid school chronically because of their irrational fear of (a) separation from parents/caregivers, (b) school-related persons or events, or (c) other unknown elements (Kearney, Eisen, & Silverman, 1995). There is a history of terms in this area: school phobia, **school refusal, separation anxiety,** and delinquent and nondelinquent **truancy.** In the 19th century, the United States enacted compulsory school attendance laws and thereby created "truancy," and in the 1930s a distinction was made between "delinquent" and "nondelinquent" truancy (Kearney, 2003). This text uses the umbrella term *school refusal.*

**School refusal:** A general category of chronic avoidance of attending school.

## FORMAL IDENTIFICATION

### Definitions

**Separation anxiety:** An intense fear of separation from a parent or surrogate (guardian or parent substitute); the term is often used interchangeably with *school anxiety* (Kearney, 2003).

#### IDEA

IDEA defines this group of children under the category of EBD (see the Section V overview).

#### DSM-IV-TR

*DSM-IV-TR* (APA, 2000, p. 125) defines separation anxiety disorder as follows:

**Truancy:** A specific type of school refusal in which the child leaves the school and goes into the community but does not go home. The term *truant* is used mainly to describe children who miss school without parental consent (Kearney, 2003).

*Defining characteristics:* Developmentally inappropriate and excessive anxiety concerning separation from home or from those to whom the individual is attached, as evidenced by three (or more) of the following:

- Recurrent excessive distress when separation from home or major attachment figures occurs or is anticipated
- Persistent and excessive worry about losing, or about possible harm befalling, major attachment figures
- Persistent and excessive worry that an untoward event will lead to separation from a major attachment figure (e.g., getting lost or being kidnapped)
- Persistent reluctance or refusal to go to school or elsewhere because of fear of separation
- Persistently and excessively fearful or reluctant to be alone or without major attachment figures at home or without significant adults in other settings

- Persistent reluctance or refusal to go to sleep without being near a major attachment figure or to sleep away from home
- Repeated nightmares involving the theme of separation
- Repeated complaints of physical symptoms (such as headaches, stomachaches, nausea, or vomiting) when separation from major attachment figures occurs or is anticipated

*Impairment:* "Significant distress or impairment in social, academic (occupational), or other important areas of functioning."

*Exclusions and conditions:* The duration of the disturbance is at least 4 weeks. Onset is before age 18 years; early onset occurs before age 6. Not with Pervasive Developmental Disorder, Schizophrenia, or other Psychotic Disorder and not if better accounted for by Panic Disorder with Agoraphobia.

### Possible Co-Occurring Conditions and Differences Among Related Disorders

Co-occurring with school phobia are social anxiety, oppositionality, and depressive symptoms (Kearney et al., 1995). Although school phobia can be confused with truancy, truants respond to pressure to attend to school, whereas children with school phobia refuse to attend or stay at school regardless of pressure, punishment, or blame from parents or school administration (Chitayo & Wheeler, 2006). See Table 12.1 and Figure 12.5.

## Etiology

*Biogenetic.* See the discussion in the etiology subsection above for anxiety disorders.

*Environmental.* Behavioral theory suggests that school phobia consists of two separate factors—an extreme fear of school that is maintained by secondary reinforcements, mostly attention from parents, siblings, and counselors (Lazarus, Davison, & Polefka, 1965). Family contributors are parents who have unrealistic expectations of academic success (Jenni, 1997) and mothers who are more likely to be diagnosed with anxiety disorders and who discourage autonomy in their children (Phelps, Cox, & Bajorek, 1992). Other environmental factors include life-changing events at home, such as death in the family, birth of a sibling, a move to a new house or school, a parent losing a job, or parental marital instability or divorce (e.g., Akande et al., 1999). Related school factors for both school phobics and truants include stressful conditions, for example, bullying or **failure-oriented classrooms** (Pilkington & Piersel, 1991).

**Failure-oriented classrooms:** Classrooms in which children are punished for trying and not succeeding in addition to being punished for not trying. As well, there may be overuse of strategies that involve making comparisons among children's performance (e.g., by posting children's graded work) or focusing on what is wrong rather than on what is correct.

**Table 12.1**  Comparison of School Refusal Subtypes

| School phobia (internalizers) | Truancy (externalizers) |
| --- | --- |
| Typically a good student | Typically not a good student |
| Avoids school and stays home | Avoids school and home |
| May stay out of school for weeks | Typically misses school for less extended periods of time |
| Parents are aware of the absence | Parents are most often not aware of the absence |

**Figure 12.5**  A Comparison Between a Child with School Phobia and a Second Child with Truancy

*Functional.* Following from the above environmental factors, a functional analysis could identify that school phobia functions *to avoid negative* school social situations or academic tasks (Akande et al., 1999; Evans, 2000). Transitions are especially difficult, such as starting kindergarten, middle school, or high school (Brulle, McIntyre, & Mills, 1985) or returning to school after school breaks, holidays, or summer vacations (Evans, 2000). In contrast, some children with school phobia try *to get positive* attention from parents or siblings by staying at home, going with parents to work, or gaining special activities, such as sleeping in, watching television, playing games. Truants also attempt to get positive outcomes through delinquent behavior or to use illicit substances (Kearney, 2006). An instrument called the School Refusal Assessment Scale–Revised can be used to assess possible functions; it includes 24 questions designed to measure the strength of each function (Kearney, 2006).

## Prevalence, Gender, Age, and Cultural Factors

*Prevalence.* Approximately 10% of school refusal cases have school phobia. School phobias represent only about 1–8% of school-age children (Lee & Miltenberger, 1996).

*Gender.* School phobias are more common among boys than among girls (Kearney & Beasley, 1994), and girls are often younger, more emotionally disturbed, and may have been labeled with separation anxiety (see Wenar & Kerig, 2006).

*Age.* School phobias are found in 5–15-year-olds (Freemont, 2003).

*Culture.* Anxiety is more common in children from single-parent/divorced families (Akande et al., 1999; Lee & Miltenberger, 1996). Boys with school phobias are typically from higher economic backgrounds than are girls with such phobias (Wenar & Kerig, 2006).

# INFORMAL EDUCATOR IDENTIFICATION OF CHARACTERISTICS

## Behavioral

Very young children with school phobia physically cling to their parents (Pilkington & Piersel, 1991); older students may cry and hide before and during school, or use aggression or noncompliance to get expelled (Kearney, 2001).

## Social-Emotional

School-phobic children are more likely to have negative self-images and low self-esteem; they fear criticism and do not respond well to reprimands (Akande et al., 1999; Jenni, 1997). In other words, these children can be hypersensitive to criticisms. Typically their emotional reactions are acute panic and apprehension, feelings of terror, depression, hopelessness, and shame (Chitayo & Wheeler, 2006). School phobia predicts social problems (Kearney et al., 1995), such as withdrawal from peers and difficulty making and keeping friends (e.g., Evans, 2000; Paccione-Dyszlewski & Contessa-Kislus, 1987). However, these students are eager to please and conscientious conformers with adults (McAnanly, 1986). In fact, some of these children wield too much power with adults, showing willful domination and manipulation of their parents to avoid school.

## Cognitive

Children with school phobia have average or above-average intelligence (Akande et al., 1999), and they can even recognize that their fears are unreasonable (Phelps et al., 1992). Still they cannot go to school, which may relate to their cognitive distortions: (a) "If I go to school, everyone will make fun of me" (expects negative outcomes), (b) "I am not able to go to school. I can't do it" (negatively evaluates personal abilities), (c) "If I can't leave school right now, I will go crazy. I have to get out of here" (needs to escape), and (d) "I will be a failure in life. I can't even go to school" (Akande et al., 1999).

## Motor, Physical, and Somatic

In children with school phobia, intense anxiety produces nightmares or somatic complaints that are nonexistent during weekends, breaks, and vacations (Evans, 2000). The physical reactions are diarrhea, dizziness, nausea, headaches, vomiting, drowsiness, abdominal pain, headaches, and stomachaches—similar to those associated with stage fright (Pilkington & Piersel, 1991). These children are *not* faking illness; they feel as if they have no control over their feelings of terror or their physiological reactions (Jenni, 1997).

## Academic

About half the number of children with school phobia underachieve (Bernstein, Hektner, Borchardt, & McMillan, 2001) due to poor concentration and high rates of absence that involve incomplete assignments and missed instruction. These children *want* to go to school but are just unable to do so. Their psychosomatic and avoidance symptoms are worse on Sunday evenings and Monday mornings.

# SOCIAL PHOBIA

Children with social phobia are described as "shy," "timid," "lonely," and "isolated" (APA, 2000, p. 719). Social phobia is considered to be one of the most painful anxiety disorders, because it is isolating and rarely recognized in school contexts. See Figure 12.6. The fears of those with social phobia are observed across social settings, but fears commonly associated with the disorder are fear of speaking in public or to strangers, fear of meeting new people, and fear of specific types of performance that could be embarrassing, such as writing, working at the board, reading aloud, eating or drinking in public, or using a public restroom.

**Figure 12.6**   A Young Girl with Social Phobia and Her Perceptions of Others

## FORMAL IDENTIFICATION

### Definitions

#### *IDEA*

IDEA defines this group of children under the category of EBD (see the Section V overview).

#### *DSM-IV-TR*

*DSM-IV-TR* (APA, 2000) defines social phobia, generalized type, as follows:

*Defining characteristics:*

- A marked and persistent fear of one or more social or performance situations in which the person is exposed to unfamiliar people or to possible scrutiny by others. The person fears that he or she will act in a way (or show anxiety symptoms) that will be humiliating or embarrassing. **Note:** In children, there may be evidence of the capacity for age-appropriate social relationships and the anxiety must occur in peer settings, not just in interactions with adults.

- Exposure to the feared social situation almost invariably provokes anxiety, which may take the form of a panic attack. **Note:** In children, the anxiety may be expressed by crying, tantrums, freezing, or shrinking from social situations with unfamiliar people.
- The person recognizes that the fear is excessive or uncontrollable. **Note:** In children, this feature may be absent.
- The feared social or performance situations are avoided or else are endured with intense anxiety or distress.

*Impairment:* Social avoidance, anxious anticipation, or distress.

### *Frequently Occurring Subtypes*

**Performance anxiety:** Anxiety characterized by high physiological arousal in achievement contexts, excessive fear of negative evaluations, and escape or avoidance from these situations (Faust, Ashcraft, & Fleck, 1996).

Within the category of social phobia, there are specific fears of evaluation (**performance anxiety**) in public settings, such as in restrooms and while speaking. There are also general fears associated with public settings, for example, fears related to groups, crowds, hallways, or transitions.

Elective or selective mutism (SM) is a relatively rare subtype of social phobia that is somewhat more common in females than in males and is manifested as a persistent (more than 1 month) failure to speak in certain settings (Chavira, Shipon-Blum, Hitchcock, Cohan, & Stein, 2007). Because children with social phobia avoid conversation, they may be mislabeled with SM (Hollander & Bakalar, 2005). Children with SM understand spoken language and have the ability to speak and to learn age-appropriate academic skills. However, there is evidence that they do not perform as well as their peers on various language measures (Manassis et al., 2007). Most do not speak at school or in other large social situations, even though they express a desire to speak; they are unable to do so due to anxiety, fear, shyness, and embarrassment. In typical cases, children with SM speak to their parents and a few selected others but not necessarily to all individuals in the home. There is a significant association between SM and social phobia; it is estimated that 37% of first-degree relatives of persons with SM have SM themselves, and 70% have social phobia (Chavira et al., 2007).

SM does not represent a choice of whether or not to speak; rather, children with SM are so anxious and uncomfortable in some situations that they are unable to speak. Many do participate in activities nonverbally, and they can make their needs known by nodding their heads, by pointing, by remaining expressionless or motionless until someone guesses what they want, "or, in some cases, by monosyllabic, short, or monotone utterances, or in an altered voice" (APA, 2000, p. 126). Their withdrawn behavior and lack of verbalizations are not usually disturbing until these children begin school, at which time their inability to speak interferes with education.

By the time SM is recognized, the child has usually had several years in which non-verbalization has become a pattern and several years exposed to teasing by peers.

### *Possible Co-Occurring Conditions and Differences Among Related Disorders*

Around 90% of children with social phobia have other anxiety disorders (Curtis, Kimball, & Stroup, 2004) or depression (10%), substance abuse, speech and language LD, or ADHD (Sweeney & Rapee, 2001). Children with giftedness can develop social phobias—fearing external criticism when they have early and easy successes and have not learned to cope with failure. Alternatively, they may become perfectionistic, with fears of failing to meet their own overly high internal expectations and standards (Webb et al., 2005).

It can be challenging to separate social phobia from normal shyness. Shyness and brief periods of social anxiety are common in childhood and adolescence, but the symptoms tend to be outgrown as children age (Webb et al., 2005). Shyness is initial discomfort or inhibition in interpersonal situations that interferes with pursuing personal or professional goals. It may be chronic (not decreasing over age levels) or it may be specific to social performance situations that are potentially evaluative. Social phobia, in contrast, involves an exaggerated fear of most social situations. The strong social avoidance of children with social phobia can be expressed as oppositionality, with a "will of iron," or aggressive, with off-putting negative behavior (see the subsection on behavioral characteristics below). Thus, they may be incorrectly labeled ODD.

## Etiology

*Biogenetic.* More than half of the population of children with social phobia has at least one shy parent, in contrast to 5% of comparison children. There is a high rate of psychiatric disturbance in the families of these children (i.e., leading to related communication difficulties at home).

*Environmental.* Children with social phobia generally have a close alliance with one parent, usually the mother, who is often overprotective. These children tend to live in a home atmosphere that does not welcome the expression of feelings. Fathers of these children tend to communicate in the home on a limited basis and may react to situations with angry outbursts.

*Functional.* For selective mutism, it is important to assess the types of communications used and the settings and persons with whom the child does and does not speak (Gortmaker, Warnes, & Sheridan, 2004). Similarly, a functional assessment will document antecedents that trigger social phobia, which are often one-on-one interactions, opposite-gender interactions, intimacy, interactions with authorities or strangers, having to assert oneself in a group, or unstructured settings in which social interactions are expected (transitions, such as in hallways, and at the beginnings and endings of classes).

Robert presented some confusing types of behavior to his teacher. This behavior included moaning, mumbling, inappropriate laughing, refusal to respond verbally, and simply walking away from her. These were labeled noncompliance, depression/anxiety, and more generally as outcomes of his LD in language arts, set in contrast to his giftedness in mathematics and computers. It was only when his teacher examined the triggers or antecedents of his "strange" behavior and how others responded to him (being left alone, no requirements to produce) that she began to understand the payoffs for Robert's bizarre behavior (avoid social interactions/conversations, evaluations, and possible failure).

## Prevalence and Cultural Factors

*Prevalence.* Most children with social phobia are identified in late childhood or early adolescence. Social phobia is found in an estimated 1–2% of children at the elementary level and 6% of adolescents from a community population, and 27–32% of children referred to clinics (Sweeney & Rapee, 2001; Wenar & Kerig, 2006). Some individuals with social phobia become increasingly shy and avoidant during adolescence and go on to develop adult avoidant personality disorder in early adulthood (APA, 2000).

*Culture.* Immigrant children who are unfamiliar with or uncomfortable in the official language of their new host country may refuse to speak to strangers in their new environment. This behavior should not be diagnosed as SM or social phobia.

## INFORMAL EDUCATOR IDENTIFICATION OF CHARACTERISTICS

### Behavioral

Avoidant behavioral responses associated with social phobia are crying, tantrums, freezing, or pulling away from social situations (Sweeney & Rapee, 2001). However, some children show "off-putting" behavior to keep people away, such as growling and grumbling, making negative statements to others, or speaking only in a foreign language when others attempt conversation. Some may exhibit a lack of cleanliness and/or poor dental hygiene. More commonly, they show oppositional, manipulative, and unresponsive behavior by refusing to participate in activities suggested by teachers or adults. A self-report instrument for children called the School Refusal Assessment Scale–Revised offers a good way to measure students' needs to avoid school-based stimuli, to avoid social or performance evaluation stimuli, or to get reinforcing stimuli outside of school (see Kearney, 2002).

## Social-Emotional

These children have low self-esteem (Hollander & Bakalar, 2005), fewer interpersonal relationships than other children, fears of being viewed as "awkward" (Walsh, 2002), and difficulty being assertive. They are less likely, therefore, to learn social skills, because they do not practice these skills. In addition, they are overly sensitive to evaluation. They respond emotionally to attention (blushing or crying, apathetic, or timid/anxious fearful responses) and especially to criticism (Kearney, 2005; Morris & Masia, 1998). Finally, they are more likely to be ignored by their peers than are other children (Sweeney & Rapee, 2001), and some may state that they prefer not to get attention from others.

## Cognitive

There is evidence of lower-than-average verbal memory span (Manassis et al., 2007) in children with social phobia, although the majority of these children fall within the normal range of IQ. Social phobia is sometimes observed in children with intellectual disabilities (ID).

## Communication and Somatic

Students with social phobia will avoid communicating and avoid eye contact (Hollander & Bakalar, 2005; Kearney, 2005; Morris & Masia, 1998). Increased heart rate has been documented (Leary, 1995), as have more somatic side effects (e.g., sweating, blushing, trembling, dizziness) (Curtis et al., 2004). However, in structured role play their language production is relatively normal (see Sweeney & Rapee, 2001), and they are more likely to talk in calm, low-demand settings.

## Academic

Because school is a social situation, students with social phobia have impairment in academic performance (Sweeney & Rapee, 2001). There is also a high dropout rate for this group (Rappaport, 2005).

# DISABILITY IN THE CLASSROOM

## Implications for Accommodations in General Education Settings: Tier I

Anxiety disorders have a high rate of recovery if treated appropriately and early (Jenni, 1997). The overall goal for children with school phobia is to increase attendance and decrease the stress associated with school. The longer the student avoids school, the more difficult it is for him or her to go back to school, and this develops into a long-term pattern for later work life. However, educators should remember that avoidance behavior of any type should never be punished, because punishment increases avoidance. Unfortunately, anxious mothers have been found to be more critical of the inhibited behavior of their own children. The evidence also suggests that pushing children too hard toward challenges, such as confronting the objects of their fears, being overly protective are not useful (for a review of family effects, see Wenar & Kerig, 2006). If a child exhibits anxiety, educators should recognize that the school environment may be causing that anxiety and should investigate the child's fears; the reduction of anxiety predicts improved school performance and social functioning (Wood, 2006). A good relationship with the teacher can make a difference in helping a student with social phobia return to school—just as a bad relationship can keep the child away (Paul, 1998).

**Relaxation techniques:** Strategies designed to reduce anxiety (e.g., slow breathing).

When children's fears are associated with school performance, educators should reduce pressure by giving practice tests and teaching **relaxation techniques** in the classroom (Jenni, 1997; Paul, 1998). Teaching children to make positive self-statements during panic attacks (e.g., "This will last only 10 minutes," "I have done this before successfully") can be helpful. It may be critical to allow these children to take part in extracurricular activities even when they miss school, to reduce their isolation from peers and make returning to school easier. Educators might allow children with social phobia to sit by the door, so they can leave the room or go to a quiet space in the classroom when feeling anxious (Jenni, 1997). The use of music has been documented to reduce physiological symptoms associated with anxiety and depression, even though the child may not report differences in feelings (Field et al., 1998).

## Implications for Interventions in Small-Group and Individual Settings: Tier II

Each student in this group should have a support team including a special educator, behavioral consultant, therapist, school counselor, and so on. Since the child's fear will continue to build, school phobia should be treated immediately, even if the problem arises near the end of the semester (Kearney & Beasley, 1994). Major interventions for anxiety disorders in general include the following:

- *Reconditioning* through role play, reinforcement for facing objects of fear, matter-of-fact statements (e.g., that the child will "go back to school"), removal of reinforcers for avoiding fears (e.g., not allowing the child to watch TV if at home).
- *Guided participation* or practice in which other persons are introduced as models with the feared stimulus (e.g., videotape of person with a dog and then exposure to a dog under highly supervised conditions).
- *Systematic desensitization* in which the child is gradually and repeatedly exposed to the fear-producing stimuli (in real life, with pictures, with books, or in guided fantasy) in the presence of an activity that is incompatible with anxiety (relaxing in a favorite chair, eating ice cream).
- *Self-control training* involving relaxation techniques, self-reinforcement, self-instruction, visual imagery, and problem-solving strategies. Children are taught to recognize anxious feelings and physical reactions, to modify cognitions (e.g., "I can't do this") and misperceptions that contribute to anxiety, and finally to reinforce themselves for making change.
- *Expressive therapies* of art, music, drama, dance, and **bibliotherapy.**

**Bibliotherapy:** The use of books to reduce anxiety associated with some situations or conditions (e.g., divorce, moving, disability awareness) and to provide a human child model (character in the book) who must problem solve alternative responses to a threatening situation or loss.

**Cognitive behavior modification** has been shown to be very successful in the treatment of school phobia. The behavioral component of this approach involves contracting for "baby steps" in the fear-provoking setting, using gradual reintroduction into school. These baby steps may be implemented by providing support personnel who escort the child to school or by using a written family contract to increase incentives for school attendance (Kearney, 2006). Because the pace of returning to school may be slow, teachers need to focus on the child's long-term goals, such as attending school full-time, rather than on immediate academic concerns. This includes reinforcing attendance and discouraging the child from crying or complaining about physical symptoms. (If a student complains of a physical ailment, send him or her to the nurse; if there is no verifiable illness, return the student to class and ignore further complaints. Be firm but gentle. (See Evans, 2000.) The child may be gradually reintroduced into school by staying for an hour at first. The duration of the stay would increase steadily until the child is ready to attend all day, or the majority of the school day (King & Ollendick, 1997).

In a study of social phobia, a school-based multidisciplinary individualized treatment plan targeted adolescents by promoting realistic thinking, social skills

**Cognitive behavior modification:** A type of behavior modification that involves instruction in the use of self-talk to modify one's own behavior (e.g., "I am brave," "I am not afraid," "I have a 1, 2, 3 strategy").

training, exposure to social interactions, and relapse training. Pizza parties were included for practice of social skills. These techniques were found to be successful in reducing fear and avoidance ratings (Masia, Klein, Storch, & Bernard, 2001).

## Long-Term Outcomes

"Childhood anxiety disorders, if left untreated, can include chronic anxiety, depression, and substance abuse" (Kendall et al., 2004, p. 277). Anxiety involves avoidance of risk/challenge, which creates a whole set of new problems over time. For example, half the number of adolescents with school phobia meet criteria for an anxiety, depression, conduct, personality, or other psychiatric disorder later in life, and school phobia can specifically predict agoraphobia and difficulty maintaining employment (Jenni, 1997; Kearney, 2006; Kearney et al., 1995). For this reason, it is important for educators to understand the child's stressors before anxiety spreads or generalizes (e.g., from a specific area such as reading to all schoolwork, and even to riding the school bus). Also during the school years there may be behavioral outcomes, such as dropping out of school (Evans, 2000) or suicidal behavior (Jenni, 1997).

Parents see school phobia as more debilitating than CD, depression, or separation anxiety (Phelps et al., 1992). Parents may have to quit jobs to stay home with a child or constantly have to pick up a child from school. Parental disagreements over how to best help a child can lead to short-term worry, guilt, impatience, and frustration and long-term marital problems (Evans, 2000; Kearney & Beasley, 1994). These, in turn, increase the child's anxiety and school phobia (Cerio, 1997). Siblings are also affected when parents' attention is focused on the child with school phobia (Cerio, 1997).

## OBSESSIVE-COMPULSIVE DISORDER

**OCD:** Obsessive-compulsive disorder; an anxiety disorder causing the sufferer to experience repeated unwanted thoughts and behaviors.

**OCD** is an anxiety disorder with repetitive thinking and a repetitive behavioral component. The thoughts are intrusive and distressing (Adams, 2004) and are associated with rituals, superstitious behavior, or compulsive actions that the individual performs to protect him- or herself from possible harm. These can range from overeating or overexercising to checking and rechecking to make sure windows or doors are locked or to counting objects. For example, an 11-year-old boy was terrified of germs and "used his magic number 4 for protection in a variety of ways: He touched his fork 4 times before eating; counted to 4 when entering the locker room in the school gym, got in and out of bed 4 times before going to sleep, and lined up his perfectly sharpened pencils in groups of 4. When he became worried that a ritual might not have worked, he repeated it 4 times" (Wenar & Kerig, 2006, p. 231). Compulsions can be as minor as that depicted in Figure 12.7: unreasonable anxiety accompanying the possibility of being late.

**Figure 12.7** A Child with Obsessive-Compulsive Disorder Related to Punctuality

## FORMAL IDENTIFICATION

### Definitions

The most common measure in the assessment of OCD is the Yale-Brown Obsessive Compulsive Scale (see Pignotti & Thyer, 2011).

#### *IDEA*

IDEA defines this group of children under the category of EBD (see the Section V overview).

#### *DSM-IV-TR*

*DSM-IV TR* (APA, 2000, p. 729) defines obsessive-compulsive personality disorder as follows:

*Defining characteristics:* A pervasive pattern of preoccupation with orderliness, perfectionism, and mental and interpersonal control, at the expense of flexibility, openness, and efficiency, beginning by early adulthood and present in a variety of contexts, as indicated by four (or more) of the following:

- Is preoccupied with details, rules, lists, order, organization, or schedules to the extent that the major point of the activity is lost

- Shows perfectionism that interferes with task completion (e.g., is unable to complete a project because his or her own overly strict standards are not met)
- Is excessively devoted to work and productivity to the exclusion of leisure activities and friendships (not accounted for by obvious economic necessity)
- Is overconscientious, scrupulous, and inflexible about matters of morality, ethics, or values (not accounted for by cultural or religious identification)
- Is unable to discard worn-out or worthless objects even when they have no sentimental value
- Is reluctant to delegate tasks or to work with others unless they submit to exactly his or her way of doing things
- Adopts a miserly spending style toward both self and others; money is viewed as something to be hoarded for future catastrophes
- Shows rigidity and stubbornness

### Frequently Occurring Subtypes

One subtype that educators can recognize is *perfectionism,* which involves a compulsive redoing of work to get it "just right." Striving for perfection is based on the belief that self-worth is equated with performance. That is, the child is worthy only if he or she can perform excellently. Other symptoms of perfectionism are frequent procrastination, repeatedly starting over, inflexibility, and preoccupation with details, rules, and lists. The perfectionist is afraid to do something unless he or she is certain it can be done completely and perfectly; failure is unacceptable. "These students have exaggerated reactions to mistakes. . . . They have a tendency to focus exclusively on their negative qualities and on anything that they perceive to be less than perfect about themselves" (Kottman & Ashby, 2000, p.185). Perfectionists perceive others as achieving success with minimum effort, few errors, little emotional stress, and maximum self-confidence and view their own efforts as unending and forever inadequate. Trying to be perfect is a way to protect themselves from criticism, rejection, or disapproval.

Pete, whose case study appears at the end of this chapter, was described as a perfectionist who often engaged in black-and-white thinking—all right or all wrong. These items from his observer's log illustrate his way of thinking:

- Showed me his math test, got an A. Not happy because he'll "never get them all right."
- Performed shot put, but immediately down on himself for not doing well.

- Ran away from class.
- Yelled at classmates for encouraging him 3 times.
- Ran into wall of building 6 times.
- He said he has to be the best.

Perfectionists can also have qualities that result in positive outcomes, referred to as *adaptive perfectionism.* Perfectionist students, for example, often have tidy desks, are very committed to their schoolwork, and have high standards (Kottman & Ashby, 2000).

### Possible Co-Occurring Conditions and Differences Among Related Disorders

In childhood, OCD cuts across a number of other disabilities, including other anxiety disorders, especially generalized anxiety disorder and panic disorder, as well as Tourette's syndrome and sometimes ADHD (Thomsen, 2001). Depression co-occurs with OCD at rates of 20–50%, and eating disorders are frequently found in girls (Thomsen, 2001). OCD has been diagnosed in children with Asperger syndrome but differs in that children with Asperger's are not distressed by their OCD symptoms (Thomsen, 2001). OCD involves worrying about trivial and less likely-to-occur concerns (germs, unlocked windows), whereas generalized anxiety disorder involves worrying about ordinary life circumstances, such as schoolwork and peer relations (Barlow, 1991).

## Etiology

*Biogenetic.* Evidence of genetics is particularly strong, with 52% of children with OCD having a family history of OCD in first-degree relatives (Thomsen, 2001). Positron emission tomography (PET) brain scans have shown that the brain patterns of individuals with OCD are different from those of non-OCD persons, and their brain chemistry involves less **serotonin.**

**Serotonin:** A neurotransmitter in the brain that affects mood and its regulation.

*Environmental.* There has been no evidence of environmental contributors to OCD, such as perinatal problems or abnormal birth (Wenar & Kerig, 2006).

*Functional.* Functional analysis shows that the antecedents that encourage OCD are stress related. Stress does not cause OCD, but a stressful event, such as the death of a loved one or school failure, can trigger the onset and typically worsen existing OCD symptoms. The function of the behavior of OCD is to maintain a sense of control to reduce stress; for perfectionists it is to avoid failure or possible criticism. Thus, for perfectionists any setting where comparisons can be made can trigger problem behavior.

## Prevalence, Gender, Age, and Cultural Factors

*Prevalence.* For every 1,000 students, 2–5 have OCD, making it the fourth most common disorder among students (Leininger, Dyches, Prater, Heath, & Bascom, 2010). However, this disorder is often undiagnosed and undertreated, since students attempt to hide their symptoms.

*Gender and age.* OCD is found in boys more often than in girls, at a rate of two to three times the number (Kalra & Swedo, 2009). Sometimes OCD can be difficult to identify, since there are developmentally appropriate examples of OCD. For example, normal children have rituals (compulsive behavior), such as going to bed with a favorite teddy bear, insisting on wearing certain clothes, and even compliance with the familiar expression "Step on a crack, break your mother's back." However, such rituals typically disappear by the age of 8, whereas the onset of OCD occurs around the age of 7 (Thomsen, 2001). OCD can have a gradual or an abrupt onset; it can be identified in preschool but typically is identified during adolescence or early adulthood. Overall, adolescents experience more depression, anxiety, and substance abuse than younger children (Wenar & Kerig, 2006). Children are more likely to have just compulsions without obsessions, whereas adults are more likely to show the opposite pattern (Thomsen, 2001). Approximately 40% of children who exhibit compulsive behavior deny that those compulsions are driven by obsessive thoughts (Kalra & Swedo, 2009).

*Culture.* All ethnic and cultural groups are represented, but OCD is identified more often in high-SES groups (Thomsen, 2001).

## INFORMAL EDUCATOR IDENTIFICATION OF CHARACTERISTICS

### Behavioral

**Form rituals:** Patterns of behavior that involve multiple repetitions of particular sequences. These include physical rituals (frequently washing hands, brushing teeth, checking repeatedly if a door is locked, placing objects just right, touching things, erasing or writing and rewriting letters until perfect) and mental rituals (repeating words, counting objects, or calculating answers) (Adams, 2004; Szechtman & Woody, 2004).

The range of symptoms seen in OCD is so wide that it is considered a heterogeneous condition (Pignotti & Thyer, 2011). Common **form rituals** in children are washing or cleaning, checking, repeating, ordering, arranging, touching, and counting. Less obvious types of behavior are nail biting, picking at cuticles, picking at sores or scabs, and pulling out eyelashes or hairs. Form rituals differ from compulsions, in that compulsions are more often accompanied by obsessions (repeated unwanted thoughts). OCD symptoms can be divided into four categories: symmetry/order compulsions, contamination/washing compulsions, hoarding, and checking (Pignotti & Thyer, 2011). Students with OCD may also be overly thrifty, conscientious, or obsessed with the mistakes of others (Webb et al., 2005). Almost everyone has some characteristics of OCD. However, counting stairs hardly interferes with one's life, whereas continuously counting most environmental objects does.

## Social-Emotional

Thoughts of suicide are frequent in individuals with OCD, and 15% commit suicide (Fenske & Schwenk, 2009). Peers tease these children in response to their odd behavior; children with OCD may line up school supplies in a certain order, repeat words or behaviors, touch objects multiple times, reenter rooms, or wash or clean themselves or objects frequently. Older children especially are secretive about their obsessions and compulsions (Salkovskis et al., 2000). Because they fear ridicule, children with OCD often withdraw and are isolated from peers; they find social situations stressful and find it difficult to focus on relationships. This results in a lack of social competence and few friendships (e.g., Adams, 2004). Furthermore, "they are oblivious to the fact that other people tend to become very annoyed at the delays and inconveniences that result from this behavior" (APA, 2000, p. 725). Parents whose children have OCD frequently complain about the children's failure to complete assigned chores, settle into bed, concentrate on homework, and get along with family members (Wenar & Kerig, 2006).

The emotional consequences of OCD include shame and denial of the obsessions and compulsions, as well as an "inflated sense of responsibility" (Salkovskis et al., 2000). Individuals with OCD "are prone to become upset or angry in situations in which they are not able to maintain control of their physical or interpersonal environment, although the anger is typically not expressed directly" (APA, 2000, p. 727).

## Cognitive

There is a normal range of intelligence among children with OCD (Adams, 2004), and most studies find no differences between these children and others in memory or attention and no differences on tasks requiring spatial perception/orientation or on reaction time or decision-making time (Thomsen, 2001). Most individuals in the general population have intrusive negative thoughts that are similar in content to the obsessive thoughts associated with OCD. The difference lies in the frequent and chronic nature of the thoughts, behavior, and emotional reactions of persons with OCD, which impair functioning. Additionally, there is consistent evidence of cognitive distortions in individuals with OCD, including black-and-white thinking, "hairsplitting" (making overly fine distinctions of what is correct), and indecisiveness that can take the form of severe doubting (Thomsen, 2001). Their performance of rituals is evidence of their tendency toward **magical thinking.**

**Magical thinking:** Believing that specific behavior, such as rituals, can offer protection.

## Communication and Somatic

Some of these children repeat words or sounds (e.g., "um"), similar to the verbal tics of children with Tourette's syndrome (a related disability discussed in Chapter 15). Some students may not get enough rest because the rituals they perform before bed or in the morning cause them to be very tired or lethargic during school hours.

## Academic

The fears of these students detract from their attending to and completing tasks and making decision without continually weighing pros and cons (Thomsen, 2001). They may never get started on a task because they may have so much difficulty deciding what to do first or the "best way" of proceeding. They are likely to under-perform and to avoid such things as open-ended tasks and specific objects, places, or situations, including school (e.g., they may be tardy or absent). In addition, their self-imposed high standards of performance cause them significant dysfunction and distress. For example, their "time is poorly allocated, the most important tasks being left to the last moment" (APA, 2000, pp. 725, 727). Unfortunately, these children are often mistakenly judged to be lazy, oppositional, or poorly motivated.

# SUMMARY OF STRENGTHS AND NEEDS: ALL ANXIETY DISORDERS

| Possible strengths | Probable needs |
|---|---|
| • Conscientious and conforming<br>• Learn simple tasks easily and well; probably good memory<br>• Socially responsive to adults and/or peers | • Opportunities to practice new learning in safe environments, especially if performance evaluation will be public<br>• Assistance with breaking complex tasks (e.g., written compositions, problem solving) into manageable chunks<br>• Rehearsal of positive self-statements about their ability to cope to reduce their tendency to overestimate threat (e.g., "I did this last time, when . . . ," "It always looks difficult in the beginning, but once I get started. . . .") |

# DISABILITY IN THE CLASSROOM

## Implications for Accommodations in General Education Settings: Tier I

For students with OCD and perfectionism, it is important that educators keep stress levels low, capitalize on the students' strengths and talents, and establish private two-way signals they can use to give these children permission to leave stressful settings temporarily. The educator's job is to provide acceptance and help for the child in reducing the inappropriate behavior to acceptable levels. For example, a child who needed to do hand "bumps" in threes was told that she could do a "fist bump" with her teacher at each of the three periods she had with the teacher throughout the day. This helped ease the tension the child would feel if she was not allowed to perform hand bumps and reduced her fear of not being accepted. Other possible types of accommodations include the following:

- *Bibliotherapy:* Reading about other children with fears can help these children realize they are not alone (for a list of books, see Leininger et al., 2010).
- *Increased time for tasks:* Perfectionism reduces a child's available time to complete tasks, so educators should provide extra time on tests or testing breaks and reduce the amount of homework (Adams, 2004).
- *Physical movement:* There is evidence that exercise reduces the anxiety of adults with OCD (for a review, see Allison et al., 1995).
- *Education of peers:* If peers make fun of a child with perfectionism when he or she goes over answers multiple times, or if a child with OCD is suffering socially, it is important for educators to intervene by educating the class. They need to work with parents early and, with the permission of parents, educate the class about the child's need to get things "just right" (Adams, 2004).

## Implications for Interventions in Small-Group and Individual Settings: Tiers II and III

Educators can help those children who are perfectionistic to redefine success as outcomes with shades of gray rather than black and white. This could involve reinforcing times when they perform less than perfectly rather than reinforcing correct performance.

*Tier III.* Anti-OCD drugs (selective serotonin reuptake inhibitors, or SSRIs) reduce unwanted thoughts (obsessions) by restoring the brain chemical serotonin; this treatment is effective in about 50% of children with OCD. A combination of SSRIs and cognitive-behavioral therapy or behavioral therapy (i.e., exposure to anxiety conditions paired with preventing compulsive behavior) has been found to be useful ("Treating," 2009). Support personnel can be used for cognitive-behavioral therapy. For example, support personnel can give the child homework to take control over distressing symptoms for brief periods of time; this works for about half of children with OCD (see Thomsen, 2001). The technique involves exposure to potentially threatening cues, learning to tolerate the associated anxiety, and response prevention (e.g., touching "contaminated objects," recognizing the anxiety, and not responding with hand washing). Even with such treatment, however, most children with OCD continue to experience half or more of their obsessive and compulsive symptoms.

## Long-Term Outcomes

Only about 10% of adult OCD patients completely recover, although 40–60% improve in response to intervention, which includes medication ("Treating," 2009). OCD is considered a chronic condition with high rates of reoccurrence of symptoms (Fenske & Schwenk, 2009).

Age of onset and symptom severity do *not* appear to predict outcome (Thomsen, 2001). Among the factors that do influence outcome is the presence or absence of other anxiety disorders or secondary symptoms (e.g., depression, perfectionism, guilt, anger, aggression, phobias, procrastination). Individuals with hoarding obsessions are less likely than others with OCD to seek treatment, which could mean they "have less insight" into these symptoms (Cullen et al., 2008) or they have a greater ability to hide the symptoms. As children with OCD age, they encounter more personal difficulties of hopelessness and pessimistic thoughts; marital, work, family, and social life/relationship difficulties; and high suicide ideation, plans, and attempts (Adams, 2004).

*Continuance.* Long-term follow-up studies of adults who had OCD as children found that approximately 25% were symptom-free, 25% had minor nonimpairing symptoms, 25% experienced periods of being disorder-free with reappearing symptoms under stressful conditions, and 25% had chronic impairment and continued to live with their parents (Thomsen, 2001).

## DEPRESSIVE DISORDERS

Depression affects the way a person eats, sleeps, feels, and thinks. It is *not* the same as a passing blue mood; the symptoms can last for weeks, months, or years. It is *not* a personal weakness due to laziness, and children with depression cannot simply "pull themselves together" and get better. See Figure 12.8.

## FORMAL IDENTIFICATION

### Definitions

#### IDEA

IDEA defines this group of children under the category of EBD (see the Section V overview).

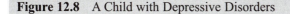

**Figure 12.8**    A Child with Depressive Disorders

### DSM-IV-TR

*DSM-IV-TR* (APA, 2000) defines clinical depression as follows:

*Defining characteristics:* Five of the following symptoms, which must be present during the same 2-week period and must represent a change from a previous level of functioning; at least one of the symptoms is either (1) depressed mood or (2) loss of interest or pleasure:

- Depressed mood, nearly every day during most of the day
- Marked diminished interest or pleasure in almost all activities
- Significant weight loss (when not dieting), weight gain, or a change in appetite
- Insomnia or hypersomnia (excessive sleep)
- Psychomotor agitation or psychomotor retardation
- Fatigue or loss of energy
- Feelings of worthlessness or inappropriate guilt
- Impaired ability to concentrate or indecisiveness
- Recurrent thoughts of death, recurrent suicidal ideation

### Frequently Occurring Subtypes

Subtypes of depression include three subtypes of unipolar depressive disorders: major depressive disorder; dysthymic disorder (persistent depressed mood or symptoms for 2 years or more), which appears in childhood/adolescence; and "depression not otherwise specified" (NOS), a categorization used when symptoms do not meet a sufficient number of criteria (APA, 2000).

Another subtype is classified as bipolar disorder. In past decades, bipolar was referred to as *manic-depression* because of characteristic "cycling" between the emotional extremes of **mania** and depression. However, children with mania are more likely to be irritable and prone to destructive tantrums than to be overly happy. Children with bipolar disorder have more anxiety, worry, frustration, grief, remorse, and difficulty identifying emotions than peers (Olvera et al., 2005). Children and young adolescents with bipolar disorder can experience rapid mood swings between depression and mania many times a day, unlike 80% of adults with the disorder (Geller et al., 2000, cited in Wenar & Kerig, 2006).

**Mania:** Mood that is persistently elevated, abnormally expansive, or irritable.

### Possible Co-Occurring Conditions and Differences Among Related Disorders

Depression co-occurs with 90–95% of other disorders, such as anxiety disorders, behavioral disorders, ID, and LD (Chrisman, Egger, Compton, Curry, & Goldston, 2006; Cole & Carpentieri, 1990; Markward & Bride, 2001; Quinn, 1997). "Up to 20%–25% of individuals with certain general medical conditions (e.g., diabetes, myocardial infarction, carcinomas, stroke) will develop Major Depressive Disorder during the course of their general medical condition" (APA, 2000, p. 371).

The main difficulty in diagnosis is differentiating bipolar disorder from ADHD. Children with bipolar are often initially identified as ADHD when they are assessed while in an "up" state and are identified as depressed when they are assessed while in a "down" state. In fact, 60–90% of bipolar adults have been diagnosed with ADHD, and up to 22% of children with ADHD been diagnosed with bipolar disorder (e.g., Singh, Delbello, Kowatch, & Strakowski, 2006). Differential diagnosis is particularly important, because the psychostimulant medication used for ADHD can increase the irritability of children with bipolar, and the antidepressants used for students with depression can increase the mania in those with bipolar disorder (see Wenar & Kerig, 2006). Although both groups can show hyperactivity, distractibility, risk taking/impulsivity, and depression, children with ADHD show a more consistent, noncyclical, pattern of overactivity that is intensified by specific tasks and settings of low stimulation. As previously described in Chapter 9, students with ADHD, especially adolescent girls, emotionally overreact to the good and bad events in their lives, making differential diagnosis even more difficult at that age.

The verbal fluency, racing thoughts, and emotional intensity of gifted children can be misdiagnosed as bipolar. However, the gifted child is sensitive and responsive to specific life events, which is not true for children with bipolar disorder (Webb et al., 2005). Similarly, children with CD and ODD show irritability and impulsivity, but they do not have the excessive guilt, flight of ideas, or cluttered speech found in children with bipolar (Weller, Weller, & Fristad, 1995).

## Etiology

*Biogenetic.* Overall heritability for depression is estimated to be between 37% and 45% (see Garrett, 2011; Wenar & Kerig, 2006). Children with depressed parents are 3 times more likely to experience depression than children without depressed parents, and major depressive disorder is 1.5 to 3 times more common among first-degree biological relatives of persons with this disorder than among the general population (APA, 2000). Brain-imaging studies also provide evidence of decreased activation of the left hemisphere in children with depression (for a review, see Wenar & Kerig, 2006).

*Environmental.* Having a depressed parent doubles an individual's likelihood of developing depression over the life span. The adverse effects of parental depression on infants can be measured as early as 8 months (Fields, 1992, cited in Wenar & Kerig, 2006). Parents who are depressed themselves are also less positively involved with their child's activities, less affectionate, more negative, unavailable, unresponsive, and unsupportive (Shirk, Gudmundsen, & Burwell, 2005). In fact, a depressed parent is more likely to produce depressed offspring than parents with bizarre behavior or more severe psychopathology.

Traumatic life experiences, including abuse, predate depression in adolescents (Gied & Pine, 2002). Ongoing life stressors associated with depression include (a) having LD or having difficulty in school, (b) family loss (in one research sample, 41% of depressed patients had lost a parent by divorce or absence before age 15), (c) parental pathology or family conflict (divorce, blended families, low SES), and (d) experiencing some type of disaster, abuse, medical problems, or pregnancy, or being gay or lesbian or alcohol/cocaine dependent (Harrington, 1993; Sarafolean, 2000). Overall, research indicates that any significant loss in childhood can be associated with depression.

*Functional.* For depression, functional assessment is less useful than it is with other disorders. The behavior of children with depression appears to function generally to avoid future pain associated with loss, disappointment, or punishment that has *already* occurred. This would explain the decreases in verbal and motor activity (lack of engagement) and slowed rate of responding that characterize these students. Depression could represent a "flight" rather than a "fight" response to threat or stress. It is for this reason that perceived and real successes are important as interventions.

## Prevalence, Gender, Age, and Cultural Factors

*Prevalence.* The incidence of depression has been increasing in recent decades for all children, especially among adolescents (for a review, see Wenar & Kerig, 2006). The rates for depressive disorder in children in the United States are 1% for children identified as young as 4 years, 2.5% of children, and 8% of adolescents. The rates for children identified in clinical populations are considerably higher (i.e., up to 57%).

*Gender.* During childhood, the proportions of boys and girls with depression are almost equal. During adolescence and adulthood, "Major Depressive Disorder (Single or Recurrent) is twice as common in adolescent . . . females as in adolescent . . . males" (APA, 2000, p. 372). Depressed mood occurs in about 10–20% of all boys (20–46% of adolescents) and 15–20% of all girls (25–59% of adolescent girls). Boys with depression are more likely than their female counterparts to use illicit substances and to exhibit denial. Girls are more likely to cope with stress through repetitive thinking, or **rumination,** rather than denial (Sarafolean, 2000), and rumination may increase depression. Girls are also more likely to attempt suicide, but boys are more likely to complete suicide, because they tend to use more violent (error-proof) means. Girls with depression may be described as vulnerable, anxious, and overly concerned about somatic functioning and about their adequacy; boys may be described as indulgent, antagonistic, aggressive, antisocial, deceitful, and mistrustful (Wenar & Kerig, 2006).

**Rumination:** Repetitive negative thinking; going over and over the same negative event.

*Age.* Children are being identified as depressed at earlier and earlier ages (Webb et al., 2005), and depression increases in magnitude with age and with each prior depressive episode (Wenar & Kerig, 2006). Depression looks different depending on the age of the child. Preschool children show **regressive behavior;** school-aged children may complain and exhibit disobedience/tantrums, truancy, and lethargy; and adolescents may be irritable and asocial or antisocial, may have low self-esteem, may abuse illicit substances, and may have school problems.

**Regressive behavior:** Behavior associated with an earlier stage of development (e.g., acting babyish, such as thumb sucking, whining, complaining).

*Culture.* Rates of depression are higher in low-SES populations. Even when economic class is statistically controlled, it is also higher in Mexican American families in which the mothers use repetitive thinking as an individual coping style and believe in fatalism ("things are beyond our control") (see O'Connor et al., 1998, cited in Wenar & Kerig, 2006). However, suicide rates are higher among white males than among other groups (rates for young African American males are on the rise).

# INFORMAL EDUCATOR IDENTIFICATION OF CHARACTERISTICS

## Behavioral

Overall, depressed children tend to emit more negative and aggressive types of behavior than nondepressed children (Segrin, 2000). They are more likely to act out sad feelings through behavior, because they have difficulty using words to describe feelings (Hyde & Forsyth, 2002). For example, depressed preschoolers show less play and more nonplay behavior (e.g., reading, observing) (Annemieke et al., 2000). Depressed children, more than depressed adults, are responsive/reactive to their environments. In other words, they can be cheered for periods of time (e.g., at a party) but fall back into depression, unlike adults, whose mood is relatively constant across setting conditions.

## Social-Emotional

Children with depression initiate fewer social interactions and are alone more often than nondepressed children; they lack interest in playing with other children and don't enjoy participating in organized activities (e.g., sports, games). They also suffer more rejection from other children (Gied & Pine, 2002). In fact, one-third of suicide attempts are associated with peer difficulties (Wenar & Kerig, 2006). Children with depression also have more difficulty identifying and regulating their emotions or the intensity of their emotions, especially sadness and anger (Wenar & Kerig, 2006). Of depressed preschoolers, 98% are sad and irritable, 78% have low self-esteem, and 61% exhibit death- or suicide-related talk or play. Elementary school-age children show a loss of interest in others and in most activities (**anhedonia**). They more often feel discouraged and have lower self-esteem than their nondepressed peers. Externalizing sadness can be seen as bad temper, irritability, and emotional outbursts—shouting or complaining (Chrisman et al., 2006; Gied & Pine, 2002).

> **Anhedonia:** The lack of capacity to experience pleasure.

Preadolescents who are depressed frequently look sad, tired, or ill; they are irritable and often have reduced appetite and weight loss or increased appetite and weight gain. These children express depression nonverbally, showing less facial animation than nondepressed people and less gesturing and head nodding.

They also hold their heads in a downward position more often. They have low frustration tolerance and are demanding; nothing can make them happy and they complain about "everything." They say they do not feel well or complain of frequent stomachaches or headaches; they may become increasingly clingy and dependent and may regress (e.g., Peacock, 2000; Segrin, 2000). Depressed adolescents are ill-tempered, touchy, and overreactive. Boys in particular are likely to externalize sadness with behavior that is aggressive, disruptive, or delinquent; these children may also show excessive party going and extreme thrill seeking (Quinn, 1997).

## Cognitive

**Self-efficacy:**
Feelings of personal
competence in
producing outcomes
(the opposite of
learned helplessness).

Children with depression have cognitive distortions that involve negatively biased interpretations. They have negative thoughts about themselves and others and have lower academic and social **self-efficacy** than their performance actually warrants (Wenar & Kerig, 2006). These negative biases are self-renewing and lead to increased depression through (a) self-devaluation, (b) social devaluation (feeling inadequate in social relationships, which leads to withdrawal from social support), and (c) difficulty controlling depressive thoughts and negative thinking. They also have biases in what they remember. Specifically, they are less able than nondepressed children to recall past positive experiences. Children with depression also have poorer-than-average concentration (Wenar & Kerig, 2006).

## Communication and Somatic

Compared with nondepressed peers, children with depression speak less often, more slowly, with longer pauses, more softly, at a lower pitch, and with less inflection (monotone), and they take longer to respond to the speech of others. Because of these language features, their speech is less clear and more difficult for others to hear and understand. The language content of children with severe depression can be described as resigned and resentful: "Life isn't worth living." "I have no future." "Why get out of bed?" "Who do you think would come to my funeral?" "Maybe things would be better if I weren't around." These children also tend to withhold their negativity when talking to strangers, introducing negative topics only when talking with friends (Segrin, 2000). This suggests that they are aware that their negative thinking is atypical. Children with bipolar disorder who are in a manic state will not stop talking and speak rapidly, but when they are in a depressive state, they are not talkative (Hillegers et al., 2005).

Preschool children who are depressed show somatic and sleep problems, and school-aged children show somatic problems. Depressed adolescents show increased incidence of smoking and bingeing with alcohol (on-and-off drinking of large quantities) (Gied & Pine, 2002).

## Academic

Children with depression generally lose interest in academics, show poor coopera-tive skills, and frequently skip school (e.g., Hyde & Forsyth, 2002). They can show specific problems in mathematics, which may be related to their inability to sustain attention or concentrate (see LaGace et al., 2003, cited in Olvera et al., 2005).

# DISABILITY IN THE CLASSROOM

## Implications for Accommodations in General Education Settings: Tier I

Accommodations for depressed children include using an active curriculum and encouraging them to participate and to exercise. "There is considerable evidence that exercise reduces depression" (for a review, see Allison et al., 1995, p. 296).

Educators can also increase these children's perceptions of having control and being successful by breaking tasks down into increments and starting with easy subparts. They can then use task feedback, such as charts for self-monitoring, and self-reward.

## Implications for Interventions in Small-Group and Individual Settings: Tiers II and III

Support personnel can be especially effective with Tier II interventions. These strategies can include providing rewards (e.g., free time, special projects) for behavioral improvements or the development of social skills, such as assertive-ness, and the use of cognitive techniques to teach positive self-statements designed to change the child's negative belief system.

*Tier III.* Medications for depression include Prozac and Paxil, which inhibit the reuptake of serotonin. Antidepressant drugs and medications used to treat bipolar disorder, such as lithium, valproic acid, and carbamazepine, are effective for changing behavior in 30–50% of cases (Wenar & Kerig, 2006). However, no long-term studies have yet determined the possible effects of these drugs on the brain development of children.

## Long-Term Outcomes

The greatest impairments associated with depression are in social functioning and in accomplishing daily activities (Yatham et al., 2004). Some individuals, especially those with bipolar disorder, may suffer severe interpersonal, social, and vocational consequences, such as job loss or marital conflict or separation (Schweitzer, Maguire, & Ng, 2005).

The earlier the onset of depression, the greater the chances that a child will be separated from peers for long periods of time. That is, younger children have fewer resources and life experiences to cope with depression. Without treatment, depressed adolescents are also more likely to fail academically and socially to become promiscuous and to self-medicate with drugs and alcohol. For every adolescent suicide there may be 20 attempts (suicide is the second leading cause of death among teens). "Up to 15% of individuals with severe Major Depressive Disorder die by suicide" (APA, 2000, p. 371). Outcomes of bipolar disorder are also severe: Less than 25% have full recovery and about 15% commit suicide.

*Prevention.* Suicide prevention programs are successful at increasing knowledge but are not successful in changing the negative attitudes of students with depression and suicidal thoughts (see Wenar & Kerig, 2006). Educators can, however, identify the following early suicide warning signs to refer children for individual counseling:

1. Sudden changes in behavior or affect

2. Giving away of possessions or talk of not being present in the future

3. Academic, social, or disciplinary problems at school

4. Family problems (separation, divorce, child abuse)

5. A situational crisis (death, pregnancy or abortion, arrest, loss of employment of self or family member, peer rejection, breakup of a romantic relationship)

6. Health problems (insomnia, loss of appetite, sudden weight change)

It is important for educators to take suicide threats and attempts seriously. If an educator has reason to believe that a child or adolescent has current ideas or plans of suicide and a counselor is not immediately available, the educator must ask the child for a written promise not to engage in suicidal behavior for specified period of time, such as 2 weeks, while getting outside help.

*Continuance.* Symptoms of depression and mania continue into adulthood (Wenar & Kerig, 2006).

## CHAPTER SUMMARY

**Specific anxiety disorders:** Disorders characterized by fears of particular events, experiences, animals, or objects (e.g., spiders, escalators).

- The *subtypes* within the broad category of anxiety disorders are generalized and **specific anxiety disorders.** The specific anxiety disorders often seen in classrooms are social and school phobias. OCD and depressive disorders may not be seen until middle childhood. These disorders can be differentiated according to the ways in which children attempt to handle their anxiety (e.g., anxiety with avoidance, OCD with behavioral rituals, depression with passivity).

- Among these disabilities there is a very high rate of co-occurrence. That is, children with one type of anxiety disorder often have others, OCD, or depression. The children's worry topics can indicate subtype. That is, children with OCD worry about unlikely events (unlocked windows, germs), whereas children with anxiety and depressive disorders worry about ordinary life events, such as school or social failure (past or future).

- The etiology of ED is related to an overly sensitive temperament combined with negative life experiences (failure, lack of control, disaster, parental divorce, death). Genetics plays a strong role in OCD and major depressive disorder. Children with high trait anxiety are especially sensitive to threats involving possible failure, pain, or loss. For each of the subtypes, immediate antecedents of anxiety can be analyzed and may be related to social experiences (adult evaluations, peers) or specific classroom experiences (school tasks). Furthermore, there may be positive consequences that reinforce fears, such as increased attention for school phobics who stay at home.

- Fears and even compulsive rituals follow an age course. Depression increases in magnitude with each experienced loss.

- Emotional disorders are among the most common childhood disorders. Most anxiety disorders are not identified until students reach middle childhood, but girls show chronic anxiety earlier and have higher prevalence rates of both anxiety and depression than do boys during adolescence. In contrast, school phobias are found more often in males than in females and more often in single-parent families. Different cultures may express anxiety cognitively through worrying or somatically through muscle tension; low-SES families have higher rates of depression.

- Anxiety can be recognized by behavior that is typically avoidant. For children with depression this can also be seen in their verbal communications (e.g., less talking, slower, softer, monotone). Other types of behavior that suggest anxiety are crying/clinging and repetitive behavior (e.g., excessive talking, eating, hand rubbing, perfectionism, preoccupation with details, OCD compulsions). Young children may express anxieties through tantrums and express depression through irritability and by playing less. School-age children who are depressed play less with other children and also show more negative and aggressive behavior. Preadolescents and adolescents externalize depression through complaints and aggressive behavior.

- Anxiety is associated with poor social adjustment. Most of these children are characterized by negative and/or obsessive thoughts—worrying about the future and negative judgments about the past (depression). More severe social outcomes are reported for social phobics, who are oversensitive to evaluation and tend to be socially isolated. In the absence of intervention, a child's fears and anxieties can spread to new areas or settings.

- Even though these children can range from average to gifted in intelligence, high levels of anxiety disrupt their performance of complex but not simple academic tasks. Depression also takes energy away from concentrating on even simple academic performance.

- Cognitive distortions are seen in both anxiety and depressive disorders. These include exaggerated expectations of threat; feelings of being unable to cope socially or academically ("I can't do it"), despite actual performance; beliefs that self-worth is based on perfect performance; biases in recalling threatening experiences (anxiety); and failure to recall past positive experiences (depression).

- Fears and anxiety disorders are often expressed somatically, with trembling, dizziness, stomachaches, and sleep problems. Young children may display physical reactions (e.g., drowsiness, vomiting) and older children may engage in smoking and binge drinking. Children with social phobias may have physical off-putting characteristics (e.g., lack of cleanliness).

- If interventions are applied early, there is a high rate of recovery. Anxiety is well treated through gradual introduction of the child to fearful settings while guaranteeing comfort, safety, and pleasure, with escape opportunities available, and through cognitive techniques such as bibliotherapy, relaxation, and self-reinforcement. Helping children redefine success and increasing their experiences with real success are important interventions for children who are anxious or depressed.

## CHAPTER QUESTIONS

### Phobias

1. School phobia is often triggered by what kinds of events in a child's life?

2. School phobics can be manipulative of adults. Does this indicate that they are able to control their own fears?

3. What is the cognitive distortion that is involved in anxiety and in school phobia?

4. What is the probable cognitive distortion of social phobia?

5. What kinds of tasks are more difficult for children with high anxiety?

6. How might poor school attendance be related to later employment and vocational outcomes?

7. How does shyness differ from social phobia?

8. Brittany is a Caucasian female, 11 years old, from a two-parent household, with one younger brother. For yelling inappropriate words, she has been labeled and placed in a self-contained ED classroom. Brittany fails to speak in social situations, specifically in academic settings; she is chatterbox at home. Her educational achievements are of concern, and her relationships with others are minimal. She does have a few close friends and is considered compliant, although she can be verbally aggressive when pressed. Brittany has good verbal language skills; she enjoys school and is eager to attend, is quiet and nondisruptive, and smiles occasionally. She sings in the school choir and has a good relationship with the school principal. Based on this information and that in the table below, identify Brittany's possible anxiety disorders.

| *What Brittany does* | *What Brittany rarely does* |
|---|---|
| Copies, draws, listens | Reads aloud to teacher |
| Writes on a self-selected topic | Verbalizes answers to questions |
| Selects answers to recognition-type questions (multiple-choice, true/false, and the like) | Writes answers to recall questions (short answer, essay) |
| "Chatterbox" and compliant at home | Verbalizes with peers in nonacademic and academic settings |
| Sings in school choir | Verbalizes with adults |
| Smiles occasionally; quiet, not disruptive | Eats lunch in the cafeteria |
| Completes homework | Participates in special activities |

## OCD

1. How can the perfectionism of Andy (the student with TBI whose case study appears in Chapter 8) be compared with the general subtype of perfectionism in OCD?

2. How are anxiety disorders and OCD similar? How are they different?

3. How and why is secretive behavior related to OCD?

4. How do rituals, superstitions, and compulsive behavior indicate magical thinking or the belief that individuals can protect themselves with specific types of behavior?

5. Is it a good idea to place children with severe behavior disorders (BD) together with children with severe emotional disorders (ED) in an EBD self-contained classroom? Why or why not?

## Depression

1. Why is having depressed parents a stronger predictor of clinical depression in children than having schizophrenic or bizarre parents?

2. What kind of losses are associated with depression?

3. In what ways do boys and girls express depression differently?

4. How can educators help children with depression focus on positive experiences?

### TRUE/FALSE AND MULTIPLE-CHOICE

1. Specific fears are more common in young children, whereas fears about evaluation from others are more common in older students.

2. A student who enters classrooms late and leaves early may be suffering from
   A. social phobia
   B. agoraphobia
   C. school phobia

3. A developmentally early innate basis of fear is the
   A. Cliff edge reflex
   B. Moro reflex
   C. Gag reflex

4. Anxiety should be highest in which disability groups?
   A. CD & ADHD
   B. LD & ID

5. School phobia is often "triggered" by
   A. a life-changing event, such as a divorce
   B. a failure-oriented classroom
   C. transitions back to school after holidays
   D. all of the above

6. Anxiety improves performance on
   A. complex problem-solving tasks
   B. simple detailed tasks
   C. reading and communication tasks
   D. incidental learning tasks

7. Cognitive biases are brought out by ambiguous conditions. These biases may be seeing
   A. sad or loss outcomes (associated with depression)
   B. threatening outcomes (associated with anxiety)

C. hostile outcomes (associated with aggression)

D. all of the above

E. A & C

8. Indecisiveness is common in children with

A. aphasia

B. social phobia

C. depression

9. Women are more likely to use denial than ruminations in dealing with anxious situations from the past.

## SHORT ANSWER

1. Repeated functional actions (reordering items) and rituals are examples of _____.

2. Extremely high expectations for a child can lead to_____.

3. Significant loss seems to be a past experience that is associated with this disorder, and activity programs are a good intervention.

4. Repeated ideas that "haunt" individuals

5. Loss of interest in most activities, including those that are pleasurable

6. Both social phobia and truancy are types of school _____.

7. Anxiety leads to average or better performance on _____tasks, such as calculations.

8. A neurotransmitter involved in many anxiety types of disorders

## PROBLEM-BASED CASE APPLICATIONS AND QUESTIONS

### CASE STUDY 12.1: PETE

*"I'm not smart at all. I didn't get 100%. I'm not smart at all."*
(adapted from a report submitted by Joy Cedarquist)

*Background.* Pete is a 9-year-old boy in a general education classroom with 20 other students. The female teacher has more than 20 years of experience in teaching the fourth grade. Pete has been previously diagnosed as having Asperger syndrome (AS) and a communication disorder. His IEP was written at the end of third grade. Now, as a fourth grader in a different school, he is having problems adjusting; for example, he seems to be having problems following directions.

His original IEP states the following:

1. He can spend 0–20% of his day in the resource room.

2. He avoids fine motor skills (FMS) and his cursive is more legible than his print. (Observation shows that he prefers to print.)

3. He finds noisy and busy environments challenging and is not to use the gym for inside recess due to sensory overload.

4. He loves attention and is down on himself frequently.

5. He is very literal.

6. He is to have a paraprofessional in the classroom in the afternoon to help him understand social language cues.

7. He has excellent verbal skills.

8. He can take short sensory breaks as needed.

## ABC Analysis

*Table 1: Evaluative Setting in a Nonsocial Environment*

When given an evaluative task without possible peer evaluations, Pete will either perform well because he feels competent or ask specific questions in order to avoid failure at the task. Overall, he wants to get competence about half the time and to avoid failure or get clarification the other half. The following table provides examples of his behavior in this setting.

| Antecedent | Behavior | Result | Payoff |
|---|---|---|---|
| Art | Went to teacher with practice drawing for approval to start final. | Positive interaction with teacher. | Get competence |
| Art | Received individual instruction from teacher on how to make drawing better. | Positive interaction with teacher. | Get competence |
| Science/IN history | Started labeling map, sitting quietly, no complaints. | | Get competence |
| Science/IN history | Wanted me to cut it out for him, then asked the teacher. (Now a social setting, see Table 3.) | Told it didn't have to be perfect. | Avoid failure |

| Antecedent | Behavior | Result | Payoff |
|---|---|---|---|
| Transition, math homework | Told teacher "I'm just too sad" to be doing his homework. | Given choice to work on math in class or spend rest of day in resource room. | Avoid failure |
| Individual instruction with OT | He was instructed to open a document and complied. | Positive reinforcement from OT. | Get competence |
| Individual instruction with OT | Seemed to have run out of patience to do what was asked on the computer. | Positive reinforcement from OT. | Avoid failure |
| Social studies | Sat at desk to take the test. | | Get competence |
| SS | Asked if the test was timed. | Told no. | Avoid failure |
| SS | Asked teacher about printing or cursive. | Told to write what's easier. | Avoid failure |
| SS | Worked on test quietly. | | Get competence |

*Table 2: Evaluative Setting in a Social Environment With Perceived 100% Success*

When Pete perceived that he could achieve a 100% success rate in a given social setting, he was comfortable showing competence. For example, in the presence of the paraprofessional, he perceived that success was guaranteed, so he let the paraprofessional do the work for him. He took little or no responsibility for his learning. Instead he used this time to socialize with his classmates and made minimal or no work effort. (Notes in italics in the following table were made with a paraprofessional in the classroom.)

| Antecedent | Behavior | Result | Payoff |
|---|---|---|---|
| Reading/ language arts | Raised hand to answer question. | Called on. | Get competence |
| Reading/ language arts | Volunteers for reading for both scenes | Not called on. | Get competence |
| Reading/ language arts | Didn't raise hand to answer questions. | Ignored. | Get competence |
| Art | Raised hand with question—idea for joke of the day. | Positive feedback from teacher. | Get competence |

*(Continued)*

(Continued)

| Antecedent | Behavior | Result | Payoff |
|---|---|---|---|
| Art | Tablemates wanted to see his drawing. | Positive interaction with peers. | |
| Art | Showed me drawing and explained it to me. | Positive interaction with adult. | Get relatedness |
| Math | Showed me his math test, got an *A*. Not happy because he'll "never get them all right." | Positive encouragement for doing well. | Get relatedness |
| Math | Volunteered for several questions early on. | Not called on. | Get competence |
| Math | Corrected mispronunciations by classmates while they were reading the math problems. | Ignored. | Get competence |
| Science | *Looked around the classroom while a peer was reading* | | Avoid failure |
| Science | *Corrected the teacher.* | Shushed by paraprofessional. | Get competence |
| Science | *Told paraprofessional to build his DNA.* | | Avoid failure |
| Science | *Told paraprofessional, "All I care is that I get an A."* | | Get competence |
| Science | *Answered teacher's questions correctly.* | Ignored; he wasn't called on. | Get competence |
| IN history | Answered questions. | Positive reinforcement by teacher. | Get competence |
| IN history | Started labeling map, sitting quietly, no complaints. | | Get competence |
| Chess Club | Match ended in a stalemate, he was glad he didn't lose. | Told "good match" by classmates. | Get competence |
| Science (video) | Answered question by teacher during pause. | | Get competence |
| Science | Answered question. | Teacher gave positive feedback. | Get competence |

*Table 3: Evaluative Setting in a Social Environment With Perceived Less Than 100% Success*

The following observations were made in a social setting where Pete had less than 100% perceived success. When he felt he had already failed, his response was to avoid the social attention his failure might bring. When the evaluation was imminent and he perceived his success to be less than 100%, he responded by avoiding the task to avoid failure. (Notes in italics in the table were made with a paraprofessional in the classroom.)

| Antecedent | Behavior | Result | Payoff |
|---|---|---|---|
| Math | Told me, "I'm not smart at all. I didn't get 100%. I'm not smart at all." | I didn't respond. | |
| Math | Told me, "I got two 0s for turning in work late. I'm not smart at all." | I didn't respond. | |
| PE | Performed shot put, but immediately down on himself for not doing well. | Encouragement from classmates. | Avoid social attention |
| PE | Ran away from class. | Encouragement from classmates. | Avoid social attention |
| PE | Yelled at classmates for encouraging him 3 times. | Encouragement from teacher. | Avoid social attention |
| PE | Ran into wall of building 6 times. | Classmates yelling at him not to, he'd get hurt. | Avoid social attention/ rejection |
| PE | He said he has to be the best. | I had conversation with him about Michael Phelps. | Get competence |
| PE | Ran off screaming in frustration. | Ignored. | Avoid social attention/ rejection |
| PE | Stayed outside an extra 5 minutes after class went in. | | Avoid social attention |
| PE | Went in, didn't join class on floor. | Teacher asked for his scores. | Avoid social attention |
| PE | Walked away from class 2 times. | Ignored. | Avoid social attention |
| PE | Ran loudly across gym, away and back. | Ignored. | |
| IN history | (Continued from Table 1) Said he has to cut it out perfectly, repeated 4 times. | Asked to be quiet. | Avoid failure |

*(Continued)*

(Continued)

| Antecedent | Behavior | Result | Payoff |
|---|---|---|---|
| IN history | Said he can't do it. | Teacher said he could— that it doesn't have to be perfect. | Avoid failure |
| IN history | He said he can't repeatedly and argued with the teacher about his ability. | She reiterated that it didn't have to be perfect. | Avoid failure |
| IN history | Told me, "I have to be right all the time." | I didn't respond. | Get competence |
| Timed writing activity | He went into the hall—"I can't do it, it's time." He wouldn't even try. | Finally had him call his mom to get him to calm down. | Avoid failure |
| Math | *He wanted someone to write the answers for him.* | *Teacher said no.* | Avoid failure |
| Individual instruction with OT | Yelled at paraprofessional. | Resource room teacher told him to be quiet. | Avoid failure |
| Individual instruction with OT | Yelled again. | Received positive reinforcement from OT. | Avoid failure |
| Individual instruction with OT | Kicked a trash can next to the desk. | Told to relax. | Avoid failure |
| Individual instruction with OT | Ran out of the room in anger. | When the OT followed, he ran further down the hall. | Avoid failure |
| Individual instruction with OT | Slapped at OT's hands several times as she tried to get him to come back into the resource room. | | Avoid social attention |
| Individual instruction with OT | Dragged back into the classroom by the OT. | OT asked if there was a behavior plan in place. Told no. | Avoid social attention |
| Individual instruction with OT | When back in the resource room, he commented that "I could just destroy myself. That'd be the best way." | Positive encouragement from OT and paraprofessional. | Avoid social attention |
| Individual instruction with OT | OT gave him and a classmate squeeze balls to relieve frustrations, anger. He wanted nothing to do with it. | Encouraged by OT to try. | Avoid failure |
| Individual instruction with OT | Began trying to hit the OT as she attempted to work with him. | Told that wasn't appropriate behavior. | Avoid failure |

## *Table 4: Responses to Direct Commands by the Teacher*

Another problem Pete has is with directions, specifically direct commands given by the teacher, whether to him individually or to the class as a whole. While many children choose to disregard requests from authority figures from time to time, Pete disregards those requests on a regular basis. The following table shows that when Pete was given a direct command from the teacher, almost half of his responses are to avoid failure. Often it seemed that the paraprofessional took care of the activity/assignment simply because it was easier to do so than to fight to get Pete on track. (Notes in italics in the table were made with a paraprofessional in the classroom.)

| Antecedent | Behavior | Result | Payoff |
|---|---|---|---|
| Reading/ language arts | Teacher instructed him to get book, complied. | | Get preferred activity |
| Reading/ language arts | Got in line when instructed (going to art). | | Get preferred activity |
| Assigned homework from skills book | He told another student that his parents get mad when he has homework. | Student asked him if they were mad at him or teacher. | Get relatedness |
| Math | He was asked to help his seatmate with a problem, did as asked. | | Get competence |
| Science | *Told to sit down after walking away from paraprofessional, complied.* | | Avoid failure |
| Science | *Ignored paraprofessional when she asked him questions.* | | Avoid failure |
| Science | *Told by paraprofessional to sit after leaving seat to look at classmate's mutated marshmallow, complied.* | | Avoid failure |
| Science | *Followed directions from paraprofessional in getting supplies.* | | Get relatedness |
| Science | Didn't follow instruction until after the third time. | | Avoid failure (of task) |

*(Continued)*

(Continued)

| Antecedent | Behavior | Result | Payoff |
|---|---|---|---|
| IN history | Knew what to do even though he had looked like he wasn't paying attention as the instructions were given. | | Get competence |
| IN history | Didn't listen to instruction until it was repeated. | | Avoid failure (of task) |
| IN history | Told to sit, complied. | | |
| IN history | Was jumping around in from of me, didn't listen to teacher. | Ignored by teacher. | Was trying to get relatedness |
| IN history | Sat after being told many times to do so. | | Still trying to get relatedness |
| Chess Club | May not have heard the instructions to reset the board before leaving or may have been ignoring them. | | Get preferred activity (peer relatedness) |
| Math homework | Teacher gave verbal instructions, rest of kids complying, he ignored. | | Avoid failure |
| Math homework | *Didn't follow directions.* | | Get preferred activity |
| Math homework | *Supposed to return to seat, but didn't follow directions 3 times.* | *Paraprofessional tried to rationalize with him about doing as told.* | Avoid failure |
| Independent work. | Didn't follow instruction. | Ignored. | Avoid failure |
| Science | Followed directions as asked. | | Get preferred activity |
| End-of-day cleanup | Followed instructions to return to desk, then started to wander. | | Avoid boredom |
| End-of-day cleanup | Followed directions to get backpack. | | Avoid failure |
| Science | *Teacher told him to sit up (he was lying), complied.* | | Get preferred activity |

| Antecedent | Behavior | Result | Payoff |
|---|---|---|---|
| Science | *Picked up computer off floor when asked.* | | |
| Science | Went to teacher to ask question. | Told to sit 2 times before complying. | Get preferred activity |
| Social studies | Tried to give the test to the teacher (not following previous instruction). | Told to put it in the basket. | |
| Social studies | Went to desk to follow teacher's instructions about putting worksheet in specific folder. | | Avoid failure |
| End-of-day cleanup | Listened and started listing homework. | | Avoid failure |
| | Left room when dismissed to get backpack. | | Avoid failure (miss bus) |

## ABC Analysis

Overall, Pete spends most of his time avoiding failure or avoiding the social attention he might receive as a result of possible failure. See Figure 12.9.

Pete has been previously diagnosed with AS and a communication disorder. However, his ABC analysis is not consistent with this diagnosis. The main antecedent for much of his inappropriate behavior is his perceived level of success. When he feels he can be totally successful, he displays competence, whether it is answering whole-class questions from the teacher (social setting) or taking a test (nonsocial).

What defines Pete are settings where his success will be anything less than 100%. In these task settings, he responds as if he will fail and avoids the task at all costs (whether cutting out continents in science in a social setting or working on a timed writing activity in a nonsocial setting). If he believes he can't succeed, whether his peers are aware of his grade or not, he won't try; he's unwilling to even attempt.

While his unwillingness to try may be a problem, a bigger problem exists in his definition of success. For Pete anything less than 100% is a failure. This can be seen directly in comments such as "I'm not smart at all. I didn't get 100%. I'm not smart at all." And "I have to be right all the time." Another example is the math test: He scored an *A,* but he wasn't happy because it wasn't 100%. While most students view grades as a sliding gray scale from *A* to *F,* Pete sees grades as black or white, white being a 100%, black being everything else. So his comment "All I care is that I get an *A*" really means, "All I care is that I get 100%."

**Figure 12.9**   Pete's Payoffs in an Environment With Perceived Success Less Than 100%

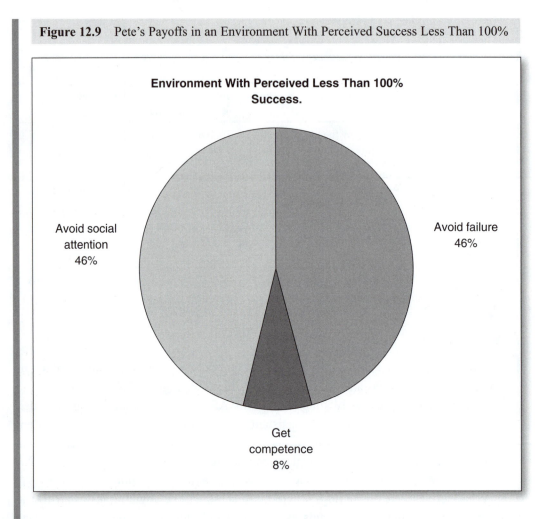

When he feels he has a chance at evaluative success, he pays close attention and gives the expected response. Examples of this are his listening to the list of homework reviewed at the end of the day to make sure he has all the needed books and getting his backpack from the hall when instructed in order to not miss the bus, a point of great anxiety for him. Other times when he shows great ability to respond as requested is when the task involves reading. When Pete is given a choice, his preferred activity is reading, and he will typically do as requested when the response will give him the chance to read, even if from a text.

As noted, Pete has a previous diagnosis of AS, a subtype of ASD. However, he seems to display only characteristics specifically related to evaluation anxiety. He has close friends, interacts well with peers, and generally shows appropriate social behavior. The other students in his class seem to like him and respond to him in a positive manner.

If AS were ruled out, another possibility would be ADHD-IN. However, he doesn't have sufficient characteristics of ADHD-IN. His defiance of direct commands could result in a label of ODD. However, Pete is defiant only when he feels destined to fail. From the inappropriate behavior noted in the observation, the best conclusion is that Pete has a form of performance anxiety, specifically in social settings. One can see generalized anxiety play out minute by minute in his constant finger and fingernail chewing. He was never observed to draw blood, but his fingers were in his mouth constantly. While fourth grade may seem early to be displaying this type of anxiety, it is possible that Pete's internal dialogue is actually making the anxiety worse. His mind is now trained to feel threatened by all evaluation, timing, and grading experiences.

## Interventions Derived From ABC Analysis

First, an intervention is needed to change Pete's perception of what success is and what failure is. Currently, he sees this as black and white; even an *A* isn't a success unless it's 100%. He needs to be taught about shades of gray on the success continuum. One possible way of doing this would be to show him a grayscale line with one end white and marked *A* (which Michael Phelps would represent) and then going darker and darker gray (and marked at each grade *B* through *D*) until the line is black, signifying an *F*. Having the Pete compare his score to the line to determine how gray the grade really is may teach him that even a *C* isn't a failure.

Also related to his perceived social failure, an accommodation the teacher could make for him would be to change his class job to being "the paper pusher." If he has a problem with turning in his homework because someone else will see his grade, taking away the social embarrassment should decrease his anxiety with the situation and increase his chances of turning in the assignment. If this is really the source of his anxiety, the teacher should see a rapid turnaround in his failure to turn in his homework.

## Case Questions

1: Does this child have any "insight" into his own fears? What is your evidence?

2 (problem-based small-group assignment): Currently does this child receive positive attention for his low self-esteem statements and behavior? Is this the outcome of the teacher's behavior or the behavior of Pete's peers? How would you address this problem?

3: What might the teacher do to increase Pete's compliance?

# Chapter 13

## Autism Spectrum Disorders

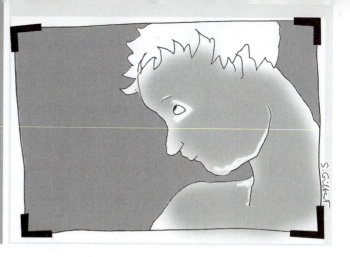

For comparison purposes only, this chapter considers two subtypes of autism spectrum disorders (ASD) concurrently: Asperger syndrome (AS) and autism. Students with **autism** are at the low end of the IQ distribution, with low cognitive and language development (Mayes & Calhoun, 2003). These children would be considered within an intense intervention program or as moderately to severely disabled and thus would not typically be presented in a text addressing mild exceptionalities. However, they provide a basis for understanding the milder symptomology of AS at the middle to higher end of the IQ distribution, with normal cognitive and language development (Mayes & Calhoun, 2003). For example, children with autism display abnormal ritualistic stereotyped behavior (known as **stereotypies**), such as a preoccupation with nonfunctional parts of objects (e.g., spinning the wheels of a toy car) (APA, 2000). In contrast, students with AS have an insistence on routines (e.g., the ordering of classroom tasks and activities) and a focus on special topics of interest (e.g., **perseveration** on such topics as weather, tractors, trains).

Children with both subtypes appear almost otherworldly—some even with a quirky sense of humor. It is quite surprising to see the delight expressed by a child with AS when he finds a fake apple that his mother has put into his lunch box. In spite of this apparent "with-it-ness," children with AS can be naive, socially reclusive, and "locked up." This could be explained by their high levels of anxiety and arousal, which are even higher than for the anxiety disorders discussed in Chapter 12. Such levels of high arousal in AS, especially social anxiety, are associated with social deficits. The social deficits in children with autism are even more severe due to these children's additional language and cognitive deficits.

**Autism:** A disorder characterized by severe social, behavioral, and communication deficits and lower IQ than is found in children with Asperger syndrome. The word *autism,* which is derived from the Greek word *autos,* meaning "self," connotes isolation within the self.

**Stereotypies:** Repetitive movements (e.g., hand clapping, finger shaking) are typically observed in children with autism, which function to structure time in the absence of other activities or to reduce arousal (Zentall & Zentall, 1983).

**Perseveration:** Repetition of the same motor or verbal responses.

**Figure 13.1**  A child with Autism Spectrum Disorders

## FORMAL IDENTIFICATION

### Definitions

#### *IDEA*

IDEA defines autism follows:

a developmental disability significantly affecting verbal and nonverbal communication and social interaction, generally evident before age three, that adversely affects a child's educational performance. Other characteristics often associated with autism are engagement in repetitive activities and stereotyped movements, resistance to environmental change or change in daily routines, and unusual responses to sensory experiences. The term does not apply if a child's educational performance is adversely affected primarily because the child has an emotional disturbance, as defined in paragraph (c)(4) of this section. (34 C.F.R. Section 300.7 [c][1][1999])

#### *DSM-IV-TR*

*DSM-IV-TR* (APA, 2000, p. 84) defines Asperger's as follows:

*Defining characteristics:*

A. Qualitative impairment in social interaction, as manifested by at least two of the following:

- Marked impairment in the use of multiple nonverbal behaviors such as eye-to-eye gaze, facial expression, body postures, and gestures to regulate social interaction
- Failure to develop peer relationships appropriate to developmental level
- Lack of spontaneous seeking to share enjoyment, interests, or achievements with other people (e.g., by a lack of showing, bringing, or pointing out objects of interest to other people)
- Lack of social or emotional reciprocity

B. Restricted repetitive and stereotyped patterns of behavior, interests, and activities, as manifested by at least one of the following:

- Encompassing preoccupation with one or more stereotyped and restricted patterns of interest that is abnormal either in intensity or focus
- Apparently inflexible adherence to specific, nonfunctional routines or rituals

- Stereotyped and repetitive motor mannerisms (e.g., hand or finger flapping or twisting, or complex whole-body movements)
- Persistent preoccupation with parts of objects

*Impairment:* Social

*Exclusions and conditions:* No general delay in language (single words by and phrases by 3 years); no significant delay in cognitive development or adaptive behavior ("other than in social interaction"); not pervasive developmental disorder or schizophrenia

### Frequently Occurring Subtypes

Within the category of ASD are autism, AS, **Rett syndrome, childhood disintegrative disorder,** and pervasive developmental disorder (PDD) not otherwise specified (insufficient number of symptoms to be classified). Except for AS, these subtypes have intellectual disabilities. Currently there is no conclusive evidence about whether AS is an entirely separate category of exceptionality or a mild form of autism. To date, and as planned for the future, AS falls within the category of autism spectrum disorders. However, the proposed definition for *DSM-V* may include criteria specifying that children with ASD function at the more severe end of the continuum. Changes in criteria, however, will not eliminate those students with characteristics of ASD in general education settings.

### Possible Co-Occurring Conditions and Differences Among Related Disabilities

AS is "associated with a number of other mental disorders, including Depressive Disorders" (APA, 2000, p. 81). In addition, NVLD may co-occur; ID is *"not"* usually observed in Asperger's Disorder, although occasional cases" have been noted (APA, 2000, p. 81). Both AS and autism have similar atypical social skills and anxiety-reducing (repetitive) types of behavior. Children with AS have routines and repetitive or restricted interests that make them relatively easy to identify (Rogers, Dziobek, Hassenstab, Wolf, & Convit, 2007). Their interests can include games, such as Monopoly and video games, or topics such as insects or TV programs. NVLD can also be mistaken for AS. In both disorders there may be a similar lack of understanding of nonverbal social interactions, similar poor motor skills, and poor speech inflection (Rourke, 1995). Adult-provided verbal explanations can normalize much of the social awkwardness of NVLD and sometimes can reduce the anxiety of students with AS. However, math concepts (time, distance, math symbols) are difficult for children with NVLD but not necessarily for those with AS. Also associated are disorders with high levels of anxiety, such as OCD and Tourette's syndrome (TS). Examples are the

**Rett syndrome:** A condition that occurs in young females and is characterized by marked degrees of impairment in intelligence, language, and communication, with a characteristic loss in head growth from the ages of 5 months to 48 months and loss of previously acquired socialization skills and fine motor and gross skills (Hagin, 2004).

**Childhood disintegrative disorder:** A disorder characterized by marked degrees of intellectual disability and loss of previously acquired skills, with losses in language, social skills, and adaptive behavior occurring more gradually (Hagin, 2004).

barking and physiological noises (tics) that Greg (whose case study appears at the end of this chapter) produces when another child gets physically too close:

> When the students were playing a math game, another student got pretty close in proximity to Greg. Greg started to make farting noises, and the student moved away from him. . . . While Greg was reading, another student came and sat next to him. Greg made barking noises at him. The classmate moved seats and Greg was redirected. . . . During the discussion of the day's lesson, Greg started to make burping noises. The teacher gave him a disappointed look and directed him to look at the board. A minute later Greg started the burping noises again. He was given a verbal warning and told it was inappropriate.

Children with autism and AS do not resist or keep hidden their repetitive behaviors and interests; in fact, they appear to enjoy their behavior (Frith, 1991). This is different from the resistance of children with OCD to their compulsive behavior and of children with TS, who attempt to hide their tics. See Table 13.1 for a disability comparison of types of repetitive behavior. Note that what appears to be nonfunctional to the observer may be functional for the child.

Finally, *DSM-IV-TR* notes that "symptoms of overactivity and inattention are frequent in Asperger's Disorder, and indeed many individuals with this condition receive a diagnosis of Attention-Deficit/Hyperactivity Disorder prior to the diagnosis of Asperger's Disorder" (APA, 2000, pp. 82–83). However, the behavioral

**Table 13.1**  Comparison of Repetitive Behaviors Associated with Asperger Syndrome, Autism, Tourette Syndrome, and Obsessive-Compulsive Disorder

| Tourette syndrome[a] | Asperger syndrome | Autism | Obsessive-compulsive disorder |
|---|---|---|---|
| Multiform, frequently changing motor and vocal tics that are nonfunctional and repetitive (e.g., head tossing) | Nonfunctional routines or rituals (carrying around a button or making repeated verbal statements, such as, "is it cookies?") and preoccupation with restricted interests and activities (e.g., trains) | Stereotyped and repetitive nonfunctional motor mannerisms, often called stereotypies (e.g., hand shaking) | Functional repetitive compulsive behaviors that serve an apparent purpose of cleanliness, orderliness, safety, or the like (e.g., hand washing) |

a. For full discussion of Tourette's syndrome, see Chapter 15.

**Table 13.2**   Comparison of Characteristics of Students with Asperger Syndrome and Students with Attention Deficit Hyperactivity Disorder

| *Asperger syndrome* | *Attention Deficit Hyperactivity Disorder* |
|---|---|
| Higher scores than students with ADHD in self-directedness, responsibility, purposefulness, harm avoidance, fear of uncertainty, and shyness (Anckarsäter et al., 2006). | Higher scores than students with AS in seeking attachments with others, impulsivity, novelty seeking, disorderliness, and reward dependence (Anckarsäter et al., 2006). |
| More anxious about change than peers; they attempt to preserve sameness and predictability. | Seek change (novelty) and frequently change activities and topics of conversation. |
| Typically engage in repetitive activity. They self-report more passive behavior. | Hyperactivity is variable in nature, often with more assertion or aggression than is seen in peers. |
| Attention is biased toward restricted, personal interests and toward familiar individuals and activities (Anckarsäter et al., 2006). | Attention is biased toward novelty (for a review, see Zentall, 2006). |

responses of students with ADHD are typically not repetitive, unless there is too high a dose of medication or stress accompanying co-occurring LD. See Table 13.2 for a comparison of ADHD and AS. Thus, type of activity and response to novelty should serve to differentiate between these two disabilities.

Also sometimes confused with AS or autism are schizophrenia, selective mutism, OCD, social phobia (social anxiety) and other anxiety disorders, and giftedness. Schizophrenia, however, usually develops after years of normal, or near normal, development and is characterized by hallucinations, delusions, and disorganized speech. Children with selective mutism usually exhibit appropriate communication skills in certain contexts without the severe impairment in social interaction or restricted patterns of behavior associated with AS. Children with AS can be talkative, especially about their restricted interests. In OCD, obsessive topics are the source of anxiety, whereas special "obsessive interests" are sources of pleasure or comfort in students with AS. Although children with social phobia and other anxiety disorders may show heightened and debilitating anxiety in social settings similar to children with AS, only AS is accompanied by restricted interests. AS may be mistaken for giftedness in part because 22% of children with AS demonstrate giftedness (Barnhill, Hagiwara, Myles, & Simpson, 2000). Similarities between children with AS and those with GT are excellent memory, intellectualized talking at an early age, perseveration on special interests or topics and amassing information on these topics, quirky sense of humor, and hypersensitivity to stimuli, such as noises and textures (Webb et al., 2005). "The child may be described as talking before walking, and indeed parents may believe the child to be advanced (e.g., with a rich or 'adult' vocabulary)" (APA, 2000, pp. 80–84). Unlike students with AS, however, students with GT are concerned with broad issues (justice), are socially aware and engage in social reciprocity, are emotionally intense and empathetic, and are able to see both sides of an issue, to generalize, and to understand metaphors (e.g., "Don't jump the gun") (Webb et al., 2005).

## Etiology

*Biogenetic.* There is "an increased frequency of Asperger's Disorder among family members of individuals who have the disorder. There may also be an increased risk for Autistic Disorder as well as more general social difficulties" (APA, 2000, p. 82). Recent evidence finds that older fathers are more likely than younger fathers to pass genetic mutations to their offspring and thus increase the risk of autism and schizophrenia (Callaway, 2012). This could also contribute to the evidence that siblings of children with autism are 25% more likely to be diagnosed with autism than are other children (see Garrett, 2011). Interestingly, and opposite to ADHD, individuals with autism and AS have *larger* brain volume or weight, especially white matter, which makes for more efficient connections in the brain and may create sensory overload for the child (Redcay & Courchesne, 2005). This sensory overload may then contribute to higher arousal/anxiety in this population (see Zentall & Zentall, 1983).

*Environmental.* No evidence has been found that environmental factors such as childhood vaccination or family dynamics contribute to the development of ASD.

**Neophobia:** Fear of new and unfamiliar people and situations.

*Functional.* Functional analysis would identify the following as triggers of abnormal responding for students with autism and AS: changes of routine, loss of predictability or order, stress/anxiety, failure, change/transitions, and noise. Children with AS often have a fear of new persons or situations or tasks (**neophobia**).

## Prevalence, Gender, and Age Factors

*Prevalence.* The rate of autism diagnosis has increased dramatically in recent years, from 1 in 10,000 to 1 in 88 individuals, a 78% increase since 2007 and twice the rate since 2002 according to statistics from the U.S. Centers for Disease Control and Prevention. This increase has partially been explained by the advanced ages that fathers are having children, although other biological factors are yet to be identified (Callaway, 2012).

*Gender.* AS can be 15 times more prevalent in males than in females. Boys with AS have more emotional deficits (e.g., lack of emotional sensitivity and empathy) than do girls with AS, yet they also demonstrate more skills (e.g., math and engineering) (APA, 2000; Wenar & Kerig, 2006).

*Age.* These children are identified later in development, partly because their accumulation of knowledge at early ages can give the appearance of advanced skills.

# INFORMAL EDUCATOR IDENTIFICATION OF CHARACTERISTICS

## Behavioral

Around 79% of children with AS can be described as being active but odd (Ghaziuddin, 2008). Their activity includes verbal and behavioral routines and has been described as obsessive-compulsive (Wenar & Kerig, 2006). They have "restricted, repetitive patterns of behavior, interests, and activities. . . . These interests and activities are pursued with great intensity often to the exclusion of other activities" (APA, 2000, p. 80).

## Social-Emotional

Children with AS score significantly higher than other children on the Personal Distress Test and show greater anxiety, especially in response to interpersonal settings (Rogers et al., 2007). This social-emotional oversensitivity can lead to exaggerated behavioral reactions of avoidance or even extreme aggression when they are faced with crowding, noise, or perceived social threat (Reynolds, Bendixen, Lawrence, & Lane, 2011). Some researchers have suggested that stimulus avoidance may be a "driver" of the social deficits of this population (Reynolds et al., 2011; Zentall & Zentall, 1983).

AS is all about the lack of social appropriateness, even though there is *no* significant delay in language or cognitive development. Children with AS do not mature socially at the same rate as peers. They are also more likely to engage in solitary play, reading or writing, video games, and play with computers and less likely to engage in dramatic imaginative role play, such as "playing school" or "playing army" (Reynolds et al., 2011). Their social behavior can be defined by their (a) approaching others to have their own needs met, (b) having a clumsy social approach, and (c) having difficulty understanding and empathizing with other children's emotions (Garrett, 2011). However, there are no differences between children with AS and normal peers in emotion identification (i.e., recognition of emotions from tone of voice and facial expression), and both AS and normal peers are better at emotion identification than children with autism (Mazefsky & Oswald, 2007). Additional impairments are listed above in the section on "qualitative impairment in social interaction" in *DSM-IV-TR*'s definition.

*Friendships.* Across ages, children with AS show naive, inappropriate, one-sided interactions. Unfortunately, many of these students are victimized by bullies (Webb et al., 2005). However, it is possible for adolescents with AS to form friendships with those peers who have similar restricted interests (e.g., they may join computer or math clubs or take part in science fairs). Some students with AS may pass socially as "nerds," a group they actually resemble. According to *DSM-IV-TR:*

> Younger individuals may have little or no interest in establishing friendships. Older individuals may have an interest in friendship but lack understanding of the conventions of social interaction and may more likely make relationships with individuals much older or younger than themselves. . . . Interest in forming social relationships may increase in adolescence as the individuals learn some ways of responding more adaptively to their difficulties, for example, the individual may learn to apply explicit verbal rules or routines in certain stressful situations (APA, 2000, p. 82).

## Cognitive

**Savant:** A child who has special talents or abilities in spite of a disability. The term comes from the French word *savoir,* meaning "to know." Savants generally excel in one of the following areas: mathematical calculations, memory feats, artistic abilities, or musical abilities.

The attention of students in the autism spectrum involves attending to details and ignoring the big picture more than normal peers and than students with ADHD, ID, or LD of equivalent IQ (Webb et al., 2005; Wenar & Kerig, 2006). Together with their repetitive interests, this may contribute to the relatively rare so-called **savant** abilities seen in some (10% prevalence in autism versus 1% prevalence in those with ID, major mental illness, and other disorders). The source for these savant abilities is unknown, although repeated practice (e.g., with calculations, dates) accounts for some. However, the ability to play a complicated piece of music immediately after hearing it for the first time is less easily explained.

For students with AS, learning is primarily in the form of *memorization,* "often with strengths in areas of verbal ability (e.g., vocabulary, rote auditory memory)" (APA, 2000, p. 81). However, many children with AS have weaknesses in auditory processing with relative strengths in visual-spatial skills), in contrast to their strength (for review see Baranek, 2002; Goldberg et al., 2005; 2008). By definition, children with AS have average to above-average IQ, with no significant delay in age-appropriate self-help skills (adaptive behavior). However, they may have difficulties with cognitive abstractions, specifically in planning/organizing and applying information and skills across settings. This failure to generalize typifies children who are connected to the concrete world more than to abstract principles and ideas (Webb et al., 2005). Across the range of intelligence and severity levels, children with ASD have more difficulty with planning and flexibility or shifting sets and multitasking (Myles & Adreon, 2001).

## Communication

Students with AS talk repeatedly about their special interests (e.g., dinosaurs, TV programs) in a perseverative or obsessive manner. However, their language is normal in structure (e.g., word order, use of pronouns) and in development (e.g., single words by age 2, communicative phrases by age 3, speaking fluently by age 5). Even so, they have poor pragmatic everyday communication that is "odd in its use for communication" and often accompanied by "little professor" monologues that fail to consider the listener's interest or lack of interest (Frith, 1991, p. 3). See Table 13.3 for a comparison between AS and autism in the areas of cummunication, cognition, emotion, and socialization.

**Echolalia** and delayed echolalia are frequently seen in students with autism; the contents of these repeated conversations are often "worry topics," such as an overheard argument, the presence/absence of sprinklers, an accident that occurred at a stop sign, a program on television. In addition, these children do not signal changes of topics and show greater literalness in interpretations of events. Also, a delay in the use of nonverbal communication (gestures) has been found to be an indicator of autism (Mitchell et al., 2006). Children with autism co-occurring with ID show even fewer types of behavior that signal joint social attention (eye gazing, vocalization) than do children who have only ID (Shumway & Wetherby, 2009). In contrast, the sharing of attention (e.g., pointing) has been found in association with good spoken language at age 3 (Shumway & Wetherby, 2009).

> **Echolalia:** The repetition or echoing of others' words or phrases, which can be immediate or delayed (e.g., from a TV program heard the night before).

## Motor, Physical, and Somatic/Sensory

Unusual sensory responses, such as preoccupations with sensory features of objects, have been reported in 42–88% of older children with autism (for a review, see Baranek, 2002). These children show heightened "responsiveness" to sensations of sight, sound, and touch (i.e., eight times more sensitive to and more avoidant of sensations than typical children; Reynolds et al., 2011), especially to loud sounds. Greg's sensitivity to sound can be seen in his actions:

The classroom started to get very noisy before class officially began. The teacher asked students to be seated and Greg shouted out for everyone to be quiet.

Oversensitivity may also contribute to these children's avoidance when faced with unpleasant stimuli (Reynolds et al., 2011). For example, students with AS may try to avoid art materials and gluing projects that expose them to strong sights, smells, and textures.

"Motor clumsiness and awkwardness may be present but usually are relatively mild, although motor difficulties may contribute to peer rejection and social isolation (e.g., inability to participate in group sports)" (APA, 2000, p. 81). Fine motor skills may also be less well developed in children with AS, and motor planning may contribute to these dificulties (for review, see Baranek, 2002). Sleep disturbances are reported more often than for typical children or than children with autism. For example, in one research sample, children with AS (5–17 years of age) slept less than 7 hours per night, took more than 30 minutes to fall asleep, and, in comparison with non-AS peers, had more sleep-related fears, more frequent awakenings and problems going back to sleep, and greater daytime tiredness (Paavonen et al., 2008).

## Academic

Academic progress is an area of relative strength for students with AS in the early grades. For example, their rote reading is usually quite good, their calculation skills may be similarly strong, and many acquire high levels of factual information (for a review, see Mayes & Calhoun, 2006). In addition, the amount of time they devote to gathering information in their interest areas can contribute to their classroom skills.

However, their poor fine motor skills make pencil and drawing tasks difficult, and their handwriting skills are worse than those of IQ- and age-matched peers (Reynolds et al., 2011). Children with ASD also have difficulties applying their knowledge in the advanced academic areas of written language, reading comprehension, and math problem solving (e.g., a 4-year-old girl with autism may be able to decode "written materials with minimal understanding of the meaning of what is read"; APA, 2000, pp. 71–72). In other words, the low IQ of autism makes reading comprehension impossible, even though reading decoding may be an easier skill for these children. For students with AS, written language skill deficits are more typical, as were recorded for 11-year-old Greg:

> He stated that he does not like to write, read, or do homework. . . . He stated that his favorite subjects are science and technology education and that his *least* favorite subjects are communications and social studies. When Greg was asked why communications was his least favorite class, he stated that he could never finish the amount of work and that he could not concentrate in that class.

Greg's deficits may be related to requirements to apply information, to fine motor difficulties needed for handwriting, or to the social nature of the communication in social studies classes.

**Table 13.3**    Comparison of Characteristics of ASD Subtypes

|  | Asperger syndrome | Autism |
|---|---|---|
| Social | "Although the social deficit in Asperger's Disorder is severe and is defined in the same way as in Autistic Disorder, the lack of social reciprocity is more typically manifest by an eccentric and one-sided social approach to others (e.g., pursuing a conversational topic regardless of others' reactions)" (Macintosh & Dissanayake, 2006).<br><br>Can form friendships based on common interests. Play is often rule based, and friendships can dissolve when rules are broken. | Little awareness of social behavior. "Typical social interaction patterns are marked by self-isolation or markedly rigid social approaches" (APA, 2000, p. 83). |
| Emotional | Situationally appropriate and often with intense emotions (e.g., laughter, anger) (Wenar & Kerig, 2006). | Typically emotionally flat, indicated by monotone speech and lack of facial expression. Sometimes facial expressions reflect fear or agitation. |
| Cognitive | "In the first 3 years of life, there are no clinically significant delays in cognitive development as manifested by expressing normal curiosity about the environment or in the acquisition of age-appropriate learning skills and adaptive behaviors (other than in social interaction)" (APA, 2000, p. 80–84). | In the majority of cases, there is lower IQ with ID from mild to profound. |
| Communication | Normal development in the structure of language. "No clinically significant delays or deviance in language acquisition (e.g., single non-echoed words are used communicatively by age 2 years, and spontaneous communicative phrases are used by age 3 years . . . although more subtle aspects of social communication (e.g., typical give-and-take in conversation) may be affected" (APA, 2000, p. 80).<br><br>Little understanding of **figurative language** (e.g., humor, idioms, metaphors, irony) (Saalasti et al., 2008). | Language delays and marked echolalia.<br><br><br><br><br><br><br><br><br><br>Little understanding of figurative language (Saalasti et al., 2008) |

*(Continued)*

**Table 13.3** (Continued)

|  | Asperger syndrome | Autism |
|---|---|---|
|  | No significant imagination or communication impairments.<br><br>No delays in speech (Mayes & Calhoun, 2003).<br><br>Fixation on specific topics. For example: "Fred is really afraid of storms. He likes to know all about storms and remembers them in detail. On a day when it looked like rain, Fred tried to see out the window several times." | Imagination and communication impairments.<br><br>May or may not show speech difficulties (Mayes & Calhoun, 2003). |

## SUMMARY OF STRENGTHS AND NEEDS

| Possible strengths | Probable needs |
|---|---|
| • General information in specific interest areas<br>• Concrete memory tasks<br>• Good calculation skills<br>• Good reading decoding skills<br>• Ability to complete procedural tasks—following steps<br>• Can be successful in careers that emphasizes their special interests and strengths | • Assessment of written language to determine skills in handwriting, comprehension, and application of information<br>• Reduced requirements or accommodations for pencil skills (see Chapter 15)<br>• Social stories that help in applying knowledge in multiple settings<br>• Interventions for developing adaptive responses to social settings (e.g., with scripted responses) |

## DISABILITY IN THE CLASSROOM

### Implications for Accommodations in General Education Settings: Tier I

Educators can take the following steps to accommodate students with AS:

- Provide a predictable everyday environment and a safe place these children can retreat to when overstimulated.
- Establish a schedule early and provide a visual representation of that daily schedule during instruction (e.g., task cards, transition cards, homework

checklists), especially for adjusting to a new activity. Write notes in advance for the children if the schedule is going to change, set clear expectations and boundaries and post them on the wall, ask questions to check the children's understanding of the instructions, use a timer to limit perseveration/echolalia and allow the children to earn "free time" in their chosen areas of interest, such as art or computers.

- Create visual cue cards of expected social behavior and place them in the areas where those behaviors are expected. More generally, visual instruction and visual structuring of the environment can be effective (Stichter et al., 2008).
- Use a strength- and interest-based approach to teaching (Bianco, Carothers, & Smiley, 2009).

## Implications for Interventions in Small-Group and Individual Settings: Tier II

Interventions for children with AS include technological and behavioral approaches:

- *Technological interventions:* Use selected applications for iPads and other tablet computers as well as smart phones. The number of apps appropriate for use with the ASD population has grown considerably in recent years, and the touch screen as well as the mechanical (nonsocial) interface offered by tablets and smart phones make these particularly useful tools. Even for nonverbal children with autism, the iPad app called FindMe encourages players to focus on others and can be used from the age of 18 months up. Useful smart phone apps include TappyTunes, which lets a child tap out a favorite song; iEarnedThat, a puzzle-based reward system that uses custom images; First-Then Visual Schedule, which creates digital visual schedules with several format options; and Stories2Learn, which creates custom social stories from the user's own photos, text, and voice over.
- Behavioral interventions—social skills training:
  - ○ Teach specific socially acceptable phrases for use in certain situations.
  - ○ Model and role-play social situations demonstrating appropriate behavior for upcoming social events.
  - ○ Use social stories, comic strips, and video modeling paired with simple sentences to improve understanding of situational social cues (Rogers & Myles, 2001; Scattone, 2008). A social story is a brief story describing a situation (e.g., changes in daily routine, such as having a substitute

teacher) and providing appropriate responses for that setting for an individual child (Sansosti & Powell-Smith, 2006); social stories are typically used with students with autism (Scattone, Wilczynski, Edwards, & Rabian, 2002) to help them interpret social situations and decrease their anxiety, anger, frustration, and disruptive behavior (e.g., Pierson & Glaeser, 2005; Scattone et al., 2002). Such stories focus first on the perception of cues and then on how to respond.

## Long-Term Outcomes

Many children with co-occurring ID will acquire a variety of additional psychiatric disorders that involve depression, anxiety, and tic and eating disorders (LoVullo & Matson, 2009). Furthermore, 73% of individuals with autism require close supervision and are unable to function on their own. However, individuals with AS more often live independently, with some economic self-sufficiency (i.e., 5–44% are employed and 16–50% live independently) (for a review, see Wenar & Kerig, 2006). These employment figures suggest that finding the right job and work situation may be a critical task for individuals with AS. Often this involves finding careers that emphasize their strengths, such as interest in and talent for mathematics, physics, and engineering. However, guidance toward an appropriate field needs to begin early, and this requires a correct diagnosis. See the following e-mail from a father:

Good morning Dr. Zentall,

I was searching through Purdue's website and came across your name and a link to your work *Characteristics of Mild Exceptionalities.* My wife and I have a son, soon to be 21, who seems to demonstrate many of the characteristics of Asperger's Syndrome. Over the years, he has been "diagnosed" as ADD, ODD, and Gifted, and our journey through K–12 grades was challenging, to say the least. Now, he is an adult whose primary interests are Legos, SciFi, and things German. He has been involved in Karate for over 10 years, and is currently a volunteer instructor, however, that is his only extracurricular activity. Our challenge is moving him towards adulthood and associated responsibilities, and frankly, my wife and I are at a loss as to what to do. He is aware that he should get a job, but he is so restrictive and particular about the where/what, that he hasn't had any success. So, I was searching the Purdue website to see if there was anyone who researches in this area, and your name seemed to be appropriately associated. Do you have any advice you can give us, or alternatively, could you point us in any direction?

Sincerely,

C.

Unfortunately, C.'s son did not receive a correct diagnosis early. Asperger's seems the correct diagnosis now (given the father's description), and the young man's characteristic of oppositionality makes sense for someone anxious about and avoidant of change. However, neither ADHD–inattentive subtype nor GT appears to have been a correct diagnosis. At this point, it will be difficult to set a 21-year-old on an appropriate career path. For those students identified early with ASD, whose skills are less advanced or are more resistant to change, supportive settings, such as in rural, smaller, less complex towns and in family businesses, are often the best choice.

## CHAPTER SUMMARY

- AS and autism are subtypes of ASD, both of which have social deficits related to high levels of arousal or anxiety. High arousal explains the nature of the repetitive and avoidant behavior of children with ASD, which is greater than that observed in children with anxiety or depressive disorders.

- Co-occurring conditions include generalized anxiety disorder, TS, and OCD. The repetitive types of behavior seen in ASD can make the differential diagnosis of these related disabilities difficult. That is, TS is characterized by variable nonfunctional tics and OCD by functional compulsive rituals. Both ASD and ADHD have high rates of activity, but the nature of their activity (repetitive versus variable) and their attention (narrow versus wide focus) differentiates between these groups. ASD may co-occur with NVLD or be confused with NVLD. However, children with NVLD respond excellently to verbal explanations of events, which is not typical of students with ASD (unless verbal explanations are used to reduce anxiety), and students with ASD typically do not have difficulties with math.

- The etiology of ASD is genetic, associated with large brain volume and more efficient connections in the brain, which may create sensory overload (overarousal). Functional assessments document "change" as a major antecedent, as well as crowding, loud noises, novel individuals or settings, and unpredictability.

- AS is identified later in age than autism and more frequently in males than in females.

- Educators can identify children with ASD through observation of behavior, including the rituals in AS and stereotypies in autism. Characteristics that are markers for both subtypes are greater feelings of anxiety and discomfort in social settings, with a failure to share attention (eye contact, pointing, games) or difficulty taking the perspective of the other (empathy). Children with AS may make friendships at older age levels around special interests.

- IQ is a major factor that distinguishes autism from AS. Children with both subtypes, however, are more sensitive to visual, touch, and auditory sensations, especially to loud sounds. Children with AS typically have skills in rote auditory memory and the ability to accumulate facts (in their special interest areas). These memory abilities may be related to their ability to sustain attention to details. Motor clumsiness and poor fine motor writing skills can be observed. In addition, planning and flexibility are more difficult for them. They also have weaknesses in multitasking and applying information across settings. The language of students with AS is normal in structure and development, but pragmatic deficits are apparent in their use of language for everyday communication. In classroom settings, when basic skills are taught, the academic performance of children with AS can appear normal. At the older age levels, when applications of skills are taught (reading comprehension, math problem solving), these students may appear less proficient.

- Accommodations for children with AS involve the use of their special interest areas in the content of instruction, predictable schedules with advance warnings of upcoming changes, and methods that allow the children to escape from or avoid crowding and noise (e.g., through the use of earplugs or headphones). Interventions include social skills training and the use of social stories.

## CHAPTER QUESTIONS

1. What one characteristic makes AS so difficult to differentiate from other disorders?

2. How would you describe the preferences of children with AS?

3. How would you summarize the social dysfunctions of these students?

4. What accommodations would you suggest to a teacher who has learned that children with AS can be overstimulated by their peers and therefore wants to exclude a student with AS from all social interactions?

## TRUE/FALSE AND MULTIPLE-CHOICE

1. Children with AS have below-average IQ.

2. Children with AS differ from those with autism in the performance of routines and rituals rather than stereotypies.

3. Parents may be confused and may even blame the teacher if their child with AS shows a lack of academic growth. The reason some student's with AS plateau around the fourth-grade level is probably related to

A. difficulties with tasks that require fine motor skills (e.g., poor handwriting)
B. difficulties with reading decoding and math calculations
C. difficulties with comprehension tasks
D. all of the above

4. Children with AS are likely to have

A. a strong sense of justice
B. skills in applying information
C. skills in reading comprehension
D. skills in math calculations and reading decoding

5. The ability to infer or grasp the probable mental states of others is called

A. working memory
B. desensitization
C. theory of mind
D. neophobia

6. The most easily observed characteristic that differentiates between AS and ADHD:

A. response to novelty or change
B. social difficulties
C. size of brain

## SHORT ANSWER

1. Fear of new things or change

2. Saying "The tree is like a poem" is using _____ language.

3. Repeating others' words

4. Term from the French word meaning "to know," applied to some individuals with ASD

5. Students with AS are similar to students with ID in that they have difficulty applying learnings across settings, which is a failure to _____.

6. Repeated *non*functional actions (e.g., hand shaking) are examples of _____.

7. An intervention that scripts social interactions in specific settings is called _____.

8. What increases the frequency of some kinds of repetitive behavior?

## PROBLEM-BASED CASE APPLICATIONS AND QUESTIONS

### CASE STUDY 13.1: GREG

*"Smart cookies."*
(adapted from a report submitted by Melissa Savage-Bowling)

*Background.* Greg is an 11-year-old male who is in the sixth grade. He has been diagnosed with autism and a language disorder. Greg, along with his 9-year-old sister, currently lives in two different households throughout the week. On Mondays and Tuesdays he lives with his mother, on Wednesdays and Thursdays he lives with his father, and on Fridays through Sundays he switches dependent on which parent's weekend it is to have the two children. When asked about his parents' recent divorce, Greg stated that he was mad at first because he couldn't get the schedule right, but now he understands where he is going and on what days. Changes were noted in Greg's behavior at school as well when his dad moved out of the house. Teachers stated that Greg was shouting out more and not completing any work. Both of Greg's parents are supportive of his schooling. They are present at meetings and request information regularly on his academic and social progress. Greg is currently on one antidepression medication. He takes this regularly.

Greg's current placement is the general education setting for 80% of the school day and special education services for the other 20% of the day. He attends English class in an inclusion setting; the class is co-taught by a language arts general education teacher and a special education teacher. Greg's math instruction takes place in a resource setting. Greg also receives occupational and speech therapy services. For speech therapy he receives services 10 minutes monthly to work on socially appropriate responding. Strengths for Greg include being talkative and sharing knowledge; in addition, he has a strong interest in fixing things, he is articulate, he is interested in electronics and technology education.

Greg's teachers indicated that he responds inappropriately in the classroom and has a difficult time staying on topic, determining what is relevant in a situation, and paying attention. Greg prefers not to interact in social situations unless they involve topics that interest him, such as electronics or fixing things. He prefers to sit and do class work by himself and acts inappropriately when he feels threatened by his peers or when he is overstimulated.

Currently, Greg is having a difficult time with some of his academics. He is not passing his science, social studies, or communications classes. His teachers state that his failing grades are due to incomplete class work and not turning in homework assignments. He stated that he does not like to write, read, or do homework.

Greg is doing well in his English, technology, band, and math classes. He has acquired and maintained grade-level concepts in math and is ready to move into the general education math classroom. He stated that his favorite subjects are science and technology education and that his *least* favorite subjects are communications and social studies. When Greg was asked why communications was his least favorite class, he stated that he could never finish the amount of work and that he could not concentrate in that class.

### Behavioral Log

### Tuesday, February 16, Period 3: Math

When the bell rang for class to begin, Greg sat at his desk and pulled out his weekly problems worksheet and began working on the problems for Tuesday with no prompt from the teacher. Once the students were finished with their worksheets, they went over the answers. Another student gave an incorrect response and Greg made a buzzing sound to indicate the student was wrong. The teacher marked Greg's behavior down in the behavior log. The other student also told Greg it was wrong and that the sound made him feel dumb. Greg apologized and raised his hand to answer the next question. He was called on and answered correctly. The teacher gave Greg verbal praise for raising his hand before responding.

### Wednesday, February 17, Period 1: English

Class began with the media specialist giving instructions for checking out books. Greg stated that he didn't care about the instructions and shouted, "This is stupid." Some of his classmates started to laugh, and Greg shouted, "I don't want to." His classmates laughed again. The teachers ignored him, and he began searching for a book to check out. Once he found a book and started to read, he was making noises at his table. Other students were making noises as well. The teachers ignored this behavior. While Greg was reading, another student came and sat next to him. Greg made barking noises at him. The classmate moved seats and Greg was redirected.

### Wednesday, February 17, Period 3: Math

When the bell rang, Greg began his daily problems with no prompting from the teacher. She praised him for starting his work. Once they went over the daily problems, the teacher asked her students to write down their homework for the night in their assignment books. When the students were playing a math game, another student got pretty close in proximity to Greg. Greg started to make farting noises, and the student moved away from him.

### Wednesday, February 17, Period 6: Social Studies

After the teacher gave instructions Greg commented on the assignment they were about to do. He shouted out that it would be boring and did not raise his hand. Greg began the assignment and asked the teacher for a pencil. He was given a pencil. The teacher asked the students to watch the video and write down five important facts. Greg watched the video and wrote down two things. When the class discussed the first video, Greg did not respond or interact with the class. While the teacher was preparing the next video, students began to talk. Greg shouted for the class to be quiet. This action was ignored and the teacher gave the same instructions for the second video as he did the first. Greg wrote down three notes this time.

### Thursday, February 18, Period 3: Math

After the bell rang, Greg sat down. The teacher had to give him a verbal prompt to take out his daily problem worksheet. The teacher asked the students to raise their hands if they had the answers to the problems, but Greg shouted them out. The teacher ignored his behavior and called on a student with their hand raised to answer. All the students got the answer correct, and the teacher called the students "smart cookies." Greg started to bite his arm and the teacher explained that she meant that they did a good job on the math problem. When the teacher announced the homework assignment, one of the students started to complain. Greg shouted, "Someone's getting cranky" and made a face at the student. The student told Greg to stop and Greg did stop.

### Thursday, February 18, Period 8: Communications

While the teacher was giving instruction for the assignment, another student was singing. Greg shouted, "Shut up!" to the student and the student returned the shout out. The teacher ignored this behavior and continued with instructions. Greg shouted out once more during instructions, "I don't wanna." This was also ignored. When the teacher gave Greg a pencil for the assignment he shouted, "I hate this assignment," which was ignored as well. The class began typing and started to research their assignment. Greg shouted, "Shut up everybody." He received redirection from his teacher and his classmate called him a psycho.

### Friday, February 19, Period 8: Communications

The classroom started to get very noisy before class officially began. The teacher asked students to be seated and Greg shouted out for everyone to be quiet. A classmate mentioned that it was crazy hat day. Greg decided to pull his coat over his head and tell everyone it was crazy hat day. Some students called him an idiot. The teacher began giving instructions for a dictionary assignment they were to do with small groups. She told them she did not have enough red dictionaries so they could use red or blue. Greg shouted that he did not want a red one. The teacher stated that she didn't want him talking and continued with her instructions. Greg interrupted once more and asked her to look up the word *diarrhea.* She let him know that was inappropriate. She gave instructions for them to form small groups, up to five students, and Greg did not attempt to find classmates to work with. Greg shouted out during the assignment. He shouted that he was bored and then shouted, "Shut up." When he shouted "Shut up" the classroom had become very noisy. Classmates told him to shut up and the teacher gave redirection. Another classmate told Greg his face was scary. Greg responded by telling him his face was even more scary. Both were given redirection. When the teacher checked on progress on the assignment Greg told her it made no sense. She helped him for the remainder of the class.

### Tuesday, February 23, Period 3: Math/Acuity Testing

Greg walked into the computer lab for acuity testing. He sat down, put headphones on, and began testing after instructions. He was given a red card and verbal praise. After testing he stated to his teacher that the test was really hard, but that he still got half of them right. The teacher gave him verbal praise for trying his hardest.

### Wednesday, February 24, Period 3: Math

When class began, the teacher wrote the daily math problems on the board. Greg completed the problems with no prompting. The teacher gave him verbal praise and a red card. During the discussion of the day's lesson, Greg started to make burping noises. The teacher gave him a disappointed look and directed him to look at the board. A minute later Greg started the burping noises again. He was given a verbal warning and told it was inappropriate.

### Thursday, February 25, Period 8: Study Hall

Greg came into class and got out his assignment book after the teacher prompted the class to do so. Once he was done he was able to take out his iPod touch. He showed it to a classmate and they started to talk about electronics.

## ABC Analysis

In large-group settings Greg's highest payoff is avoiding the task, occurring 26.6% of the time. Trying to receive attention from peers and teachers in the form of relatedness occurs 20.6% of the time. Greg is shouting out in class in order to avoid the task at hand and in attempts to gain relatedness from his peers. Other times Greg is shouting out because he is overstimulated due to a loud environment.

Greg's math class is the only class he currently has that is a small-group setting. His most frequent payoff in this setting is to get competence, occurring 48% of the time. Greg works well in small-group settings and his behaviors are manageable. Greg spent time making comments to other classmates about how simple problems were. Greg had a hard time comprehending why other classmates were not able to grasp the concepts the same way he could. Greg was moved into a higher math class at the completion of the functional assessment.

Greg is excited to show his study hall teachers passing grades he received that day and has transitioned well, following expectations and completing his assignments during study hall. His highest-frequency payoff is to get competence, occurring 41.7% of the time. Greg has made important strides in attempting to get appropriate relatedness. He has connected with another classmate, and they have been talking to each other appropriately about their knowledge of electronics as well as sharing their electronic devices.

## Diagnosis Versus ABC Analysis

Greg is a sixth-grade student diagnosed with autism and a language disorder. Greg exhibits many classic signs and symptoms of Asperger's rather than autism, including intense and narrow interests, inability to cope well with change, sensory issues, distinguishing relevant details, mild intellectual disability, misreading of social cues, and an inability to express emotions well. Clearly communication is difficult for him, but he does have adequate language.

Greg is shouting out for a variety of functions, making it complicated to understand his needs at one time. It would be impossible to understand the function of Greg's behaviors without paying careful attention to his surrounding environment. He is shouting out to show competence, to get relatedness with peers and teachers, to get control of situations, to avoid unwanted/uncomfortable social interactions, to avoid overstimulation, and to avoid certain tasks. He has a difficult time expressing emotions and uses shouting out to get what he wants and needs and to avoid as well.

Greg's most frequent payoff is getting competence, occurring 31.5% of the time. Greg enjoys sharing his academic accomplishments with all teachers and answering questions in math class. A majority of Greg's getting competence is done appropriately. Teachers stated that he has made a big improvement over the first three quarters with raising his hand, answering questions, and being prepared for class. Greg is also trying to relate with his peers and teachers, relatedness occurring 20.5% of the time. Many times he is relating inappropriately by shouting out during instructions.

Classmates tend to laugh at Greg's comments, encourage him, and also make comments about the teacher's instructions, all of which give Greg an impression that he should continue. Also, when Greg wants to avoid a task, which occurs 16.4% of the time, he tends to shout out inappropriately, ask off-topic questions, or make off-topic comments to both peers and teachers. Greg has been successful with these techniques and has verbally expressed that he doesn't have to do as much work when he gets off topic. He stated that he likes to "stall."

The behavior in the following table was reorganized into "uncomfortable" social situations after Greg answered the question of what made him feel uncomfortable. He responded: "For me it's when it's really loud like annoying noises around me or people are standing next to me. The damn noise kills my ears and they feel like they're going to explode." He currently uses shouting out and inappropriate social interactions, such as farting noises, to remove himself from situations that bother him and to gain control of the situation. Greg also does not participate well in group activities. He chooses to work individually, and when that is not an option, he acts inappropriately to avoid group work. Avoiding social situations and avoiding overstimulation account for 11.0% of his payoffs.

| Antecedent | Behavior | Consequence | Payoffs |
|---|---|---|---|
| Classmate sat next to him to read | Made barking noises | Redirection from teacher, classmate moved seats | Avoid social situation<br>Get self-determination |
| Classmates typing in computer lab | Shouted, "Shut up everybody" | Teacher: redirection<br>Classmate: told Greg he's psycho | Avoid overstimulation |
| Classmate singing during instruction | Shouting out "Shut up" | Teacher: ignored<br>Classmate: told him to shut up | Avoid overstimulation |
| Teacher asks students to be seated, loud classroom environment | Shouting out "Shut up everybody" after teacher asked students to be quiet | Ignore | Get self-determination<br>Avoid overstimulation |
| Classroom environment loud | Shouted, "Shut up" | Redirection from teacher, classmates told him to shut up | Avoid overstimulation |
| Classmate stood next to him in very close proximity | Made farting noises | Student moved away | Avoid social situation<br>Get self-determination |

**Figure 13.2**   Greg's Uncomfortable Social Situations

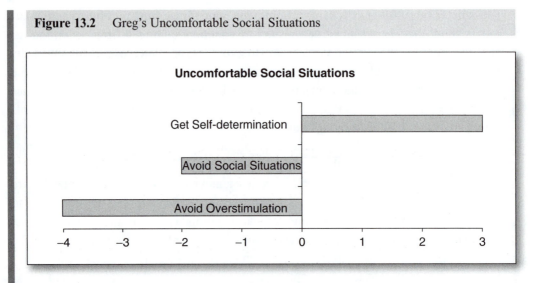

Greg has difficulties appropriately removing himself from these uncomfortable social situations. His highest payoff in these situations is avoiding overstimulation, occuring 44.4% of the time. When Greg's environment gets loud he deals with it by shouting "Shut up." Greg has stated that certain noises really bother his ears, even something like pencil tapping that is pretty far away. When classmates get too close to him he currently deals with it by making farting and burping noises in order to avoid the social aspect and gain control of the situation. Self-determination or control accounts for 33.3% of the payoffs.

## Interventions Derived From ABC Analysis

The functional assessment revealed that Greg does not have the ability to exit appropriately those social situations in which he feels uncomfortable or threatened. The intervention chosen for Greg includes using social stories to address his challenges with uncomfortable social situations and training him in the use of earplugs.

### Goal 1: Changes in Greg's Environment/Accommodations

*Changes/accommodations:* Preferential seating, schedule change, access to alternative setting for assemblies, access to earplugs. Training for Greg's use of earplugs took place over a 3-day period. Greg's parents gave permission for him to use earplugs in the classroom. Greg and I spent 15 minutes during study hall each day, during which I instructed him on how to insert the earplugs and we tested out his ability to hear a lecture and the degree to which the earplugs minimized sensory distractions. While using the earplugs and sitting farthest from the blackboard, Greg was still able to hear a lecture. Also, the earplugs blocked out the sensory distractions around Greg, so that he was not bothered by loud typing next to him, tapping pencils, a fan, or humming. Greg stated that he really liked wearing them. He stated he could hear the teacher but "annoying things" were not loud anymore.

## Goal 2: Replacement Behavior

*Current behavior:* When noises are overwhelming or classmates stand too close to Greg, he yells "Shut up" or makes barking and farting noises at them.

*Replacement behavior:* Training will enable Greg to respond appropriately when he feels uncomfortable or threatened.

The intervention phase took place over a 3-week period. During the first part of the intervention phase, I introduced Greg to social stories. Greg and I wrote three social stories together (see Table 1), and I assessed his comprehension by asking him a set of questions related to the social stories. Greg answered all questions correctly. During the second part of the intervention phase, Greg read each social story aloud once each day during study hall. During the third week of the intervention phase, Greg read each social story aloud twice each day, once in first period and once during study hall.

**Table 13. 1** Teacher–Student–Created Social Stories to Help Greg Exit Uncomfortable Situations Appropriately

**Social Story 1**

    I have classes with a lot of students in them.

    Sometimes students get too close to me and I get irritated.

    I will remember to ask them to please give me some space.

    If a student says no I will let the teacher know about the situation.

    I know I can handle this appropriately.

**Social Story 2**

    I have classes with a lot of students in them.

    Sometimes the classroom gets noisy.

    Sometimes my classmates make noises that irritate me.

    I will remember to put my earplugs in if noises are making me mad.

    If the earplugs don't help enough, I will ask my teachers to be excused to work in the hallway.

    I need to handle my needs appropriately.

**Figure 13.3**    Greg's Intervention Data

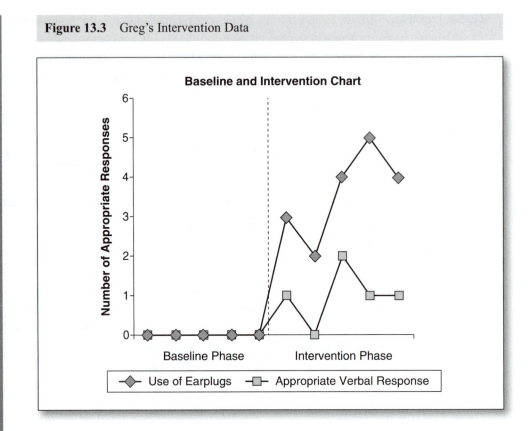

*Summary.* Before the start of the intervention phase, Greg was *unable* to respond appropriately in uncomfortable social situations (see Figure 13.3). He scared students away with his farting and barking noises when they got too close to him. He was also unable to respond appropriately when the environment around him became noisy. Greg is extremely sensitive to different noises in his environment. The tapping of a pencil across the room or the soft sounds of a fan can send Greg into a shouting fit.

Our first goal was to change setting conditions to make it easier for Greg to get needed payoffs. If we could lessen the effects of the noisy classroom environment, then Greg would not have to avoid overstimulation by shouting out for everyone to "shut up." Greg was given preferential seating for each of his classes. He chose to sit in the back, by the door, for each class. In two of his classes where there was a round table a bit further from the desks, he chose to sit at the table.

Changes were made to Greg's schedule to reduce his time in large-group settings. Greg was also placed into a higher-functioning math class to closer match his ability level. This math class is also a small-group setting. In addition, Greg was taken out of his communications class and given a resource study hall. This study hall takes place at the end of the day and has several functions for Greg: It's a smaller group setting, it allows him 42 more minutes in his day to complete assignments and to get organized for going home, it enables him to work on social skills with his teacher and peers, and it provides built-in time for incentives. Greg has many motivators that he is willing to work toward, including fixing things, electronics, sharing knowledge with adults, talking in different voices, and computer games.

Greg was given earplugs as an accommodation as well. He used the earplugs appropriately in the intervention phase, and teachers stated that Greg appeared less irritated and decreased his shouting out in the classroom when wearing them. Results show that he used the earplugs appropriately in 18 occurrences throughout the intervention phase. He did not use earplugs appropriately at all during baseline data collection. One of his teachers stated that Greg was putting the earplugs in and telling everyone he was Frankenstein. Social Story 2 worked to teach Greg to use the earplugs appropriately. Greg stated that he really likes how the noises around him are not very noticeable anymore.

Our second goal was to teach Greg appropriate verbal responses to use when he felt threatened or overwhelmed. The use of social stories to teach Greg appropriate responses showed success. He responded appropriately using a verbal response five times during the intervention phase, which was an improvement from the baseline phase, in which he did not verbally respond appropriately in any occurrence. Greg stated that he liked the social stories; he stated that they remind him of what he is supposed to do.

Results of the intervention phase show success. Throughout the 5 follow-up days of the intervention phase Greg responded appropriately 23 times, 18 times by choosing to put in earplugs and 5 times using verbal responses when he was uncomfortable. Greg's teachers stated that Greg appears to be more calm, has completed more assignments, and has significantly decreased his shouting of "shut up" since implementation of the intervention.

## Case Questions

1: How can you explain the following interaction as representing AS? "All the students got the answer correct, and the teacher called the students 'smart cookies.' Greg started to bite his arm and the teacher explained that she meant that they did a good job on the math problem."

2: How do you understand the following interaction? "The teacher began giving instructions for a dictionary assignment they were to do with small groups. She told them she did not have enough red dictionaries so they could use red or blue.

Greg shouted that he did not want a red one. The teacher stated that she didn't want him talking and continued with her instructions. Greg interrupted once more and asked her to look up the word *diarrhea*. She let him know that was inappropriate."

3: How would you as a teacher deal with the following situation? "Classmates tend to laugh at Greg's comments, encourage him, and also make comments about the teacher's instructions, all of which give Greg an impression that he should continue."

4: How could you balance Greg's avoidance of groups and loud social settings with his need to learn how to interact appropriately with other children?

5 (problem-based small-group assignment): Make a case for why Pete, whose case study appears in Chapter 12, does not have Asperger syndrome. Compare Pete and Greg and their characteristics using a table of similarities and differences.

# Chapter 14

## Abuse and Addictions

The disorders of abuse and addictions are placed together in this chapter because they have high rates of co-occurring anxiety disorders and depression (Crosse, Kaye, & Ratnofsky, 1993). As discussed in Chapter 12, specific ED diagnoses often depend on the way that the child deals with anxiety (e.g., compulsive activities, avoidance, passive nonresponding). For students with substance abuse, anxiety occurs prior to their initiating the abuse of substances (i.e., to relieve stress), and depression may follow (Wenar & Kerig, 2006). Anxiety can also be temporarily relieved through addictive control *over the self* (e.g., the self-starvation of anorexia and the self-cutting behavior of some adolescents; see Carroll, Shaffer, Spensley, & Abramowitz, 1980); cutting behavior is often found in association with a history of abuse (Carroll et al., 1980). Somewhat more controversial is a conceptualization of an abuser as one attempting to relieve anxiety through the control of *others* (e.g., physical, sexual, or emotional abuse of others). This could explain why so many children who have been abused become abusers themselves—to reclaim the control they lost as victims of abuse. See Figure 14.1.

It may be difficult for educators to identify with students who have been abused or who are addicted, as these types of disorders seem so far beyond the range of typical experience. Furthermore, there is shame associated with addiction and abuse, which keeps the behavior hidden and increases the social isolation of these students from their teachers and from their peers.

---

**Figure 14.1**   A Child Who Has Been Abused May Respond to Others with Angry Behavior.

## ABUSE

## FORMAL IDENTIFICATION

### Definitions

#### IDEA

IDEA provides no definition of childhood abuse, but 67% of children who have been abused are later diagnosed with EBD, when they are identified and services become needed (Crosse et al., 1993).

#### DSM-IV-TR

*DSM-IV-TR* defines subtypes of abuse as follows:

- *Physical abuse* is injury to the child, usually inflicted by a caregiver. It is sometimes seen in multiple bruises or abrasions, injuries to soft-tissue areas (e.g., upper arm, thigh, buttocks), or bruises, burns, or other marks in the shape of fingers, hands, or other objects. Unexplained multiple fractures are sometimes detectable on X rays.
- *Emotional abuse* occurs when children are repeatedly insulted, belittled, intimidated, rejected, criticized, called names, or terrorized by those who are supposed to provide nurturance. Emotional abuse may also be the result of actions not directed specifically at the child. Children who observe violence react with many of the same psychological symptoms as children who have experienced it directly.
- *Sexual abuse* is any interaction between a child and adult in which the child is used for sexual stimulation. Subtle forms of sexual abuse are (a) suggestive language, innuendos, and (b) being viewed while naked.
- *Neglect* occurs when children are not provided basic food, shelter, and clothing to the best of their parents' abilities. Not surprisingly, neglect is more prevalent in areas of extreme poverty than in other socioeconomic strata. Neglect may be evidenced in undernourishment or failure to thrive.

### Possible Co-Occurring Conditions

Data from the National Incidence Study of Child Abuse and Neglect indicate a 67% increase in reported cases of abuse from 1986 to 1993, with a majority of these cases involving children with disabilities (37% BD, 25% ID, 16% LD, 11% health related) versus 9% of nondisabled children (for a review, see Gore & Janssen, 2007). For example, out of 226 children brought to a hospital for physical abuse, 160 had a disability (Sullivan & Knutson, 2000a), and 76% had a physical health problem, such as being confined to a wheelchair or deafness (Crosse et al., 1993).

## Etiology

*Biogenetic.* Biology is associated with abuse in that abused children typically have disabilities (as noted above). These disabilities are often complicated by difficult behavior, including resistance to caregivers' child-rearing attempts (e.g., ADHD, ODD, CD) and behavior that requires "extraordinary physical care and supervision" (Gore & Janssen, 2007, p. 50).

*Environmental.* Some abusers were abused themselves as children. Other stress-related factors within the environment that can stretch families beyond their resources are poverty, lack of education, and family size. For one abuse victim, James, his teacher reported:

> James is an only child of a single mother from a lower economic housing development in Chicago. . . . He has been a victim of inconsistent parenting, which varied from punitive and unsupportive to extremely permissive.

*Functional.* Since most abuse has already occurred in a child's past (i.e., that an educator cannot see), a functional analysis of symptoms in school contexts is less likely to determine specific antecedents. However, children who have been physically abused may respond with anger or rage if touched, hurt, or challenged, and children who have been emotionally abused may be particularly sensitive and overreact to verbal threats or innuendos. These may act as triggers for their behavior.

In all cases of abuse, the abuser has taken control away from the child, who is left powerless with respect to his or her own body and self-regard. For this reason, these children may have particularly strong needs for self-determination/control in settings in which they feel physically or emotionally vulnerable or undervalued. James, for example, shows a high need for control, especially in relation to female staff members.

## Prevalence, Age, and Cultural Factors

**Affinity system:**
A child's family members, friends, neighbors, teachers, and significant others.

*Prevalence.* Adult females who report themselves as victims of sexual abuse were most often abused by males within their own **affinity system** (75–80% of cases involve relatives, friends of family, neighbors, or other authority figures with legitimate routine access to the child); only 7% were molested by strangers (Kvam, 2000). However, victimization is underreported, in part because child victims of abuse often have communication disorders (e.g., very young children and children who are deaf, physically disabled, ID) (e.g., Embry & Grossman, 2006/2007).

*Age.* Two-thirds of childhood abuse occurs before age 12, with a large percentage of those cases occurring from 2 to 4 years of age (Kvam, 2000).

*Culture.* Lower-SES families are more likely to report child abuse to authorities, even though the incidence is thought to be the same across SES levels. However, punitive disciplinary practices that turn into physical abuse are more common in low-income, mother-headed families (for a review, see Olson et al., 2002).

## INFORMAL EDUCATOR IDENTIFICATION OF CHARACTERISTICS

### Behavioral

Extreme compliance in children may be a signal that parental physical or emotional abuse is occurring; such children may be afraid to express independence of thought or action (Wenar & Kerig, 2006). This pattern of internalizing behavior represents only superficial cooperation and a suppression of anger. At least 81% of abused children with disabilities try to run away from home, and more than half of children who are runaways have disabilities (Sullivan & Knutson, 2000b). Anger and aggressive externalizing behavior are also probable, and many of these students show oppositional behavior, as in the case of A.B., whose case study appears at the end of this chapter. A.B. has been neglected and emotionally abused:

> Teacher's directions appear to be the major antecedent for his noncompliance. A.B. argues with the teacher-authority about everything he is told to do and makes his own decisions about what he will do. He just does not listen to the teacher's instruction no matter what it is. He argues, doesn't listen, or simply does nothing. Once he makes a decision about what he will do, he insists on that. Sometimes he has disruptive and externalizing behaviors, such as aggression (yelling and stomping).

Similarly, James does *not* show compliant behavior in response to the physical abuse he has received from his mother. Instead he throws objects, yells, and verbally threatens and assaults his peers.

Some children who have been physically abused try to avoid being identified by wearing clothes that cover their bruises and avoiding medical intervention; by doing this they escape from suffering additional shame. Children who have been sexually abused may show inappropriate sexual behavior or language at school. The common warnings signs of sexual abuse are as follows:

1. Abrupt changes in behavior (e.g., loss of appetite, sleep, failing school)

2. Inappropriate seductive behavior with others

3. Knowledge of or unusual interest in sexual matters

4. Promiscuity

5. Anger directed everywhere

6. Avoidance of certain persons

7. Regressive behavior

8. Depressive, passive, withdrawn, and compliant behavior

9. Having few friends

10. Repeated running away

## Social-Emotional

Children reared in homes where they were exposed to threat and physical abuse develop heightened arousal and oversensitivity to conflict, anger, and distress (Maughan, 2001). For example, Sara would not play with her peers, especially when physical contact was involved. When someone would tap her or touch her in a friendly manner, she would startle and walk away. These students are more likely to have a meltdown, even in situations that are only remotely threatening (e.g., reading). For other children who have been abused there is a cutting off of painful feelings or an absence of emotions and a greater likelihood of developing internalizing disorders (Wenar & Kerig, 2006). Guilt and shame are frequent feelings of children who have been abused. Alternating mood states can also be observed:

Since his admission to the unit, his affect and demeanor have vacillated between pensiveness and anger. There are also periods of time where he displays a calm curiosity and a sense of humor.

## Cognitive

Lowered IQ in physically abused children can be explained by physical damage to the brain. Thus, delays in cognitive development are typical, and lowered verbal

**Cortisol:** A chemical secreted by the body when a person is under chronic stress.

**Psychosomatic:** Involving the interrelationship between mind and body (e.g., getting headaches in response to mental stress).

IQ is related to the severity of abuse. Chronic stress produces increased **cortisol** secretion, which in turn produces short-term memory vulnerability.

## Motor, Physical, and Somatic

**Psychosomatic** symptoms are common in children with abuse histories. These can include sleep disturbances, such as nightmares, bedwetting, and changes in eating habits. Physical abuse can, of course, result in bruises or injuries that a child may be unwilling or unable to explain, and for children with sexual abuse there may be changes in gait (i.e., they "walk funny") due to lacerations or tears. Some children develop rashes and infections that go untreated.

## Academic

Children who have been abused are more likely to have difficulty concentrating or learning in school, because they lack food or sleep or have emotional or physical concerns about prior or future abuse. Failure of parents to send children to school or otherwise provide for their education can be considered neglect, which would also contribute to gaps in learning.

## SUMMARY OF STRENGTHS AND NEEDS

| Possible strengths | Probable needs |
|---|---|
| • Personality characteristics that improve long-term outcomes:<br>  o empathy<br>  o sense of identity, purpose, and independence<br>  o communication skills<br>  o humor about oneself (Frankl, 1959; Thompson, 2001): | • Early identification, using school-based procedures, leading to therapy<br>• Consistent rule-based consequences, without anger, in a safe environment<br>• Educators who are willing to share power (e.g., give choices, allow student-directed activities)<br>• Empathy and communication training<br>• Interventions that focus on student strengths<br>• Tutoring for those students who miss a lot of school<br>• Help in understanding how to get along with peers or with teachers who are the same gender as the abuser |

## DISABILITY IN THE CLASSROOM

### Implications for Accommodations in General Education Settings: Tier I

Whether children have been formally identified as abused or are in process, it is critical for educators to listen to and validate these students' feelings. These are "turnaround" teachers, who also convey support by encouraging the expression of opinions, choice making, and problem solving (Kohn, 1993). It may be especially helpful for educators to teach to students' strengths and to share power, create safe places, provide positive expectations, and deal with anger calmly (e.g., give students space and speak to them in a quiet voice) (Benard, 1997).

## Implications for Interventions in Small-Group and Individual Settings: Tier II and III

Educators are not typically involved in primary interventions for abused children, although they can and should address many of these children's probable needs as listed above. School counselors are better trained than teachers to undertake individual interventions with these children.

## Long-Term Outcomes

Adolescents and young adults with histories of maltreatment have been found to be three to four times more likely to become depressed and/or suicidal than individuals without such histories. Furthermore, 67% undergo changes in personality that worsen as they continue to be abused (Crosse et al., 1993). Maltreatment in childhood is also associated with an increased risk of conduct problems and criminality (Maughan, 2001). For example, in one sample, 26% of abused and neglected youth were arrested compared with 17% of youth in a well-matched comparison group. The risk of repeated suicide attempts in sexually abused individuals has been found to be eight times greater than the risk for their peers (Brown, 1999).

**Risk factors** that increase negative outcomes for sexually and physically abused children include the following:

**Risk factors:** Those events, attitudes, life experiences, or traits associated with negative outcomes.

1. Little social or community support

2. High family psychopathology and stress (e.g., unrealistic parental expectations, parent perceptions of child as difficult, family isolation or substance abuse)

3. Close relationships with their offenders

4. High degree of guilt (i.e., older children are likely to feel more guilt than are younger children)

5. Low degree of support and assurance provided by parents after disclosure (i.e., lack of reaction/support increases the trauma, and so does overreaction)

6. Poor emotional health of the child prior to abuse (for a review, see Gore & Janssen, 2007)

In addition to risk factors, there are protective factors that are known to characterize resilient people. Long-term studies that have followed children born into extremely high-risk environments (including environments of physical and sexual abuse, alcoholism, war, and poverty) have found that 50–70% of these children grow up to be successful. Those likely to survive and prosper after exposure to such environments have what has been called an innate self-righting mechanism (Werner & Smith, 1992). Among the protective characteristics that can improve the outcomes for children who have been abused are the following:

1. Easy temperament or disposition

2. Empathy and caring about others and the ability to elicit positive response from others

3. The ability to communicate and use problem-solving skills

4. Sense of humor about oneself

5. Sense of one's identity and sense of purpose or future

6. The ability to act independently and to separate from unhealthy situations or people (Frankl, 1959; Thompson, 2001)

## ADDICTIONS

There is a normal developmental progression in children from dependence to independence. Early dependence is important to the survival of individuals and to the continuance of the species. The prolonged period of dependence on caretakers from infancy through childhood helps to support the physical, emotional, educational, and social needs of young children and forms the basis for independence. During adolescence, when youth begin to experiment with autonomy, this dependence is transferred from caretakers to peers and eventually to self-reliance (reliance on one's own skills and experiences) and to physical resources in the environment. When children appropriately abandon dependence on parents and move away into experimentation and rule-breaking behavior (rebellion), these normal experimentations may become ends in themselves rather than a temporary means for promoting identity and autonomy. This can contribute to the development of addictions; see Figure 14.2.

Failure to progress from dependence to independence can be attributed to factors within the environment and/or within the child. Factors that protect "normal" adolescents from substance abuse include "achievement of a developmentally appropriate sense of identity" (Wenar & Kerig, 2006, p. 396). However, some children's environments may not provide sufficient growth opportunities (e.g., in the case of

**Figure 14.2** A Child with Addictive Behavior

overcontrolling or overprotective parents), or children may lack skills (e.g., because of disabilities or significant failure experiences). When children do not have growth opportunities or skills, they are more likely to learn that it is safer to depend on others, to stay in close proximity to others, to wait, and to be more passive, avoid decisions, and ask for reassurances (e.g., "Did I do a good job?"). For example, a study of students at risk for reading disabilities, with presumed histories of reading failure, found that they were more likely to depend on external persons and standards and less likely than equivalent-IQ peers to learn through curiosity or interests, use their own judgment, or work independently (Zentall & Beike, 2012).

At the extreme of this kind of dependence are addictions (e.g., eating, sex, gambling, shopping), which reflect a disturbance of identity and autonomy (i.e., not of appetite). The term *addiction* typically refers to dependence on substances (drugs, such as alcohol or tobacco). In other words, addictions in children are not *initially* about a physiological need for a substance or a behavior; they are initially about failing to develop independence and a personal identity. The physiological dependence on a substance continues in spite of the fact that there are negative physiological and adaptive outcomes.

Substance abuse and eating disorders have been selected for discussion in this text because they represent addictions common in youth—primarily in adolescents.

**Anorexia nervosa:** A condition causing self-starvation. However, as *DSM-IV-TR* points out, "The term *anorexia* is a misnomer because loss of appetite is rare"; APA, 2000, p. 583).

Eating disorders are of two types: the *binge-eating/purging type* (i.e., self-induced vomiting or the misuse of laxatives, diuretics, or enemas) and the *restricting type* (**anorexia nervosa**), which does *not* involve binge eating or purging behavior. It is not clear why obesity is not also considered an addiction, since identity issues appear to be involved, and for obese children eating can temporarily relieve anxiety. However, obesity is considered a metabolic problem (Wenar & Kerig, 2006). Given the ever-increasing rate of obesity in the United States, it may even be considered a cultural problem.

## FORMAL IDENTIFICATION

### Definitions

#### IDEA

IDEA provides no definitions for eating disorders or substance abuse, but the category of EBD may be used for children with these disorders when services become needed.

#### DSM-IV-TR

*DSM-IV-TR* (APA, 2000, p. 589) defines anorexia nervosa as follows:

*Identifying characteristics:*

A. Refusal to maintain body weight at or above a minimally normal weight for age and height (e.g., weight loss leading to maintenance of body weight less than 85% of that expected; or failure to make expected weight gain during period of growth, leading to body weight less than 85% of that expected).

B. Intense fear of gaining weight or becoming fat, even though underweight.

C. Disturbance in the way in which one's body weight or shape is experienced, undue influence of body weight or shape on self-evaluation, or denial of the seriousness of the current low body weight.

D. In postmenarcheal females, amenorrhea, i.e., the absence of at least three consecutive menstrual cycles. (A woman is considered to have amenorrhea if her periods occur only following hormone, e.g., estrogen, administration.)

*DSM-IV-TR* (APA, 2000, p. 594) defines bulimia nervosa as follows:

*Identifying characteristics:*

A. Recurrent episodes of binge eating. An episode of binge eating is characterized by both of the following:

- Eating, in a discrete period of time (e.g., within any 2-hour period), an amount of food that is definitely larger than most people would eat during a similar period of time and under similar circumstances
- A sense of lack of control over eating during the episode (e.g., a feeling that one cannot stop eating or control what or how much one is eating)

B. Recurrent inappropriate compensatory behavior in order to prevent weight gain, such as self-induced vomiting; misuse of laxatives, diuretics, enemas, or other medications; fasting; or excessive exercise.

C. The binge eating and inappropriate compensatory behaviors both occur, on average, at least twice a week for 3 months.

D. Self-evaluation is unduly influenced by body shape and weight.

E. The disturbance does not occur exclusively during episodes of Anorexia Nervosa.

*DSM-IV-TR* (APA, 2000, p. 725) defines dependent personality disorder as follows:

*Identifying characteristics:* A pervasive and excessive need to be taken care of that leads to submissive and clinging behavior and fears of separation, beginning by early adulthood and present in a variety of contexts, as indicated by five (or more) of the following:

- Has difficulty making everyday decisions without an excessive amount of advice and reassurance from others
- Needs others to assume responsibility for most major areas of his or her life
- Has difficulty expressing disagreement with others because of fear of loss of support or approval. **Note:** Does not include realistic fears of retribution.
- Has difficulty initiating projects or doing things on his or her own (because of a lack of self-confidence in judgment or abilities rather than a lack of motivation or energy)
- Goes to excessive lengths to obtain nurturance and support from others, to the point of volunteering to do things that are unpleasant

- Feels uncomfortable or helpless when alone because of exaggerated fears of being unable to care for himself or herself
- Urgently seeks another relationship as a source of care and support when a close relationship ends
- Is unrealistically preoccupied with fears of being left to take care of himself or herself

### Possible Co-Occurring Conditions

In community samples, 58% of females with bulimia also have anxiety disorders. Eating disorders can also be found in children with giftedness (Webb et al., 2005), and these disorders have co-occurrence rates around 73% with depression. However, depressive symptoms may be produced by the physiological outcomes of semistarvation (APA, 2000). As well, "obsessive-compulsive features, both related and unrelated to food, are often prominent. Most individuals with Anorexia Nervosa are preoccupied with thoughts of food. Some collect recipes or hoard food. . . . When individuals with Anorexia Nervosa exhibit obsessions and compulsions that are not related to food, body shape, or weight, an additional diagnosis of Obsessive-Compulsive Disorder may be warranted" (APA, 2000, p. 584).

Adolescent drug and alcohol use is correlated with psychopathology (e.g., low self-esteem, crime, delinquency, truancy, anxiety, depressive disorders, suicide; Angold & Costello, 2001). With substance abuse, especially for boys, the highest co-occurrence is with conduct disorders (95%; see Brown et al., 1996, cited in Wenar & Kerig, 2006), and for girls substance abuse co-occurs with depression. Also seen in association with substance abuse are ADHD and anxiety disorders (Wenar & Kerig, 2006).

## Etiology

*Biogenetic.* Even though anorexia and bulimia tend to run in families, evidence of heritability is inconsistent (0–70%), and a genetic mechanism has not been identified. Evidence of heritability in bulimia is supported by higher rates of mothers' obesity and self-dissatisfaction with body shape. There is also some evidence of biochemical differences. That is, restricted food intake, purging, and bingeing appear to be compensatory mechanisms to regulate the depressed mood associated with depleted serotonin. Dieting further decreases serotonergic activity and is associated with subsequent eating in an attempt to correct depleted serotonin. For alcoholism, there is a well-established heritability connection, even though the exact gene has not been identified. For example, if one parent is an alcoholic, the chances of the child becoming addictive are 50–50, and if both parents are alcoholics, the odds are even greater. For illegal drugs, heritability estimates are from 10% to 25%, and for nicotine dependence they are 40% to 60% (for a review of the above information, see Wenar & Kerig, 2006).

*Environmental.* **Psychosocial** factors have been linked to eating disorders. The families of children with eating disorders have been characterized as highly involved in an intrusive way, with confusion or overlapping of parent/child roles, overprotectiveness, and rigidity. The intrusive behavior and family's focus on appearances undermine the child's autonomy. Also observed in families of children with bulimia are depression and substance abuse; conflict and hostility; mothers who interfere with children's attempts to assert individuality and who make critical comments about the children's weight, body, or eating habits. Students with eating disorders may sense high expectations to be perfect, and being perfect in today's society means being thin. Dieting, exercise, and purging offer ways to rigidly control weight and to regain a sense of self-esteem. However, these are temporary, and the child may again resort to ever more rigid controls over food or to **binge** eating (see Wenar & Kerig, 2006).

Environmental factors specific to alcoholism are the easy availability of substances, stressors (anxiety), and impairment in the ability to obtain real satisfactions from life. Other family factors implicated in substance abuse are parental depression; parental substance abuse and child abuse; family conflict; and low levels of family support, discipline, or monitoring (for a review of the above, see Wenar & Kerig, 2006)

*Functional.* In a functional assessment, we would expect addictive behavior to be worse under conditions of physical or psychosocial stress (e.g., before tests or presentations). In short, addictions to substances and to behavior function to reduce or escape from uncomfortable feelings of anxiety or depression. As stated in *DSM-IV-TR:* "Binge eating is typically triggered by dysphoric mood states, interpersonal stressors, intense hunger following dietary restraint, or feelings related to body weight, body shape, and food. Binge eating may transiently reduce **dysphoria,** but disparaging self-criticism and depressed mood often follow" (APA, 2000, p. 590). Anxiety effects may be especially evident in girls, who are more likely than boys to relieve stress through drinking and to suffer more negative physiological effects due to drinking (Wenar & Kerig, 2006). Addiction begins when an individual uses something to feel good and to "help" him or her avoid painful feelings. Over time, the person feels less pleasure from the use, and a feeling of "I don't care, as long as I can . . ." often follows.

**Psychosocial:** Intrapersonal (within the person) and interpersonal (in relations with other persons).

**Binge:** "A *binge* is defined as eating in a discrete period of time an amount of food that is definitely larger than most individuals would eat under similar circumstances. . . . A 'discrete period of time' refers to a limited period, usually less than 2 hours. A single episode of binge eating need not be restricted to one setting. For example, an individual may begin a binge in a restaurant and then continue it on returning home. Continual snacking on small amounts of food throughout the day would not be considered a binge" (APA, 2000, p. 589).

**Dysphoria:** Depressed mood.

428  SECTION V: SOCIAL DISORDERS

## Prevalence, Gender, Age, and Cultural Factors

*Prevalence.* Failure to develop independence is a difficult diagnosis to make in children, for whom dependence is developmentally appropriate and must be viewed within the context of culture and age group.

*Gender.* For anorexia, the ratio is 1 male to 10 females; however, these data include adults, which may exaggerate gender differences. For bulimia, age of onset is later for males (between the ages of 18 and 26), who represent only 10–15% of individuals with this disorder. For substance abuse, prevalence rates range from 2% for girls to 3% for boys. Dependent personality disorder is seen more often in females than in males. (See Wenar & Kerig, 2006, for a full review of prevalence and gender differences.)

*Age.* Onset for anorexia is typically around 17 and rarely is seen before puberty or after 40; for bulimia, age of onset is around 18 years. Overall prevalence rates for substance abuse are around 1% for children 12 years or younger; however, by age 16, prevalence rates jump to around 8%. Overall, 3% of adolescents have addictions, about 1% of which are eating disorders. These figures are most likely underestimates, given the secretiveness of children with addictive disorders.

*Culture.* Higher rates of substance use and abuse have been reported for higher-SES youth and may be related to achievement pressure and alienation from parents. The environment explains 41% to 66% of contributors to substance abuse, and having friends who are substance abusers is the greatest risk factor. "Anorexia Nervosa appears to be far more prevalent in industrialized societies, in which there is an abundance of food and in which, especially for females, being considered attractive is linked to being thin" (APA, 2000, p. 587). Furthermore, the United States has the highest level of illicit drug use of any industrialized nation, with substance use and abuse climbing, especially at the high school level. Epidemiological studies in Norway and England have found that individuals with eating disorders (and substance abuse) have equivalent prevalence rates across economic classes, but in the United States, ethnicity and culture are factors in substance abuse, with higher prevalence rates for specific types of drugs in specific cultures. For example, rates of heroin and cocaine use are higher among Hispanic youth than among other groups, and Native American youth also have higher overall prevalence rates. (For references related to the above summary, see Wenar & Kerig, 2006.)

# INFORMAL EDUCATOR
# IDENTIFICATION OF CHARACTERISTICS

## Behavioral

*Eating addictions.* Commonly observed among children with eating disorders are sharp restrictions of food intake (nibbling or picking at food) and compulsive exercise. As *DSM-IV-TR* describes:

> Although individuals may begin by excluding from their diet what they perceive to be highly caloric foods, most eventually end up with a very restricted diet that is sometimes limited to only a few foods. . . . Some individuals feel globally overweight. Others realize that they are thin but are still concerned that certain parts of their bodies, particularly the abdomen, buttocks, and thighs, are "too fat." They may employ a wide variety of techniques to estimate their body size or weight, including excessive weighing, obsessive measuring of body parts, and persistently using a mirror to check for perceived areas of "fat." (APA, 2000, p. 584)

According to *DSM-IV-TR*: "Binge eating usually occurs in secrecy, or as inconspicuously as possible. An episode may or may not be planned in advance and is usually (but not always) characterized by rapid consumption. Binge eating often continues until the individual is uncomfortably, or even painfully, full" (p. 590). Individuals with bulimia may fast for a day or more or exercise excessively to compensate for binge eating. Exercise is considered excessive when (a) it significantly interferes with important activities, (b) it occurs at inappropriate times or in inappropriate settings, or (c) the individual continues to exercise despite injury or other medical complications (pp. 589–590).

*Substance abuse.* Behavioral characteristics that predict substance abuse in children include sensation-seeking behavior (e.g., risk taking) (Wenar & Kerig, 2006).

## Social-Emotional

Among children with eating disorders, negative self-perceptions and the secretiveness needed to hide their addictions often lead to social isolation from peers. Similarly, substance abuse eventually interferes with social development by reducing social support and increasing loneliness.

Early differences in emotional temperament (e.g., poor adaptability to change) may be seen in children with eating disorders (see Strober, 1995, cited by Wenar & Kerig, 2006). They are more likely to be anxious, conforming, perfectionistic, obsessional, and unassertive, and to have low self-esteem. During adolescence, conforming social behavior can include increased sexual activity, especially for individuals with bulimia, even though there is evidence these young people enjoy sex less (Garfinkel & Garner, 1986, cited in Wenar & Kerig, 2006). For the binge-purge type of disorder, adolescents may be more extroverted and emotionally dysregulated (see Wenar & Kerig, 2006).

## Cognitive

Across types of eating disorders, there is consistent evidence of cognitive distortions. These take the form of "all or none" thinking, such that the individuals see themselves as completely in control or powerless. Adolescents with anorexia interpret the restriction of food intake as a sign of self-discipline and control, which brings feelings of empowerment and escape from negative self-judgments. Thus, their behavior of food restriction does not signal to them that there is a need for behavioral change (i.e., they *are* in control). In contrast, individuals with bulimia recognize that there is a need for behavioral change (Wilson et al., 2003, cited in Wenar & Kerig, 2006). Cognitive characteristics that predict substance abuse in children include EF factors, such as poor planning, failure to anticipate consequences, and poor judgment (Wenar & Kerig, 2006). Cognitive distortions of "mental bookkeeping" occur when addicts incorrectly (irrationally) weigh the positives of their addiction against the negatives. In other words, the addict places increasing emphasis on the positive aspects of the addictive behavior (i.e., a form of denial), with a need for higher doses and frequency of dosage, even when the effects are devastating to the addicted person and to significant others. Furthermore, "drug use can affect cognition by making thinking more disorganized and bizarre" (Wenar & Kerig, 2006, p. 398).

## Motor, Physical, and Somatic

Eating disorders result in muscle loss, erosion of the periodontal layer of teeth, brittle nails, alterations of bone marrow, extreme fatigue, frequent bruising, and dry skin or rashes. "Many of the physical signs and symptoms of Anorexia Nervosa are attributable to starvation. In addition to amenorrhea [cessation of menstruation], there may be complaints of constipation, abdominal pain, cold intolerance, lethargy, and excess energy" (APA, 2000, p. 585).

## Academic

Children with eating disorders generally show average to above-average school achievement. However, substance abusers are more likely to have disorganized thinking and to miss significant amounts of schooling, thus reducing their learning opportunities.

# DISABILITY IN THE CLASSROOM

## Implications for Accommodations in General Education Settings: Tier I

For children who are overly dependent as a result of overcontrolling or over-protective parenting, an appropriate strategy is to attempt to have them transfer dependencies from adults to selected peers or to resources, such as PDAs or cell phones. For children with dependence due to repeated failures (e.g., for children with ID or LD), educators can change tasks from complex to simple, highlight relevant information, encourage the development or expansion of hobbies, allocate more time for them to complete work, and provide advance warnings to respond, clear structure, self-selected goals, and personally meaningful content.

## Implications for Interventions in Small-Group and Individual Settings: Tiers II and III

Children with eating disorders are often treated with medications, psychotherapy, behavior modification, cognitive therapy, or family therapy. Children with addictions are treatable but not curable. Total abstinence is the appropriate treatment, but the risk of relapse is present throughout life no matter how long the recovery. Educational programs that target drug abuse prevention (e.g., "Just say no" programs) can be effective, as can self-help groups (for a review of evidence related to interventions, see Wenar & Kerig, 2006).

## Long-Term Outcomes

Substance abusers often drop out of school in favor of immediate entry into the workforce; they often have conflicts with the law and enter into early marriages, thereby reducing advanced career opportunities and increasing the risks of divorce. For students with both depression and substance abuse, there is an increased risk of suicide, with 42% of attempters reporting this combination (for a review, see Wenar & Kerig, 2006). Among children with anorexia, research indicates that 10% of those who are hospitalized as a result of the disorder die (APA, 2000). Furthermore, as few as 25% fully recover, and 50% partially recover with continued symptomology of depression, anxiety, OCD, substance abuse, and so on. Individuals with bulimia do not die from starvation, but they risk other physical consequences from repeated vomiting (e.g., stomach acid erosion of tooth enamel, electrolyte imbalances, kidney problems).

*Continuance.* "Substance abuse is best conceptualized as a life-span problem" (Wenar & Kerig, 2006, p. 399). For anorexia, educational and vocational outcomes are unaffected, but social and opposite-sex relationships remain problematic over the life span. Although bulimia is more treatable, 30% of these individuals have been found to be at risk for continued binge eating and/or purging (for a review, see Wenar & Kerig, 2006). Even with early intervention, half will continue to have eating difficulties and psychological problems (e.g., depression, anxiety, social problems).

## CHAPTER SUMMARY

- Childhood abuse victims, children with eating disorders, and young substance abusers suffer from social disorders that are related in that all involve attempts to control anxiety. These attempts take the form of abuse of substances or obsessive control and self-abuse of the body.

- Abuse victims are not formally defined by IDEA. It is the social and emotional consequences of abuse and addictions that place these children within the EBD category. *DSM-IV-TR* defines multiple subcategories of substance abuse, eating disorders, and abuse (physical, emotional, sexual, neglect). Co-occurring disabilities are common in abuse victims, making them vulnerable (deaf, physically disabled) or difficult to manage (e.g., ADHD or physical disabilities).

- Peak ages of identification are 8–13 years, and the reporting of abuse is highest in lower-SES groups. In addition to disability groups being victimized, etiology is primarily environmental (e.g., poverty, large families, parental psychopathology). Immediate antecedents for children who have been abused depend on the nature of their abuse. For example, children who have been emotionally abused overreact to verbal threats or criticism.

- Informal identification of children who have been abused is difficult because of the children's own attempts at concealment. However, abuse is similar to anxiety and depression in emotional markers (e.g., anger expressed everywhere, rage, passivity/apathy) and in somatic problems (nightmares, eating disorders, stomachaches). More specific behavioral indicators of abuse are avoidance (e.g., running away), the extremes of compliance or defiance/rage, and oversensitivity to conflict and stress. Children who have been sexually abused may exhibit overly sexualized language and behavior.

- Basic intelligence may be good in most children who have been abused. However, physical insults to the brain can lower IQ, and sustained stress can decrease memory. Lowered cognitive skills may affect the academic achievement of these children, and worries about possible past or future threats may disrupt their concentration. Parental neglect that keeps children from attending school can also produce learning gaps. Substance abuse contributes to cognitive disorganization that reduces learning opportunities.

- Possible implications for treatment of children who have been abused are similar to those for anxiety and depression. These include accommodations that create a safe, nonangry, and predictable environment with a focus on supporting student strengths and on acceptance of feelings in collaboration with psychological and health professionals. Interventions for substance abusers include support in the development of individual identities, independence, and feelings of competence.

## CHAPTER QUESTIONS

### Abuse

1. What programs might you request of school counselors if you have a self-contained classroom of children with disabilities?

2. How can failure to comply (ODD) and being overly compliant both act as signs of abuse/neglect?

3. What are some types of statements you can make to students that support their feelings, opinions, and strengths and generally empower them?

4. Children who have been abused are often more sensitive than their peers. How might you see this sensitivity in the classroom?

### Addiction

1. Can you explain addictions as a challenge in achieving independence?

2. How might you recognize whether a child has a sense of his or her own identity?

3. How is Andy, whose case study appears in Chapter 8, afraid of his own dependency needs?

4. Eating disorders are commonly associated with what other disorders? How do boys with eating disorders differ from girls with these disorders?

5. How do family factors contribute to addictions?

6. Why do students with anorexia not realize that they need to begin eating, given that they experience so many negative physical consequences?

## TRUE/FALSE AND MULTIPLE-CHOICE

1. I often talk to my peers about sex; I could be
   A. conduct disordered
   B. sexually abused
   C. anorexic
   D. socially phobic

2. Probable co-occurring condition(s) with abuse:
   A. overly compliant behavior
   B. oppositional/angry behavior
   C. depression
   D. all of the above

3. "Turnaround teachers" are likely to listen to students' opinions and allow them to make choices (cognitive support) but not to support their feelings (emotional support).

4. Children with abuse histories and with addictions are similar in their attempts to control.

5. It is appropriate and supportive to react with a strong emotional response when you learn of a child's abuse history.

6. A "funny walk" is a symptom of sexual abuse.

7. Children who react with rage to perceptions of threat are most likely addicted children.

8. Children who experience significant failure are more likely to depend on others.

9. Identity issues lie at the basis of most addictions (i.e., failure to "grow up" and establish a sense of self).

10. In class I wait for others and ask the teacher if I did a good job or not. I have
    A. ADHD
    B. dependency
    C. ODD

11. Match each disorder listed on the right with the appropriate cognitive distortion on the left.

    • The world is a dangerous place.          A. addictions

    • Mental bookkeeping.                       B. depression

- I am in control of my body and therefore of my life.
- The glass is half empty.
- Others are hostile to me.

C. aggression

D. anxiety

E. self-abuse (e.g., bulimia)

## SHORT ANSWER

1. A sexual relationship within the _____ system has especially bad outcomes for a child.

2. Anger directed everywhere, problems with concentration, and memory losses are signs of _____ .

3. Anorexia is characterized by restriction of food intake and compulsive _____ .

4. A physiological and psychological dependency

## PROBLEM-BASED CASE APPLICATIONS AND QUESTIONS

### CASE STUDY 14.1: A.B.

(adapted from an assignment submitted by Karly Gibson)

*Background.* A.B. is a seventh-grade student who has attended B Middle School for 2 years. He has been diagnosed with an emotional disability. He lives with his father, stepmother, and younger stepbrother. A.B.'s stepmother is not very supportive, nor is she understanding of his need for attention. As far as she is concerned, the problems in her marriage are because of him. She refuses to take responsibility for his actions, yet at the same time, she refuses to help him deal with his ongoing problems. She doesn't feel as though it's her responsibility to manage his behavior, so it's hard to get any cooperation in order to work on these behaviors at home. The mind-set of the stepmother has been to let the school system deal with his behavior. A.B. was removed from school for 2 weeks last year to be with his biological mother out of state. However, his biological mother has a reputation for neglecting A.B. and not wanting to take responsibility for his upbringing. She blames all of A.B.'s disobedient behaviors on his dad and stepmother. There was a 2-week period that A.B. was removed from school, which included time spent driving out of state to meet his mom. However, she never showed. Now we were back to square one with him because his behaviors returned. However, A.B. hasn't become physically cruel or deceitful.

## Behavioral Log

| Time, Date, Location | Antecedent | Behavior | Social Consequence/ Outcome | Payoffs |
|---|---|---|---|---|
| 1:20 p.m., 8/26, Study Hall (SH) | A.B. was reading and was instructed to get a book. | He started getting agitated, saying that he didn't have one. I told him that he needed to bring one on Monday. | Class looking at him because he was getting loud. | |
| 12:38 p.m., 8/30, English | Given assignment to do a comic strip of their life. | A.B. had about 25 half-inch boxes at the top of his page, so I asked him to make his boxes bigger and he laid his head down on the desk. | I walked away and he turned it over and began working. | He got me to walk away! Get self-determination |
| 3:28 p.m., 8/31, SH | Many assignments that needed to be done, but didn't want to do any of them. | A.B. had three different things to work on, but one of them consisted of using a dictionary. He wanted to take home the dictionary and didn't want to do anything else until he checked it out, even though the class had just started. | I talked to him about starting some of his other work, and he still refused to do anything until he was able to check out the dictionary. | I told him to get busy, and he did once I left. Get self-determination |
| 11:50 a.m., 9/1, Comm. | Told to finish overdue assignment. | He refused to finish the overdue assignment until he finished today's work. I sat beside him and wouldn't let him continue with the work until he finished his old assignment. | He didn't get anything done. | He escaped doing any work?! Get self-determination |
| 3:00 p.m., 9/1, SH | Wanted to go to library without work finished. | AB still didn't have his assignment done, even though he sat in SH two periods ago and did nothing. I told him he had to finish his overdue assignment first. He fought me and said he didn't want to do it and I told him that was fine, but he couldn't go to the library until it was completed. Then I left him alone. | He got to argue with me. But eventually he sat and did it. He was allowed to go to the library. | Get self-determination |
| 11:30 a.m., 9/7, English | Didn't have yesterday's DOL done. | We were working on DOL, which we do every day at the beginning of class, and he | He didn't get anything done. | Avoid work and get self-determination |

| Time, Date, Location | Antecedent | Behavior | Social Consequence/ Outcome | Payoffs |
|---|---|---|---|---|
|  |  | didn't have it done from the day before. He refused to do today's work when he didn't have yesterday's done. I ignored him. |  |  |
| 11:40 a.m., 9/7, English | I told another student to stand up because he was tipping his chair back, so A.B. started tipping his back too. | I told A.B. to stop and he said, "No, I want to stand up too." I told him that wasn't an option for him. He then proceeded to pound his fists and his head on the desk. I ignored him. He got up from his seat and began stomping and yelling. Again, I ignored him. I was calling on other students to answer my questions and he started raising his hand while standing and I again ignored him. | He got what he wanted for a short period of time, although other students ignored him. | Get self-determination |
| 11:20 a.m., 9/8, English | Class deciding what page we were on for reading. | He wanted to argue about what page we were on. | I asked him to read it again so it would refresh our memory. | Get self-determination |

## ABC Analysis

Teacher's directions appear to be the major antecedent for his noncompliance. A.B. argues with the teacher-authority about everything he is told to do and makes his own decisions about what he will do. He just does not listen to the teacher's instruction no matter what it is. He argues, doesn't listen, or simply does nothing. Once he makes a decision about what he will do, he insists on that. Sometimes he has disruptive and externalizing behaviors, such as aggression (yelling and stomping). Finally, he is not willing to show his academic difficulties and tries to hide them.

## Interventions Derived From ABC Analysis

The payoff of most of A.B.'s behaviors is getting self-determination or control. A.B. does not like authority. He wanted to continue a task he preferred (e.g., going to library) and he argued with the teacher about what page they were on for reading.

**Figure 14.3**   A.B.'s Behaviors

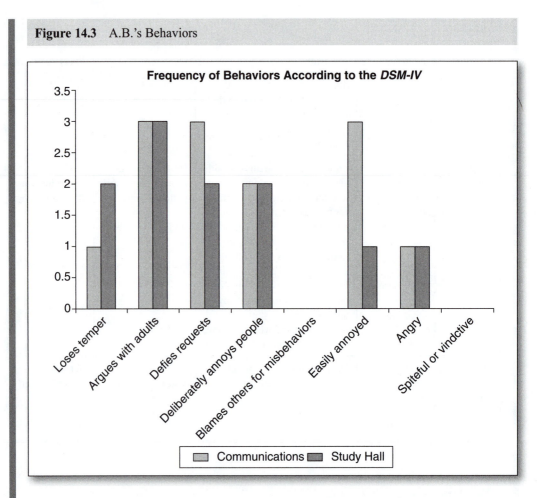

**Figure 14.4**   A.B.'s Academic Preferences Ratings

His strength was that he might know that what the teacher told him to do was right and he would do it when the teacher left him. For example, he did turn in his assignment of comic strips when the teacher left. Furthermore, he never actually refused to do an assignment, but he wanted to choose what he would do first. See Figure 14.3 for A.B.'s behavior. Rather than confronting him with behavior he needs to change, I suggest making accommodations for him as an initial step.

Possible accommodations for A.B. include the following:

1. Have a male teacher for him, whenever possible.

2. Have the teacher give his instructions and then leave him to do the work by himself.

3. Give him options of choosing what to do first. See Figure 14.4 for A.B.'s academic preferences. For example, in Language Arts, allow him a choice of assignment order and allow him extra time to finish these assignments.

4. Finally, assess him in language learning to see if he should be provided with special education services in Language Arts or English.

## Case Questions

1: What related disorder(s) might A.B. have?

2: When is A.B. more defiant–in Communcations (Language Arts) or Study Hall–and how is this related to his subject area preferences? See figures 14.3 and 14.4

3: What additional accommodations would you put into place for A.B., especially given his needs for self-determination and given his academic preferences?

4 (problem-based small-group assignment): Describe how as educators you will manage a child's need for empowerment and self-determination as well as your own need for the child's compliance.

**Chapter 15**

Motor Disabilities

This section focuses on children whose motor skills do not allow them to respond adequately to the school requirements of speaking or writing or whose primary difficulty is inhibiting motor responses. These response output problems are different from the focus in previous chapters on the input and processing requirements of attending, learning, and socialization. Motor disorders can be subdivided into (a) gross motor response impairments, or lack of coordination of the large muscles of the legs and arms; and (b) fine motor response impairments, or difficulties involving the small muscles in the hands and mouth. See Figure VI.I. When children have gross motor difficulties, they often also have fine motor control problems, which explains developmental coordination disorder (DCD) and difficulties with both the large muscles of mobility and the small muscles of handwriting (Kirby & Sugden, 2007). Dysgraphia involves only the small muscles in the hands required for handwriting. Dyspraxia is an impairment of sensorimotor skills of the small speech muscles of articulation, which are among the finest motor mechanisms in the human body; apraxia is lack of ability to *plan* a motor response and to coordinate and sequence the speech muscles for the production of speech sounds. From an educational perspective, these disorders belong together, because they involve the same

441

functional motor response outcomes. Equally important, all children with motor disorders devote considerable energy to attempting to hide or control their motor responses, thus limiting the energy they can spend learning (disability fatigue).

This section also includes discussion of children whose motor responses are involuntary, as in Tourette's syndrome (TS). TS could be placed in several other sections in this volume; for example, it could be addressed in the discussion of OHI, which is where it is classified under IDEA, or it could be placed within social disorders, especially emotional disorders, because it shares genetic roots with OCD (Garrett, 2011). TS is discussed in this section because it involves the disinhibition of motor responses—both vocal and motor. See Figure IV.I.

**Figure VI.1**  Disorders of Motor Response

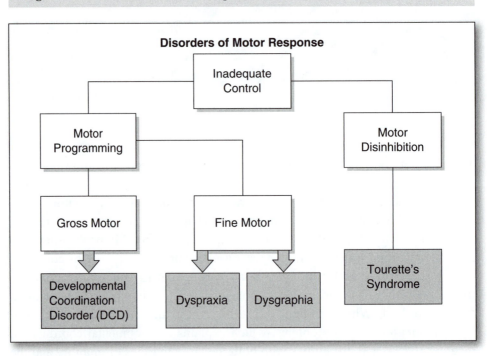

## LEARNING GOALS

In this section you will learn the following:

- Subtypes of motor disorders
- The causes or etiology and prevalence of each motor disorder and how age, culture, and gender can influence outcome

- How educators can informally identify children with motor disorders through observations of their (a) behavior, (b) responses to social and communication settings, (c) responses to academic tasks, and (d) responses to motor and physical tasks
- Possible implications for treatment
- How to apply the information you have learned to the behavior of case study children with and without diagnoses

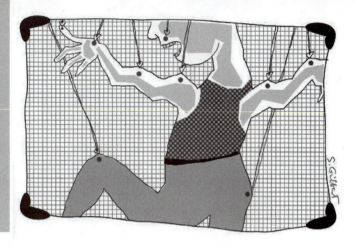

# Chapter 15
## Motor Disabilities

The first part of this chapter presents a discussion of disorders involving gross motor skills and disorders involving the smallest motor muscles of articulation. The more common fine motor disorder of dysgraphia is then addressed, and finally Tourette's syndrome is discussed.

## DEVELOPMENTAL COORDINATION DISORDER AND DYSPRAXIA

## FORMAL IDENTIFICATION

**DCD** is a failure to acquire both gross and fine movements (Kirby & Sugden, 2007). Assessment of motor difficulties can be made with the Bruininks-Oseretsky Test of Motor Proficiency (for a review, see Kirby & Sugden, 2007).

**DCD:** Developmental coordination disorder.

### Definitions

#### IDEA

IDEA defines speech disorders (apraxia/dyspraxia) as communication disorders (see Chapter 3):

Speech or language impairment means a communication disorder, such as stuttering, impaired articulation, a language impairment, or a voice impairment, that adversely affects a child's educational performance.(34 C.F.R. Section 300.7[a][c][11])

---

**Figure 15.1**  A child with Developmental Coordination Disorder who struggles to control his large muscles

## DSM-IV-TR

*DSM-IV-TR* (APA, 2000, p. 58) defines developmental coordination disorder and apraxia/dyspraxia as follows:

> *Identifying characteristic:* Performance in daily activities that requires motor coordination is substantially below that expected given the person's chronological age and measured intelligence. This may be manifested by marked delays in achieving motor milestones (e.g., walking, crawling, sitting), dropping things, "clumsiness," poor performance in sports, or poor handwriting.
>
> *Impairment:* Academic achievement or daily living activities.
>
> *Exclusions and conditions:* Not a general medical condition (e.g., cerebral palsy, hemiplegia, or muscular dystrophy) and not PDD.

### Possible Co-Occurring Conditions and Differences Among Related Disabilities

The two conditions that co-occur with DCD most frequently are ADHD and LD. DCD overlaps with about 50% of each of these populations (Jongmans, Smits-Engelsman, & Schoemaker, 2003). However, students "with ADHD may fall, bump into things, knock things over, but this is usually due to hyperactivity and impulsiveness, rather than to a large motor muscle impairment. If criteria for both disorders are met, both diagnoses can be given" (APA, 2000, p. 57). Gross motor difficulties are also common in children with ID, but a separate diagnosis of DCD can be given "only if the motor difficulties are in excess of those usually associated with [ID]" (APA, 2000, p. 57). That is, students with ID are also likely to have motor immaturity that causes difficulties with the small muscles involved in dressing (buttons, snaps, tying shoes), handwriting, and speech (Taylor et al., 2005). Further, diagnosing DCD requires distinguishing between motor programming of large muscles from motor impairments that are caused by medical conditions or "specific neurological disorders (e.g., cerebral palsy, progressive lesions of the cerebellum), but in these cases there is definite neural damage and abnormal findings on neurological examination" (APA, 2000, p. 57). In other words, these medical conditions involve physiological damage of structure.

**Dyspraxia:** Poor ability to plan fine motor movements of speech.

**Dyspraxia** involves motor programming of the articulatory muscles and is easily distinguished from DCD by the types of muscles involved. Dyspraxia co-occurs with RD, especially when there is disorganization of language (Nicolson, 2000). Because dyspraxia involves the finest motor skills of articulating speech, it can also involve the fine motor skills required in handwriting (dysgraphia). Speech intelligibility can also be a problem for students with ID (Roberts et al.,

2007). Other disorders similar to dyspraxia include stuttering or stammering, which involves hesitations or repetitions of primarily the beginning sounds of words. **Apraxia,** or failing to produce any speech, can be confused with selective or elective mutism (see Chapter 12, which involves mutism in specific situations only (e.g., at school but not at home). Apraxia can also be confused with hearing impairments, so a hearing assessment may be necessary.

**Apraxia:** Lack of ability to plan the motor movements involved in speech.

## Etiology

*Biogenetic.* Both apraxia/dyspraxia and DCD stem from the same neurological problem in the motor programming system of the cerebellum (Nijland, 2003). That is, the child's brain sends a signal to produce sound or movement, but the message is disrupted or lost in the circuitry of the brain, and the result is little or no control of muscles. The basis for these difficulties is found in the cortical and subcortical areas of the brain, where higher-level functions are dedicated to organizing muscular events (Ferrand & Bloom, 1997).

*Functional.* A functional assessment may find that the antecedents that set the occasion for motor planning are physical education, playground activities, and sports that require large motor skills and subject areas with requirements to speak (Jongmans et al., 2003). Under these setting conditions, many children with DCD will avoid or become angry/frustrated, especially in a social context, or they will pretend to be clowns during those activities (i.e., intentionally bumping into things). Children with dyspraxia may find classroom discussions and verbal response requirements stressful because they require clear articulation, but they may enjoy the playground, as the example of Taylor illustrates:

> When the teacher asked the kids to retell the story, he avoided it. . . . yet on the playground he became very excited when he was playing on the swing. He shouted and yelled for fun and to scare other boys by making monster or animal sounds.

## Prevalence and Age Factors

*Prevalence.* Around 6% of the population between the ages of 5 and 11 years have a motor programming disorder such as DCD or dyspraxia (APA, 2000). Estimates for individual nations vary, from 3% of the population in the Netherlands to 16% in Singapore (Jongmans et al., 2003). Higher rates of DCD have been reported in special education school populations (36%) (Jongmans et al., 2003) than in general education populations (about 4–5% of students), with greater prevalence among boys (Kirby & Sugden, 2007).

*Age.* Infants and toddlers with DCD may display clumsiness or delays in the development of motor milestones (e.g., walking, crawling, sitting, tying shoelaces, buttoning shirts, zipping pants). Identification of DCD "usually occurs when the child first attempts such tasks as running, holding a knife and fork, buttoning clothes, or playing ball games. . . . Older children may display difficulties with the motor aspects of assembling puzzles, building models, playing ball, and printing or handwriting" (APA, 2000, p. 57). By adolescence, many children appear to grow out of these difficulties (i.e., they improve over time through practice and experience) until they need to learn new motor skills (Kirby & Sugden, 2007). Young children with apraxia or dyspraxia may be able to produce only simple sounds that infants use, such as *b* and *d*.

## INFORMAL EDUCATOR IDENTIFICATION OF CHARACTERISTICS

### Behavioral and Communication

Children with DCD and those with dyspraxia are likely to be behaviorally behind their classmates (i.e., show immature behavior) (Velleman, 2002). The primary characteristics, however, include unsequenced sounds or syllables, inconsistent speech, and loss of sounds or words during articulation. Examples of speech errors are (a) "shif" instead of "fish," (b) "miskate" instead of "mistake," and (c) pronouncing "gate" as it should be one day and then replacing the *g* sound the next day with *k* or *d*. For example, when the teacher asked Taylor how many cubes there were in a particular tower, he answered " sis, si" (six).

As might be expected, compared with their peers these children tend to vocalize less, avoid reading aloud, and speak with simpler vocabularies, especially in social contexts, due to fear of failure and extreme frustration at not being understood (Hall, 2000; Velleman, 2011). Taylor's case illustrates:

> Even in speaking to his only two friends, he speaks little. Yet, Taylor sings songs with other kids while they walk.

The majority of the time, Taylor's teacher would ignore his silence. For example, when the teacher asked everyone to retell a story, Taylor avoided it and his teacher just ignored him without making any further demands. Students with dyspraxia may use other ways to extend their verbal production; for example, by using the sounds that objects make:

> Outside on a walk, Taylor saw a plane fly overhead and said "I like planes" and imitated the engine sound.

## Social-Emotional

Children with DCD show decreased self-esteem in any social setting involving an extended use of **gross motor skills** or **fine motor skills** (Piek, Dworcan, Barrett, & Coleman, 2000). General locomotor difficulties, such as problems with running, contribute to the finding that, compared with their non-DCD peers, "children with DCD spend more playground time in isolation" (Wang, Tseng, Wilson, & Hu, 2009). In addition to being socially excluded during activities involving fine motor skills, children with dyspraxia exhibit social and emotional characteristics that result from their being misunderstood and and often mimicked or laughed at by classmates. Perhaps because of these social responses, children with dyspraxia are more likely than other children to engage in socially deviant behavior and have poor socialization skills (Kanioglou, Tsorbatzoudis, & Barkoukis, 2005).

**Gross motor skills:** Physical skills involving the large muscles of the legs and arms, especially needed for coordination in walking and balance. Good gross motor skills are needed for adequate performance in physical education at school.

**Fine motor skills:** Physical skills involving the small muscles of the hands and the articulation muscles of the mouth and tongue.

## Motor, Physical, and Somatic

There is evidence of increased health problems for children with DCD (Kirby & Sugden, 2007), and some students with apraxia or dyspraxia alter the positions of their tongues, lips, or jaws when speaking as they attempt to produce the correct sounds.

Students with DCD, who have difficulties with balance and gross motor skills (running, skipping, hopping, walking, riding bicycle), are likely also to have difficulties writing (dysgraphia), coloring, using scissors, and managing self-care (e.g., they may have messy clothes or unfastened clothes), and they may even have difficulties with speaking (dyspraxia) (Jongmans et al., 2003; Orloff, 2005; Peters & Henderson, 2008). In Taylor's case, his gross motor skills appear to be his strength, as suggested by his playground behavior: "Running everywhere and playing a chasing game with three kids." However, he appears to have fine motor difficulties in addition to dyspraxia: "When he paints, he does it very carefully."

## Cognitive and Academic

Children with dyspraxia are typically average or above in IQ (Velleman, 2002). However, a disorder with motor origins may have long-term cognitive consequences (i.e., a failure to "do" may contribute to failure to experience and thus a failure to "know"). This area awaits further research (Velleman, 2011). Students with DCD are likely to have difficulty organizing independent activities for school (Jongmans et al., 2003) as well as problems participating in physical education and playground activities. Additional difficulties can be observed in art classes as these children attempt to draw shapes, color, or form clay.

# DISABILITY IN THE CLASSROOM

## Implications for Accommodations in General Education Settings: Tier I

Accommodations for children with DCD and dyspraxia might include helping them to avoid tasks and social settings that require the public use of the gross and fine motor movements by assigning them alternate activities or "jobs" not involving specific movements. Educators might also provide low-tech assistive technologies for these children, such as Velcro and tape (for a list of adaptations for toys, see Beard et al., 2007, p. 63).

## Implications for Interventions in Small-Group and Individual Settings: Tiers II and III

Children with DCD and dyspraxia should receive training on the specific motor components of particular tasks and then on the sequencing of those components (Kirby & Sugden, 2007). For children with dyspraxia, adaptive equipment such as a bite plate may improve vowel quality.

*Tier III.* Motor training with an occupational therapist or physiotherapist can be helpful for children with DCD. One study found that 27 out of 31 children showed significant improvement in motor skills following such training (Sugden & Chambers, 2003). In relatively severe cases of apraxia, students may need to learn a system of gestures and nonspeech symbol systems.

## Long-Term Outcomes

Around 58% of participants with motor-coordination planning disabilities of dyspraxia or DCD also have co-occurring ADHD; when DCD overlaps with ADHD, the long-term prognosis is less positive (Kirby & Sugden, 2007). One longitudinal study found that poor outcomes for individuals with ADHD and DCD, compared with an ADHD-only group, included more alcohol abuse, more criminal offenses, and lower educational levels after 28 years (Rasmussen & Gillberg, 2000).

**Memory dysgraphia:** Poor recall of the written forms of letters. Individuals with memory dysgraphia can copy letters.

# HANDWRITING DISABILITIES (DYSGRAPHIA)

Dysgraphia involves motor control of the hand that is guided by the eyes, following the planning of the brain. Some children with dysgraphia cannot recall the shapes of the letters of the alphabet (**memory dysgraphia**) but can

**Figure 15.2**   The Awkward Pencil Grip of a Child with Dysgraphia

copy them; others have poor handwriting and do not perceive that their letters are misshapen (**perceptual or spatial dysgraphia**). Children with perceptual dysgraphia have normal fine motor skills but poor perceptual abilities.

**Perceptual or spatial dysgraphia:** Poor ability to form letters accompanied by an inability to recognize that the letters are badly formed.

## FORMAL IDENTIFICATION

Studies that examine dysgraphia generally look at features of handwriting such as poor spatial arrangement of letters and letters erased or overwritten, as well as the number of letters a child forms in the first minute of writing. Children with **motor dysgraphia** (see Figure 15.2) can accurately assess their own handwriting disability; that is, their self-ratings are significantly correlated with computerized assessments (Computerized Penmanship Evaluation Tool; see Engel-Yeger, Nagauker-Yanuv, & Rosenblum, 2009). Individuals with motor dysgraphia can see that their own writing is poor (adequate perceptual skills). Writing long passages can be painful for them, and they are unable to sustain legibility; letter shape and size become increasingly inconsistent and illegible.

**Motor dysgraphia:** Poor ability to form letters (owing to poor fine motor skills).

### Definitions

#### IDEA

IDEA *could* include dysgraphia within the category LD, because the dysfunction involves the use of written language. However, the IDEA definition of LD is typically interpreted to *exclude* academic problems due to motor disabilities, as stated: "but does not include learning problems resulting from visual, hearing, *or motor disabilities,* of mental retardation, of emotional disturbance, or of environmental, cultural, or economic disadvantage" (H.R. 1350, Section 602 [30]; italics added).

### DSM-IV-TR

*DSM-IV-TR* (APA, 2000) includes all subtypes of motor disorders (e.g., dysgraphia, apraxia/dyspraxia) under the category of developmental coordination disorder (see the definition above in the section on DCD and dyspraxia).

### Subtypes

Three subtypes of dysgraphia have been identified: memory dysgraphia, motor dysgraphia, and perceptual-spatial dysgraphia.

### Possible Co-Occurring Conditions and Differences Among Related Disabilities

Dysgraphia can be found in the company of other fine motor disabilities (dyspraxia), and it is often accompanied by dyslexia, aphasia, math disabilities, or ADHD. In particular, the writing of students with ADHD is more illegible than that of non-ADHD peers (Zentall & Kruczek, 1988).

## Etiology

*Biogenetic.* Parents or close relatives of children with dysgraphia are often dysgraphic themselves (Miceli, Capasso, Ivella, & Caramanza, 1997). Thus, there is a genetic contribution to this disability.

*Environmental.* Dysgraphia may be acquired as the consequence of a stroke or TBI (Miceli et al., 1997).

*Functional.* A functional assessment may document that the immediate antecedents that set the occasion for dysgraphia are those that require handwriting and other small motor tasks (tying shoes), which can be set in contrast to the children's greater skill on tasks with verbal response requirements or even with gross motor tasks.

## Prevalence and Age Factors

Around 10–34% of the general population fails to develop efficient handwriting performance required for adequate school performance (for a review, see Rosenblum, Aloni, & Josman, 2010). Children are typically diagnosed soon after they learn to write, between 7 and 10 years.

# INFORMAL EDUCATOR IDENTIFICATION CHARACTERISTICS

## Behavioral

Children with dysgraphia typically try to avoid tasks that involve writing and show a preference for verbal tasks.

## Social-Emotional

Many adults assume that children with dysgraphia are lazy, careless, or impulsive, and these social judgments appear to be particularly harmful. Students with dysgraphia are more likely to be punished by having to stay in for recess to complete assignments or take home excessive amounts of homework. Seth, whose case study appears at the end of this chapter, has been diagnosed with a communication disorder but not dysgraphia; that he has not received this secondary diagnosis could explain why his teacher has concluded that he lacks interest—a common misunderstanding about these students. However, this appears to be an incorrect assumption from the evidence presented in the behavioral log of Seth's initial genuine attempts in responding to writing activities:

*Day 1.* Started off well with handwriting, following directions and interacting well with classmate. Seth quickly lost interest and began scribbling in his book with his pencil.

- Paraprofessional took notice and asked Seth to stop and hand over his book.
- Seth said no and started to scribble harder in his book.
- Paraprofessional seized the book from Seth.
- When he did work on something, he would rush through it and turn in sloppy results.
- Rushed through his work to get done faster.
- Seth began to crumple paper and destroy his materials.

*Day 2.* Started worksheet with eagerness: Seth sat still, traced his picture well, and interacted with teacher. After 2 minutes, Seth quickly lost interest, picked up a pencil, and attempted to throw it at the paraprofessional.

## Perceptual/Motor, Physical, and Somatic

Children with visual memory dysgraphia can copy but *cannot recall* the shapes of letters; children with visual-spatial/perceptual dysgraphia *do not see* that their writing is poor, owing to poor visual-spatial perception. Children with motor dysgraphia see that their writing is poor but *cannot make the muscles* in their hands produce letters correctly, whether they are copying letters or writing from recall. Many of these children have strong verbal skills and may carefully "watch" or coach the hand that is writing (i.e., they need external verbal cues to plan and execute written responses). For these students, the rate of writing is slow—whether in response to verbal directions, when writing independently, or even when copying. Additionally, the mechanics of their writing involve awkward or cramped fingers and odd wrist placement, finger positions, or paper positions. Many children with dysgraphia experience pain while writing, which usually starts in the center of the forearm and spreads along the nervous system to the entire body. The pain can get worse or appear when these children are stressed, but they may not report it because they do not know that it is unusual to experience pain while writing, do not think that others will believe them, or think that they just have muscle aches or cramps.

## Cognitive and Academic

Typically children with dysgraphia have average to above-average IQ, although dysgraphia can occur across the IQ distribution. Given these children's difficulty with the mechanics of handwriting, they experience academic outcomes that are influenced by decreased production of written language (e.g., in spelling and composition) (Engel-Yeger et al., 2009). These problems are made worse by classroom requirements. That is, in second-, fourth-, and sixth-grade classrooms, 30–60% of classroom activities require fine motor skills; 85% of these activities involve paper-and-pencil tasks (McHale & Cermak, 1992). Children with dysgraphia respond to these requirements with avoidance. For example, see Figure 15.3, which displays data on Seth's behavior.

The specific handwriting problems seen with dysgraphia are inconsistent spaces between words and letters, inconsistent letter formations and slant, irregular letter shapes and sizes, on-the-line and margin errors, and poor organization on the page. Children with dysgraphia also tend to mix lowercase and uppercase letters as well as printed and cursive letters, and they have problems with the sequencing of letters and with the "mechanics" of writing (spelling, punctuation, and so on). (Figure 15.4 shows an example of the handwriting of a child with dysgraphia.) Because of these problems, dysgraphia can have a negative influence on a child's grades and can affect performance in a range of areas (e.g., spelling, alignment of numbers in math, neatness on compositions), including homework and completion of assignments on time (Engel-Yeger et al., 2009; May-Benson, Ingolia, & Koomar, 2002). Parents of children with dysgraphia report that these children fail to be organized for school (e.g., ready on time and with learning materials) (Rosenblum et al., 2010).

**Figure 15.3** Seth's Overall Avoid Payoffs During Handwriting

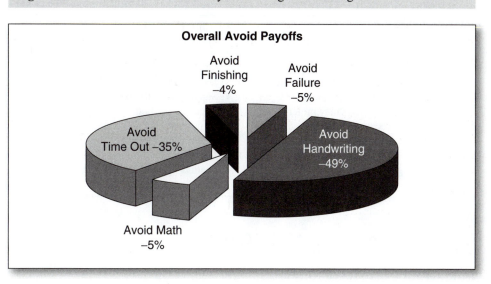

**Figure 15.4** An Example of Dysgraphia

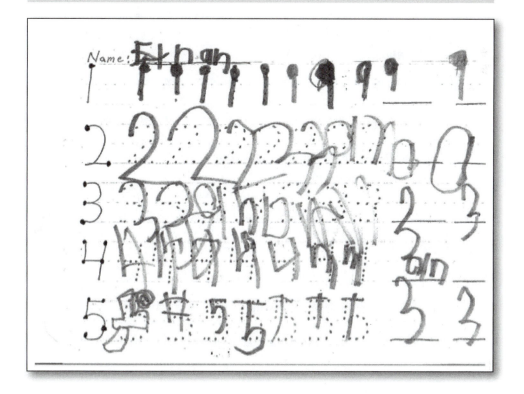

## SUMMARY OF STRENGTHS AND NEEDS

| *Possible strengths* | *Probable needs* |
|---|---|
| • Intelligence.<br>• Students with dysgraphia may prefer verbal tasks and can respond adequately in this domain.<br>• Students with dyspraxia may prefer tasks requiring nonvocal, motor responses and can respond adequately in this domain. | • Accommodations that include increased time to respond and alternate ways to respond.<br>• Support for activities promoting organization, both of objects (e.g., homework materials) and of events and assignments that are due in a time sequence.<br>• Grading systems that separate content from form. |

## DISABILITY IN THE CLASSROOM

### Implications for Accommodations in General Education Settings: Tier I

Accommodations for students with dysgraphia should involve changing the methods by which they can respond (including the use of low-tech devices to help with poor motor control) as well as changing the standards for handwriting.

*Change methods for responding:*

- Keyboarding is best, but when handwriting is necessary, the use of pencil grips, clipboards or angled boards, tactile boundaries for writing (e.g., raised lines), and writing devices (markers) of different colors can be helpful (Imhof, 2004).
- Allow oral answers to questions/discussion.
- Provide graph paper for math.
- Provide notes, assign buddy scribes to take notes using carbon paper or NCR paper, or have the child write only key words and fill in the details later.
- Use cooperative writing projects where different students assume roles, such as "brainstormer," "organizer of information," "writer," "proofreader," and "illustrator."
- Add colors to specific difficult-to-form letters; this can significantly improve the writing performance of attention-problem elementary-age children (Zentall & Kruczek, 1988) and of attention-problem adolescents, with little effect on the performance of typical adolescents (Zentall et al., 1985).

- High-tech computer-animated interface designs known as rotoscopy can be helpful for engaging students and improving the handwriting skills of older students (see Othman & Keay-Bright, 2011). Less expensive are apps, such as iWriteWords, that guide handwriting with a reinforcing interface.

### *Change standards for handwriting:*

- Extend time for responding.
- Allow printing instead of cursive or whichever is preferred.
- Reduce the need for copying from the board or for editing papers.
- Remove neatness and correct spelling as grading criteria, or separate the grading of content and form.
- Use self-evaluation checklists to ensure that students are aware of the various skills involved in writing (e.g., checklists can encourage students to evaluate their sitting position, their formation of letters, and their spacing of letters).

(For additional ideas for accommodations for children with dysgraphia, see Jones, 1999.)

## Implications for Interventions in Small-Group and Individual Settings: Tiers II and III

Many students with dysgraphia can benefit from the use of low-tech devices, such as tape recorders, that allow them to avoid fine motor movements. Students with severe motor impairment will need high-tech interventions, such as voice-activated speech-recognition software (e.g., Dragon Naturally Speaking) (Silverman, 2003, p. 541). High-tech assistive devices for complex motor tasks, similar to those used by children with cerebral palsy (e.g., laptop computers with large keyboards and pointers), are also helpful (Orloff, 2005).

*Remediation.* Practicing specific letters with a verbal self-instructional procedure has been found to improve the handwriting of students with LD, with results maintained over time (Graham, 1983, 1999). To improve students' formation of letters:

1. Compare and contrast features of the target letter with other letters that share common formational characteristics, especially for children with perceptual dysgraphia.

2. Overtly model how to form the letter, use visual cues (e.g., numbered arrows that describe where to begin writing and where to end), or use physical

assistance in forming the letters, with an adult guiding the child's hand, especially for children with motor dysgraphia.

3. Provide practice tracing, copying, and writing the letters from memory, especially for children with memory dysgraphia.

4. Praise and provide corrective feedback on letter formation.

5. Encourage students to evaluate their own efforts by identifying correctly formed letters and correcting poorly formed letters.

6. Dramatize student progress through use of charts or graphs.

*Discrimination learning* is especially useful for children with perceptual dysgraphia. This example, illustrating point 1 above, is from the case study of Andy, the student with TBI in Chapter 8:

> I asked Andy to point to letter *T*. Then, I asked him to compare it to letter *F*. He noticed that the only different piece was the cross in the middle. Andy had little difficulty writing the word *Friday* after that point.

Note that for students with ADHD and dysgraphia, practice alone can *increase* the number of errors over time (Zentall & Kruczek, 1988) because of the repetition in one setting. Thus, different low-tech techniques are warranted, as well as the use of self-monitoring for increased production and somewhat increased accuracy (for a review regarding students with ADHD and dysgraphia, see Zentall, 2006, p. 253).

## Long-Term Outcomes

It is estimated that dysgraphia costs American industry and business billions of dollars per year due to errors in business records, accounting, prescriptions, and so on. The long-term costs to the individual have not been researched.

# TOURETTE SYNDROME

At the age of 8, Tom self-reported these observations:

> I was devastated when I found out I had TS. I thought I was going to be a normal boy. But I'm not. My life is awful. I feel like I'm missing out on a lot of things because of my tics. I will feel a lot better if my tics go. If they don't, I will learn to put up with them.

**Figure 15.5** Two children with Tourette Syndrome, each Expressng Vocal and Motor Tics

Tourette syndrome (TS) is characterized by **tics,** or involuntary repetitive movements, which may be motor and/or vocal; motor tics are often described as twitches See Figure 15.5. Children with TS have noted that just prior to expressing a tic, they may have a physical feeling of needing to stretch their shoulder or clear their throat; they also report uncomfortable, nervous, weird, **prescient feelings** (which may be experienced as feelings of fear, disgust, or doubt), or they may feel like they are going to explode (Leckman, 2002; Walter & Carter, 1997). TS is often mistaken for a behavioral or emotional disorder, but it is a neurological condition. Steve, whose case study appears at the end of this chapter, represents a child with Tourette's.

**Tourette syndrome (TS):** A disorder characterized by both vocal and motor tics and typically associated with an inherited pattern (Silver, 2004).

**Tics:** Repetitive, brief, stereotypical movements (motor tics) or vocalizations (vocal tics), including eye blinking, shoulder shrugging, grimacing, head jerking, yelping, sniffing, and making grunting noises.

## FORMAL IDENTIFICATION

### Definitions

#### *IDEA*

IDEA includes TS within the other health impairment (OHI) category, with the following wording (italics added here to indicate relevance to this section):

**Prescient feelings:** Sensations that occur just prior to tics that act as warnings (Walter & Carter, 1997).

having limited strength, vitality, or alertness, including a heightened alertness to environmental stimuli, that results in limited alertness with respect to the educational environment, that (a) is due to chronic or acute health problems such as asthma, attention deficit disorder or attention deficit hyperactivity disorder, diabetes, epilepsy, a heart condition, hemophilia, lead poisoning, leukemia, nephritis, rheumatic fever, sickle cell anemia, and *Tourette syndrome;* and (b) adversely affects a child's educational performance. (34 C.F.R. Section 300.8[c][9][i])

## DSM-IV-TR

*DSM-IV-TR* (APA, 2000, p. 114) defines Tourette's syndrome as follows:

*Defining characteristics:*

A. Both multiple motor and one or more vocal tics have been present at some time during the illness, although not necessarily concurrently. (A tic is a sudden, rapid, recurrent, nonrhythmic, stereotyped motor movement or vocalization.)

B. The tics occur many times a day (usually in bouts) nearly every day or intermittently throughout a period of more than 1 year, and during this period there was never a tic-free period of more than 3 consecutive months.

*Exclusions and conditions:* Not due to postviral encephalitis, TBI, brain tumors, epilepsy, ASD, muscular dystrophy, CP, Parkinson's, etc. Onset before 18 years.

## Frequently Occurring Subtypes

**Tic disorder:** A disorder typically involving just motor or vocal tics.

TS differs from other **tic disorders** in that it involves both motor and vocal tics (**multiform,** frequently changing, nonfunctional repetitive behaviors, often described as twitches).

## Possible Co-Occurring Conditions and Differences Among Related Disabilities

Many individuals with TS have other disorders, most often anxiety disorders. Also, 20–50% have sleep problems (e.g., frequent awakening, nightmares, difficulty falling/staying asleep, walking/talking in sleep) (Dreher, 1996; Robertson, 2006). When TS is accompanied by other disorders, it is called Tourette's plus, or TS+ (e.g., Lue, 2001). In one study of clinic-referred children with TS, 50% also had OCD symptoms, 50–60% had ADHD, 25–35% had tantrums and aggression, and 33% had LD (Denckla, 2006). (These frequencies exceed 100% because many of these children had co-occurring disabilities.) The motor types of behavior seen in OCD (Bloch et al., 2006) differ from those associated with TS in that the repetitive behavior of OCD is related to "purposeful" form rituals or compulsions (e.g., repeated checking or hand washing).

Although ADHD can overlap with TS, TS can also be misidentified as ADHD, because many of the tics, especially the vocal tics, can be viewed as purposeful classroom disturbances. Children with tics prefer to look as though they are trying to disturb others rather than look like they have no control over their behavior. It is especially difficult to differentially diagnose students when some of their behavior is caused by TS and some vocal and motor behavior looks like ADHD, as with Steve, who is only 6 years old:

> While walking in line he lost his shoe on the way to the restroom and then he continued to fall down several times while making a short trip to the restroom with the whole class.

## Etiology

The etiology of tics is both biochemical and environmental. That is, "the child receives the genetic or constitutional basis for developing a Tic Disorder; the precise type or severity of disorder may be different from one generation to another and is modified by nongenetic [environmental] factors" (APA, 2000, p. 113).

*Biogenetic.* TS is an inherited brain disorder with biochemical differences (i.e., an excess of or oversensitivity to dopamine) (Munson, 2005). Specifically, 50–70% of the cases diagnosed with TS are genetically based. In other words, with one parent with TS, a boy has a 50% chance of inheriting TS.

*Environmental.* "Even when both members of identical twins inherit TS, the tics may differ in intensity and frequency; these differences are also explained by nongenetic factors. However, not everyone who inherits this genetic vulnerability will have TS . . . and for some individuals who have TS, there is no evidence of heritability" (APA, 2000, p. 113). Environmental factors include prenatal exposure to drugs and to severe stress on the mother (Leckman, 2002).

*Functional.* A functional assessment of individuals with TS would find that their tics increase as a function of stress or anxiety (being teased by peers). Tics may function to reduce stress, similar to the function of the repetitive compulsive behavior of OCD. For many children with TS, stress may occur during less predictable settings (e.g., transitions); for others it may be highest in situations involving specific academic subject areas, as in the case of Steve during handwriting and math:

> Disrupts teacher's math lesson when returning from the restroom by making disturbing noises (sounds similar to someone gagging). . . . Constantly disrupted other students throughout the math lesson by jumping around his desk, making noises, touching, and talking to them.

Furthermore, calling attention to tics actually increases their frequency. Tics are also made worse by the ingestion of caffeinated beverages, cough syrup, recreational drugs, and diet medications, as well as by hay fever, allergies, and viral illnesses. Tics infrequently occur during sleep or during activities that absorb the child's concentration.

## Prevalence, Gender, Age, and Cultural Factors

TS was once thought to be rare, but the incidence of this disorder is now estimated to be between 31 and 157 cases per 1,000 in children 13–14 years old (Leckman, 2002).

*Gender.* Boys are three times more likely than girls to have TS (Clarke, Bray, Kehle, & Truscott, 2001; Leckman, 2002).

*Age.* Symptoms are visible by 7 years, but some signs, such as eye blinking, can be seen as early as 2–5 years, followed in several years by phonic tics (e.g., throat clearing or sniffing) (Crawford, Channon, & Robertson, 2005; Leckman, 2002). Tics typically start around age 5 and reach their peak at about 10–12 and then gradually decrease during adolescence, with less than a quarter of those affected continuing with mild or more severe symptoms (Bloch et al., 2006).

*Culture.* Caucasian students are more likely than African American or Hispanic students to have TS.

## INFORMAL EDUCATOR IDENTIFICATION OF CHARACTERISTICS

### Behavioral

Most children with TS develop tics in this sequence: (a) eye tics, (b) facial tics or involuntary sounds, and (c) other tics within weeks or months, such as head

jerks, grimaces, and hand-to-face movements. These behavioral tics change over
time and can vary in frequency/intensity and type (grunting to yelling out), similar
to the example of Steve, who would yell out "Balloon quilt."

**Multiform:** Of different-appearing forms.

Steve had additional "apparently" socially noncompliant behavior ("When the
whole class was asked to stretch he started doing push-ups; the teacher and students seemed to ignore him"). Although his teachers assumed he performed such
behavior to get attention or a social reaction, it is probable that Steve could not
inhibit these motor responses.

## Social-Emotional

The social and emotional difficulties of TS are more problematic in day-to-day
adaptations than the motor and vocal tics themselves (Carter et al., 2000). Children
with TS are embarrassed and teased and made to feel stupid, different, and
unwanted. Peers' negative responses to tics can cause anxiety in students with TS,
which in turn increases tics and generates self-doubt. As stated by Jeff:

> I used to get asked why I blinked all the time and everyone used to get angry at
> me because I couldn't help looking at them, and I was always getting harassed.

In Steve's case, his unpopularity was observed as early as the first grade
("Didn't find a partner during partner sharing time. Teacher found one for him").
However, Steve also had some positive behavior ("He tried helping Ben sound out
a word") and he was also very socially directed.

In particular, adolescence is a period with a strong emphasis on physical attrac-
tiveness. For this reason, TS creates more social/emotional difficulties during this
period than any other developmental period, with a higher risk of poor peer relationships or no relationships and withdrawn or aggressive social behavior (Chang,
Tu, & Wang, 2004).

## Cognitive

Most individuals with this syndrome have normal IQ scores (Munson, 2005).
However, they may have visual perceptual problems (e.g., noticing similarities
and differences in objects, letters) and visual-motor problems, such as handwriting
(Chiu et al., 2001; Hendren, 2002; Shannon, 2003). For Steve, tapping was a
motor tic that occurred during stressful handwriting practice: "While the teacher
was giving direct instruction on the writing lesson, Steve tapped his pencil on his
desk in an obnoxious manner."

## Communication: Verbal/Vocal

**Coprolalia:** Using obscene or socially inappropriate words (cursing); this most disruptive and disturbing of TS symptoms is found in less than 15% of cases and occurs late in childhood (Jay, 2000).

The verbal characteristics of children with TS are related to their vocal tics, which can be simple or complex. Simple vocal tics include throat clearing, sniffing, coughing, grunting, spitting, yelling, belching, and stuttering. Complex vocal tics are wide-ranging and may include animal sounds, repeating words or phrases out of context ("Oh boy," "I don't know"), **coprolalia, palilalia,** and echolalia. Steve shows complex vocal tics:

> Steve often made animal noises or gagging sounds. For instance, on September 12th he shouted out "balloon quilt" while doing seatwork and on September 14th he started barking like a dog during a transition.

**Palilalia:** The repetition or echoing of one's own spoken words; may sound like stuttering (e.g., "Do my work work work").

## Motor, Physical, and Somatic

**Echopraxia:** Involuntary repetition or imitation of the observed movements of another.

Physical or motor tics can also be divided into simple and complex. Simple motor tics include blinking, which is the most common, and jerking neck, shrugging shoulders, flipping head, kicking, swinging or tapping feet, tensing muscles, sticking tongue out, and finger movements. Complex motor tics take the form of facial gestures such as eye rolling, grooming behaviors, smelling things, touching other people or things, tapping, jumping, squatting, retracing steps, doing deep knee bends, twirling when walking, hitting, biting, **echopraxia,** and **copropraxia.** Rarely are tics self-injurious, such as hitting or biting oneself (Woods, Koch, & Miltenberger, 2003). In addition to motor tics, there is evidence to suggest that individuals with TS may feel compelled to touch others or objects or perform specific action sequences. For example, Steve was observed "spinning in his chair or running a figure eight around the room in the middle of a lesson . . . on a regular basis."

**Copropraxia:** Using obscene or socially inappropriate gestures, similar to coprolalia.

## Academic

Tic disorders can also affect the control of the muscles involved in handwriting. Thus, tics can make simple activities difficult (e.g., copying from the blackboard, working on long written assignments, completing assignments on time and neatly) (Chiu et al., 2001; Hendren, 2002). Repetitive writing is particularly difficult for a child with TS, especially when the child also has characteristics of ADHD, as in the case of Steve:

> His avoidance of boredom was trying to get out of mind-numbing work, such as writing the letter *Q* or reading a story that may not interest him or activities that involve more waiting.

Although children are able to suppress tics for limited periods of time, especially as they get older, this suppression takes great effort away from the immediate task and learning (Walter & Carter, 1997). This effort at suppression (disability fatigue) can explain why Lyle, who is 9 years old with both AS and TS, reports that he feels like he's in prison when he is at school. Tic disorders are also associated with both reading and math difficulties. A good example of difficulties with math can be seen in the case Steve, who has already learned to avoid math and to produce less work:

> For instance, on September 19 Steve was redirected three times during a math lesson and then finally sent into the hall. The final consequence did not even seem to bother him, based on the fact that he played with garbage in the hallway.

## SUMMARY OF STRENGTHS AND NEEDS

| *Probable strengths* | *Probable needs* |
|---|---|
| • Intelligence.<br>• Usually free of tics during activities of high interest and child engagement.<br>• Tics usually decrease in severity during adolescence. | • Ways to cope with situational stress or the stress brought on by disability fatigue, such as the option to leave a situation briefly.<br>• Educators who do not allow others to tease these students.<br>• Educational evaluation of possible difficulties in math, handwriting, and reading.<br>• Other ways for the child to respond aside from handwriting or public verbal presentations.<br>• Help in developing structured responses to transitions or other nonstructured times |

## DISABILITY IN THE CLASSROOM

### Implications for Accommodations in General Education Settings: Tier I

Children with TS experience fewer tics when they are relaxed or when they are focused on absorbing tasks (Shannon, 2003). Therefore, providing tasks that are of interest to the child will reduce tic activity. Further, educators need to model acceptance of these children and not allow peer teasing. One student with TS, Tom, stated:

> My teacher manages my TS really well. The other students try to be understanding as my teacher has told them all about TS.

Other Tier I accommodations include (a) allowing short breaks (e.g., breaking longer assignments into smaller parts), movement around the room, access to a private room or permission to run an errand when the child sees a private signal from the teacher); (b) providing access to oral presentations and reports that can be taped; and (c) providing access to exams in a private room for tension and tic release and to allow more time (Lue, 2001).

## Implications for Interventions in Individual Settings: Tier III

Anti-tic drugs block the activity of the neurotransmitter dopamine and decrease the expression of tics. Unfortunately, there is no medication that completely eliminates tics (Clarke et al., 2001). Many people with TS choose tics over medications, because the side effects of the drugs include sleepiness and weight gain.

## Long-Term Outcomes

Regarding the long-term outcomes for individuals with TS, *DSM-IV-TR* states:

The duration of the disorder may be lifelong, though periods of remission lasting from weeks to years may occur. In most cases, the severity, frequency, disruptiveness, and variability of the symptoms diminish during adolescence and adulthood. In other cases, the symptoms actually disappear entirely, usually by early adulthood. In a few cases, the symptoms may worsen in adulthood. The predictors of this course are not known. (APA, 2000, p. 113)

Higher IQ has been found to predict the development of OCD symptoms in individuals with TS later in life (Bloch et al., 2006).

## CHAPTER SUMMARY

- Subtypes of motor disorder involving planning and motor control, that are not due to physiological damage of structure or hearing loss, can be categorized by the types of muscles that are involved: (a) gross motor skills, DCD, defined only under *DSM-IV-TR* as "DCD and Apraxia/Dyspraxia"; (b) fine motor control, dysgraphia, defined under *DSM-IV-TR* as "DCD and Apraxia/Dyspraxia," and possibly under IDEA as "Disorder of Written Expression" (however, this label is generally not given if there is only poor handwriting or poor spelling); (c) planning fine motor articulation responses, dyspraxia, identified under IDEA as a communication disorder and under *DSM-IV-TR* as "DCD and Apraxia/Dyspraxia"; (d) lack of control

over some fine or gross motor (vocal or motor) responses, labeled TS, and identified under IDEA as OHI and under *DSM-IV-TR* as "Tourette Disorder."

- Frequently co-occurring disabilities that often involve fine motor difficulties are ADHD,
  LD (dyslexia, MLD, aphasia), and MID for fine and gross motor difficulties. Students
  who have difficulties with balance and gross motor skills (running, riding a bicycle) are
  also likely to have problems with fine motor skills (writing, coloring). TS often co-occurs
  with and can be confused with ADHD, because many gross motor tics (e.g., running in
  circles) and vocal tics can be viewed as purposeful classroom disturbances.

- The etiology of DCD and dyspraxia/apraxia is genetically based neurological problems in the motor programming system of the cerebellum. Antecedent tasks and settings are physical education, playground activities, and sports that require large motor
  skills; art and handwriting tasks that require small motor skills; and subject areas with
  verbal participation requirements. The etiology of TS for most individuals is genetic,
  but prenatal exposure to drugs and maternal stress are also contributors. Furthermore,
  tics are triggered by antecedent classroom conditions of stress and do not occur when
  the child is engaged or asleep.

- Age level and school requirements for motor control are factors in identification.
  About a third of the population has handwriting difficulties (dysgraphia) that interfere
  with school performance. Boys are three times as likely as girls to have TS.

- Educators can informally identify students with dyspraxia by listening to their
  unsequenced sounds or syllables, inconsistent speech, and loss of sounds or words
  during articulation. Children with dysgraphia, on the other hand, can be quite talkative to compensate for poor handwriting skills.

- The behavioral characteristics that lead to informal identification of students with DCD
  and dyspraxia are primarily avoidance of social and physical activities and tasks that
  will reveal their motor problems. In students with TS, tics develop in a sequence that
  often begins with eye tics and change over time in intensity and type. The social consequences of motor deficits include peer teasing and rejection (for odd speaking and for
  vocal and motor tics), adult punishment stemming from judgments about the child's
  laziness and attention seeking, and social exclusion during activities that require motor
  skills (physical education). These social responses contribute to low self-efficacy in
  children with these disorders, especially during adolescence, when physical appearance
  is especially important, and can lead to the development of socially deviant behavior.

- The intelligence of children with motor disabilities and TS is typically average.
  However, the learning processes involved in dysgraphia can sometimes be traced to
  poor visual perceptual or visual memory skills; similarly, children with TS often have
  visual perception and visual-motor difficulties.

- Academic problems associated with the motor difficulties of children with dysgraphia include poor organization. Both children with TS and those with dysgraphia show poor handwriting, which can make it difficult for them to complete assignments and tests on time, since half of classroom activities require the use of fine motor skills (especially spelling and compositions). Disability fatigue can be seen in children with these motor disorders, as they attempt to control their motor responses.

- Accommodations include allowing methods of responding that do not involve writing or speaking (depending on type of motor disorder); adding color to difficult-to-form letters; using assistive technology; and changing standards, such as allowing printing, extending time, and not grading on the basis of handwriting. In addition, for children with motor disorders, educators need to make the classroom environment safe by providing information about the disorder to classmates (with parental permission) and not allowing teasing. Interventions for dysgraphia include short sessions of practice/feedback with praise and self-checklists and self-graphing.

## CHAPTER QUESTIONS

### Apraxia/Dyspraxia

1. Why is dyspraxia so difficult to identify in children?

2. What are the academic outcomes of apraxia/dyspraxia?

3. How can it be that in today's technological society we still have disabilities defined by poor motor responding? Do we still have disabilities defined by sensory-based visual impairment?

### Dysgraphia

1. When is attention a factor in handwriting?

2. How would you determine whether a child has dysgraphia or is just careless, when in both cases rushing through assignments may occur?

3. If a child has dysgraphia, might he or she have another disorder?

4. How would you determine the extent of motor, memory, and/or perceptual contributions to handwriting problems?

5. In what ways might students with dysgraphia compensate for their handwriting deficits?

## Tourette's Syndrome

1. In what types of settings would you expect children with TS to show increased tics?

2. How do tics, TS, and tic disorders differ?

3. Why is the behavior of children with TS in the classroom thought to be volitional?

4. What can educators expect from children with TS in the classroom?

5. What have you learned from this chapter, and what questions remain for you about Tourette's syndrome?

## TRUE/FALSE AND MULTIPLE-CHOICE

1. Students with gross motor difficulties are more likely to also have fine motor difficulties, whereas fine motor difficulties are not necessarily paralleled by large motor difficulties.

2. Dyspraxia is
   A. a lack of coordination in the large muscles
   B. a poor ability to plan fine motor movements
   C. an impaired capacity to plan a motor response and to coordinate and sequence the speech muscles for the production of speech sounds
   D. all of the above

3. Students with developmental coordination disorder
   A. perform worse academically then their peers with apraxia or dyspraxia
   B. perform worse on IQ tests than their peers
   C. have difficulty in physical education because of the motor movements required to throw or catch a ball

4. The expression of both motor and vocal tics would be labeled a tic disorder.

5. Children with motor dysgraphia cannot see that their letters are incorrectly formed.

6. Nonspeech (gesture or picture) methods to facilitate communication are best for students with
   A. apraxia
   B. dyspraxia
   C. dysgraphia
   D. DCD

7. A student who copies or writes very slowly, carefully watches the hand he or she is writing with, and holds the pencil awkwardly while writing, with odd wrist and finger placement and paper position, probably has

A. memory dysgraphia
B. motor dysgraphia
C. perceptual-spatial dysgraphia

8. A non-language-based sensorimotor disorder of articulation that is characterized by an impaired capacity to motor plan, coordinate, and sequence the speech muscles for the volitional production of speech sounds is

A. dyspraxia
B. dysgraphia
C. DCD
D. dyscalculia

9. A student who mixes upper- and lowercase letters and printed and cursive letters, inconsistently shows letter formations and slant, produces irregular letter sizes and shapes, misuses lines and margins, and organizes writing poorly on the page probably has

A. memory dysgraphia
B. motor dysgraphia
C. perceptual-spatial dysgraphia

10. A child who has difficulty with gross motor activities, such as walking, running, and riding a bicycle, as well as difficulty with fine motor skills, such as writing, coloring, and using scissors, probably has

A. apraxia/dyspraxia
B. dysgraphia
C. DCD

## SHORT ANSWER

1. _____ motor skills use the large muscles.

2. This disorder can result in gross motor problems as well as problems with fine motor tasks.

3. Some children with dysgraphia experience _____, especially after writing for a long time.

4. Poor ability to plan the finest motor movements of speech

5. Failure to recall the form of letters is called _____ dysgraphia.

6. For children with ADHD and dysgraphia, _____ can make their writing *more illegible.*

7. Imitating others' movements is called _____.

8. What increases the frequency and/or intensity of tics?

9. The warning feeling that an individual with TS has immediately prior to expressing a tic is called a _____ _____.

## PROBLEM-BASED CASE APPLICATIONS AND QUESTIONS

### CASE STUDY 15.1: STEVE

*("Balloon quilt.")*
(adapted from a report submitted by Kate Rohder)

*Background.* Steve is a first-grade student at a typical public city school. He is highly verbal, expressive, and very creative and loves to talk to his peers and teachers. However, he can be very competitive, often bossy, and may be considered a "know-it-all." On a regular basis he can be observed disrupting the class by talking, making noises, moving, or otherwise bothering others. Sometimes he has a difficult time dealing with authority, which leads to arguments with his teacher. Currently he has *not* been diagnosed with any disorder or disability.

## ABC Table and Analysis

### Setting 1: Direct Instruction

| *Behavior* | *Antecedent* | *Consequence* | *Payoff* |
|---|---|---|---|
| **Writing lessons** | | | |
| Made loud animal noises. | | Teacher ignored him. | Avoids writing |
| Tapped his pencil on his desk in a loud and obnoxious manner. | | Teacher redirected him to continue writing *Q*s. | Avoids writing |
| Talked loudly. | | Teacher told him to stop shouting at her. | Gets self-determination over teacher |

*(Continued)*

(Continued)

| Behavior | Antecedent | Consequence | Payoff |
|---|---|---|---|
| Started shouting out "Balloon quilt." | | Told by teacher to be quiet and got his desk moved farther away from other students. | Avoids writing |
| **Math lessons** | | | |
| Stuck his tongue out at Amy because she was asked to turn on the lights. | | Teacher conferenced with both students. | Gets emotional stimulation |
| Shouted answer at teacher. | | Teacher told him to stop shouting at her. | Gets emotional stimulation |
| Constantly continued to disrupt lesson by jumping around his desk/making noises/bothering other students. | | Redirected by teacher two different times, and she also threatened to talk to his parents after school. | Gets emotional stimulation |
| Continued to disrupt class by smacking his shoes together loudly. | | Finally he was sent into the hall until the lesson was over. | Gets emotional stimulation |
| Ran a figure eight around the entire classroom. | Direct instruction | Teacher told him to sit down. He replied by saying he was trying to find the garbage can. | Gets self-determination—power over teacher and peer attention |
| Threw pencil across the room and then proceeded to dive from his desk to retrieve it. | | Teacher asked him if she should invite his parents in to see his behavior. | Avoids math |
| Collected garbage off the ground and then held it in front of the air conditioner in order to make it fly in the air. | While in the hall | Teacher was in the classroom teaching the rest of the math lesson. | Avoids math and gets stimulation |

## Setting 2: Transition (from carpet to seat, seat to carpet, walking in hall)

| Behavior | Antecedent | Consequence | Payoff |
|---|---|---|---|
| Jumped on other students. | During transition to writing | Teacher did not notice. | Gets stimulation-activity/play or avoids writing |

| Behavior | Antecedent | Consequence | Payoff |
|---|---|---|---|
| Collected garbage from the floor, then threw the pieces in air like confetti. | Transition to restroom | Teacher didn't notice. | Gets stimulation-play |
| Lost his shoe. | While walking to the restroom | Teacher didn't say anything. | Gets activity/play stimulation |
| After finding his shoe continued to fall down. | In line on the way to the restroom | Teacher didn't say anything. | Gets activity/play stimulation |
| Spun around on the floor when asked to be seated. | Transition to math | Redirected by teacher to return to his seat. | Gets stimulation |
| Barked like a dog. | At desk when asked to clear off his desk | Teacher asked, "Are you a dog?" | Avoids task |
| Fell down several times. | In line to the restroom | Asked by the teacher why he does that, he said nothing, then he later said, "To be stupid." | Gets emotional stimulation |
| Made disturbing and very disruptive noises. | While washing his hands in the restroom | Teacher said nothing. | Gets play stimulation |
| Disrupted teacher's lesson by making gagging noises. | Returning from restroom (he went alone) | Teacher does not address. | Gets emotional stimulation |
| Kicked Jacob and attempted to kick other students as they walked by his desk. | At the end of the day | Teacher told his parents after school. | Gets emotional stimulation |
| Took 3 minutes to put his homework away. | Transition from carpet to desk | Nothing. | Gets self-determination |
| Knocked all his papers off his desk onto the ground; it took him 5 minutes to pick them up. | | Nothing. | Gets emotional stimulation |
| Talked to his hand, as though it were an imaginary friend. | While in line at the restroom | Teacher said nothing. | Gets play stimulation |
| Ran out of the room in excitement. | When asked to go with Mrs. H. | Teacher said nothing. | Gets activity/play stimulation |

### Setting 3: Teacher-Instructed Small Reading Group (with four other students)

| Behavior | Consequence | Payoff |
|---|---|---|
| Stood up while playing tic-tac-toe. | Teacher said nothing. | Gets activity stimulation |
| Tried to help another student sound out a word. | Teacher said nothing. | Gets relatedness |
| Stood often and constantly leaned on the table. | Teacher said nothing. | Gets activity stimulation |
| When another student was reprimanded for getting out of the chair, he shouted that he would watch Donnie to make sure he didn't get out of his seat again. | Teacher stated that she could watch Donnie herself. | Gets competence |

*Antecedents.* Direct instruction and transition seemed to be the most difficult times for Steve. Most of his misbehavior, 45%, occurred during direct instruction (e.g., story time or listening to the teacher, writing lessons, math lessons), and 37% occurred during transitional times (e.g., carpet moving to desks, desks to carpet, between lessons, waiting in line, end of day, getting papers and bags together). Thus, more than 80% of Steve's misbehaviors occurring during these two settings.

*Consequences.* Steve's teacher simply redirected Steve back on task, which lasted for only a few minutes before he fell into some other type of misbehavior. For instance, on September 19 Steve was redirected three times during a math lesson and then finally sent into the hall. The final consequence did not even seem to bother him, based on the fact that he played with garbage in the hallway. Mrs. B. mentioned to me that she had conferenced with his parents on a few occasions already, but it did not seem to make a difference.

*High-frequency payoffs.* Steve is trying to avoid boredom 22% of the time and to get stimulation 62% of the time. Most of the stimulation he is seeking is emotional or activity. He appears to want attention or a reaction from peers (get social/emotional stimulation). However, these responses could also be those of TS and thus may be mislabeled. His avoidance of boredom was trying to get out of mind-numbing work, such as writing the letter $Q$ or reading a story that may not interest him or activities that involved waiting.

## Diagnosis Versus ABC Analysis

Steve is a first-grade general education student who can be observed disrupting the class by talking, making inappropriate noises, moving or bothering others, and inappropriate movement.

**Figure 15.6** Steve's Payoffs

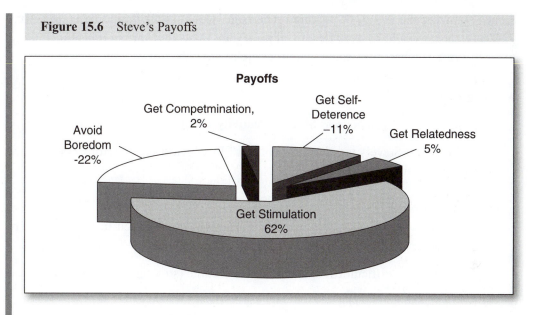

**Payoffs**

Get Competmination, 2%

Get Self-Deterence −11%

Avoid Boredom -22%

Get Relatedness 5%

Get Stimulation 62%

Steve makes animal noises or gagging sounds. For instance, he shouted out "Balloon quilt" while doing seatwork and started barking like a dog during a transition. Gagging noises also seemed to be an issue. These types of behavior are consistent with vocal tic disorder. Steve also may have difficulty inhibiting motor responses (moving inappropriately); he may feel compelled to touch other children or perform specific action sequences (e.g., "Spinning in his chair or running a figure eight around the room in the middle of a lesson was observed on a regular basis"). As well, talking out of turn is routine for Steve. It appears that Steve wants to ensure that everyone is listening to him, including the teacher. However, this may be related to TS.

There is some evidence of co-occurring ADHD, the hyperactive/impulsive subtype. When Steve was not entertained by the teacher's lesson, he seemed to quickly look for other forms of stimulation; this accounted for 63% of his behavior. Steve attempts to interact with other students by talking to them, by fighting, by throwing garbage on them, or by playing with other students' shirts. However, it is unclear whether these types of behavior are related to TS or ADHD. It is clear that Steve has characteristics of TS, and this would be the first diagnosis to consider.

## Interventions Derived From ABC Analysis

Some interventions to try first with Steve are peer tutoring, since he seemed to take pleasure in the small-group interaction with his teacher during literacy stations and he also seemed to like helping students. This might also help him make more friends, and it would allow him to be in control of the activity. Assigning him special chores, such as organizing the library or picking up garbage, would allow him to be more active. These chores would be most beneficial if they are to be done during transitional times or *before* Steve begins to show inappropriate motor behavior.

## Case Questions

*1:* How would you address Steve's creativity strength?

*2:* What are Steve's vocal and motor tics? In which tasks or settings does Steve emit vocal tics?

*3:* Could Steve have fine or gross motor difficulties? What is your evidence?

*4:* What is the emotional immaturity that might be observed in Steve? Is there evidence as well of cognitive maturity?

*5:* Steve has difficulties with direct instruction (structured). How would you explain this?

*6 (problem-based small-group assignment):* In which setting(s) does Steve show the greatest approach to tasks? In other words, what motivates Steve? In which setting(s) does he show the greatest avoidance of tasks? How could his teacher accommodate for these problems?

*7 (problem-based small-group assignment):* Review the case study of Elliot in Chapter 5 and see if you can find characteristics in Elliot of a tic disorder or TS. How is Elliot's expression of these tics similar to and different from Steve's case?

### CASE STUDY 15.2: SETH

(adapted from an assignment submitted by Amy Wilson)

*Background.* Seth is 6 years old and currently a first grader. Seth's mother is single and raises him and his siblings. Seth loves to swing, draw, and play with other children on the playground. Seth is considered mildly mentally disabled (MID) and has also been diagnosed with a speech communication disorder. However, "communication disorder" does not fully explain the nature of his problems. It is clear that Seth struggles; he has unusually long pauses between syllables and will replace difficult sounds with easier syllables.

On a regular basis Seth can be observed ignoring directions. Destroying materials and pushing away in his chair are also most frequently observed behaviors. Seth appears to do these behaviors as a way to avoid the task on hand. When he begins to go off track, he also begins to "doodle" or purposely mark up his paper.

*Behavioral Log*

### Handwriting Day 1

a. Started off well with handwriting, following directions and interacting well with classmate.

b. Seth quickly lost interest and began scribbling in his book with his pencil.
   - Paraprofessional took notice and asked Seth to stop and hand over his book.
   - Seth said no and started to scribble harder in his book.
   - Paraprofessional seized book from Seth.

c. The paraprofessional asked Seth to work on something else.
   - Seth refused and said he wanted to play.

d. Seth climbed onto the desk on all fours.
   - Paraprofessional verbally warned Seth to remove himself from the desk; warned him of time-out and set the timer for a 2-minute warning.

e. Seth was asked to get back into his chair.
   - While on the desk, Seth kicked away his chair.
   - Paraprofessional guided Seth into his chair.

f. Seth was asked again to get to work and stay busy.
   - Seth repeatedly ignored her requests.
   - When he did work on something, he would rush through it and turn in sloppy results.
   - Rushed through work to get done faster.

g. Seth began to crumple paper and destroy his materials.
   - Paraprofessional told Seth to stop and reminded him of the timer for time-out.

h. Seth soon got back to work and began working properly.

i. Soon after, Seth began flipping his pencil (i.e. tapping, flipping in fingers, throwing on table).
   - Paraprofessional asked Seth to stop; requests were ignored.

### Handwriting Day 2

a. Started worksheet with eagerness.
   - Seth sat still, traced his picture well, and interacted with teacher.

b. After 2 minutes, Seth quickly lost interest, picked up a pencil, and attempted to throw it at the paraprofessional.
   - Paraprofessional warned Seth about his behavior and asked him to get to work.

c. Seth flipped around in his chair facing away from the paraprofessional.

- Paraprofessional warned Seth about his behavior and asked him to turn around in his chair four times; each request was ignored by Seth.

d. Seth got up from his chair and climbed onto the desk on all fours.

- Paraprofessional warned Seth about his behavior and set timer for 2-minute warning.

e. Attempted to throw pencil at the paraprofessional.

- Warned about 2-minute warning before time-out.

f. Seth got down from desk and said he could do what he wanted; began to crumple up worksheets and destroy materials.

- Timer went off.
- Paraprofessional ignored behavior and began to place Seth into time-out without making a visible response.

### Handwriting Day 3

a. Was able to get back to work; told the paraprofessional he was tired.

b. Seth asked the paraprofessional if he could work independently at another desk.

c. Seth worked for a bit but quickly regressed and began scribbling on paper, purposely going outside of lines.

- Seth turned paper over and began destroying back side with same behavior.
- Paraprofessional told Seth to stop.

d. Seth refused other work, saying he is not going to listen; crumpled paper and threw it at the paraprofessional.

## ABC Analysis

Avoidance of handwriting is Seth's major payoff (see Figure 15.3, above). A majority of consequences for this behavior were attempts to redirect him back to his work. Seth, at times, would be successfully redirected, but for only a few minutes. Mostly Seth ignored the directions and continued or increased his behavior.

## Diagnosis Versus ABC Analysis

Seth's ABC analysis supports his diagnosis of speech disorder—specifically the diagnosis of dyspraxia. However, Seth has another disability; he also has dysgraphia. In other words, he has difficulty with the fine motor tasks of both speaking and writing.

Because Seth has difficulty with fine motor skills, he avoids writing or quickly becomes frustrated. Seth knows what he wants to communicate but has trouble expressing it. He struggles in combining words, taking unusually long pauses, and will replace difficult sounds with easier syllables.

The school has an intervention plan but not an accommodation plan for Seth. He attends occupational therapy for fine motor skills once a week, adaptive PE once a week for flexibility through yoga, physical therapy every other week, and speech therapy twice a week. Intervention involves practice; unfortunately, in the area of handwriting, it does not improve his skills.

## Case Questions

1: Is there evidence that Seth has other motor problems aside from handwriting?

2 (problem-based small-group assignment): Why are there only interventions for Seth? What accommodations would you put into place?

3: What is your evaluation of the consequences that Seth is receiving in terms of their effectiveness?

# Appendix I

*Council for Exceptional Children (CEC) Standards for Core Competencies Represented in This Text (CEC, 1998)*

**Standard II**  Development and Characteristics of Learners

| Knowledge (chapter subtopics addressing the standard; italics represent special emphasis) | | *Chapters Addressing Standard II* | | | | | | | | | | | | | | |
|---|---|---|---|---|---|---|---|---|---|---|---|---|---|---|---|---|
| | | 1 | 2 | 3 | 4 | 5 | 6 | 7 | 8 | 9 | 10 | 11 | 12 | 13 | 14 | 15 |
| **Typical and atypical human growth and development**<br><br>Chapter 1: Group Norms: Societal Definitions<br><br>Other chapters: Formal Identification (*Etiology*; Prevalence, Gender, *Age,* and Cultural Factors) | CC2K1 | ✓ | | ✓ | ✓ | ✓ | ✓ | ✓ | ✓ | ✓ | ✓ | ✓ | ✓ | ✓ | ✓ | ✓ |
| **Educational implications and characteristics of various exceptionalities**<br><br>Informal Educator Identification of Characteristics (Behavioral; Social-Emotional; Cognitive; Communication; Academic) | CC2K2 | ✓ | | ✓ | ✓ | ✓ | ✓ | ✓ | ✓ | ✓ | ✓ | ✓ | ✓ | ✓ | ✓ | ✓ |

*(Continued)*

**Standard II** (Continued)

| Knowledge (chapter subtopics addressing the standard; italics represent special emphasis) | | Chapters Addressing Standard II | | | | | | | | | | | | | | |
|---|---|---|---|---|---|---|---|---|---|---|---|---|---|---|---|---|
| | | 1 | 2 | 3 | 4 | 5 | 6 | 7 | 8 | 9 | 10 | 11 | 12 | 13 | 14 | 15 |
| **Characteristics and effects of the cultural and environmental milieu of the individual with exceptional learning needs and the family**<br><br>Formal Identification (Prevalence, *Gender,* Age, and *Cultural Factors*) | CC2K3 | | | ✓ | ✓ | ✓ | ✓ | ✓ | ✓ | ✓ | ✓ | ✓ | ✓ | ✓ | ✓ | ✓ |
| **Family systems and role of families in supporting development**<br><br>Disability in the Classroom (Implications for Interventions in Small-Group and *Individual Settings*: Tiers II and III) | CC2K4 | | | | | | | | | | | ✓ | ✓ | ✓ | ✓ | |
| **Similarities and differences among individual with and without exceptional learning needs**<br><br>Formal Identification (Definitions) | CC2K5 | | | ✓ | ✓ | ✓ | ✓ | ✓ | ✓ | ✓ | ✓ | ✓ | ✓ | ✓ | ✓ | ✓ |
| **Similarities and differences among individual with exceptional learning needs**<br><br>Formal Identification (Definitions: *Possible Co-Occurring Conditions*) | CC2K6 | | | | | ✓ | ✓ | ✓ | ✓ | ✓ | ✓ | ✓ | ✓ | ✓ | ✓ | ✓ |
| **Effects of various medications on individuals with exceptional learning needs**<br><br>Disability in the Classroom (Implications for Interventions in Small-Group and Individual Settings: Tiers II and *III*) | CC2K7 | | | | | | | | | ✓ | ✓ | ✓ | ✓ | ✓ | ✓ | |

## Standard III  Individual Learning Differences

| Knowledge (chapter subtopics addressing the standard; italics represent special emphasis) | | Chapters Addressing Standard III | | | | | | | | | | | | | | |
|---|---|---|---|---|---|---|---|---|---|---|---|---|---|---|---|---|
| | | 1 | 2 | 3 | 4 | 5 | 6 | 7 | 8 | 9 | 10 | 11 | 12 | 13 | 14 | 15 |
| **Effects exceptional conditions can have on an individual's life**<br><br>Informal Educator Identification of Characteristics<br><br>*Summary of Strengths and Needs*<br><br>Disability in the Classroom (*Long-Term Outcomes*) | CC3K1 | | | ✓ | ✓ | ✓ | ✓ | ✓ | ✓ | ✓ | ✓ | ✓ | ✓ | ✓ | ✓ | ✓ |
| **Impact of learner's academic and social abilities, attitudes, interests and values on instruction and career development**<br><br>Disability in the Classroom (Implications for Interventions in Small-Group and Individual Settings: Tiers II and III) | CC3K2 | | | ✓ | ✓ | ✓ | ✓ | ✓ | ✓ | ✓ | ✓ | ✓ | ✓ | ✓ | ✓ | ✓ |

## Standard IV  Instructional Strategies

| Knowledge (chapter subtopics addressing the standard; italics represent special emphasis) | | Chapters Addressing Standard IV | | | | | | | | | | | | | | |
|---|---|---|---|---|---|---|---|---|---|---|---|---|---|---|---|---|
| | | 1 | 2 | 3 | 4 | 5 | 6 | 7 | 8 | 9 | 10 | 11 | 12 | 13 | 14 | 15 |
| **Select, adapt, and use instructional strategies and materials according** | CC4S3 | | | ✓ | ✓ | ✓ | ✓ | ✓ | ✓ | ✓ | ✓ | ✓ | ✓ | ✓ | ✓ | ✓ |

*(Continued)*

## Standard IV  (Continued)

| Knowledge (chapter subtopics addressing the standard; italics represent special emphasis) | | Chapters Addressing Standard IV | | | | | | | | | | | | | |
|---|---|---|---|---|---|---|---|---|---|---|---|---|---|---|---|
| **to characteristics of the individual with exceptional learning needs.**<br><br>Disability in the Classroom (*Implications for Accommodations* in General Education Settings: Tier I; *Implications for Interventions* in Small-Group and Individual Settings: Tiers II and III) | | | | | | | | | | | | | | | |

## Standard V   Learning Environments/Social Interactions

| Knowledge (chapter subtopics addressing the standard; italics represent special emphasis) | | Chapters Addressing Standard V | | | | | | | | | | | | | |
|---|---|---|---|---|---|---|---|---|---|---|---|---|---|---|
| | | *1* | *2* | *3* | *4* | *5* | *6* | *7* | *8* | *9* | *10* | *11* | *12* | *13* | *14* | *15* |
| **Create a safe, equitable, positive, and supporting learning environment in which diversities are valued.**<br>Chapter Summary<br>*Chapter Questions*<br>*Problem-Based Case Applications and Questions* | CC5S1 | | | ✓ | ✓ | ✓ | ✓ | ✓ | ✓ | ✓ | ✓ | ✓ | ✓ | ✓ | ✓ | ✓ |
| **Design learning environments that encourage active participation in individual and group settings.**<br>Chapter Summary<br>*Chapter Questions*<br>*Problem-Based Case Applications and Questions* | CC564 | | | ✓ | ✓ | ✓ | ✓ | ✓ | ✓ | ✓ | ✓ | ✓ | ✓ | ✓ | ✓ | ✓ |

| Knowledge (chapter subtopics addressing the standard; italics represent special emphasis) | | Chapters Addressing Standard V | | | | | | | | | | | | | | |
|---|---|---|---|---|---|---|---|---|---|---|---|---|---|---|---|---|
| | | 1 | 2 | 3 | 4 | 5 | 6 | 7 | 8 | 9 | 10 | 11 | 12 | 13 | 14 | 15 |
| **Use the least intensive behavior management strategy consistent with the needs of the individual with exceptional needs.**<br><br>Disability in the Classroom (*Implications for Accommodations* in General Education Settings: Tier I; *Implications for Interventions* in Small-Group and Individual Settings: Tiers II and III)<br><br>Chapter Summary<br><br>*Chapter Questions*<br><br>*Problem-Based Case Applications and Questions* | CC5S11 | | | ✓ | ✓ | ✓ | ✓ | ✓ | ✓ | ✓ | ✓ | ✓ | ✓ | ✓ | ✓ | ✓ |

## Standard VI    Language

| Knowledge (chapter subtopics addressing the standard; italics represent special emphasis) | | Chapters Addressing Standard VI | | | | | | | | | | | | | | |
|---|---|---|---|---|---|---|---|---|---|---|---|---|---|---|---|---|
| | | 1 | 2 | 3 | 4 | 5 | 6 | 7 | 8 | 9 | 10 | 11 | 12 | 13 | 14 | 15 |
| **Effects of cultural and linguistic differences on growth and development**<br><br>Informal Educator Identification of Characteristics (Behavioral; Social-Emotional; Cognitive; *Communication*; Academic) | CC6K1 | | | ✓ | ✓ | ✓ | ✓ | ✓ | ✓ | ✓ | ✓ | ✓ | ✓ | ✓ | ✓ | ✓ |
| **Augmentative and assistive communication strategies** | CC6K4 | | | ✓ | ✓ | ✓ | ✓ | ✓ | ✓ | ✓ | ✓ | ✓ | ✓ | ✓ | ✓ | ✓ |

*(Continued)*

## Standard VI  (Continued)

| Knowledge (chapter subtopics addressing the standard; italics represent special emphasis) | | Chapters Addressing Standard VI | | | | | | | | | | | | | |
|---|---|---|---|---|---|---|---|---|---|---|---|---|---|---|---|
| | | 1 | 2 | 3 | 4 | 5 | 6 | 7 | 8 | 9 | 10 | 11 | 12 | 13 | 14 | 15 |
| Disability in the Classroom (*Implications for Accommodations* in General Education Settings: Tier I; *Implications for Interventions* in Small-Group and Individual Settings: Tiers II and III) | | | | | | | | | | | | | | | | |

## Standard VII    Instructional Planning

| Knowledge (chapter subtopics addressing the standard; italics represent special emphasis) | | Chapters Addressing Standard VII | | | | | | | | | | | | | |
|---|---|---|---|---|---|---|---|---|---|---|---|---|---|---|---|
| | | 1 | 2 | 3 | 4 | 5 | 6 | 7 | 8 | 9 | 10 | 11 | 12 | 13 | 14 | 15 |
| **Use functional assessments to develop intervention plans.** <br><br> Chapter Summary <br><br> *Chapter Questions* <br><br> *Problem-Based Case Applications and Questions* | CC7S4 | | ✓ | ✓ | ✓ | ✓ | ✓ | ✓ | ✓ | ✓ | ✓ | ✓ | ✓ | ✓ | ✓ | ✓ |
| **Use task analysis.** <br><br> Functional Analysis of Antecedents, Behavior, Consequences, and Payoffs <br><br> Chapter Summary <br><br> *Chapter Questions* <br><br> *Problem-Based Case Applications and Questions* | CC7S5 | ✓ | | | | | | | | | | | | | | |

# Appendix II

*Data for Case Study 11.1: Lily ("She shouted, 'NO!'") (adapted from an assignment submitted by Jia Liu)*

*Background.* The S Preschool has two classrooms. One is for 3-year-old children and the other is for 4-year-olds. Usually there are around 10 children in the morning in the 3-year-old class; 7 of the children come from China, and the others come from countries such as Egypt and Puerto Rico. In the classroom there are four little tables with several chairs where children sit to do art projects, to play with blocks or puzzles, and to have snacks. The classroom also has a rug area where they play with toys, listen to instructions, and read books. Other items in the classroom are a cage in which a big white rabbit is kept and a little house that imitates a home with furniture. Mary is the young female American teacher of this class. Two adult assistants are also in the class every day. Among the Chinese children, Lily is the only girl. She is the only child of her family.

## Setting 1: Free Play Time

| Antecedent | Behavior | Observable Consequence | Payoff |
|---|---|---|---|
| **Day 1** | | | |
| When Lily entered the room in the morning. | She said "No!" to the first child she met. | No one said anything about it. | Gain emotional stimulation |
| A boy just began drawing on a piece of paper. | She pointed at the boy and shouted "No" to him repeatedly. | Was not noticed. | Gain emotional stimulation |

*(Continued)*

(Continued)

| Antecedent | Behavior | Observable Consequence | Payoff |
|---|---|---|---|
| Mary came to the table to ask if Lily also wanted to draw on a piece of paper: "Do you want the paper? You should say 'Thank You.'" | She said: "Thank you." | No response. | Gain competence |
| When Lily was sitting on a chair about to draw, Mary asked: "Do you want me to put the feather in your mailbox?" | She said, "No." | Mary put the feather away. | Gain self-determination |
| In the middle of drawing she began stripping the paper on the crayon. "Do you need help?" Mary asked. | She did not respond. | Mary put the stripped pieces aside. | Gain self-determination |
| While drawing. | She was humming to herself. | No response. | Gain sensory/ activity stimulation |
| A boy next to her was holding his drawing. | She shouted "No" repeatedly to the boy. | No response. | Gain emotional stimulation |
| The boy tried to hit her hand. | She intentionally put her hand on the table in front of the boy and pulled back quickly to make him unable to touch her. | No response. | Gain emotional/ play stimulation |
| While drawing. | She hit the paper with a crayon. | No response | Gain activity stimulation |
| A boy was holding two toys in his hands. | She shouted to the boy and pointed to the horse toy and shouted something and then pointed to the carpet where most toys were put. | The boy looked down at his toys. | Gain self-determination |
| A crying boy was held by Mary and was doing some puzzles. | Lily came to the boy and began to play with his puzzles. | She was told by Mary to go back to coloring a kangaroo. | Gain play stimulation<br><br>Gain relatedness |
| A crying boy was held by Mary and was doing some puzzles. | She came to puzzles very soon and said "No" to the boy and kept talking about how to do it. | The boy cried again. | Gain self-determination |

| Antecedent | Behavior | Observable Consequence | Payoff |
|---|---|---|---|
| The boy cried again. | She took the puzzles to the drawer where they belong. | No response. | Gain self-determination |
| Free play time. | She shouted "No" to a boy and hit him. | She was stopped by Mary. | Gain emotional stimulation |
| Doing arts. | She grabbed a glue. | An assistant tried to get it back. | Gain tangible stimulation |
| An assistant tried to get it back. | She held it tight to herself. | The assistant got the glue from her. | Gain self-determination |
| A boy was holding a paper with animals on it. | She shouted "Put it down" and scratched him. | She was punished to sit by the wall individually. | Gain self-determination |
| She was punished to sit by the wall individually. | She quickly apologized: "Sorry, sorry." | She was still required to sit by the wall. | Avoid punishment<br>Avoid boredom |
| She was still required to sit by the wall. | Very soon she went back to a table. | She was taken back by an assistant. | Gain activity stimulation |
| While drawing. | She was talking and humming to herself and said "done" loudly when she finished. | No response. | Gain activity/sensory stimulation<br>Gain competence |
| In the middle of playing interlocking blocks. | She shouted and jumped. | No response. | Gain activity stimulation |
| After connecting the blocks. | She shouted "Na—" to the teacher to get her to see it. | Mary turned around and said, "Beautiful." | Gain competence<br>Gain relatedness |
| Mary turned around and said, "Beautiful." | Lily jumped for a while. | No response. | Gain activity stimulation |
| A boy was holding several pieces of puzzles. | She said "No" to him and shouted something to him. | No response. | Gain emotional stimulation |
| Free play time. | She held blocks in the shape of a flower and sang "green flowers" and put it in front of everyone in the room and asked, "Do you want flowers?" | One boy wanted to get it. | Gain play stimulation |

*(Continued)*

(Continued)

| Antecedent | Behavior | Observable Consequence | Payoff |
|---|---|---|---|
| One boy wanted to get it. | She pulled it back and said "no." | No response. | Gain emotional/ play stimulation |
| Free play time. | She used a "plane" made by blocks to hit other boys. | She was told to say sorry. She said it. | Gain relatedness<br>Gain play stimulation |
| **Day 2** | | | |
| She put two little plastic toy bears in a box. The girl next to her tried to see what was inside the box. | She shouted "No." | She was reprimanded by Mary, who called, "Lily." | Avoid relatedness |
| While playing with the toys. | She and another girl hit their heads together. She then walked to the other side of the girl and picked up a toy and threw it to the girl. Then she threw several more toys to her. | The girl yelled. Mary came to ask Lily to say sorry. | Gain emotional stimulation |
| The girl yelled. Mary came to ask Lily to say sorry. | She refused by saying no. | No response. | Gain self-determination |
| Playing. | She took a toy bear from the girl and held it tightly. | The girl tried to get it back. | Gain emotional stimulation |
| The girl tried to get it back. | Lily ran away. | The girl cried. Mary came and managed to get the bear out of her hand and taught her not to take bears from others and keep them to herself. | Gain emotional stimulation<br>Gain play stimulation |
| While she was playing next to the girl. | She shouted "No" repeatedly as if the girl wanted to grab her bears. She put one bear in front of the girl and grabbed it to herself and shouted "No." | Was not noticed. | Gain activity stimulation<br>Gain emotional stimulation |
| While playing. | She grabbed a little box from the hand of an assistant. | The assistant called, "Lily." | Gain self-determination |

| Antecedent | Behavior | Observable Consequence | Payoff |
|---|---|---|---|
| While playing. | She then came between the assistant and another girl and yelled for a while. | The assistant called, "Lily." | Gain sensory stimulation |
| An assistant was playing toys with two girls on another table. | She took two toys from their table. She connected the toys together and put them on the previous table with different toys. | No response. | Gain activity stimulation |
| Mary was cutting a spider out of paper for preparation of their arts today. | Lily came to Mary and put a picture of a spider on the floor. | Mary asked her to pick it up. She did so. | Gain activity/ play stimulation |
| A girl was also there watching Mary cutting things. | Lily shouted "Away" repeatedly to the girl. | She was reprimanded by Mary. | Avoid relatedness |
| Arts time. | She watched a girl sticking pieces of paper with different shapes together to make a spider. | Mary asked if she wanted to make one by herself. | Gain sensory stimulation |
| Mary asked if she wanted to make one by herself. | She walked back with smile. | Mary asked again. | Avoid task |
| Mary asked again. | She pulled out a chair and sat on it with smile. | Mary helped her make a spider. | Gain competence |
| She was asked by Mary to draw a spider web following an example. | She drew the example. | She was complimented by Mary. | Gain competence |
| Play and art time. | She said something to herself and jumped. | No response. | Gain activity/ sensory stimulation |
| Play and art time. | She watched a boy making a spider and pointed where to stick the feet. | Mary told her to go play and let others finish by themselves several times. | Gain relatedness |
| Mary told her to go play and let others finish by themselves several times. | She turned back every time and would not leave. | No response. | Gain self-determination |

*(Continued)*

(Continued)

| Antecedent | Behavior | Observable Consequence | Payoff |
|---|---|---|---|
| Play and art time. | She laughed at the boy when he scribbled lots of black circles at random where a net was supposed to be drawn. | No response. | Gain emotional stimulation |
| Play and art time. | She pushed a little chair around the room. | Mary asked her to stop. She stopped. | Gain activity stimulation |
| A boy chewed a little toy bear. | She said, "NO . . . in your mouth" twice to him. | An assistant told the boy not to put toys in his mouth. | Gain relatedness |
| When she saw a boy put a bear in a tiny little box. | She smiled and said, "Ya . . ." | No response. | Gain play/sensory stimulation |
| Play time. | She played with balls on the rug and threw them into the small house through the window. | She was stopped by Mary and was asked to get them back. She did so. | Gain activity stimulation |
| A boy was trying to glue a spider. | She pointed on the boy's paper. | She was asked by Mary twice to leave. | Gain play stimulation<br>Gain relatedness |
| Play time | She put a little toy box twice to the boy doing the spider. | Mary got a box from her. | Gain relatedness<br>Gain emotional/play stimulation |
| Mary held her hand and asked if she wanted to play with two other girls and the assistant. | She refused all. | Then Mary asked where she wanted to play. | Gain self-determination |
| Then Mary asked where she wanted to play. | She pointed to the boy doing the spider. | No response. | Gain self-determination |
| Play time | She walked around the room and shook the cage of the rabbit. | She was told by Mary to stop. | Gain activity stimulation |
| Some boys were shouting something not nice in Chinese. | She shouted "No" to them and ran away. | Mary asked one of the boys if he was saying something impolite. | Gain self-determination |

| Antecedent | Behavior | Observable Consequence | Payoff |
|---|---|---|---|
| While playing with another girl in the small house. | She said something not understandable. | No response | Gain sensory stimulation |
| Play time | She pushed a girl's belly. | The girl tried to avoid her. | Gain relatedness<br>Gain tangible/ play stimulation |
| The girl tried to avoid her. | She followed the girl and grabbed her arms. | She was stopped by an assistant. The assistant held her and told her how to behave. | Gain relatedness<br>Gain tangible/ play stimulation |
| The assistant held her and told her how to behave. | She tried to get out of the assistant's hands and shouted "No." | She said "sorry" finally as the assistant told her to do. | Avoid relatedness<br>Gain self-determination |
| A boy played near her while she was lying there. | She hit the boy's knee with a toy car. | She was told by the assistant to say sorry and she did. | Gain activity stimulation<br>Gain relatedness |
| She was asked by the assistant if she wanted to play with the puzzle. | She said "No." | No response. | Gain self-determination |
| A boy was sitting on a chair and doing the spider. | She tried to climb on the boy's chair. | She was told by Mary not to sit on another's chair and she nodded. | Gain activity stimulation<br>Gain relatedness |
| Two girls were playing with toy bears by a table. | She took away a toy bear from the table. | They did not respond. | Gain negative emotional stimulation |
| They did not respond. | She grabbed two more bears and ran away. | The two girls said "No" and held the rest of the bears in their arms. | Gain negative emotional stimulation |
| A girl was doing a puzzle. | She grabbed one piece of puzzle from the girl. | The girl shouted. Mary got the puzzle back from her. | Gain negative emotional stimulation |

## *Setting 2: Group Instruction*

| Antecedent | Behavior | Observable Consequence | Payoff |
|---|---|---|---|
| **Day 1** | | | |
| Group instruction. | She touched the braids of another girl. | The girl shook her head to avoid her. She was held by an assistant in her arms. | Gain relatedness Gain tangible stimulation |
| Mary was giving instructions about baby animals. | She shouted, "What is that?" | Mary answered her question. | Gain relatedness Gain competence |
| Group instruction. | She got out of the assistant's arms and talked to a girl. | No response. | Gain play stimulation Gain relatedness |
| Children sat and sang with Mary. | Lily took off her shoes, then lay down, then got up and shook her head heavily. | She stood up and turned around. | Gain activity stimulation |
| Group instruction. | She sang ABC song with others well. | No response. | Gain competence |
| **Day 2** | | | |
| Children were singing. | She shook her head heavily and tried to turn around and stand up. | She was held by an assistant in her arms. | Gain activity stimulation |
| Instruction began. | She looked at the book in Mary's hand and listened carefully and said something in the process. | No response. | Gain competence Gain sensory stimulation |
| Instruction | She came to a boy and put her face close to him. | She was stopped by the assistant immediately. | Gain relatedness |
| Mary showed the pictures to them and asked what the animals are. | She first shouted, "Pig, dog, cat, duck." | No response. | Gain competence |
| **Day 3** | | | |
| While children were sitting on the rug waiting for the instruction. | She said to the boy who cries every morning when his mother leaves that his mother would come to pick him up and do not be sad in Chinese. | She was told by Mary to stop talking. She said, "Okay." | Gain relatedness |

| Antecedent | Behavior | Observable Consequence | Payoff |
|---|---|---|---|
| Mary showed animals' pictures with songs describing animals. | She asked a boy in Chinese what happened to the turtle they just saw in the book during instruction period. | Mary asked her to stop talking. | Gain relatedness Gain competence |
| Mary taught them to say "Go, go, go" with a picture and music from the recorder. | Lily lay on the rug and stretched out her legs high. | An assistant called her to stop. | Gain activity stimulation |
| The music stopped and Mary showed them pictures and gave instructions. | Lily crawled. | She was stopped by an assistant, who called her name. | Gain activity stimulation |
| A boy sat quite close to her. | She touched his back and put her face quite close to his and said something in Chinese about the picture in Mary's hand. | Mary said, "Lily." She stopped. | Gain play stimulation Gain relatedness |
| The boy moved away from her. | She tried to reach him. | She was held by an assistant in her arms. | Gain relatedness |
| When the instruction was over. | She followed the boy crawling around the rug and touched him and helped him get his shoes. | No response. | Gain play stimulation Gain relatedness |

## Setting 3: Snack

| Antecedent | Behavior | Observable Consequence | Payoff |
|---|---|---|---|
| **Day 1** | | | |
| A boy was holding his napkin. | She shouted to the boy. | Some other boys shouted following her. | Gain emotional stimulation |
| Snack. | She drank and ate quietly and later talked and hummed to herself. | No response. | Gain sensory stimulation |
| Snack. | She held up her cup and said, "I don't have juice" in Chinese. | Mary taught her to say, "More juice, please" and she did it. | Gain relatedness |

*(Continued)*

(Continued)

| Antecedent | Behavior | Observable Consequence | Payoff |
|---|---|---|---|
| Snack. | She dropped the rest of the juice on the napkin and ate a little bit of the wet napkin and threw it up immediately. | No response. | Gain sensory stimulation<br><br>Gain activity stimulation |
| Snack. | She put the rest of her cereal by the boy next to her and asked him to eat hers. | He did not notice her. | Gain relatedness |
| Snack. | She cleaned her trash by herself. | No response. | Gain competence |
| **Day 2** | | | |
| Snack. | She ate quietly and then said something to the boys at the same table in Chinese. | No response. | Gain relatedness |
| Snack. | She pointed to the juice and made a sound. | She was told by the assistant to say, "More please," and she did so. | Gain relatedness |
| She and a boy threw their trash at the same time. | She, with smile, shouted "Woo" to the boy. | No response. | Gain play stimulation |
| **Day 3** | | | |
| The boy next to her said he had no more cookies in Chinese. | She gave half of her cookie to him. | Was not noticed. | Gain relatedness |
| After her snack. | She came to a boy and kissed his head and smelled it and came to smell another boy's head. | She was stopped by an assistant, who told her to read on the rug. | Gain sensory stimulation<br><br>Gain relatedness |

## Setting 4: Reading Plus Other Activities

| Antecedent | Behavior | Observable Consequence | Payoff |
|---|---|---|---|
| **Day 1** | | | |
| A girl came near her while she was reading. | She said "No" to the girl and stretched out her arms to keep her away. | No response. | Avoid relatedness |

| Antecedent | Behavior | Observable Consequence | Payoff |
|---|---|---|---|
| Mary was reading stories to several children. | She came to touch Mary. | No response. | Gain relatedness |
| Mary was reading stories to several children. | She pulled the cotton out of a broken chair with another child. | She was stopped by Mary. | Gain play stimulation Gain tangible stimulation |
| Mary was reading stories to several children. | She asked a boy to sit down on the chair. | He did not listen to her. | Gain self-determination |
| He did not listen to her. | She tried to grab him. | He avoided her. | Gain relatedness Gain self-determination |
| Reading time. | She jumped up off the carpet and played with other toys and then fought with a boy. | Asked by an assistant to say sorry. | Gain activity/ emotional stimulation |
| Asked by an assistant to say sorry. | She shouted, "NO!" | She was asked again by Mary and she said sorry. | Gain self-determination |
| Little instruction: Mary gave some instructions and the children were required to sit on their bottoms. | She jumped. | She was stopped and sat down quietly. | Gain activity stimulation |
| Little instruction. | She took off her shoes and threw them in the air and jumped again. | She was taken to sit in a corner. | Gain activity stimulation |
| The instruction finished. | She shouted, "Where are my shoes?" | No response. | Gain relatedness |
| **Day 2** | | | |
| After she did some reading. | She touched the heads of three boys. | No response. | Gain relatedness Gain tangible/play stimulation |
| Reading time began. | She climbed on Mary's chair. | Mary asked her to get off. | Gain activity stimulation |
| Mary asked her to get off. | She said, "No." | Mary picked her up off the chair. | Gain self-determination |

*(Continued)*

(Continued)

| Antecedent | Behavior | Observable Consequence | Payoff |
|---|---|---|---|
| Reading time was over. | She helped organize the bookshelf. | She was complimented by Mary. | Gain competence |
| Dancing: Mary gave instructions on how to dance with the music from the recorder. | She danced as Mary told them to do. | No response. | Gain competence |
| Dancing time. | She did some extra actions at will. | She was stopped by the assistant most of the time. | Gain activity stimulation |

## Setting 5: Playground

| Antecedent | Behavior | Observable Consequence | Payoff |
|---|---|---|---|
| **Day 1** | | | |
| A girl after her was trying to climb up the slide. | She gave her hand to the girl. | The girl pushed her hand aside. | Gain relatedness |
| The girl pushed her hand aside. | She tried to grab the girl's head and shoulder. | The girl kept pushing her away. | Gain relatedness |
| A girl was on the same ladder with her. | She shouted "No" to the girl, "It's mine!" She tried to get the girl's hand off the ladder. | No response. | Avoid relatedness |
| A boy slid down the slide. | She stood by the end of the slide and yelled to him. | No response. | Avoid relatedness |
| A boy wanted to slide down behind her. | She shouted, "No." She did not slide down until he left. | No response. | Avoid relatedness |
| **Day 2** | | | |
| She climbed up the ladder and got into the inner side of the ladder. An assistant came and asked if she needed help. | She said no. | Then the assistant tried to carry her to get up the ladder. | Gain self-determination |
| Then the assistant tried to carry her to get up the ladder. | She shouted, "No help." | The assistant said, "Okay, okay, I'm not helping." | Gain self-determination |

| Antecedent | Behavior | Observable Consequence | Payoff |
|---|---|---|---|
| On a slide. | She pushed a girl who was in front of her on the slide to hurry her to slide down quickly. | No response. | Gain self-determination |
| While playing. | She pushed a girl's belly. | Mary said, "No, Lily." Lily said, "Sorry." | Gain relatedness<br>Gain tangible/play stimulation |
| **Day 3** | | | |
| While children were waiting to go play outside. | She pushed a boy. | Mary put her to sit on a chair and go out last for punishment. | Gain emotional stimulation |
| Mary made her sit on a chair and go out last for punishment. | She said, "I'll apologize" in Chinese and ran from the chair to the boy and shouted sorry. | Mary thanked her for saying sorry, but still took her back to sit for a little while. | Avoid punishment<br>Avoid boredom |
| While sitting there. | She ran again when she saw Mary did not notice her. | Was not noticed. | Gain activity stimulation |

# Glossary

**AAC:** Augmentative and alternative communication. AAC devices provide technological support for the language that the child has: verbal (speech) or nonverbal/gestural modes of communication (pointing or mechanical output systems) and alternative communication methods that bypass the oral system of communication. (Section II)

**Abreaction:** The release of emotions by acting out; often a reaction against a set of circumstances. (Section III)

**Abstract thinking:** The ability to go beyond visually based concrete events or objects to form visual concepts, such as greater than, and symbols, such as understanding that one thing can represent many. For example, a picture of a chair can represent a chair and a color (e.g., red and green) can represent an action (stop/go). Verbal abstract processing involves making categories, such that a word or group of words can represent an idea (e.g., fairness). (Section III)

**Abstract verbal language:** The degree to which language involves more than the concrete naming of things and moves to descriptions of objects (adjectives), descriptions of actions (adverbs), and use of abstract prepositions, along this continuum: (a) single words—nouns (objects, concepts, categories), verbs (simple verbs, verb tense), adjectives, prepositions; (b) phrases and sentences (following directions); (c) paragraphs and stories; (d) cause and effect, (e) drawing of inferences; (f) fact versus opinion; (g) absurdities and humor; (h) idioms and figures of speech ("on the rocks," "over the hill"). (Section II)

**Accommodations:** Changes in the setting or task that are made by the teacher to bring out optimal responding from the child. (Section I)

**Acquired language disorder:** A type of language disorder in which an impairment occurs after a period of normal development as the result of a neurological or other general medical condition (e.g., encephalitis, irradiation, TBI) (APA, 2000). (Section II)

**Acute:** Immediate and typically short-term. (Section II)

**Adaptive behavior:** Behavior in the areas of practical everyday functioning that are needed to live independently, care for oneself, and interact with others. Adaptive areas include communication, community use, functional academics, school/home living, health and safety, leisure, self-care, self-direction, social interaction, and work. (Section III)

**ADHD:** Attention deficit hyperactivity disorder. (Section II)

**ADHD-HI:** Attention deficit hyperactivity disorder, hyperactive/impulsive subtype. (Section IV)

**ADHD-IN:** Attention deficit hyperactivity disorder, inattentive subtype. (Section IV)

**Affinity system:** A child's family members, friends, neighbors, teachers, and other significant others. (Section V)

**Agoraphobia:** A condition causing fear and avoidance of leaving one's home. (Section V)

**Alpha commands:** Commands that have a clearly stated outcome (e.g., "When you have finished your math homework, you may select one TV program to watch"). (Section V)

**Amnesia:** Loss of memory of immediate or distal events. (Section III)

**Analytic:** Taking apart information; critically breaking information into component parts or logical sequences. (Section III)

**Androgynous:** Having the behavioral or social/emotional characteristics of both gender groups (male and female). (Section III)

**Anhedonia:** The lack of capacity to experience pleasure. (Section V)

**Anomia:** The inability to name objects. *See also* Dysnomia. (Section II)

**Anorexia nervosa:** A condition causing self-starvation. However, as *DSM-IV-TR* points out, "The term *anorexia* is a misnomer because loss of appetite is rare"; APA, 2000, p. 583). (Section V)

**Antecedents:** What precedes a particular behavior (time, setting, task, and so on). (Section I)

**Antisocial:** Against the social order (e.g., breaking social rules). (Section II)

**Apathetic:** Indifferent (without emotion). (Section V)

**Aphasia:** A specific language disorder that involves problems with the structure and formulation of spoken language. (Section II)

**Apraxia:** Lack of ability to plan the motor movements involved in speech. (Section VI)

**Aptitude:** A natural ability or intelligence. Different types of aptitude can be assessed, such as verbal-linguistic, logical-mathematical, musical, spatial, bodily-kinesthetic, interpersonal, intrapersonal, and naturalistic (Gardner, 1983). (Section II)

**Arousal:** Physiological activation of the child, which has trait qualities (inborn individual differences) and state qualities that depend on setting conditions (e.g., number of people in a setting). Arousal cannot be observed, but it can be assessed through psychophysiological measures, such as heart rate and skin conductance, and can be inferred from the amount of stimulation in the setting or the anxiety that the child communicates. (Section I)

**Asperger syndrome (AS):** A syndrome within the autism spectrum disorders category that has been considered a mild form of autism (high-functioning autism). Children with AS have a greater capacity to achieve normal-like behavior and functioning than do children with autism. (Section V)

**Assistive technology:** "An item or piece of equipment or product system acquired commercially, off the shelf, modified, or customized, and used to increase, maintain, or improve functional capability for an individual with a disability" (Beard et al., 2007, p. 4). Provisions for assistive technology are funded by grants to states from the Technology-Related Assistance to Individuals with Disabilities Act of 1968, amended (the Tech Act). (Section I)

**Attentional bias:** Preference for certain types of stimuli. All humans selectively attend to their own names, and most attend to information that signals potential danger (e.g., loud sounds). Students with the inattentive subtype of ADHD are more likely than their peers to selectively attend to novelty (movement, color, emotion, and so on). (Section IV)

**Auditory errors in composition and spelling:** Errors in which the words within sentences, sentences within paragraphs, and ideas within compositions are out of order or poorly organized. Also, sounds, syllables, and words are missing or have omissions, additions, substitutions, or ending errors (agreement, tense, plural, possessives). (Section II)

**Auditory perception:** The ability to identify words/sentences from the sensations of sound. Perception can also require a synthesis or blending of sounds and an analysis or breaking of words into syllables. (Section I)

**Aura:** A somatic or sensory feeling or a motor response that precedes a seizure and acts as a kind of warning. (Section III)

**Autism:** A disorder characterized by severe social, behavioral, and communication deficits and lower IQ than is found in children with Asperger syndrome. The word *autism,* which is derived from the Greek word *autos,* meaning "self," connotes isolation within the self. (Section V)

**Behavior modification:** Strategies aimed at changing behavior that involve the application of learning principles, such as the use of reward. (Section IV)

**Bibliotherapy:** The use of books to reduce anxiety associated with some situations or conditions (e.g., divorce, moving, disability awareness) and to provide a human child model (character in the book) who must problem solve alternative responses to a threatening situation or loss. (Section V)

**Binge:** "A *binge* is defined as eating in a discrete period of time an amount of food that is definitely larger than most individuals would eat under similar circumstances. . . . A 'discrete period of time' refers to a limited period, usually less than 2 hours. A single episode of binge eating need not be restricted to one setting. For example, an individual may begin a binge in a restaurant and then continue it on returning home. Continual snacking on small amounts of food throughout the day would not be considered a binge" (APA, 2000, p. 589). (Section V)

**CD:** Conduct disorder. (Section V)

**Central auditory processing disorders:** Listening disorders that are severe and involve, for example, poor awareness of, attention to, and discrimination of sounds; poor association of sounds with symbols; poor recall of sound sequences; and overall slowed processing rate. (Section II)

**Childhood disintegrative disorder:** A disorder characterized by marked degrees of intellectual disability and loss of previously acquired skills, with losses in language, social skills, and adaptive behavior occurring more gradually (Hagin, 2004). (Section V)

**Chronic:** Persisting over time. Chronic behavioral problems differ from short-term acute behavioral difficulties. (Section IV)

**Circumlocution:** Saying something in a roundabout way (e.g., by describing an object or saying it is like something else rather than actually naming it). (Section II)

**Clinical range:** The level at which a child's disability is severe enough for the child to be labeled and to receive services. (Section II)

**Cognitive behavior modification:** A type of behavior modification that involves instruction in the use of self-talk to modify one's own behavior (e.g., "I am brave," "I am not afraid," "I have a 1, 2, 3 strategy"). (Section V)

**Cognitive distortion:** A bias in interpreting events, typically produced by a set of past experiences (e.g., an expectation of negative or hostile interactions, or failure experiences). This is included within the category of cognitive characteristics because it is a thinking bias. (Section III)

**Community-based learning:** Method of education that uses structured lessons in actual settings (e.g., workplace, home). (Section III)

**Comorbidity:** The occurrence of two or more medical or psychological conditions in a single individual. Clinical professionals use this term when referring to students with co-occurring disorders. (Section II)

**Compensatory behavior:** The reliance by individuals with weaknesses on their stronger areas of functioning. For example, difficulties understanding gestures, tones of voice, and facial expressions can be offset by stronger verbal skills. Such individuals compensate for or work around their weak areas of functioning. (Section I)

**Compliance:** The capacity to delay achieving one's own goals in response to the implicit or stated goals/standards of authority figures (Greene et al., 2002). (Section V)

**Compulsions:** Seemingly purposeful types of behavior that individuals perform to relieve, prevent, or undo the anxiety or discomfort created by their obsessions or to "magically" prevent some dreaded event or situation (Adams, 2004). (Section V)

**Concussion:** The most common brain injury, which generally occurs either when the head accelerates rapidly and then is stopped suddenly or when the head is shaken. (Section III)

**Conditioned fear:** Fear that is learned from observing another person's fearful or avoidant response or from direct experience with a traumatic event (e.g., being bitten by a dog). (Section V)

**Confabulation:** The reporting of events that never happened (e.g., false memories) although the individual describing them believes them to be true events. Confabulation is a way that people with TBI fill in for losses in memory that typically occur in cases involving damage to the frontal lobes of the brain (Garrett, 2011). (Section II)

**Context cues:** The meanings of words and pictures that surround unknown words, which children may use to decode the unknown words and capture meaning. (Section II)

**Contingent:** Dependent upon. For example, giving a child attention specifically when he or she is performing appropriate behavior (e.g., compliance) is giving a reward contingent on compliance behavior. (Section IV)

**Contusion:** Bruising of brain tissues. Contusions of the brain can cause bleeding and toxic effects. (Section III)

**Coprolalia:** Using obscene or socially inappropriate words (cursing); this most disruptive and disturbing of TS symptoms is found in less than 15% of cases and occurs late in childhood (Jay, 2000). (Section VI)

**Copropraxia:** Using obscene or socially inappropriate gestures, similar to coprolalia. (Section VI)

**Correlation:** The positive association of one factor, *A,* with another, *B,* such that the higher the amount of factor *A* (e.g., intelligence), the higher the amount of factor *B* (e.g., achievement). One factor does not necessarily cause the other; the two are simply related. (Section V)

**Cortisol:** A chemical secreted by the body when a person is under chronic stress. (Section V)

**Creativity:** The ability to sustain a wide array of interests, openness to novel experiences and to tangential ideas, and the ability to apply existing knowledge to novel problems. (Section III)

**Cuing/prompting:** The use of cues that precede the desired behavior in time and act as reminders of what is required. (Section II)

**DCD:** Developmental coordination disorder. (Section VI)

**Decoding:** The process of translating visual symbols (letters) into auditory equivalents (sounds and words) or the achievement of accurate and/or fluent word recognition. (Section II)

**Delinquency:** Involvement with the legal system. (Section IV)

**Detailed cue:** A part of the whole (e.g., a tree that is one of many that make up the forest). (Section IV)

**Developmental expressive language disorders:** Language disorders characterized by their appearance at different developmental stages. Children with such disorders "often begin speaking late and progress more slowly than usual through the various stages of expressive language development" (APA, 2000, p. 59). (Section II)

**Developmental tasks:** Accomplishments in life specific to particular ages (e.g., inhibition of activity, attention, establishing peer networks, developing autonomy). (Section IV)

**Differential diagnosis:** The ability to identify a child at risk for a disability as different from related disabilities with similar or overlapping characteristics. (Section I)

**Disability fatigue:** The tiredness or lack of energy a child with a disability feels as the result of the effort he or she must expend in attempting to overcome skill deficits or to conform with school requirements. (Section II)

**Discrimination learning and training:** Discrimination learning involves the ability to perceive differences between two stimuli presented for comparison. Training involves presenting stimuli with few irrelevant details and only a few relevant dimensions, and then directing attention to these relevant dimensions or teaching rules for identifying relevant dimensions (Beirne-Smith et al., 2006). For example, a teacher asked a student with MID to compare the letters *T* and *F.* When the student noticed the cross in the middle of the *F,* he had little difficulty thereafter writing the word *Friday.* (Section III)

**Disinhibition:** The inability to stop verbal or motor responses that are often socially inappropriate (e.g., cursing, removing all clothes after a seizure). (Section V)

**Dopamine:** A chemical that helps transmit signals from one nerve cell in the brain to the next. (Section IV)

**Drug holidays:** Periods (often during vacation time) when students with ADHD are taken off their psychostimulant medications. (Section IV)

***DSM-IV-TR***: The fourth edition, text revised, of the *Diagnostic and Statistical Manual of Mental Disorders,* which presents the most widely used medical/psychological classification system (APA, 2000). (Section I)

**Dysarthria:** A condition that results in unintelligible speech that sounds like gibberish. (Section III)

**Dyscalculia:** A specific learning disability (SLD) in math; also called a math disability (MD) or math learning disability (MLD). (Section II)

**Dysgraphia:** Difficulty with the task of handwriting. *See also* Memory dysgraphia; Motor dysgraphia; Perceptual dysgraphia. (Section VI)

**Dyslexia:** A disorder of reading or decoding that is often accompanied by spelling problems. The name in Greek means "difficulty with words." The main problem for those diagnosed with the disorder in English-speaking countries is an understanding of how sounds fit together to make words (Lyon et al., 2003). (Section II)

**Dysnomia:** Difficulty in recalling the names of objects (nouns) or people. (Section II)

**Dysphoria:** Depressed mood. (Section V)

**Dyspraxia:** Poor ability to plan fine motor movements of speech. (Section VI)

**Dysthemia:** A persistent depressed mood or symptoms of depression lasting 2 or more years. (Section V)

**EBD:** Emotional behavioral disorder or disability. (Section V)

**EBP:** Empirically based practice (also known as evidence-based practice)—that is, scientifically tested practice that has demonstrated effectiveness. (Section I)

**Echolalia:** The repetition or echoing of others' words or phrases, which can be immediate or delayed (e.g., from a TV program heard the night before). (Section VI)

**Echopraxia:** Involuntary repetition or imitation of the observed movements of another. (Section VI)

**ED:** Emotional disturbance; more commonly referred to as EBD or emotional and behavioral disorder. (Section V)

**Emotional intelligence (EQ):** The ability to identify and understand one's own and others' emotions by "reading" faces, gestures, and tones of voice—in essence to read between the lines of what is spoken. EQ can also be defined by the child's ability to make sense of things (i.e., common sense) and to understand the emotional aspects of everyday social interactions (Stuss et al., 2001). (Section I)

**Empathy:** The ability to feel with or identify with the feelings of another. (Section V)

**Endowment:** The abilities an individual is born with (congenital). (Section II)

**Epidemiological samples:** In research studies, groups of individuals recruited from the general population or from community samples and not from special schools or mental health clinics. (Section V)

**Etiology:** The cause of disability, which is biological/genetic, environmental, or, most frequently, a combination of the two. (Section I)

**Exclusionary time-out:** A period during which a child is removed from the group and placed away from the ongoing activities (so the child cannot see, hear, or learn from the activities). (Section IV)

**Executive functions (EF):** Self-regulatory processes involved in such tasks as identifying problems, goal setting, developing plans, executing plans, and evaluating or self-monitoring the implementation of plans. EF also encompasses the cognitive flexibility, attention, and working memory systems that guide the individual throughout these regulatory processes. (Section I)

**Exogenous factors:** Factors in a disability that have their etiology outside the person (acquired). (Section II)

**Expressive language:** Talking (spoken language) and composition/spelling (written language). (Section I)

**Externalizing disorders:** Disorders that cause children to act out emotions through aggressive or disruptive behavior. (Section V)

**Extrinsic motivation:** Impetus to action that is directed toward the goals of others; the evaluation of progress in relation to others' standards. (Section III)

**Extroversion:** Demonstration of active, talkative, and acting-out types of behavior (e.g., hyperactivity). (Section I)

**Failure-oriented classrooms:** Classrooms in which children are punished for trying and not succeeding in addition to being punished for not trying. As well, there may be overuse of strategies that involve making comparisons among children's performance (e.g., by posting children's graded work) or focusing on what is wrong rather than on what is correct. (Section V)

**FAPE:** Free, appropriate program of education, legally required under IDEA. (Section I)

**FAS:** Fetal alcohol syndrome. (Section III)

**Figurative language:** Abstract, nonliteral language, such as idioms and metaphors. (Section V)

**Fine motor skills:** Physical skills involving the small muscles of the hands and the articulation muscles of the mouth and tongue. (Section VI)

**Fluency:** The ability to read text accurately and quickly (automatically). (Section II)

**fMRI:** Functional magnetic resonance imaging, a type of neuroimaging technology that is used to conduct assessments. An individual performs a task requiring specific skills while undergoing an MRI, and the brain activity associated with performing the task can be nonintrusively assessed. (Section II)

**Focal damage:** Damage affecting specific areas of the brain. (Section III)

**Form rituals:** Patterns of behavior that involve multiple repetitions of particular sequences. These include physical rituals (frequently washing hands, brushing teeth, checking repeatedly if a door is locked, placing objects just right, touching things, erasing or writing and rewriting letters until perfect) and mental rituals (repeating words, counting objects, or calculating answers) (Adams, 2004; Szechtman & Woody, 2004). Form rituals differ from compulsions, in that compulsions are more often accompanied by obsessions (repeated unwanted thoughts). (Section V)

**Frontal lobes:** That part of the brain that plays an important role in human behavior, with damage to that region affecting high-level cognitive functions (intelligence) as well as social behavior, personality, personal memories, and self-awareness (for a review, see Stuss et al., 2001). (Section III)

**Functional analysis or functional assessment (FA):** Assessment of a child's behavior in specific settings, during specific tasks, or with specific persons that produces a better understanding of how the child attempts to adapt his or her behavior to the specific setting, task, or person (e.g., to avoid a difficult task, to get relatedness with peers). (Section I)

**Functional etiology:** The immediate antecedents of behavior or performance, which typically can be used to understand the short-term purpose of that behavior. (Section I)

**Functional math skills and curriculum:** Skills and curriculum related to the use of money, time, and measurement. Functional reading involves basic word recognition and comprehension of literal meanings. Functional skills in general might be considered the skills necessary for adaptive behavior. (Section III)

**G factor:** General intelligence factor. A measure of efficient processing across a number of brain areas, distributed across the frontal, parietal, and temporal lobes, which involves the brain's ability to pull together different functions and types of processing. G is more heritable than specific talents (Garrett, 2011). (Section III)

**Generalization:** The application of information, elements, or problem-solving processes to novel situations or tasks (e.g., from addition to multiplication). Children who fail to generalize fail to extract commonalities across prior learning experiences, tasks, or settings. *See also* Transference. (Section III)

**Global (or gestalt) cues:** Cues to the big picture that can be presented as advance organizers, concept maps, general descriptions, or comparisons (e.g., "It is like X"). (Section IV)

**Global damage:** Damage affecting large areas of the brain and causing major changes in cognitive functions and adaptive behavior. (Section III)

**Global fears:** Anxieties attached to a wide range of related objects, experiences, animals, or events. (Section V)

**Grandiosity:** Feelings of superiority and entitlement often accompanied by fantasies of winning, becoming powerful, or gaining revenge for perceived injustice. (Section V)

**Graphic organizers:** Tools such as mind maps and outlines that allow students to visualize their ideas. (Section II)

**Gross motor skills:** Physical skills involving the large muscles of the legs and arms, especially needed for coordination in walking and balance. Good gross motor skills are needed for adequate performance in physical education at school. (Section VI)

**GT:** Gifted and talented. (Section III)

**Heritability:** The percentage of a characteristic that can be explained by genetics. (Section II)

**Homogeneous groupings:** Groupings of students who are similar in one or more characteristic(s). For example, in the gifted area, groups that encourage the development and achievement of gifted students are those "cluster" groups with the most advanced learners. (Section III)

**Hyperlexia:** Reading disability involving the failure to understand the meanings of the words (encoding) even when difficult words are easily decoded. (Section II)

**ID and MID:** Intellectual disability and mild intellectual disability, previously labeled "mild mental retardation" or "educable mental retardation." (Section III)

**IDEA:** The Individuals with Disabilities Educational Act of 2004, the main U.S. federal law for special education, which mandates schools to find, evaluate, and provide a free, appropriate program of education for each child with a disability. (Section I)

**IEP:** Individualized education program, a requirement of IDEA. An IEP is a written document with special instructions detailing related services designed for a student with a diagnosed disability; it is a legal document that represents the accountability of the school to the student. (Section I)

**Impairment:** The outcome of a disability in terms of reduced functioning (academic or social). (Section I)

**Impulsivity:** Personality trait that involves overly fast responding, difficulty waiting to respond or inhibiting responses, and acting without considering possible consequences. (Section III)

**Incidental learning:** Gains in knowledge that are unplanned or unintended; informal learning. Most children with average IQs "pick up" information from their own observations and from direct experiences. Children with ID are unlikely to experience much incidental learning; they need direct instruction with relevant information highlighted. (Section III)

**Inclusionary time-out:** A period in which a child is pulled back from the ongoing activity but is allowed to remain in the room and learn from the interactions. (Section IV)

**Inclusion classes:** Classrooms in general education that include students who have disabilities or who are at risk for disabilities. (Section I)

**Individuals with Disabilities Educational Act:** *See* IDEA.

**Instrumental:** Directed toward obtaining a goal. (Section V)

**Insular:** Isolated socially. (Section V)

**Intelligence:** Two types of intelligence are generally assessed: performance intelligence, using novel visual stimuli (pictures, blocks, objects, mazes); and verbal intelligence, using auditory stimuli (vocabulary, statements). The Wechsler Intelligence Scale for Children (WISC) includes both verbal and performance scales. When the verbal and performance intelligence scales are combined they form a single score called an intelligence quotient (IQ) or the full-scale IQ. Scores from this test are normally distributed, typically with a mean score of 100 and a range that defines "average" from 85 to 115. (Section III)

**Internal cues:** Thoughts, feelings, strategies, values, and the like. (Section IV)

**Internalizing disorders:** Disorders that cause individuals to express feelings inwardly and thus increase the likelihood of anxiety and/or depression. (Section IV)

**Internalizing symptoms:** Symptoms that are directed inward. Somatic internalizing symptoms include stomachache, insomnia, and nausea; mood symptoms include worrying and depression; and behavioral symptoms include crying, withdrawal, and phobias. (Section IV)

**Interventions:** Treatments used to change a child with disabilities (e.g., medications or skill training in weak areas, such as remedial phonics training for reading). Interventions based on functional analysis do not target weak areas but target high-frequency payoffs (e.g., needed stimulation). This might involve teaching the child to perform replacement behavior (alternate methods to get stimulation that are not disruptive) (Stahr et al., 2006). (Section I)

**Intrinsic motivation:** Impetus to action that is directed toward self-selected interests and goals; the evaluation of progress in relation to one's own standards or past performance. (Section III)

**Introversion:** Demonstration of internalizing behavior (e.g., shyness, anxieties). (Section I)

**Language production:** The quantity or amount of language spoken or written. (Section II)

**Language quality:** The content, structure, and pragmatic social (everyday) use of language. (Section II)

**LD:** Learning disability, also termed *specific learning disability* (SLD). (Section II)

**LEA:** Local educational agency, such as a local school. (Section I)

**Learned helplessness:** A condition in which individuals attribute their successes to external factors (not to their own efforts) and their failures to their lack of ability (not to lack of effort). (Section II)

**Learning processes:** Psychological processes or abilities that contribute to the learning of academic skills; these learning processes are intelligence, memory, perception/discrimination, and attention. (Section I)

**Long-term memory:** The ability to recall information, such as math facts, learned last week, last month, or years earlier. (Section I)

**LRE:** Least restrictive environment. The LRE for a child is typically the general education classroom, in contrast to, for example, a self-contained classroom for students with disabilities. (Section I)

**Magical thinking:** Believing that specific behavior, such as rituals, can offer protection. (Section V)

**Mania:** Mood that is persistently elevated, abnormally expansive, or irritable. (Section V)

**Manifest determination:** The determination of whether a child's "misconduct" is an outcome of the child's disability. (Section I)

**Marker variable:** Distinguishing characteristic. (Section IV)

**Masking:** The hiding of a disability by giftedness or of giftedness by a disability. (Section II)

**Mathew effect:** The spreading of reading difficulties to other subject areas (e.g., math problem solving), accompanied by a cyclical downward spiral of motivation. Often characterized as "the rich get richer and the poor get poorer" (Cunningham & Stanovich, 199:7). (Section II)

**MD or MLD:** Math learning disability. (Section II)

**Memory dysgraphia:** Poor recall of the written forms of letters. Individuals with memory dysgraphia can copy letters. (Section VI)

**Memory strategies:** Strategies for retaining material in memory. These include rehearsal or repetition; clustering, or grouping similar items to make recall easier (all animals, all things that are red); and associational learning, or the pairing of the meaning of the items to be recalled with past experiences (using the situation or setting as a cue to recall behavior, such as an acronym with each letter representing a word or a mental picture prompting the recall of a word). (Section III)

**Metacognitive skills:** Abilities concerning awareness of one's own mental states, beliefs, strategies, opinions, experiences, and so on and the relation of these to the mental states, motives, intentions, and experiences of others. Such skills include the ability to reflect on one's own thinking strategies, attentional strategies, emotional and social strategies, problem-solving strategies, and the like. Metacognition is often described as "thinking about thinking." Subcomponents may include thinking about one's own specific mental abilities, such as memory (metamemory) or comprehension (metacomprehension). Awareness of *others'* states, which has been termed *theory of mind,* is thought to be relatively absent in individuals with autism spectrum disorders and in individuals with right-hemispheric brain dysfunction. (Section III)

**Mnemonics:** Memory "tricks" such as acronyms, crazy phrases, or cartoons that act as global or abbreviated cues and can be used to recall more complex and detailed verbal information. (Section II)

**Modeling:** The observed demonstration of responses to particular objects or events. When a child observes an adult or another child with characteristics similar to his or her own interacting with a feared object or in a feared situation, the child learns responses from the behavior modeled. (Section II)

**Monotone:** Speech without inflection. (Section II)

**Mood lability:** Ups and downs in feelings that appear to be unpredictable. (Section V)

**Moro reflex:** The inherited startle reflex. (Section V)

**Motor dysgraphia:** Poor ability to form letters (owing to poor fine motor skills). Individuals with motor dysgraphia can see that their own writing is poor (adequate perceptual skills). Writing long passages can be painful for them, and they are unable to sustain legibility; letter shape and size become increasingly inconsistent and illegible. (Section VI)

**MTBI:** Mild traumatic brain injury. MTBI can result from an injury to the head that results in a brief alteration of mental state (e.g., transient confusion or disorientation, loss of memory around the time of the injury) or loss of consciousness for less than 30 minutes. *See also* TBI. (Section III)

**Multiform:** Of different-appearing forms. (Section VI)

**Negative entitlement:** The feeling that one "deserves" to be protected from bad outcomes or unpleasant experiences because one is special. (Section V)

**Neophobia:** Fear of new and unfamiliar people and situations. (Section V)

**Neutral cues:** Information that is not salient and is difficult to notice, such as the organization of a room or the structure of an assignment. (Section IV)

**Nonverbal communication:** Communication without verbal language, through gestures, postures, facial expressions, visual symbols, and concepts. (Section II)

**Nonverbal IQ:** Performance IQ, which is often assessed through testing that involves speeded processing during the manipulation of novel stimuli (mazes, blocks). (Section III)

**Norm:** A statistical average or the most frequently occurring score or response in a setting or during the performance of a task. (Section I)

**NPD:** Narcissistic personality disorder. (Section V)

**Number concepts:** Quantity, more/less (relative magnitude)—related to numerosity. (Section II)

**Numerosity:** Number sense, or the ability to understand the properties of numerical problems or expressions without doing precise computations, such as would be involved in estimations of quantity (Gersten & Chard, 1999). (Section II)

**NVLD:** Nonverbal learning disability. Difficulty with the visually based concepts of time, space, gesture, distance, age, and so on, including mathematics and social interactions. (Section II)

**Obsessions:** Repeated unwanted thoughts involving feelings, images, or experiences that cause anxiety (e.g., "I am going to drive into the river"). (Section V)

**OCD:** Obsessive-compulsive disorder; an anxiety disorder causing the sufferer to experience repeated unwanted thoughts and behaviors. The repetitive behaviors, which are called compulsions, can range from overeating or overexercising to checking and rechecking to make sure windows or doors are locked. (Section V)

**ODD:** Oppositional defiant disorder. (Section V)

**OHI:** Other health impairment, a category of exceptionality under IDEA. (Section IV)

**Palilalia:** The repetition or echoing of one's own spoken words; may sound like stuttering (e.g., "Do my work work work"). (Section VI)

**Perception:** The ability to take sensory input and convert that input into a recognition of meaningful objects, persons, symbols, and so on. Perception is often assessed through tasks in which students are asked to tell which objects/letters/sounds are different from or the same as other objects/letters/sounds. (Section I)

**Perceptual dysgraphia:** Poor ability to form letters accompanied by an inability to recognize that the letters are badly formed. Children with perceptual dysgraphia (also known as spatial dysgraphia) have normal fine motor skills but poor perceptual abilities. (Section VI)

**Performance anxiety:** Anxiety characterized by high physiological arousal in achievement contexts, excessive fear of negative evaluations, and escape or avoidance from these situations (Faust, Ashcraft, & Fleck, 1996). (Section V)

**Performance deficit:** Lack of motivation or ability to sustain effort or attention to an area the child already has the skills to perform. (Section IV)

**Perinatal:** During the time of childbirth. (Section II)

**Perseveration:** Repetition of the same motor or verbal responses. (Section V)

**Phobia:** Irrational fear, such as fear of snakes or of the dark, that is *not* based on direct or observed experiences and may be associated with, or representative of, a past experience that was fear inducing (e.g., passing too near a cliff edge while driving). Some phobias are temporary and specific to a normal developmental period (e.g., fear of going into the attic). (Section V)

**Phoneme:** The smallest unit of sound, which may be composed of one or several letters. (Section II)

**Phonological code system:** A method of teaching children to read in which they learn the visual letter symbols, their corresponding sounds, and their governing rules in order to decode words and to spell (hundreds of component graphemes, phonemes, syllable types, prefixes, suffixes, and roots). Typically, after a word has been learned through a phonological method, it is placed in long-term memory and recalled visually as the whole word, which produces reading that is fluent; phonics is then used as a backup strategy (i.e., when a child forgets a word or encounters a new word). (Section II)

**Phonology/phonetics and phonics:** Phonology is the study of how sounds are organized and used within and across languages; phonetics deals with the physical production of sounds. In contrast, phonics involves awareness or sensitivity to the sound structure within words (hearing individual beginning, middle, and ending sounds within words) and making discriminations between words and their sounds (rhyming or finding similar words), blending sounds, and separating sounds into segments. More generally, it concerns the ability to translate visual symbols into sounds in order to pronounce words. (Section II)

**Plasticity:** The ability of the brain, especially the brain of a young child, to form new connections between intact areas, with uninjured brain tissue taking over the functions of lost neurons. (Section III)

**Positive entitlement:** The feeling that one is "owed" good things, such as respect and positive outcomes. (Section V)

**Posttraumatic stress disorder (PTSD):** A condition characterized by continual reexperiencing of an earlier traumatic experience that involved death or serious injury or threat to the self or others. In children, behavioral responses to trauma include agitation or disorganization (APA, 2000). In a sense, anxiety stemming from trauma is rationally based and might be considered an example of conditioned responding. (Section V)

**Pragmatics:** Everyday, practical language that is used for social communication. For students with LD, deficient areas of pragmatics include the use of nonspecific referents and ambiguous messages, failure to take the perspectives of others, nonassertive responding, and difficulty asking questions or seeking clarification. (Section II)

**Precarious:** Dangerous or risky. (Section IV)

**Prescient feelings:** Sensations that occur just prior to tics that act as warnings (Walter & Carter, 1997). (Section VI)

**Primary and secondary disability:** A primary disability "causes" or contributes to a secondary disability; for example, inattention can contribute to secondary academic outcomes. (Section IV)

**Prognosis:** Predicted or expected long-term outcome, usually described as positive or negative. (Section III)

**Protective factors:** Those events, attitudes, life experiences, or individual traits that are associated with positive long-term outcomes (e.g., sense of humor). (Section V)

**Psychosocial:** Intrapersonal (within the person) and interpersonal (in relations with other persons). (Section V)

**Psychosomatic:** Involving the interrelationship between mind and body (e.g., getting headaches in response to mental stress). (Section V)

**PTSD:** *See* Posttraumatic stress disorder (PTSD).

**RD:** Reading disability. This broad term is used to refer to many problems associated with reading, including reading comprehension problems or hyperlexia, but most often it refers to dyslexia. (Section II)

**Reading comprehension:** The ability to gain meaning from text that is read (understanding or encoding). (Section II)

**Receptive language skills:** Listening skills (in the area of spoken language) and reading and math skills (in the area of written language). (Section II)

**Regressive behavior:** Behavior that reflects the behavior associated with an earlier stage of development (e.g., acting babyish, such as thumb sucking, whining, complaining). (Section V)

**Relaxation techniques:** Strategies designed to reduce anxiety (e.g., slow breathing). (Section V)

**Relevant information:** Information that is important to correct task performance. (Section IV)

**Remediation training:** Intervention that takes the form of asking the child directly to practice or learn skills in his or her weak areas of functioning. (Section II)

**Replacement activities:** Different and socially more appropriate ways to achieve the same goals (e.g., asking questions rather than talking excessively). (Section IV)

**Response to intervention (RTI):** An assessment of achievement (e.g., reading) as it changes over time as the result of intervention. RTI changes the definition of LD to include diagnosed students as those who do *not* respond to empirically based intervention strategies and thus need more intense interventions, placing more responsibility on educators to provide empirically based interventions before labeling children. (Section I)

**Rett syndrome:** A condition that occurs in young females and is characterized by marked degrees of impairment in intelligence, language, and communication, with a characteristic loss in head growth from the ages of 5 months to 48 months and loss of previously acquired socialization skills and fine motor and gross skills (Hagin, 2004). (Section V)

**Revisualization:** Seeing something again in one's mind (visual memory). (Section II)

**Right-hemispheric functions:** Functions of the right side of the brain. Damage to this area can impair pragmatics in language and in the nonverbal aspects of communication (e.g., understanding sarcasm, humor, irony). This area may be particularly important to the development of "theory of mind" or inferences about the intentions and feelings of others (empathy) (Stuss et al., 2001). Students with problems in right-hemispheric functions are often those with nonverbal learning disabilities, traumatic brain injury, and autism. (Section I)

**Risk factors:** Those events, attitudes, life experiences, or traits associated with negative outcomes. (Section V)

**Rote tasks:** Repetitive tasks that lack variation or novelty, such as math calculations, spelling drills, and handwriting practice. (Section IV)

**RTI:** *See* Response to intervention.

**Rumination:** Repetitive negative thinking; going over and over the same negative event. (Section V)

**Savant:** A child who has special talents or abilities in spite of a disability. The term comes from the French word *savoir,* meaning "to know." Savants generally excel in one of the following areas: mathematical calculations, memory feats, artistic abilities, or musical abilities. The source for these abilities is unknown, although repeated practice (e.g., with calculations, dates) accounts for some. However, the ability to play a complicated piece of music immediately after hearing it for the first time is less easily explained. (Section V)

**School phobia:** A specific disorder of school refusal wherein children avoid school in favor of staying home because of an irrational fear of separation from parents or caregivers. (Section V)

**School refusal:** A general category of chronic avoidance of attending school. (Section V)

**Section 504:** A section of the Vocational Rehabilitation Act of 1973 that guarantees physical access and access to the content of instructional programs to all students. (Section I)

**Selective attention:** Preference for attending to some things. For students with ADHD, selective attention is directed toward external stimulating sights, sounds, smells, tastes, movement, emotion, and aggression, and internally to exciting daydreaming, thought, and emotionality. This can be called an attentional bias rather than an attentional deficit. Average children find it easier to selectively attend to relevant task information—to the underlying structure of a task, the details, the relevant information in directions. (Section IV)

**Self-determination:** The state of feeling in control (empowered) and able to make one's own decisions and have one's own plans. This is the opposite of learned helplessness. (Section III)

**Self-efficacy:** Feelings of personal competence in producing outcomes (the opposite of learned helplessness). (Section V)

**Self-monitoring:** The focusing of attention on aspects of the self (e.g., thoughts, behavior, feelings). In an intervention with a child with disabilities, auditory signals (e.g., taped beeps) may be used to cue the child to self-monitor by recording current behavior or feelings at the sound of each signal. (Section III)

**Semantics:** The meanings underlying verbalizations (substance). (Section II)

**Sensation-seeking behavior:** Behavior that is highly variable and produces additional stimulation for the child. (Section IV)

**Sensorimotor systems:** Visual systems that guide motor responses. (Section III)

**Separation anxiety:** An intense fear of separation from a parent or surrogate (guardian or parent substitute); the term often is used interchangeably with *school anxiety* (Kearney, 2003). (Section V)

**Serotonin:** A neurotransmitter in the brain that affects mood and its regulation. (Section V)

**SES:** Socioeconomic status; that is, the economic class of an individual. (Section II)

**Setting-specific responses:** Responses that occur only at certain times or in certain situations. (Section IV)

**Shearing:** A form of damage to the brain in which layers of the brain ride up on each other, cutting nerve pathways. (Section III)

**Sight approach:** A method of teaching reading that relies on visually based retrieval (sometimes called the basal reading approach). Children are taught to recognize and associate meanings with whole words or word pictures, often using high-frequency grade-level words. (Section II)

**Short-term memory:** Immediate recall (within seconds when rehearsal is prevented) of from three to nine elements (words, digits, or letters) (Miller, 1956). Short-term memory differs from working memory in that working memory involves holding information in mind in order to reorganize, summarize, or change that information in some way (e.g., mental mathematics). (Section I)

**Simultaneous verbalizations:** Verbal explanations presented concurrently with visuals. (Section II)

**Skill deficit:** Lack of ability or lack of educational experience in "how" to do something. (Section IV)

**SLD:** Specific learning disability (e.g., in math, reading). (Section I)

**Social interpersonal problem solving:** The generation of multiple strategies for responding in a social situation and the selection of a good strategy that is more effective than others (Edeh, 2006); also could be termed *social brainstorming.* (Section III)

**Social skills training:** Direct instruction in the subcomponents of individual social skills (e.g., social greetings involve eye contact, smiling, handshake, verbal statement), which are modeled and reinforced for each step that approximates correct achievement (successive approximation). (Section III)

**Specific anxiety disorders:** Disorders characterized by fears of particular events, experiences, animals, or objects (e.g., spiders, escalators). (Section V)

**State:** Behavior, thinking, or mood that is temporary and depends on the conditions within the setting, such as time, task, persons, and amount of light or noise. (Section I)

**Stereotypies:** Repetitive, apparently "nonfunctional" movements (e.g., hand clapping), the function of which is to structure time in the absence of other activities or to reduce arousal; typically observed in children with autism (Zentall & Zentall, 1983). (Section V)

**Strategic reprimands:** Short, firm, immediate, and consistent reprimands. (Section IV)

**Sustained attention:** The ability to maintain a consistent behavioral or cognitive response during continuous or repetitive activity (Sohlberg & Mateer, 1989). Damage to the right frontal lobe of the brain has been reported to produce deficits in sustained attention (for a review, see Stuss et al., 2001). (Section IV)

**Syntax:** Grammar and sentence construction, or the correctness of the form of language. Syntax includes rules of morphology, such as how plurals and possessives are formed. (Section II)

**Synthetic intelligence:** Form of intelligence that involves assembling, or synthesizing, information into whole categories or ideas. (Section III)

**Systematic desensitization:** The graduated exposure of an individual to feared objects/experiences/persons/animals in a pleasant or relaxed context, until the phobic individual can tolerate exposure. (Section V)

**Talent:** Exceptional level of performance in verbal-linguistic, logical-mathematical, musical, spatial, bodily-kinesthetic, interpersonal, intrapersonal, and naturalistic areas of functioning. Talent is less heritable than the g factor. (Section III)

**Task analysis:** The breaking down of a task (e.g., how to make a peanut butter-and-jelly sandwich) into its component parts, typically as they can be arranged sequentially, to achieve the overall task. Task analysis can also involve a determination of input (visual or auditory), learning process (e.g., memory, reasoning), and response requirements of a task (e.g., fine motor skill). (Section I)

**TBI:** Traumatic brain injury. TBI can result from severe injuries to the brain that cause long periods of loss of consciousness, including lengthy periods of coma and frequent seizures. (Section III)

**Temperament:** Biologically based behavioral style that has a number of components, including (a) emotionality, or the degree to which a person can become upset; (b) sociability, or the degree to which a person prefers the presence of others; (c) activity, or the degree to which a person is restless; and (d) shyness, or the degree to which a person is uneasy in unfamiliar social situations (Masi et al., 2003). (Section I)

**Theory of mind:** The ability to infer the mental states of others, such as their intentions (Stuss et al., 2001). (Section V)

**Tic disorder:** A disorder typically involving just motor or vocal tics. (Section VI)

**Tics:** Repetitive, brief, stereotypical movements (motor tics) or vocalizations (vocal tics), including eye blinking, shoulder shrugging, grimacing, head jerking, yelping, sniffing, and making grunting noises. (Section VI)

**Tourette's syndrome (TS):** A disorder characterized by both vocal and motor tics and typically associated with an inherited pattern (Silver, 2004).

**Trait:** Habitual pattern of behavior that is associated with personality characteristics (e.g., extroversion) and is relatively enduring over time. Traits can also be physical, such as height and eye color. (Section I)

**Transference:** The implementation of what has been learned in one setting, context, or task in another setting, context, or task (e.g., from a school to a work environment, from reading to social studies). This term is often considered to have the same meaning as *generalization,* but the two can be distinguished according to the level of abstraction that is required. Transference is the direct application (copying) of a skill across contexts, whereas generalization is more broadly the application of elements, such as those used in problem solving or in "if-then" thinking. (Section III)

**Traumatic brain injury:** *See* TBI; MTBI.

**Truancy:** A specific type of school refusal in which the child leaves the school and goes into the community but does not go home. The term *truant* is used mainly to describe children who miss school without parental consent (Kearney, 2003). (Section V)

**Twice exceptional:** Having both giftedness and co-occurring disabilities, such as LD or ADHD. (Section III)

**UDL:** Universal Design for Learning, a philosophy related to designing and delivering products and services within a classroom that are usable by people with the widest range of capabilities. UDL should be in place before any student enters the classroom (Beard et al., 2007). (Section I)

**Underachiever:** A child for whom there are discrepancies between aptitude or IQ and actual performance on everyday schoolwork. (Section III)

**Underrepresented GT:** Gifted children whose families are economically disadvantaged or are members of a minority or linguistically different culture. (Section III)

**Vandalism:** The destruction of another's property. (Section V)

**Verbal LD (VLD):** Verbal learning disability; difficulty with language-based subject areas of reading, spelling, and composition. Problems with talking and listening may be early indicators. Children with VLD are sometimes referred to as having language learning disabilities (LLD). (Section II)

**Visual errors in reading, composition, and spelling:** Letter reversals, punctuation and capitalization errors, and spelling that reflects poor recall of sound/symbol inconsistencies with a reliance on good sound analysis (e.g., writing "nite" for the word *knight*). In other words, students spell words exactly the way they sound and not the way they look. (Section II)

**Visual perception:** The ability to take what the eyes see (color, form, and size) and give these visual sensations meaning (to identify objects, words). Visual perception also involves completing figures (identifying the whole from a part or blending parts into a whole) and finding a small part in a whole (visual analysis, such as identifying hidden pictures). (Section I)

**Visual reasoning and concepts:** The ability to understand visual symbols (plus signs, division signs), pictured information (block designs, humor in pictures), and the functions of everyday common objects, such as a hammer or a light switch. (Section II)

**Whole language approach:** A method of teaching reading that involves using a context of meaningful experiences, which are dictated by the child, written by the adult, illustrated by the child, and subsequently reread by the child. This method is often used with older students who have been unable to make gains through the phonics method. (Section II)

**Working memory (WM):** Memory that involves holding information in mind to bring hindsight and forethought into decision making (Greene, 2006), to consider personal history and possible future consequences for the purposes of planning, sequencing, summarizing, reorganizing, problem solving, and the like. Visual working memory, which resides in the right frontal lobe (Stuss et al., 2001), involves identifying visual patterns, sequences, mapping, following visual directions, and other nonverbal skills. (Section I)

**Yerkes-Dodson law:** Developed by psychologists Robert M. Yerkes and John D. Dodson (1908), this law posits that performance improves with increased alertness (arousal), but only up to a certain level, and when arousal is too high, performance decreases. Furthermore, different tasks require different levels of arousal for optimal performance. For example, difficult tasks may require lower arousal, and repetitive tasks requiring persistence are performed better with higher arousal or activation. (Section I)

# References

Abelson-Mitchell, N. (2008). Epidemiology and prevention of head injuries: Literature review. *Journal of Clinical Nursing, 17,* 46–57.

Abikoff, H. B., Courtney, M. E., Szeibel, P. J., & Koplewicz, H. S. (1996). The effects of auditory stimulation on the arithmetic performance of children with ADHD and nondisabled children. *Journal of Learning Disabilities, 29,* 238–246.

Abikoff, H. B., Jensen, P. S., Arnold, L. L., Hoza, B., Hechtman, L., Pollack, S., et al. (2002). Observed classroom behavior of children with ADHD: Relationship to gender and comorbidity. *Journal of Abnormal Child Psychology, 30,* 349–359.

Adams, G. B. (2004). Identifying, assessing, and treating obsessive-compulsive disorder in school-aged children: The role of school personnel. *Teaching Exceptional Children, 37*(2), 46–53.

Advokat, C. (2009). What exactly are the benefits of stimulants for ADHD? *Journal of Attention Disorders, 12,* 495–498.

Akande, A., Osagie, J., Mwaiteleke, P., Botha, E., Ababio, T., & Chipeta, K. (1999). Managing children's fears and anxieties in classroom settings. *Early Child Development and Care, 158,* 51–69.

Alessandri, S. M. (1992). Attention, play, and social behavior in ADHD preschoolers. *Journal of Abnormal Child Psychology, 20,* 289–302.

Allison, D. B., Faith, M. S., & Franklin, R. D. (1995). Antecedent exercise in the treatment of disruptive behavior: A meta-analytic review. *Clinical Psychology, 2,* 279–304.

American Association on Intellectual and Developmental Disabilities. (2010). Intellectual disability. Retrieved from http://www.aamr.org

American Psychiatric Association. (2000). *Diagnostic and statistical manual of mental disorders* (4th ed., text rev.). Washington, DC: Author.

Anckarsäter, H., Stahlberg, O., Larson, T., Hakansson, C., Jutblad, S., Niklasson, L., et al. (2006). The impact of ADHD and autism spectrum disorders on temperament, character, and personality development. *American Journal of Psychiatry, 163,* 1239–1244.

Andreou, G., Agapitou, P., & Karapetsas, A. (2005). Verbal skills in children with ADHD. *European Journal of Special Needs Education, 20,* 231–238.

Ang, R. P., & Yusof, N. (2005). The relationship between aggression, narcissism, and self-esteem in Asian children and adolescents. *Current Psychology, 24,* 113–122.

Angold, A., & Costello, E. J. (1993). Depressive comorbidity in children and adolescents: Empirical, theoretical, and methodological issues. *American Journal of Psychiatry, 150,* 1779–1791.

Angold, A., & Costello, E. J. (2001). The epidemiology of disorders of conduct: Nosological issues and comorbidity. In J. Hill & B. Maughan (Eds.), *Conduct disorders in childhood and adolescence* (pp. 126–168). Cambridge: Cambridge University Press.

Annemieke, M. L., de Wit, C. A. M., de Bruyn, E. E. J., Riksen-Walraven, J. M., & Rost, H. (2000). Depression and play in early childhood: Play behavior of depressed and nondepressed 3- to 6-year-olds in various play situations. *Journal of Emotional and Behavioral Disorders, 8,* 249–260.

Antshel, K. M., & Khan, F. M. (2008). Is there an increased familial prevalence of psychopathology in children with nonverbal learning disorders? *Journal of Learning Disabilities, 41,* 208–217.

Armstrong, T. (1995, October 18). ADD as a social invention. *Education Week,* pp. 33, 40.

Artiles, A. J., Rueda, P., Salazar, J. J., & Higareda, I. (2005). Within group diversity in minority disproportionate representation: English language learners in urban school districts. *Exceptional Children, 76,* 283–300.

Ashcraft, M. H., Krause, J. A., & Hopko, D. R. (2007). Is math anxiety a mathematical learning disability? In D. M. Berch & M. M. M. Mazzocco (Eds.), *Why is math so hard for some children? The nature and origins of mathematical learning difficulties and disabilities* (pp. 329–348). Baltimore: Paul H. Brookes.

Assouline, S. G., Foley Nicpon, M., & Whiteman, C. (2010). Cognitive and psychosocial characteristics of gifted students with written language disability. *Gifted Child Quarterly, 54,* 102–115.

August, G. J. (1987). Production deficiencies in free recall: A comparison of hyperactive, learning-disabled, and normal children. *Journal of Abnormal Child Psychology, 15,* 429–440.

August, G. J., Realmuto, G. M., MacDonald, A. W., III, Nugent, S. M., & Crosby, R. (1996). Prevalence of ADHD and comorbid disorders among elementary school children screened for disruptive behavior. *Journal of Abnormal Child Psychology, 24,* 571–595.

Babyak, A. E., Koorland, M., & Mathes, P. G. (2000). The effects of story mapping instruction on the reading comprehension of students with behavioral disorders. *Behavioral Disorders, 25,* 239–258.

Baranek, G. T. (2002). Efficacy of sensory and motor interventions for children with autism. *Journal of Autism and Developmental Disorders, 32,* 397–422.

Bardenstein, K. (2009). The cracked mirror: Features of narcissistic personality disorder in children. *Psychiatric Annals 39,* 147–155.

Barkley, R. A. (1998). *Attention-deficit hyperactivity disorder: A handbook for diagnosis and treatment* (2nd ed.). New York: Guilford Press.

Barkley, R. A. (2003). Issues in the diagnosis of attention-deficit/hyperactivity disorder. *Brain and Development, 25,* 77–83.

Barkley, R. A. (2006). *Attention-deficit hyperactivity disorder: A handbook for diagnosis and treatment* (3rd ed.). New York: Guilford Press.

Barkley, R. A., DuPaul, G. J., & McMurray, M. B. (1990). Comprehensive evaluation of attention deficit disorder with and without hyperactivity as defined by research criteria. *Journal of Consulting and Clinical Psychology, 58,* 775–789.

Barlow, D. H. (1991). Disorders of emotions: Clarification, elaboration, and future directions. *Psychological Inquiry, 2,* 97–105.

Barnhill, G., Hagiwara, T., Myles, B. S., & Simpson, R. L. (2000). Asperger syndrome: A study of the cognitive profiles of 37 children and adolescents. *Focus on Autism and Other Developmental Disabilities, 15,* 146–153.

Barron, K., Evans, S., Baranik, L., Serpell, Z., & Buvinger, E. (2006). Achievement goals of students with ADHD. *Learning Disability Quarterly, 29,* 137–158.

Barry, C. T., Frick, P. J., & Killian, A. L. (2003). The relation of narcissism and self-esteem to conduct problems in children: A preliminary investigation. *Journal of Clinical Child and Adolescent Psychology, 32,* 139–152.

Barry, T. D., Lyman, R. D., & Klinger, L. G. (2002). Academic underachievement and attention-deficit/hyperactivity disorder: The negative impact of symptom severity on school performance. *Journal of School Psychology, 40,* 259–283.

Baum, S. M., Rizza, M. G., & Renzulli, S. (2006). Twice-exceptional adolescents: Who are they? What do they need? In F. A. Dixon & S. M. Moon (Eds.), *The handbook of secondary gifted education* (pp. 137–164). Waco, TX: Prufrock Press.

Bazarian, J. J., & Townend, W. (2009). Mild traumatic brain injury. In B. H. Rowe et al. (Eds.), *Evidence-based emergency medicine* (pp. 307–315). Oxford: Wiley-Blackwell..

Beach, R., Appleman, D., & Dorsey, S. (1994). Adolescents' uses of intertextual links to understand literature. In R. Ruddell, M. Ruddell, & H. Singer (Eds.), *Theoretical models and processes of reading* (pp. 695–714). Newark, DE: International Reading Association.

Beard, L. A., Carpenter, L. B., & Johnston, L. B. (2007). *Assistive technology: Access for all students* (2nd ed.). Boston: Pearson.

Beike, S. M., & Zentall, S. S. (in press). "The snake raised its head": Content novelty alters the reading performance of students at-risk for reading disabilities and ADHD. *Journal of Educational Psychology.* Advance online publication. doi:10.1037/a0027216

Beirne-Smith, M., Patton, J., & Kim, S. (2006). *Mental retardation: An introduction to intellectual disabilities* (7th ed.). Baltimore: Paul H. Brookes.

Beljan, P., Webb, J. T., Amend, E. R., Webb, N. E., Goerss, J., & Olenchak, F. R. (2006). Misdiagnosis and dual diagnosis of gifted children and adults: ADHD, bipolar, OCD, Asperger's, depression, and other disorders. *Gifted and Talented International, 21,* 83–86.

Benard, B. (1997). *Turning It Around for All Youth: From Risk to Resiliency.* ERIC/Clearinghouse on Urban Education Digest 126.

Benedict, G. C. (1997). Behavior problems: A little recognized but common cause. *Contemporary Education, 1,* 52–53.

Benner, G. J., Nelson, J. R., & Epstein, M. H. (2002). Language skills of children with EBD: A literature review. *Journal of Emotional and Behavioral Disorders, 10,* 43–59.

Bental, B., & Tirosh, E. (2007). The relationship between attention, executive functions, and reading domain abilities in attention deficit hyperactivity disorder and reading disorder: A comparative study. *Journal of Child Psychology and Psychiatry, 48,* 455–463.

Berkout, O. V., Young, J. N., & Gross, A. M. (2011). Mean girls and bad boys: Recent research on gender differences in conduct disorder. *Aggression and Violent Behavior, 16,* 503–511.

Berninger, V. W. (2001). Understanding the "lexia" in dyslexia: A multidisciplinary team approach to learning disabilities. *Annals of Dyslexia, 51,* 23–48.

Bernstein, G. A., Hektner, J. M., Borchardt, C. M., & McMillan, M. H. (2001). Treatment of school refusal: One-year follow-up. *Journal of the American Academy of Child and Adolescent Psychiatry, 40,* 206–213.

Bever, L. M. (2005). Heterogeneity in reading impairment and attention deficit hyperactivity disorder: Search for a common element. *Dissertation Abstracts International: Section B. Sciences and Engineering, 66*(6B), 3397.

Beyda, S. D., & Zentall, S. S. (1998). Administrative responses to AD/HD. *Reaching Today's Youth, 2,* 31–36.

Beyda, S. D, Zentall, S. S., & Ferko, D. J. K. (2002). The relationship between teacher practices and the task-appropriate and social behavior of students with behavioral difficulties. *Behavior Disorders, 27,* 236–255.

Bianco, M., Carothers, D. E., & Smiley, L. R. (2009). Gifted students with Asperger syndrome: Strategies for strength-based programming. *Intervention in School and Clinic, 44,* 206–215.

Bianco, M., & Leech, N. L. (2010). Twice-exceptional learners: Effects of teacher preparation and disability labels on gifted referrals. *Teacher Education and Special Education, 33,* 319–334.

Blackorby, J., & Wagner, M. (1996). Longitudinal postschool outcomes of youth with disabilities: Findings from the National Longitudinal Transition Study. *Exceptional Children, 62,* 399–413.

Blankenship, T. L., Ayres, K. M., & Langone, J. (2005). Effects of computer-based cognitive mapping on reading comprehension of students with emotional disorders. *Journal of Special Education Technology, 20*(2), 15–23.

Bloch, M. H., Peterson, B. S., Scahill, L., Otka, J., Katsovich, L., Zhang, H., & Leckman, J. F. (2006). Adulthood outcome of tic and obsessive-compulsive symptom severity in children with Tourette syndrome. *Archives of Pediatrics and Adolescent Medicine, 160,* 65–69.

Bloom, L., & Lahey, M. (1978). *Language development and language disorders.* New York: John Wiley.

Boden, J. M., Fergusson, D. M., & Horwood, L. J. (2010). Risk factors for conduct disorder and oppositional/defiant disorder: Evidence from a New Zealand birth cohort. *Journal of the American Academy of Child and Adolescent Psychiatry, 49,* 1125–1133.

Bogels, S. M., & Zigterman, D. (2000). Dysfunctional cognitions in children with social phobia, separation anxiety disorder, and generalized anxiety disorder.

*Journal of Abnormal Child Psychology, 28,* 205–211.

Booth, J., Farrell, A., & Varano, S. P. (2008). Social control, serious delinquency, and risky behavior: A gendered analysis. *Crime & Delinquency, 54,* 423–456.

Bottage, B. A. (2002). Weighing the benefits of anchored math instruction for students with disabilities in general education classes. *Journal of Special Education, 35,* 186–200.

Bouck, E. C., Bassette, L., Taber-Doughty, T., Flanagan, S. M., & Szwed, K. (2009). Pentop computers as tools for teaching multiplication to students with MID. *Education and Training in Developmental Disabilities, 44,* 367–380.

Bouras, N. (Ed.). (1999). *Psychiatric and behavioural disorders in developmental disabilities and mental retardation.* New York: Cambridge University Press.

Bowen, J. M. (2005). Classroom interventions for students with traumatic brain injury. *Preventing School Failure, 4,* 34–41.

Boysen, S. T., & Capaldi, E. J. (Eds.). (1993). *The emergence of numerical competence: Animal and human models.* Hillsdale, NJ: Lawrence Erlbaum.

Braaten, E. B., & Rosen, L. A. (2000). Self-regulation of affect in attention deficit-hyperactivity disorder (ADHD) and non-ADHD boys: Differences in empathic responding. *Journal of Consulting and Clinical Psychology, 68,* 313–321.

Brandau, H., Daghofer, F., Hollerer, L., Kaschnitz, W., Kellner, K., Kirchaier, G., Krammer, I., & Schlagbauer, A. (2007). The relationship between creativity, teacher ratings on behavior, age, and gender in pupils from seven to ten years. *Journal of Creative Behavior, 41,* 91–113.

Bright child vs. gifted child. (n.d.). Retrieved from http://gleigh.tripod.com/brightvG.htm

Brown, J. (1999). Childhood abuse and neglect: Specificity of effects on adolescent and young adult depression and suicidality. *Journal of the American Academy of Child and Adolescent Psychiatry, 38,* 1490–1496.

Brulle, A., McIntyre, T., & Mills, J. (1985). School phobia: Its educational implications. *Elementary School Guidance and Counseling, 20,* 19–28.

Bryan, T., Burstein, K., & Ergul, C. (2004). The social-emotional side of learning disabilities: A science-based presentation of the state of the art. *Learning Disability Quarterly, 27,* 45–51.

Burgess, D. M., & Streissguth, A. P. (1990). Educating students with fetal alcohol syndrome or fetal alcohol effects. *Pennsylvania Reporter, 22,* 1–6.

Burkhardt, S. (2005). Non-verbal learning disabilities. *Advances in Special Education, 16,* 21–33.

Bussing, R., Zima, B. T., Perwien, A. R., Belin, T. R., & Widawski, M. (1998). Children in special education: Attention deficit hyperactivity disorder, use of services, an unmet need. *American Journal of Public Health, 88,* 1–7.

Butterworth, B., & Reigosa, V. (2007). Information processing deficits in dyscalculia. In D. M. Berch & M. M. M. Mazzocco (Eds.), *Why is math so hard for some children? The nature and origins of mathematical learning difficulties and disabilities* (pp. 65–81). Baltimore: Paul H. Brookes.

Butterworth, B., Varma, S., & Laurillard, D. (2011). Dyscalculia: From brain to education. *Science, 332,* 1049–1053.

Callaway, E. (2012). Fathers bequeath more mutations as they age. *Nature, 488,* 439.

Camahalan, F. M. (2006). Effects of a metacognitive reading program on the reading achievement and metacognitive strategies of students with cases of dyslexia. *Reading Improvement, 43,* 77–93.

Cardon, L. R., DeFries, J. C., Fisher, S. E., Francks, C., Gayan, J., Monaco, A. P., et al. (2005). Bivariate linkage scan for reading disability and attention-deficit/hyperactivity disorder localizes pleiotropic loci. *Journal of Child Psychology and Psychiatry, 46,* 1045–1056.

Carlson, C. L., Booth, J. E., Shin, M., & Canu, W. H. (2002). Parent-, teacher-, and self-rated motivational styles and ADHD subtypes. *Journal of Learning Disabilities, 35,* 104–113.

Carlson, C. L., Tamm, L., & Gaub, M. (1997). Gender differences in children with ADHD, ODD, and co-occurring ADHD/ODD identified in a school population. *Journal of the American Academy of Child and Adolescent Psychiatry, 36,* 1706–1714.

Carmichael, M. (2008, May 26). Welcome to Max's world. *Newsweek.*

Carroll, J., Shaffer, C., Spensley, J., & Abramowitz, S. I. (1980). Family experiences of self-mutilating patients. *American Journal of Psychiatry, 137,* 852–853.

Carter, A. S., O'Donnell, D. A., Schultz, R. T., Scahill, L., Leckman, J. F., & Pauls, D. L. (2000). Social and emotional adjustment in children affected with Gilles de la Tourette's syndrome: Associations with ADHD and family functioning. *Journal of Child Psychology and Psychiatry, 41,* 215–223.

Cartledge, G. (1999). African-American males and serious emotional disturbance: Some personal perspectives. *Behavioral Disorders, 25,* 76–79.

Castellanos, F. X., Lee, P. P., Sharp, W., Jeffries, N. O., Greenstein, D. K., Clasen, L. S., et al. (2002). Developmental trajectories of brain volume abnormalities in children and adolescents with attention-deficit/hyperactivity disorder. *Journal of the American Medical Association, 288,* 1740–1748.

Cerio, J. (1997). School phobia: A family systems approach. *Elementary School Guidance and Counseling, 31,* 180–191.

Chan, W. S., Hung, S. F., Liu, S. N., & Lee, C. K. (2008). Cognitive profiling in Chinese developmental dyslexia with attention-deficit/hyperactivity disorders. *Reading and Writing, 21,* 661–674.

Chang, H., Tu, M., & Wang, H. (2004). Tourette's syndrome: Psychopathology in adolescents. *Psychiatry and Clinical Neurosciences, 58,* 353–358.

Chavira, D. A., Shipon-Blum, E., Hitchcock, C., Cohan, S., & Stein, M. B. (2007). Selective mutism and social anxiety disorder: All in the family? *Journal of the American Academy of Child and Adolescent Psychiatry, 46,* 1464–1472.

Cherry, R., & Rubinstein, A. (2006). Comparing monotic and diotic selective auditory attention abilities in children. *Language, Speech, and Hearing Services in School, 37,* 137–142.

Chitayo, M., & Wheeler, J. J. (2006). School phobia: Understanding a complex behavioral response. *Journal of Research in Special Educational Needs, 6,* 87–91.

Chiu, N. T., Chang, Y. C., Lee, B. F., Huang, C. C., & Wang, S. T. (2001). Differences in 99m Tc-HMPAO brain SPET perfusion imaging between Tourette's syndrome and chronic tic disorder in children. *European Journal of Nuclear Medicine, 28,* 183–190.

Chrisman, A., Egger, H., Compton, S. N., Curry, J., & Goldston, D. B. (2006). Assessment of childhood depression. *Child and Adolescent Mental Health, 11,* 111–116.

Cicci, R. (1984). Dyslexia: Tips for parents. *Journal of Rehabilitation, 36,* 89–101.

Ciuffreda, K. J., Kapoor, N., Rutner, D., Suchoff, I. B., Han, M. E., & Craig, S. (2007). Occurrence of oculomotor dysfunctions in acquired brain injury: A retrospective analysis. *Journal of the American Optometric Association, 78,* 155–161.

Clark, B. (2002). *Growing up gifted* (6th ed.). Upper Saddle River, NJ: Prentice Hall.

Clark, E. (1996). Children and adolescents with traumatic brain injury: Reintegration challenges in educational settings. *Journal of Learning Disabilities, 29,* 549–560.

Clarke, M., Bray, M., Kehle, T., & Truscott, S. (2001). A school-based intervention designed to reduce the frequency of tics in children with Tourette's syndrome. *School Psychology Review, 30,* 11–22.

Cole, C. L., Marder, T., & McCann, L. (2000). Self-monitoring. In E. S. Shapiro & T. R. Kratochwill (Eds.), *Conducting school-based assessments of child and adolescent behavior* (pp. 121–149). New York: Guilford Press.

Cole, D. A., & Carpentieri, S. (1990). Social status and the comorbidity of child depression and conduct disorder. *Journal of Consulting and Clinical Psychology, 58,* 748–757.

Cole, D. A., Peeke, L. G., Martin, J. M., & Truglio, R. (1998). A longitudinal look at the relation between depression and anxiety in children and adolescents. *Journal of Consulting and Clinical Psychology, 66,* 451–460.

Combs, M. L., & Slaby, D. A. (1977). Social skills training with children. *Advances in Clinical Child Psychology, 1,* 161–201.

Cook, A., Cooper, S. A., Miller, E., & Petch, A. (2008). Outcomes important to people with intellectual disabilities. *Journal of Policy and Practice in Intellectual Disabilities, 5*(3), 150–158.

Copeland, S. R., & Hughes, C. (2002). Effects of goal setting on task performance of persons with mental retardation. *Education and Training in Mental Retardation and Developmental Disabilities, 37,* 40–54.

Cornoldi, C., Rigoni, F., Tressoldi, P. E., & Vio, C. (1999). Imagery deficits in nonverbal learning disabilities. *Journal of Learning Disabilities, 32,* 48–57.

Cotugno, A. J. (1987). Cognitive control functioning in hyperactive and nonhyperactive learning disabled children. *Journal of Learning Disabilities, 20,* 563–567.

Coulter, G., & Jantz, P. (2007). Child and adolescent traumatic brain injury: Academic, behavioral, and social consequences in the classroom. *Support for Learning, 2,* 84–89.

Council for Exceptional Children. (1998). *Core competencies: Knowledge and skills for beginning special educators.* Reston, CA: Author.

Covington, M. V. (1992). *Making the grade: A self-worth perspective on motivation and school reform.* New York: Cambridge University Press.

Crain-Thoreson, C. (1999). Enhancing linguistic performance: Parents and teachers as book reading partners for children with language delays. *Topics in Early Childhood Special Education, 19,* 28–39.

Crawford, S., Channon, S., & Robertson, M. (2005). Tourette's syndrome: Performance on tests of behavioral inhibition, working memory, and gambling. *Journal of Child Psychology and Psychiatry, 46,* 1327–1336.

Crepeau-Hobson, F., & Bianco, M. (2010). Identification of gifted students with learning disabilities in a response-to-intervention era. *Psychology in the Schools, 48,* 102–109.

Crosse, S. G., Kaye, E., & Ratnofsky, A. C. (1993). *A report on the maltreatment of children with disabilities.* Washington, DC: U. S. Department of Health and Human Services.

Cullen, B., Samuels, J. F., Pinto, A., Fyer, A. J., McCracken, J. T., Rauch, S. L., et al. (2008). Demographic and clinical characteristics associated with treatment status in family members with obsessive-compulsive disorder. *Depression and Anxiety, 25,* 218–224.

Cunningham, A. E., & Stanovich, K. E. (1997). Early reading acquisition and its relation to reading experience and ability 10 years later. *Developmental Psychology, 33,* 934–945.

Curtis, R. C., Kimball, A., & Stroup, E. L. (2004). Understanding and treating social phobia. *Journal of Counseling and Development, 82,* 3–9.

Dadds, M., & Barrett, P. (2001). Practitioner review: Psychological management of anxiety disorders in childhood. *Journal of Child Psychology and Psychiatry, 42,* 999–1011.

Dahlin, K. (2011). Effects of working memory training on reading in children with special needs. *Reading and Writing, 24,* 479–491.

Daleiden, E. L. (1998). Childhood anxiety and memory functioning: A comparison of systemic and processing accounts. *Journal of Experimental Child Psychology, 68,* 216–235.

de Bildt, A., Serra, M., Luteijn, E., Kraijer, D., Systema, S., & Minderaa, R. (2005). Social skills in children with intellectual disabilities with and without autism. *Journal of Intellectual Disability Research, 49,* 317–328.

Deci, E. L., & Ryan, R. M. (1985). *Intrinsic motivation and self-determination in human behavior.* New York: Plenum.

Dehaene, S. (1992). Varieties of numerical abilities. *Cognition, 44,* 1–42.

Deidrick, K., & Farmer, J. (2005). School reentry following traumatic brain injury. *Preventing School Failure, 4,* 23–33.

DeKroon, D., Kyte, C., & Johnson, C. (2002). Partner influence on the social pretend play of children with language impairments. *Language, Speech and Hearing Services in Schools, 33,* 253–267.

Delcourt, M. A. B., Cornell, D. G., & Goldberg, M. D. (2007). Cognitive and affective learning outcomes of gifted elementary school students. *Gifted Child Quarterly, 51,* 359–381.

Denckla, M. B. (2006). Attention-deficit hyperactivity disorder (ADHD) comorbidity: A case for "pure" Tourette syndrome? *Journal of Child Neurology, 21,* 701–703.

Denham, S. A., Caverly, S., Schmidt, M., Blair, K., DeMulder, E., Caal, S., Hamada, H., & Mason, T. (2002). Preschoolers' understanding of emotions: Contributions to classroom anger and aggression. *Journal of Child Psychology and Psychiatry, 43,* 901–916.

Derr, A. M. (1985). Conservation and mathematics achievement in the learning disabled child. *Journal of Learning Disabilities, 18,* 333–336.

Deshler, D. D., Schumaker, J. B., Lenz, B. K., Bulgren, J. A., Hock, M. F., Knight, J., & Ehren, B. J. (2001). Ensuring content-area learning by secondary students with learning disabilities. *Learning Disabilities Research and Practice, 16,* 96–108.

Diamantopoulou, S., Verhulst, F. C., & van der Ende, J. (2011). The parallel development of ODD and CD symptoms from early childhood to adolescence. *European Child and Adolescent Psychiatry, 20,* 301–309.

DiCecco, V. M., & Gleason, M. M. (2002). Using graphic organizers to attain relational knowledge from expository text. *Journal of Learning Disabilities, 35,* 306–320.

Dick, D. M., Viken, R. J., Kaprio, J., Pulikkinen, L., & Rose, R. J. (2005). Understanding the covariation among childhood externalizing symptoms: Genetic and environmental influences on conduct disorder, attention deficit hyperactivity disorder, and oppositional defiant disorder symptoms. *Journal of Abnormal Child Psychology, 33,* 219–229.

Didden, R., Korzilius, H., van Oorsouw, W., Sturmey, P., & Bodfish, J. (2006). Behavioral treatment of challenging behaviors in individuals with mild mental retardation: Meta-analysis of single-subject research. *American Journal on Mental Retardation, 111,* 290–298.

Dietz, S., & Montague, M. (2006). Attention deficit hyperactivity disorder comorbid with emotional and behavioral disorders and learning disabilities in adolescents. *Exceptionality, 14,* 19–33.

DiSarno, N. J., Schowalter, M., & Grassa, P. (2002). Classroom amplification to enhance student performance. *Teaching Exceptional Children, 34*(6), 20–26.

Dobbins, M., Sunder, T., & Soltys, S. (2007). Nonverbal learning disabilities and sensory processing disorders. *Psychiatric Times, 24*(9), 1–14.

*Doe* v. *Withers.* (1992). Civil action no. 92-C-92. Retrieved from http://www.wrightslaw.com/law/caselaw/case_Doe_Withers_Complaint.html

Drabick, D. A. G., Ollendick, T. H., & Bubier, J. L. (2010). Co-occurrence of ODD and anxiety: Shared risk processes and evidence for a dual-pathway model. *Clinical Psychology: Science and Practice, 17,* 307–318.

Drecktrah, M. E., & Chiang, B. (1997). Instructional strategies used by general educators and teachers of students with learning disabilities: A survey. *Remedial and Special Education, 18,* 174–181.

Dreher, N. (1996). What is Tourette syndrome? *Current Health, 23,* 21–23.

Ducharme, J. M., Harris, K., Milligan, K., & Pontes, E. (2003). Sequential evaluation of reinforced compliance and graduated request delivery for the treatment of noncompliance in children with developmental disabilities. *Journal of Autism and Developmental Disorders, 33,* 519–526.

DuPaul, G. J. (2007). School-based interventions for students with attention deficit hyperactivity disorder: Current status and future directions. *School Psychology Review, 36,* 183–194.

DuPaul, G. J., Ervin, R. A., Hook, C. L., & McGoey, K. E. (1998). Peer tutoring for children with attention deficit hyperactivity disorder: Effects on classroom behavior and academic performance. *Journal of Applied Behavior Analysis, 31,* 579–592.

DuPaul, G. J., & Henningson, P. N. (1993). Peer tutoring effects on the classroom performance of children with attention deficit hyperactivity disorder. *School Psychology Review, 22,* 134–143.

DuPaul, G. J., Jitendra, A. K., Tresco, K. E., Vile Junrod, R. E., Volpe, R. J., & Lutz, J. G. (2006). Children with attention deficit hyperactivity disorder: Are there gender differences in school functioning? *School Psychology Review, 35,* 292–308.

Durrant, J. E., Cunningham, C. E., & Voelker, S. (1990). Academic, social, and general self-concepts of behavioral subgroups of learning disabled children. *Journal of Educational Psychology, 82,* 657–663.

Dykeman, B. F. (2003). School-based interventions for treating social adjustment difficulties in children with traumatic brain injury. *Journal of Instructional Psychology, 30,* 225–230.

Edeh, O. M. (2006). Cross-cultural investigation of interest-based training and social interpersonal problem solving in students with mental retardation. *Education and Training in Developmental Disabilities, 41,* 163–176.

Education for All Handicapped Children Act of 1975, P.L. 94-142. Retrieved from http://www.scn.org/~bk269/20usc1400.html

Eisen, A. R., Brien, L. K., Bowers, J., & Strudler, A. (2001). Separation anxiety disorders. In C. A. Essau & F. Petermann (Eds.), *Anxiety disorders in children and adolescents: Epidemiology, risk factors, and treatment* (pp. 111–141). New York: Taylor & Francis.

Elder-Hinshaw, R., Manset-Williamson, G., Nelson, J. M., & Dunn, M. W. (2006). Engaging older students with reading disabilities: Multimedia inquiry projects supported by reading assistive technology. *Teaching Exceptional Children, 39*(1), 6–11.

Embry, R. A., & Grossman, F. D. (2006/2007). The Los Angeles County response to child abuse and deafness: A social movement theory analysis. *American Annals of the Deaf, 151,* 488–500.

Engel-Yeger, B. E., Nagauker-Yanuv, L., & Rosenblum, S. (2009). Handwriting performance, self-reports, and perceived self-efficacy among children with dysgraphia. *American Journal of Occupational Therapy, 63,* 182–192.

Englert, C. S., Garmon, A., Mariage, T., Rozendal, M., Tarrant, K., & Urba, J. (1995). The early literacy project: Connecting across the literacy curriculum. *Learning Disability Quarterly, 18,* 253–275.

Epstein, M. A., Shaywitz, S. E., Shaywitz, B. A., & Woolston, J. L. (1991). The boundaries of attention deficit disorder. *Journal of Learning Disabilities, 24,* 78–86.

Estell, D. B., Jones, M. H., Pearl, R., & Van Acker, R. (2009). Best friendships of students with and without learning disabilities across late elementary school. *Exceptional Children, 76,* 110–124.

Evans, L. (2000). Functional school refusal subtypes: Anxiety, avoidance, and malingering. *Psychology in the Schools, 37,* 183–191.

Executive summary. (1995). *ISEAS Cable, 16*(3), 5.

Eysenck, H. J. (1967). *The biological basis of personality.* Springfield, IL: Thomas.

Fairweather, J. S., & Shaver, D. M. (1990). Making a transition to postsecondary education and training. *Exceptional Children, 57,* 264–270.

Faris, R., & Felmlee, D. (2011). Status struggles: Network centrality and gender segregation in same- and cross-gender aggression. *American Sociological Review, 76,* 48–73.

Famy, C, Streissguth, A. P., & Unis, A. S. (1998). Mental illness in adults with fetal alcohol syndrome or fetal alcohol effects. *American Journal of Psychiatry, 155,* 552–554.

Faust, M. W., Ashcraft, M. H., & Fleck, D. E. (1996). Mathematics anxiety effects in simple and complex addition. *Mathematics Cognition, 2,* 25–62.

Feindler, E. L., & Ecton, R. B. (1986). *Adolescent anger control: Cognitive-behavioral techniques.* New York: Pergamon Press.

Feldhusen, J. F. (1998a). Programs and services at the elementary level. In J. VanTassel-Baska (Ed.), *Excellence in educating gifted and talented learners* (3rd ed., pp. 211–223). Denver: Love.

Feldhusen, J. F. (1998b). Programs and services at the secondary level. In J. VanTassel-Baska (Ed.), *Excellence in educating gifted and talented learners* (3rd ed., pp. 225–240). Denver: Love.

Feldhusen, J. F. (1998c). Strategies and methods for teaching the talented. In J. VanTassel-Baska (Ed.), *Excellence in educating gifted and talented learners* (3rd ed., pp. 363–379). Denver: Love.

Feldman, E., & Dodge, K. A. (1987). Social information processing and sociometric status: Sex, age, and situational effects. *Journal of Abnormal Child Psychology, 15,* 211–227.

Fenske, J. N., & Schwenk, T. L. (2009). Obsessive-compulsive disorder: Diagnosis and management. *American Family Physician, 80,* 139–245.

Ferrand, C. T., & Bloom, R. L. (1997). *Introduction to organic and neurogenic disorders of communication: Current scope of practice.* Needham Heights, MA: Allyn & Bacon.

Fidler, D. (2006). The emergence of a syndrome-specific personality profile in young children with Down syndrome. *Down Syndrome Research and Practice, 10,* 53–60.

Field, T., Martinez, A., Nawrocki, T., Pickens, J., Fox, N. A., & Schanberg, S. (1998). Music shifts frontal EEG in depressed adolescents. *Adolescence, 33,* 109–116.

Finn, J. D. (1989). Withdrawing from school. *Review of Educational Research, 59,* 117–142.

Fisher, N. J., & DeLuca, J. W. (1997). Verbal learning strategies of adolescents and adults with the syndrome of nonverbal learning disabilities. *Child Neuropsychology, 3,* 192–198.

Fletcher, K. L., Blair, C., Scott, M. S., & Bolger, K. E. (2004). Specific patterns of cognitive abilities in young children with mild mental retardation. *Education and Training in Developmental Disabilities, 39,* 270–278.

Flint, L. J. (2001). Challenges of identifying and serving gifted children with ADHD. *Teaching Exceptional Children, 33*(4), 62–69.

Foley Nicpon, M., Allmon, A., Sieck, B., & Stinson, R. D. (2011). Empirical investigation of twice-exceptionality: Where have we been and where are we going? *Gifted Child Quarterly, 55,* 3–17.

Foltz, R. (2008). Behind the veil of conduct disorder: Challenging current assumptions in search of strengths. *Reclaiming Children and Youth, 16,* 5–9.

Foss, J. M. (2001). *Nonverbal learning disability: How to recognize it and minimize its effects.* ERIC/Clearinghouse on Disabilities and Gifted Education Digest E619.

Fossati, A., Maffei, C., Bagnato, M., Donati, D., Donini, M., Fiorilli, M., & Novella, L. (2000). A psychometric study of *DSM-IV* passive-aggressive (negativistic) personality disorder criteria. *Journal of Personality Disorders, 14,* 72–83.

Frankl, V. E. (1959). *Man's search for meaning.* New York: Basic Books.

Freeman, S. F. N., & Alkin, M. C. (2000). Academic and social attainments of children with mental retardation in general education and special education settings. *Remedial and Special Education, 21,* 3–18, 26.

Freemont, W. P. (2003). School refusal in children and adolescents. *American Family Physician, 68,* 1555–1560.

Freer, B. D., Hayden, A., Lorch, E. P., & Milich, R. (2011). The stories they tell: Story production difficulties of children with ADHD. *School Psychology Review, 40,* 355–366.

French, B. F., Zentall, S. S., & Bennett, D. (2003). Short-term memory of children with and without characteristics of attention deficit hyperactivity disorder. *Learning and Individual Differences, 13,* 205–225.

Frith, U. (1991). Asperger and his syndrome. In U. Frith (Ed.), *Autism and Asperger syndrome* (pp. 1–36). London: Cambridge University Press.

Fuchs, L. S., Compton, D. L., Fuchs, D., Paulsen, K., Bryant, J. D., & Hamlett, C. L. (2005). The prevention, identification, and cognitive determinants of math difficulty. *Journal of Educational Psychology, 97,* 493–513.

Fuchs, L. S., & Fuchs, D. (2001). Principles for the prevention and intervention of mathematics difficulties. *Learning Disabilities Research and Practice, 16,* 85–95.

Fuchs, L. S., Fuchs, D., & Speece, D. L. (2002). Treatment validity as a unifying construct for identifying learning disabilities. *Learning Disability Quarterly, 25,* 33–45.

Furner, J. M., & Marinas, C. A. (2007). Geometry sketching software for elementary children: Easy as 1, 2, 3. *Eurasia Journal of Mathematics, Science, and Technology Education, 3,* 83–91.

Gallagher, J. J. (2003). Issues and challenges in the education of gifted education. In N. Colangelo & G. A. Davis (Eds.), *Handbook of gifted education* (pp. 11–23). Boston: Pearson Education.

Gallivan, N. P., & Kottler, E. (2007). Eight types of graphic organizers for empowering social studies students and teachers. *Social Studies, 98,* 117–128.

Gardner, H. (1983). *Frames of mind: The theory of multiple intelligences.* New York: Basic Books.

Garrett, B. (2011). *Brain and behavior: An introduction to biological psychology.* Thousand Oaks, CA: Sage.

Geary, D. C. (2003). Learning disabilities in arithmetic: Problem-solving differences and cognitive deficits. In H. L. Swanson, K. R. Harris, & S. Graham (Eds.), *Handbook of learning disabilities* (pp. 199–212). New York: Guilford Press.

Geary, D. C. (2004). Mathematics and learning disabilities. *Journal of Learning Disabilities, 37,* 4–15.

Geary, D. C., Hoard, M. K., Nugent, L., & Byrd-Craven, J. (2007). Strategy use, long-term memory, and working memory capacity. In D. M. Berch & M. M. M. Mazzocco (Eds.), *Why is math so hard for some children? The nature and origins of mathematical learning difficulties and disabilities* (pp. 83–105). Baltimore: Paul H. Brookes.

Gerberding, J. L., & Binder, S. (2003). *Report to Congress on mild traumatic brain injury in the United States: Steps to prevent a serious public health problem.* Atlanta, GA: Centers for Disease Control and Prevention.

Gersten, R., Beckmann, S., Clarke, B., Foegen, A., Marsh, L., Star, J. R., & Witzel, B. (2009). *Assisting students struggling with mathematics: Response to intervention (RtI) for elementary and middle schools.* Washington, DC: U.S. Department of Education, Institute of Education Sciences. Retrieved from http://ies.ed.gov/ncee/wwc/pdf/practice_guides/rti_math_pg_042109.pdf

Gersten, R., & Chard, D. (1999). Number sense: Rethinking arithmetic instruction for students with mathematical disabilities. *Journal of Special Education, 33,* 18–28.

Gersten, R., Compton, D., Connor, C. M., Dimino, J., Santoro, L., Linan-Thompson, & Tilly, W. D. (2009). *Assisting students struggling with reading: Response to intervention and multi-tier intervention in the primary grades.* Washington, DC: National Center for Education Evaluation and Regional Assistance, Institute of Education, U.S. Department of Education. Retrieved from http://ies.ed.gov/ncee/wwc/publications/practice guides

Gettinger, M. (1985). Effects of teacher-directed versus student-directed instruction and cues versus no cues for improving spelling performance. *Journal of Applied Behavior Analysis, 18,* 167–171.

Ghaziuddin, M. (2008). Defining the behavioral phenotype of Asperger syndrome. *Journal of Autism and Developmental Disorders, 38,* 138–142.

Ghelani, K., Sidhu, R., Jain, U., & Tannock, R. (2004). Reading comprehension and reading related abilities in adolescents with reading disabilities and attention-deficit/hyperactivity disorder. *Dyslexia, 10,* 364–384.

Gied, S., & Pine, S. D (2002). Consequences and correlates of adolescent depression. *Archives of Pediatrics and Adolescent Medicine, 156,* 1009–1014.

Goldberg, M. C., Mostofksy, S. H., Cutting, L. E., Mahone, E. M., Astor, B. C., Denckla, M. B., et al. (2005). Subtle executive impairment in children with autism and children with ADHD. *Journal of Autism and Developmental Disorders, 35,* 279–293.

Goldberg, M.C., Mostow, A.J., Vecera, S.P., Gidley Larson, J.C., Mostofsky, S.H., Mahone, E.M., & Denkla, M.B. (2008). Evidence for impairments in using static line drawings of eye gaze cues to orient visual-spatial attention in children with high functioning autism. Journal of Autism and Developmental Disorders, 38, 1405–1413.

Goldstein, D. (n.d.). *Screening tool: Nonverbal learning disability (NVLD).* Retrieved from http://www.emental-health.ca/index.php?m=survey&ID=30

Gore, M. T., & Janssen, K. G. (2007). What educators need to know about abused children with disabilities. *Preventing School Failure, 52,* 49–55.

Gortmaker, V. J., Warnes, E. D., & Sheridan, S. M. (2004). Conjoint behavioral consultation: Involving parents and teachers in the treatment of a child with selective mutism. *Proven Practice, 5,* 66–72.

Gottfredson, L. S. (2003). The science and politics of intelligence in gifted education. In N. Colangelo & G. A. Davis (Eds.), *Handbook of gifted education* (pp. 24–40). Boston: Pearson Education.

Gould, K. R., Johnston, L., Ponsford, J. L., & Schonberger, M. (2011). Predictive and associated factors of psychiatric disorders after traumatic brain injury: A prospective study. *Journal of Neurotrauma, 28,* 1155–1163.

Graham, S. (1983). The effect of self-instructional procedures on LD students' handwriting performance. *Learning Disability Quarterly, 6,* 231–234.

Graham, S. (1999). Handwriting and spelling instruction for students with learning disabilities: A review. *Learning Disability Quarterly, 22,* 78–98.

Graham, S., & Harris, K. R. (2003). Students with learning disabilities and the process of writing: A meta-analysis of SRSD studies. In H. L. Swanson, K. R. Harris, & S. Graham (Eds.), *Handbook of learning disabilities* (pp. 323–344). New York: Guilford Press.

Graham, S., & Harris, K. R. (2009). Almost 30 years of writing research: Making sense of it all with *The Wrath of Khan. Learning Disabilities Research & Practice, 24,* 58–68.

Graves, A., & Hauge, R. (1993). Using cues and prompts to improve story writing.

*Teaching Exceptional Children, 25*(4), 38–40.

Green, J. H., & Gillen, P. (2002). *Cognitive disabilities and associated features of fetal alcohol spectrum disorders.* Poster presentation at the Coleman Institute Workshop.

Greene, R. W. (2006). Oppositional defiant disorder. In M. Hersen & J. C. Thomas (Eds.), *Comprehensive handbook of personality and psychopathology* (Vol. 3, pp. 285–298). Hoboken, NJ: John Wiley.

Greene, R. W., & Ablon, J. S. (2006). *Treating explosive kids: The collaborative problem-solving approach.* New York: Guilford Press.

Greene, R. W., Ablon, J. S., Monuteaux, M. C., Goring, J. C., Henin, A., Raezer-Blakely, L., et al. (2004). Effectiveness of collaborative problem solving in affectively dysregulated children with oppositional-defiant disorder: Initial findings. *Journal of Consulting and Clinical Psychology, 72,* 1157–1164.

Greene, R. W., Biederman, J., Zerwas, S., Monuteaux, M. C., Goring, J. C., & Faraone, S. V. (2002). Psychiatric comorbidity, family dysfunction, and social impairment in referred youth with oppositional defiant disorder. *American Journal of Psychiatry, 159,* 1214–1224.

Greenwood, C. R., Horton, B. T., & Utley, C. A. (2002). Academic engagement: Current perspectives on research and practice. *School Psychology Review, 31,* 328–349.

Gresham, F. M., MacMillan, D. L., & Bocian, K. M. (1996). Learning disabilities, low achievement, and mild mental retardation: More alike than different? *Journal of Learning Disabilities, 29,* 570–581.

Grskovic, J. A., & Zentall, S. S. (2010). Understanding ADHD in girls: Identification and social characteristics. *International Journal of Special Education, 25,* 171–184.

Gumpel, T. P., & David, S. (2000). Exploring the efficacy of self–regulatory training as a possible alternative to social skills training. *Behavioral Disorders, 25,* 131–141.

Gureasko-Moore, S., DuPaul, G. J., & White, G. P. (2007). Self-management of classroom preparedness and homework: Effects of school functioning of adolescents with attention deficit hyperactivity disorder. *School Psychology Review, 36,* 647–664.

Hagin, R. A. (2004). Autism and other severe pervasive developmental disorders. In F. M. Kline & L. B. Silver (Eds.), *The educator's guide to mental health issues in the classroom* (pp. 55–73). Baltimore: Paul J. Brookes.

Hahn, L. V. (2004). What is a nonverbal learning disability? *Exceptional Parent, 34,* 49–51.

Hall, A. M., & Zentall, S. S. (2000). The effects of learning station on the completion and accuracy of math homework for middle school students. *Journal of Behavioral Education, 10,* 123–137.

Hall, P. K. (2000). A letter to the parent(s) of a child with developmental apraxia of speech, Part III: Other problems often associated with the disorder. *Language, Speech, and Hearing Services in Schools, 31,* 176–178.

Hallowell, E. M., & Ratey, J. J. (1995). *Driven to distraction: Recognizing and coping with attention deficit disorder from childhood through adulthood.* New York: Simon & Schuster.

Hann, P., Penney, C. G., & Power, B. (1999). A possible contribution of word-retrieval difficulties to reading and spelling impairments. *Learning and Individual Differences, 11,* 377–400.

Hanna, F. J., Hanna, C. A., & Keys, S. G. (1999). Fifty strategies for counseling defiant, aggressive adolescents: Reaching, accepting, and relating. *Journal of Counseling and Development, 77,* 395–405.

Harnadek, M. C. S., & Rourke, B. P. (1994). Principal identifying features of the syndrome of nonverbal learning disabilities in children. *Journal of Learning Disabilities, 27,* 144–154.

Harrington, R. (1993). *Depressive disorder in children and adolescents.* New York: John Wiley.

Harris, K. R., & Graham, S. (1999). Programmatic intervention research: Illustrations from the evolution of self-regulated strategy development. *Learning Disability Quarterly, 22,* 251–262.

Harrison, J., Thompson, B., & Vannest, K. J. (2009). Interpreting the evidence for effective interventions to increase the academic performance of students with ADHD: Relevance of the statistical significance controversy. *Review of Educational Research, 79,* 740–775.

Hart, K. C., Massetti, G. M., Fabiano, G. A., Pariseau, M. E., & Pelham, W. E. (2011). Impact of group size on classroom on-task behavior and work productivity in children with ADHD. *Journal of Emotional and Behavioral Disorders, 19,* 55–64.

Hartley, S. L., & MacLean, W. E., Jr. (2005). Perceptions of stress and coping strategies among adults with mild mental retardation: Insight into psychological distress. *American Journal on Mental Retardation, 110,* 285–297.

Hasselbring, T., Sherwood, R., Bransford, J., Fleenor, K., Griffith, D., & Goin, L. (1988). Evaluation of a level-one instructional videodisc program. *Journal of Educational Technology Systems, 16,* 151–169.

Hatton, C. (1998). Pragmatic language skills in people with intellectual disabilities: A review. *Journal of Intellectual and Developmental Disabilities, 23,* 79–100.

Hawken, L., Vincent, C., & Schumann, B. (2008). Response to intervention for social behavior: Challenges and opportunities. *Journal of Emotional and Behavioral Disorders, 16,* 213–225.

Hawley, P. (2002). Social dominance and prosocial and coercive strategies of resource control in preschoolers. *International Journal of Behavioral Development, 26,* 167–176.

Hay, I., Elias, G., Fielding-Barnsley, R., Homel, R., & Freiberg, K. (2007). Language delays, reading delays, and learning difficulties: Interactive elements requiring multidimensional programming. *Journal of Learning Disabilities, 40,* 400–409.

Hecker, L., Burns, L., Elkind, J., Elkind, K., & Katz, L. (2002). Benefits of assistive reading software for students with attention disorders. *Annals of Dyslexia, 52,* 243–273.

Heiervang, E., Stevenson, J. Lund, A., & Hugdahl, K. (2001). Behaviour problems in children with dyslexia. *Nordic Journal of Psychiatry, 55,* 251–256.

Hendren, G. (2002). Tourette syndrome: A new look at an old condition. *Journal of Rehabilitation, 68,* 22–27.

Herpertz, S. C., Huebner, T., Marx, I., Vloet, T. D., Fink, G. R., Stoecker, T., et al. (2008). Emotional processing in male adolescents with childhood-onset conduct disorder. *Journal of Child Psychology and Psychiatry, 49,* 781–791.

Higgins, E. L., & Raskind, M. H. (2005). The compensatory effectiveness of the Quicktionary Reading Pen II on the reading comprehension of students with learning difficulties. *Journal of Special Education Technology, 20*(1), 31–37.

Hillegers, M. H. J., Reichart, C. G., Wals, M., Verhulst, F. C., Ormel, J., & Nolen, W. A. (2005). Five-year prospective outcome of psychopathology in the adolescent offspring of bipolar parents. *Bipolar Disorders, 7,* 344–350.

Ho, C. S., Chan, D. W., Leung, P. W., Lee, S., & Tsang, S. (2005). Reading-related cognitive deficits in developmental dyslexia, attention-deficit/hyperactivity disorder, and developmental coordination disorder. *Reading Research Quarterly, 40,* 318–337.

Hodgins, S., Cree, A., Alderton, J., & Mak, T. (2008). From conduct disorder to severe mental illness: Associations with aggressive behaviour, crime and victimization. *Psychological Medicine, 38,* 975–987.

Hollander, E., & Bakalar, N. (2005). Children and adolescents. In *Coping with social anxiety: The definitive guide to effective treatment options* (pp. 73–89). New York: Henry Holt.

Holmes, J., Gathercole, S. E., & Dunning, D. L. (2009). Adaptive training leads to sustained enhancement of poor working memory in children. *Developmental Science, 12,* F9–F15.

Houck, C. K., & Billingsley, B. S. (1989). Written expression of students with and without learning disabilities: Differences across the grades. *Journal of Learning Disabilities, 22,* 561–567.

Huffman, L. F., Fletcher, K. L., Bray, N. W., & Grupe, L. A. (2004). Similarities and differences in addition strategies of children with and without mental retardation. *Education and Training in Developmental Disabilities, 39,* 317–325.

Humphrey, N. (2002). Teacher and pupil ratings of self-esteem in developmental dyslexia. *British Journal of Special Education, 29,* 29–36.

Humphreys, K. L., & Lee, S. S. (2011). Risk taking and sensitivity to punishment in children with ADHD, ODD, ADHD+ODD, and controls. *Journal of Psychopathology and Behavioral Assessment, 33,* 299–307.

Hyde, M. O., & Forsyth, E. H. (2002). *Depression: What you need to know.* New York: Scholastic.

Imhof, M. (2004). Effects of color stimulation on handwriting performance of children with ADHD without and with learning disabilities. *European Child and Adolescent Psychiatry, 13,* 191–198.

Individuals with Disabilities Education Improvement Act of 2004, P.L. 108-446. Retrieved from http://nichcy.org/wp-content/uploads/docs/PL108-446.pdf

Jarvinen, D. W., & Sprague, R. L. (1995). Using ACTeRS to screen minority children for ADHD: An examination of item bias. *Journal of Psychoeducational Assessment, 1,* 172–184.

Jay, T. (2000). *Why we curse: A neuro-psychosocial theory of speech.* Philadelphia: John Benjamins.

Jenni, C. (1997). School phobia: How home-school collaboration can tame this frightful dragon. *School Counselor, 44,* 206–218.

Jensen, P. S., Hinshaw, S. P., Kraemer, H. C., Nilantha, L., Newcorn, J. H., Abikoff, H. B., et al. (2001). ADHD comorbidity findings from the MTA study: Comparing comorbid groups. *Journal of the American Academy of Child and Adolescent Psychiatry, 40,* 147–158.

Jepsen, J. R. M., & Mortensen, E. L. (2009). Do attention deficits influence IQ assessment in children and adolescents with ADHD? *Journal of Attention Disorders, 12,* 551–562.

Jiménez, J. E., Siegel, L. S., & López, M. R. (2003). The relationship between IQ and reading disabilities in English-speaking Canadian and Spanish children. *Journal of Learning Disabilities, 36,* 15–23.

Jones, S. (1999). *Dysgraphia accommodations and modifications.* LD online. Retrieved from http://www.ldonline.org/article/6202

Jongmans, M. J., Smits-Engelsman, B. C. M., & Schoemaker, M. M. (2003). Consequences of comorbidity of developmental coordination disorders and learning disabilities for severity and pattern of perceptual-motor dysfunction. *Journal of Learning Disabilities, 36,* 528–537.

Jordan, N. C. (2007). Do words count? Connections between mathematics and reading difficulties. In D. M. Berch & M. M. M. Mazzocco (Eds.), *Why is math so hard for some children? The nature and origins of mathematical learning difficulties and disabilities* (pp. 107–120). Baltimore: Paul H. Brookes.

Kalra, S. K., & Swedo, S. E. (2009). Children with obsessive-compulsive disorder: Are they just "little adults"? *Journal of Clinical Investigation, 119,* 737–746.

Kang, H., & Zentall, S. S. (2011). Computer-generated geometry instruction: A preliminary study. *Educational Technology Research and Development, 59,* 783–797.

Kanioglou, A., Tsorbatzoudis, H., & Barkoukis, V. (2005). Socialization and behavioral problems of elementary school pupils with developmental coordination disorder. *Perceptual and Motor Skills, 101,* 163–173.

Kapalka, G. M. (2004). Longer eye contact improves ADHD children's compliance with parental commands. *Journal of Attention Disorders, 8,* 17–23.

Kats-Gold, I., Besser, A., & Priel, B. (2007). The role of simple emotion recognition skills among school-aged boys at risk of ADHD. *Journal of Abnormal Child Psychology, 35,* 363–378.

Katsiyannis, A., Zhang, D., & Archwamety, T. (2002). Placement and exit patterns for students with mental retardation: An analysis of national trends. *Education and Training in Mental Retardation and Developmental Disabilities, 37,* 134–145.

Kavale, K. A., & Forness, S. (1995). *The nature of learning disabilities: Critical elements of diagnosis and classification.* Mahwah, NJ: Lawrence Erlbaum.

Kearney, C. A. (2001). *School refusal behavior in youth: A functional approach to assessment and treatment.* Washington, DC: American Psychological Association.

Kearney, C. A. (2002). Identifying the function of school refusal behavior: A revision of the School Refusal Assessment Scale. *Journal of Psychopathological Behavioral Assessment, 24,* 235–245.

Kearney, C. A. (2003). Bridging the gap among professionals who address youths with school absenteeism: Overview and suggestions for consensus. *Professional Psychology: Research and Practice, 34,* 57–65.

Kearney, C. A. (2005). *Social anxiety and social phobia in youth.* New York. Springer Science and Business.

Kearney, C. A. (2006). Dealing with school refusal behavior: A primer for family physicians. *Journal of Family Practice, 55,* 685–692.

Kearney, C. A., & Beasley, J. F. (1994). The clinical treatment of school refusal behavior: A survey of referral and practice characteristics. *Psychology in the Schools, 31,* 128–132.

Kearney, C. A., Eisen, A. R., & Silverman, W. K. (1995). The legend and myth of school phobia. *School Psychology Quarterly, 10,* 65–85.

Kellam, S. G., Rebok, G. W., Mayer, L. S., Ialongo, N., & Kalodner, C. R. (1994). Depressive symptoms over first grade and their response to developmental epidemiologically based preventive trial aimed at improving achievement. *Development and Psychopathology, 6,* 463–481.

Kempes, M., Walter, M., Han, V., & Engeland, H. (2005). Reactive and proactive aggression in children: A review of theory, findings and the relevance for child and adolescent psychiatry. *European Child and Adolescent Psychiatry, 14,* 11–19.

Kendall, P. C., Pimentel, S., Rynn, M., Angelosante, A., & Webb, A. (2004). Generalized anxiety disorder. In T. Ollendick & J. March (Eds.), *Phobic and anxiety disorders in children and adolescents.* New York: Oxford University Press.

Kercood, S., & Grskovic, J. A. (2009). The effects of highlighting on math computation performance and off-task behavior of students with attention problems. *Education and Treatment of Children, 32,* 231–241.

Kercood, S., Zentall, S. S., Vinh, M., & Tom-Wright, K. (2012). Attentional cuing in math word problems for girls at-risk for ADHD and their peers in general education settings. *Contemporary Educational Psychology, 37,* 106–112.

Kerns, K. A., Don, A., Mateer, C. A., & Streissguth, A. P. (1997). Cognitive deficits in nonretarded adults with fetal alcohol syndrome. *Journal of Learning Disabilities, 30,* 685–693.

Kerns, K. A., Eso, K., & Thomson, J. (1999). Investigation of a direct intervention for improving attention in young children with ADHD. *Developmental Neuropsychology, 16,* 273–295.

Keyser-Marcus, L., Briel, L., Sherron-Targett, P., Yasuda, S., Johnson, S., & Wehman, P. (2002). Enhancing the schooling of students with traumatic brain injury. *Teaching Exceptional Children, 34*(4), 62–67.

King, N. J., & Ollendick, T. H. (1997). Treatment of childhood phobias. *Journal of Child Psychology and Psychiatry, 38,* 389–400.

Kirby, A., & Sugden, D. A. (2007). Children with developmental coordination disorders. *Journal of the Royal Society of Medicine, 100,* 182–186.

Klecan-Aker, J. S., & Kelty, K. R. (1990). An investigation of the oral narratives of normal and language-learning disabled children. *Journal of Childhood Communication Disorders, 13,* 207–213.

Kohn, A. (1993). Rewards versus learning: A response to Paul Chance. *Phi Delta Kappan, 74,* 783–786.

Konrad, M., Fowler, C., Walker, A., Test, D., & Wood, W. (2007). Effects of self-determination interventions on the academic skills of students with learning disabilities. *Learning Disability Quarterly, 30,* 89–113.

Kooistra, L., Crawford, S., Dewey, D., Cantell, M., & Kaplan, B. J. (2005). Motor correlates of ADHD: Contribution of reading disability and oppositional defiant disorder. *Journal of Learning Disabilities, 38,* 195–205.

Kopecky, C. C., Sawyer, C. R., & Behnke, R. R. (2004). Sensitivity to punishment and explanatory style as predictors of public speaking state anxiety. *Communication Education, 53,* 281–285.

Kottman, T., & Ashby, J. (2000). Perfectionistic children and adolescents: Implications for school counselors. *Professional School Counseling, 3,* 182–188.

Krupski, A. (1980). Attention processes: Research, theory, and implications for special education. In B. K. Keogh (Ed.), *Advances in special education* (Vol. 1, pp. 101–140). Greenwich, CT: JAI Press.

Kuester, D. A., & Zentall, S. S. (2012). Social interaction rules in cooperative learning groups for students at risk for ADHD. *Journal of Experimental Education, 80*(1), 69–95.

Kvam, M. H. (2000). Is sexual abuse of children with disabilities disclosed? A retrospective analysis of child disability and the likelihood of sexual abuse among those attending Norwegian hospitals. *Child Abuse and Neglect, 24,* 1073–1084.

Lahey, B. B., Applegate, B., McBurnett, K., Biederman, J., Greenhill, L., Hynd, G. W., et al. (1994). *DSM-IV* field trials for attention deficit hyperactivity disorder in children and adolescents. *American Journal of Psychiatry, 151,* 1673–1685.

Lahey, B. B., Moffitt, T. E., & Caspi A. (Eds.). (2003). *Causes of conduct disorder and juvenile delinquency.* New York: Guilford Press.

Lahey, B. B., Pelham, W. E., Loney, J., Lee, S. S., & Willcutt, E. G. (2005). Instability of the *DSM-IV* subtypes of ADHD from preschool through elementary school. *Archives of General Psychiatry, 62,* 896–902.

Lambert, N. M., Sandoval, J., & Sassone, D. (1978). Prevalence of hyperactivity in elementary school children as a function of social system definers. *American Journal of Orthopsychiatry, 48,* 447–463.

Lanza, H. I., & Drabick, D. A. G. (2011). Family routine moderates the relation between child impulsivity and oppositional defiant disorder symptoms. *Journal of Abnormal Child Psychology, 39,* 83–94.

Larkby, C. A., Goldschmidt, L., Hanusa, B., & Day, N. L. (2011). Prenatal alcohol exposure is associated with conduct disorder in adolescence: Findings from a birth cohort. *Journal of the American Academy of Child and Adolescent Psychiatry, 50,* 262–271.

Lawrence, V., Houghton, S., Tannock, R., Douglas, G., Durkin, K., & Whiting, K. (2002). ADHD outside the laboratory: Boy's executive function performance on tasks in videogame play and on a visit to the zoo. *Journal of Abnormal Child Psychology, 30,* 447–462.

Lazarus, A. A., Davison, G. C., & Polefka, D. A. (1965). Classical and operant factors in the treatment of a school phobia. *Journal of Abnormal Psychology, 70,* 225–229.

Leary, M. R. (1995). *Social anxiety.* New York: Guilford Press.

Leckman, J. F. (2002). Tourette's syndrome. *The Lancet, 360,* 1577–1586.

Lee, D. L., & Zentall, S. S. (2002). The effects of visual stimulation on the mathematics performance of children with attention deficit/hyperactivity disorder. *Behavior Disorders, 27,* 272–288.

Lee, M., & Miltenberger, R. (1996). School refusal behavior: Classification, assessment, and treatment issues. *Education and Treatment of Children, 19,* 474–486.

LeFever, G. B., Villers, M. S., Morrow, A. L., & Vaughn, E. S. (2002). Parental perceptions of adverse educational outcomes among children diagnosed and treated with ADHD: A call for improved school/provider collaboration. *Psychology in the Schools, 29,* 63–71.

Leininger, M., Dyches, T. T., Prater, M. A., Heath, M. A., & Bascom, S. (2010). Books portraying characters with obsessive-compulsive disorder. *Teaching Exceptional Children, 42*(4), 22–28.

Lerner, J., & Kline, F. (2006). *Learning disabilities and related disorders: Characteristics and teaching strategies* (10th ed.). Boston: Houghton Mifflin.

Lesh, R., & Doerr, H. (1998). Symbolizing, communicating, and mathematizing: Key components of models and modeling. In P. Cobb & E. Yackel (Eds.), *Symbolizing, communicating and mathematizing.* Mahwah, NJ: Lawrence Erlbaum.

Leuven, E., Oosterbeek, H, & van Ophem, H. (2004). Explaining international differences in male skill wage differentials by differences in demand and supply of skill. *Economic Journal, 114,* 466–486.

Lilienfeld, S. O., & Penna, S. (2001). Anxiety sensitivity: Relations to psychopathy, *DSM-IV* personality disorder features, and personality traits. *Journal of Anxiety Disorders, 15,* 367–393.

Linemann, T. O., & Reid, R. (2008). Using self-regulated strategy development to improve expository writing with students with attention deficit hyperactivity disorder. *Exceptional Children, 74,* 471–487.

Little, T. D., Jones, S. M., Henrich, C. C., & Hawley, P. H. (2003). Disentangling the "whys" from the "whats" of aggressive behaviour. *International Journal of Behavioural Development, 27,* 122–133.

Loe, I. M., & Feldman, H. M. (2007). Academic and educational outcomes of children with ADHD. *Journal of Pediatric Psychology, 32,* 643–654.

Loeber, R., Burke, J., & Pardini, D. A. (2009). Perspectives on oppositional defiant disorder, conduct disorder, and psychopathic features. *Journal of Child Psychology and Psychiatry, 50,* 133–142.

Long, N. J., & Long, J. E. (2001). *Managing passive-aggressive behavior of children and youth at school and home: The angry smile.* Austin, TX: Praeger.

Lorch, E. P., O'Neil, K., Berthiaume, K. S., Milich, R., Eastman, D., & Brooks, T. (2004). Story comprehension and the impact of studying on recall in children with attention deficit hyperactivity disorder. *Journal of Clinical Child and Adolescent Psychology, 33,* 506–515.

LoVullo, S. V., & Matson, J. L. (2009). Comorbid psychopathology in adults with autism spectrum disorders and intellectual disabilities. *Research in Developmental Disabilities, 30,* 1280–1296.

Lubinski, D. (2009). Exceptional cognitive ability: The phenotype. *Behavioral Genetics, 39,* 350–358.

Lue, M. S. (2001). *A survey of communication disorders for the classroom teacher.* Needham Heights, MA: Allyn.

Lynam, D. R., & Henry, B. (2001). The role of neuropsychological deficits in conduct disorders. In J. Hill & B. Maughan (Eds.), *Conduct disorders in childhood and adolescence* (pp. 235–263). Cambridge: Cambridge University Press.

Lyon, G. R. (1996). Learning disabilities: The future of children. *Special Education for Students with Disabilities, 6,* 54–75.

Lyon, G. R. (2003). Reading disabilities: Why do some children have difficulty learning to read? What can be done about it? *International Dyslexia Association, 29,* 1–14.

Lyon, G. R., Shaywitz, S. E., & Shaywitz, B. A. (2003). Defining dyslexia, comorbidity, teachers' knowledge of language and reading: A definition of dyslexia. *Annals of Dyslexia, 53,* 1–14.

MacArthur, C. A. (1996). Using technology to enhance the writing process of students with learning disabilities. *Journal of Learning Disabilities, 29,* 344–354.

Maccini, P., & Gagnon, J. C. (2006). Mathematics instructional practices and assessment accommodations by secondary special and general educators. *Exceptional Children, 72,* 217–234.

Maccoby, E. E. (1998). *The two sexes: Growing up apart, coming together.* Cambridge, MA: Belknap Press of Harvard University Press.

Machin, S., & Pekkarinen, T. (2008). Global sex differences in test score variability. *Science, 322,* 1331–1332.

Macintosh, K., & Dissanayake, C. (2006). Social skills and problem behaviours in school aged children with high-functioning autism and Asperger's disorder. *Journal of Autism and Developmental Disorders, 36,* 1065–1076.

MacMillan, D. L., Siperstein, G. N., & Gresham, F. M. (1996). A challenge to the viability of mild mental retardation as a diagnostic category. *Exceptional Children, 62,* 356–371.

Maehler, C., & Schuchardt, K. (2009). Working memory functioning in children with learning disabilities: Does intelligence make a difference? *Journal of Intellectual Disability Research, 53,* 3–10.

Manassis, K., Tannock, R., Garland, J., Minde, K., McInnes, A., & Clark, S. (2007). The sounds of silence: Language, cognition, and anxiety in selective mutism. *Journal of the American Academy of Child and Adolescent Psychiatry, 46,* 1187–1195.

Mann, V. A., & Brady, S. (1988). Reading disability: The role of language deficiencies. *Journal of Consulting and Clinical Psychology, 56,* 811–816.

Markward, M. J., & Bride, B. (2001). Oppositional-defiant disorder and the need for family-centered practice in schools. *Children and Schools, 23,* 73–83.

Marshall, R. M., Schafer, V. A., O'Donnell, L., Elliott, J., & Handwerk, M. J. (1999). Arithmetic disabilities and ADD subtypes: Implications for *DSM-IV. Journal of Learning Disabilities, 32,* 239–247.

Martin, N. C., Levy, F., Pieka, J., & Hay, D. A. (2006). A genetic study of attention deficit hyperactivity disorder, conduct disorder, oppositional defiant disorder, and reading disability: Aetiological overlaps and implications. *International Journal of Disability, Development, and Education, 53,* 21–34.

Martinussen, R., Hayden, J., Hogg-Johnson, S., & Tannock, R. (2005). A meta-analysis of working memory impairments in children with attention-deficit/hyperactivity disorder. *Journal of the American Academy of Child and Adolescent Psychiatry, 44,* 377–384.

Martinussen, R., & Tannock, R. (2006). Working memory impairment in children with attention-deficit hyperactivity disorder with and without comorbid language learning disorders. *Journal of Clinical and Experimental Neuropsychology, 28,* 1073–1094.

Marzocchi, G. M., Oosterlaan, J., Zuddas, A., Cavolina, P., Geurts, H., Redigolo, D., et al. (2008). Contrasting deficits on executive functions between ADHD and reading disabled children. *Journal of Child Psychology and Psychiatry, 49,* 543–552.

Masi, G., Mucci, M., Favilla, L., Brovedani, P., Millepiedi, S., & Perugi, G. (2003). Temperament in adolescents with anxiety and depressive disorders and in their families. *Child Psychiatry and Human Development, 33,* 245–259.

Masia, C. L., Klein, R. G., Storch, E. A., & Bernard, C. (2001). School-based behavioral treatment for social anxiety disorder in adolescents. *Journal of the American Academy of Child and Adolescent Psychiatry, 40,* 780–786.

Masterson, J. J. (1993). The performance of children with language-learning disabilities on two types of cognitive tasks. *Journal of Speech and Hearing Research, 36,* 1026–1036.

Mather, D. S. (2003). Dyslexia and dysgraphia: More than written language difficulties in common. *Journal of Learning Disabilities, 36,* 207–317.

Matheson, E., & Jahoda, A. (2005). Emotional understanding in aggressive and nonaggressive individuals with mild or moderate mental retardation. *American Journal on Mental Retardation, 110,* 57–67.

Maughan, B. (2001). Conduct disorder in context. In J. Hill & B. Maughan (Eds.), *Conduct disorders in childhood and adolescence* (pp. 169–201). Cambridge: Cambridge University Press.

May-Benson, T., Ingolia, P., & Koomar, J. (2002). Daily living skills and developmental coordination disorder. In S. A. Cermak & D. Larkin (Eds.), *Developmental coordination disorder* (pp. 140–156). Albany, NY: Delmar.

Mayes, S. D., & Calhoun, S. L. (2003). Relationship between Asperger syndrome and high-functioning autism. In M. Prior (Ed.), *Learning and behavior problems in Asperger syndrome* (pp. 15–35). New York: Guildford Press.

Mayes, S. D., & Calhoun, S. L. (2006). Frequency of reading, math, and writing disabilities in children with clinical disorders. *Learning and Individual Differences, 16,* 145–157.

Mayes, S. D., Calhoun, S. L., & Crowell, E. W. (2000). Learning disabilities and ADHD: Overlapping spectrum disorders. *Journal of Learning Disabilities, 33,* 417–424.

Mayfield, J., & Homack, S. (2005). Behavioral considerations associated with traumatic brain injury. *Preventing School Failure, 4,* 17–22.

Mazefsky, C. A., & Oswald, D. P. (2007). Emotion perception in Asperger's syndrome and high-functioning autism: The importance of diagnostic criteria and cue intensity. *Journal of Autism and Developmental Disorders, 37,* 1086–1095.

McAnanly, E. (1986). School phobia: The importance of prompt intervention. *Journal of School Health, 56,* 433–436.

McGee, R., Brodeur, D., Symons, D., Andrade, B., & Fahie, C. (2004). Time perception: Does it distinguish ADHD and RD children in a clinical sample? *Journal of Abnormal Child Psychology, 32,* 481–490.

McGuire, J., Scott, S., & Shaw, S. (2006). Universal Design and its application in educational environments. *Remedial and Special Education, 27,* 166–175.

McHale, K., & Cermak, S. A. (1992). Fine motor activities in elementary school: Preliminary findings and provisional implications for children with fine motor problems. *American Journal of Occupational Therapy, 46,* 892–898.

McKinlay, A., Grace, R. C., Horwood, L. J., Fergusson, D. M., Ridder, E. M., & MacFarlane, M. R. (2008). Prevalence of traumatic brain injury among children, adolescents and young adults: Prospective evidence from a birth cohort. *Brain Injury, 22,* 175–181.

McKinney, C., & Renk, K. (2006). Similar presentations of disparate etiologies: A new perspective on oppositional defiant disorder. *Journal of Child and Family Therapy, 2,* 37–49.

McNab, F., Varrone, A., Farde, L., Jucaite, A., Bystritsky, P., Forssberg, H., & Klingberg, T. (2009). Changes in cortical dopamine D1 receptor binding associated with cognitive training. *Science, 323,* 801–802.

McNulty, M. A. (2003). Dyslexia and the life course. *Journal of Learning Disabilities, 36,* 363–381.

Menghini, D., Carlesimo, G. A., Marotta, L., Finzi, A., & Vicari, S. (2010). Developmental dyslexia and explicit long-term memory. *Dyslexia, 16,* 213–225.

Meyer, M. J., & Zentall, S. S. (1995). Influence of loud behavioral consequences on attention deficit hyperactivity disorder. *Behavior Therapy, 26,* 351–370.

Miceli, G., Capasso, R., Ivella, A., & Caramanza, A. (1997). Acquired dysgraphia in alphabetic and stenographic handwriting. *Cortex, 33,* 355–367.

Milich, R., & Landau, S. (1988). Teacher ratings of inattention/overactivity and aggression: Cross-validation with classroom observations. *Journal of Clinical Child Psychology, 17,* 92–97.

Miller, G. A. (1956). The magical number seven, plus or minus two: Some limits on our capacity for processing information. *Psychological Review, 63,* 81–97.

Millon, T., & Radovanov, J. (1995). Passive-aggressive (negativistic) personality disorder. In W. J. Livesley (Ed.), *The DSM-IV personality disorders* (pp. 312–325). New York: Guilford Press.

Mitchell, S., Brian, J., Zwaigenbaum, L., Roberts, W. K., Szatmari, P., Smith, I., & Bryson, S. (2006). Early language and communication development of infants later diagnosed with autism spectrum disorder. *Developmental and Behavioral Pediatrics, 27,* S69–S78.

Moffitt, T. E., Arseneault, L., Jaffee, S. R., Kin-Cohen, J., Koenen, K. C., Odgers, C. L., et al. (2008). *DSM-V* conduct disorder: Research needs for an evidence base. *Child Psychology and Psychiatry, 49,* 3–33.

Montague, M., & Fonseca, F. (1993). Using computers to improve story writing. *Teaching Exceptional Children, 25*(4), 46–49.

Moon, S. M., & Reis, S. M. (2004). Acceleration and twice-exceptional students. In N. Colangelo, S. G. Assouline, & M. U. M. Gross (Eds.), *A nation deceived: How schools hold back America's brightest students* (Vol. 2, pp. 109–119). Iowa City: Connie Belin & Jacqueline N. Blank International Center for Gifted Education and Talent Development.

Moon, S. M., Zentall, S. S., Grskovic, J., Hall, A. M., & Stormont, M. (2001). Social and family characteristics of boys with giftedness and/or attention deficit/hyperactivity disorder. *Journal for the Education of the Gifted, 24,* 207–247.

Morris, S. (2002). Promoting social skills among students with nonverbal learning disabilities. *Teaching Exceptional Children, 34*(3), 66–70.

Morris, T. (2010). Traumatic brain injury. In C. L. Armstrong (Ed.), *Handbook of medical neuropsychology: Applications of cognitive neuroscience* (pp. 17–32). New York: Springer Science and Business.

Morris, T. L., & Masia, C. L. (1998). Psychometric evaluation of the Social Phobia and Anxiety Inventory for Children: Concurrent validity and normative data. *Journal of Clinical Child Psychology, 27,* 452–459.

Most, T., & Greenbank, A. (2000). Auditory, visual, and auditory-visual perception of emotions by adolescents with and without learning disabilities and their relationship to social skills. *Learning Disabilities Research and Practice, 15,* 171–178.

Mrug, S., Hoza, B., & Gerdes, A. C. (2001). Children with attention-deficit/hyperactivity disorder: Peer relationships and peer-oriented environments. *New Directions for Child and Adolescent Development, 91,* 51–76.

Munkvold, L. H., Lundervold, A. J., & Manger, T. (2011). Oppositional defiant disorder: Gender differences in co-occurring symptoms of mental health problems in a general population of children. *Journal of Abnormal Child Psychology, 39,* 577–587.

Munson, B. L. (2005). About Tourette's syndrome. *Nursing, 35,* 29–29.

Murray-Leslie, C. (2000). Confronting traumatic brain injury. *British Medical Journal, 321,* 456.

Myklebust, H. R. (1965). *Picture story language test: A diagnostic test of written language.* New York: Grune & Stratton.

Myles, B. S., & Adreon, D. (2001). *Asperger syndrome and adolescence.* Kansas: Autism Asperger Publishing.

Myrbakk, E., & von Tetzchner, S. (2008). Psychiatric disorders and behavioral problems in people with intellectual disability. *Research in Developmental Disabilities, 29,* 316–332.

Nabuzoka, D., & Smith, P. K. (1995). Identification of expressions of emotions by children with and without learning disabilities. *Learning Disabilities Research and Practice, 10,* 91–101.

Nampiaparampil, D. E. (2008). Prevalence of chronic pain after traumatic brain injury: A systematic review. *Journal of the American Medical Association, 300,* 711–719.

National Council of Teachers of Mathematics. (2000). *Principles and standards for school mathematics.* Reston, VA: Author.

National Dissemination Center for Children With Disabilities. (2012). *Other health impairment* (NICHCY Disability Fact Sheet 15). Washington, DC: Author. Retrieved from http://nichcy.org/disability/specific/ohi#IDEA

Neef, N. A., Marckel, J., Ferreri, S. J., Bicard, D. F., Endo, S., Aman, M. G., et al. (2005). Behavioral assessment of impulsivity: A comparison of children with and without attention deficit hyperactivity disorder. *Journal of Applied Behavioral Analysis, 38,* 23–37.

Neef, N. A., Nelles, D. E., Iwata, B. A., & Page, T. J. (2003). Analysis of precurrent skills in solving mathematics story problems. *Journal of Applied Behavior Analysis, 36,* 21–33.

Nicolson, R. (2000). Dyslexia and dyspraxia: Commentary. *Dyslexia, 6,* 203–204.

Nigg, J. T. (2001). Is ADHD a disinhibitory disorder? *Psychological Bulletin, 127,* 571–598.

Nijland, L. (2003). Evidence of motor programming deficits in children diagnosed with DAS. *Journal of Speech, Language, and Hearing Research, 46,* 437–450.

Nota, L. Ferrari, L., Soresi, S., & Wehmeyer, M. (2007). Self-determination, social abilities and the quality of life of people with intellectual disability. *Journal of Intellectual Disability Research, 51,* 850–865.

Numminen, H., Service, E., & MacLean, I. (2002). Working memory, intelligence, and knowledge base in adult persons with intellectual disability. *Research in Developmental Disabilities, 23,* 105–118.

Nussbaum, N. L., Grant, M. L., Roman, M. J., Poole, J. H., & Bigler, E. (1990). Attention deficit hyperactivity disorder and the mediating effect of age on academic and behavioral variables. *Developmental Behavioral Pediatrics, 11,* 22–26.

Olenchak, F. R. (1994). Talent development: Accommodating the social and emotional needs of secondary gifted/learning disabled students. *Journal of Secondary Gifted Education, 5,* 40–52.

Ollendick, T. H., Grills, A. E., & Alexander, K. L. (2001). Fears, worries, and anxiety in children and adolescents. In. C. A. Essau & F. Petermann (Eds.), *Anxiety disorders in children and adolescents: Epidemiology, risk factors, and treatment* (pp. 1–35). New York: Taylor & Francis.

Olson, S. L., Ceballo, R., & Park, C. (2002). Early problem behavior among children from low-income, mother-headed families: A multiple risk perspective. *Journal of Clinical Child and Adolescent Psychology, 31,* 419–430.

Olvera, R. I., Semrud-Clikeman, M., Pliszka, S. R., & O'Donnell, L. (2005). Neuropsychological deficits in adolescents with conduct disorder and comorbid bipolar disorder: A pilot study. *Bipolar Disorders, 7,* 57–67.

Orloff, S. N. S. (2005). Motor-apraxia: Transitioning in school. *Exceptional Parent, 11,* 82.

Othman, M. F., & Keay-Bright, W. (2011, February). Rotoscopy-handwriting interface for children with dyspraxia [Abstract]. *Fourth International Conference on Advances in Computer-Human Interactions,* pp. 254–259.

Paavonen, E. J., Vehkalahti, K, Vanhala, R., von Wendt, V., Nieminen-von Wendt, T., & Aronen, E. T. (2008). Sleep in children with Asperger syndrome. *Journal of Autism and Developmental Disorders, 38,* 41–51.

Paccione-Dyszlewski, M., & Contessa-Kislus, M. (1987). School phobia: Identification of subtypes as a prerequisite to treatment intervention. *Adolescence, 22,* 377–383.

Palombo, J. (1996). The diagnosis and treatment of children with nonverbal learning disabilities. *Child and Adolescent Social Work Journal, 13,* 311–332.

Pardini, D. A., & Fite, P. J. (2010). Symptoms of conduct disorder, oppositional defiant disorder, attention-deficit/hyperactivity disorder, and callous-unemotional traits as unique predictors of psychosocial maladjustment in boys: Advancing an evidence base for *DSM-V. Journal of the American Academy of Child and Adolescent Psychiatry, 49,* 1134–1144.

Passolunghi, M. C., Marzocchi, G. M., & Fiorillo, F. (2005). Selective effect of inhibition of literal or numerical irrelevant information in children with attention deficit hyperactivity disorder (ADHD) or arithmetic learning disorder (ALD). *Developmental Neuropsychology, 28,* 731–753.

Passolunghi, M. C., & Pazzagliab, F. (2004). Individual differences in memory updating in relation to arithmetic problem solving. *Learning and Individual Differences, 14,* 219–230.

Paul, T. (1998). Do schools make students fearful and phobic? *Journal for a Just and Caring Education, 4,* 193–211.

Peacock, J. (2000). *Depression: How to recognize it, where to get help.* Mankato, MN: Capstone Press.

Pearson, D. A., Yaffee, L. S., Loveland, K. A., & Lewis, K. R. (1996). Comparison of sustained and selective attention in children who have mental retardation with and without attention deficit hyperactivity disorder. *American Journal on Mental Retardation, 100,* 592–607.

Penley, J. A., Tomaka, J., & Wiebe, J. S. (2002). The association of coping to physical and psychological health outcomes: A meta-analytic review. *Journal of Behavioral Medicine, 25,* 551–563.

Pennington, B. F. (1991). *Diagnosing learning disorders: A neuropsychological framework.* New York: Guilford Press.

Peters, J. M., & Henderson, S. E. (2008). Understanding developmental coordination disorder and its impact on families: The contribution of single case studies. *International Journal of Disability, Development and Education, 55,* 97–111.

Peterson, J. S., & Ray, K. E. (2006). Bullying and the gifted: Victims, perpetuators, prevalence, and effects. *Gifted Child Quarterly, 50,* 148–168.

Peterson, P. L., Carpenter, T., & Fennema, E. (1989). Teachers' knowledge of students' knowledge in mathematics problem solving: Correlational and case analyses. *Journal of Educational Psychology, 81,* 558–569.

Petti, V. L., Voelker, S. L., Shore, D. L., & Hayman-Abello, S. E. (2003). Perception of nonverbal emotion cues by children with nonverbal learning disabilities. *Journal of Developmental and Physical Disabilities, 15,* 23–35.

Phelps, L., Cox, D., & Bajorek, E. (1992). School phobia and separation anxiety: Diagnostic and treatment comparisons. *Psychology in the Schools, 29,* 384–392.

Piazza, M., Facoetti, A., Trussardi, A. N., Bertelletti, I., Conte, S., Lucangeli, K. D., et al. (2010). Developmental trajectory of number activity reveals a severe impairment in developmental dyscalculia. *Cognition, 116,* 33–41.

Piek, J. P., Dworcan, M., Barrett, N., & Coleman, R. (2000). Determinants of self-worth in children with and without developmental coordination disorder. *International Journal of Disability Development and Education, 47,* 259–271.

Pierson, M. R., & Glaeser, B. C. (2005). Extension of research on social skills training using comic strip conversations to students without autism. *Education and Training in Developmental Disabilities, 40,* 279–284.

Pignotti, M., & Thyer, B. A. (2011). Guidelines for the treatment of obsessive compulsive disorder. *Best Practices in Mental Health, 7,* 84–93.

Pilkington, C., & Piersel, W. (1991). School phobia: A critical analysis of the separation anxiety theory and an alternative conceptualization. *Psychology in the Schools, 28,* 290–301.

Pincus, A. L., & Lukowitsky, M. R. (2009). Pathological narcissism and narcissistic personality disorder. *Annual Review of Clinical Psychology, 6,* 421–446.

Pintrich, P., & Schunk, D. (1996). *Motivation in education: Theory, research, and applications.* Englewood Cliffs, NJ: Prentice Hall.

Plata, M., Trusty J., & Glasgow, D. (2005). Adolescents with learning disabilities: Are they allowed to participate in activities? *Journal of Educational Research, 98,* 136–143.

Plomin, R., & Price, T. S. (2003). The relationship between genetics and intelligence. In N. Colangelo & G. A. Davis (Eds.), *Handbook of gifted education* (pp. 113–145). Boston: Pearson Education.

Polloway, E. A., Patton, J. R., Smith, J. D., Lubin, J., & Antoine, K. (2009). State guidelines for mental retardation and intellectual disabilities: A re-visitation of previous analyses in light of changes in the field. *Education and Training in Developmental Disabilities, 44,* 14–24.

Poulton, A. S. (2011). Time to refine the diagnosis of oppositional defiant disorder. *Journal of Paediatrics and Child Health, 47,* 332–334.

Powell, J. W. (2000). Traumatic brain injury in high school athletes. *Journal of the American Academy of Child and Adolescent Psychiatry, 282,* 958–963.

President's Commission on Excellence in Special Education. (2002, October 2). A new era: Revitalizing special education for children and their families. *ISEAS Cable, 23*(10), 1–2.

Quinn, B. P. (1997). *The depression sourcebook.* Los Angeles: Lowell House.

Quinn, P. D. (2005). Treating adolescent girls and women with ADHD: Gender-specific issues. *Journal of Clinical Psychology, 61,* 579–587.

Rappaport, N. (2005). Treating social phobia: Making a case for school-based intervention. *Brown University Child and Adolescent Behavior Letter, 21,* 1–7.

Rasmussen, P., & Gillberg, C. (2000). Natural outcome of ADHD with developmental coordination disorder at age 22 years: Controlled, longitudinal, community-based study. *Journal of the American Academy of Child and Adolescent Psychiatry, 39,* 1424–1431.

Reaser, A., Prevatt, F., Petscher, Y., & Proctor, B. (2007). The learning and study strategies of college students with ADHD. *Psychology in the Schools, 44,* 627–638.

Redcay, E., & Courchesne, E. (2005). When is the brain enlarged in autism? A meta-analysis of all brain size reports. *Biological Psychiatry, 58,* 1–9.

Redmond, S. M. (2004). Conversational profiles of children with ADHD, SLI and typical development. *Clinical Linguistics and Phonetics, 18,* 107–125.

Reeves, W. (1980). Auditory learning disabilities and emotional disturbance: Diagnostic differences. *Journal of Learning Disabilities, 13,* 30–33.

Reid, R., Trout, A. L., & Schartz, M. (2005). Self-regulation interventions for children with attention deficit/hyperactivity disorder. *Exceptional Children, 71,* 361–377.

Reis, S. M., & Renzulli, J. S. (2010). Is there still a need for gifted education? An examination of current research. *Learning and Individual Differences, 20,* 308–317.

Renzulli, J. S. (1979). *The enrichment triad model.* Mansfield Center, CT: Creative Learning Press.

Resta, S. P., & Eliot, J. (1994). Written expression in boys with attention deficit disorder. *Perceptual and Motor Skills, 79,* 1131–1138.

Reynolds, S., Bendixen, R. M., Lawrence, T., & Lane, S. J. (2011). A pilot study examining activity participation, sensory responsiveness, and competence in children with high-functioning autism spectrum disorder. *Journal of Autism and Developmental Disorders, 41,* 1496–1506.

Riccio, C. A., & Hynd, G. W. (1993). Developmental language disorders in children: Relationship with learning disability and attention deficit hyperactivity disorder. *School Psychology Review, 22,* 696–710.

Richards, P. O., Thatcher, D. H., Shreeves, M., Timmons, P., & Barker, S. (1999). Don't let a good scare frighten you: Choosing and using quality chillers to promote reading. *Reading Teacher, 52,* 830–840.

Ridgway, A., Northup, J., Pellegrin, A., LaRue, R., & Hightshoe, A. (2003). Effects of recess on the classroom behavior of children with and without attention-deficit hyperactivity disorder. *School Psychology Quarterly, 18,* 253–268.

Rivera, D. (1997). Mathematics education and students with learning disabilities: Introduction to special series. *Journal of Learning Disabilities, 30,* 2–19.

Roberts, J. E., Price, J., & Malkin, C. (2007). Language and communication development in Down syndrome. *Mental Retardation and Developmental Disabilities Research Reviews, 13,* 26–35.

Robertson, M. (2006). Attention deficit hyperactivity disorder, tics and Tourette's syndrome: The relationship and treatment implications. *European Child and Adolescent Psychiatry, 15,* 1–11.

Rogers, K., Dziobek, I., Hassenstab, J., Wolf, O. T., & Convit, A. (2007). Who cares? Revisiting empathy in Asperger syndrome. *Journal of Autism and Developmental Disorders, 37,* 709–715.

Rogers, M. F., & Myles, B. S. (2001). Using social stories and comic strip conversations to interpret social situations for an adolescent with Asperger syndrome. *Intervention in School and Clinic, 38,* 310–313.

Ronningstam, E. F. (2005). *Identifying and understanding the narcissistic personality.* New York: Oxford University Press.

Rosenberg, M. S., Westling, D. L., & McLeskey, J. (2008). *Special education for today's teachers: An introduction.* Upper Saddle River, NJ: Pearson Merrill Prentice Hall.

Rosenblum, S, Aloni, T., & Josman, N. (2010). Relationships between handwriting performance and organizational abilities among children with and without dysgraphia: A preliminary study. *Research in Developmental Disabilities, 31,* 502–509.

Rourke, B. P. (1995). *Syndrome of nonverbal learning disabilities: Neurodevelopmental manifestations.* New York: Guilford Press.

Rowe, R., Maughan, B., Costello, E. J., & Angold, A. (2005). Defining oppositional defiant disorder. *Journal of Child Psychology and Psychiatry, 46,* 1309–1316.

Rowland, A. S., Lesesne, C. A., & Abramowitz, A. J. (2002). The epidemiology of attention-deficit/hyperactivity disorder (ADHD): A public health view. *Mental Retardation and Developmental Disabilities Research Reviews 8,* 162–170.

Rubinsten, O., & Tannock, R. (2010). Mathematics anxiety in children with developmental dyscalculia. *Behavioral and Brain Functions, 6*(46), 1–13.

Rydell, M. (2010). Family factors and children's disruptive behavior: An investigation of links between demographic characteristics, negative life events, and symptoms of ODD and ADHD. *Social Psychiatry Epidemiology, 45,* 233–244.

Saalasti, S., Lepistö, T., Toppila, E., Kujala, T., Laakso, M., Nieminen-von Wendt, T., et al. (2008). Language abilities of children with Asperger syndrome. *Journal of Autism and Developmental Disorders, 38,* 1574–1580.

Sabornie, E. J., Evans, C., & Cullinan, D. (2006). Comparing characteristics of high-incidence disability groups. *Remedial and Special Education, 27,* 95–104.

Salkovskis, P. M., Wroe, A. L., Gledhill, A., Morrison, N., Forrester, E., Richards, C., et al. (2000). Responsibility attitudes and interpretations are characteristics of obsessive-compulsive disorder. *Behavior Research and Therapy, 38,* 347–372.

Sansosti, F. J., & Powell-Smith, K. A. (2006). Using social stories to improve the social behavior of children with Asperger syndrome. *Journal of Positive Behavior Interventions, 8,* 43–57.

Sarafolean, M. H. (2000). Depression in school-aged children and adolescents: Characteristics, assessment, and prevention. *Gillette Children's Specialty Healthcare, 9,* 1–4.

Saunders, M. D. (2001). Who's getting the message? Helping your students understand in a verbal world. *Teaching Exceptional Children, 33*(4), 70–74.

Sayal, K. (2000). Case study: Bipolar disorder after head injury. *Journal of the American Academy of Child and Adolescent Psychiatry, 39,* 525–528.

Scattone, D. (2008). Enhancing the conversational skills of a boy with Asperger's disorder through social stories and video modeling. *Journal of Autism and Developmental Disorders, 38,* 395–400.

Scattone, D., Wilczynski, S. M., Edwards, R. P., & Rabian, B. (2002). Decreasing disruptive behaviors of children with autism using social stories. *Journal of Autism and Developmental Disorders, 32,* 535–543.

Scheuermann, A. M., Deshler, D. D., & Schumaker, J. B. (2009). The effects of the explicit inquiry routine on the performance of students with learning disabilities on one-variable equations. *Learning Disability Quarterly, 32,* 103–120.

Schmidt, A. T., Hanten, G. R., Li, X, Orsten, K. D., & Levin, H. S. (2010). Emotional recognition following pediatric traumatic brain injury: Longitudinal analysis of emotional prosody and facial emotion recognition. *Neuropsychologia, 48,* 2869–2877.

Schoenbrodt, L., Kumin, L., & Sloan, J. M. (1997). Learning disabilities existing concomitantly with language disorder. *Journal of Learning Disabilities, 30,* 264–281.

Schweitzer, I., Maguire, K., & Ng, C. H. (2005). Should bipolar disorder be viewed as a manic disorder? Implications for bipolar depression. *Bipolar Disorders, 7,* 418–423.

Schweitzer, J. B., & Sulzer-Azaroff, B. (1995). Self-control in boys with attention-deficit hyperactivity disorder: Effects of added stimulation and time. *Journal of Child Psychology and Psychiatry, 36,* 671–686.

Seeley, K. (1998a). Giftedness in early childhood. In J. VanTassel-Baska (Ed.), *Excellence in educating gifted and talented learners* (3rd ed., pp. 67–81). Denver: Love.

Seeley, K. (1998b). Underachieving and talented learners with disabilities. In J. VanTassel-Baska (Ed.), *Excellence in educating gifted and talented learners* (3rd ed., pp. 83–93). Denver: Love.

Segrin, C. (2000). Social skills deficits associated with depression. *Clinical Psychology Review, 20,* 379–403.

Semrud-Clikeman, M., & Hynd, G. W. (1990). Right hemispheric dysfunction in nonverbal learning disabilities: Social, academic, and adaptive functioning in adults and children. *Psychological Bulletin, 107,* 196–209.

Semrud-Clikeman, M., Walkowiak, J., Wilkinson, A., & Christopher, G. (2010). Neuropsychological differences among children with Asperger syndrome, nonverbal learning disabilities, attention deficit disorder, and controls. *Developmental Neuropsychology, 35,* 582–600.

Senf, G. (1986). LD research and sociological and scientific perspective. In J. K. Torgesen & B. Y. L. Wong (Eds.), *Psychological and educational perspectives on learning disabilities* (pp. 27–53). San Diego: Academic Press.

Settle, S. A., & Milich, R. (1999). Social persistence following failure in boys and girls with LD. *Journal of Learning Disabilities, 32,* 201–212.

Shalev, R. S. (2004). Developmental dyscalculia. *Journal of Child Neurology, 19,* 765–771.

Shalev, R. S., Auerbach, J., Manor, O., & Gross-Tsur, V. (2000). Developmental dyscalculia: Prevalence and prognosis. *European Child and Adolescent Psychiatry, 9* (Suppl. 2), 58–64.

Shalev, R. S., Manor, O., Kerem, B., Ayali, M., Badichi N., Friedlander, Y., & Gross-Tsur, V. (2001). Developmental dyscalculia is a familial learning disability. *Journal of Learning Disabilities, 34,* 59–65.

Shanahan, M. S., Pennington, B. F., Yerys, B. E., Scott, A., Boada, R., Willcutt, E. G., et al. (2006). Processing speed deficits in attention deficit/hyperactivity disorder and reading disability. *Journal of Abnormal Child Psychology, 34,* 585–602.

Shannon, J. B. (2003). *Movement disorders sourcebook.* Detroit, MI: Omnigraphics.

Shaw, G., & Brown, G. (1990). Laterality and creativity concomitants of attention problems. *Developmental Neuropsychology, 6,* 39–56.

Shaw, G., & Brown, G. (1999). Arousal, time estimation, and time use in attention-disordered children. *Developmental Neuropsychology, 16,* 227–242.

Shaywitz, S. E., Morris, R., & Shaywitz, B. A. (2008). The education of dyslexic children from childhood to young adulthood. *Annual Review of Psychology, 59,* 451–475.

Shaywitz, S. E., & Shaywitz, B. A. (1988). Attention deficit disorder: Current perspectives. In J. F. Kavanagh & J. T. J. Truss (Eds.), *Learning disabilities: Proceedings of a national conference* (pp. 369–567). Parkton, MD: York Press.

Shirk, S., Gudmundsen, G., & Burwell, R. (2005). Links among attachment-related cognitions and adolescent depressive symptoms. *Journal of Clinical Child and Adolescent Psychology, 1,* 172–181.

Shumway, S., & Wetherby, A. M. (2009). Communicative acts of children with autism spectrum disorders in the second year of life. *Journal of Speech, Language, and Hearing Research, 52,* 1139–1156.

Sideridis, G. D. (2009). Motivation and learning disabilities. In K. R. Wentzel & A. Wigfield (Eds.), *Handbook of motivation at school* (pp. 605–625). New York: Routledge.

Siegler, R. S. (1991). *Children's thinking: Developmental function and individual differences.* (2nd ed.). Englewood Cliffs, NJ: Prentice Hall.

Siegler, R. S. (2007). Foreword. In D. B. Berch & M. M. M. Mazzocco (Eds.), *Why is math so hard for some children? The nature and origins of mathematical learning difficulties and disabilities* (pp. xvii–xxii). Baltimore: Paul H. Brookes.

Silver, L. B. (2004). Brain-mind emotional interactions in the classroom. In F. M. Kline & L. B. Silver (Eds.), *The educator's guide to mental health issues in the classroom* (pp. 9–23). Baltimore: Paul H. Brookes.

Silverman, L. K. (1998). Developmental stages of giftedness: Infancy through adulthood. In J. VanTassel-Baska (Ed.), *Excellence in educating gifted and talented learners* (3rd ed., pp. 145–171). Denver: Love.

Silverman, L. K. (2003). Gifted children with learning disabilities. In N. Colangelo & G. A. Davis (Eds.), *Handbook of gifted education* (3rd ed., pp. 533–543). Boston: Pearson Education..

Simonoff, E., Pickles, A., Wood, N., Gringras, P., & Chadwick, O. (2007). ADHD symptoms in children with mild intellectual disability. *Journal of the American Academy of Child and Adolescent Psychiatry, 46,* 591–600.

Singer, E. (2005). The strategies adopted by Dutch children with dyslexia to maintain their self-esteem when teased at school. *Journal of Learning Disabilities, 38,* 411–423.

Singh, M. K., Delbello M. P., Kowatch R. A, & Strakowski S. M. (2006). Co-occurrence of bipolar and attention-deficit hyperactivity disorders in children. *Bipolar Disorder, 8,* 710–720.

Skoulos, V., & Tryon, G. S. (2007). Social skills of adolescents in special education who display symptoms of oppositional defiant disorder. *American Secondary Education, 35,* 103–114.

Snowling, M. (2009). Changing concepts of dyslexia: Nature, treatment and comorbidity. *Journal of Child Psychology and Psychiatry, 52,* 205–213.

Soenen, S., van Berckelaer-Onnes, I., & Scholte, E. (2009). Patterns of intellectual, adaptive and behavioral functioning in individuals with mild mental retardation. *Research in Developmental Disabilities, 30,* 433–444.

Sohlberg, M. M., & Mateer, C. A. (1989). *Introduction to cognitive rehabilitation: Theory and practice.* New York: Guilford Press.

Sonuga-Barke, E. J. S., Williams, E., Hall, M., & Saxton, T. (1996). Hyperactivity and delay aversion III: The effect on cognitive style of imposing delay after errors. *Journal of Child Psychology and Psychiatry, 37,* 189–194.

Sparks, S. D. (2011, May 18). "Math anxiety" explored in studies. *Education Week,* pp. 1–2.

Stage, S. A., Abbott, R. D., Jenkins, J. R., & Berninger, V. W. (2003). Predicting response to early reading intervention from verbal IQ, reading-related language abilities, attention ratings, and verbal IQ-word reading discrepancy: Failure to validate discrepancy method. *Journal of Learning Disabilities, 36,* 24–34.

Stahr, B., Cushing, D., Lane, K., & Fox, J. (2006). Efficacy of a function-based intervention in decreasing off-task behavior exhibited by a student with ADHD. *Journal of Positive Behavior Interventions, 8,* 201–211.

Sternberg, R. J. (1985). *Beyond IQ: A triarchic theory of human intelligence.* Cambridge: Cambridge University Press.

Stevens, L. J., Zentall, S. S., Deck, J. L., Abate, M. L., Watkins, B. A., & Burgess, J. R. (1996). Omega-3 fatty acids in boys with behavior, learning, and health problems. *Physiology and Behavior, 59,* 915–920.

Stichter, J. P., Conroy, M. A., & Kauffman, J. M. (2008). *An introduction to students with high-incidence disabilities.* Upper Saddle River, NJ: Pearson Merrill Prentice Hall.

Stipek, D., & Mac Iver, D. (1989). Developmental change in children's assessment of intellectual competence. *Child Development, 60,* 521–538.

Stormont-Spurgin, M., & Zentall, S. S. (1995). Contributing factors in the manifestation of aggression in preschoolers with hyperactivity. *Journal of Child Psychology and Psychiatry, 36,* 491–509.

Stormont-Spurgin, M., & Zentall, S. S. (1996). Child-rearing practices associated with aggression in youth with and without ADHD: An exploratory study. *International Journal of Disability, Development, and Education, 43,* 135–146.

Streissguth, A. P., Sampson, P. D., Carmichael O. H., Bookstein, F. L., Barr, H. M., Scott M., et al. (1994). Maternal drinking during pregnancy and attention/memory performance in 14-year-old children: A longitudinal prospective study. *Alcoholism: Clinical and Experimental Research, 18,* 202–218.

Stuss, D. T., Gallup, G. G., & Alexander, M. P. (2001). The frontal lobes are necessary for "theory of mind." *Brain, 124,* 279–286.

Sugden, D. A., & Chambers, M. E. (2003). Intervention in children with developmental coordination disorder: The role of parents and teachers. *British Journal of Educational Psychology, 73,* 545–561.

Sullivan, P. M., & Knutson, J. F. (2000a). Maltreatment and disabilities: A population-based epidemiological study. *Child Abuse and Neglect, 24,* 1257–1273.

Sullivan, P. M., & Knutson, J. F. (2000b). The prevalence of disabilities and maltreatment among runaway children. *Child Abuse and Neglect, 24,* 1275–1288.

Swanson, H. L., & Sáez, L. (2003). Memory difficulties in children and adults with learning disabilities. In H. L. Swanson, K. R. Harris, & S. Graham (Eds.), *Handbook of learning disabilities* (pp. 182–198). New York: Guilford Press.

Swanson, J., Baler, R. D., & Volkow, N. (2011). Understanding the effects of stimulant medications on cognition in individuals with attention-deficit hyperactivity disorder: A decade of progress. *Neuropsychopharmacology Reviews, 36,* 207–226.

Sweeney, L., & Rapee, R. M. (2001). Social phobia. In C. A. Essau & F. Petermann (Eds.), *Anxiety disorders in children and adolescents: Epidemiology, risk factors, and treatment* (pp. 163–192). New York: Taylor & Francis.

Szechtman, H., & Woody, E. (2004). Obsessive-compulsive disorder as a disturbance of security motivation. *Psychological Review, 111,* 111–127.

Tannenbaum, A. J. (1992). Early signs of giftedness: Research and commentary. *Journal of the Education of the Gifted, 15,* 104–133.

Tannock, R. (2000). Attention-deficit/hyperactivity disorder with anxiety disorders. In T. E. Brown (Ed.), *Attention-deficit disorders and comorbidities in children, adolescents, and adults* (pp. 125–170). Washington, DC: American Psychiatric Press.

Taylor, H. G., Yeates, K. O., Wade, S. L., Drotar, D., Stancin, T., & Minich, N. (2002). A prospective study of short- and long-term outcomes after traumatic brain injury in children: Behavior and achievement. *Neuropsychology, 17,* 15–27.

Taylor, R. L., Richards, S. B., & Brady, M. P. (2005). *Mental retardation: Historical perspectives, current practices, and future directions.* Boston: Pearson.

Taylor, R. L., Smiley, L. R., & Richards, S. B. (2009). *Exceptional students: Preparing teachers for the 21st century.* Boston: McGraw-Hill.

Teicher, M. H., Ito, Y., Glod, C. A., & Barber, N. I. (1996). Objective measurement of hyperactivity and attentional problems in ADHD. *Journal of the American Academy of Child and Adolescent Psychiatry, 35,* 334–342.

Thomas, A., & Chess, S. (1977). *Temperament and development.* New York: Brunner-Mazel.

Thompson, K. (2001). *Building resilient students: Integrating resiliency into what you already know and do.* Thousand Oaks, CA: Corwin Press.

Thomsen, P. H. (2001). Obsessive-compulsive disorder. In C. A. Essau & F. Petermann (Eds.), *Anxiety disorders in children and adolescents: Epidemiology, risk factors, and treatment* (pp. 261–284*).* New York: Taylor & Francis.

Tiffin-Richards, M. C., Hasselhorn, M., Richards, M. L., Banaschewski, T., & Rothenberger, A. (2004). Time reproduction in finger tapping tasks by children with attention-deficit hyperactivity disorder and/or dyslexia. *Dyslexia, 10,* 299–315.

Torgesen, J. (2000). Individual differences in response to early interventions in reading: The lingering problem of treatment registers. *Learning Disabilities Research and Practice, 15,* 55–64.

Treating obsessive-compulsive disorder. (2009, March). *Harvard Mental Health Letter,* pp. 4–5.

Tremblay, R. E., Japel, C., Perusse, D., Boivin, M., Zoccoliollo, M., Montplaisir, J., & McDuff, P. (1999). The search for the "onset" of physical aggression: Rousseau and Bandura revisited. *Criminal Behavior and Mental Health, 9,* 8–23.

Tryon, A. S., & Keane, S. P. (1991). Popular and aggressive boys' initial social interaction patterns in cooperative and competitive settings. *Journal of Abnormal Child Psychology, 19,* 395–406.

Tsaousides, T., & Gordon, W. A. (2009). Cognitive rehabilitation following traumatic brain injury: Assessment to treatment. *Mount Sinai Journal of Medicine, 76,* 173–181.

Tseng, M. H., Henderson, A., Chow, S. M., & Yao, G. (2004). Relationship between motor proficiency, attention, impulse, and activity in children with ADHD. *Developmental Medicine and Child Neurology, 46,* 381–388.

U.S. Department of Education. (2006). *Twenty-sixth annual report to Congress on the implementation of the Individuals with Disabilities Education Act* (2 vols.). Washington, DC: Author.

van Lier, P. A. C., Muthén, B. O., van der Sar, R. M., & Crijnen, A. A. M. (2004). Preventing disruptive behavior in elementary schoolchildren: Impact of a universal classroom-based intervention. *Journal of Consulting and Clinical Psychology, 72,* 467–478.

Vanlint, S., & Nugent, M. (2006). Vitamin D and fractures in people with intellectual disability. *Journal of Intellectual Disability, 50,* 761–767.

Vansteenkiste, M., Lens, W., & Deci, E. L. (2006). Intrinsic versus extrinsic goal contents in self-determination theory: Another look at the quality of academic motivation. *Educational Psychologist, 41,* 19–31.

VanTassel-Baska, J. (1998a). Disadvantaged learners with talent. In J. VanTassel-Baska (Ed.), *Excellence in educating gifted and talented learners* (3rd ed., pp. 95–114). Denver: Love.

VanTassel-Baska, J. (Ed.). (1998b). *Excellence in educating gifted and talented learners* (3rd ed.). Denver: Love.

VanTassel-Baska, J. (1998c). Girls of promise. In J. VanTassel-Baska (Ed.), *Excellence in educating gifted and talented learners* (3rd ed., pp. 129–143). Denver: Love.

Vaughn, S., Hogan, A., Kouzekanani, K., & Shapiro, S. (1990). Peer acceptance, self-perceptions, and social skills of learning disabled students prior to identification. *Journal of Educational Psychology, 82,* 101–106.

Velleman, S. L. (2002). *Childhood apraxia of speech resource guide.* Clifton Park, NY: Thompson.

Velleman, S. L. (2011). Lexical and phonological development in children with childhood apraxia of speech: A commentary on Stoel-Gammon's "Relationships between lexical and phonological development in young children." *Journal of Child Language, 38,* 82–86.

Vellutino, F. R., Scanlon, D. M., Sipay, E. R., Small, S. G., Pratt, A., Chen, R., & Denkla, M. B. (1996). Cognitive profiles of difficult-to-remediate and readily remediated poor readers: Early intervention as a vehicle for distinguishing between cognitive and experiential deficits as basic causes of specific reading disability. *Journal of Educational Psychology, 88,* 601–638.

Vogel, C. (2006). A field guide to narcissism. *Psychology Today, 39,* 68–74.

Vogel, S. A. (1998). Adults with learning disabilities: What learning disabilities specialists, adult literacy educators, and other service providers want and need to know. In S. A. Vogel & S. Reder (Eds.), *Learning disabilities, literacy, and adult education* (pp. 5–28). Baltimore: Paul H. Brookes.

Volkow, N. D., Wang, G.-J., Newcorn, J., Telang, F., Solanto, M. V., Fowler, J. S., et al. (2007). Depressed dopamine activity in caudate and preliminary evidence of limbic involvement in adults with attention-deficit/hyperactivity disorder. *Archives of General Psychiatry, 64,* 932–940.

von Aster, M. (2000). Developmental cognitive neuropsychology of number processing and calculation: Varieties of developmental dyscalculia. *European Child and Adolescent Psychiatry, 9*(Suppl. 2), 41–57.

Wahler, R. G., Vigilante, V. A., & Strand, P. S. (2004). Generalization in a child's oppositional behavior across home and school settings. *Journal of Applied Behavior Analysis, 37,* 43–51.

Walsh, Joseph. (2002). Shyness and social phobia. *Health and Social Work, 27,* 137–145.

Walter, A. L., & Carter, A. S. (1997). Gilles de la Tourette's syndrome in childhood: A guide for school professionals. *School Psychology Review, 26,* 28–46.

Wang, T., Tseng, M., Wilson, B. N., & Hu, F. (2009). Functional performance of children with developmental coordination disorder at home and at school. *Developmental Medicine and Child Neurology, 51,* 817–825.

Waschbusch, D. A, Pelham, W. E., Jennings, J. R., Greiner, A. R., Tarter, R. E., & Moss, H. B. (2002). Reactive aggression in boys with disruptive behavior disorders: Behavior, psychology, and affect. *Journal of Abnormal Child Psychology, 30,* 641–56.

Webb, J. T. (2000). *Misdiagnosis and dual diagnosis of gifted children: Gifted and LD, ADD/ADHD, OCD, oppositional defiant disorder.* ERIC Digest 448-382.

Webb, J. T., Amend, E. R., Webb, N. E., Goerss, J., Beljan, P., & Olenchak, F. R. (2005). *Misdiagnosis and dual diagnosis of gifted children and adults: ADHD, bipolar, OCD, Asperger's, depression, and other disorders.* Scottsdale, AZ: Great Potential Press.

Wehmeyer, M. L., & Agran, M. (2005). *Mental retardation and intellectual disabilities.* Boston: Pearson.

Weintraub, N., & Graham, S. (1998). Writing legibly and quickly: A study of children's ability to adjust their handwriting to meet common classroom demands. *Learning Disabilities Research and Practice, 13,*146–152.

Weller, E. B., Weller, R. A., & Fristad, M. A. (1995). Bipolar disorder in children: Misdiagnosis, underdiagnosis, and future directions. *Journal of the American Academy of Child and Adolescent Psychiatry, 34,* 709–714.

Wenar, C., & Kerig, P. (2006). *Developmental psychopathology: From infancy through adolescence* (5th ed.). New York: McGraw-Hill.

Werner, E. E., & Smith, R. S. (1992). *Overcoming the odds: High risk children from birth to adulthood.* Ithaca, NY: Cornell University Press.

Westen, D., Dutra, L., & Shedler, J. (2005). Assessing adolescent personality pathology. *British Journal of Psychiatry, 186,* 227–238..

Wheeler, J., & Carlson, C. L. (1994). The social functioning of children with ADD with and without hyperactivity: A comparison of their peer relations and social deficits. *Journal of Emotional and Behavioral Disorders, 2,* 2–12.

White, S. W., Keonig, K., & Scahill, L. (2007). Social skills development in autism spectrum disorders: A review of the intervention research. *Journal of Autism and Developmental Disorders, 37,* 1858–1868.

Widiger, T. A. (1992). Generalized social phobia versus avoidant personality disorder: A commentary. *Journal of Abnormal Psychology, 101,* 340–343.

Wilens, T. E., Biederman, J., & Spencer, T. J. (2002). Attention deficit/hyperactivity disorder across the lifespan. *Annual Review of Medicine, 53,* 113–131.

Willcutt, E. G., Doyle, A. E., Nigg, J. T., Faraone, S. V., & Pennington, B. F. (2005). Validity of the executive function theory of attention-deficit/hyperactivity disorder: A meta-analytic review. *Biological Psychiatry, 57,* 1336–1346.

Willcutt, E. G., & Pennington, B. F. (2000). Psychiatric comorbidity in children and adolescents with reading disability. *Journal of Child Psychology and Psychiatry, 41,* 1039–1048.

Willcutt, E. G., Pennington, B. F., Boada, R., Ogline, J. S., Tunich, R. A., Chhabildas, N. A., et al. (2001). A comparison of the cognitive deficits in reading disability and attention-deficit/hyperactivity disorder. *Journal of Abnormal Psychology, 110,* 157–172.

Willcutt, E. G., Pennington, B. F., Olson, R. K., Chhabildas, N., & Hulslander, J. (2005). Neuropsychological analyses of comorbidity between reading disability and attention deficit hyperactivity disorder: In search of the common deficit. *Developmental Neuropsychology, 27,* 35–78.

Willerman, L. (1973). Activity level and hyperactivity in twins. *Child Development, 44,* 288–293.

Wong, B., Butler, D., Ficzere, S. A., & Kuperis, S. (1996). Teaching low achievers and students with learning disabilities to plan, write, and revise opinion essays. *Journal of Learning Disabilities, 29,* 197–212.

Wood, A. C., Saudino, K. J., Rogers, H., Asherson, P., & Kuntsi, J. (2007). Genetic influences on mechanically-assessed activity level in children. *Journal of Child Psychology and Psychiatry, 48,* 695–702.

Wood, J. (2006). Effect of anxiety reduction on children's school performance and social adjustment. *Developmental Psychology, 42,* 345–349.

Woods, D. W., Koch, M., & Miltenberger, R. G. (2003). The impact of tic severity on the effects of peer education about Tourette's syndrome. *Journal of Developmental and Physical Disabilities, 15,* 67–78.

Woodward, J. (2002). Meeting the challenge of mathematics reform for students with LD. *Journal of Special Education. 36,* 89–101.

Woodward, J. (2004). Mathematics education in the United States: Past and present. *Journal of Learning Disabilities, 37,* 16–31.

Woodward, J., & Brown, C. (2006). Meeting the curricular needs of academically low-achieving students in middle grade mathematics. *Journal of Special Education, 40,* 151–159.

Wu, K. K., Anderson, V., & Castiello, U. (2006). Attention-deficit/hyperactivity disorder and working memory: A task-switching paradigm. *Journal of Clinical and Experimental Neuropsychology, 28,* 1288–1306.

Xin, Y. P. (2008). The effect of schema-based instruction in solving word problems: An emphasis on pre-algebraic conceptualization of multiplicative relations. *Journal for Research in Mathematics Education, 39,* 526–551.

Xin, Y. P., Wiles, B., & Lin, Y. (2008). Teaching conceptual model-based word-problem story grammar to enhance mathematics problem solving. *Journal of Special Education, 42,* 163–178.

Xin, Y. P., & Zhang, D. (2009). Exploring a conceptual model-based approach to teaching situated word problems. *Journal of Educational Research, 102,* 427–441.

Yatham, L. N., Lecrubier, Y., Fieve, R. R., Davis, K. H., Harris, S. D., & Krishnan, A. A. (2004). Quality of life in patients with bipolar depression: Data from 920 patients. *Bipolar Disorders, 6,* 379–385.

Yeates, K. O., Armstrong, K., Janusz, J., Taylor, H. G., Wade, S., Stancin, T., & Drotar, D. (2005). Long-term attention problems in children with traumatic brain injury. *Journal of the American Academy of Child and Adolescent Psychiatry, 44,* 574–584.

Yerkes, R. M., & Dodson, J. D. (1908). The relation of strength of stimulus to rapidity of habit-formation. *Journal of Comparative Neurology and Psychology, 18,* 459–482.

Zentall, S. S. (1975). Optimal stimulation as theoretical basis of hyperactivity. *American Journal of Orthopsychiatry, 45,* 549–563.

Zentall, S. S. (1988). Production deficiencies in elicited language but not in the spontaneous verbalizations of hyperactive children. *Journal of Abnormal Child Psychology, 16,* 657–673.

Zentall, S. S. (1989). Attentional cuing in spelling tasks for hyperactive and comparison regular classroom children. *Journal of Special Education, 23,* 83–93.

Zentall, S. S. (2005a). Contributors to the social goals and outcomes of students with ADHD with and without LD. *International Journal of Educational Research, 43,* 290–307.

Zentall, S. S. (2005b). Theory- and evidence-based strategies for children with attentional problems. *Psychology in the Schools, 42,* 821–836.

Zentall, S. S. (2006). *ADHD and education: Foundations, characteristics, methods, and collaboration.* Upper Saddle River, NJ: Pearson Merrill Prentice Hall.

Zentall, S. S. (2007). Math performance of students with ADHD: Cognitive and behavioral contributors and interventions. In D. B. Berch & M. M. M. Mazzocco (Eds.), *Why is math so hard for some children? The nature and origins of mathematical learning difficulties and disabilities* (pp. 219–243). Baltimore: Paul H. Brookes.

Zentall, S. S., & Beike, S. M. (2012). Achievement and social goals of younger and older elementary students: Response to academic and social failure. *Learning Disability Quarterly, 35,* 39–53.

Zentall, S. S., Cassady, J. C., & Javorsky, J. (2001). Social comprehension of children with hyperactivity. *Journal of Attention Disorders, 5,* 11–24.

Zentall, S. S., Falkenberg, S. D., & Smith, L. B. (1985). Effects of color stimulation and information on the copying performance of attention-problem adolescents. *Journal of Abnormal Child Psychology, 13,* 501–511.

Zentall, S. S., & Ferkis, M. A. (1993). Mathematical problem-solving for ADHD children with and without learning disabilities. *Learning Disability Quarterly, 16,* 6–18.

Zentall, S. S., & Gohs, D. E. (1984). Hyperactive and comparison children's response to detailed vs. global cues in communication tasks. *Learning Disability Quarterly, 7,* 77–87.

Zentall, S. S., Hall, A. M., & Lee, D. L. (1998). Attentional focus of students with hyperactivity during a word-search task. *Journal of Abnormal Child Psychology, 26,* 335–343.

Zentall, S. S., & Javorsky, J. (1997). Attention deficit/hyperactivity disorder research-to-practice through distance education. *Teacher Education and Special Education, 20,* 146–155.

Zentall, S. S., & Kruczek, T. (1988). The attraction of color for active attention problem children. *Exceptional Children, 54,* 357–362.

Zentall, S. S., Kuester, D. A., & Craig, B. A. (2011). Social behavior in cooperative groups: Students at risk for ADHD and their peers. *Journal of Educational Research, 104,* 28–41.

Zentall, S. S., & Lee, J. (2012). A reading motivation intervention with differential outcomes for students at risk for reading disabilities, ADHD, and typical comparisons: "Clever is and clever does." *Learning Disability Quarterly, 35,* 248–259. doi:10.1177/0731948712438556

Zentall, S. S., & Meyer, M. J. (1987). Self-regulation of stimulation for ADD-H children during reading and vigilance task performance. *Journal of Abnormal Child Psychology, 15,* 519–536.

Zentall, S. S., Moon, S. M., Hall, A. M., & Grskovic, J. (2001). Learning and motivational characteristics of boys with giftedness and/or attention deficit/hyperactivity disorder. *Exceptional Children, 67,* 499–519.

Zentall, S. S., Tom-Wright, K., & Lee, J. (in press). Psychostimulant and sensory stimulation interventions that target the reading and math deficits of students with ADHD. *Journal of Attention Disorders.* Advance online publication. doi:10.1016/j.lindif.2012.05.010

Zentall, S. S., & Zentall, T. R. (1983). Optimal stimulation: A model of disordered activity and performance in normal and deviant children. *Psychological Bulletin, 94,* 446–471.

Zimmerman, B., & Conant, J. (1994). Powerful tools for students with learning disabilities. *TECH-NJ: Technology, Educators, and Children with Disabilities, New Jersey, 5,* 14–15.

# Index

# About the Author

**Sydney S. Zentall** is professor of educational studies at Purdue University. Her academic training includes a foundation in psychology, a master's degree in the area of emotional/behavioral disorders, and a doctorate in the area of learning disabilities from the University of California at Berkeley and the University of Pittsburgh. Her background experiences teaching children include both general and special education, and she has more than three decades of experience in educating teachers. She is a national/international educational expert in the area of ADHD, and she has published several books and numerous scientific articles in psychology, special education, and education. In 1995 she was inducted into the ADD Hall of Fame by the national organization Children and Adults with ADD (Ch.ADD). Dr. Zentall has also been the recipient of grants from the National Institute of Mental Health and from the Office of Special Education and is past president of the Division for Research of the Council for Exceptional Children (CEC).

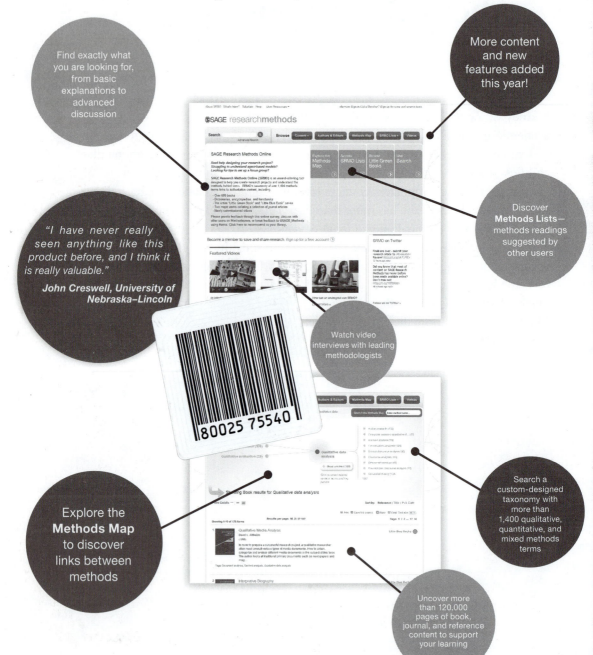